EXTERIOR MAINTENANCE & IMPROVEMENTS

EXTERIOR MAINTENANCE & IMPROVEMENTS

Created and editorially produced for Petersen Publishing Company by Allen D. Bragdon Publishers, Inc., Home Guides Division

STAFF FOR THIS VOLUME:

Editorial Director — Allen D. Bragdon
Managing Editor — Michael Donner
Art Director — John B. Miller
Assistant Art Director — Lillian Nahmias
Text Editors — Charles Johnson, James Wyckoff
Copy Editor — Jill Munves
Production Editor — Jayne Lathrop
Contributing Artists — Pat Lee, Clara Rosenbaum, Jerry Zimmerman
Contributing Photographers — Monte Burch, Norma Chacona, Chérie Francis, Michael Mertz, John B. Miller, Clara Rosenbaum, Tim Snyder
Cover design by — "For Art Sake" Inc.
Technical Consultant — Monte Burch

ACKNOWLEDGEMENTS

The Editors wish to thank the following firms for their help in the preparation of this book: Asphalt Roofing Manufacturers Association; California Redwood Association; Dow Chemical USA, Functional Products and Systems Dept.; Georgia-Pacific Corp.; Johns-Manville Sales Corp.; Little Giant Pump Company; National Paint & Coatings Association, Inc.; Rockwell International, Power Tool Division; Stanley Tools, Division of the Stanley Works; U.S. Department of Agriculture; U.S. Department of Housing and Urban Development; Walpole Woodworkers, Inc.; R.D. Werner Co., Inc.; Westinghouse Electric Corporation, Lamp Division.

Petersen Publishing Company

R. E. Petersen/Chairman of the Board
F. R. Waingrow/President
Alan C. Hahn/Director, Market Development
James L. Krenek/Director, Purchasing
Louis Abbott/Production Manager
Erwin M. Rosen/Executive Editor,
Specialty Publications Division

Library of Congress Catalog Card
No. 77-076147
Paperbound Edition:
ISBN 0-8227-8005-4
Hardcover Edition:
ISBN 0-8227-8017-8

Table of Contents

1. THE PROUD HOUSE

The purpose of this book is to save you time and money. It will accomplish this by helping you do things to the exterior of your house that you might otherwise have to pay a tradesman to do for you—or else not tackle at all.

It is one thing to fix something, say a leaky rain gutter, but it is far less time consuming and costly to prevent the problem from arising. So in addition to enabling you to take on repair and improvement projects, this book will help you spot trouble in its early stages. You'll be fixing little things before they become big ones, thanks to a simple program of periodic inspections and maintenance.

This book has been designed to be used by beginners. As you will see, its organization is project by project. When you have a job you need to do, just look it up in the table of contents. When you turn to that page, you will find everything you need there: list of tools, recommended materials, planning hints, and step-by-step directions in ordinary language, backed up by photo-graphs and illustrations that show you key techniques.

Here are some other helpful devices to watch for throughout the book as you use it. "Planning hints" help cut down on frustrating traps and will help you avoid wasting costly materials. "Stopgaps and copouts" show you how to make temporary repairs or fix something you might have thought you had to replace. And there is a cartoon character, "Practical Pete," who makes the same kind of mistakes most inexperienced do-it-yourselfers make. So he is a good "flag" for school-of-hard-knocks advice. "New wrinkles" describes new tools and materials you may not have heard of yet, or know how to use.

Your house may well be your largest financial asset and best investment as well. You yourself have a good measure of control over its market value, which is greatly affected by its appearance and condition. Keep them up, and your house will appreciate in value. That kind of appreciation you can take to the bank!

Preventive maintenance

The checklist below encompasses inspections you need to complete a top-to-bottom examination of your home's exterior. In addition to helping you to spot problems, present or potential, the chart refers you to directions you can follow to remove the cause.

As you will see, some of the inspections should be made at a stated frequency; others can be made only when nature cooperates, for example, by raining. To insure that you make the periodic inspections, pencil them in on your calendar or incorporate them in a list of things you want to do each fall and spring.

You may be able to make additional use of this checklist: Take the book along when you are going to look at a house you might buy. By inspecting it systematically, you might detect defects you otherwise could have missed. The list also suggests some questions to ask the present owner.

Top-to-bottom inspection

Chimney
Install chimney cover to keep out birds and rain. (Page 15)
Inspect concrete cap for cracks. Patch if necessary. (Page 15)
Inspect joints for missing or crumbling mortar, and loose bricks. Tuck-point. (Page 15)
Inspect flashing for cracks or gaps where it has pulled away from mortar. (Page 13)
Clean every three or four years—every year if you have a fireplace or wood-burning stove. (Page 15)

Roof
Check attic and attic crawl space during rain for signs of leaks. (Page 8)
Check for loose or broken shingles. Replace. (Page 9)
Observe asphalt shingles in high wind to see if tabs are blowing up. Cement down. This prevents lost shingles. (Page 9)
Check attic vents and repair any holes in the screening. (Page 17)
Inspect flashing in valleys and around dormers for holes and tears. Patch. (Page 14)
After snow, look for fast-melting areas, revealing excessive heat loss. Add insulation. (Page 48)
When temperatures just below freezing follow heavy snow, look for ice dams on uninsulated overhang. If observed, correct by melting or removing causes. (Page 16)

Gutters
Inspect during rain for water pouring over sides. Correct. (Page 19)
Inspect after rain for pools of water. Correct. (Page 19)
Look for damp spots on the ground below or for erosion of top soil. Correct. (Page 20)
Check for blistered paint. Treat and repaint. (Page 19)
Every fall and spring remove leaves, twigs, balls, and other obstructions. (Page 19)

Downspouts
Observe during heavy rain for water pouring out at connection with gutter and between joints of downspouts. Correct. (Page 20)
Observe movement of water to make sure it is not flowing into basement or washing away soil. Correct. (Page 20)
Make sure metal cage covers top and is not clogged. (Page 20)

Walls and siding
Test to determine need for repainting. Sides exposed to sun go first. (Page 30)
Probe for rotten wood. (Page 30)
Look for blistered or peeling paint, revealing that moisture is getting into wood. (Page 30)
Inspect bricks for white, dusty discoloration, revealing moisture inside wall.
Remove sources of moisture causing rot or discoloration. (Page 30)
Look for mildew. Remove and prevent. Shady sides are susceptible. (Page 40)
Probe for shriveled or brittle caulking in seams around windows, doors, air conditioners, and other openings. Recaulk. (Page 36)
Inspect joints in brick wall for missing or crumbling mortar. Tuck-point. (Page 70)
Inspect stucco for holes and hairline cracks. Patch. (Page 34)
Look for strips of siding that have pulled loose, shingles that have curled up at edges or slipped out of place. Correct. (Page 31)
Cut shrubs back 18 inches from wall and pull down ivy, wisteria, and other creeping vines. In northern climes shut off and drain outside faucets each fall or install nonfreeze type.

Windows
Replace missing or peeling putty.
Replace cracked glass.
Oil hinges and crank handles of casement windows annually.

Storm windows
Make sure vents in frame carry off condensed water that collects on sill.

Basement windows
Check areaway during or right after rain to see if water has collected. Remove leaves and other debris in areaway and/or drain.

Doors, locks, and hinges
Inspect sticking doors for sources of moisture causing expansion. Correct.
Adjust threshold weather strip.
Inspect top and bottom surfaces to see if they are protected from moisture.
Tighten drip cap.
Look for glued joints that have opened up.
Clean channels of sliding doors with steel wool.
Lubricate locks.
Lubricate pins and tighten hinge screws.
Lubricate hinges, rollers, and tracks on garage doors.

Porches, decks, and stoops
Inspect undersides for signs of wood rot, termites, and carpenter ants. (Page 82)
Check paint to make sure it's in good condition. (Page 82)
Make sure cracks between boards are filled. (Page 82)
Install drains in floors where water can collect.

Driveways and walks
Inspect concrete for cracks.
Patch cracks in concrete. (Page 58)
Inspect concrete for rough surfaces caused by chemical ice melters. Smooth. (Page 58)
Reseal blacktop every other year. (Page 76)
Inspect blacktop for holes and cracks. Patch. (Page 76)

Grounds
Inspect fences for needed repair and repainting after the shrubs have died back each fall. (Page 78)
Check galvanized steel fencing for rust. (Page 78)
Inspect trees to make sure no limbs touch house or overhang power lines.

Termite detection/prevention
Look under porches, wood steps, and near crawl spaces for mud tunnels. (Page 56)
Check plumbing access hole on concrete-slab houses. (Page 56)
Remove any accumulations of wood near the house. (Page 56)

Septic tank
Make sure downspouts do not run into septic tank system.
Remove shrubs or trees near tank or in drainage field.
Have tank inspected annually and cleaned every two or three years.
Take steps to prevent heavy vehicles from running over the drainage field.

Lawn and garden equipment
Fall
Store garden tools, preparing motors on all powered equipment for storage.
Drain and store hoses.
Disconnect sprinkler timer.

Winter/Spring
Sharpen cutting tools.
Clean, adjust, and/or overhaul motors on powered equipment.
Repaint lawn furniture as needed.
Replace missing or burst webbing on lawn chairs and lounges.

2. THE TOOLS

Light maintenance tools:

1. Electric hand drill: ¼″ chuck, variable speed, reversing
2. Drill bits: 1/64″ to ¼″
3. Brace and screwdriver bit: 5/16″
4. Center punch and nail set
5. Electric saber saw with carbide-tipped blade
6. Pliers: slip joint, 8″
7. Pliers: locking grip, 10″
8. Wrenches: open end
9. Utility knife
10. Hacksaw blade and frame
11. Hammer: 16 oz., curved claw
12. Screwdrivers: flat tipped, 4″, 6″, and 10″
13. Surform planing tool
14. Wrench: adjustable, 8″
15. Screwdrivers: Phillips, sizes 1 and 2
16. Wood chisels: ⅜″ to ¾″
17. Files: round, half round, rasp
18. Rule: wooden, 6′ with slide extension
19. Carpenter's square

Heavy maintenance tools:

20. Crosscut saw
21. Combination square
22. Drop cord with light: 20′
23. Extension cord: grounded, 20′
24. C-clamp: 4″
25. Smoothing plane: 8″ to 10″
26. Safety goggles
27. Metal shears: straight cutting
28. Tape measure: 16′, ¾″ wide
29. Hammer: ball peen, 20 oz.
30. Caulking gun: cartridge
31. Cold chisel
32. Carpenter's level: 24″
33. Step ladder: 5′ or 6′
34. Extension ladder: 24′

Specialized tools:

35. Wrecking bar: 24″
36. Paint scraper: hook type
37. Utility bar
38. Putty knife: 1½″ wide
39. Mason's trowel
40. Sanding block: rubber
41. Circular saw: 7¼″ blade, minimum 1½ horsepower
42. Mini-hacksaw
43. Mortar joiner (for smoothing fresh mortar in pointing between bricks, blocks, etc.)
44. Offset screwdriver
45. Square-shank screwdriver
46. Whetstone: combination, 7″
47. Staple gun: heavy duty
48. Pipe-bar clamps
49. Pop rivet tool

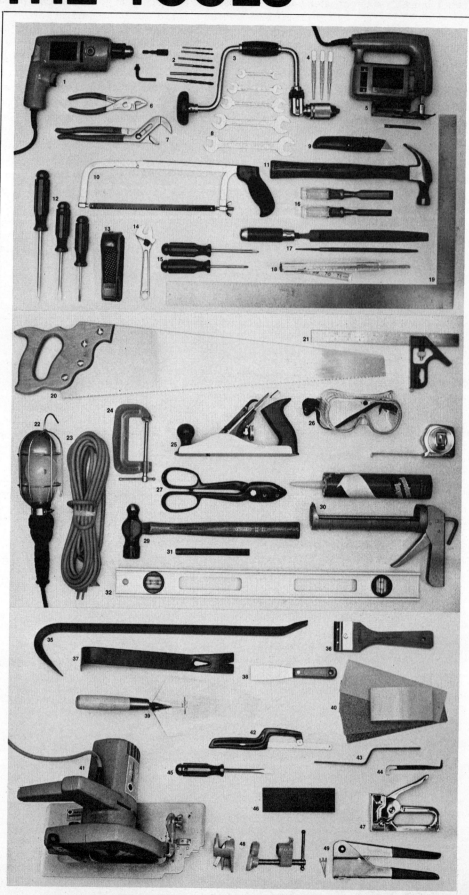

Ladder use and safety

In maintaining and improving the exterior of your house, sooner or later you'll find yourself on a ladder, perhaps even an extension ladder. As even a short fall can be—and often is—disastrous, special precautions are in order. Consider the following for your future safety:

When purchasing an extension ladder, select one with safety treads. Before extending a ladder to the height you want, get it in position. If you are going to shift its position any distance, lower it first. It's dangerous to yourself, others, and your windows to try to waltz an extended ladder around your lawn. The best way for a lone worker to raise a ladder is to pin its feet against the base of the house and push the ladder up from the other end, hand over hand, until it is upright.

Before you climb a ladder, jump on its bottom rung a few times to make sure it is solidly footed. If the ground slopes, put a broad board or beam—never bricks—under the lower foot until it is level with the other one. If the ground is soft or muddy, place both of the ladder's feet on a wide board. If you are planning to work on a ladder extended to its full length, you can gain stability by lashing the bottom rung to a stake driven into the ground under the ladder. If yours is an aluminum ladder, watch out for power lines. Electricity flows readily through aluminum. Make sure the ladder has firm support at the top. Never place it against a window sash or so close to an edge that a slight shift would send it and you sailing. For comfort, don't wear soft-soled shoes if you are going to work on a ladder for a long spell. The rungs will be hard on your arches.

Don't knock it
The front stoop seemed just the spot to place the ladder when I was cleaning out a clogged gutter. Wasn't it firm and level? I had reached the top and begun to scoop away when my teenage son decided to come out of the house. He pushed open the door, knocking the ladder clean off the stoop. That's me clinging to the gutter until he could get the ladder back up, and thinking "never again put up a ladder in front of an unlocked door."

Practical Pete

Position your ladder so that the distance of its feet from the base of the house is about one-quarter its length. Measure the distance between rungs so you can estimate the ladder's extended length.

Keep your hips within the ladder's rails. Extend the ladder two rungs higher than the place you are working on.

Here's a way to free both hands when you need them. Note how the heel is locked against the rung. Have somebody else brace the ladder when you use it this way.

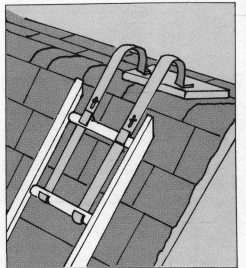

A ladder makes it safer for you to work on a pitched roof—also easier on the shingles. You can buy brackets that hook over the ridge, holding your ladder in place.

TIP: This ladder stabilizer comes in handy when you're painting or working on gutters.

3. ROOF REPAIRS

Finding leaks

Repairing roofs usually involves fixing leaks. To fix a leak you first have to find it, and this can be the most time-consuming part of the job, especially when the leak is in a sloping roof. Often it is not located directly over the damage that it produced in the ceiling. What happens is this: the water flows in through the hole, runs diagonally down the sheathing or a rafter until it meets something—say, a knot or the end of a nail—and only then drops straight down. This can happen three or four feet from the hole and be very misleading.

The common causes of leaks are loose, torn, cracked, or missing shingles, and defective flashing around a chimney or vent, or in a valley between gables. Shingles along the ridge or hip of a roof tend to get cracked or blown away because the wind lifts them, causing the nails to pop.

To find a leak, go up to the attic or crawl space during a rainstorm. Take along a flashlight, felt-tip pen, and several pieces of wire about a foot long. **TIP:** Paint the wire a bright color; it will be easier for you to spot when you are looking for it later on the roof. Once in the area of the leak, shine your flashlight along the sheathing and rafters. Work in the dark. It will be easier for you to spot the gleam of the water when your flashlight illuminates it. When you locate the hole, push a wire up through it and draw a circle around the hole as a permanent record. On the next day, locate the wire from the outside and make the repair as shown on the following pages.

If your roof is insulated and you have reason to suspect a leak, take off the batts one by one until you find one that is damp or discolored. Then start looking above it for the hole.

If you can't examine your roof from below, you'll have to wait for a dry day and examine it from the outside. Crawl over the suspected area, examining it for loose or missing shingles, cracks in flashing, and popped or missing nails.

If dripping water is not localized but appears over a wide area, check the flashing around the chimney. This can pull away from the mortar. Instead of deflecting water, it collects it. Water then flows down *under* the shingles and spreads out before getting into rooms below.

If you live in a northern region, your house may develop mysterious water spots and dripping in winter. When ice dams form in gutters, melting water can back up the roof and under the shingles, then seep through the sheathing into your house.

If you have a flat roof, finding a leak is simplified by the fact that water from a hole tends to fall directly below. Leaks generally develop in low spots where water collects, around a chimney or vent pipe, or in the flashing where the roof joins a vertical wall. Also check for popped nails, especially along the seams.

The solvent solution
I was pleased with the job I did patching cracked shingles along the ridge of my house. I was sure the leak was stopped. But when I climbed down to admire my work from the ground, I saw that I had left smears of black roofing cement on my beautiful, silvery shingles. I quickly called the lumber yard where I bought the stuff. A clerk told me to soak a rough rag or brush in kerosene and scrub the stains off right away. It beats having to paint the whole roof black.
Practical Pete

Fixing leaks in asphalt shingles

1. If the leak comes from a cracked, loose, or raised shingle, your task is usually simple. A small crack can be filled with asphalt roof paint. To repair a badly torn shingle or one with curled edges, first lift its bottom portion. On "stick-down" shingles, you may need a putty knife to pry the edge up. But be careful not to push the knife through the shingle.

2. Smear roof cement on the exposed underside of the shingle as well as the area on which the shingle will rest. You can use a caulking gun for this step. Then push the shingle back into position. On cold days place a flat board over the repair and press down until the shingle is firmly in place. If you have to nail into the exposed portion of the shingle, do so sparingly; cover nailheads with cement.

What it takes

Approximate time: Once the leak is located and you have all your materials assembled on the roof, allow 5 to 10 minutes per shingle. The preliminaries are what take time, and they cannot be predicted.

Tools and materials: Hammer, putty knife, pry bar, hacksaw blade or nail ripper, caulking gun, roof cement or asphalt paint, 1½-inch galvanized or aluminum roofing nails, and replacement shingles.

To remove a badly damaged shingle, lift the surrounding shingles to expose the nails in the flawed one. Pull the nails out (gently!) with a pry bar or chisel. After extracting the shingle, scrape away any old roofing cement. Round off the corners of the new shingle before inserting it so it will slip into place more easily. Fold back the next higher shingle with one hand and hammer with the other. Nail only into that portion of shingle to be overlapped.

Replacing a course. A big wind can rip several shingles off your roof. Replacing them is no more complicated a job than putting in a single shingle. When you are replacing more than one row or "course" of shingles, be sure before you nail the first one in the bottom course that its lower edge is properly aligned with the other shingles in the same course and that its joints are staggered with the joints in the courses above and below it. Then nail succeeding shingles in place.

Planning hints:

- Wait for a sunny day if you can. Shingles will be easier to work with. A wet roof is dangerously slippery.
- Wear sneakers or soft-soled shoes.
- Buy a tool holster in which to carry your hammer, putty knife, and other tools.
- A carpenter's or roofer's apron is handy for keeping nails, small cans, and tools.
- If you're new to a house, search the attic, basement, and garage for leftover shingles before buying a new bundle. It may be hard to match the old color.

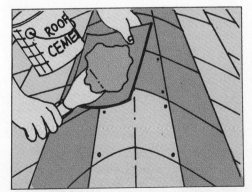

Ridge shingles. Shingles along the ridge of your house are whipped by the wind and are most prone to cracking or blowing away. To replace one, first nail down the corners of the ones below it. Apply a coat of roof cement to the underside of the new shingle. Space it so its overlap is proportionate to the others on the ridge; then nail it in place and cover nailheads with dabs of roof cement.

Stopgaps and copouts

Sheet-metal shingle. For an emergency repair, until you can get a permanent replacement shingle, you can make a patch from a piece of sheet metal. Cut it to fit over the damaged area and slip it well under the shingle above it. Apply a coat of roof cement to the bottom of the patch, smoothing down any beads with your putty knife. Tack in place. Be sure to cover the heads of the tacks with cement. When you get the proper size and type of shingle, pry up the patch.

Fixing leaks in wood shingles

The most common causes of leaks in a wood-shingle roof is that one or more shingles have become warped or split. If so, they can let in a lot of water. Some houses roofed with wood shingles have no attic sheathing underneath the shingles. You may even see cracks between the shingles, but these will not admit water if the roof has been well laid and the shingles are solid.

Leaky wood shingles usually have to be replaced. They can't often be repaired or patched. Replacing one isn't a particularly hard job, but it does require care so you don't split or damage surrounding shingles. The job will look better and go faster if you can replace it with one of exactly the same size and shape. The raw wood color will weather and blend in after about a year. If you are new to the house, explore the attic, cellar, and garage. The builder or previous owner may have left a supply to be used as replacements when needed.

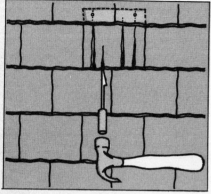

1. To replace a wood shingle, remove the defective shingle (without pulling out the nails that hold it) by splitting it into strips with a sharp wood chisel and a hammer. When the shingle splits at the nail holes, you can dislodge it from beneath the shingle above. Measure the opening left by the removed shingle and trim a new shingle about ⅜ inch narrower so it won't buckle when it swells in the rain.

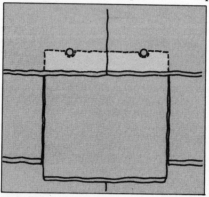

2. Push the new shingle gently into the opening and under the shingle above until it meets the nails left by the old one. Force the shingle up against these nails hard enough to mark their positions in the end. Withdraw the shingle and inspect it to make sure you can see the indentations made by the nails.

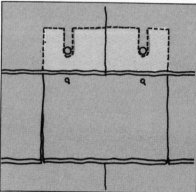

3. Measure the depth of the nail holes in the original shingle. Put the new shingle in a vise and cut slots to these depths with gentle strokes of a coping saw so it doesn't split. Push the new shingle up under the ones above it so the bottom lines up with the adjacent shingles. Tap in a couple of roofing nails, but since they will be in the exposed portion of the shingle, set the nails and cover the heads with caulking compound.

Fixing leaks in slate shingles

Because slate shingles crack so easily, major repairs on a slate roof should be made only by an experienced roofer. But you can repair a loose or slightly cracked shingle yourself. Lift off the damaged piece and coat its underside with roof cement. Then fit it exactly back into position. If you have a cracked shingle, cover the crack with cement and smooth the bead down with a putty knife.

1. To replace a slate shingle, first remove nails with a nail ripper. Hook the ripper over the nail and hammer on it until the nail comes out. Starting the nail from inside the house will shorten this step.

2. Position and nail two metal strips as shown. Strike the nail sharply and it will go through the slate without splitting it. Cover the nail heads with cement and leave the excess on.

3. Slide the new slate into position and fold back the metal strips so that each fits snugly to the slate. (If you don't have a supply of slates, have them cut to size for you.)

Fixing leaks in flat roofs

Most flat roofs are covered with layers of felt paper saturated with asphalt. (The surface of some older roofs is covered with gravel or stone chips to protect the roof from the sun.) If the leak comes from a small hole or crack, the remedy is to seal it with roof cement. If the roof is in bad shape with many leaks, cover it with a coat of roof paint. This will do the job and costs less than roof cément. If the roof has pebbles, brush them off; no need to replace them. Apply the paint in sections measuring about 25 feet square. Since even flat roofs have some slope, work from highest point.

What it takes

Approximate time: From half an hour to a couple of hours, depending on extent and depth of damage.

Tools and materials: Hammer, putty knife, sharp knife, long-handled brush, 1½-inch galvanized or aluminum roofing nails, roof cement, roof paint (5 gallons cover 100 sq. feet), 15-pound roofing felt, building paper, tar paper or shingles.

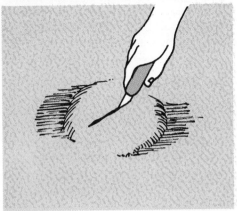

1. If you have a cracked blister, slice it down the middle, being careful not to cut into the layer below. Raise the flaps to allow the area to dry. Then force roof cement under both edges with a putty knife or caulking gun.

2. Nail down the edges with roofing nails and place a tar-paper or shingle patch over the blistered area. Nail the patch down with roofing nails every ½ inch. Cover entire patch with roof cement.

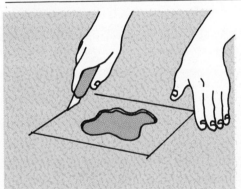

1. If you have a long rip or extensively damaged area, cut away the top layer of the entire area. Measure this to the nearest full inch so it will be easier to cut a patch that fits exactly.

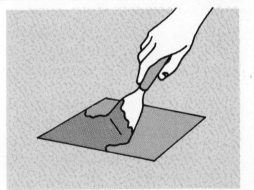

2. Fit patch of 15-pound roofing felt into cutaway section. Coat this with roof cement. No need to nail.

3. Cut patch to overlap inset patch about 2 inches on all sides. Nail, and cover nail heads with roof cement to prevent new leaks.

Patching a deep hole

Flat roofs are more vulnerable to damage than pitched roofs because they absorb rather than deflect the blow of falling objects. If your flat roof suffers a deep puncture, repair it this way:

1. Cut away all materials down to the sheathing. Replace the broken sheathing if necessary.
2. Cover sheathing with building paper and lay a piece of 15-pound roofing felt over the paper. Coat with roof cement.
3. Repeat this until felt is level with roof.
4. Patch with overlapping piece as shown above and at left.

Repairing flashing

One of the main causes of leaks on older roofs is faulty or damaged flashing. It can also be the source of leaks in new homes. If a flashing is not properly installed, gallons of water can pour in from an otherwise perfect roof. Flashing is used to provide a watertight joint wherever shingles won't do the job: around chimneys and vent pipes, in valleys where two planes of the roof meet or where a dormer meets the roof, along the peak of the roof, and where a flat roof meets a vertical wall. You will also find flashing around window and door jambs.

Flashing is now made from a number of different materials: roll roofing, roofing felt, galvanized steel, aluminum, and rubber. If your home is an older one, the flashing may be copper, which is the best

—and worth salvaging. You'll find it especially around the chimney and in the valleys. Boots of other metals are used for flashing around vent pipes. Whichever flashing material you use, you will often be sealing joints with roofing cement or tar.

It is worth the effort to inspect your flashing once a year, especially around the chimney, a common place for leaks to develop. It won't be hard to spot large cracks in your flashing or gaps between it and other elements of your roof, such as bricks in the chimney. But a flashing can also develop pinhole leaks or cracks which can admit quantities of water. If the flashing looks old, give it a coat of roofing cement or roof paint. Fill any large holes with roofing felt and coat with cement.

What it takes

Approximate time: Three hours.

Tools and materials: Putty knife, caulking gun, hammer, mason's trowel, asphalt roof cement, roof paint, and patching mortar.

Preventing leaks around chimneys

Flashing around chimneys is commonly embedded in mortar. But the mortar can age or the flashing pull away. In either case the old mortar must be cleaned out and

replaced. Chisel out the old mortar, reposition the flashing, and embed it in new patching mortar. This will create a tight, waterproof joint.

When the flashing material is roofing felt or paper, fill holes and cracks by smearing roof cement over them with a putty knife.

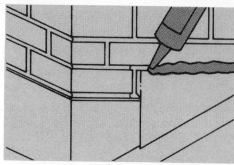

If your flashing is metal, use a caulking gun loaded with roof cement to refill the joint between the cap of the flashing and mortar.

TIP: Corrosion can weaken metal—even rot it away. Since problems frequently start where two different metals meet, use nails made of the same metal as the flashing you are repairing.

Preventing leaks around vents

Vents may be flashed with a metal boot or tightly fitted shingles. On some new homes, the vent flashing is a plastic boot

cemented or nailed to the sheathing. In any event, the flashing must be closely fitted and tightly sealed, or water is sure to enter.

What it takes

Approximate time: One hour.

Tools and materials: Putty knife, caulking gun, screwdriver or cold chisel, hammer, asphalt roof cement, and roof paint.

Water can run down the vent pipe and into the house if the lead flashing around the pipe's neck becomes loose. Tamp it with a cold chisel or screwdriver so that the boot grips the pipe tightly all around its circumference.

Caulk vent flashing with roof cement, covering partway up the pipe. Pick up the covering shingles where you can and apply roof cement underneath them. Then press them back in place.

Replacing flashing

Metal chimney flashing should usually be replaced outright as soon as it begins to leak. Holes tend to develop in the corners of metal flashing and in rust areas. Flashing made of asphalted felt or roll-roofing paper begins to melt after a while. When you see tarry streaks running down the chimney inside the house, you know it's time to replace felt or paper flashing, even if it isn't leaking. If you are laying a new roof you should install new flashing because this job is much easier to do when the new shingles are being applied. Metal flashing is so much more durable, leak-resistant, and easier to maintain than the felt-and-paper types that it is worth the investment.

What it takes

Approximate time: Varies with the job. Allow a full day to replace flashing around chimney, half a day around vent pipe. Fitting the new flashing is often time consuming and trying.

Tools and materials: Flat chisel, pry bar, putty knife, hammer, mason's trowel, pointer, wire brush, 1½-inch roofing nails, sheet metal, roof cement, patching mortar, shingles, sheet-metal shears, and boot-type vent flashing.

Repairs around chimneys

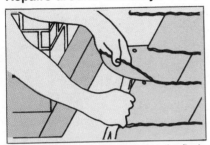

1. Remove the shingles covering the flashing. Get under the nail heads with a wide, thin chisel; then lift them out with a pry bar. Chip away the mortar and caulking that secure the flashing to the chimney.

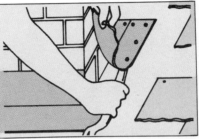

2. Remove the nails that fasten the flashing to the sheathing. Then pull the flashing away from the chimney. But keep the old flashing intact; you will use it as a pattern for cutting out a replacement.

3. If the old flashing was of soft material, cut a pattern out of heavy cardboard. You will need separate patterns for base flashing and cap flashing. Try your patterns for size on the chimney. Adjust until they fit.

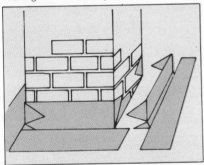

4. Cut the new flashings with sheet-metal shears and adjust each section of base flashing to the chimney for a snug fit. Trim as necessary. Then assemble, cementing mating surfaces and undersides. Nail bottom flange to sheathing.

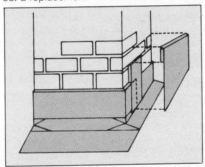

5. Bend lips in cap flashing to fit two inches into horizontal space between bricks; bend flaps around sides of bricks. Cut bottom of cap flashing to match roof's pitch.

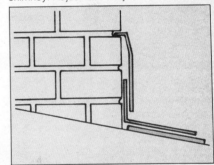

6. Fasten cap in place by filling space between bricks with patching mortar. After mortar has cured, caulk space with roof cement. Replace shingles, coating nail heads.

Repairs around vents

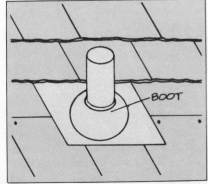

1. Remove shingles around pipe. Chip off cement holding boot to roof. Lift off boot. Wire-brush cement off pipe. If you tore roofing paper, patch with 15-pound roofing felt.

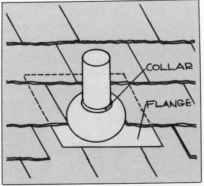

2. Slide new boot down pipe. Adjust flange until it is flush with roof; then cement. Do not nail. Slip collar down pipe and push into tight union with boot. Replace shingles, coating nail heads with cement.

New wrinkles

Plastic boots are now available for flashing vent pipes. They are easier to install than metal ones. Leaks around electrical service masts can also be stopped with boot flashing.

Valley flashing

What it takes

Approximate time: Will vary from an hour (roll-roofing an open valley) to several hours, depending on material and extent of damage.

Tools and materials: Hammer, putty knife, pry bar, metal shears, roofing cement, 1½-inch roofing nails, sheet metal, 15-pound roofing felt, and roll roofing.

Two different methods are used to waterproof the valleys formed where two slopes of a roof meet. When the shingles border the valley but do not enter it, the flashing is called open valley. But when the shingles cover the flashing entirely, it is called a closed valley.

The flashing used in valleys may be roll roofing or sheet metal. Either material may develop cracks or holes from age, damage,

or decomposition. Open-valley flashing is of course easier to work with than closed valley. Replacing the latter is a big job because the covering shingles must be replaced with new ones. However, leaks in closed-valley flashing can be patched (without any need to tear and replace the shingles) by forcing overlapping squares of sheet metal under the shingles as shown in the second sequence below.

Open valley

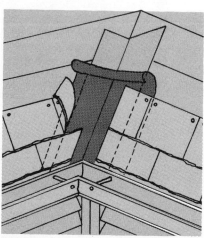

To patch a hole in a valley flashed with metal, cut a piece from the same kind of metal. Make it big enough to overlap the hole at least an inch. Coat the area with roofing cement. Press the patch in place and hold it down for several minutes. To patch a hole in roll roofing, cut the patch from 15-pound roofing felt and apply as above.

To patch a strip of metal flashing, remove the holding nails from adjacent shingles. Do not remove the old metal flashing. Cut a strip of roll roofing to cover the flashing and extend at least 4 inches under the shingles on either side of the valley. Nail the shingles back in place, and seal the nail heads with roofing cement.

To replace roll-roofing flashing, pry out the holding nails. The flashing will be cemented to the shingles, so separate them carefully with a broad-bladed putty knife, and pull out the old flashing. Cut a strip of roll roofing the same size as the old flashing. Slip it back under the shingles and nail it in place along each side so the nail heads are covered by the overlapping shingles. Cement the nail heads and shingle tabs to the new flashing.

Closed valley

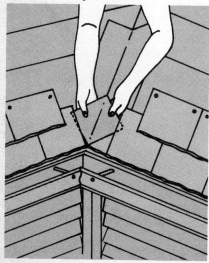

1. To patch holes in a closed valley, cut squares of metal large enough to extend at least 2 inches under the second shingle on each side. Bend squares to fit the angle of the valley.

2. Start at the bottom of the valley and slip the squares under the shingles and over the old flashing until all the leaky areas have been covered. Insert roofing cement with a caulking gun between the metal squares and the shingles.

3. Lift out any nails that prevent you from pushing a square into place. Use a pry bar. Replace the nails and seal nail heads with roofing cement.

Chimney repairs

Chimneys should be inspected each year just before the cold season. Inspection reduces chances of fire and increases chimney efficiency. You will see more if you inspect the chimney from the top. If it's a bright day, reflect sunlight down it with a mirror. Or use a flashlight. If you can't look down a chimney, inspect it with a strong flashlight and a mirror from a fireplace, from the cleanout door at the base, or through a flue opening for a stove pipe.

Look for obstructions such as birds' nests and for thick deposits of soot and tar. A hot fire can ignite these, turning your chimney into a torch.

To clean a chimney, weight a burlap bag with a chain and stuff it with paper or old clothes. Seal off the fireplace with wrapping paper and masking tape. Tie a strong rope around the neck of the bag and lower it all the way down the chimney. Extract the bag by giving the rope short, vigorous tugs. Lowering the bag should knock down any obstructions. Tugging it up will loosen tar and soot. When you are finished, dispose of the wrapping paper carefully so as not to track soot through the house.

If rain or drafts come down your chimney, you can install a deflector. This item is available in a variety of styles and material: concrete, wire, and conical caps in sizes to fit standard-size flues. In addition to keeping out wind and rain, a chimney deflector can end a bird's-nest problem and trap flying sparks.

If you see smoke oozing out from between your chimney bricks, you may have a cracked flue. Don't use the chimney until the flue is checked and fixed by a pro.

Sooner or later the mortar between the bricks in chimneys begins to bake dry or weather away. If cracks are allowed to form, water can get in and cause serious leaks. And if the mortar deteriorates beyond a certain point, a strong wind could topple a section of the chimney.

Electrical heating tapes

After a heavy snow, ice dams can easily form on roof overhangs, causing trapped water to back up under shingles and enter the house. You can forestall this by cleaning gutters and drains in late fall and providing soffit ventilation (page 16) and extra insulation so roof snow melts evenly. Another method is to install electrical heating tapes that keep the overhang warm enough to prevent ice from forming. These usually come in pairs, one for the overhang and the other for the gutter and downspout.

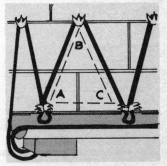

To determine how much tape you will need for your overhang, measure off the length of line **a-b-c** on your roof. Point **b** lies at the upper limit of the overhang; points **a** and **c** are a shingle's width apart. Then divide line **a-c** into the length of the gutter. Multiplying line **a-b-c** by this factor will give you the length you need for the overhang cable. The length of the gutter-downspout cable can be determined by direct measurement.

Lay one tape along the gutter and down the full length of the downspout. Zigzag the other across the overhang. Hold it in place by affixing clips to the asphalt shingles. If your shingles are slate or wood, use epoxy cement.

Tuck-pointing

1. Check your chimney for crumbling mortar. If you need to repair it, go easy as you chip away cracked, loose mortar in preparation for tuck-pointing, or remortaring. A chimney in bad shape could topple over at any time.

2. Wear safety goggles to protect your eyes against flying chips when you chip out old mortar with a hammer and cape chisel. Brush joints to remove dust and mortar fragments, then hose down the chimney to prevent the fresh mortar from drying out too quickly.

What it takes

Approximate time: Three hours.

Tools and materials: Goggles, 3/8-inch cape chisel, 2½-pound mason's hammer, trowel, pointer, rubber gloves, stiff brush, old broom, premixed mortar or your own mix (1 part portland cement, 1 part hydrated lime, 6 parts sand), and muriatic acid solution (10 parts water, 1 part acid).

3. Trowel smooth but not soupy mortar into the joints; then smooth neatly indented seams with a pointer. Let the mortar harden overnight; then, wearing rubber gloves, wash the bricks down with a solution of 1 part muriatic acid and 10 parts water to clean cement stains from the brick. Flush down chimney exterior with fresh water.

Preventing ice dams

What it takes

Approximate time: Inserting insulation—2 hours; installing strip vent—4 hours; installing vented soffit—3 hours; installing single vent—1 hour.

Tools and materials: Depending on the job, a hammer, wood chisel, saber or keyhole saw, chalk line, 10-penny nails, soffit vents or fully vented soffit, and insulation with vapor barrier.

Install insulation between rafters in the attic. Use insulation with a vapor barrier and leave air space between the vapor barrier and roof boards under an overhang. Insulation should be 6 inches deep.

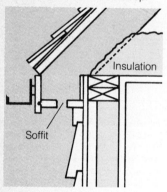

Heating tapes keep ice dams from forming, but they have several disadvantages. They consume electricity; somebody has to remember to turn them on when it starts to snow—and off when the roof is bare; and if you have to install an electrical box, you will incur additional expense (page 15).

You can avoid these problems by removing the conditions that cause ice dams to form in the first place. This can be done by adding insulation and by providing ventilation for the attic through the soffit, the wooden panel beneath the roof overhang.

There are three types of soffit ventilation: single vent units that fit into openings cut in the soffit; vented strips that fit into channels cut the full length of the soffit; and soffits that come with vent holes in them.

An additional benefit of vented soffits is that air flowing through them will keep the attic cooler in hot, sunny weather and allow it to cool more quickly at night. Vents in the gables or roof are essential for proper attic ventilation throughout the year.

Fitting a full-length vent

1. Mark cutting lines in the soffit for the channel into which you will fit the vent. The channel should be the width of the vent and begin 3 inches from the overhang. Snapping chalk lines is a quick, professional step.

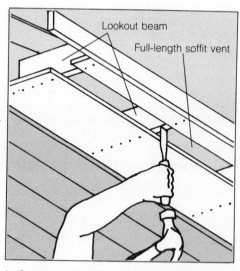

2. Cut the strip out of the soffit with a saber or keyhole saw. Chisel out the lookout beams so the vent will seat properly. When vent is in place, nail it to the lookouts.

Single vent units

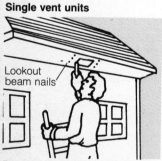

Pencil an outline of the single soffit vent in the soffit where you will place it. Be sure to position it between lookout beams; you can locate them by nail heads in the soffit. Cut the hole with a saber saw or keyhole saw. Screw the vent in position.

Installing a vented soffit

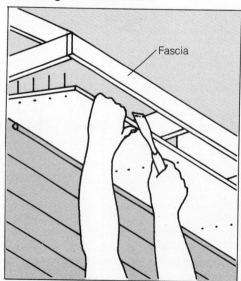

1. Pull the nails holding the present soffit to the lookouts and remove any molding; then remove the soffit with a pry bar.

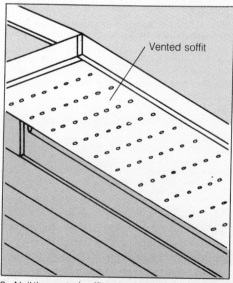

2. Nail the vented soffit to the lookouts and put back any molding. **TIP:** Paint the new soffit before you put it in place.

Gable vents

For adequate under-roof ventilation, air flowing in through soffit or eave vents must be able to get back out. Therefore vents are needed in the gables or roof. Proper air flow will not only forestall ice dams, but by allowing the escape of warm, moist air rising from living areas, it will also prevent rafters and roof sheathing from rotting. Good air circulation helps in another way, too. During the summer, an unvented attic can get as hot as 150 degrees Fahrenheit. This hot blanket radiates heat after the sun has set, keeping the house uncomfortable and putting an extra strain on the air conditioning downstairs.

Adequate circulation of attic air requires louvers in the gables or vents in the roof. If the pitch of your roof is shallow, you may need to install an electrically powered fan. As a rule of thumb, every 300 square feet of attic floor area requires a square foot of louver. (Add 50 percent more louver area, if you plan to screen them.) Two louvers in opposite gables are more efficient than one large one. You can purchase either rectangular or triangular louvers at lumber yards. The triangular type is more efficient and less evident, being fitted up under the roof. Get one with the same pitch as your roof. (See page 26 for measuring pitch.) Adjustable types are available. Installing a triangular louver is more difficult, but because it is more desirable, directions are given for installing this type. They can easily be adapted to the less difficult task of installing a rectangular louver.

What it takes

Approximate time: Six hours.

Tools and materials: Carpenter's rule, pencil, drill with 1-inch bit, saber or keyhole saw, hammer, 3-inch common nails, 2x4s, louvered vent unit, and roofing cement.

1. Draw a triangle on the inside wall to mark the opening. Its top should be as close to the bottom of the ridge beam as you can saw. At the three corners, drill starter holes.

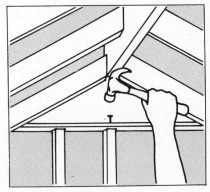

2. Cut out the opening with a saber or keyhole saw. Saw enough off the tops of any studs to fit in a 2x4 header as the base of the triangle. Nail two more 2x4s to the rafters to complete the frame.

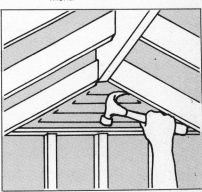

3. Slide the vent in place to ensure a snug fit. If necessary, adjust the 2x4s. Then apply roofing cement to the flange or lip on the outside of the vent. Insert in place and nail. Caulk the outside edges of the vent with roofing cement.

Roof vents

Another way to get adequate attic ventilation is to install a roof vent. Being on the roof, such a vent allows more air to escape than a comparable vent in the gables. Attics of any size require two roof vents, unless you use a unit with an electric fan. One such vent will suffice for areas as large as 2,000 square feet. The directions here apply to either type of unit, except that a fan will of course require electrical power.

Approximate time: Eight hours.

Tools and materials: Carpenter's rule, compass, pencil, drill with ½-inch bit, roofer's knife, hammer, 1½-inch roofing nails, and roof vent unit.

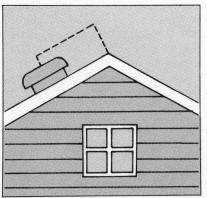

1. Lay the vent in position on the roof, as close to the ridge line as possible. If installing only one vent, position it as close to the center of the roof as possible. When the fan is in position, measure from the ridge line to the center of the fan.

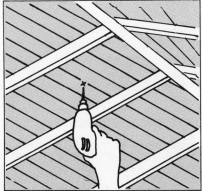

2. Measure down from the ridge line inside the attic. Drill a hole on center between two rafters. Back on top of the roof, scribe a circle equal to the diameter of the vent housing. Remove shingles and roofing paper within this circle.

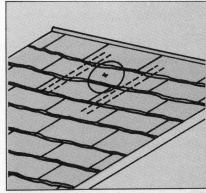

3. Cut away sheathing with a keyhole or saber saw. Do not cut rafters. Nail headers between rafters on either side of the hole. After caulking the base, slide the vent up under the loosened shingles. Fasten base to sheathing with roofing nails. Caulk the edges and restore the shingles around the vent.

Gutters and downspouts

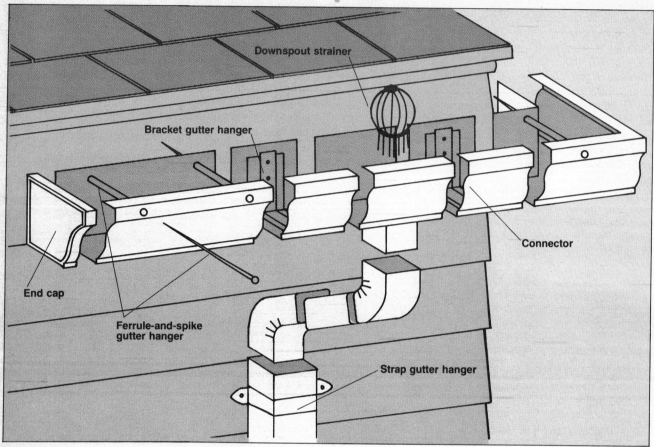

Downspout strainer

Bracket gutter hanger

Connector

End cap

Ferrule-and-spike
gutter hanger

Strap gutter hanger

Gutters and downspouts, also called leaders, have an important job to do in maintaining your house—its solidity as well as its exterior appearance. If your gutter/downspout system doesn't do its job of collecting and carrying water away, runoff can wash the topsoil away from the foundation below, cause basement flooding, and rot siding and fascia boards. Moreover, gutters and downspouts that are not properly maintained will have to be prematurely repaired or replaced. You can forestall these time-consuming and costly problems by adopting the following measures:

General maintenance

1. Insert strainers at the tops of all downspouts.
2. Cover gutters with leaf guards.
3. Correct overflowing and drips as soon as they are observed.
4. Paint galvanized steel gutters and downspouts; treat the exterior of wooden gutters with preservative.
5. Be sure that no downspout feeds onto a lower roof; connect it directly to a gutter.
6. Install splash blocks beneath open-ended downspouts.
7. Seal joints at connectors and end caps with caulking compound.

Fall / Spring maintenance

1. Remove debris from all gutters.
2. Clean strainers.
3. Rod out downspouts.
4. Look for evidences of gutter sags and improper pitch; test with a pail of water or a garden hose at full blast.
5. Check all hangers for loose nails and bent straps.
6. Inspect gutter alignment with fascia.
7. Tighten elbows from gutters to downspouts.
8. Inspect straps holding downspouts to the siding; hammer down any loose or popped nails.
9. Tighten elbows at the tops and the ends of downspouts.
10. Inspect topsoil under gutters and downspouts for erosion.

The case of the mysterious sags
I couldn't keep my gutters from sagging. Every time it rained, pools of water would collect in the low spots. Up the ladder I would go to bend them back into shape and hammer the spikes back into the rafters. But the problem persisted. One day a neighbor came by to see why I was spending so much of my spare time on a ladder. "You're the problem," he announced. That's when I learned not to rest a ladder on a gutter. It bends the gutter out of shape.
Practical Pete

Maintaining gutters

Some of the leaves, twigs, and other debris that land on your roof make their way into your gutters. Most of the light material is carried to the downspouts. But even swiftly flowing water does not carry everything along. Leaves rot, seeds sprout, balls and rocks impede. After a while, a neglected gutter along your roof can resemble a gutter in a neglected city street.

Gutters should be cleaned at least twice a year: in the autumn after most of the leaves have fallen, and again in the spring after seed pods and leaf buds have dropped. If a number of large trees are nearby, it may be necessary to clean your gutter more frequently. There is another reason for semi-annual cleaning: it gives you a chance to inspect your gutters. They are subject to considerable force in a heavy rain. And if you live in a cold climate, ice can form in gutters and as it expands, push them out of alignment or loosen joints.

What it takes

Approximate time: Two hours to clean and inspect the gutters of a typical two-story house. Twice as long to paint them.

Tools and materials: Rubber glove, ladder (with stabilizer if necessary), garden hose, hammer, screwdriver, metal shears, paintbrush, wire brush, leaf screen (hardware cloth or expanded metal screening), primer for galvanized steel, and paint.

Cleaning gutters

1. Muck out gutters by hand. Wear a rubber glove or old work glove for protection. Remember, do not rest the rails of the ladder on the gutter; this can push the gutter out of alignment and strain hangers. Keep an eye open for water or discolored spots that reveal sags or inadequate gutter pitch.

2. Hose down the gutter after you have removed most of the debris. This will flush out the last remnants while giving you an opportunity to observe the flow of water and look for low spots or improper pitch. Check for leaks at the joints and end caps. Be alert also for leaks caused by rust holes.

Inspect each hanger as you work your way along the gutter. You may spot bent straps and popped nails. If your house has fascia or board trim, check the gutter's alignment with it. The gutter should rest firmly against it for maximum support.

Keeping out debris

1. Install leaf guards in gutters under trees. The type shown comes in 3-foot sections. It is made of semirigid hardware cloth. You fit it into the gutter by compressing it. Once in the gutter, the screen snaps into place.

2. Fit rolled leaf guard by cutting sections of expanded metal screening to fit. One edge goes up under the shingles and the other down under the front lip of the gutter. This type is lighter than the snap-in type and can thus bend and crush more readily.

Paint galvanized steel gutters and downspouts, but only after they have been up for a year. Paint will blister on galvanized steel unless you first apply a special primer. Painting extends the life of galvanized steel greatly. If paint has begun to peel, wire-brush, prime, and paint the spots.

Maintaining downspouts

Being enclosed and vertical, downspouts are not subject to the same stress and wear that gutters are. But downspouts require regular maintenance and inspection. They become clogged; they develop leaks; they pull away from the house; they come apart; water from a heavy rain gushing out can force an elbow off.

Water from a defective gutter usually cascades over a fairly wide stretch. That's bad enough, but water from a defective downspout pours in a concentrated stream. In a very short period it can carry off topsoil, flood a window well, or put several inches of water in a cellar. It is no fun to have to clean up one of these messes; likewise to have to go out in a heavy rain and try to put a downspout back together again. A stitch in time saves nine. Here are five key aspects of preventive maintenance.

What it takes

Approximate time: One hour or less.

Tools and materials: Leaf strainer, hammer, caulking compound and gun, splash block, and downspout sleeve are among the items that may be useful.

1. Put strainers into the mouths of all downspouts. But don't force them deep into the neck; set them just far enough in so they remain in place. Because so much debris flows to downspouts, strainers should be inspected and cleaned more frequently than gutters.

2. Rod out the upper elbows of downspouts with a bent coat hanger. Use a plumber's snake if you have one. Even with strainers, debris can get into downspouts and build up in the bends.

Vulnerable parts of a downspout

Downspout fitting

Elbow

End elbow

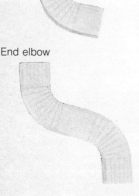

3. Grasp the elbow linking the gutter to the downspout. Make sure it is secure. When you are hosing down the gutters, look for leaks in the downspout, particularly in the joints of elbows. If you spot any leaks, seal them with caulking compound.

4. Check the nails or screws in the straps holding the downspout to the house. These can work themselves loose when a downspout has been used as a ladder support, or as a result of use and age.

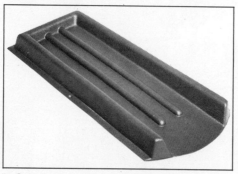

5. Control the direction in which water flows out of downspouts—unless it goes directly into a storm sewer, dry well, or underground drainage system. A splash block like the one shown will divert water in the desired direction. The open end of the downspout should be only a few inches above the splash block.

New wrinkle

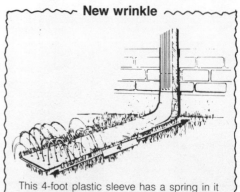

This 4-foot plastic sleeve has a spring in it that will coil it up and out of the way when rainwater stops flowing out the downspout. Water seeps from holes in the sleeve rather than streaming out from the downspout. An 8-foot model is available without the spring.

Repairing gutters and downspouts

Water from a leaky gutter can drip onto the cornice and down the siding. Over a period of years the resultant dampness can blister paint and cause the siding to rot. One response to a leaky gutter is to pull it off. But this is not a remedy. The fact that your house has gutters probably means that it needs them.

Often the water that leaks from gutters and downspouts comes from cracked seams or holes that have rusted through. In repairing gutters and downspouts, remember to use nails, screws, and sheet metal of the same material as the existing system—galvanized steel with galvanized steel, aluminum with aluminum, and copper with copper. If you mix metals, galvanic corrosion will take place where the two metals meet. This will eat new holes in your gutter or downspout.

Occasionally a gutter will leak even though it is free of holes and cracks. It leaks at its joints because the sections were not assembled correctly. Upper sections must overlap lower sections, not vice versa. The solution to this problem is to take the run down and lap the sections correctly: the open joint facing the direction the water will flow. The wrong and right ways are illustrated below:

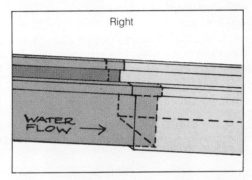

Wrong — WATER FLOW →

Right — WATER FLOW →

What it takes

Approximate Time: One hour.

Tools and materials: Wire brush, putty knife, sheet-metal shears, pliers, 100-grit sandpaper, roof cement, and sheet metal to match existing gutter.

Sealing holes

1. Wire-brush or sandpaper around the hole after first sweeping away the debris adjacent to the area. Clean the spot with paint thinner or other solvent.

2. Spread roof cement around the hole and in it with a putty knife. Be sure to keep the surface smooth; globs of cement in a gutter can catch twigs and leaves, damming water.

Patching holes

1. If a hole or crack is too large to be filled with roof cement, cut a matching pattern out of heavy paper to serve as a template for a patch. The patch must completely line the gutter and have a lip that fits over the gutter's outer edge.

2. Lay down a layer of roof cement before you fit in the patch, then crimp the lip of the patch over the gutter, and coat the patch with roof cement. Be sure to fill the joints between the patch and the gutter.

New wrinkles

A mixture of fiberglass and epoxy provides a quick, effective way to stop leaks in gutters and downspouts. It comes in a repair kit with mixing instructions. Application is similar to that used for roofing cement.

New gutters and downspouts

Calculating your needs

- A gutter section for every 10 feet of run.
- A hanger for every 3 feet of run; if you use the ferrule-spike type, one spike for every other rafter.
- Downspouts for both ends of runs 30 feet or longer. (Shorter runs can feed into a single downspout.)
- A connector for each joint between sections of the gutter.
- A drop outlet or downspout fitting for each downspout.
- An elbow for the top of each downspout.
- An elbow for the bottom of each downspout.
- An end cap for gutters next to downspouts.
- An outside corner wherever a gutter wraps around the house.
- One downspout strap for every 10 feet of run.

TIP: Get a helper. Lifting long gutter sections into place requires four hands.

Some gutters become so rusty and damaged that they should be replaced. Often it makes sense to put up an entire gutter run rather than fit in a single section or two. The finished run will look better and will eliminate repair work you would otherwise have to do later. If your house is an older one, you may want to install a complete new gutter-downspout system. This will give you an opportunity to select the material you want.

If you are replacing only a section or two, take a cross-sectional piece of the old gutter along when you buy the new one. You need an exact match of shape and metal. The standard length of a gutter section is 10 feet, but some gutters also come in longer lengths.

Should you decide to put up an entirely new system, consider the various materials in which gutters and downspouts are available, and select the best one for your needs. **Plastic** is simple to install and easy to maintain. The joints are sealed by a special mastic. Plastic gutters and downspouts expand on hot days and will buckle unless room is allowed at the joints.

Aluminum can be cut with a hacksaw, and its lightness makes it easier to lift into place. Because aluminum gutters and downspouts lack structural strength, they are easily dented. However, they resist corrosion well. In addition to their natural finish, they also come in white enamel.

Galvanized steel gutters and downspouts require priming and painting after a year, as detailed on page 18. You can avoid painting by buying enameled units, but these are more costly.

Copper leaders and gutters should be put up by a professional because the joints must be soldered. Copper is the most expensive material but the most durable and, when aged, the most handsome. Leaks in the seams, however, have to be resoldered occasionally.

Assembling the parts

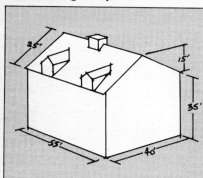

1. Make a sketch of the roof, if you plan to put up a new run or a complete system. To determine what and how much to buy, consult the requirements list above. Don't simply replace old elements; they may have been incorrect in the first place.

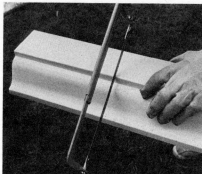

2. Cut a gutter section to length with a hacksaw. Support aluminum or plastic gutters from the inside with wood blocks. If the gutter is metal, remove the burrs with a file.

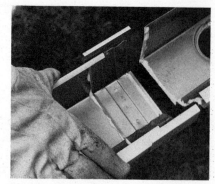

3. Assemble the gutter on a workbench. An important part of the job is fitting the connectors so that the joints don't leak. Apply caulking to gutter and connector before joining.

4. Tap the two sections together; then crimp the connector down over both sections. If you lap sections of the gutter instead of using connectors, put a ½-inch sheet-metal screw through each joint to keep the parts linked. Remember, the opening in the joint must face downstream.

5. Fasten the downspout fitting to the gutter after first applying caulking compound. Install this fitting on the *outside* of the gutter, rather than on the inside.

6. Crimp the end cap to the gutter, then secure with sheet-metal screws and caulking compound. The screws go through each side of the cap and into the gutter at the top. The gutter is now ready to be hung in place.

Pitching gutters

The water in gutters should flow swiftly enough to carry along leaves and other light debris to the downspouts. When it does not, a soggy mass builds up in the bottom of the gutter; if this is not cleaned out frequently, it promotes rust and corrosion; it can also cause damaging overflows.

For water to flow fast enough, gutters must have the proper pitch. The following instructions show how to repitch existing gutters and hang new ones correctly. Neither project calls for special skill.

Adjusting old gutters

1. Snap an absolutely level line on the trim board a few inches below the gutter from end to end. Use a carpenter's level to ensure accurate measurement.

2. Snap another line along the bottom of the gutter from end to end. **TIP:** If the gutter slopes below the trim, mark the lines on the ends of the rafters or along the eaves.

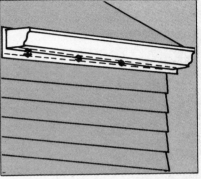

3. Measure the distance at intervals between the level line and the one marking the gutter's pitch. The gutter should slope ¼ inch toward the downspout for every 5 feet of run. Where it does not, adjust the gutter until it conforms to the proper pitch.

Hanging new gutters

1. Install the high end of the gutter in its permanent position. It should just touch the shingles. Support the downspout end in a sling of twine or wire wrapped around a nail.

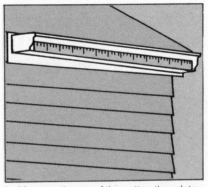

2. Measure the run of the gutter; then determine what the total drop should be. The standard slope is ¼ inch per 5 feet of run.

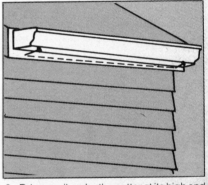

3. Drive a nail under the gutter at its high end and another at the downspout end where the bottom of the downspout must be to produce the required slope. Snap a chalk line between the two nails.

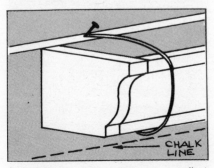

4. Loosen the sling so that you can adjust the slope of the gutter. Beginning at the high end, you will secure the gutter at 30-inch intervals or fasten it to every other rafter. As you work your way across, be sure the bottom of the gutter stays even with the sloping chalk line.

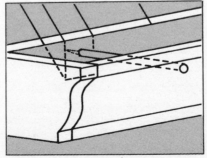

5. When the gutter is in position, pierce holes for the spikes—if you use ferrule-and-spike hangers. Drive the spikes into the ends of the rafters, rather than into the trim board or fascia.

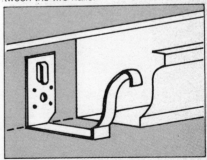

6. Screw the brackets into the fascia, if you are use to this type of hanger. To fasten the brackets, you will have to take down the gutter temporarily. The lower lip of the bracket goes on the chalk line.

Creating underground drainage

Over several rainy days, thousands of gallons of water can pour out of a downspout. If the ground slopes away from your house, splash blocks or downspout sleeves will usually distribute the water so that it does no damage. But if your house rests on level ground or in a slight basin, a heavy rain can flood your basement; light rains will keep it dank and mildewy. Strangely enough, an absolutely waterproof foundation poses an even greater problem. What can happen is this: As water seeps down and collects around the foundation, pressure builds up. This can become intense; one cubic foot of water weighs about 63 pounds. The force can reach the point where it will crack a concrete foundation or floor. Then the water floods in.

To prevent damp or flooded basements, it is necessary to have a means of carrying the water off underground. If your house is on a street that has a storm sewer, investigate the cost of linking up with it. This is often the simplest and least expensive solution. But if it is not feasible, you can create your own underground dispersal system in either of two ways. One is by digging a dry well. The other is by laying perforated plastic tubing under the ground. Water seeps from the perforations over a wide area, feeding the lawn as well as any nearby plants, shrubs, and trees. **CAUTION:** Building codes and health-department rules often control the use of storm sewers and the digging of dry wells. Check with the authorities before you dig. Keep dry wells and perforated tubing out of septic-tank fields. Do not run perforated tubing near trees, as this can attract roots. Hooking up with a sanitary system is not recommended.

What it takes

Approximate time: Up to four hours per 10-foot length of tubing, depending on soil type. A full day for a dry well.

Tools and materials: Shovel, rule, string, stakes, 4-inch-diameter flexible plastic tubing (perforated and non-perforated), downspout adapter, and pea gravel or 6A stone. For a dry well, you'll also need a trowel, plastic or terra cotta tile, a 55-gallon drum, gravel, rubble, planks or a concrete slab, and cement mix.

Laying tubing or drainage tile

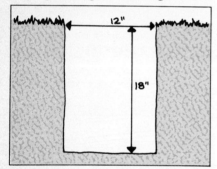

1. Dig a ditch from the downspout leading directly away from your house, following the dimensions shown above. A slope of 2 inches per 10 feet will promote rapid drainage. Make the slope continuous over the entire line, with no reversals in grade.

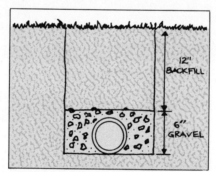

2. Bed the tubing or tile in a gravel or stone envelope as shown. You can also bed with backfill, but use only small, loose particles of earth that will flow around the tubing, and remove stones and clods to avoid excessive settling. Link tubing firmly to downspout with an adapter.

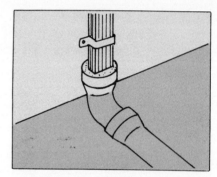

3. Make the first 10-foot section of tubing solid, not perforated, to divert water from the house. Use all solid tubing if you are connecting with a dry well or storm sewer. You can feed several downspouts into a single line to a dry well or storm sewer.

Digging a dry well

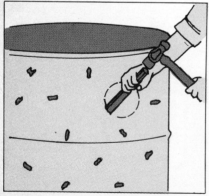

1. Chisel the top and bottom out of a 55-gallon drum, and make an opening in its side for 4-inch tubing. Then punch about three dozen holes around the sides of the drum for adequate drainage.

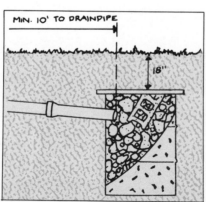

2. Place the drum in a hole dug to the depth shown and fill it with rubble: stones, bricks, broken cinder blocks. Insert the tubing into the drum; then cover the top with a slab or planks. Replace earth and sod.

Alternative method: Use cinder blocks alone instead of a steel drum. Dig a hole about 3 feet by 6 feet and line it with the blocks, leaving gaps of several inches and an opening for the tubing. Fill the hollow space with rubble, cover with planks, and replace earth and sod.

Reshingling a roof

Sometimes it becomes necessary or desirable to reshingle a roof. The old shingles may have become brittle or curled. With asphalt shingles, loss of the mineral granules speeds deterioration. Reshingling a roof is a project that demands careful planning and execution. It also involves hard work. On a multistory house, it is *hazardous* work. But putting asphalt shingles on a roof is within the capabilities of the homeowner who is willing to plan, take pains, and move cautiously when on the roof or ladder. The reward is saving 50 percent or more of what a roofing contractor would charge for the job.

A package of asphalt shingles usually contains a set of step-by-step directions for laying that particular type of shingle. While such directions were prepared by the manufacturer for professional roofers, you will be able to follow them once you have grasped the procedures and techniques explained on this and the following pages.

Several factors affect your choice of shingles and method of application: slope of the roof, wind velocity, and direction. The priority consideration, however, is your physical safety and that of anybody helping you. If yours is a two-story house, you would do well to obtain special scaffolding from a rental outlet, or construct or buy the ladder hooks shown on page 7.

ladder hooks shown on page 7.

Planning hints:

Before starting to reshingle:
- Inspect the chimney and tuckpoint if necessary.
- Realign the gutters, replacing defective ones.
- Repair or replace any rotting wooden trim.
- Check for signs of moisture condensing on the sheathing caused by inadequate ventilation in the attic or crawl space.
- Obtain scaffolding, ladder hooks, etc., needed to make reroofing less risky.
- Obtain tarp or other cover for roofs overnight.
- Wait for a weather prediction of zero percent rain probability over the next 48 to 72 hours.

When and how to remove old shingles

New asphalt shingles can be put down over old asphalt shingles, wood shingles, and roll roofing. Cedar shakes, however, must be taken off as must slate shingles. Here are the general tests for whether or not you have to remove the old shingles:

1. Are the roof supports strong enough to carry the added weight of the new shingles, plus that of yours and any helpers who will be on the roof with you? Usually, yes.
2. Is the deck solid enough to provide anchorage for the nails? (Nails should go into sheathing at least ¾ of an inch and go completely through ⅝-inch plywood.)
3. Does the decking provide a continuous nailing surface, with solid sheathing?

If you can't answer yes to all three of these questions, the old shingles must go.

1. Remove old shingles with a wide, flat shovel. You can take the old felts off the same way. **TIP:** If the deck under the old shingles is spaced sheathing, begin at the ridge so that debris does not fall through the spaces into the house.

2. Use a pry bar to remove the soil stack and the vent flashings. The old shingles, flashings, and felt create a large volume of debris. Sweep the deck clean periodically and remove debris from the gutters. Loose material underfoot is especially hazardous on a pitched roof.

What it takes

Approximate time: The time it will take you to tear off shingles from a roof depends on the roof size and whether your house has one or two stories. A good worker can rip up 200-300 shingles an hour.

Tools and materials: Claw hammer, pry bar, shovel, No. 15 asphalt-saturated felt, 1-inch roofing nails, ladder, and scaffolding.

3. Inspect the deck for holes, rotted or broken sheathing, and loose or protruding nails. Patch over the holes with sheet metal. Hammer down the nails. Replace defective sheathing. If the old deck was spaced sheathing, cover it with ⅝-inch plywood.

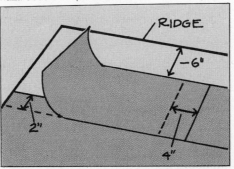

4. Apply No. 15 asphalt-saturated felts to the deck. Lay the felts horizontally, lapping each course 2 inches over the lower one; where ends join, lap them 4 inches. Lap the felt 6 inches from both sides of hips and ridges. Nail every 2 inches along the outside edges. Note: This underlayment is for roofs having a pitch of 4 inches per foot or greater.

Calculating your shingle needs

What it takes

Approximate time: Under an hour.

Tools and materials: Carpenter's rule, pencil, and pad of grid paper, or house plans if available.

Shingle requirements are estimated in *squares*. A square of roofing covers 100 square feet of roof. The number of packages of shingles making up a square varies according to the type of shingle, as does the number of shingles in a package. To find out the number of squares you need, you have to compute the area of the roof in square feet, divide by 100, and then add 10 percent for waste and cutting.

To compute the area of your roof, you need to know the dimensions of its sloping plane. This can involve you in dangerous scampering, unless you have a copy of the plans. A much safer, simpler way is to determine the horizontal area your roof covers by taking direct measurements on the ground, and calculate its pitch, as shown below. Then take these figures to your roofing supplier, who will convert them into slope area and then into squares.

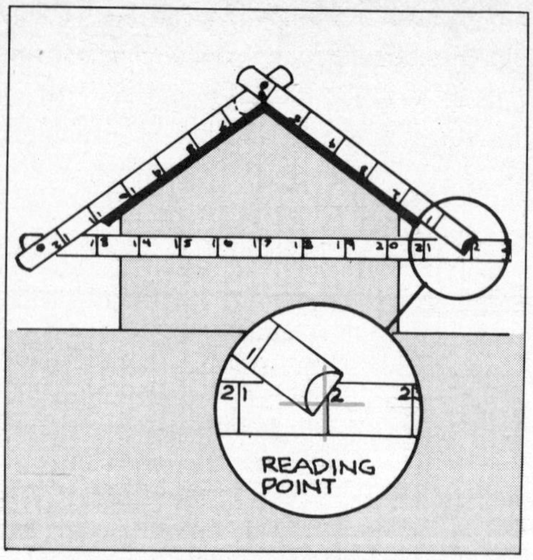

1. Step back from your house until you can frame it within a triangle formed by a carpenter's rule, as shown. Keeping the base of the triangle horizontal, adjust its sides until they align with the roof. Read the base of the rule at the reading point.

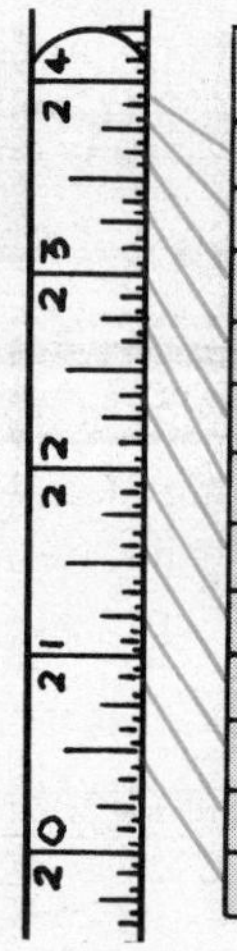

Rule reading	Pitch fraction	Rise-in. per foot
23 15/16	1/24	1
23 13/16	1/12	2
23 5/8	1/8	3
23 3/8	1/6	4
23 1/16	5/24	5
22 3/4	1/4	6
22 3/8	7/24	7
22	1/3	8
21 5/8	3/8	9
21 1/4	5/12	10
20 7/8	11/24	11
20 1/2	1/2	12

2. Locate the reading on the line marked Rule Reading in this chart. In the example, the reading on the rule is 22; this represents a 1/3 pitch with 8 inches of rise per horizontal foot. For any given horizontal area and pitch, a roof has the same slope area, regardless of its design or type.

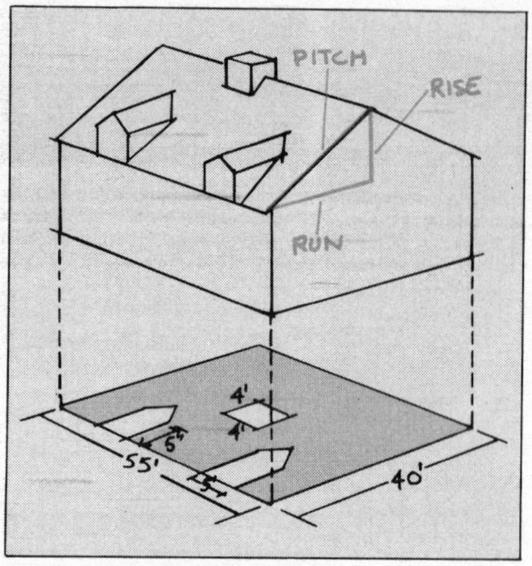

Map the horizontal area covered by your roof, leaving out areas occupied by a chimney and where one element of the roof projects over another. Be sure to figure the pitch over dormers separately.

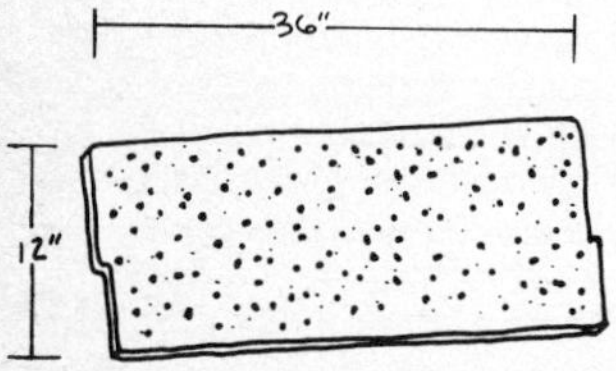

One-tab shingle (no cutout)

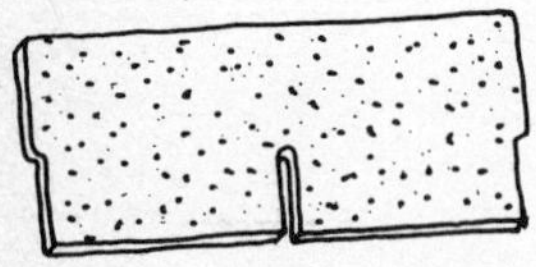

Two-tab shingle

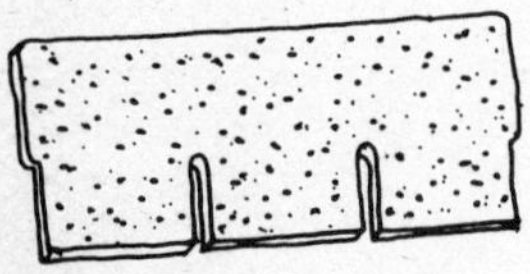

Three-tab shingle

Selecting shingles

Shingles are a simple product that have several difficult and essential jobs to do. They have to shed water. They must not blow off and away. They should resist fire from chimney sparks. They ought to look nice and last long. In recent years many shingle manufacturers have devoted large sums to research; as a result, you now have a variety of improved asphalt shingles to select from. For example, white asphalt shingles often turned a gray-green from algae and fungi. Several manufacturers now use granules on white shingles that repel mildew-forming organisms.

A local building code may specify the rating of the shingles you put on. Chances are it will be an Underwriters' Laboratory Class C. Even if you are not covered by a building code, you should purchase nothing less fire resistant than a Class C shingle. If your roof is exposed to high winds, consider buying a self-sealing shingle whose flaps won't raise even in a 60-knot gale. You can, however, seal down shingles yourself with a technique shown opposite.

Maintaining proper alignment is difficult, particularly when putting new shingles down over old. If the latter is the case, try to find shingles that have the same dimensions as the old. Fitting and applying shingles will be simplest for you if you select one of the square-butt types.

Preparing old surfaces

When you are planning to put asphalt shingles down over old wood shingles, you have to prepare the surface to receive the new roofing. Here are the things you should do beforehand:

1. Replace missing shingles with new ones.
2. Nail down all loose shingles.
3. Remove all loose or protruding nails; drive new nails but not into the old nail holes, as this will cause them to pop.
4. Split badly warped or curled shingles and nail down the segments.

When the shingles along the eaves and up the rakes—the outside edges of the roof—are badly weathered, prepare the surface according to the steps below. Feathering strips nailed as shown will produce a more professional job.

Cut the shingles back far enough so that wood strips can be fitted in. Nail these strips in place with the outside edges projecting beyond the deck the same distance the wood shingles did.

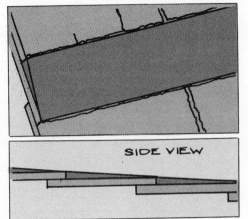

SIDE VIEW

Build a smooth deck for asphalt shingles by nailing beveled feathering strips along the butt of each course of the old shingles. This will give the new roof a more even appearance and anchor the nails better.

What it takes

Approximate time: Maximum times are likely to be 2 hours to prepare surface, 8 hours to cut and fit edges, 4 hours to put down feathering strips, 4 hours to install drip edge, and 3 hours to apply eave flashing.

Tools and materials: Claw hammer, wood chisel, metal shears, ladder, broom, 1x4 or 1x6 boards, noncorrosive metal, 1½-inch roofing nails of same material, and 8-penny wire nails.

The preparation procedure is simpler when you are reshingling over asphalt shingles. Nail down or cut away all loose, curled, or lifted shingles. Remove all loose and protruding nails. Replace all badly worn edges with new edging. Just before you apply the new shingles, sweep the surface clean of all debris.

One advantage of tearing off shingles is that you can install a drip edge along the eaves and the rakes. But you can also install a drip edge on the wood strips you fit when preparing to cover wood shingles. A drip edge provides a neater, more watertight corner. Water drips from it more readily than from wood.

Another advantage of applying roofing to a clean deck is that you can apply flashing at the eaves if you live in a region where ice dams are a problem. (See pages 15–16.)

UNDERLAYMENT

Cut a strip of corrosion-resistant metal wide enough to cover the edge and extend 3 inches back on the roof. Apply it over the No. 15 asphalt-saturated felt used as underlayment. Bend the strip down over the edges. Secure with roofing nails of the same metal as the strip. Drive a nail every 10 inches along the strip.

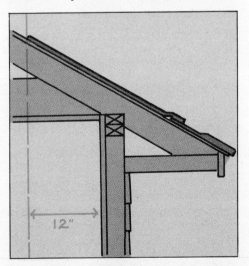

Lay a strip of roll roofing, smooth or mineral surface, over the roofing felt and drip edge. The flashing should be wide enough to extend up the roof at least 12 inches inside the interior wall line.

Applying shingles

A smooth, well-patterned, asphalt-shingle roof is within the reach of anybody who can carefully follow the directions below. They are written for the application of three-tab shingles but could easily be adapted for other types as well.

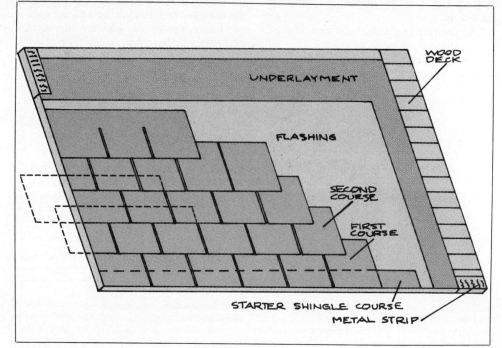

It didn't take me long to catch on
There I was working from a ladder, trying to get a shingle in place in the very first course. I forgot myself and reached out to the side. The ladder started to slide, and I grabbed for the gutter. I didn't fall, but my hammer did. As soon as my wife got the ladder back in place, I climbed right down and bought a ladder stabilizer like the one you can see back on page 7.

Practical Pete

What it takes

Approximate time: Two hours to apply a square (100 square feet); roof area will determine total time.

Tools and materials: Hammer, carpenter's rule, chalk line, ladder, scaffolding, special tab cement, and galvanized steel or aluminum roofing nails with ⅜-inch heads. Nail length will vary from 1½ inches on a clean deck, to 1¾ inches over old asphalt shingles, to 2 inches over wood shingles.

TIPS:
Do not store asphalt shingles directly on the ground or on the roof overnight.
Cover shingles with a tarp, not with plastic (moisture can condense underneath plastic).
Stack shingles no higher than 4 feet.

1. Remove the tabs from shingles needed for a starter course, which should be placed under the first visible course. Cut 3 inches off the side of the first shingle so that cutouts of shingles in this course will not coincide with those of the first course. Place starter-course shingles so they overhang eaves and rakes ¼ inch.
2. Start the first course with a full-length shingle. Its top edge should line up with the butt edge of the old shingle in the next higher course. If it doesn't, make it fit by cutting along its top edge. Trim the remaining shingles in the course to make the same fit.
3. Cut 4 inches (or half a tab) from the first shingle in the second course and 8 inches (or a full tab) from the first shingle in the third course. On the fourth course, begin to repeat the process that you started with the first course. Continue it for the rest of the roof. Varying the length of starting shingles over three courses ensures that joints and cutouts in one course are not aligned with those in the next.
4. Apply shingles across and up, rather than completely laying one course before starting the next one up. This method will make less noticeable any package-to-package color variation by spreading shingles from one package fanlike over several courses rather than stringing them out in a few rows.
5. Align each shingle carefully. Make sure that cutouts and end joints are no closer than 2 inches from any nail in the underlying course. Follow the manufacturer's specifications for exposure. Lay the butt edge of the tabs even with the top of the cutouts in the course below.
6. Start nailing from the end of the shingle that adjoins the shingle you just laid, and move across the shingle from there, using four nails per shingle. Drive nails straight so the edge of the nail head does not cut into the shingle. Hammer nail heads flush, not into the asphalt surface. Replace immediately any shingle you cut into or rip.
7. Begin to shingle at the rake that is most visible and work toward the other one. Where a roof is interrupted by a valley or dormer, begin at the rake and lay shingles toward the break.
8. If your roof is exposed to high winds and the shingles you bought don't have factory-applied adhesive, put a spot of special tab cement about the size of a 50-cent piece under each tab. Use a putty knife or caulking gun. Don't bend shingles back more than is neccessary. Press the tab down. Cement should not come out beyond edge of tab.

Shingling hips and ridges

Before applying new shingles at a ridge, remove the old ridge cap. Do the same for hips. Replace any badly deteriorated shingles with new shingles to provide a good nailing surface. Do not use metal material on hips or ridges. Corrosion may discolor and ruin the appearance of the roof.

To cover hips and ridges, you can buy shingles made specially for that purpose, or you can cut rectangular pieces not less than 9x12 inches from the shingles you are applying to the main roof. Here is the fitting and nailing procedure.

1. Bend a shingle lengthwise along the center so that it will have equal coverage on each side of the hip or ridge. In cold weather, warm the shingles inside the house before bending them.
2. Begin at the lower end of a hip, or at either end of a ridge, and lay the shingles over the edge, securing each side with a nail 5½ inches from the exposed end and 1 inch up from the edge. Lay the succeeding shingles to obtain a 5-inch exposure. On ridges, apply laps away from the direction of the prevailing wind.

Flashing valleys

If you are covering old shingles, it is not necessary to replace the valley flashing unless it leaks or is deteriorating badly. But in working on a roof, do not step in the valleys. When you put down new flashing in valleys, the following procedure, known as open-valley flashing, is recommended. It works equally well on a roof whose shingles you have just torn off, on one where you are covering old shingles, or on a new roof.

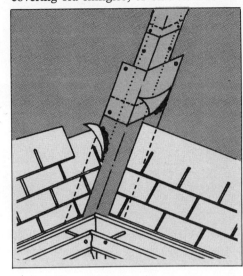

1. Lay an 18-inch-wide strip of mineral-surface roll roofing, surfaced side down, along the full length of the valley. Cut the lower edge flush with the eave flashing. Secure with two rows of nails, 1 inch in from the sides. Nail one entire row before you begin the second. As you proceed along the second row, press the roofing firmly in place in the valley.

2. Place a 36-inch-wide strip of the roll roofing, surfaced side up, centered in the valley. Secure it the same way you did in the first strip. On both strips use only enough nails to hold the paper in place. If you have to splice a strip, make the ends of the upper segment overlap the lower segment by 12 inches and secure with asphalt cement.

3. Snap two chalk lines the full length of the valley. The lines should be 6 inches apart at the ridge and diverge at the rate of ⅛ inch per foot. Thus a valley 8 feet long, for example, will be 7 inches wide at the eaves. Trim the shingles to the chalk line. Cut off the upper outside corner of each shingle to deflect water into the valley. Secure the shingles with asphalt cement. Do not nail within the chalk lines.

Flashing and shingling dormers

Open-valley flashing is a good way to obtain waterproof, water-shedding roofing in the joint between a dormer and the main roof. Follow the procedure described above for flashing the valley between two roofs, but note the following special techniques that apply to flashing a dormer valley:

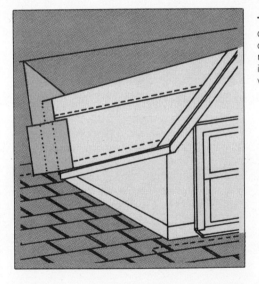

1. Continue the courses of main-roof shingles to a point just above the lower end of the valley. Then lay the 18-inch strip of roll roofing. Extend its bottom end ¼ inch below the edge of the dormer deck.

2. Fit the second strip of roll roofing, cutting the dormer side to match the lower end of the underlying strip. Cut the side that lies on the main deck to overlap the course of shingles. Make this overlap the same as the shingle-to-shingle overlap.

3. Snap vertical and horizontal lines to ensure proper alignment of courses above the dormer. You want the edges of shingles to be in line and any cutouts to be vertical.

Flashing a vertical wall

When reshingling a roof that abuts a vertical wall, you face a special flashing problem. But you can handle it with the simple technique described below.

1. Lay a strip of smooth roll roofing 8 inches wide over the old shingles next to the wall. Nail this strip down with a row of nails along each edge, spaced about 4 inches apart.

2. Cover the strip with asphalt cement just before you apply a shingle over it. The end of each new course is secured by bedding the shingle in asphalt cement. No nails are used in the finish course. When you have completed the roof, lay a bead of asphalt cement in the joint with a caulking gun. It will tighten the joint and improve its appearance.

What it takes

Approximate time: To flash a valley, 2 hours; to flash and shingle a dormer, 3 hours; to flash a joint between a vertical wall and roof, 1½ hours.

Tools and materials: Hammer, caulking gun, carpenter's rule, chalk lines, mineral-surface roll roofing, smooth-surface roll roofing, asphalt cement, and galvanized or aluminum roofing nails.

4.SIDING

Unlike roofing, siding can and should last as long as the house itself. But regardless of the material it consists of—even aluminum or vinyl—siding requires maintenance.

It pays to inspect siding once a year. The early spring is a good time. You can spot any winter damage; shrubs around the foundation will not yet have leafed, so you can see more. Look for peeling paint, blisters, loose or warped boards, cracks, shrunk caulking, and evidence of termites. While you're at it, prune back shrubs that have grown closer than two feet to the house, and pull down all climbing vines.

Maintaining wood siding

Wood is the most common siding and has a number of advantages over the newer materials: ease of repair and replacement, higher insulation and soundproofing value, and greater resistance to dents. On the other hand wood is subject to decay and deterioration. During your annual inspection, check for signs of rotting in your siding. If you spot the decay early enough, you can often prevent real damage. Look also for peeling or blistered paint. Water is usually the culprit. Often it is not water from the outside but from the inside. Warm, moist vapor from the house flows through the walls and, reaching the cold sheathing, condenses. Even a few drops of water between the siding and the film of paint will cause paint to blister and peel. Moisture doesn't reveal itself on unpainted wood siding, but if present will start wood rotting. The answer to such a problem is to install vents in the siding. There are several different types available. The two below are the most popular.

What it takes

Approximate time: Two or three hours for preventive maintenance of an average house.

Tools and materials: Brace and bit, hammer, scraper, paintbrush, vents, latex caulk, and latex paint.

Venting wood siding

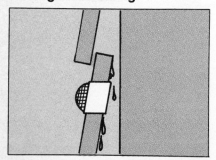

Drill holes in the siding the same diameter as the vent you are installing. Locate the holes between the studs and 6 inches below the ceiling level. Line the holes with latex caulk. Insert the vent. Plug-type vents can be used on flat siding as well.

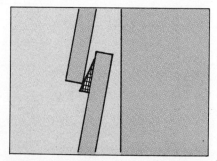

Push a wedge-shaped vent under the lower edge of clapboard siding. This type of vent is made of plastic or aluminum. It is permanent, being held in place by pressure from the clapboard. The vents should be 2 feet apart in the problem area.

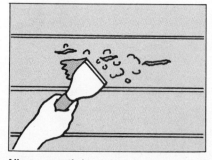

Allow a month for moisture to escape and the siding to dry. Then scrape off the blistered and peeling area, and repaint with latex exterior paint.

Repairing wood siding

One of the advantages of wood siding is that it's easy to repair or splice a replacement piece into any gaps. A wood shingle in a siding is repaired or replaced in the same way as a wood shingle on a roof. See the directions on page 10. In addition to shingles, wood siding comes in a variety of boards. The siding type will govern how the repair or replacement is made.

The most common wood siding is clapboard. There are two types. One has a tapered profile, thicker at the bottom and gradually narrowing toward the top. This is called beveled siding. The other type has a uniform thickness.

A course of clapboard overlaps the one below it. Nails in the bottom of the upper course go through the top of the clapboard below. Despite the overlapping, it is easy to replace a piece of defective clapboard.

Your house, or portions of it, may also have vertical board-and-batten siding. This is the easiest type of siding to replace.

Holes occasionally occur in wood siding. Regardless of the type of siding, they are patched the same way.

What it takes

Approximate time: One-half hour per defective board.

Tools and materials: Hammer, chisel, putty knife, wooden wedges, electric drill with ⅛-inch bit, finishing nails, waterproof glue, wood putty, and oil-based caulking and gun.

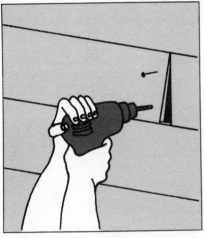

Straighten warped or buckled clapboards by first removing nails. Then sandpaper any joints that were too tight. The board will now need new nails to hold it in place. But to avoid splitting the wood, drill pilot holes for the nails. Set the nails and fill holes with wood putty or caulking.

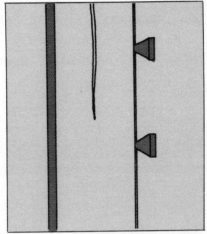

Repair splits in board-and-batten siding by forcing waterproof glue into cracks. To close a large split, remove the strip of batten and force one or more wooden wedges into the exposed joint along the length of the split.

Clean all dust and debris from a hole in wood siding. Deepen the hole around the edges if it is too shallow there to retain a filling. Fill the hole with several layers of wood putty, allowing each layer to dry for several hours. This will prevent the center from sinking as it dries. Sand and paint the next day.

Closing splits in clapboard

1. Close gaps by gluing the parted sections together. Remove the nails in the lower section, then pry it out, being careful not to split the board more. Coat exposed edges of both sections with waterproof glue and work some into the crack.

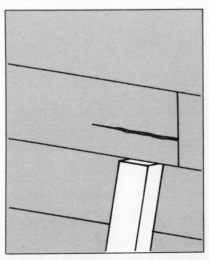

2. Wedge a 2x4 between the ground and the clapboard to hold it tight until the glue sets. Wipe off excess glue. If wedging is impractical, nail a board under the split to clamp the crack tightly.

Stopgaps and copouts

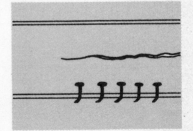

Cracked, warped, or loose siding should be repaired as soon as you notice it. Water works its way through such defects into the interior wall, where rotting can take place undetected. If you don't have time for a thorough repair, seal the splits with oil-based caulking compound and clamp them together by driving nails and clinching them over the boards. This method is recommended as a temporary expedient only.

Replacing wood siding

Some wood siding becomes so badly split, warped, or rotted that the boards can no longer be made weatherproof by repairing them. Such boards should be replaced. Because of their overlapping pattern, clapboards must be replaced differently from board-and-batten siding. Replacing the latter is simpler, but neither job is difficult.

The ideal time to replace siding is just before you are going to paint the house. This is because the spliced-in piece will have to be painted or treated, and if you cover only it, the contrast with the rest of the siding will be of the sore-thumb variety.

Patching clapboard

What it takes

Approximate time: One or two hours per patch.

Tools and materials: Hammer, backsaw, 2-inch chisel, ½-inch chisel, screwdriver, nail set, paintbrush, 1¼-inch galvanized or aluminum finishing nails, wood putty, and paint or stain to match existing siding.

1. Cut the board at each end of the deteriorated section. If a joint is nearby, use it to save a saw cut even though the section contains some good wood. Start the cutting with a backsaw and finish it with a large, flat chisel.

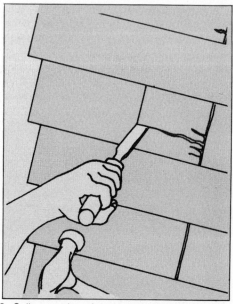

2. Split out strips of the deteriorated section with the chisel, being careful not to damage the building paper and sheathing underneath. Pull out the nails in the overlapping board and chisel out the remains of the damaged board beneath it.

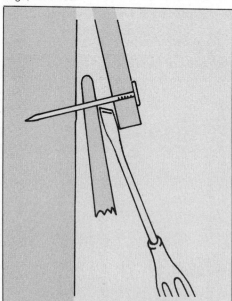

3. Trim the hidden edges of the cut-out section with a small chisel so that they are even with the exposed edges. You can push a screwdriver up under the overlapping board so you have room to work and to see what you are doing. Replace any building paper you cut into.

4. Measure the new board so that it makes a tight patch. Drive it into place so that its butt edges line up with those of the boards on either side. Drive nails and set. Fill the nail holes with wood putty. When putty is dry, paint or stain the board.

Patching vertical siding

Most vertical siding is either board or strips of plywood, and batten. The boards are generally 1x12 feet in size. Except for removing the batten strips, the same procedure can be used for patching any defective piece of vertical siding. **TIP:** If your siding is plywood, be sure to make the patch out of exterior grade plywood.

What it takes

Approximate time: One hour per patch.

Tools and materials: Claw hammer, small pry bar, saber saw, 1¼-inch galvanized or aluminum finishing nails, and wood putty.

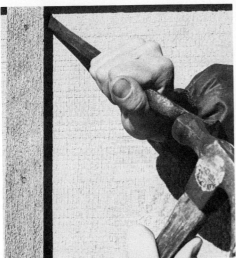

1. Remove the battens on both sides of the board, using a small pry bar. Then pull out the nails that hold the board to the studs. Be careful when pulling the nails not to scar the exposed surface, nor enlarge any holes you are not going to reuse. Then lift out the board or plywood section.

2. Trim off the defective portion and place it over the new board or plywood. Using the old piece as a pattern, mark cutting lines on the new one. Cut the patch with a saber saw. Nail the patch and remaining section of the old wood in place. Fill the joint between the two pieces with wood putty. Replace the battens.

Repairing aluminum

Aluminum is one of the most popular materials for nonwood siding. Aluminum siding does not need repainting and lasts indefinitely. But it is susceptible to denting; a baseball, even a heavy hailstorm can mar it. Fortunately such dents are usually easy to remove. A more serious but less common problem with aluminum siding is that if not correctly applied, sections may buckle from the heat of the summer sun. Then it is necessary to remove the siding and install it correctly, straightening or replacing the buckled section. This process is simple if the correct sequence is followed.

What it takes

Approximate time: One-half hour for a dent; two hours to replace a section.

Tools and materials: Screwdriver, pair of pliers, file, small self-tapping screw with rubber ferrule, tube of plastic aluminum material, aluminum paint, and brush.

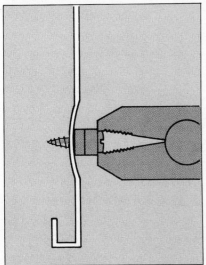

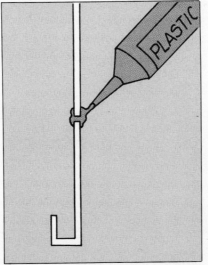

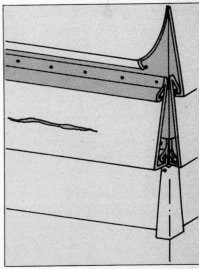

1. Twist a small self-tapping screw into the center of the dent. Place a rubber ferrule or a few washers around the screw's shank as a spacer. Grasp the end of the screw with a pair of pliers and pull until the dent has popped or flattened out.

2. Squeeze plastic aluminum, a hardware-store item, into the hole made by the screw. Allow this to harden, then file and sand smooth. Touch up with matching paint. The same technique can of course be used to patch small holes in aluminum.

To replace aluminum siding remove the corner caps and pry up the overlapping piece. Pull out the nails in the top flange and both end flanges. Lift out the piece. With some siding you may have to start at the top piece and remove each succeeding piece.

Repairing stucco

Repairing a stucco wall usually means filling a crack or patching a hole. The nature of the defect determines the treatment required. You can deal with a hairline crack by painting over it with a cement water paint. A somewhat larger crack must be caulked first, then painted. But large holes must be filled with mortar in stages over several days.

Any crack or cavity in stucco should be repaired as soon as you notice it. Otherwise water will seep in. If your house has a wooden frame, the dampness will rot the wood. If you live in a cold climate, water in the crack will freeze in the winter and enlarge the opening. If your house walls are masonry block, the moisture will keep them damp.

There is little you can do to prevent cracks in stucco. They result from a number of irremediable causes. The original mortar may have been incorrectly mixed, may have lacked the proper ingredients, or dried too rapidly; or walls may have settled due to poor foundations. Stucco over brick or stone can crack because different materials expand and contract differently.

What it takes

Approximate time: One half hour to prepare a hole, and half-hour sessions over three days to patch it.

Tools and materials: Dull knife, wire brush or whisk broom, trowel, bucket, striker board, wire cutters, wire, lath, white silica sand, and white portland cement.

1. Scrape away all loose materials in large cracks and holes. A dull knife works well. Then undercut the edges so that the patch will be wider inside than at the surface, securing it better to the old stucco. Clip out and replace any wire lath that has rusted through. Brush out all dust and particles.

2. Mix a mortar using the same ingredients and proportions as the existing stucco. If this is unknown, use one part white portland cement to four parts white silica sand, adding just enough water for a puttylike consistency. The mortar should stand on its own when pulled up with a trowel.

3. Spray the damaged section with water, then force mortar in and around the wire lath. Fill the hole less than halfway, blending the mortar into the surrounding stucco with a wire brush. Scratch up the surface with the tip of the trowel and allow to set up, but not dry out completely.

4. Apply a second layer the next day, almost filling the hole. Allow the mortar to set overnight. On the third day, apply the final coat, using a small wooden striker board to smooth it off flush with the surrounding surface. Texture the surface to match the old stucco surrounding it. After allowing it to dry for a couple of days, paint the patch to match the old stucco's appearance.

Replacing asbestos siding

Because of their rigidity, asbestos shingles tend to pop nails. Since they are brittle, they crack easily. When hammering a nail back into place, exercise care. It's safer to use a nailset to drive it home. Do not try to start a nail through an asbestos shingle; they come with nail holes in them. If you need a new hole, drill it; locate it at least an inch from an existing hole to avoid cracking the shingle.

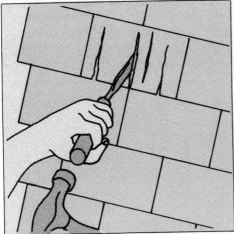

1. Break up a shingle that needs to be replaced. Being brittle, it will fragment readily and you can extract it piece by piece. Then pull out the exposed nails with a pair of pliers. If there are nails in the overlapping shingle, cut them off from behind with a hacksaw blade.

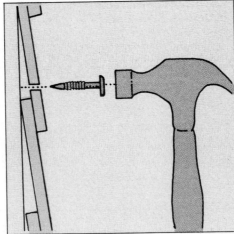

2. Slide the new shingle into place until its bottom edge is aligned with those of the others in its course. Its nail holes may or may not line up with the ones in the shingles above and below. If you can't line them up with minor readjustments, drill new holes.

What it takes

Approximate time: One-half hour to reinforce a cracked shingle; one hour to replace a shingle.

Tools and materials: Hammer, chisel, hacksaw blade, pair of pliers, and 1-inch galvanized or aluminum annular-ring roofing nails.

Stopgaps and copouts

You don't have to replace a cracked asbestos shingle if all pieces are still in place. After pulling out the obstructing nails, slide a piece of roofing felt or roll roofing under the shingle until it is behind the cracks. Drill holes for the new nails needed; drive the nails gently.

Replacing vinyl siding

Vinyl siding—polyvinyl chloride—needs little maintenance or repair. Unlike aluminum siding, it does not dent. But like aluminum, it will buckle during hot weather if any pieces were not correctly measured and fitted together. In addition to expanding from heat, vinyl siding contracts markedly from the cold, and can become brittle enough to be cracked by a sharp blow. The limb of a tree crashing into vinyl siding can do extensive damage in any season. People in vinyl-sided houses should be prepared to replace pieces. Here is a simple method.

1. Pull off the blocks at the corners. A piece of vinyl siding interlocks with the one above and below it. Being brittle, it can't be pried like aluminum siding. So start at the top, removing the nails and lifting off each piece. Work your way down to the damaged piece, numbering the pieces you remove so that you can replace them in the same order.

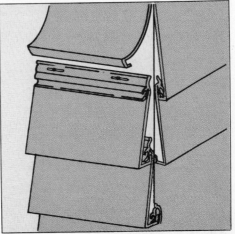

2. Remove the damaged piece or pieces and replace with new ones, then reassemble the rest of the siding, being careful to interlock the pieces and nail them so there's no gap between courses. The color of the replacement may differ from that of the others at first but will gradually blend in.

What it takes

Approximate time: Two hours for a simple repair.

Tools and materials: Hammer, screwdriver, pair of pliers, and pieces of replacement siding.

Caulking your house

Caulking is one of the simplest jobs a homeowner can undertake. It requires no special skills or expensive tools. And it does not consume much time. Working a few hours a day, you can recaulk all the seams in your house in two or three weekends. Once the job is done, it should last for four or five years. And the rewards are many. Caulking keeps water, drafts, dirt, and insects such as termites out of your house. It also keeps heat from escaping in cold weather.

Cracks and holes that need caulking exist in every house. You will find them wherever two parts of your house come together or different materials meet. Common trouble spots are: areas around door and window frames; areas between siding and chimney; where the house foundation and siding meet; where a wing or garage intersects the main part of the house; around a water pipe or electrical conduit that penetrates the foundation or siding; around vents set in the siding; at all points where the siding meets the trim. Caulking is also necessary in repairing roof leaks (pages 9 and 12). It is one of the homeowner's greatest allies.

(pages 9 and 12)

What it takes

Approximate time: A few minutes for small patching jobs; 30 minutes to prepare and recaulk the seams around one door or window frame.

Tools and materials: Wire brush, old screwdriver, putty knife, squeeze tube of the caulking compound (or cartridge and cartridge gun), recommended cleaner/solvent (see chart), a clean rag.

Types of caulking and uses

Caulking is now available in a variety of materials and forms. It comes in bulk form and in disposable cartridges which are used with an applicator gun. Use the chart below to select the type best suited to the job you have to do.

TYPE	USED FOR	SPECIAL REQUIREMENTS	SOLVENT CLEANER	COMMENTS
Oil-based	Routine caulking and glazing	Needs priming and painting	Turpentine or paint thinner	Shrinks; maximum life: five years. Least expensive.
Oakum	Very wide or deep cracks	Must be pounded in	None needed	Needs to be covered with additional compound.
Polybutane cord	Wide or deep cracks	Does not adhere, must be pressed in	None needed	Can't be painted.
Butyl rubber	Metal-to-wood or metal-to-masonry joints	None.	Paint thinner	Hard to use. Can be painted over immediately.
Neoprene	Cracks in concrete	Requirements vary from brand to brand	Toluene	Fumes are toxic.
Silicone	Joints that must be waterproof	Follow manufacturer's instructions	Paint thinner	Does not stick well to painted surfaces; costly. Lasts 15-20 years.

Caulking roundup

Most of the compounds listed above are available in three forms: bulk (one- or five-gallon cans); disposable cartridges for use in cartridge guns; and squeeze tubes. The latter are meant for special applications, so the choice is usually between the first two. Bulk form is the least expensive—but also the least convenient. The barrel of the caulking gun must be loaded and cleaned with each use. With cartridges, loading and cleaning the gun means merely slipping the cartridge in and out of it.

How to caulk

Caulking is not difficult if you take a few preparatory steps and follow the application techniques on the next page. To begin, work with clean seams. Using a scraper or screwdriver, chip off the exposed caulking. If it has not dried completely, try pulling it out in strips. After you have removed the caulking, wire-brush the seams to remove dust and chips. Then wipe them with a rag dipped in the indicated solvent or cleaner. **TIP:** Digging dried caulking out of deep seams takes time. In such cases, your best choice may be to leave the old caulking in place and apply oil-based caulking over it. While the oil-based material has a limited life (five years or less), it is inexpensive, will stick well to the caulking beneath it, and is relatively easy to apply. It's a good idea to check your house's caulking periodically.

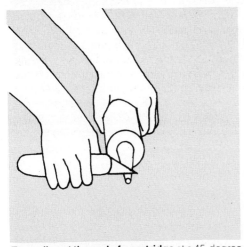

To caulk, cut the end of a cartridge at a 45-degree angle, using a sharp knife. Push a nail down the nozzle to break the inner seal. Leave the nail in place until you are ready to begin working.

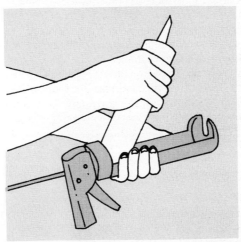

Place the cartridge in the gun, and twist the plunger until the ratchet side is down. Pulling the gun's trigger forces the ratchet forward, squeezing compound out the nozzle.

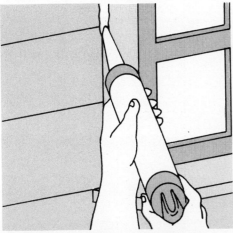

Work from top to bottom on vertical seams and in the direction of your stronger arm on horizontal ones. Slant the gun at a 45-degree angle, with the base pointing toward the direction you're working in. This keeps the nozzle level with the seam and creates an even bead of caulking.

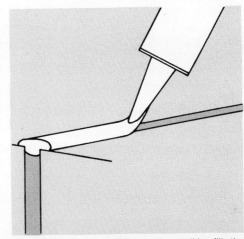

Draw the gun along slowly, so the caulking fills the crack and the bead overlaps both sides. The trick is to keep even pressure on the trigger. If you have to stop before you complete a seam, quickly release the trigger. **TIP:** To keep the caulking soft, plug the nozzle of the cartridge with a nail when done.

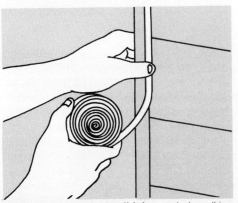

For emergencies or small jobs unwind caulking rope as shown, and force it into the crack with your fingers. You can unroll more than one strand at a time if the crack is large.

Planning hints

Caulk in warm weather, never when the temperature is below 80 degrees Fahrenheit. For an emergency job in cold weather, use polybutane cord.

On hot summer days, caulking gets runny. Chill the tube or cartridge in the refrigerator for an hour or so to firm it up.

A cartridge will cover about 100 feet of seam with a ¼-inch bead.

The best time to caulk is when you are painting your house. Apply primer to the seams first; then caulk. (The primer helps the caulking stick.) Let the caulking cure for several days. Then apply the finish coat. Remember to use a compound that will take paint without bleeding.

Runaway caulk?
I remembered too late that on a warm day, caulk should be placed in the refrigerator for an hour or two before using, or it will get runny. (Change to a fresh tube each time you go in for a beer.)

Practical Pete

5.EXTERIOR PAINTING

Sequence to follow when painting your house

1. Wash the siding and trim with warm water and detergent. **2.** Scrape off loose and peeling paint. Sand the wood. **3.** Prime bare wood; set exposed nails. **4.** Sand glossy surfaces under the eaves and other protected places. **5.** Wire-brush loose paint from gutters and downspouts. **6.** Remove loose caulking from around windows, doors, and other joints. Replace. **7.** Remove loose putty from windows. Reglaze. **8.** Cover exposed roofs, steps, and shrubs with drop cloths. **9.** Paint the trim, gutters, and downspouts first, beginning at the top. **10.** Paint the siding, working across the house from left to right. Always end at a door, window, or edge.

Planning hints:

- Spring and fall are good times to paint a house.
- Don't paint until all gutters, downspouts, and siding have been repaired and all joints have been caulked.
- Preparing the surface is the essential first step.
- Buy your paint and brushes from a store with an experienced sales clerk.

Painting the outside of a house is not for the lazy or slapdash. Pushing a brush back and forth is hard on the forearm. Climbing up and down a ladder is hard on the feet. The job requires planning and patience, too. There are many small jobs to complete before you pick up a brush. BUT . . .

On the plus side, it is not a job that requires technical skill or the use of complicated equipment. And painting your house can save you quite a bit of money. When painting is done by a professional contractor, labor represents about 75 percent of the cost. These days, it can cost $750 or $1,000 to have even a small house painted. As you can see, the savings are substantial.

If you prefer not to spend time on a ladder, have a professional paint the gables and other upper parts of your house; then paint the lower sections yourself.

Paint is designed to preserve as well as beautify your house. Physically, it is a coating of film. What is underneath must be solid and in good shape. Thus painting can't be done until gutters, downspouts, and siding are repaired, and joints and cracks are caulked. It will also be necessary to sand and even wash the surface.

Avoiding common paint problems

Shown below are six common paint problems, along with information that will help you avoid them—or deal with them correctly should one confront you.

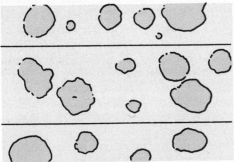

Blistering. This is caused by gas or liquid pressure under the paint. Most blisters are caused by moisture resulting from poor household ventilation; to correct this, install vents in the siding (page 30). Blisters that appear a few hours after the paint is applied arise from unevaporated solvent. The surface of the paint dried too rapidly, trapping the solvent. This can happen when you paint on a surface exposed to direct sunlight or on a very hot day. Dark paints are especially susceptible to blistering because they absorb more heat than light paints do.

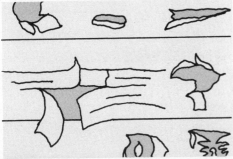

Peeling. Peeling occurs because the paint did not bond with the underlying surface. This can happen when the surface is wet, dirty, oily, or glossy. Paint will not bond with a surface that is wet from morning dew or with a prime coat that was not given time to dry thoroughly.

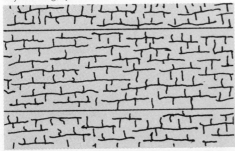

Alligatoring. This somewhat fanciful term refers to paint that has separated into rectangular segments. The result is a surface that resembles the hide of an alligator. Alligatoring results from surface paint and underlying paint that fail to expand and contract at the same rate. This condition arises when paint is applied over an incompatible surface, and when it has been thinned with an incompatible solvent. It can also occur if the paint is applied before the prime coat has dried.

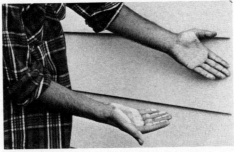

Chalking. If you've ever brushed up against dry paint and gotten covered with powder, you know what chalking is. The powder is pigment that is shed by the paint. Some chalking is desirable, especially in white paint, and is formulated into the mixture. One benefit of chalking is that it cleans the surface, making the paint look fresh for a long time. Another is that by gradually wearing away, it eliminates the need to sand. When it's time to paint again, the coat is thin enough to take new paint without buildup.

Excessive chalking, however, is bad. The pigment washes away too quickly, exposing the siding it should protect. This has three possible causes: The paint was of poor quality and lacked sufficient binder; the undersurface was not sufficiently primed and was so dry it soaked up all the binder; or the paint was applied in cold weather.

Chalking is undesirable on siding above bricks, as the pigment will streak the bricks. (To remove streaks, wash the bricks with a strong solution of hot water and dish detergent.)

Crawling. With this problem, the paint fails to form a continuous coat. Instead it gathers in globules, like water on an oily surface. Crawling occurs when latex is applied over a high-gloss surface that has not been sanded. An oily or dirty surface will also make paint crawl. Such surfaces are apt to be found under eaves and in other sheltered places.

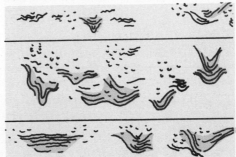

Wrinkling. This occurs when too much paint is applied or when the paint itself is too thick. It is especially likely to take place in cold weather. Wrinkles develop soon, and you can quickly correct them. Sand the surface and brush on paint of a lighter consistency.

House pox
A week after I'd finished painting my house, it began to look sick. A month later, it *was* sick. The paint was blotched and peeling. I had bought "one-coat-covers-all" bargain paint and hurried it on. Well, I had to sand it off and begin the job from scratch. But then I got smart. I bought the best paint I could find and applied it right.

Practical Pete

Preparing the surfaces

What it takes

Approximate time: Three hours to wash an average one-story house; eight hours for a two-story house.

Tools and materials: Push broom, garden hose, aspirator, dish detergent, trisodium phosphate (a paint-store item).

Not all painting errors reveal themselves in problems like those shown on the previous page. A common and expensive problem is that the whole coat of paint deteriorates rapidly—and soon you're back on the ladder, repainting the entire house. The most common causes for this general deterioration are: inadequate preparation of the surfaces to be painted; use of poor-quality paint; and errors in applying the paint. The following pages deal with each, starting with how to prepare surfaces.

Washing a house

All surfaces to be painted must be scrupulously clean. The first step is washing down the house. (There's an unexpected bonus in this first step, by the way. You may find that your house doesn't need repainting at all. It may only have needed a thorough cleaning to rid it of dust, soil, and mildew that made the paint appear dingy.) You will need a high-pressure spray cleaner to wash the house. You can rent one from a paint store, hardware store, or equipment-rental company. You can also make your own, as shown in step 1, below. It will do the necessary job of removing both dirt and loose, peeling paint. In performing this operation, keep the work area clean.

What it takes

Approximate time: Two hours to clean a wall 6 feet high and 15 feet long.

Tools and materials: Heavy rubber gloves, thick rubber apron, goggles, muriatic acid, wire or other stiff brush.

Acid tips

- When mixing acid and water, always add the acid to the water, never vice versa.
- For heavy deposits, double the strength of the solution and the length of time left on.
- Put on the gloves, goggles, and apron before you mix the solution; leave them on until after you rinse it off.

Identifying and preventing mildew

Blotches of what appears to be dirt on siding may actually be mildew. It grows on the north side of houses and on other shaded surfaces, especially damp ones. Washing will remove the mildew stains but not its spores. These are embedded in the surface of the paint. To determine if a stain is mildew, dab chlorine laundry bleach on it. If the stain disappears in a few minutes, it is mildew. Ordinary soil will not come off.

To remove mildew, scrub the surface with a bleach-and-water solution (1 cup of bleach to a gallon of warm water). Flush the area with clear water, and allow it to dry well before painting. **TIP:** If you are using an oil-based paint, add a mildew inhibitor to it when you are painting the area. This is not necessary with water-based paints because they don't have the oil that the fungus feeds on.

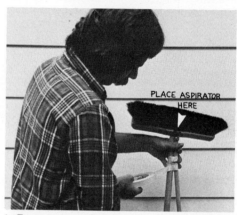

1. To make a spray cleaner, tape your garden hose to a stiff-bristled push broom. Fill an aspirator/sprayer with a concentrated solution of dish detergent and TSP (trisodium phosphate), and place it between the hose and the nozzle. Attach the hose to a hot-water faucet, and brush vigorously.

2. Flush off the detergent solution before it dries. Whether or not you remove the hose from the broom for better control, hold the nozzle about 6 inches from the wall, and at a sharp angle to it, so the jet can knock off loose paint and soil. Use clear water; it does not have to be hot. Let the wall dry.

3. To remove white, powdery deposits on brick or concrete surfaces, go over them with a stiff, dry brush, Then wet the surface with a weak (5 percent) solution of muriatic acid and water. After the solution has been on five minutes, brush the wall and immediately rinse with clear water. Work 4-foot-square sections.

Preparing wood surfaces

Most siding and trim is made of wood. It presents a fine surface for paint, provided it is in good shape. Cracked boards should be repaired (page 31) or replaced (page 32), and loose boards nailed tight. Popped nails should be hammered home. It is building practice to use nonrusting flathead nails on exterior siding and trim. If these nails were used on your house, caulking is not necessary. But if you see signs of rust, correct the problem as soon as possible and as it is described below.

Dealing with rust

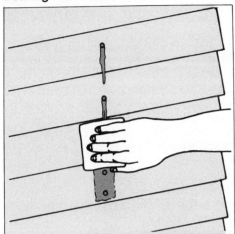

1. Sand the rust stains around the nail and the nail itself until it shines. Then set the nail about ⅛ inch below the surface. Prime the nailhead with a rust-inhibiting paint. When this has dried, caulk the hole. When the caulking has dried, prime it.

2. Paint over rust stains that are too deep to be sanded off. **TIP:** Using an opaque stain will help obscure the rust and may keep it from bleeding through the paint. Do not try to set flathead nails.

What it takes

Approximate time: About 10 minutes per nail.

Tools and materials: Sanding block, medium-grit sandpaper, wire brush, nail set, putty knife, 2-inch paintbrush, rust-inhibiting metal primer, caulking compound, opaque stain.

Removing paint

For painting, the surface must be smooth and firm. To start, scrape off all loose and peeling paint that the hosing did not remove. Generally, all you'll need for this is a wire brush, scraper, or putty knife. However, where a deeper paint problem exists—blisters, alligatoring, or cracking, for example—you may have to remove large areas of paint down to the bare wood. This calls for specialized tools and materials. What you use will depend on the thickness of the paint, its extent, and your own schedule. A sanding block will do for small areas. For larger ones, use a power sander, an electrical paint remover, or a chemical paint remover.

What it takes

Approximate time: About two hours for a section 4 feet wide by 8 feet long.

Tools and materials: Hook-shaped scraper, putty knife, and either an orbital power sander, sanding block, electrical paint remover, or semipaste chemical paint remover. Also needed: solvent, steel wool, open-coat—60- or 80-grit—sandpaper (for the sander), brush, and clean rag.

Rent a vibrating sander if you need to remove large areas of blistered and peeling paint. Get one with legs that prevent gouging. Maintain even pressure on the device so that the entire sanding surface is flat against the siding. Never hold it motionless over one spot. **TIP:** Don't use a sander with a revolving disc. It will gouge the surface.

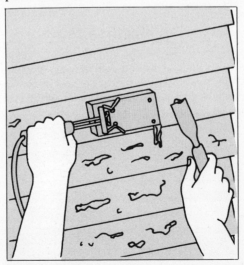

Remove wrinkles and other thick, rough paint with an electrical paint remover. The higher its wattage, the faster the unit will work. While the unit scrapes as well as softens paint, you will have to scrape off paint remnants and sand the surface smooth before you paint it. **TIP:** Don't use a flame to soften paint; you may ignite the siding.

Where there's flame . . .
It happened this way: I had a huge patch of alligatored paint on my house. It would have taken a week to sand. I'd seen painters use a blowtorch to soften old paint. So I rented a propane torch. It took off the paint fine. But a fire took off the siding. Firemen told me that the flame probably shot into a crack and ignited the sheathing.

Practical Pete

Stripping paint

What it takes

Approximate time: Half an hour to remove paint from a 2-foot-square area, including washing and sanding.

Tools and materials: Old brush, putty knife, scraper, paint remover, solvent, sandpaper.

Use chemical paint remover for cleaning off large areas of paint. Apply it in 2-foot sections. Use a semipaste type on vertical surfaces. Lay it on in thick, short strokes, all going in the same direction. Wait about 20 minutes before you scrape it off. When you have finished, use the indicated solvent—water or benzene—to remove all traces of the chemical. Then sand the wood smooth with fine-grit paper.

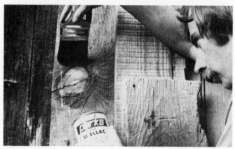

Feather the edges of paint that border an area you have cleaned down to bare wood. Rub the edges first with coarse sandpaper, then with fine. This will enable you to smoothly blend the new paint with the old. Paint stripping is only necessary on especially problematic areas, where ordinary scraping leaves an irregular surface.

Knots and resins

You can locate knots under old paint. The paint just over the knot will be discolored. This is caused by resin bleeding through the paint. Resin will discolor the new paint, too, unless you take steps to prevent it. This is easily done, as is dealing with knots on new wood. It's a good point not to just order lumber, but if you can, to select it.

What it takes

Approximate time: 15 minutes to treat a knot.

Tools and materials: Putty knife, sanding block, chisel, sharp knife, 2-inch paintbrush, shellac, alcohol.

To prepare new wood, scrape off soft resin with a knife blade or putty knife. If the resin has hardened, chip it off with a chisel or sharp knife. Once you have removed all resin, clean the area with alcohol and seal it with thinned shellac or a sealer designed for resinous wood. The sealer is not a primer; limit it to the affected area.

To prepare old wood for paint, simply seal all knots with thinned shellac, and sand when dry. (It is not necessary to remove the old paint.) If the knot is loose, do not remove it. Tighten it with wood caulking. After the caulking has dried, shellac the area, let dry, and then sand it smooth.

Preparing metal surfaces

Remove loose paint and rust from metal surfaces. You don't have to remove paint to the bare metal, but the surfaces must be free of dirt and oil. Application of a rust-inhibiting primer is advisable. Of course, the most useful thing is to keep up your maintenance. Checking periodically can save you a lot of time and effort.

What it takes

Approximate time: Two hours to prepare railings on front step.

Tools and materials: Wire brush, scraper or putty knife, small mirror, electric drill with wire brushes.

Use a wire brush to remove loose and peeling paint from curved metal surfaces. A scraper or putty knife will take such paint off flat surfaces. Use steel wool on rust spots. Inspect under surfaces with a mirror.

Prepare large areas like those on gutters and downspouts with an electric drill fitted with a wire brush. If they are made of aluminum, wash the surface with a specially formulated aluminum cleaner available at hardware stores. While aluminum is not subject to rust, it does oxidize and will pit if left exposed.

Selecting and buying paint

Paints are formulated to adhere to specific surfaces and to possess certain performance characteristics. Thus, there are surfaces to which a paint will not adhere and performance characteristics which it will lack. The chart below summarizes the qualities of various exterior paints. Use it to select the type best suited for your house and job.

There are three different types of paint you can apply to trim and siding: oil-based, alkyd-based, and latex. Oil-based paint was the standard paint for many years. It has been made less popular by developments in paint chemistry. Its big handicap is that it is difficult to apply and lacks durability. Nowadays, it is used primarily for painting trim when a high gloss is desired.

There are two widely used types of latex paint. One has a polyvinyl-acetate binder; the other has an acrylic-latex binder. The latter is more durable and is used in expensive paints. Latex paint of both types has many advantages. It can be applied to damp surfaces, goes on easily and usually dries within an hour. Since it is thinned with water, you can clean the brushes in water. It is especially well adapted to siding that has blistered, as it lets trapped moisture escape. The major drawback of latex paint is that it does not adhere well to surfaces already coated with a different type of paint.

Alkyd-based paint contains a resin-and-oil binder. It spreads easily and covers better than latex paint, especially on chalky surfaces. It must, however, be applied to dry surfaces and thinned with paint thinner or turpentine. Brush cleaning is a chore.

. Exterior siding paint in all types is available in flat and semigloss styles; paint for trim in semigloss and gloss.

TIP: When you buy paint, open the cans first. If there is a cake of pigment on the bottom or the paint is lumpy, reject it. The paint is not fresh, and it will be hard to apply. Have every can of paint you buy mixed in the store's agitator. This will save you time. Get a supply of free mixing sticks, painting hats, and hooks for hanging paint cans from the ladder.

What paint to use and where

A dot indicates that a primer or sealer is necessary before the finish coat (unless surface has been previously finished).

	House paint (oil)	Transparent sealer	Cement-based paint	Exterior clear finish	Aluminum paint	Wood stain	Roof coating	Roof cement	Asphalt emulsion	Trim and trellis paint	Awning paint	Spar varnish	Porch and deck paint	Primer or undercoat	Metal primer	Latex types	Water-repellant preservatives
Clapboard siding	✓•				✓									✓		✓•	
Brick	✓•	✓	✓		✓									✓		✓	
Cement & cinder block	✓•	✓	✓		✓									✓		✓	
Asbestos cement	✓													✓		✓	
Stucco	✓•	✓	✓		✓									✓		✓	
Natural wood siding & trim				✓		✓						✓					
Metal siding	✓•				✓•					✓•					✓	✓•	
Wood-framed windows	✓•				✓					✓•				✓		✓•	
Steel windows	✓•				✓•					✓•					✓	✓•	
Aluminum windows	✓•				✓					✓•					✓	✓•	
Shutters & other trim	✓•									✓•				✓		✓•	
Canvas awnings											✓						
Wood-shingle roof				✓													✓
Metal roof	✓•														✓	✓	
Coal-tar felt roof							✓	✓	✓								
Wood porch floor													✓				
Cement porch floor													✓			✓	
Copper surfaces												✓					
Galvanized surfaces	✓•				✓•					✓•	✓			✓		✓•	
Iron surfaces	✓•				✓					✓•					✓	✓	

Choosing the colors

Deciding on the color—or colors—to paint your house is a process directed by personal taste. There are, however, some practical matters to consider. If the house is now a dark color and you are thinking about painting it white, you may be converting a one-coat job into a two-coat process. You may have to apply two coats anyway, but using white paint over dark will make a second coat more likely.

The following tips can help you make color serve your purposes:
• If you want your house to appear larger, choose a light color. A dark color will reduce its apparent size.
• Painting the trim and window and door frames in a contrasting color will add interest to the house. But if there are a number of different materials on the outside of the house—clapboard, shingles, bricks, and stucco, for example—using a single color will unify the house and reduce the clash between textures.
• When you select a color, you may be working from color swatches. When using

them, remember that printing inks can only approximate the color of the paint. There will be further variations due to the surface of the house, the method of application, and the lighting. The color of the paint, seen in its container, is not a reliable guide either. Here are some facts to remember when you select a color from paint in a container:
1. Paint always appears darker in the container than it will on a surface.
2. Artificial light darkens color; the paint will look lighter in daylight. If in doubt, take the container outside.
3. All paint dries to a lighter shade than the one you see when it is first applied.
4. A color can saturate your eyes. To insure accuracy when you are mixing paints, look away from the mix for several minutes to let your eyes readjust.
5. When you are seeking a particular shade, it is a good idea to paint a test patch about 2 feet by 2 feet, and let it dry. What appeared to be the lemon yellow you want may dry to a washed-out tint.

Estimating how much paint you need

It is better to buy too much paint than too little. Running out of paint in the middle of a job is no joke. Any leftover paint (in unopened cans) can probably be returned to the store for a refund or credit. Be sure to

have an understanding on this before you buy; have it written on the sales slip.

It is better still to estimate your needs accurately. Using this formula, you'll be able to come close:

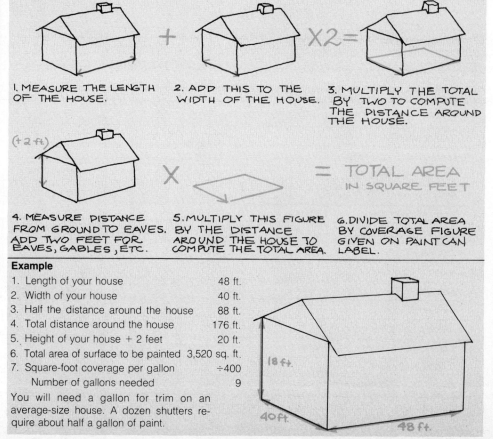

1. MEASURE THE LENGTH OF THE HOUSE.
2. ADD THIS TO THE WIDTH OF THE HOUSE.
3. MULTIPLY THE TOTAL BY TWO TO COMPUTE THE DISTANCE AROUND THE HOUSE.
4. MEASURE DISTANCE FROM GROUND TO EAVES. ADD TWO FEET FOR EAVES, GABLES, ETC.
5. MULTIPLY THIS FIGURE BY THE DISTANCE AROUND THE HOUSE TO COMPUTE THE TOTAL AREA.
6. DIVIDE TOTAL AREA BY COVERAGE FIGURE GIVEN ON PAINT CAN LABEL.

Example

1. Length of your house	48 ft.
2. Width of your house	40 ft.
3. Half the distance around the house	88 ft.
4. Total distance around the house	176 ft.
5. Height of your house + 2 feet	20 ft.
6. Total area of surface to be painted	3,520 sq. ft.
7. Square-foot coverage per gallon	÷400
Number of gallons needed	9

You will need a gallon for trim on an average-size house. A dozen shutters require about half a gallon of paint.

Looks larger

Looks smaller

Looks more interesting

Looks more harmonious

Buying brushes

The type of paint you are to apply will determine the type of brush you need. Do not use natural-bristle brushes for applying latex or water-based paint. The bristles will absorb the water and swell. These brushes are better for oil- and alkyd-based paints, epoxies, varnish, shellac, and lacquer. Use brushes with nylon bristles for applying latex and water-based paint. Do not use them with shellac, lacquer, or varnish; all will make the bristles soften or dissolve.

If you are buying a natural-bristle brush, look for one made of imported hog bristles. These are superior because the end of each bristle is split into many tiny branches. This "flagging" enables the brush to carry a great deal of paint and leave very fine brush marks that flow together to create a smooth finish. The bristles of good nylon brushes are artificially flagged. Horsehair bristles are used in poor-quality brushes. The bristles hold little paint, do not spread it well, and soon become limp.

Before you buy a brush, apply the following tests: **1.** Press it against a flat surface; the bristles should not fan out. **2.** Squeeze the bristles; they should feel full and spongy. **3.** Poke your fingers into the brush to determine fullness of the bristles. **4.** Look at the bristle ends; they should be split into a number of fine branches. **5.** Inspect the length of the bristles; they should be varied. This permits the brush to carry larger paint loads and increases the life of the brush. As the tip wears, new bristle ends replace worn ones. **6.** Squeeze and jar the brush; few loose bristles should fall out. **7.** Examine the metal band, or ferrule around the bristles. It should be made of aluminum or stainless steel.

For painting siding, you will need a 4- or 5-inch brush; for window frames, sashes, and other narrow boards, a 2-inch trim brush. A 1½-inch trim brush with a beveled end is excellent for painting narrow strips like the muntins in windows. If you will be painting stucco or masonry, get a brush designed for those surfaces. Choose one with nylon bristles because they can resist abrasive surfaces.

Caring for brushes

Brushes with nylon and other synthetic bristles are ready for use when you buy them. But you will lengthen the life and improve the performance of the brush if you soak it in thinner before first using it. This removes loose bristles and tightens the others. **TIP:** Do not soak any brush in water. That can split the handle and may rust the ferrule.

Before you use a natural-bristle brush for the first time, soak it in linseed oil for 48 hours. In addition to tightening the bristles, the oil makes them more flexible. It also removes the loose bristles.

When you are done painting for the day, clean all brushes thoroughly—even if you intend to resume painting the first thing in the morning. Any paint left on the brush will thicken, stiffening the bristles and making it difficult to draw the brush over the surface. When you clean brushes, be sure to use the solvent appropriate for the type of paint used:

Paint	Solvent
Oil-based or alkyd	Turpentine followed by benzene or paint thinner
Latex or water-based	Warm water and detergent

What it takes

Approximate time: An average of 10 minutes to clean a 4-inch siding brush.

Tools and materials: Clean can, appropriate solvent, metal paint-brush comb, clean rags.

1. Lower the brush into the solvent up to the ferrule. Withdraw it and let the bristles drip. Repeat several times; then place the brush on newspapers, and squeeze the paint out by dragging a mixing stick down the bristles, from ferrule to tip. Turn the brush over and squeeze the other side.

2. Spin the brush in the solvent, ferrule-deep, rinsing it thoroughly. Remove and run a paintbrush comb through the bristles. Spin the brush in the solvent a second time, and comb it out again. Repeat until the brush is free of paint.

3. Suspend the brush overnight in a clean can filled with the solvent. For this, drill a 1/16-inch hole in the handle of the brush and run a stiff wire through it. The can must be tall enough to keep the bristles from resting on the bottom. (This is also a good way to soften dried paint on old brushes.)

Applying paint

Approximate time: Figure on eight days—four weekends—to paint an average-size house.

Tools and materials: Drop cloths, ladders, scaffolding (planks plus an extension ladder and ladder jack, or planks plus two A-ladders), mixing bucket, mixing sticks, 4- to 5-inch siding brush, 2-inch trim brush, 1½-inch trim brush with taper tip, paint-can hooks, siding paint, trim paint, primer paint, appropriate solvent, clean rags.

Planning hints:

• Take down screens and storm windows.
• Fold newspaper over the tops of doors and shut them.
• Having a helper will more than halve the time required.
• Protect walks and driveways with weighted-down newspapers.
• Don't paint in direct sunlight.
• Wait for a no-rain forecast before you paint.
• Prime new wood and all surfaces you have taken down to bare wood.

Before you begin painting, be sure you have all the necessary materials at hand. Check that all surfaces have been properly prepared. If possible, also enlist a helper. This does more than cut your working time in half. It provides a safety factor and takes a lot of the chore out of the job. For bigger jobs, you may need more than one helper.

Mixing paint

Even though you have bought fresh paint and have had the cans agitated, you will have to mix the paint throughout the project. As you work, stir the paint frequently to keep the pigment from settling to the bottom. Lower a mixing stick to the bottom and move it in a figure-eight pattern. Paint will thicken in a can as the thinner evaporates. If necessary, add the appropriate thinner and stir as above. When you open a can of paint, fix it as described below. Pour the paint into a clean can, the larger the better. Pour the paint back and forth from one can to the other. Professionals call this *boxing* the paint. Continue this procedure until the color and consistency are uniform. If there is pigment caked at the bottom, break it with a mixing stick and pour in a little paint at a time. And of course, keep stirring.

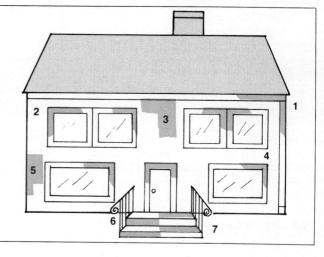

Follow this sequence when painting your house:
1. Gutters—use appropriate paint on the outside (see page 43); asphalt paint on the inside.
2. Top trim: eaves, window frames, and any other edges.
3. Upper siding. **4.** Lower trim.
5. Lower siding. **6.** Ornamental iron railings. **7.** Steps.
By painting trim first, you avoid ladder marks on freshly painted siding. Top-to-bottom painting covers drips.

Scaffolding

If your house has two stories or more, you will need an extension ladder. Follow the procedures for ladder safety given on page 7. If the house is large, you can paint it more quickly from a scaffold. Scaffolding enables you to paint large areas at one time, and planking is easier on your feet than are ladder rungs. For safety, do not raise scaffolds above 10 feet. And be sure always to work with a helper.

To make a scaffold, separate an extension ladder into its two segments. Fit each with ladder jacks, which you can rent from a paint store or equipment-rental firm. Despite the length of the planks, keep the ladders within 10 feet of each other.

A better scaffold consists of two A-ladders with a plank resting on the rungs. To adjust the height, just move the plank to different rungs, a much faster process than adjusting ladder jacks. Keep the ladders positioned so that the working length of planking is not longer than 10 feet.

Practical pointers and procedures

Dip the brush into the paint at least one-third the length of the bristles but not more than one-half. This loads the brush so the paint flows on easily. Remove excess paint by tapping the brush against the lip of the can. **TIP:** Don't wipe the brush against the lip. It will soon fill up and the paint will run down the side and drip off.

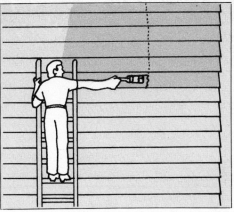

Work across the siding in a horizontal band, from left to right if you are right-handed; from right to left if you are left-handed. Progress by painting squares. If you are on a ladder, the size of the squares will be determined by how far you can safely reach. If you are on the ground or a scaffold, paint squares roughly 2 feet high and 3 feet wide.

TIP: Removing the lip from an empty paint can will give you a good container to paint from. Take the lip off with a cold chisel. This lets you wipe excess paint off your brush without creating a dripping rim. You'll be able to paint faster and with less mess.

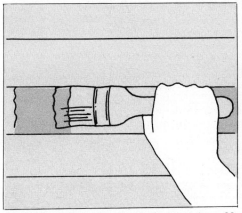

Apply the paint in brush-wide strokes, about 20 inches long. Then, starting about a foot from the wet edge, paint back toward it. Painting dry into wet saves you the work of rebrushing an area you've already painted. Blend the paint evenly into the wet area with a light stroke, lifting the brush as you end. Smooth off excess paint with a long, even stroke.

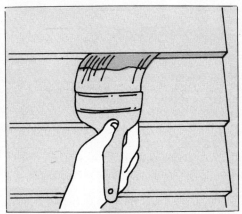

Paint clapboard with a brush as wide as the face of the board, if possible. First cover the undersides of four or five boards. Then paint the face of each one, working one board at a time. Follow the procedure of painting into the wet. Brush pads are good for painting clapboard, especially for the hard-to-reach undersides.

No more holidays
From the ladder, I seemed to be covering the surface thoroughly. But when I got down and looked up, I saw that I had skipped the lower edges of clapboards. Professional painters call skipped spots *holidays*. It sure was no holiday for me, having to put the ladder back up. Now I inspect my work *as* I work.

Practical Pete

Paint window frameworks from an angle that allows you to see the tip of the bristles meeting the wood. Use a tapered trim brush. Work from the inside of the frame out toward its edges. If you get paint on the glass, wipe it off with a rag wrapped around your finger. **TIP:** Drive nails in the bottoms of the upper and lower sash so that you can move the windows without marring the wet paint.

Keep stairs in use by painting every other tread. When the paint on the first set has dried, paint the treads you skipped. Paint the risers and other elements when you paint the first half of the treads. Instead of painting every other tread, you can paint half of each step and when this has dried, paint the the other half.

6.INSULATION

Insulation is the most functional and cost-effective way to conserve energy in the home to date. It cuts heat loss in winter—and heat gain in summer—by creating dead air spaces between temperature-controlled indoor air and the weather outside.

Yet, as important a role as it plays, many homes, particularly those built before 1960, have little or no insulation. While most older homes have some attic insulation, the majority of homes built before 1960 have nothing in the walls. Homes built between 1960 and 1970 often have only a thin 1½-inch layer of insulation in the walls. Those built later generally have 2½ to 3½ inches.

One contractor's rule of thumb is: If the home is more than 10 years old, you can assume it needs some insulation. How much varies from house to house and from locality to locality.

The R system

Insulation materials are evaluated in terms of *R values*. The R value of a material is a measure of how effectively it can hold heat in—or out. R values are given in terms of numbers; the higher the number, the more effective the insulation. For example, glass fiber, in sheet or blanket form, has an R value of 3.2 per inch, whereas glass fiber in loose-fill form has an R value of 2.2 per inch. As indicated in the chart below, R values vary by material as well as form. When you purchase insulation, specify what R value you need to install, not the number of inches of thickness.

R VALUES OF DIFFERENT INSULATION TYPES					
TYPE	**Batts or blankets**		**Loose fill (poured in)**		
R VALUE	Glass fiber	Rock wool	Glass fiber	Rock wool	Cellulosic fiber
R-11	3½″-4″	3″	5″	4″	3″
R-19	6″-6½″	5¼″	8″-9″	6″-7″	5″
R-22	6½″	6″	10″	7″-8″	6″
R-30	9½″-10½″*	9″*	13″-14″	10″-11″	8″
R-38	12″-13″*	10½″*	17″-18″	13″-14″	10″-11″

*Two batts or blankets required

Types of insulation

Batts or blankets. Thick sheets of insulation are known as *batts.* Like blanket insulation, batts are usually made of glass fiber or rock wool. Both fit between joists, studs, or rafters with standard spacing. Batts come in 4- and 8-foot lengths. Blanket insulation is cut to the desired length. Both are available with or without a vapor barrier on one side. Batts and blankets are commonly used for insulating attic floors and ceilings, sidewalls, basement walls, and crawl-space ceilings.

Loose fill. Generally made of glass fiber, rock wool, cellulosic fiber, vermiculite, or perlite, this insulating material is either poured in by hand or pneumatically blown into closed spaces. It is used in finished and unfinished attic floors and finished walls.

Rigid board. Rigid-board insulation is made of extruded polystyrene, urethane, glass fiber, or expanded polystyrene beads. It is available in thicknesses ranging from ¾ inch to 4 inches and offers a high insulation value for a relatively thin material. Rigid-board insulation can be applied to finished interior walls, basement walls, and crawl spaces. If used inside the home, it should be covered with gypsum board for fire safety. On outside walls, extruded-polystyrene board can be applied to the foundation wall all the way to the footer.

Foam insulation. Urea-formaldehyde insulation can be pumped in place through holes drilled in finished walls and finished attic floors. This is usually done by contractors because the equipment is expensive. Be sure to use a qualified contractor who will guarantee his work.

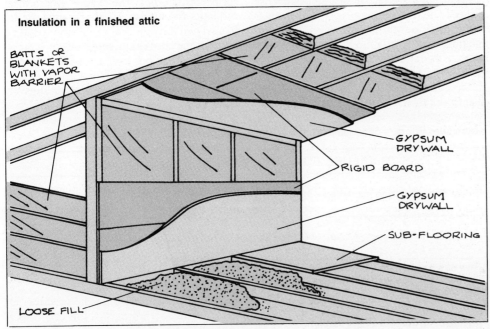

Insulation in a finished attic

BATTS OR BLANKETS WITH VAPOR BARRIER

GYPSUM DRYWALL

RIGID BOARD

GYPSUM DRYWALL

SUB-FLOORING

LOOSE FILL

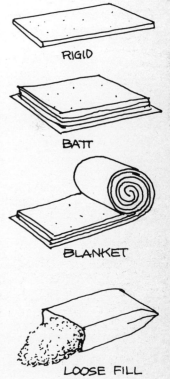

RIGID

BATT

BLANKET

LOOSE FILL

Checking your home for insulation

Once you know how much insulation you need (page 48), find out how much you have. This can be tricky in areas, such as finished sidewalls that are not readily accessible. There, you'll have to take a guess or have a professional look into the matter. But for the most part, you can check insulation yourself. Here's what to look for:

Attic floor and roof. Insulation material will generally lie between joists or trusses. You may want to add more insulation yourself (see chart on page 50). If so, the kind of insulation that is already there will determine what kind you add. If the attic floor is finished, pry up a board and look under it.

Sidewalls. A tough place to inspect if the house is already finished. Your best bet is to locate the contractor who built the house and check his specifications. If that isn't possible, you can have an energy audit made. In this process, called thermography, a heat-sensitive camera is used to determine if areas of your house are losing too much heat. To locate a firm offering this service, check your hardware dealer.

Another way to check is to feel the inside wall of a finished room on a cold day. It should be room temperature. If it's cold, insulation is in order.

Crawl spaces. These are easy to assess because the insulation is often exposed. Be sure to check all crawl-space ceilings, even if they may already be insulated.

Basement walls. Finished or unfinished, it's an easy matter to insulate a basement against heat loss. If your basement is finished, remove a ceiling or wall panel so you can check for insulating material.

Adding insulation

What it takes

Approximate time: Depending upon the kind of insulation material used and the size of the area of work, anywhere from a few hours to a full day.

Tools and materials: Linoleum knife or heavy-duty shears, wooden rake or board (to level loose fill if you use it), heavy-duty staple gun and staples, gloves, breathing mask (when using mineral-wool or glass-fiber materials), hammer, nails, ruler, insulation material of your choice, vapor-barrier material, wire holders (if necessary).

Starting at the top of the house, the following material will show you how to add insulation to your home and how to get the most value for it.

Attic floor. Use fibrous batts, blankets, or loose fill, referring to the chart below for ideal R values. If you are using a batt or blanket with a vapor barrier, place the material so the vapor barrier faces the floor below. Otherwise, lay polyethylene sheeting over the flooring before you install the insulation. You can staple it. For more on vapor barriers, see pages 52-53.

If you already have batt or blanket insulation, you can add more by laying batts or blankets—without vapor barriers—over the existing material, or simply pour loose fill over it. Make sure you don't cover ventilation louvers in the eaves, and remember that insulation must be 3 inches away from recessed light fixtures.

Attic walls. Place batts or blankets between rafters, and staple them in place. You can also secure them by attaching wire fasteners between the rafters.

Sidewalls. For new construction, use batts, blankets, or rigid-board insulation. On finished walls, have a contractor pump loose fill or foamed-in-place material into the walls. (The contractor makes and repairs the holes.) Another option is to install extruded-polystyrene rigid board on inside surfaces and cover it with gypsum board. If you are installing new siding, you can also use rigid-board insulation underneath it.

Crawl spaces. When it comes to crawl spaces, you can insulate either the ceiling or walls; it is not necessary to do both. For ceilings, place batts or blankets between joists and support them with wire fasteners, available at hardware stores. For walls, use 1-by-1½-inch nailers (strips of wood) to secure insulation to the header. Make sure the batts fit snugly. Allow the material to hang down the wall. For even better protection let the insulation come out at least 2 feet across the floor from the wall. The size and height of your crawl space will determine whether it's easier to do ceilings or walls. Whichever you choose to do, place a polyethylene vapor barrier across the earth before you install floor insulation.

R VALUES FOR UNFINISHED ATTIC FLOORS				
Thickness of existing insulation	0″	0″-2″	2″-4″	4″-6″
How much to add	R-22	R-11	R-11	none
How much to add if you have electric heat or if you have oil heat and live in a cold climate	R-30	R-22	R-19	R-11
How much to add if you have electric heat and live in a cold climate	R-38	R-30	R-22	R-19

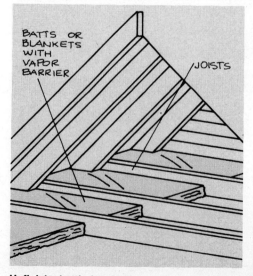

Unfinished attic insulation

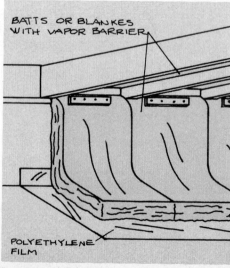

Crawl-space insulation

Basement walls. The easiest way to insulate basement walls is with extruded-polystyrene boards. You can apply them directly to masonry walls, using mastic, and then cover them with gypsum dry wall. An alternative is to have the walls framed out, place batt or blanket insulation between the studs, and cover it with extruded-polystyrene board and gypsum dry wall.

Basement floors. To insulate concrete floors, apply extruded-polystyrene boards directly to the floor with mastic paste. Then regular flooring must be installed over the insulation to finish the job.

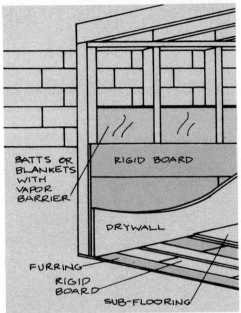

Basement insulation

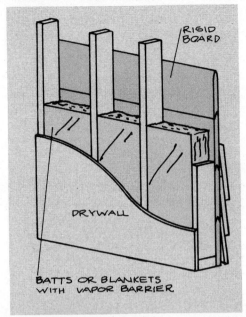

Insulation in new construction

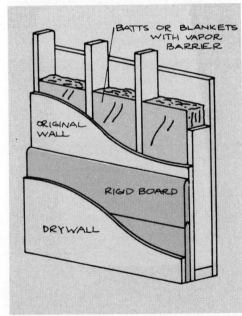

Insulation in existing inside walls

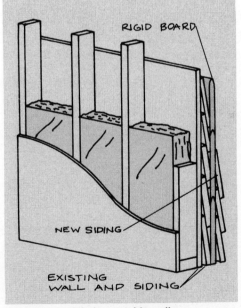

Insulation in existing outside walls

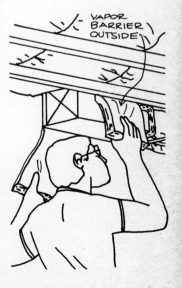

Ducts. If you have ducts for either air conditioning or heating running through your attic, garage, or any other space that is not heated or cooled, and they are exposed, then you should insulate them.

Generally, duct insulation comes in blankets 1 or 2 inches thick. It's sensible to get the thicker kind, especially if the ducts are rectangular. The important thing is to do the job thoroughly; after all, it's energy and money that you will be saving—or losing, as the case may be.

For air conditioning ducts, you should have the kind of insulation that has a vapor barrier. The vapor barrier goes on the outside. Seal the joints of the insulation tightly with tape to avoid condensation. Also, it is important to check before you start, to see if there are any leaks in the duct. If there are, tape them tightly.

In addition to insulation

While insulation plays a very important part in conserving energy in the home, it is not the only answer. There are a number of supplementary steps the homeowner can take, some of which are:

Storm windows and doors can save a lot of energy. If you have a choice between wood and aluminum frames, choose wood. It transfers heat more slowly than metal. An alternative step is to place plastic sheeting over windows. This is an inexpensive and effective way to block cold air.

You can also install combination storms. That is, storm doors and screens, and storm windows and screens. These are becoming more and more popular and they do save all that taking down and storing, and then putting up again every spring and fall.

Weather stripping placed around windows and doors is another heat saver. It comes in a variety of materials and there are numerous application techniques. Weather stripping is excellent for blocking drafts through joinings; where the floor and door meet or at the center of a double window where the two frames join, for example.

There are several types of weather stripping for doors and windows. You can buy it by the running foot or in kit form. Foam rubber with adhesive backing, spring metal, rolled vinyl, and foam rubber with wood backing are some of the materials that you will find available.

You won't need many tools, and installation is quite simple. For doors, installation is similar for the two sides and the top. The threshold may offer a variety of methods of installation; a vinyl tubing threshold, a sweep, an interlocking threshold are some.

Caulking, in tubes or cords, can be used around outside window frames and door frames to close gaps that let drafts into your living area. Caulking can be applied at any opening where two different materials meet. (See page 36 for caulking details.)

Efficient use of energy in the home will in part determine the size of your heating or cooling bill. There are dozens of small ways to cut down on your energy costs: Closing off unused rooms, turning down the thermostat at night, closing the fireplace flue when it is not in use are simple examples.

FOAM-EDGED WOOD

ADHESIVE-BACKED FOAM

METAL-BACKED VINYL

FOAM-FILLED GASKET

CASEMENT STRIPPING

TUBULAR GASKET

FELT

SPRING METAL

Weather stripping is available in many forms, both flexible and rigid, for either doors or windows.

BRACKETS

HOOK   EYE

Traditional storm sashes generally hang on brackets on the house exterior. The brackets are secured with screws.

Vapor barriers

Since heat is lost more easily through water than through air, insulation that is damp loses its effectiveness. Vapor barriers prevent water from condensing in the insulation material and in the wooden frame of your house.

Always use vapor barriers in sidewalls. Proper alignment is shown on page 51.

You may not need a barrier in your attic, however, provided there is adequate ventilation. Batt and blanket insulation can be purchased with the vapor barrier already attached to one side. Always install a vapor barrier *toward* the living space so the insulation is between it and the *cold* wall or area. Use 2-mil or thicker polyethylene as a vapor barrier for any insulation material, such as loose fill, that is not supplied with one. Extruded-polystyrene board serves as its own vapor barrier, but some other rigid boards require one.

Caution: Never use vapor barriers between layers of insulation. If, for example, you plan to add fibrous batts over existing batts in your attic floor, get them *without* a vapor barrier. Otherwise, moisture will gather in the existing insulation, causing wood rot and substantial loss of heat.

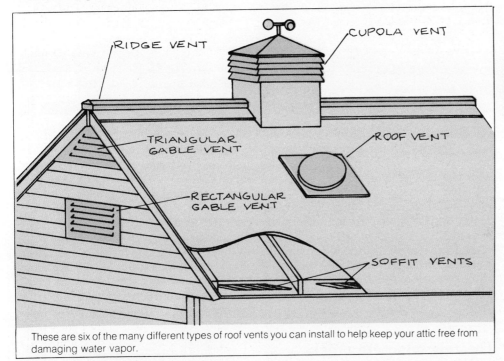

How a vapor barrier works

Ventilation

Whenever you add insulation you may also need to add ventilation. Adequate ventilation, especially in the attic, removes water vapor before it gets a chance to condense into drops of water, which mat down insulation and also rot beams and rafters.

A ventilated attic will also keep your house cooler in summer. If you live in the cold northern part of the country, your attic ventilation area should equal 1/300th of your attic floor area if you do not have a vapor barrier and if you notice any condensation. In the warmer south, you should have both ventilation and vapor barrier. If your house is air-conditioned, however, you'll only need half as much ventilation area to be effective. For how to install vents, see pages 16 and 17.

Street scene
My roof vent cools the attic just fine but I should have had a helper down on the ground when I positioned it. I got the dern thing so far up front that it can be seen from the street. A few feet back and it would have done the job just as well but out of sight.

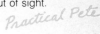
Practical Pete

RIDGE VENT — CUPOLA VENT — TRIANGULAR GABLE VENT — ROOF VENT — RECTANGULAR GABLE VENT — SOFFIT VENTS

These are six of the many different types of roof vents you can install to help keep your attic free from damaging water vapor.

Point of diminishing returns

There comes a point at which you have the perfect kind and amount of insulation for your home and for the geographic location you live in. After this, additional insulation will not save you any money on fuel bills. Your local or regional Federal Energy Administration office can give you the maximum recommendations for your area. It's a good idea to check with them *before* you purchase and install insulation because geographical areas do have different insulation requirements.

You can get the names of reputable local insulation contractors from the local FEA, FHA office, or Better Business Bureau.

For detailed information and reliable instructions on step-by-step installation of all kinds of insulation, write for *In the Bank or up the Chimney?*, a book prepared under contract H-2179R for the Office of Policy Development and Research; Division of Energy, Building Technology, and Standards; U.S. Department of Housing and Urban Development; Washington D.C.

In Canada, write for: *Keeping the Heat In*, published by the Office of Energy Conservation, Department of Energy, Mines and Resources, Ottawa, Canada.

7. FOUNDATIONS AND MASONRY

The foundation is the support for your house; without proper care and maintenance it can cause some drastic and expensive problems.

Taking worst things first, a foundation can crack. This can be caused by several things, but the most common factors are water pressure on the foundation or having the building located on unstable ground. If your home has been built on ground that is not reasonably solid, it may settle and shift to such an extent that the foundation cracks badly no matter how it is repaired. In this case, there isn't really anything you can do except call in a professional firm.

On the other hand, if water is the problem, you can correct it. Excessive water pressure is caused by large amounts of water seeping into the ground. Like any fluid, water will flow downhill, taking the path of least resistance. If there is a foundation in its path, you can count on trouble. The pressure of the water may be great enough to actually lift the house out of the ground like a giant boat, or it may crack the foundation wall and flood the basement. Of course, in a situation that extreme you would call in professional help.

What it takes

Approximate time: Depends on the extent of the damage, but allow at least 30 minutes.

Tools and materials: Hammer, cold chisel, old screwdriver and wire brush (for cleaning crack), garden hose, trowel, putty knife, gloves, goggles, and patching material.

UNDERCUTTING

Treating concrete cracks

Concrete cannot be used to repair concrete. It will not bond properly. Grout, mortar, premixed cement, latex compounds, and cement-sand-epoxy compounds are all good repair materials. Which you use depends on the job at hand. Of course, you could do a whole section of wall over with concrete (see page 55).

For small jobs, you can use a masonry-paste patcher. These come in handy cartridges, ready for use. (For cartridge-gun how-tos, see page 36.) On larger jobs, one of the premixed cements is best.

For any job, first clear out all loose material to a depth of at least 1 inch. If the crack is more than the width of a hairline, it should be undercut. As shown at left, this results in a cut that is wider at the bottom than on the surface, and helps lock the cement or patching compound in place.

It is essential that the cut be thoroughly clean. Hose it out with water. Then press the compound into the area with a trowel, making sure to fill each crevice. (If you're using the cartridge and gun, press down with the tip of the nozzle.) Be sure not to leave any air bubbles. Smooth the compound with a putty knife, and allow it to cure according to the manufacturer's directions. It's a good idea to wear gloves when working with concrete, and goggles when breaking up the surface.

Waterproofing

No repair, no matter how professionally executed, will stop water from leaking into your house if there is excessive water pressure on the foundation. In order to avoid this kind of problem, have the soil around your house graded so that water flows away from the house. You should also waterproof the foundation.

Waterproofing interior basement walls is a relatively simple matter. Exterior waterproofing, however, requires digging. You will need to expose at least some of the foundation; how much depends on the extent of the leak.

To waterproof the top of the foundation, have a trench, 4 feet wide and 2 feet deep, dug all around the house. Make sure the trench slopes downward, away from the house. Using a trowel, apply asphalt foundation coating to the wall, from the bottom of the trench up to grade level. Smooth the asphalt and press a sheet of polyethylene plastic against it. At the same time, extend the sheeting to line the bottom of the ditch. Fill in the trench with a 1½-foot layer of rocks; cover with topsoil.

If the leak is lower on the foundation, it is necessary to excavate right down to the footing. This is the time to call in a professional. He will do the excavating and waterproof the entire wall with concrete. At that point, either you or your contractor can lay drain tile to carry underground water away from the house.

What it takes

Approximate time: Indeterminate, depending on the extent of the area. From minutes to days.

Tools and materials: Pick and shovel (if you do the digging yourself), trowel, stiff brush, asphalt foundation coating, heavy hammer, polyethylene plastic, rocks.

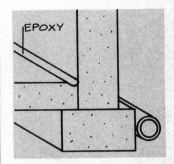

Foundation seam

The seam of the foundation is a vulnerable area. Under pressure, water may be forced up through the joint where the wall and floor meet. This condition is not difficult to remedy. Undercut the surface of the joint with a cold chisel, and fill the cavity with a two-part epoxy mix that will seal the joint. Check with your hardware dealer on the most desirable epoxy. Do this job during a dry spell, and allow at least 24 hours for the epoxy to cure.

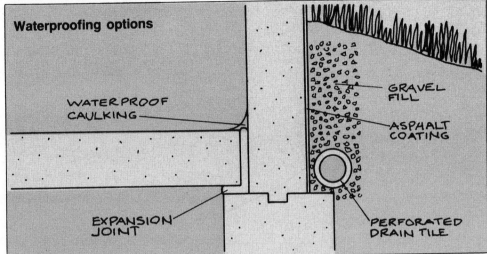

Waterproofing options

WATERPROOF CAULKING — GRAVEL FILL — ASPHALT COATING — EXPANSION JOINT — PERFORATED DRAIN TILE

Splash blocks

In a heavy rainstorm, the water running off your house and down the guttering can become a torrent. When it comes out of the downspout, it can both damage your lawns and can act as an environmental pollutant, by washing sediment from your yard into city storm drains. It can also soak the area beneath the pipe and create enough water pressure to weaken the foundation. By placing splash blocks under the downspout, you can slow the water and control it as well. There are basically two kinds of splash blocks. Both are described below.

But how do you keep it repaired?
I followed all the instructions on the sealing-compound package, but I forgot that for any crack in the foundation wall that's bigger than a hairline, you've got to make an undercut. Otherwise the compound will just fall out.

Practical Pete

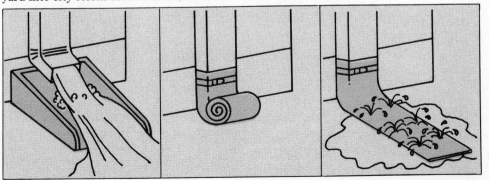

The type of splash block shown at left is simply a concrete or plastic trough with one end open. Placed under the downspout, it directs water away from the house foundation and takes some of the force from the water as it spreads. A better type of diverter is similar to a loaded hose. During dry weather, the hose automatically rolls up against the end of the downspout, out of the way, as shown in the center illustration. As water comes down the downspout, it forces the hose out, which then spreads the water evenly and without force over a wider portion of the yard, as shown at right.

Drainage

What it takes

Approximate time: Figure your time in days, depending on the size of the job.

Tools and materials: Pick and shovel (if you plan to do your own digging), gravel, drain tiles.

If waterproofing and patching don't solve the problem, the entire drainage system may be at fault. Proper drainage is essential to problem-free foundations. Indeed, the only sensible approach lies in intelligent preparation during house construction. But you may not have built your own home, in which case you could be the inheritor of certain problems in this area. Here are a few points to consider:

1. Make sure that the grade around your house slopes *away* from the foundation.
2. There will very likely be some natural drainage around your house, small channels which were created when the property was first graded or which formed by themselves. These should not be filled in, nor should they be dammed.
3. Check flower beds next to the house to make sure that they slope away from it. Also check that the edge of the bed does not act as a trap for water.
4. Water lawns and flower beds equally so that the moisture content around the house will be uniform.
5. Do not plant shrubs or trees right next to the house. They take moisture out of the soil, and you can have a foundation problem from too little moisture as well as from too much. Moreover, tree roots can crack a foundation wall.
6. Check gutters and downspouts to be sure they are working effectively and that the water is being routed far enough away from the foundation.
7. Check that any water outlets in the foundation are in good shape, and in case of a problem, deal with it immediately.

You can tell if there is unequal settling of the house or upheaval by noticing if there are spaces developing between the doors and walls and windows, if there are cracks in the inside walls, doors that all at once don't fit properly in their frames, and certainly if there are cracks in the foundation itself. Many of these you can handle.

Drains

Drainpipe, known as tile, is similar to storm-sewer pipe, but is perforated. It is available in many lengths and has various types of connectors, including elbow fittings for corners. The easiest kinds of tiles to use are those made of rigid plastic or the asphalt-impregnated type.

If your house is on level land, you will need to create a slope so the water drains away. Put a 4-inch layer of gravel in the trench, alongside the foundation footing (see page 55). Arrange the gravel so it slopes from the foundation; then set the tiles on top of it, letting them slope slightly with the gravel. Connect the tiles to a dry well (see page 24 for digging instructions).

On the other hand, if your house is on land that slopes, you can probably lay out the tiles without connecting them to a dry well. Lay the tiles around the three sides of the house that are uphill, and let the open ends extend 12 feet beyond the foundation on the lower side. This will cause the water to flow away from the house. You will need a dry well only if the soil has especially poor drainage or your house is in a crowded area.

To finish the job, in either type of installation, bury the tile in gravel, fill the trench with soil and gravel, and replace the sod carefully.

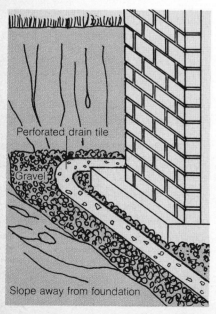

Perforated drain tile

Gravel

Slope away from foundation

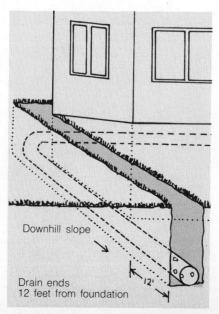

Downhill slope

Drain ends 12 feet from foundation

Bury tile in gravel —then backfill

Termite protection

So respected has the termite become, and so feared, that in the current vocabulary, his name is a synonym for silent, invisible destruction. More than 40 species can be found in the United States and Canada. The most destructive type is the subterranean termite, a tiny animal that requires moisture for its survival. The termite is highly social, living in colonies that are composed of three groups: reproductive termites, soldiers, and workers. It is the workers—wingless, blind, and white—who are the providers for the community; and they can and do eat one out of house and home.

Where and what to look for

1. Foundation walls, inside as well as outside the house, should be checked periodically. Notice cracks or any looseness in the areas around basement windows and doors. Look for wings, rotted wood. Check floor-wall joinings closely.
2. Check crawl spaces in the basement. Remove any scrap lumber stored in such areas, and any old boxes.
3. During spring and early summer look for shed wings at any of these sites. They are a sure sign of termites.
4. Look for earthen tunnels or tubes that connect the colony in the moist soil with the wood that the workers convert into food for themselves and their fellows. The tunnels are half-round in shape and about ½ inch wide. They may be found on foundation walls, basement walls, porches, and openings where pipes enter the house through the foundation. Seal such openings with caulking compound.
5. Check suspect wood by poking it with a sharp instrument such as an awl, pocketknife, or ice pick. If the instrument sinks into the wood to about ½ inch with just gentle hand pressure, you can be fairly sure that termites or dry rot have been at work:

Preventive measures

The best defense against termites is to have copper termite shields where the foundation meets the wood. These shields deny access to all those tasty joists and sills. Since the shields must extend about 3 inches beyond each side of the masonry and be anchored to the top of the foundation every 3 feet, they must be installed while the house is being built. If your home was not provided with these shields, there are other measures you can take.

Putting down a termite barrier

You can control termites with a chemical known as chlordane. It is toxic to humans, however, and so must be used with extreme care. It comes in concentrated form and must be diluted with water to create the exact solution specified by the manufacturer. Certain states have restrictions concerning the use of chlordane. Check with your county agricultural agent before you use this chemical around your house. Be careful about children and pets in the area.

If you use chlordane, follow this procedure: Dig a shallow trench all around your house, placing it close to the foundation. Mix the chlordane with water, following the package instructions—and any local regulations that may exist. Use a watering can (with the sprinkler head removed), and carefully pour the chlordane into the trench. Wear gloves for protection.

Also apply chlordane inside the house, putting it in and around any cracks where the foundation wall meets a concrete floor, near the foundation wall of all crawl spaces, and in any area that has a soil floor.

Don't ever forget that chlordane is poisonous; when you use it indoors be sure to have adequate ventilation. Leave the room after you use the chlordane, and close it off for several days.

Soil injection. A much easier way of exterminating termites is by soil injection. Chlordane is simply shot into the ground. No digging is required. For this, a soil injector is fitted with chlordane cartridges. This costs more than the liquid method, but it is cleaner, easier, and less dangerous. It's easy enough to do yourself.

Joist
Siding
Sill
Copper termite shield

What it takes

Approximate time: Indeterminate, but you should inspect periodically.

Tools and materials: Ice pick, awl, or other sharp instrument; shovel, power drill and masonry bit, garden hose, soil-injector tube or watering can, chlordane (or liquid cartridge), concrete-patch mix, caulking compound and gun.

Caution

Since chlordane can be harmful to humans, it is a good idea to follow these instructions as well as those specified by the manufacturer:
1. Dig a trench 2 feet deep and about 6 inches wide all around your house foundation. Do not go below the footing, and make sure that the trench slants well away from the house.
2. Pour the diluted chlordane into the trench, at the rate specified in the instructions. Fill the trench and mix extra chlordane solution with the dirt.
3. Make a trench around each pillar that supports a porch or any other structure, and treat it with chlordane in the same way.
4. Treat ground beneath slabs, such as garage floors, patios, and walks, if they are near the foundation. With a power drill and masonry bit, drill holes in the slabs, 6 inches out from the foundation and a foot apart. Using a funnel, pour the chlordane into the holes at the required rate. Then fill in the holes with concrete.

Concrete

Tools for concrete work

Edger

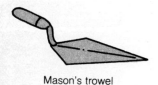

Mason's trowel

Wood float

Steel trowel

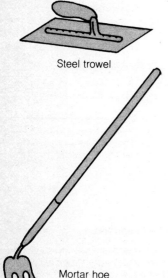

Mortar hoe

TIP: The best kind of hoe for mixing is one with holes in the blade.

TIP: Use a square-bladed shovel for mixing concrete ingredients.

Unquestionably, concrete is one of man's most useful inventions. It is also the one material you are bound to find in any house. There is good reason for its popularity. Beyond being inexpensive and relatively easy to work with, concrete is strong, fireproof, and can be formed in many shapes.

Most homeowners who are do-it-yourselfers get their hands into concrete at one point or another, either to repair existing work or to install a patio, pool, or the like. Since large repairs call for tearing the old structure apart and starting from scratch, this chapter treats all concrete installations as new projects. (For minor repairs, see page 54.)

Whether you are planning a repair or a new installation, you have to know how to buy concrete. There are two ways to purchase it: already mixed or in raw materials that you mix yourself.

Transit-mix

You can purchase concrete in this form from a concrete-manufacturing plant and have it delivered to your house ready to pour. Transported in large trucks, the concrete is held inside mixers that prevent it from hardening. The advantage of this method is apparent on large jobs such as foundations, patios, walks, and steps. Not only do you save a great deal of time and work; the resulting work will be smoother and better in all ways because the concrete was poured at one time.

The disadvantage of transit-mix is that you must have everything ready for the truck's arrival, including extra help to man shovels and wheelbarrows if the truck can't get close enough to the work site.

Here are a few points to consider when you use transit-mix concrete.
1. Get the ground ready well ahead of time. Level the work-site area and tamp it to compact the soil. If the soil is hardpan or clay, or if it has poor drainage, add a few inches of cinders or gravel as fill.
2. Build forms that are level and strong (page 62). Remember that you will be dumping tons of concrete in a few minutes, and once the work begins, you won't have time to do any adjusting. Brace the forms from the outside. If they look as if they might fall inwards, brace them internally as well, with blocks of wood you can remove as the mix flows in.
3. Prepare the route that the truck will take to your work site. You'll have perhaps 25 tons moving in there, and you'll have to allow for clearance as well as weight.

4. Be sure of your tools and the help you might require. Let the family pitch in, and ask your friends for help.
5. Estimate the amount of concrete as well as you can and place your order early.
6. Prepare some extra forms in case there is excess concrete. You may find that you have ordered more than you needed, and this way you won't waste it. Build the forms with future projects—steps, slab paths, and so on—in mind. If nothing is planned, forms 4 inches deep and 2 feet square are the most practical because that size slab is most versatile. (If you have ordered too little concrete on the other hand, you might be able to make up for it by putting small rocks into the mix. Have them handy.)

You-haul

One of the most convenient ways of getting concrete is via the you-haul system. You simply purchase the concrete in a rented trailer or pickup-size truck and haul it yourself. When done, you return the vehicle. This method is best for middle-size jobs—those calling for something between a quarter of a yard and a yard of concrete.

As with transit-mix, be sure to have everything ready before you start pouring. And remember to hose the trailer or mixer clean before you return it to the dealer. The last type of premixed concrete is known as dry-mix. It is sold ready for use with the addition of water. For very small jobs, dry-mix is an excellent choice. For anything else, its cost makes it prohibitive.

Mix-it-yourself

With all the premixed concrete available, in many cases your most practical choice is to buy the raw materials and mix the concrete yourself. The reasons are several: Many jobs are too small for transit-mix and you-haul (most companies will not deliver under a specified amount). The same jobs are frequently too large for dry-mix. Add to this the fact that many areas do not offer you-haul concrete, and you can see why you may have to mix your own. This should be a last resort, however. Never mix your own concrete when you can use transit-mix or you-haul. Not only is it unnecessary, it's impractical. The first part of the concrete may set before you can fill the form.

There are two methods for mixing your own concrete: in a wheelbarrow, or in a concrete mixer. For the first, merely shovel the specified amount of sand, gravel, and cement into a wheelbarrow, and mix thoroughly with a garden hoe. Make a hole in the center, add a little water, and mix. Continue adding small amounts of water and mixing thoroughly until the concrete is a good consistency (see "Mixing" below). Then wheel the mix over to the job.

A good alternative is to rent a portable concrete mixer from your dealer. Shovel the ingredients into the mixer, then let it do the work. The result will be a mix made in much less time, with less effort, and one that is more thoroughly blended.

Caution: If the mixer is powered by electricity, make sure that all electrical connections are correct and in good condition and that the extension cord is grounded. If possible, plug into an outside ground-fault-interrupter circuit.

The materials

Portland cement is the material used in making concrete. This is a type of material, not a brand name, and it is manufactured by several different companies. It comes in paper bags weighing 94 pounds.

Cement must be stored in a dry place; never place it on a damp floor or in a damp room. It will take up moisture and become hardened, lumpy, and useless. Once the bag is open, concrete takes up moisture more readily. Always seal the bag tightly.

The sand used in concrete should be well washed to remove any salt or organic matter. It may run from fine beach sand to coarse particles; the crucial thing is that it must be free of impurities such as soil, clay, plant life, and other foreign materials. To test it, rub some of the dry sand through your hands. If they become soiled, the sand is not suitable.

The larger particles or aggregates used in concrete range in size from ¼ inch to stones as large as 3 inches. A good rule to follow is that none of the aggregate should be larger than one-third the thickness of the concrete being poured.

The water used in mixing concrete must not have alkalies or oils in it; if it does, it won't mix properly. To be safe, use only potable water—and measure it out from a clean container.

Mixing

The secret in mixing concrete lies in using the proper materials, mixing them thoroughly, and being sure you have used them in the correct proportions. This is especially so with respect to water, which determines the strength of the concrete.

	Cement	Sand	Gravel
Walks, driveways, floors, curbs, steps, basements, etc.	1 part	2 parts	3 parts
Footings, foundations, porous walls	1 part	3 parts	4 parts

Concrete formulas

It's a good idea to mix only one sack of cement at one time; that makes it easier to figure the amounts and keep the proportions correct.

The first step is to measure out the concrete. If you're mixing only small quantities, use a shovel and count the shovelfuls to get the proper total. Then add the sand and gravel in the correct proportions. Lastly, add the water, a little at a time. For most work, you'll need about 6 gallons of water to each sack of cement.

Estimating quantities

One of the most puzzling parts of concrete work is figuring out just how much you will need. Normally slabs such as terraces and walks should be 3½ to 4½ inches thick. Driveways are usually 6 inches thick. The first step in estimating is to multiply the width times the length of the project to determine the square footage. Then multiply this by the thickness of the project. The following chart gives a rough estimate of how much of each material you will need for 100 square feet to a depth of 3, 4, and 6 inches.

Depth	3 inches	4 inches	6 inches
Cement	6 cu. ft.*	7.8 cu. ft.*	12 cu. ft.*
Sand	15 cu. ft.	19.5 cu. ft.	30 cu. ft.
Gravel	21 cu. ft.	27.3 cu. ft.	42 cu. ft.

Regardless of whether you're purchasing ready-mix concrete or making it up yourself, you can use the above formulas for purchasing materials.

*One bag of dry cement contains one cubic foot of the material.

Yards and feet

People who work around concrete often speak in terms of "yards." This standard measurement confuses some people, for in this case a "yard" is definitely *not* 3 feet. Rather, it is short talk for a cubic yard, and that's 27 cubic feet . not 3, or 9 either.

The concrete form

What it takes

Approximate time: At least a day for an average, home-handyman job.

Tools and materials: Hammer, saw, nails (regular and double-headed), 2-by-4, 2-by-6, or 2-by-8-inch wood for forms, ¾-inch plywood sheet (as needed), level.

Next in importance to the concrete mix is the form. Your project will look only as good as the form it takes, and this depends on how the moist concrete is held until it sets. Forms must be sturdy enough to hold the concrete without breaking or bulging. Of course, there should be no leakage, and the concrete must be uniformly level.

There are dozens of different kinds of forms, depending on the specific job. Drawing A shows a form that would hold a slab pouring for a patio, walk, or something similar. Drawing B shows the form used for pouring a foundation wall.

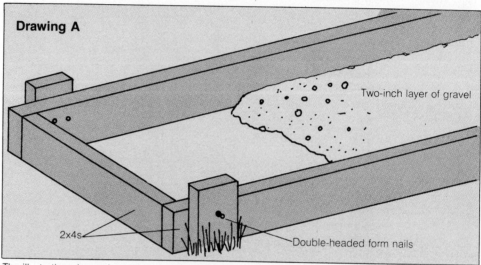

Drawing A

Two-inch layer of gravel

2x4s

Double-headed form nails

The illustration above shows the wooden form for a typical slab pouring. The drawing below pictures the form for a foundation wall. All form lumber should be straight-grained and solid. Brush it with old crankcase oil to keep the concrete from sticking to it. However, if the lumber is to remain in the concrete, use a wood preservative instead of oil.

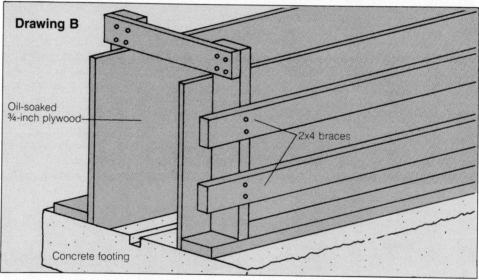

Drawing B

Oil-soaked ¾-inch plywood

2x4 braces

Concrete footing

Reinforcing the pour

With a good concrete mix and well-made form, your concrete pour is bound to give you good results. For the results to last, however, one more step is necessary— reinforcing the concrete. There are a few exceptions to the rule. A small slab that rests on solid ground does not require reinforcement. Nor does a slab broken into short segments, as in the steps shown on pages 64 and 65. But all vertical pours and long, unbroken slabs must be reinforced. Otherwise, chances are good that the concrete will buckle or crack in a few years.

The reinforcing material used for concrete is steel. It is available in two forms: a wire fabric, known as steel mesh, and steel rods. In general, steel mesh is used for ground-supported slabs; steel rod for elevated slabs and vertical pours, such as foundation walls.

Both materials are sold at lumberyards and building-supply stores. Mesh wire is available in widths of 5 and 6 feet and is sold cut to the length you specify. Steel rod is sold in a variety of lengths and diameters. For most household work, ½-inch-diameter rod is used. **Caution:** Most areas have building codes that specify the minimum rod spacing and rod diameter for freestanding structures. Check these codes before you make your purchase. Suppliers are generally knowledgeable.

Choosing and using steel mesh

Reinforcing mesh is available in many strengths. The two factors that determine this variable are the amount of space between the wires and the gauge of the wire itself. For flat areas like sidewalks and patios, 10-gauge wire spaced to create 6-inch squares is adequate. For stairwells, driveways, and other structures requiring more support, 6-gauge wire is a better choice. These figures are, of course, general. Where the subsoil offers exceptionally poor drainage, you will want to use stronger wire. Check with your dealer for the best wire for your locale and project.

There are several ways of positioning the mesh in the concrete. Since in most cases, it should be placed midway between the top and bottom of the concrete, the easiest method is to pour half the thickness of the concrete, put the precut wire on top of it, and then pour the remaining half, as shown below, left.

About mesh prices:

Steel mesh comes in rolls that look like heavy fencing wire and are usually a bulky 6 feet wide. Your supplier will cut off as many feet of it as you want. But because cutting is a chore, he'll probably quote you a much better price per foot on a full roll. If you think you can use it, buy it in quantity and save.

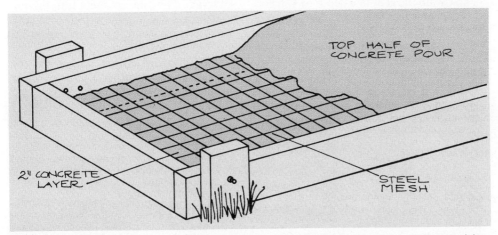

Pour concrete in the form to half the desired thickness. Lay the wire mesh on top; then pour the remaining half. Be sure to keep the mesh at least 1 inch below the surface of the concrete, and make sure that cut wire ends don't poke up through the surface. If any do, push them back in place before the concrete sets.

Using reinforcing rod

Reinforcing rod is placed in the wet concrete in much the same way as mesh wire. However, most projects in concrete that the do-it-yourselfer would engage in will not require reinforcing.

If, however, you do take on an ambitious job requiring rod, then check your local code on specifications. You can tie the rod in with wire to stone or brick. If there is overlapping, it should be about 18 inches, and tied with wire. Rod comes in 20-foot lengths and can be cut with a hacksaw.

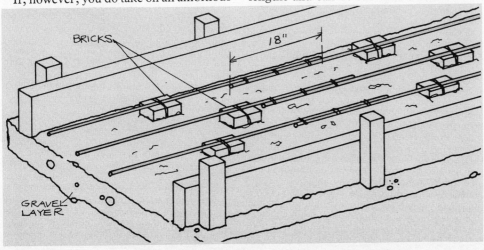

Pouring small slabs

What it takes

Approximate time: Depends on size of job and skill of homeowner. If you are new to concrete work, allow a long day even for a small job.

Tools and materials: Hammer, nails, reinforcing steel if necessary, float, edger, 2x4s for forms, one 2x4 longer than the form is wide, iron rake, steel trowel, sheet plastic or burlap bags, concrete.

From plain to fancy

There are dozens of ways to liven up concrete. It can be painted with specially formulated coatings, textured, or embedded with exposed aggregate. To paint concrete, clean it with trisodium phosphate and water (1 pound to a gallon), rinse well, and scrub with a solution of 1 gallon of muriatic acid and 3 gallons of water. **Caution:** Handle acid with extreme care, and use a long-handled shop broom for the scrubbing. Rinse well, then apply the paint according to the manufacturer's directions.

To texture concrete, go over it with a stiff-bristled broom before it sets. Cover with burlap bags until it cures.

To create exposed-aggregate concrete, mix and pour the concrete just like any other slab. After the initial smoothing, scatter washed pebbles over the surface. Using a wooden board, pound them flush with the surface. Let the surface of the concrete harden slightly. Then flush away the surrounding concrete with a soft stream of water.

Nine out of ten concrete projects involve pouring ground-supported slabs. Small slabs serve as paths, barbecue-pit supports, and like objects. Extend the length of the form and you have a sidewalk or driveway. Enlarge it all around and you have a porch or patio. The basic techniques for all slab pouring are the same.

For most slab work, figure on pouring a 4-inch layer of concrete, and thus on using 2x4s for your forms. Start by grading the work-site ground. If the slab is to join the house, grade the land so it slopes away from the house at a rate of ½ inch for every foot. Otherwise, the ground should be level.

Excavate the area to a depth of 4 inches. **TIP:** If your land has poor drainage, excavate to 6 inches and fill in with a 2-inch layer of tamped gravel or medium-coarse rock.

Lay the 2x4s in place, wedging them into the ground slightly to prevent leakage. If the slab is to be level side-to-side and back-to-front, check for level all around. If the land was graded to slope, check that opposite sides of the form are level (step 4, page 64). In both cases, check that opposite sides are parallel, and make sure the form doesn't get distorted in the following steps.

With double-headed nails, nail the form together. Reinforce it with 2-by-4-inch stakes all around. Drive the stakes at least 1 foot into the ground and make sure they rest flat against the form. Saw the stakes so they are level with the top of the form. Nail the form lumber to the stakes from inside the form, using common nails.

If you need reinforcing steel (page 61), have it cut and ready to be placed.

With the form ready and everything needed at hand, either mix or purchase the concrete. Pour the concrete into the form and settle it thoroughly, using an iron rake. Be sure you push the mix firmly against the sides of the form.

To finish the surface, follow the steps shown below. Then, to allow the concrete to cure properly, keep the surface moist for three days. You can do this either by sprinkling it with water or covering it with burlap or polyethylene plastic.

1. To remove excess concrete, use a long 2x4. Resting it on either side of the form and starting at the top, run the 2x4 down the form in short back-and-forth strokes. Have a helper man one end of the 2x4 while you hold the other.

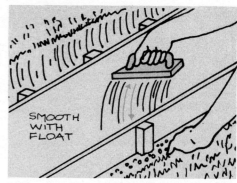

2. Use a wood float to smooth and level the surface. This also removes excess water on the surface. Work the float back and forth until you are thoroughly satisfied with the job.

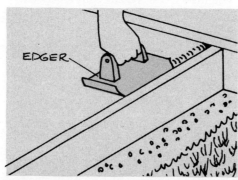

3. With an edger, round off the concrete where it meets the form. This keeps edges from chipping or getting broken. If you are pouring a long run, such as a walk, use the edger to divide the walk into sections. This will not only improve the appearance of the walk, but will help prevent it from cracking.

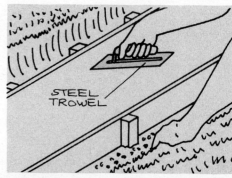

4. Finally, use a steel trowel on the surface to clear it of all water and smooth it down to a finish. Be sure to allow the concrete to cure properly before walking on it. Moisten the surface each day for three days with a fine spray of water.

Pouring concrete steps

One major home-repair job that may seem a bit difficult until you try it is pouring concrete steps. There are dozens of different kinds of concrete steps and all sorts of places where they can be put. You may want steps off the front or back porch, to connect with a walk, or to run from a patio to a swimming pool. No matter what kind of steps you have in mind, the method of pouring is the same; although with a larger job you will need reinforcing mesh. Check your local building code.

There are two things to remember when you pour concrete steps: The steps must be safe to use, and the forms you use must be sturdy enough to hold the weight of the concrete until it sets or cures.

On most entrance steps, the risers—the vertical portions of the steps—should be about 7½ inches high. The step tread or depth varies, but is usually 10 to 11 inches. On most main walks and steps, the width of the steps should be about 4 feet. When you

pour entrance steps for a door, make sure that the top step is actually a small platform at least 3 feet in depth. This prevents the possibility of someone walking out the door and having a nasty fall.

Although most homemade steps have straight up-and-down risers, the professional job will angle in about 15 degrees at the bottom. For this, the bottom edges of the risers are beveled to a 15-degree angle, so the trowel can be pushed under them.

Drawing A shows the proper method of constructing an entrance platform and steps to a front or back door. Note that the stakes are held securely in place by cross braces. This prevents the forms from bulging out at the top. Most step forms are made from 2x8s. These provide the proper strength and support, as well as the most commonly used riser height.

Drawing B shows the form used if you pour steps down a basement stairwell, and the walls are already poured.

What it takes

Approximate time: A day for the average home-handyman job.

Tools and materials: Hammer, nails, level, shovels, iron rake, hoe, cement, aggregate, water (or mix, as desired).

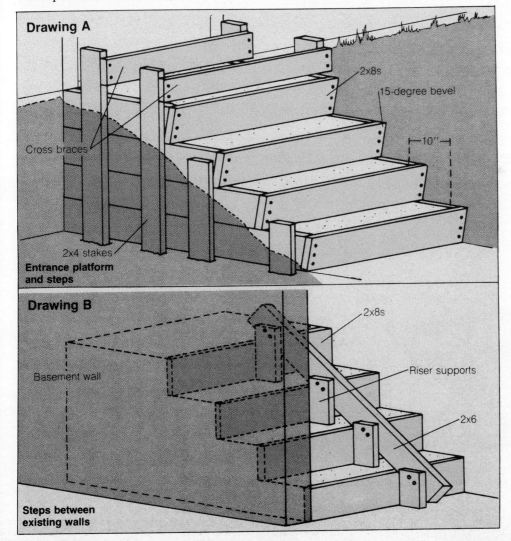

Drawing A

Cross braces

2x8s

15-degree bevel

10"

2x4 stakes

Entrance platform and steps

Drawing B

Basement wall

2x8s

Riser supports

2x6

Steps between existing walls

Step-by-step steps

1. First determine the size of the steps needed, and build individual forms for each step. On entrance steps, the norm is to build the form for the bottom step first, then the succeeding forms, so you finish at the top. Stack these forms on top of each other and put them in place. Drive 2-by-4 inch stakes at least a foot into the ground every 3 feet around the forms.

2. Make sure the stakes are driven in true and square with the form. They should not lean in or out, nor should they be twisted in relation to the side of the form. If you are pouring steps over 3 feet wide, or more than two steps high, let the stakes extend at least a foot above the forms so you can nail braces to them. Check that the form is level from all sides.

3. After you have leveled the forms, fasten them to the stakes with nails. Drive the nails from inside the form so they go through the boards, then into the stakes. All nail heads should be flush with the wood.

4. Using a long straightedge to hold the level, check across the ends of the form, which must also be square. The form for each step must fit tightly on the one below it. If there is any opening, the concrete will flow through it, creating an ugly line in the finished steps when it dries.

5. You may find, as we did, that your terrain requires special considerations. Because of the slope of the ground, this form was constructed backwards. Here the form for the bottom step is being installed under that for the top step.

6. The form is again leveled and nailed to stakes driven squarely against the sides and end of the form. If your steps are wide or high, nail cross braces to the stakes. This prevents the forms from bulging in the middle.

7. If the steps are to cross a small ditch, insert a culvert in the form to allow for water runoff. The pipe may be purchased at building-supply dealers in any length needed and in a range of diameters.

8. Once the culvert is in place, secure it to the ground with a U-shaped piece of ½-inch reinforcing rod. Any hollow object buried in concrete has a tendency to float up out of the concrete regardless of its weight.

9. With the form completed, rocks and chunks of old concrete rubble are used for fill, cutting down the amount of concrete needed. If you use this tactic, remember to keep fill away from the outer edges of the form. Otherwise, it may show when the form boards are removed.

10. You can mix the concrete yourself in a rented electric mixer. We used a formula of 1 part cement, 3 parts clean sand, and 4 parts gravel. Mix the three thoroughly, then add water until the mixture is fairly thick, but thin enough to flow. The proportion of water in the mix determines the strength of the finished project. The best method is to add water slowly until the right consistency is reached.

11. While the concrete is being poured into the form, jab a heavy rake into the concrete to help settle it. Do this especially around the edges of the form; otherwise you'll end up with air bubbles at the edges of the concrete. After using the rake to settle the concrete, you'll need to level or screed it off.

12. With a long, straight 2x4 and a helper, screed the concrete surface. Allow the edge of the 2x4 to rest on the forms, and using short back-and-forth strokes, drag off the excess concrete as you push toward the end of the form. This produces a level, fairly smooth surface, but it takes muscle and you may have to go over it a few times. This action drives the aggregates down in the mix.

13. With the surface screeded off, work the surface until it is the way you want it. Be careful when working in this position not to lock knees. This will help you maintain a free and even stroke.

14. Unless you round the edges of the steps with an edger, they will be flat and sharp and may break off. Gently drag the edger between the form boards and the concrete to round the edges and provide a nosing for the steps. After edging, trowel the concrete to smooth out any rough spots left by the edger.

15. On outdoor steps, a smooth surface is a hazard. After the concrete has set up fairly hard, but is still workable, gently drag a stiff broom across the steps to create a roughened surface. If the concrete is poured in hot weather, cover it with plastic for several days. The longer it cures, the harder and more waterproof it will be.

16. The final step is to remove the form boards and clean up any excess concrete dropped around the edges. (Wait several days for this.) Rake the area smooth and landscape as desired.

17. The actual pouring of these steps took a day, with the previous day spent in building the forms. With experience, a day would be adequate for the entire operation.

I really got horse collared!
It looked easy enough, but I should have asked my neighbor how he poured his steps. Then I would have known that any hollow object buried in concrete has a tendency to float to the surface. (Secure it with reinforcing rod.)

Practical Pete

Concrete block

This house has a concrete block foundation and a carport made of decorative blocks.

When many of us think of cinder or concrete blocks, we think of ugly commercial buildings or institutions of some sort or other. But today's concrete blocks can be decorative as well as functional. What is more, with a little practice, even the unhandy handyperson can learn to lay blocks. And although the work is physically taxing, the results can be highly rewarding when you see what you can do.

Concrete blocks come in many different shapes and sizes for a wide variety of jobs. In addition to the basic H blocks, there are a half dozen or more other types for special purposes, for instance, corner blocks which have their ends shaped flush, or jamb or joist blocks for use around door and window jambs, thin half blocks for building interiors consisting of non-load-bearing walls. There is also a great variety of decorative blocks available that can be used for anything from a carport wall to an interior divider wall.

As in any masonry work, strict attention must be paid to using the right type of mortar and to good, safe building techniques. The following sequence shows basic procedures for all block-work projects.

1. One of the most common uses of concrete blocks is in house foundations. The first step in most block work is to excavate for the footing and pour it. Normally it should be 18 inches deep, or below the frost line, and 12 to 18 inches wide.

2. You'll need something to mix the mortar in (the model shown can be rented inexpensively), a 3-foot level, string line and level, string holders, tape measure, brick chisel, hammer, trowel and jointer.

3. Position batter boards on each side of the corner wall. These can be 1x4s or 2x4s nailed to stakes 2 feet apart.

4. Determine the exact location of the wall and tie string to nails driven into the boards. Dry-lay the block in place to determine how it will lay. Drop a plumb bob down to the outside corner of the end-corner block and find its exact location.

Mixing mortar

Mortar is the basic material that holds bricks, blocks, and stones together. It also serves as a grout for repairing brick, and as a patching compound. There are basically two methods of mixing mortar. You can purchase premix mortar which is already dry mixed, or you can mix your own, using:

1 part portland cement
6 parts sand
1 part hydrated lime
Just enough water to give a puttylike consistency.

Mix the mortar in a wheelbarrow, or, if you have quite a lot of block to lay, in a concrete mixer; in this case you'll need a helper to keep the mortar mixed and hand you blocks.

Mix all the ingredients together except the water; then gradually add water until the mortar is well mixed but not soupy. It should stand up on its own when pulled up with a trowel or hoe. But it should not be dry or crumbly.

One sack of portland cement, one sack of hydrated lime, and 600 pounds of sand will lay approximately 100 regular-size blocks.

5. Spread mortar on the location of the first corner block. It is important to have your block ready before you start.

6. Position the block in place, and settle it in so that it is well seated.

7. Check with the plumb bob to make sure that the block is positioned correctly.

8. Fasten a string holder to the corner of the block. This is a wooden block which clips to the cinder block corners and holds a string taut along the outside edge of the block. Lay the two end blocks first; then position the string and lay line blocks against it.

9. Level the block and tap it into position. Of course, this must all be done before the mortar begins to set.

10. The line of blocks must follow the taut string exactly. Check with a string level every so often to see that the tops are level also.

Block options

The most common size of concrete blocks is, nominally, 16 inches long by 8 inches high by 8 inches wide. (The blocks are actually ⅜ inch shorter and lower than that, to allow for the mortar joints on two faces.) But there are also blocks that measure only 4 inches high, and their adobelike look is preferred by many designers and builders. Solid cinder blocks are available in exactly the same size as standard brick. Thinner, flatter blocks are ideal for paving jobs on patios and paths. Textured thin blocks are used on walls to give a stonelike appearance.

11. Before laying a block, prepare a bed of mortar along each side of the block position and across the end and center.

12. Stand the block up and "butter" one end. The amount of mortar shown in the illustration is about right. Apply a little pressure with the trowel, so the mortar clings to the block.

13. Then in one smooth, quick motion pick up the block and lower it onto the mortar bed and against the next block. The mortar joints should be approximately ⅜ inch wide and kept even.

14. Tap the block into position against the string line and make sure it is level with the adjoining block, as well as in every other direction.

15. The second course is also started at the corner, positioned with the string line, and of course leveled. Note that the positioning of the corner block in the second course is perpendicular to the block below it.

16. As each block is laid, the excess mortar is squeezed out of the joints and caught so that it can be used for the next block.

Painting blocks

For vivid color on concrete block, use one of the paints developed especially for masonry. The old standby for outdoor use is portland-cement paint. It comes in powder form and must be mixed with water and then applied only to a 'dampened' wall.

17. After the row or course of blocks is laid, a jointer is used to smooth out and round up the joints for a more even bond.

18. Then a quick downward swipe with the flat of the trowel knocks off any excess mortar that may be sticking to the joints.

Blocks and noise

A concrete-block wall reduces sounds by 40 decibels. This means normal speech cannot be heard through it, and loud speech can be faintly heard but not understood. Within a room, fully two thirds of the noise that strikes a block wall is absorbed and does not bounce back. Few other building materials even approach these standards.

19. To cut a block, as will sometimes be necessary, score it by tapping on a wide brick chisel with a mason's hammer or other metal-striking hammer. Don't try to break through on the first side; score across the block.

20. Then turn the block over and score the opposite side until it cracks on the scored line.

Building with brick

The tools:

Trowel

Bricklayer's hammer

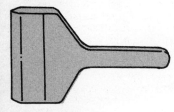

Wide chisel

Brick jointer

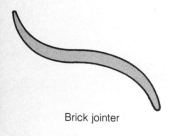

Cape chisel

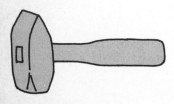

Heavy-duty hammer

For centuries brick has been the most popular masonry material for all kinds of structures: house walls, patios, fireplaces, steps. It is attractive to begin with and becomes more so with age; it is easy to handle and is solid and long lasting. Brick has been used for at least 5,000 years, and while today's bricks are made in literally thousands of combinations of size and shape, color and texture, most fit into three kinds: *building, face,* and *paving bricks.*

Building bricks. These are the standard bricks, all-purpose, reasonably priced, and they can be used for any outdoor structure. As a rule, they are red in color, and about 8 inches long by 3¾ inches wide by 2¼ inches deep. This can vary.

Face bricks. These come in many sizes, and in colors that range from purplish-black to near-white, and also in textures from very smooth to rough. Face bricks make handsome walls, steps, and bar-becues, but generally they are too expensive and too highly textured for walks and patios.

Paving bricks. These are best for patios and walks, for they have a smooth surface and are often shallow—as thin as ½ inch—so that they can be laid like tiles in a mortar bed. Paving bricks come in a variety of colors, though generally in shades of red, and they also come in many shapes and sizes, including squares and hexagons.

The chief consideration when you choose bricks for an outdoor project is the question of weather resistance. The three types mentioned above will have specifications indicated by the manufacturer. The code will read SW, MW, or NW. Bricks with an SW rating can withstand severe weathering, MW moderate weathering, and NW no weathering. SW bricks are the only kind that are fit for direct contact with the ground, so you should only do paving or patio work with bricks of this type.

How to estimate materials

To estimate your brick needs, first calculate in square feet the total area that needs to be covered. Should the area be irregular, then a good way is to divide it into squares, circles, or rectangles for easier arithmetical handling. That is to say, you can use a standard formula for each section and then add the sections together. The area of a rectangle is equal to the length times the width. The area of a circle can be computed by multiplying the radius by itself and then multiplying the product by 3.14.

Then figure the number of bricks needed to cover a square foot, as follows: For mortared paving, brick steps, and walls, add ⅜ inch to each face dimension. That is, for a brick that measures 8x2¼x3¾ inches deep, your figures would be 8⅜ and 2⅝. Then multiply these figures, and divide the result into 144 to compute the number of bricks to a square foot. For the standard brick mentioned above, the answer would be 6.55 bricks per square foot. (In the case of paving that is not mortared, do the same except for adding the ⅜-inch allowance to the brick dimensions.)

You can figure the quantity of brick needed by multiplying the number of square feet to be covered in the work area by the number of bricks to a square foot. Then add on an additional 5 percent to allow for breakage and cutting.

To estimate your mortar needs, figure as follows: For a thick (double) wall, figure 20 cubic feet of mortar for each 100 square feet of bricks. For paving, figure 8 cubic feet of mortar for each 100 square feet of bricks. Then add a little extra for waste.

Types of bonds

The pattern formed by the courses in a brick wall is called the bond. The bricks are always laid in such a way that vertical joints in two courses never fall together but are staggered. Yet, in most bonds the vertical joints of *alternate* courses should be in line. There are many kinds of bonds and you can simply take your pick. A few are shown below.

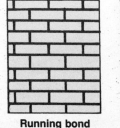

Running bond

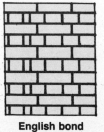

English bond

American bond

Flemish bond

How to lay brick

The techniques for laying brick are much the same as for block (pages 66-69), except for the fact that in a wall brick is normally laid in double thickness for extra strength. Another difference in handling brick is that all brick should be well moistened before laying. (Blocks, on the other hand, must be kept dry during the laying process.)

Joints. The proper mortar mix is crucial. Refer to page 67 for the basic recipe. But for brickwork, prepare a slightly moister mix, say, to about the consistency of heavy cream. The form of the joint ranks next in importance. Joints should be about ⅜ inch thick. If a joint is too thin, too wide, or just plain sloppy, it will not only spoil the appearance of the block or brick, but will weaken the wall as well.

The secret to laying bricks really lies in handling the trowel. It is essential that mortar be properly spread before the bricks are placed, and proficiency with the trowel is therefore mandatory. The techniques are the same as those shown on pages 66-69. But since you'll be working "in miniature," speed becomes more of a factor, and good work habits can only be acquired on the job. You might want to find a site where a professional bricklayer is at work and spend some time watching him.

Cutting bricks. Before cutting a brick, test it by striking it against another brick or tapping it with a hammer. If you hear a clear ring, then you'll know the brick is a good one. If the sound is dull, the brick will very likely crumble when it is cut. Before you start to work, determine how many half-bricks you will need. In this way they can be cut in batches. Use the chisel and a heavy hammer. Wear safety glasses. Place the chisel on the cutting point of the brick, tilt the handle a little toward the waste end, and strike sharply.

Line and level. To lay a course of bricks you will need a line to keep it straight, that is, level and plumb. The usual way to proceed is to build up the corners and ends first, and then attach your line, using plastic or wooden line blocks. Then lay the intermediate bricks flush with the line. (It is necessary to determine spacing by setting a course in place without mortar.)

Use a 4-foot spirit level to check your brickwork before the mortar sets. The vertical and horizontal bubbles in the level will tell you if your work is true. When necessary, you can tap the bricks into line against the level. But always keep the bottom of the level clean; even a small bit of mortar will create inaccuracies.

Tuck-pointing (brick repair)

A badly cracked wall should be repaired immediately or it may cause even more damage. First determine what caused the cracking. With a star chisel or a round-nosed cape chisel, remove all flaking debris and deepen the crack or mortar joint to about ⅝ to ¾ inch. Refill the joint with mortar and smooth it with a jointer. An alternative, if the crack persistently reopens, is to use latex patching cement.

Replacing a damaged brick

If the brick is loose in the wall and can be removed, simply chip away the loosened mortar and take it out. On the other hand, if it is in solid, you may have a good deal of trouble. If so, you may have to patch the area with mortar or patching cement rather than try to extract and replace the brick.
TIP: If you dampen a brick, it will sometimes loosen up. After the brick is out, it's a simple matter to mortar in the opening and place a new brick.

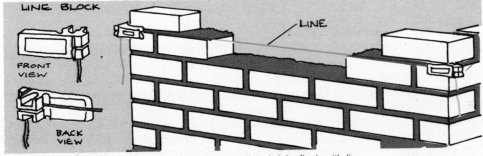

Fasten line blocks to corner bricks, and lay intermediate bricks flush with line.

Laying a brick patio in sand

One of the simplest and easiest patios you can build is the loose-laid brick-in-sand variety. There's no problem of mortar setting, or the work being spoiled if it is interrupted. You work when you wish.

The area should be smoothed and leveled as much as possible. If you like, excavate the area so that the finished patio will be flush with the surface of the yard.

Although it isn't always necessary, it's a good idea to outline the patio with redwood 2x4s. These can be fastened together with screws or nails to act as little retaining walls.

After you have secured your 2x4s, shovel a two-inch layer of sand between them and smooth it level. Then lay in the bricks in the pattern you wish, such as basket weave, or perhaps herringbone. When the bricks are in, sprinkle dry sand in the cracks and sweep away any excess.

What it takes

Approximate time: Depending on size, from a couple of hours to a day or so.

Tools and materials: Hammer, nails or screws, shovel, rake, a long level, redwood 2x4s, bricks, sand.

Paving brick patterns

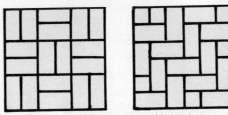

Basket weave   Herringbone

Building a stone retaining wall

What it takes

Approximate time: Plan in terms of days, not hours; but it depends, too, on the size of the wall.

Tools and materials: Wheelbarrow (for mixing mortar), a hoe, masonry trowel, garden shovel, string, string level, brick hammer, steel brush, whisk broom, muriatic acid and container for mixing it with water, gloves, goggles (if you should cut any stone), stone, mortar ingredients or mix.

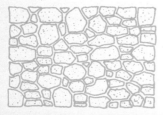

In random-rubble masonry, the crudest of all stonework, little attention is paid to laying the stone in even courses.

In coursed-rubble masonry, roughly squared stones are assembled in such a way as to produce roughly continuous horizontal layers.

Handling brick, and even cinder block, is one thing, but heavy stone is something else. Being your own stonemason is both one of the hardest and one of the simplest jobs. The techniques in stone masonry are actually quite easy to learn, but the work can be physically taxing. Let's face it: stone is heavy. Yet, few tools are needed —the same as for concrete or block work.

Take care in selecting the proper stones, and try to keep all the rocks in a project the same type, although not necessarily the same size or shape.

Basically, there are three categories of stonework construction: rubble, ashlar, and trimmings.

Rubble stonework is uncut stone, or stones that have not been cut to a specific shape. This type of masonry is used for rough work such as retaining walls or foundations. The stones can be laid in courses or at random; that is, without continuity of the joints.

Ashlar stone is cut on four sides so that it resembles, albeit roughly, brick. The surfaces can be smooth (that is, dressed), or left as they are.

Trimmings are cut on all sides, and used for moldings, sills, lintels, and ornament.

For do-it-yourself work, six kinds of natural stone are generally used: granite, limestone, slate, marble, bluestone, and sandstone, the most porous.

Natural stone can be purchased in three finishes: Dressed, the most expensive, is cut to your requirements; semidressed stones are cut to approximate sizes (you'll have to do some trimming yourself); undressed stone, the cheapest finish, is raw stone right out of the quarry.

How to buy stones

You can purchase stone from a stonemason, a quarry, or even from some lawn and garden-supply centers in the larger communities. Or, if you know a farmer, you might get all the rocks you can haul just for picking them up out of his fields.

Stones are sold by the cubic yard (except flagstone which is sold by the square foot). To determine just how much stone you will need, multiply the height of the project times the width times the length in feet. This gives the number of cubic feet. Then divide this by 27. The resulting number is the approximate cubic yardage of stone required.

In laying a wet, rubble stone wall, such as the one shown on these pages, first assemble the stones you will need to begin. Then pour the base or footing.

It is best to place the larger stones on the lower courses, so that the size of the stones will gradually grow smaller as the wall gains height.

Lay each stone on its broadest face.

Wet any porous stones before placing them in mortar so that the stone will not absorb water from the mortar and weaken the bond between stone and mortar.

Be sure that the spaces between adjoining stones are as small as practicable and that these spaces are completely filled with smaller stones and mortar.

Construction techniques

1. Pour a concrete footing for the wall. It should be at least 18 inches wide and below the frost line in your particular area. After the footing has set up, mix mortar and spread a heavy layer on the footing.

2. Now position the first inside layer of rocks, mortaring in between as you go.

3. Set the outside rocks in place; then fill in around them with rubble and mortar.

4. A string and level are essential if you want the top of the wall to be flat and even.

5. The top of the wall will tie everything together. These are the cap stones. Note the prop stick holding an unstable rock in place until the mortar sets up. Note the mortar and rubble running throughout the wall.

It wasn't just the grass that came up that spring!
I was real proud of my new wall; and it didn't take long to build. Thing is, I should've taken longer. When I do it over now, I'll know to dig below the frost line for my footing.

Practical Pete

6. A retaining wall should have pieces of pipe set in it to allow water behind the wall to drain away.

7. After the mortar has set a bit, scrub it out of the joints between the rocks with a bristle brush, and clean out any debris with a whisk broom.

8. Wash down the wall with a solution of muriatic acid and water.

9. Plantings on the upper level absorb moisture and reduce pressure against the wall.

A country dry wall

One of the most challenging, satisfying, and yet not very difficult projects a home-owner can undertake is the building of an old-fashioned dry stone wall. Moreover, if you live in a part of the country, such as New England, where fieldstone abounds, the expense is negligible.

A dry wall does not need mortar or a concrete footing because the weight and interlocking placement of the stones hold everything together. For a start, try building a wall no more than 3 feet high and a couple of feet thick. As you gain in proficiency, you can move to larger structures. Of course, you can build the wall as long as you like.

Basically, you can use stones that you find lying in fields; but these may need cutting so that they join better. Otherwise, you can buy quarried rubble. Try sandstone, bluestone, or limestone, which have fairly regular faces.

You can build your dry wall right on the ground, or in a bed of sand, which will allow for better drainage. The wall's joints will overlap. The important stone is the bonding stone, which is the first stone of the first course. Its length should equal the wall's thickness because it is set crosswise as an anchor. It ties the course on the front to the course on the back. However, if you

cannot find a stone large enough, use two stones. The space between the front and back courses must be filled with small pieces of stone, while gaps on the outside are filled with chinking; that is, little stones are hammered into crevices. The idea is that the large course stones and the smaller ones balance each other.

At the same time, the ends and faces of the wall slope slightly inward from a wide base; each successive course being set a little in from the one underneath it. This slope can be judged by eye, or you can make a simple device called a slope gauge (see step 3, opposite).

As you build, remember to let the stones tilt toward the center so that the gravitational pull against the stones will tighten the wall and help hold it together. The entire wall ties in and down toward the center.

Do not make mitered joints when you turn a corner. Always overlap joints, never stack one right above the other.

Finally, while a dry wall contains no mortar, many builders do spread mortar beneath a top surface of broad flat stones, because this cap will keep out water that may freeze and dislodge the stones. Whether you plan to mortar the top layer or not, be sure to save enough broad, flat stones for the final course.

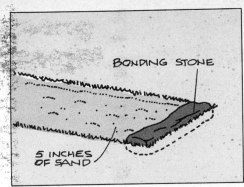

1. Your first step is to dig a trench 6 inches deep, the length and width of the wall. Fill it with 5 inches of sand. (Alternately, you can build the wall right on the ground, but a sand bed will be better for drainage.) Find a stone that is as long as the wall is thick, preferably with even faces. Place it at the end. It is your bonding stone, and it helps hold the wall together.

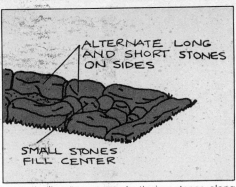

2. Start your first course by laying stones along one side, then the other. Alternate large and small stones, thin and thick. Place the long ones length-wise, and lay each stone flat. Set each stone so that any angle in the top surface will slope toward the center of the wall. For the first course use the largest stones, then as you go up the wall use smaller stones; and on top place flat stones. After you have laid about 8 feet of stone on the first course (both sides) fill the center with small stones until the first stage is more or less level.

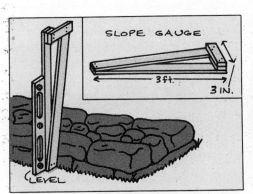

3. For the next course start at the bonding stone and lay a long stone at right angles to it so that it overlaps the joint of the stone on the course below. The top surface of this stone should tilt down slightly toward the center while its outer edges should be set in a little from the first course. Here is where you check with the slope gauge and level. Lay the second course along one side, then the other. Be sure the stones are long enough to overlap the joints in the course below. Work down each side, checking with the level and slope gauge as you go. Fill the center.

4. Because the stones will not always seat solidly, you will need to shim them with small pieces under the edges. Check each stone by trying to rock it. After you have laid a couple of courses, fill the openings between the stones with chinking—narrow stones which you can drive in with a hammer. This will lock the wall and will help it tighten toward the center. Keep checking with the slope gauge. The horizontal level does not have to be exact, but you can check it by eye as you go.

5. To turn a corner, lay the stones in the same way you would for a wall. However, for the last stone in the first course of the outer face, use a large stone to overlap the first outer course at the turn. But in the second course, set the last stone of the outer face short of the corner. This will cause its end to meet the side of the first stone on the turn. The principle is to overlap for a secure bond.

6. If you want a mortared cap as protection against water, cover the next-to-last course with a layer of mortar, 1 inch thick. A mix of 1 part cement to 3 parts sand should do it. You have been saving flat stones for the top. Set these now, filling in the gaps with mortar if you wish, and building up the center of the joint so that there will be no pockets to collect water. Finally, trowel-trim excess mortar.

A flagstone walk or patio

What it takes

Approximate time: Depends on the size of the project, but at least half a day as a start.

Tools and materials: Stonemason's hammer, chisel, goggles, rubber mallet, trowel, mortar, sand, shovel and pick, level.

Planning hints: Flagstone is sold by the square foot. Measure the space you wish to pave, and allow about 10 percent for waste.

One of the simplest do-it-yourself projects with stone is the flagstone patio or walk. Flagstone can be laid dry or wet (mortared). Dry-laid flagstone may be laid over a bed of sand with sand, not mortar, forced between the stones. Or, set the stones far enough apart to place soil between them, allowing grass or other plantings to come up for an unusual and natural-looking patio.

Dry-laid flagstone. The first thing is to stake out the area you intend to cover with flagstone. Excavate to a depth of 3 inches, and put down 2 inches of sand. Use 1½ to 2-inch-thick flagstones. Put down three or four at a time, lining up the straight edges with your outside lines, and keeping the irregular edges toward each other. Be sure to wear goggles if you do any trimming with a stonemason's hammer and chisel.

Work from one corner and tap each stone down with a rubber mallet. After you have put down a couple of rows, check with a mason's level to see if the surface is even. Put more sand under low stones, and remove sand from beneath high ones.

Shovel more sand over the flags, and sweep it across the stones so that the joints are filled. Water the surface and allow it to dry. Repeat this until the joints are compacted and completely filled.

Wet-laid flagstone. This is started in the same way as dry. After the sand has been leveled and the stones placed, a fairly dry mortar is forced down between the stones. Allow it to dry more, then sweep away the excess with a stiff-bristle broom.

Another method is to cover a level area with sand, arrange the stones on it, sweep over them with a mixture of cement and sand, and then sprinkle with a hose. The sand should be at least 2 inches deep, so that you can push the flags down into it.

If you are covering a fairly large area, then it will be necessary to allow a pitch for drainage. This is also sensible if you live in a part of the country where severe freezing occurs. Freezing and thawing of standing water can crack the cement bond.

You can put down a bed of cinders several inches deep before you put down the sand, or as an alternative, you can make the sand a good 6 inches deep.

Repair. Repairing or replacing a stone is quite simple. If dry laid, merely lift the stone up out of the sand, clean out the excess sand, and set a new stone, filling in around it with sand. If the flagstone was wet laid, chip away the surrounding mortar, replace the stone, and remortar it.

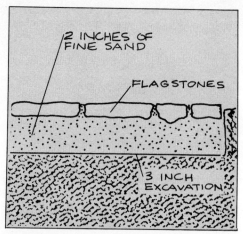

Dry-laid flagstone is a simple matter—just stone and sand. You can work at your own speed, stopping at any point for as long as you wish.

The beauty of this kind of walk is that its roughness is part of its charm. Leveling is necessary, but not difficult. You should be careful that there are no high or low points where a person can trip, or which will hold water.

Wet-laid flagstone on the other hand should not be left unfinished. It's almost as easy as putting down dry laid. All you need is mortar and a trowel, and of course, a little muscle.

Patching asphalt

Cracks and holes in your asphalt or blacktop driveway can easily be patched, and the sooner done, the better. Not only is it an annoyance when you run over a large crack or pothole with your car, but the hole can soon widen and deepen to the point where you have a major driveway problem to tackle.

The asphalt that is used on driveways is really a kind of concrete. But while ordinary concrete is a mixture of gravel with a binder of cement, asphalt is held together with a crude-oil extract.

For best protection, asphalt should be coated every four or five years with a waterproof sealer, which is also chemical resistant. You simply pour the sealer from the can onto the driveway, and spread it evenly with a push broom. It is important first, however, to make sure that the driveway is swept clean of all dirt. Most sealers come ready mixed in 5-gallon cans, and will coat from 200 to 300 square feet. This depends of course on the porousness of the driveway surface.

This coating procedure will also fill any cracks that are not over ⅛ inch wide. For larger cracks, you can thicken the sealer with sand and push it into the crack with a putty knife or trowel; then seal over it.

What it takes:

Approximate time: For most repairs allow a few hours. Extensive work could take days.

Tools and materials: Shovel, stonemason's hammer and chisel, trowel or putty knife, 2x4 tamper, sealer, asphalt mix, sand, stiff push broom.

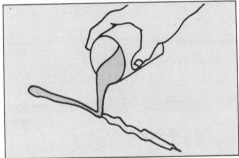

1. For small cracks, use liquid sealer; for cracks that are more than ⅛ inch wide, mix sealer with sand. It's best to do this work in warm weather.

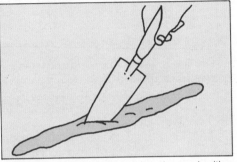

2. Press the sealer and sand into the crack with a putty knife or trowel. Then seal over it if necessary to bring it up to driveway level.

I shouldn't have brought my work home with me!
I did a real neat job patching my asphalt driveway. But I just didn't notice where I'd been standing—till I saw my wife's face when I walked into the kitchen. Next time I'll know to spread sand on that sealer so it won't stick to my shoes.

Practical Pete

Filling holes

To repair a hole, use cold-mix asphalt. Cold-mix asphalt comes in two varieties: cut-back asphalt and emulsion mix. For dry holes you may use either type, but for damp holes you should use emulsion mix only, which is made with water. The mix comes in 66-pound bags. It should be loose in the bag for best application. If it is hard, then you must warm it. Asphalt should be worked on during warm weather—never if the temperature is below 40 degrees Fahrenheit or it will be difficult to work with.

First, clean the hole thoroughly. Make certain that the sides are cut all the way back to solid asphalt and are vertical. If the hole is deep, fill it partially with coarse gravel. Then use a push broom to fill the hole with mix to within an inch of the top.

To eliminate any air pockets, slice the mix with the blade of a shovel and then tamp it with the end of a 4x4. Finish filling the hole, bringing the mix to a mound. Level the mound to the rest of the driveway surface with a roller or a 4x4 tamper. The mix must be pressed firmly against the sides of the hole. You can also drive your car over the patch to compact it. Spread sand over the new asphalt so that it won't stick to your shoes. Sweep off the sand when the asphalt dries.

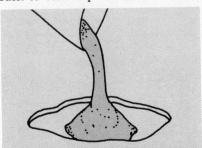

1. Pour blacktop mix into the hole, mounding it above the edges, and making sure that it fills.

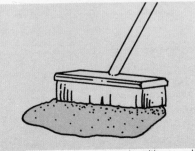

2. Alternately spread the mix with a push broom and compact it with the tip of a shovel.

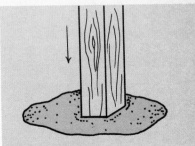

3. Then tamp it down with a 4x4 (you could also use a roller). Keep adding and tamping until it is even with the rest of the driveway.

8.FENCES

There are innumerable kinds of fences of varying designs and materials, as well as purpose. Some fences are for privacy, some for protection, and some are for looks. Many are for all three.

The first thing to take into account when you decide to put up a fence is the local building code. There may be certain restrictions as to height, materials, style, and location in relation to your property boundary lines.

Your fence can be metal, stone, wood, or, if you happen to run cattle or sheep, barbed wire. For the average homeowner, the wood fence seems to be the most popular as well as the simplest to install.

Of this type there are a great many; from the old-fashioned split rail and the picket fence, to the closed-screen type. But no matter what sort of fence you decide on, the most important thing is the durability of the posts.

Chain link

Post and rail

Old-fashioned hurdle

Screen

Salem picket

Basket weave screen

Setting posts

A wood post should be set with one-third of its length in the ground. It should first be treated with a preservative; creosote and pentachlorophenol ("penta") are the most popular.

You can dig the hole with a shovel and crowbar, or a posthole digger. Try not to disturb the ground surrounding the hole, and make the hole as narrow as possible, flaring it slightly at the bottom but keeping it small at the top.

When the hole is dug, place a flat rock or some gravel in the bottom and rest the post on top of it. Use a level to get the post plumb, and then secure it with braces. Fill around the post with concrete: 1 part portland cement, 2 parts sand, 3 parts medium gravel. (A wheelbarrow is ideal for mixing small quantities of concrete.)

When you shovel in the concrete, poke the mixture now and then to eliminate any air bubbles. Add extra concrete above ground level so that the footing slopes away from the post for drainage. Now go on to your next post. Let the concrete cure fully on all the posts before putting up your horizontals. Allow a full week if you can.

Steel posts can be set the same way, except that the lower end should be coated with asphalt paint to avoid rusting. Concrete should be set below the frost line to prevent the posts from heaving.

A simpler but less permanent way of setting a post is to dig the hole, line the bottom with gravel, or a flat rock, place the post erect and fill in with gravel and earth, tamping with a shovel handle or a piece of lumber as you go.

What it takes

Approximate time: An hour per post, if the digging is not too difficult. In rocky soil, good luck.

Tools and materials: Measuring tape, string, short sticks, level, wheelbarrow, braces, shovel, posthole digger, paint brushes, fence posts, wood (or metal) preservative, flat rocks, gravel, portland cement, sand.

1. To dig holes with a posthole digger, drive the digger's paired shovels into the ground with the handles close together. Then force the handles apart to compress the loosened earth between shovel blades. Finally, lift with the handles still spread, and trapped earth will rise.

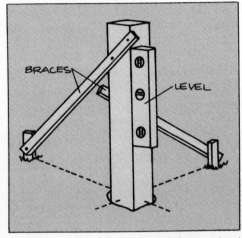

2. After positioning the post in the hole, use a level to get it plumb. Then brace the post in two directions, and stake the braces to the ground. Double-check for plumb and make final adjustments in the braces if necessary.

It turned out to be a rotten deal!

I set my fence posts good and solid. But before long the posts began to rot and my fence weakened. Then I realized that you have to slope the concrete footing so that water can drain away, and not into the posthole.

Practical Pete

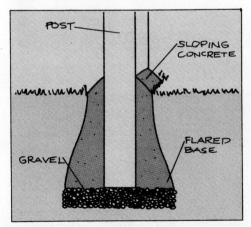

3. Fill the hole to ground level with concrete, and then add a small mound of concrete on top, sloping away from the post for good drainage.

Removable post

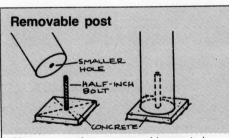

You can make a removable post by inserting a half-inch bolt into concrete before it has set. Drill a hole in the bottom of the post, slightly undersize. Then screw the post onto the bolt until it is firm. This type of post can of course be set on top of the ground and is less subject to weathering; digging is necessary only for the base. Be sure your bolt and your bolt hole are perfectly vertical.

An old-fashioned post-and-rail fence

The charm of a really rustic fence is something many homeowners wish to see on their property. You can buy such fences ready built, and all you have to do is dig the postholes, set the posts, and assemble the fence. The steps are as follows:

1. Drive stakes into the ground at each end of your proposed fence.
2. Stretch a string tightly between them, about 6 inches above the ground. This will be your guide for setting your posts in a straight line.
3. Dig your first posthole at one end of the line. For a fence that has two horizontal rails, the hole should be about 2 feet deep. For three or four rails, 30 inches is good.
4. Stand your first post in the hole so that it just touches the line you have stretched. In most kits, there will be holes in the posts to receive the cross pieces; so make sure that they face along the fence line. Then finish setting the post.
5. Insert a rail in the bottom hole of the post, and using the rail as a measure, locate the second posthole. Remove the rail and dig the second hole as detailed in step 3.
6. Reinsert the rail in the first post and in the corresponding hole in the second post. If a rail is not straight, turn it so that the bow is up.
7. If your rails are cedar, they may be slightly tapered. In this case, alternate them so that the thicker end of one is over the thin end of another. You should also place them so that the thick end of one meets the thin end of the next in the holes in the posts.
8. Plumb the second post. Make sure it is the correct height and that it touches the string. Then fill the hole and tamp it. Continue setting succeeding posts and inserting rails in like manner.

If ground is not even, make sure that you account for differences so that your fence is even. It doesn't have to be absolutely level, but it should be built up and cut back so as not to give a choppy appearance.

On sloping ground, be sure to erect the posts in a plumb position. The rails can then be tilted as necessary to follow the slope of the ground.

What it takes

Approximate time: Depends on the size or length of the fence, but, probably a couple of weekends, with help. Figure two hours per post.

Tools and materials: Fence, shovel, posthole digger, measuring tape, stakes, level, string, wheelbarrow, braces, fence and fence posts, gate hinges and latch, paint brushes, wood preservative, gravel, sand, portland cement, flat rocks.

I was plumb dumb!
My neighbor sure got a laugh when he took a look at my new fence. I'd set it straight and even, and when I got to the point where the ground began to slope, I just followed it downhill. But that's where I went wrong. So he helped me do it over, and this time I set the posts plumb no matter what the ground did.
Practical Pete

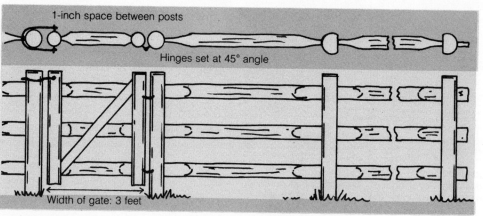

1-inch space between posts

Hinges set at 45° angle

Width of gate: 3 feet

Illustrated above is the standard configuration for a three-rail fence. Two- and four-rail styles are similar. Aerial view is shown at top. The gate is built just like the fence, but smaller; it has a diagonal brace and hook-over catch. The drawings below show the right and wrong ways to deal with uneven ground. A choppy look can be avoided by setting some posts deeper than others and then filling in or cutting back under the completed fence.

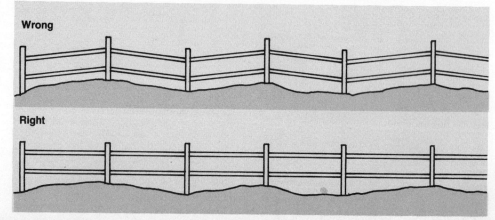

Wrong

Right

Hanging a gate

No matter what kind of fence you build, a most important aspect of the overall project—and one that is all too easy to muff after everything else has gone well—is the gate. Not every fence requires a gate, but if you elect to incorporate one into your project, follow these five steps carefully. The style of fence and gate shown here may not be at all similar to the one you are building. But if you get the basic principles right, the details (such as latch style, shape and girth of gate posts, and so on) will be of lesser importance and are simply a matter of taste and circumstances.

The essential thing, as with a door, is to hang the gate so that it opens and closes well. This means that it will have to adjust to the gate posts, even if not exactly plumb.

CHECK THAT YOUR FENCE POSTS ARE PLUMB

What it takes

Approximate time: One hour.

Tools and materials: Hammer, screwdriver, pencil and measuring tape, block of wood, level, drill, hardware, gate.

1. The essential thing is that the gate, like any door, should hang well. The fence posts must, therefore, be plumb.

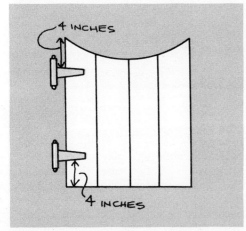

4 INCHES

4 INCHES

2. Place the gate on a flat surface—the ground or two sawhorses—while you apply the hinges. The straps should be about 4 inches from the top and bottom of the gate on the side that is to be hinged. Mark the location for the screws and drill the pilot holes. Then screw the straps into position.

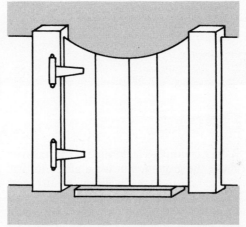

3. Place the gate in the opening, allowing the right amount of space between the bottom of the gate and the ground. You can use a wooden block under the gate to assure the correct amount of clearance. The block will act like extra hands while you work.

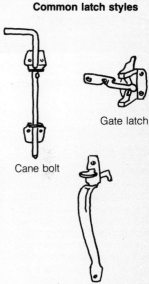

Common latch styles

Gate latch

Cane bolt

Ornamental thumb latch

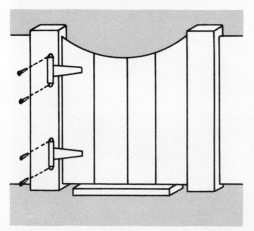

4. When you have the gate properly aligned with the adjacent posts, mark the locations of the hinge holes on the fence post. Drill pilot holes, and secure the gate with screws.

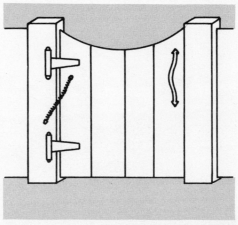

5. You may wish to add a spring to the gate and post, so that it will close by itself. Notice that the spring is always inclined to the right. You should place the spring as close to the vertical as conditions allow.

9.IMPROVEMENTS

Decks

Planning hints

The first step in planning a deck is to survey the landscaping situation and decide which problems the deck should solve. Determine a rough location for the deck and then check local building regulations to see what provisions, restrictions, or guidelines are placed on a deck of the type you want.

Building regulations may include foundation requirements, railings, load limits, height and protection limits, and other requirements. Knowing the specifics of the local code will permit more precise planning, prevent construction delays, and provide greater assurance of approval by the planning or building commission.

If the construction problem is a difficult one, if the deck area is to be extensive, or if the deck is to be more than a few feet above the ground, a building professional such as a structural engineer, architect, or contractor should be consulted.

A deck is simply a handsome platform on or above the ground. But it's a platform that can add much to the livability, beauty, and value of a house. A well-designed deck can turn a hilly site into a useful, enjoyable outdoor living area at a fraction of the cost of adding an inside room. And there's no substitute for the style of living it can provide as an area for sunbathing, entertaining, dining, conversation, container gardening, children's play and parties.

Good deck design eases the transition from deck to garden—and is part of each. Where the land slopes down and away from the foundation of a house, the deck extends the floor level of the building out into otherwise wasted space. And where paving of a flat area may be a practical expedient, a ground-level deck is often preferred for its resilient comfort and drainage advantages.

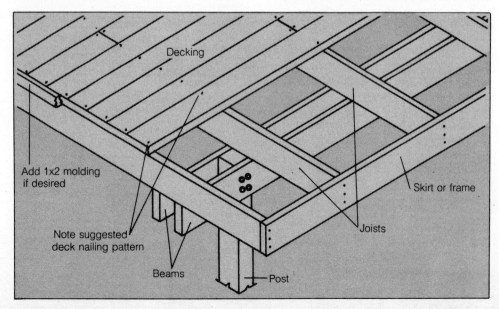

Decking

Add 1x2 molding if desired

Note suggested deck nailing pattern

Beams

Post

Joists

Skirt or frame

Structural elements

The deck structure gathers the weight and load of the deck and transmits it downward to the ground. The top layer is the *decking* itself, often decorative in pattern, but always designed to support a stated load with a minimum of deflection. The decking rests on *joists*, which are the primary structural element of the floor. The joists rest upon *beams*, which gather the load and transmit it to *posts* or other vertical supports. The posts rest on *footings* which bear the concentrated load of the deck and structure. In extremely low decks beams rest directly on footings.

Decking. The deck surface is the most visible part of the entire deck structure, and its size, grade, and placement determine the arrangement and size of the framing. Two-inch nominal redwood is recommended for most decking situations. The most common sizes are 2x4 and 2x6. Nominal 1-inch-thick material may be used where joists are placed within 16 inches of each other. Where a pattern of narrow lines is desired, 2x4s may be used on edge, with longer spans than are possible when the decking is laid flat. The decking spans possible with the common sizes and general-purpose grades of redwood are given in the table below.

Suggested decking spans

Size	Grades that may be used	Span
1x4	Clear only	16″
2x4	All grades	24″
2x6	All grades	36″

Joists. The joists (usually 2-inch dimension lumber) bear the load of the decking and whatever loads are placed upon the deck. The joist span is determined by the joist spacing and the grade of lumber. Typical joist spans for redwood general-purpose grades are given in the table below.

The joists usually rest upon a beam or header and are anchored to it. The joist can overhang slightly beyond the beam for appearance or added space if desired. Overhang depends upon joist thickness and shouldn't exceed one-fourth of length.

Suggested joist spans

		Grade	
Joist size	Clear	Select	Construction
2x6 16″o.c.	10′0″	8′0″	6′0″
24″o.c.	9′0″	7′0″	5′0″
36″o.c.	6′6″	5′6″	4′0″
2x8 16″o.c.	13′0″	12′0″	9′0″
24″o.c.	12′0″	10′0″	7′6″
36″o.c.	9′0″	8′0″	6′0″
2x10 16″o.c.	17′0″	16′0″	13′0″
24″o.c.	15′0″	12′6″	11′0″
36″o.c.	11′0″	10′0″	9′0″

o.c. means "on center"

Beams. Beams rest upon the posts and support the joists. Size of beam required depends upon the spacing and span of the beams. However, a general rule is to utilize as large a beam as necessary in order to minimize the number of posts and footings. Beams of 4-inch thickness and greater are often used. The beams can be bolted to the tops of posts. Typical beam spans are given in the table below.

Suggested beam spans

Beam size	Grade	Width of deck			
		6′	8′	10′	12′
4x6	Clear	6′6″	6′0″	5′0″	4′0″
	Construction	4′6″	4′0″	3′6″	3′0″
4x8	Clear	9′0″	8′0″	7′0″	6′0″
	Construction	6′0″	5′0″	4′6″	4′0″
4x10	Clear	11′6″	10′0″	8′6″	7′6″
	Construction	7′6″	6′6″	6′0″	5′6″

Ledgers. Where one side of the deck meets a house or other building, joists can be supported by a ledger attached to the house. Usually a ledger 2 inches thick is sufficient. But better bearing and easier toe-nailing is obtained if a thicker ledger is used. To prevent rain or snow from wetting interior floors, the ledger should be located so that the surface of the deck is at least an inch below the floor surface of the house.

Posts. The posts bear the weight of the deck, transmitting it through the footings to the ground. For most low decks, the 4x4 is an adequate post. While supporting the deck, the post can continue upward to support railing, seat, and overhead structure.

Cross bracing may be necessary to prevent lateral movement of the deck, particularly if it is elevated high above the ground.

Footings. The footing anchors the entire structure to the ground as well as transmitting the weight of the deck to the ground. Building codes are usually very specific on the subject of footings. Generally they must extend to undisturbed soil or rock, and in cold climates usually must extend below the frost line. For low-level decks, concrete blocks or precast footings may be used, by seating them firmly in the soil. If concrete footings are site-poured, metal post anchors or steel straps may be set in the wet concrete. Drift pins offer a concealed method of connecting the post to the footing when the underside of the deck is to be in view.

Location and placement of footings are determined by the design of the deck's structural members so that weight is properly transmitted to the ground. Once the perimeter of the deck has been established, refer to the table of suggested beam spans to determine the spacing of footings, based on the size of the beam to be used.

Alternative footings

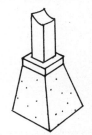

Concrete block or precast footing

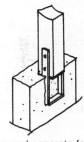

Site-poured concrete footing with metal post anchor or steel strap

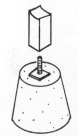

Drift pin concealing connection between post and footing

Alternative ledger placements

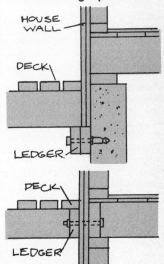

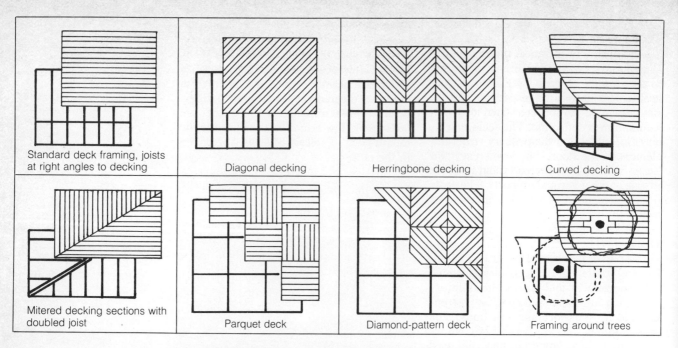

Standard deck framing, joists at right angles to decking

Diagonal decking

Herringbone decking

Curved decking

Mitered decking sections with doubled joist

Parquet deck

Diamond-pattern deck

Framing around trees

Laying out the deck

The size and pattern of the decking affects the framing plan of the deck. So determine the decking pattern first. The most common pattern is to have decking in one direction with joists at right angles to the decking. The beams are at right angles to the joists. This arrangement is referred to as *standard* framing. In standard framing, layout is simply a matter of determining decking spans, choosing joist size and span, and locating posts or other supports for beams.

But there are many other variations in surface patterns, and some require modification of the standard framing pattern.

Diagonal patterns. Decking may be laid on a diagonal to the joists at any angle greater than 45 degrees. Diagonals are often used to give visual relief to very regular deck shapes, or to give a distinctive shape to the deck. If decking is laid in a herringbone or zigzag pattern, it should be remembered that too much repetition may have a dizzying effect. Standard framing may be used for the diagonal patterns. But note that diagonal decking spans are greater, and joists may have to be set closer together than would be necessary with standard pattern decking. Where one side of the deck follows the diagonal, a header should join the joist ends to support the decking.

Laying the decking

In all situations, the decking is laid on joists and may be installed in basically the same manner regardless of pattern or shape.

First make an estimate of the lengths needed, and lay out the decking on the joists, so that any butt joints which may occur can be planned to occur at random

Geometric shapes and free forms. These are variations of standard or diagonal decking patterns, including triangles, hexagons, circles, curves, etc. Almost any form or shape can be achieved so long as a joist or joist-header lies near enough to the edge of the deck to support it properly.

Changing directions. Wherever there is a major change in the direction of the decking, a single beam or double joist must continue under the miter joining line, with joists at an angle to it and perpendicular to the decking.

Parquet and diamond pattern decks. These sectional decks require a grid pattern of support, which is achieved by blocking between the joists at a distance equal to the joist spacing. If the joists used are of 2-inch material, it may be necessary to nail a 2x2 nailer strip to the joists for better bearing and nailing.

Framing around trees. In the planning of both low and high-level decks, a friendly tree is sometimes encountered which can pierce the deck to bring its shade to the platform. Plan framing so that it permits adequate clearance for the tree. Leave room for the tree to sway in the wind and for tree growth. The higher the deck, the more room the tree needs to sway.

intervals and over joists. Joints should never occur on adjacent pieces of decking unless the pattern indicates it. It is usually better to trim the decking as it is used, rather than trimming first, in order to fit any variations caused by installation of the framing or other decking.

If the decking is laid parallel to the house, make sure the first piece is properly aligned both to the house and at the proper angle to the joists.

Vertical or flat grain. Vertical-grain redwood is recommended for decking; but if flat-grain lumber is used, make sure that the "bark side" of each piece is up (the side that was outermost on the tree). This minimizes raising of grain in flat-grain pieces. Either side of a vertical-grain piece may be up.

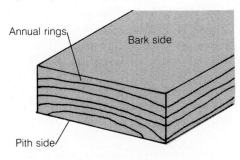

Annual rings
Bark side
Pith side

Nails and fastenings. Use only noncorroding nails and fastenings on your deck to prevent staining; these include stainless steel, aluminum alloy, and top-quality, hot-dipped galvanized materials. Nails and fastenings galvanized by the electroplating method should not be used. For 2-inch decking, use 16-penny nails. Use 8-penny nails for 1-inch decking.

Nailing. Predrill holes for nails at the end of decking pieces to avoid splitting and to achieve secure fastening. For most decks, seasoned decking materials should be spaced about ⅛ inch apart. This will be sufficient to allow drainage of water. At ends of deck plank, nail through predrilled holes. Use only one nail per bearing, alternating from one side of the piece to the other. This method is sufficient for retaining kiln-dried redwood, which does not require heavy nailing because of its stability. The nailing of alternate sides forestalls any tendency to pull or cup.

When decking rests on only two supports and each piece only completes a single span, as in herringbone and parquet decking, nail two nails at each end.

Use any handy measuring template to make sure spacing is uniform between boards. One common method is to use a nail as a spacer, pulling it out when the decking has been secured.

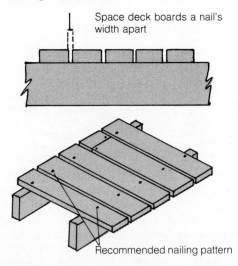

Space deck boards a nail's width apart

Recommended nailing pattern

Special situations

Decks on ground. On level ground it is often desirable to use decking as paving. The deck on the ground may serve either as a complete patio paving, or alternating with concrete, brick, grass, or plantings. This provides a quick-draining terrace at ground level and is possible only with a decay-and insect-resistant wood such as heartwood redwood.

Preparation of ground. First, a 3-inch bed of tamped sand should be laid below the planned surface of the deck to promote drainage and to help control weeds. If the soil is poorly drained, 3 inches of coarse gravel under the sand will improve drainage of a deck on the ground.

The decking should be nailed to all-heartwood 2x4 cleats, laid flat in the sand. If the decking is laid in the standard parallel pattern, the cleats should be at 2-foot intervals to allow use of random-length wood.

If the decking is laid in a parquet pattern, the squares can be fabricated separately, then laid down as large paving squares. Regular parquet or diamond design can be handled this way. Careful leveling is necessary to lay the parquet deck. When plantings or other materials are to be alternated with the parquet decking, a border strip of 2x4 heartwood on edge will suffice to contain the planting and may serve as formwork for concrete or other paving.

Downhill slopes. If the deck is begun on grade and then extends out over a slope, the transition from nailing-strip framing to joist-and-beam framing can be achieved without any interruption of the surface decking.

Decking over concrete. A deck can be laid directly over a concrete patio, and it will provide a better insulated and faster draining surface than the concrete alone. If the deck lies directly on the concrete, the same basic framing can be used as when the deck is laid directly on the ground. One modification will be required: Although the ground can be leveled, the slab probably has a slight slope, so the deck framing may have to be shimmed. If the deck is to be elevated above the slab, as in the case of a floor-level deck with a 12- to 18-inch air space below, standard framing should be used.

Plantings. Plantings are an important part of the garden picture and can be combined with the deck in a number of ways: If the deck is above ground, a planter box can be dropped in at deck level or raised above the level of the decking to provide relief in a broad expanse of deck. Portable planters can provide a changing splash of color and can be moved to the side for entertaining. **Caution:** Planters and other containers are likely to increase the load upon the deck considerably and the framing should be strengthened if such loads are planned.

Rooftop decks. The areas above first-floor rooms, carports, garages, and other flat-roofed areas offer attractive possibilities for outdoor living areas adjacent to second-floor rooms. If a rooftop deck is planned with the original construction of the building, allowance can be made for the added weight of the deck, its occupants, and planters, furniture, etc. If the deck is added in remodeling, additional bracing of the roof may be required.

For most normal, light use, decking is usually nailed into flat cleats, but one has to make sure that the nails don't penetrate the roofing beneath. The decking should maintain the previous drainage pattern of the roof. Two-inch decking will permit greater spans, and minimize nailing-cleats. One-inch decking is lighter in weight but requires supports at about 16-inch intervals.

Strip skylight

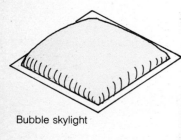

Bubble skylight

For homeowners who are planning to convert attic space into living space, lighting is perhaps the single most vexing problem. For, unless major structural changes are envisioned that would provide additional windows, attic rooms tend to resemble dungeons. And yet, getting more light into the attic via a skylight is a task most homeowners can tackle by themselves. When it is realized that a skylight will brighten a room—even on a cloudy day— far more effectively than artificial lighting, the cost is surprisingly small. You can easily install a skylight by yourself—or, prefera-

bly, with a helper—in a day's work or less, even though it means cutting a hole in your roof. It is this last point that needlessly frightens a lot of people away. But that's foolish. Simply wait for a weather forecast of zero rain-probability—and have a tarp on hand just in case. Be sure to plan the entire project carefully in advance and have all the materials on hand when you begin. Of course, no two skylight installations will be exactly the same, but the following general procedures, along with your skylight manufacturer's detailed guidelines, should cover all the basic points.

General procedures

Planning hints:

The two simplest and commonest types of skylights are the plastic bubble and glass panels. The latter are often installed in series. Prefabricated bubbles may be set into a roof wherever a source of daylight is desired—work, play, or reading areas, or in a bathroom. The bubbles come preframed in a variety of shapes and sizes. Glass panels in series—also known as strip skylights—give even more daylight and create a studio effect. For best results, plan your skylight for the north or east slope of a roof. But make sure your attic is sufficiently ventilated, because a skylight can really heat up a room on a sunny day. Glass skylights are more apt to leak than plastic ones, so they must be especially well caulked at the joints. If they are not made from insulating glass, condensation can form on them and drip down a sloping ceiling. Double-plastic bubbles on the other hand, do not form condensation.

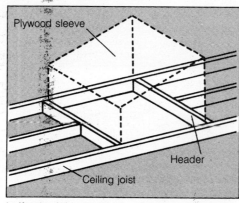

1. If your attic room has a finished ceiling with sealed space between ceiling joints and roof rafters, your first step will be to build a plywood sleeve to bridge the gap between the ceiling and the roof and to channel the light into the room. Most skylight panels span three rafters neatly, so you will have to cut a section from the center rafter and the center joist. The length of the section will be determined by the size of your skylight panel(s). Attach 2x4 headers at both ends of both cuts. Use ½-inch exterior plywood for sleeve, and slide into place as a unit.

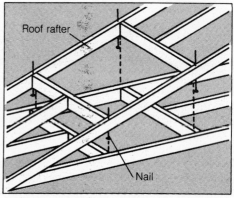

2. Whether or not you need to use a sleeve, as described in step 1, you will still have to position the skylight opening with reference to the rafters, and to install headers at opposite ends of any rafter cuts. In either case, plan your measurements carefully so the roof opening will be exactly the right size to receive the skylight panel. Then, still working from inside the attic, drive a long nail through the roof to mark each corner of the skylight.

3. Working on the roof, draw chalk lines connecting the protruding nail points to mark the size of the projected roof opening. But before cutting, double-check your measurements by setting the skylight panel in position to make sure it lines up properly with the chalk marks.

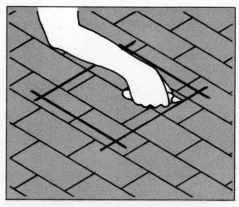

4. Use a linoleum knife or a roofing knife to cut the shingles along the chalk lines, and then remove all shingles within the rectangular area. The claw of a hammer can be used to tear up the shingles and roofing paper and to pull any roofing nails that lie on or near the cut line.

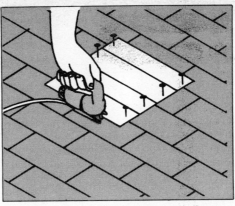

5. If your sheathing consists of a single piece of plywood, you'll have little trouble taking up the cutout as you complete the saw cut. But if you have board sheathing, drive a nail partway into both ends of each board you are about to remove. Then use the nail heads as handles to lift each cut piece and prevent it from falling into the house.

6. Cut through the sheathing boards or plywood with a saber saw. Assuming correct measurements, your saw blade will come out along the inside of the plywood sleeve (or rafter- and header-rimmed opening). But just to be sure, have a helper report to you on the progress of the saw blade within the attic.

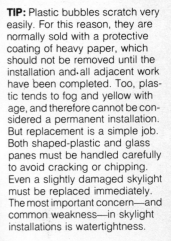

TIP: Plastic bubbles scratch very easily. For this reason, they are normally sold with a protective coating of heavy paper, which should not be removed until the installation and all adjacent work have been completed. Too, plastic tends to fog and yellow with age, and therefore cannot be considered a permanent installation. But replacement is a simple job. Both shaped-plastic and glass panes must be handled carefully to avoid cracking or chipping. Even a slightly damaged skylight must be replaced immediately. The most important concern—and common weakness—in skylight installations is watertightness.

7. Set the skylight panel in place over the opening. Note carefully the area of shingles that will have to be cut away at the top and sides to permit the base of the skylight panel to lie flat against the roof sheathing. But note also how much shingle matter must be left in place in order to overlap and seal off the flange on the bottom of the skylight.

8. After trimming away the excess, insert the skylight into place with the shingles resting above the flange along both sides and at the top. But for correct watersealing, the flange along the lower edge of the skylight must rest on top of the shingles.

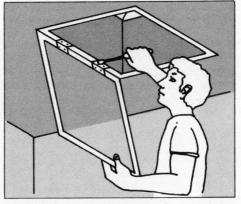

9. Seal the installation with a liberal coating of asphalt roofing cement, spreading it under the shingles at top and sides but under the flange at the bottom. Then secure the panel in place by nailing all around, through the shingles, flange, and sheathing. Finally, spread a second layer of cement all around the flange, taking particular care to cover the nail heads.

10. Many skylight installations are completed at the end of step 9. But with those that consist of both a roof and ceiling panel, install the ceiling panel last to forestall breakage due to falling debris. Clean both panels thoroughly and apply any finishing touches such as paint or trim to the area that will be enclosed. Then slip the ceiling panel inside the plywood sleeve or rafter opening, and fasten with screws or clips as provided by the manufacturer.

Picnic table

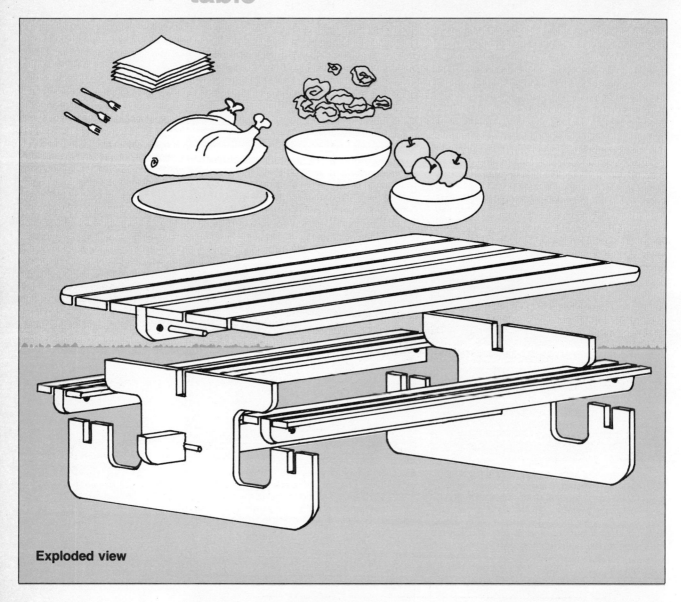

Exploded view

Perfect for casual outdoor dining, this one-piece picnic table will make an attractive addition to your patio or garden. More attractive still, the materials are relatively inexpensive, the construction is simple, and you can expect to enjoy the finished product for years to come.

First step is to draw the pattern for the end panels on the sheets of 4x8-foot plywood, two panels per sheet. Use a table saw or portable circular saw for the outside cuts and a saber saw for the inside and corner cuts. Cut as indicated in the pattern shown opposite, except for the notches and slots, which will be cut later.

Next, pair the four end panels so that their smooth surfaces face outward. Laminate each pair using a waterproof glue applied evenly to both surfaces. Fasten the

two pieces together with 1-inch wood screws, around 20 for each end-panel pair. Then cut and sand smooth the notches and slots that will accommodate the 2x8-inch cross members. Fill holes with wood putty.

Make your corner cuts on the cross members and drill ¾-inch holes in each, as indicated. Assemble the cross members and the end panels, then drive ¾-inch-by-3½-inch cut dowels into the predrilled holes.

For the table and bench tops, first make the necessary end cuts on the 2x6-inch boards; then nail the boards into place on the end panels using 3-inch galvanized nails. Leave ¼ inch between each board.

As a final step, the completed picnic table may be painted, stained or oiled to give it a weathered finish.

To make the picnic table, cut plywood and 2-inch lumber to the dimensions shown.

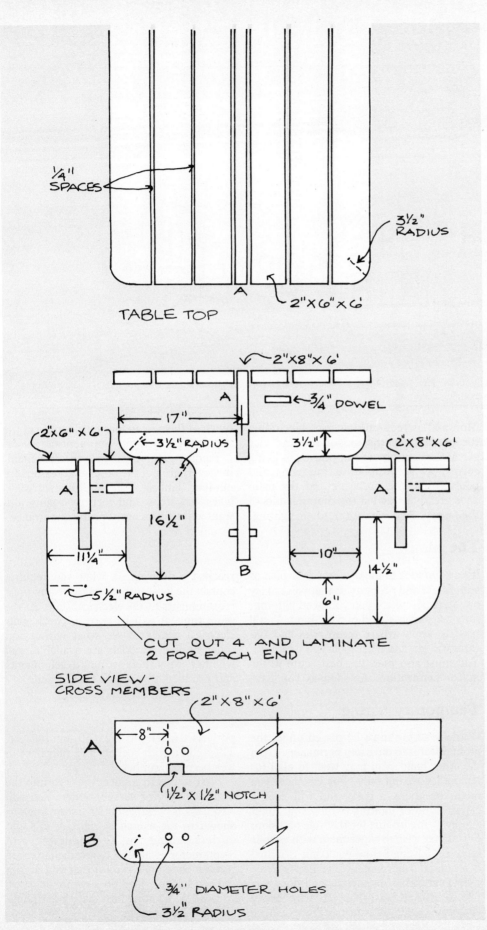

¼" SPACES

3½" RADIUS

TABLE TOP

A

2"X6"X6'

2"X8"X6'

A

←¾" DOWEL

17"

3½"RADIUS

3½"

2"X6"X6'

2"X8"X6'

A

A

16½"

B

11¼"

10"

14½"

5½" RADIUS

6"

CUT OUT 4 AND LAMINATE
2 FOR EACH END

SIDE VIEW—
CROSS MEMBERS

2"X8"X6'

A

8"

1½" X 1½" NOTCH

B

¾" DIAMETER HOLES

3½" RADIUS

What it takes

Approximate time: A full day or less, and thus an ideal Saturday project.

Tools and materials: Table saw for the outside cuts, saber saw for insides and corners. You can use a portable circular saw but it should have a minimum rating of 1½ horsepower and at least a 7¼-inch blade. You'll need two 4x8-foot sheets of ¾-inch exterior plywood, smooth on one side; four pieces 2x8-inch by 6-foot lumber; 10 pieces 2x6-inch by 6-foot lumber; 16 hardwood dowels ¾ inch by 3½ inches; 40 1-inch wood screws; 3-inch galvanized nails; waterproof glue; wood putty.

An outdoor lighting system

The components of a complete outdoor lighting system include lamp post, entryway lights, garden lights, walkway lights, eave floodlights, and step lights. You can install the entire system or select only the items that suit your needs.

What it takes

Approximate time: A day for the actual connecting work if it isn't a large job. Figure trench digging as extra time.

Tools and materials: Screwdriver, hammer, pliers, wirestrippers, electric drill and bits, shovel (spade is better if you're cutting sod), wiring and fixtures, caulking compound, electrician's tape.

More and more, homeowners are including the outdoors in the indoor life and vice versa. Gardens are now appearing in living rooms, as are miniature fountains and pools, while the barbecue and the patio have greatly extended the dining habits of the family. And without outdoor lighting, much of the new indoor-outdoor life of the home would be quite impractical.

Family gatherings and entertainment, however, are not the only good reasons for outdoor lighting. Safe, well-lighted walkways and steps, and security against unwanted intruders are of prime importance.

The plan

It's a good idea to make a sketch or plan of your house and property so that you can lay out on paper where you will need lighting, for what purpose, and of what kind. You'll need to know where receptacles and fixtures will go, and what tools you'll require. You must also plan the best route to the indoor connection. As soon as you have reached a decision on what you require, contact the local authorities to see how your requirements fit the electrical code. At the same time, it will be wise to check your electrical dealer to see what wiring and other needed materials are available, and whether or not there are new developments and products that would benefit you.

Temporary wiring

Outdoor wiring must be placed under the ground if it is to have any permanency. On the other hand, you may wish to plan for temporary wiring only. For instance, you might be giving a party and will need a certain kind of lighting, which you might simply string up just for that one occasion; or you may wish to experiment with various kinds of lighting before you come to a final decision on a permanent installation.

It is necessary in temporary outdoor wiring to use at least No. 16 wire heavy extension cords of rubber. These can be purchased in lengths of 25, 50, and 100 feet. They come with sockets and plugs set in weatherproof rubber.

First step is to connect the cord into the nearest house (or garage) outlet. You will also need a portable outlet fixture such as shown in the sketch at right. Cords and outlets come in 2-conductor and 3-conductor grounded types; the latter are recommended. Be careful that you do not put too heavy a load on any circuit, since you will be hooking into the regular house circuits already in use.

Permanent wiring

If you have had some experience with installing wiring, then you might wish to undertake your own permanent outdoor wiring. If not, call in an electrician.

The cable (type UF) is buried in trenches which will go to the various areas you wish to light. Cable should be buried at least 18 inches below the ground so that it is protected from gardening tools. It can be buried only 6 inches if it is properly protected, either in a galvanized conduit or with a piece of metal over it.

The cable will be connected to underground junction boxes to which you can install fixtures permanently, or to weatherproof outdoor outlets. Be sure to check your electrical code because most codes require that metal conduit or sheathing be installed where cable comes out of the ground. Underground-type cable, if grounded, can also be used in certain areas.

It is easy enough to locate new outlet boxes on the side of the house, or on a fence, a tree, or any number of other places. Be sure to separate circuits for outdoor lighting on the house service panel; and for con-venience, have a one-for-all switch installed inside the house.

For security purposes, you can install an electric-eye or timer that will control certain lighting units in order to light your grounds after nightfall whether or not you are home.

Try to plan your outlets and permanent lighting fixtures carefully so that you won't have to use extension cords. Measure the distance between the house and the planned outlet and fixture, and then add another 20 feet. This should give you enough slack for burying the wire. For permanent installations, it is recommended that you use No. 14 wire, or heavier.

Drill or cut any holes in the side of your house close to the circuit breaker or fuse box. Cut between studs if your house is wood. Always plug around the holes with caulking compound after the cable wiring has been run in.

It goes without saying that all your outdoor wiring must be complete, including the connection of terminals, before you connect it to the fuse or circuit-breaker box.

Additional wiring precautions

- Never work when the ground is not dry.
- Turn off the current while you are working.
- Elevate temporary wiring or any fixture, using string or tape, so that it cannot fall into a pool of water.
- Use only equipment—plugs, cords, sockets, connections—that was manufactured for the outdoors and that is waterproof.

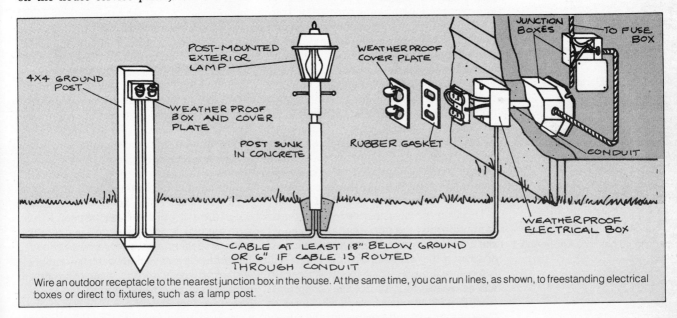

Wire an outdoor receptacle to the nearest junction box in the house. At the same time, you can run lines, as shown, to freestanding electrical boxes or direct to fixtures, such as a lamp post.

Ground fault interrupter

The ground fault interrupter (GFI) is a supplementary circuit breaker which the National Electrical Code requires in any new outdoor circuits. A GFI can detect even a slight current leak and will shut off a circuit so fast that it prevents serious shocks from happening. This receptacle with a GFI will fit an outdoor box. Except for a push button labeled R (which resets the interrupter after it trips), and another labeled T (which simulates a leakage when you want to test the device) it looks just like an ordinary receptacle. Check with your local electrical code, and electrician before installing.

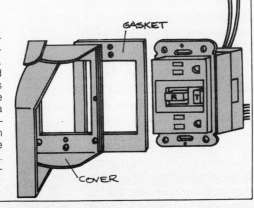

A garden pool and waterfall

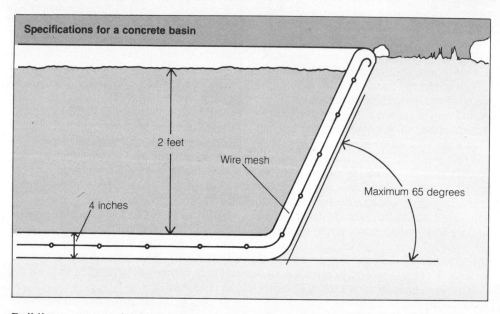

Specifications for a concrete basin

2 feet

Wire mesh

Maximum 65 degrees

4 inches

What it takes

Approximate time: One day, but add extra time for planting.

Tools and materials: Shovel, plastic liner or materials for concrete, level, pump with tubing, gravel (sand or peat moss), driftwood, rocks, electrical wiring.

Building your own backyard Shangri-La, including a pool and waterfall, is a simple and satisfying project. The pool can be either a concrete basin or a plastic-lined pit.

Concrete pool. Pouring concrete to form a bowl is easier than pouring it for a slab (see page 62), and you can create all kinds of decorative effects out of it, such as a wading pool sunk in your lawn or garden, or a pool for fish or with statuary; add a recirculating pump and you can have a waterfall.

Such pools can be built without wood forms. In general, the concrete can be poured right onto tamped earth and you will not need a gravel bed. The sides and base need only be 4 inches thick because the bowl will not bear a great deal of weight.

However, because the concrete is poured without forms, the sides of the hole should slope at an angle of not more than 65 degrees; if they are steeper the concrete will run before it has a chance to set. Wire mesh will be needed to reinforce the concrete. If your pond is for fish, you'll also need to incorporate a runoff channel in the rim so that excess water can flow out.

Plastic-lined pool. This is a great deal simpler and less costly to install. It can be removed with a minimum of effort should you wish to change your landscaping. You can purchase the plastic liner with a pump (if waterfall is desired), or separately.

The first step is to pick your location. Use a shovel to outline the pool area, which can be any shape from square, to kidney, to free form. Then dig the hole for the pool. If the pool is to be used for plants, it must be at least 2 feet deep. If you plan also to build a waterfall, then pile the excavated dirt where the waterfall will eventually be. Level the bottom of the pool, making sure it is free of sharp rocks, roots, and any other encumbrances. Spread a thin layer of sand, fine gravel, or peat moss, sufficient to cover well, over the bottom of the pool excavation. Cover the entire pool and waterfall area with the plastic liner. Secure it where necessary with rock. If you plan to introduce fish to the pool, make sure that the plastic is of a kind that won't harm them.

Installing the pump. In most cases, simply place the pump on the bottom of the pool and run a length of plastic tubing (which comes with it) up to the top of the waterfall. Cover any exposed tubing with dirt.

The waterfall. Make an uneven stairway out of the dirt you dug from the pool. Cover with the plastic liner. Then place flat rocks as steps so that the water can cascade down. Decorate the area of both waterfall and pool with driftwood, rocks, moss, and other natural materials. Cut slits in the plastic liner to accommodate poolside plants such as ground cover and cattails. Fill the pool with water and connect the pump to an electrical outlet.

Wiring for the pool. Check local codes for wiring regulations regarding pools. All electrical outlets must be grounded, and they must be weatherproof. Install a ground fault interrupter in the line as an extra precaution against shocks. Wiring of types USE or UF are best, and either of these can be run underground without enclosing them in conduit. Either type should be buried 18 inches deep as protection against accidental breakage or someone severing them with a gardening tool.

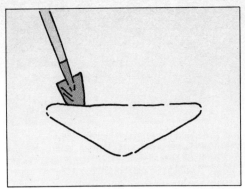

1. With a sharp instrument, or the blade of a shovel, outline on the ground the area of your pool. Let it take any shape you want.

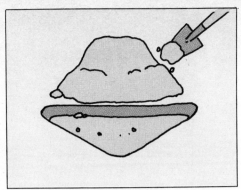

2. Dig the hole. Pile the dirt at one end of the pool, where it will eventually be formed in shelves for a series of falls. It's a good idea to first pour a slab of concrete for the dirt to rest on.

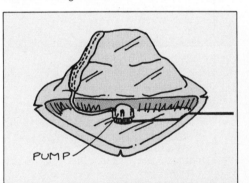

3. Make certain that the bottom of the pool is level and free of sharp rocks and other debris. It's best to spread a thin layer of sand or peat moss over the bottom—enough to cover.

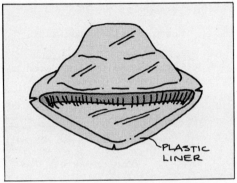

4. Cover the whole pool and falls area with a plastic liner. Excess liner may be trimmed back.

5. Install the pump in the bottom of the pool, and run the tubing up to the top of the waterfall structure. You may cover the tubing with sand so it won't show.

6. Line the edges of the plastic liner with stone, rock, and driftwood, which will help keep the liner in place and add to its attractiveness.

7. Place flat rocks as steps in the dirt you have piled for the waterfall. Wash the rocks so that muddy water won't get into your pool.

8. Add more rocks, driftwood, and plants around the pool and waterfall to finish the natural setting.

Wiring

Wiring is essential for operation of your pool and waterfall, and for lights. Either bury the electric cable, or, if this is not possible, you can fasten it with cable straps to the underside of a 1x4-inch redwood board, or lay metal over it. This will protect it from garden tools.

REMODELING KITCHENS & BATHS

REMODELING KITCHENS & BATHS

Created and editorially produced for Petersen Publishing Company by Allen D. Bragdon Publishers, Inc., Home Guides Division

STAFF FOR THIS VOLUME

Director	Allen D. Bragdon
Text Editor	James Wyckoff
Art Director	John B. Miller
Assistant Art Director	Clara Rosenbaum
Production Editor	Eileen Bossong Martines
Staff Writers	Nancy Jackson, Laura K. Palmer
Contributing Artists	Pat Lee, Gary Monteferante, Chuck Pitaro, Clara Rosenbaum, Jerry Zimmerman
Contributing Photographers	Jack Abraham, Monte Burch, Nancy Jackson
Production Coordinator	Dana P. Sephton
Production Artists	Ellen Dichner, Eleanore Fahey, Chon Vinson
Cover design by	"For Art Sake" Inc.

Technical Consultants:

Seymour Minkin comes from a long line of skilled carpenters. A licensed Master Carpenter who has worked at his trade for more than 30 years, Mr. Minkin is an instructor in woodworking at Alfred E. Smith Vocational High School and teaches Apprentice and Journeyman Retraining at Labor Technical College, both in New York City. During the summer months he takes on home remodeling and other carpentry jobs to keep his skills sharp.

John V. Vanderwende holds several Master Plumber licenses, and has 32 years' trade experience in remodeling and construction work. Since 1962 he has taught plumbing and related technical subjects at Alfred E. Smith Vocational High School. For 14 years he has served as instructor and consultant to local plumbing apprentice training programs. He works every summer as a plumber to keep in touch with new trade technology and materials.

John C. Jackson is a free-lance carpenter in New York City who builds sets for film, TV, and print advertising photography. He did the remodeling work for the "Rebuilt Kitchen" case study in this book.

ACKNOWLEDGEMENTS

The Editors wish to thank the following individuals and firms for their help in the preparation of this book: Allmilmo Corporation; American Institute of Kitchen Dealers; American Olean Tile Company; American Standard, Inc.; Argus Kitchens Incorporated; Aristocrat Kitchens Ltd.; Armstrong Cork Co.; Peter Bleckman; Celotex Division, Jim Walter Corp.; Champion Building Products, Division Champion International; Delta Faucet Company; E.I. du Pont de Nemours & Co. Inc.; Eljer Plumbingware, Division Wallace-Murray Corp.; Ernesto Tile Supply; Excel Wood Products Co., Inc.; General Electric Company; Georgia-Pacific Corp.; Goodyear Tire & Rubber Company; Kohler Co.; Lloyd Lumber Company; Kert Lundell; Mario Manstrandrea; Masonite Corporation; National Kitchen Cabinet Association; Nemo Tile Company Inc.; Owens-Corning Fiberglas Corp.; Poggenpohl USA Corp.; John Richmond; Robert Sosa; Tile Council of America; U.S. Plywood, Division of U.S. Plywood-Champion Papers, Inc.; Western Wood Products Association; Westinghouse Electric Corp.; Tom Yee

PETERSEN PUBLISHING COMPANY

R.E. Petersen / Chairman of the Board
F.R. Waingrow / President
Philip E. Trimbach / V.P. Finance
William Porter / V.P. Circulation Director
James J. Krenek / V.P. Manufacturing
Jack Thompson / Assistant Director, Circulation
Nigel P. Heaton / Director, Circulation Marketing
Louis Abbott / Director, Production
Arthur Zarin / Director, Research
Al Isaacs / Director, Graphics
Bob D'Olivo / Director, Photography
Maria Cox / Manager, Data Processing Services
Erwin M. Rosen / Executive Editor, Specialty Publications Division

Library of Congress Catalog Card No. 78-50829
Paperbound Edition:
ISBN 0-8227-8012-7

Table of Contents

1. PLANNING A DREAM

It is a rare home in which the kitchen and bathrooms look the same as they did when it was built. Someone had to have the dream and someone had to do the remodeling to make it come true. This book shows homeowners who want to save money—and do the job just right—how to go about doing the work themselves and turn their own dream into reality. Even if you will be contracting for some or all of the work, the more you know about what can, and what must, be done—the more likely you are to end up with an accurately estimated, quality job.

How to "read" a page. These pages show examples of most of the tips, guides and other helps that you will find in the pages of how-to instructions that follow.

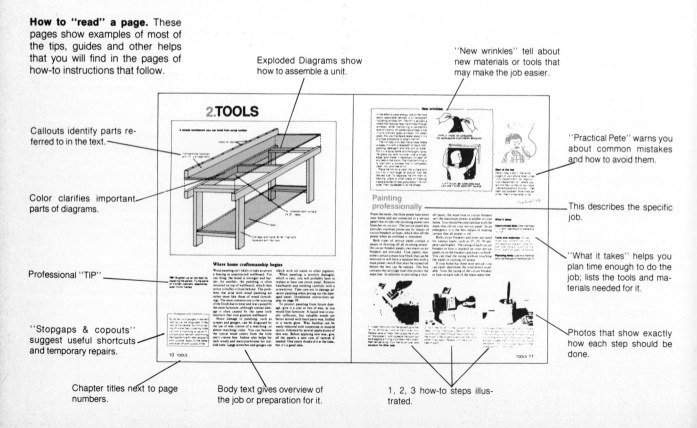

Exploded Diagrams show how to assemble a unit.

"New wrinkles" tell about new materials or tools that may make the job easier.

Callouts identify parts referred to in the text.

Color clarifies important parts of diagrams.

"Practical Pete" warns you about common mistakes and how to avoid them.

This describes the specific job.

Professional "TIP"

"What it takes" helps you plan time enough to do the job; lists the tools and materials needed for it.

"Stopgaps & copouts" suggest useful shortcuts and temporary repairs.

Photos that show exactly how each step should be done.

Chapter titles next to page numbers.

Body text gives overview of the job or preparation for it.

1, 2, 3 how-to steps illustrated.

How this book is organized

This book cannot tell you how your remodeled kitchen or bathroom will look when it is done. Only you can decide how far your tastes, pocketbook, and available space will let you go. The first two-thirds of this book shows, with step-by-step illustrations, how to do each of the jobs you are likely to have to tackle—and presents them in the general order that you will be doing them for either a kitchen or bath—from planning to hooking up your new lighting fixtures, and final decoration.

Since no two remodeling projects are exactly the same, you may be able to skip some jobs that are outlined; you may change the sequence of work; and perhaps you may wish to seek help elsewhere for elaborate effects or special situations that require professional expertise. The latter part of the book contains descriptions of how specific renovation projects were actually executed, including step-by-step instructions for creating some unusual effects.

This chapter tells you what to think about before you spend a nickel, and how to schedule the work, just as a professional contractor does, to help you keep material costs and labor time within your estimate.

Be your own contractor

Remodeling a whole kitchen or bathroom requires a kind of planning that isolated repair and maintenance jobs don't. Even if you have experience with the different trade skills—carpentry, electrical, plumbing—by planning the sequence of steps in a remodeling project carefully you can save a lot of time and expense.

For example, imagine that you've installed the kitchen cabinets, with the sink snugly in place ready to be connected, and you realize that the waste and water lines are covered by the cabinets so you can't get to them. The new acoustical tile ceiling is up and looks great, but the old ceiling fixture is not centered over the new dinette table where you wanted it so you could simply replace the fixture. So now you have to tear down enough tiles to run new cable from the old box to the spot where you want the new fixture to be—then put them all back up again. You have put up a partition wall to close off the tub and toilet and hung the new door. The new tub has been delivered and you are ready to take out the old cast iron one—but it won't fit through the door. What do you do? Tear out the door jamb? Break up the old tub with a sledgehammer? Careful planning averts such crises.

A contractor plans the sequence of jobs by working *back* from the way the finished renovation will look to the way it is now. He must line up specialists in each trade to come onto the job at the right time. Unless you are doing *all* the work yourself—rough and finish plumbing, electrical wiring, carpentry and cabinet-making, painting and decorating—you will have to tell a specialist ahead of time exactly when you will reach the stage where he will be needed to do his thing.

Once you have decided what the end result should look like, work back to see what kinds of jobs you are letting yourself in for. For example, if your plan requires that you change the dimensions of the room by moving a load-bearing wall (one that helps hold the house up rather than a partition added only to divide space), you should be prepared to relocate in-the-wall basic plumbing and electrical wiring, and expect some pretty heavy construction work, along with disrupted family activities; plus the problem of obtaining building permits.

If you don't feel your experience matches some of the steps your remodeling plan requires, talk to a contractor or to individual artisans about doing those portions of the work. Get bids from them before you abandon your plan. They may also be able to tell you whether you will need permits from the municipal building authority in your town. If you are running new wiring inside the walls, have the electrical insurance underwriters inspect it. If they don't, and a fire starts because of faulty wiring, the amount of your homeowners' insurance coverage may be affected.

A professional contractor would want to pin down when as well as how much he will be paid. If you are doing your own work, total the costs of the materials, fixtures, appliances, and new tools required (see page 7 of this book); then add a contingency of about 20% to allow for minor changes of mind or surprises along the way.

Once you have your plan, have evaluated the skills you will need, and have arranged for permits and financing, set dates to start and complete the work: Even the professionals dislike being held to a completion date. The way they get around it is to ask for more time than they believe is necessary. So should you. For

Job-sequence for remodeling a typical kitchen or bath

Most remodeling projects will require at least some of the following steps in the order given. Use this as a reminder when you plan the scope of your project. The chapters that follow provide specific detailed techniques for executing each of these steps, in this same order. See the how-to text for resequencing options in addition to those noted here. Because of the hazards and difficulty of roughing in new or relocated plumbing waste and water lines except by a professional, those techniques are not covered.

☑ Plan the extent of the job, in detail.
☑ Order and store materials, appliances, tools; after thoroughly checking.
☑ Protect the house from debris.
☑ Remove the plumbing fixtures.
☑ Remove the hanging cabinets (Note: The previous two steps can be reversed).
☑ Remove the countertops.
☑ Remove the base cabinets.
☑ Remove the old floor.
☑ Clean up the debris.
☑ Install the bathtub.
☑ Frame the walls for doorways, windows, and trimmed openings.
☑ Frame in soffits.
☑ Route the electrical wiring.
☑ Secure the electrical outlet boxes.
☑ Patch or refinish the walls (gypsum board, plastic coated fiber board, tile, etc.).
☑ Refinish the floors.
☑ Install cabinets and counter tops.
☑ Install plumbing fixtures (sinks, water closet, etc.).
☑ Connect the electrical wiring to the electrical fixtures.

Is the dream do-able?

Work back from your picture of the finished work to see if you want to tackle the kinds of jobs it will require. Here are some typical considerations.

- Replacing old appliances or plumbing fixtures is not difficult but changing their location in the room will probably mean opening a wall to extend pipes, or running new wiring, or both.

- Tearing out an existing wall and putting up a new one, or cutting openings in walls is easier, and lighter work if the walls are not load-bearing. Load-bearing walls support the structure of the house, rather than merely partition off space supported elsewhere.

- Relocating overhead electrical fixtures in a solid (not suspended) ceiling will mean cutting channels through plaster or tearing down tile or wallboard.

- Changing the location of hung cabinets requires careful measuring, locating studs, patching walls, and installing new stringers to attach them to.

- Removing a ceiling is a strenuous, very dust-producing job, especially if it is plaster. Covering it with tile or hanging a suspended ceiling is relatively easy.

- Laying new tile directly on an uneven floor will usually look worse than what was there. The old flooring usually has to be removed and the sub-flooring leveled or replaced.

- Check the voltage requirements of new electrical appliances to be sure your existing wiring is adequate. An appliance that needs 220-volt wiring or more won't work in a standard (110 or 120-volt) circuit. Also be sure the total combined wattage of all new appliances does not exceed the capacity of the circuit or circuits they must be plugged into.

example, if you estimate that you can finish the job in two weekends, you'd better not make plans for the third weekend in case something goes wrong. The less pressure you are under, the fewer mistakes you are likely to make.

Another aspect of job coordination is ordering tools, material and equipment. They will have to be delivered well in advance, so arrange for a place to store them safely. As soon as possible after delivery, unpack and inspect materials and fixtures for damage, and to be sure you have received the right model, color, size, etc. Plug in or temporarily hook up appliances and fixtures to be sure they work. Since some may have to be sent back to the supplier to be replaced, have them delivered to your home as far in advance as it would take to obtain replacements.

A contractor relies heavily on his own, or a supervisor's talents in certain specific areas. The professionals call it trade coordination. As your own contractor you will be doing that job yourself. Briefly, here are the requirements: knowing when a job is to be started and finished; seeing to it that enough time is allotted for the job; knowing when to order tools, material and equipment; checking on deliveries, as well as on quality of tools and materials; knowing how to blend the efforts of the different trades so as to expedite the work; being able and ready to devise alternative work methods when job conditions are not as expected.

Job survey checklist

General
- ☐ Plans
- ☐ Estimates
- ☐ Building Permits
- ☐ Insurance
- ☐ Financing

Appliances
- ☐ Refrigerators
- ☐ Ranges
- ☐ Ovens
- ☐ Dishwashers
- ☐ Disposal
- ☐ Freezer
- ☐ Washer
- ☐ Dryer
- ☐ Vacuum System
- ☐ Range Hood
- ☐ Exhaust Fans

Plumbing Fixtures
- ☐ Kitchen Sink
- ☐ Hot Water Heater
- ☐ Laundry Tubs
- ☐ Bathtubs
- ☐ Lavatories
- ☐ Water Closets
- ☐ Shower Cabinets
- ☐ Air Conditioner
- ☐ Disposal
- ☐ Dishwasher

Finishing
- ☐ Hardwood Flooring
- ☐ Underlayment
- ☐ Linoleum
- ☐ Floor Tile
- ☐ Ceramic Tile
- ☐ Millwork
- ☐ Doors
- ☐ Screens
- ☐ Storm Sash
- ☐ Floor Sanding
- ☐ Floor Finishing
- ☐ Blinds
- ☐ Shades
- ☐ Interior Painting
- ☐ Wallpaper
- ☐ Weatherstrip Doors
- ☐ Weatherstrip Windows
- ☐ General Clean-up
- ☐ Finish Hardware
- ☐ Medicine Cabinets
- ☐ Planters
- ☐ Stall Showers
- ☐ Tile Wainscot
- ☐ Carpets
- ☐ Drapes
- ☐ Paneling
- ☐ Shower Doors
- ☐ Patio Doors
- ☐ Bathroom Accessories
- ☐ Mirrors
- ☐ Closet Accessories

Cabinet work
- ☐ Kitchen
- ☐ Bathroom
- ☐ Laundry
- ☐ Basement
- ☐ Cabinet tops
- ☐ Counters

Framing
- ☐ Lumber
- ☐ Veneer
- ☐ Windows
- ☐ Air Conditioning
- ☐ Plastering
- ☐ Drywall
- ☐ Areawalls
- ☐ Nails
- ☐ Hardware
- ☐ Louvers
- ☐ Vents

Electrical service
- ☐ Range Circuit
- ☐ Dryer Outlet
- ☐ Convenience Outlets
- ☐ Switches
- ☐ Intercom
- ☐ Telephone
- ☐ Ceiling Lights
- ☐ Wall Lights
- ☐ Fixtures

COST ESTIMATE WORKSHEET

Quan.	Item	Rate	Outside labor		Materials		Actual results	
		Totals						

2. LAYING IT OUT

An island kitchen can be as big or as little (almost) as you like. It can include a stove, a sink, even a refrigerator; or it can be just a mix center. Here, you can also breakfast with the entire family.

Design and placement of kitchen cabinets

The first thing in planning your new kitchen is to see what the old one lacks. Very likely it is not as convenient as you would wish it to be; otherwise you wouldn't be planning a renovation.

Be specific. Do you have enough counter space? What about storage area? Can you reach things easily? Do your appliances work as they should? Does the refrigerator open in such a way that you have to walk around the door to take out the milk? How is the lighting, ventilation? Is the room attractive, a pleasant place in which to work? Do you also see your kitchen as a family center, a place for breakfast, coffee breaks, possibly lunch or dinner? There are four basic kitchen layouts that you should bear in mind: the U-shape kitchen, the L-shape, the corridor kitchen, and the one-wall.

Every kitchen is also made up of three main activity centers: storage (refrigerator), cleanup (sink), and cooking (stove). It is essential to have these three centers in a convenient work triangle.

When you realize that in order to prepare just breakfast and dinner for an average family the cook will walk 120 miles in a year, it raises the question of wasted movement which the cook will suffer due to bad kitchen planning. If you arrange the sink, the refrigerator, the stove in a good triangular relationship, you can save, the experts tell us, about 40 miles a year in walking.

The actual design of the kitchen will be regulated by three factors: the available wall space, the floor area, and your budget. You must also consider ventilation and lighting.

First, make a sketch of your existing kitchen—a "plan view." The plan view sketch will show the kitchen as though you were looking down from the ceiling. Use ¼-inch graph paper. Each square or box (¼"x¼") will represent one square foot (12"x12") of the area.

Draw the outline of the kitchen, indicating any breaks in the walls, such as doors, windows, an arch, a radiator, or boxed pipes.

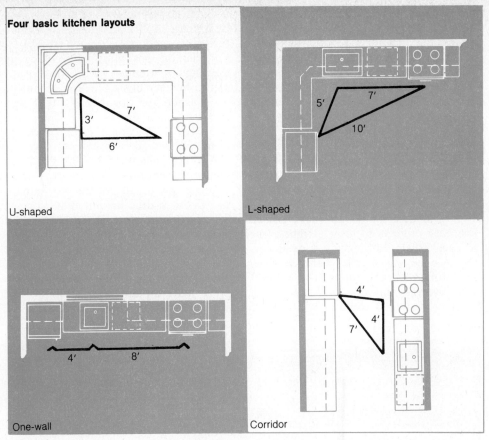

Four basic kitchen layouts

U-shaped

L-shaped

One-wall

Corridor

Base cabinets

Now sketch, still in plan view, the desired location of the new base cabinets. If you wish, use a color pencil to differentiate them from the existing kitchen.

Start with the kitchen sink. It is economically wise to put the new sink in the proximity of the existing sink. The piping may be altered to the right or left a little, but to put the new sink on the opposite wall or in an "island" in the middle of the room would involve major plumbing work. At the same time, don't eliminate a desired layout simply because of the additional work involved. Remember that you, as contractor, can sub-contract all or any part of the renovations. Moreover, a basic plan is still needed if you do wish to hire a local contractor.

The front of the base cabinets will be approximately 24 inches out from the finished wall. Count out 2 squares and draw a line parallel to the perimeter of the room where you desire the base cabinets.

You will have to decide whether to have your cabinets custom built by a cabinetmaker or buy them prefabricated. You may, of course, be able and willing to build them yourself. Of course, custom-built cabinets will offer the most flexibility, but they cost more.

Prefabricated cabinets may be constructed of wood, metal, plastic laminate, or even a combination of materials. Stock base cabinet widths start at 12 inches and increase in increments of 3 inches up to 36 inches. Beyond the 36-inch width, they increase by 6-inch increments to a maximum 60-inch width.

Locating the dishwasher
You can be flexible in placing your dishwasher. The discharge (waste pipe) from the dishwasher, and only one (hot) water supply pipe require tubing or hose of relatively small dimension. The dishwasher pump is capable of getting the drain water to the kitchen trap. The added expense of extra hose is negligible.

While a portable roll-around dishwasher has merit in an older kitchen, you would be wise to plan for an under-the-counter model. The portable type, when in use, will tie up the sink, and when not in use will present a storage problem.

The best counter height

A happy cook makes for a happy meal, is an old saying. Remember this when you consider the height of your kitchen counters. A 36-inch height is said to be average. On prefabricated cabinets you can lessen this by reducing the kick space at the bottom. If, on the other hand, you wish to raise the counter a few inches, then consider raising the upper wall cabinets to keep the kitchen height in good proportion. As a rule, the work surface that is most agreeable will be about 3 inches below your elbow.

At this point give some thought to the size and design of the kitchen sink. The sink you choose will determine the size of the sink base cabinet; and this in turn will affect the sizes of the remaining base cabinets along the same wall.

Consider that for ease of installation, as well as for the sake of efficiency, the dishwasher should be adjacent to, or at least in the proximity of the sink base cabinet. And now, too, is a good time to locate the refrigerator and range; and also the oven, garbage disposal, and other appliances.

Sketch your appliances to scale and cut them out of paper. These figures can then be pinned to the floor plan layout and if necessary can be moved.

In your design you may have placed two base cabinets to form a right angle to each other. This makes a dead corner. A good way to deal with this is by installing a "Lazy Susan"—a cabinet with revolving shelves.

U- or L-shaped cabinets will require U- or L-shaped counter tops. This could be a problem in maneuvering the countertop through the kitchen doorway. Consider the possibility of breaking up the length of counter with a strategically placed butcher block top over a built-in dishwasher, for instance. In that way you can retain the L- or U-shape and still have a functional piece of equipment.

Another means of breaking a long section of countertop is with a free-standing gas or electric range. Perhaps you desire a drop-in unit that will utilize the countertop. A cutout in the counter will of course be necessary.

Stock base and wall cabinets may not stretch from wall to wall because of an odd measurement. Filler pieces, of the same material as your cabinets, are available and are easy to install.

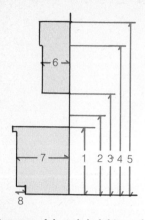

Some useful work heights and depths
1. Height of countertop—36"
2. Height of wall outlets and switches—44"
3. Bottom of wall cabinet—54"
4. Top of wall cabinet—84"
5. Ceiling—variable
6. Depth of wall cabinet—13"
7. Depth of base cabinet—24"
8. Depth of kick space—3"

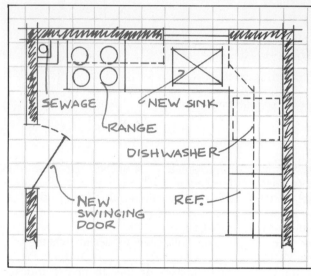

SEWAGE — NEW SINK — RANGE — DISHWASHER — NEW SWINGING DOOR — REF.

Use graph paper to draw your kitchen to scale. Each box or square of ¼"x¼" will represent 1 square foot. It is important to be exact, and as detailed as possible. Indicate breaks in the walls for windows, doors, radiators, boxed pipes. Use pencil so that you can erase if necessary. As you complete your sketch, you may wish to use color.

Wall cabinets

These should be placed above the base units, whenever possible, so that there will be a symmetrical appearance to the design. Because of the headroom space required above the kitchen sink, it is not desirable to place a wall cabinet in that location. If a window is above the sink, you have no choice anyway. Cabinets or shelves may of course go on either side of the window.

On your graph paper, indicate the distance from floor to ceiling. Sketch in the ceiling line, floor line, and adjacent wall lines. You now have a large box that will represent an entire wall. The height and width measurements of doors, windows, and other openings may now be located in their proper place on the wall. Be sure to identify the actual wall on the graph—left wall, front, right, or back.

The top of all wall-hung cabinets will be 84 inches above the floor. Count 7 squares from the floor line on your paper; draw a line from wall to wall to indicate the top of the cabinets.

A 30-inch wall cabinet will allow for 18-inch clearance between the bottom of the wall cabinet and the surface of the countertop over the base cabinets. If you place the tops of the wall cabinets higher than 84 inches it will be difficult to reach the top shelves.

Finally, your choice of cabinet finish, whether it be wood or plastic laminate, is a matter of preference. Go to the showroom or store and actually see the cabinets you are considering. Avoid choosing cabinets by photograph or brochure. While the idea may be there in a picture, the actual texture and feel of the cabinet cannot be truly appreciated.

A wall oven
If you plan a wall oven you will need a cabinet, unless you provide a "cabinet" of real or artificial brick, or fieldstone, to frame it. Be careful not to install the oven too high, and place it so that its door opens on about the same level as the countertops—36 inches from the floor.

Countertops

In any kitchen a major consideration has to be surface—walls, floors, countertops. These areas are the most visible, and the most vulnerable. Indeed, the countertop will receive almost as much punishment as the kitchen floor.

Nowadays there is an especially large variety of countertop materials to choose from. Ideally, the countertop would be attractive, stainproof, impervious to heat, moisture, scratches; it would be resilient to a certain degree, and inexpensive. Unfortunately, no one material combines all these qualities, though some do come close.

Of the many materials to choose from, about a half dozen appear to be the most popular.

- **Plastic laminate.** This is the most in demand. It's easy to maintain, comes in many colors, patterns and textures. It is resilient, non-porous, refuses grease and household chemicals. However, it should not be subjected to hot utensils, or used as a cutting surface.

- **Flexible vinyl.** It has a strong resistance to moisture, alcohol, stains, and abrasions. Don't use the surface for cutting or for placement of hot pans.
- **Laminated hardwood.** Butcher block is greatly in demand nowadays; good for cutting, but avoid prolonged moisture and hot pans.
- **Ceramic tile.** Tile wears well and comes in many patterns and colors. It resists moisture and heat, but dirt can collect in the crevices between the tiles.
- **Synthetic marble.** It is just about stainproof. However, it is less resistant to heat than tile, and it is also expensive.
- **Glass-ceramic.** This is a new heatproof material that is somewhat expensive. Yet, it is fine as a small chopping or cutting spot, or for holding hot utensils. It cleans easily and resists stains.

One-piece countertops are now available in various lengths, made from postformed plastic laminate with or without a drip-free front edge and a curved backsplash.

Countertop materials

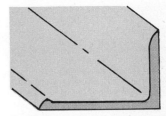

Postformed

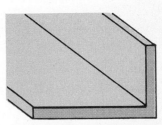

Plastic laminate, self edge

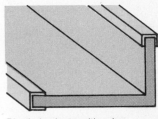

Plastic laminate with edge molding

Ventilation

When you consider the fact that some 200 pounds of smoke, moisture, and grease in the form of vapors are released in a single year's cooking, you will realize the need for adequate ventilation in your kitchen.

To handle this problem you may either vent the vapors to the outdoors or remove them by filtering the air in the kitchen.

Venting is simply done with a kitchen fan cut into a wall close to the range. There are many sizes and shapes of exhaust fans, and all require cutting through the kitchen wall for installation.

Ventilating hoods come in two types: ducted and unducted. The ducted system vents directly to the outdoors. This type of vent is most easily installed when there is major renovation work in the kitchen—renewing walls, ceiling, and cabinets, for instance.

Ductless ventilators, on the other hand, fit in a hood right over the range and can be hung on the wall, or suspended below a cabinet; and so will be part of your cabinet planning. This type of vent is not as efficient as the ducted ventilator. It draws cooking vapors through a charcoal filter, eliminating odors and grease, and then releases clean air back into the kitchen. It cannot, however, remove heat and moisture from the kitchen like a ducted system. The ductless system is favored where it is too difficult or too expensive to install a duct to the outside wall. But the filters, of aluminum mesh and fiberglass, activated carbon or granulated charcoal, should be cleaned or even replaced every few weeks. The ducted system, though, should be cleaned every six months.

It is important, in any ventilating system, that the correct fan capacity be taken into account. This must relate directly to the size of the space in which it is to operate. Check with your appliance dealer before you buy.

Suggested counter area around appliances:
- At least 15" on the latch side of the refrigerator.
- At least 30" of working counter on each side of the sink.
- 24" on each side of the range is a minimum working area.

Plumbing fixtures

The kitchen sink

Your best bet for selecting plumbing fixtures is to visit the showroom of a plumbing supply dealer or discount center specializing in building supplies.

Many of the newer sinks are self rim; this means that the unit is supported by the rim resting on the countertop. The weight of the sink and an adhesive/caulking prevent the sink from shifting. Self rim makes for an easy installation, but bear in mind that the top of the sink rim is ⅜ to ½ inch higher than the countertop. This means that if water is spilled onto the countertop it won't run into the sink.

The cast iron sink has proven its endurance over the years. The enamel is acid resistant, and the sink comes in white plus a multitude of colors, which cost about 10% more than the traditional white. The shapes and styles are also many—double compartment, triple, corner, waste disposal accommodations, and more.

The pressed steel sink (porcelain on steel) is light and not expensive. It has a coating of tar-like substance underneath the sink to deaden the sound caused by running water striking the thin body of the sink. Although pressed steel is also available in colors, the choice of shapes is limited. This is because of the manufacturer's effort to keep the price down.

The stainless steel sink offers durability, with little weight for handling problems, and it too comes in self rim. Various shapes are available, and you can get multi-compartment models. You also have a choice of gauge; that is, thickness of the steel.

Stainless steel sinks also have a soundproofing material adhered to the underside. While stainless steel will not chip, it does require more attention than cast iron. For instance, it should be wiped dry after each use to avoid water spotting.

One man's blue can be another man's gray!
My wife wanted a blue bathroom, so I shopped around at different showrooms for the fixtures. What I didn't realize was that one manufacturer's blue isn't the same shade as another's. Next time when I want color, I'll get all my fixtures from the same manufacturer.

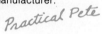
Practical Pete

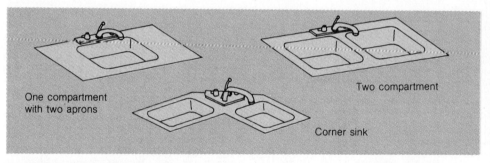

One compartment with two aprons

Two compartment

Corner sink

Types of vanities

Vanity or basin

Consider the bathroom as a whole. If you have the space, then by all means update the new bath with a vanity. You'll gain storage space, you'll have a countertop work area, and you'll have a brand new look in your bathroom.

On the other hand, if the bathroom is cramped for space, then a wall hung basin would be a sensible choice. While it is true that a small vanity will take up the same floor area as a basin, so to speak, all you actually gain with a vanity in this case is a little storage space; and the cabinet to accommodate the vanity basin will add to the cost. It could all end up looking like a small, crowded bathroom.

The wall hung lavatories are made of enameled cast iron, pressed steel, and vitreous china. Vitreous china lavatories are certainly attractive, but while serv-iceable under normal use, they are fragile. A jar falling from a medicine cabinet above a porcelain steel or an iron enamel basin might chip it, but it would crack a vitreous china one.

Vanity basins, besides coming in the above-mentioned materials, are also available in modern plastic and plastic variations. In many instances, the bowl is an integral part of the top. This is not only an attractive feature, but a sanitary one since the seams or joints formed when attaching a basin to a countertop are eliminated.

Another plus for the vanity is that the plumbing is inside the cabinet and out of view. Moreover, the vanity is probably easier to install for the home do-it-yourselfer because it does not rely on a bracket for support as does a wall hung basin. You can rely on it being firm.

Toilets

The water closet (toilet) is made of vitreous china, although some new tanks come in plastic. All modern water closets operate on the principle of siphonic action. It is the flushing and cleansing action that you pay for if you select an expensive fixture.

One-piece water closets (bowl and tank constructed as one piece) have a lower tank and are easier to clean than the conventional close-coupled bowl and tank. However, the one-piece is more than double the cost of the close-coupled combination water closet, which consists of a separate bowl and tank. The tank is bolted to the bowl by two and sometimes three bolts.

While the elongated toilet bowl is considered the most sanitary, and is required in public buildings according to strict plumbing codes, it is also the most expensive. However, a round front water closet with a reverse trap or siphon jet will be more than adequate for the average household. Most plumbing codes prohibit wash down bowls.

Before you order a water closet be sure that you know the rough-in dimension of the bowl. You can find this by measuring, at floor level, the distance from the finished wall to the center of the bolts that secure the bowl to the closet flange. You won't be able to see the flange with the bowl in place but the bolts are easily located. They may be under two china or plastic caps. In the event that you find four bolts or caps, the ones you should measure will be the rear ones, those closest to the wall. This measurement will usually be between 10 and 14 inches. But if you get a measurement of 14½ inches, figure it as 14 for purposes of roughing-in.

If you remove a 14-inch bowl and replace it with a 12-inch bowl, you will find that when you connect the tank to the bowl it will be 2 inches away from the wall. On the other hand, if you remove a 12-inch bowl and attempt to replace it with a 14-inch one, the tank just won't fit. In either case, returning the wrong tank and bowl to the dealer will present a problem. For while it is indeed "brand new" from your point of view, remember that it will be considered "used" by the dealer.

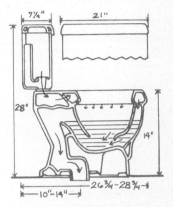

Close-coupled bowl and tank

The bathtub

The fixtures discussed so far are installed after the finished wall and floor material is secured. The bathtub, on the other hand, is built in; it is installed (set) first.

If you're planning a new tub or shower in the existing bathroom, you will have to cut the tile or plaster away from the perimeter of the present tub to free it from its recess. Of course, a very old bathroom may have a freestanding tub.

A new tub installation will almost always require alterations to the waste line and trap.

The easiest tub to install, because of its light weight, is the pressed steel tub.

Bathtubs are ordered by size; 4-foot, 4½-foot, 5-foot, 5½-foot, for example. The 5-foot tub is the most popular. In addition to the size, you must indicate whether or not the tub is to be recessed into a wall or set in a corner. The tubs that fit these requirements are called "recessed" and "corner," respectively.

You must also specify the location of the drain hole in the tub. It will be a left-hand or a right-hand waste outlet. To determine which it is, face the apron of the tub—the apron being that part of the tub that extends from the rim down to the floor. While facing the apron, if you find the tub drain is on your right, then the tub is a right-hand tub. If it is to your left, then it's a left-hand tub.

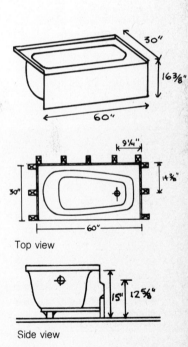

Top view

Side view

The shower

Why not plan to install a combination shower/bath fitting over the tub. The cost of the shower fitting is not high, and it will be there when you want it.

Prior to starting your bathroom remodeling, have the fixtures on hand. Ask your local dealer for rough-in sheets that give dimensions. Try to buy a lavatory or tub waste that is manufactured by the manufacturer of the fixture. Many dealers quote a price on a quality fixture, but supply competitive "trim" to keep the total cost down in order to make the sale to the customer.

You can gain space in the bathroom if you replace the tub with a shower receptor. There are many styles of shower in numerous materials, and installation is easy. Years ago the shower required a custom-made lead pad that was encased in mortar and tile. This was a little beyond the reach of the average do-it-yourselfer. Today, however, precast shower receptors and plastic shower enclosures allow the homeowners to do the job.

Only the rich can afford cheap plumbing

Remember that any money put into quality plumbing pays off. Stick to brand names, especially where you are buying small items that might need to be replaced—such as faucets. Besides long-life, quality parts are more likely to be available when needed years later.

Electrical needs

Nothing like a little light on the situation

I thought I had planned the best possible lighting in my kitchen. And, as a matter of fact I had . . . as far as the kitchen itself went. But I forgot about the kind of light needed in corners and closets. Remember that a good check is to place lighting so that you can always read the labels on jars, cans, and other items.

Practical Pete

In remodeling a kitchen or bathroom you must expect some form of electrical work. The extent of the wiring will be determined very much by the age of the house. For instance, if you have an older house you may find that the house service (electric supply cables from the utility pole outside to the electric meter and panel box where the fuses or circuit breakers are located inside the house) may not be adequate to supply sufficient power to the electrical additions you contemplate. On the other hand, an older house may have been re-wired with an eye to updating the electric service. The important thing is to remember that any extensive remodeling with new cabinets, sink, floor, and appliances, warrants a modern, safe, and well planned electrical layout. Your local utility company can tell you how to determine the load that must be handled.

All kitchens should have what is called an appliance circuit. You might very well need more than one circuit. This means new runs of electric wiring from the main panel box location. The listing on this page will serve as a check sheet of outlets you may need. Look it over carefully, and you might even add some of your own. If you outline your needs before the walls are closed in or the cabinets hung, you won't have any problem. After that, though, you'll have to work a bit harder and improvise to install the wiring you want.

Electrical outlet checklist

A suggested list of kitchen and bathroom equipment requiring electricity.

Kitchen
- ☐ Refrigerator
- ☐ Freezer
- ☐ Electric range
- ☐ Electric oven
- ☐ Gas stove
- ☐ Wall oven
- ☐ Dishwasher
- ☐ Clothes washer
- ☐ Clothes dryer
- ☐ Trash compactor
- ☐ Waste disposal
- ☐ Air conditioning units
- ☐ Exhaust fan (through wall)
- ☐ Exhaust hood with light and fan (ductless)
- ☐ Ground Fault Interrupters
- ☐ Ceiling lights
- ☐ Recessed lighting (hung ceilings)
- ☐ Fluorescent lights; under hanging cabinets, or above cabinets for diffused lighting
- ☐ 3-way switches

Wall outlets (called convenience outlets) for operation of the following kitchen equipment:
- ☐ Toaster
- ☐ Mixer/blender
- ☐ Electric coffee pot
- ☐ Electric can opener

- ☐ Radio
- ☐ T.V. outlet
- ☐ Microwave oven
- ☐ Electric skillet
- ☐ Crock pot (slow cooker)
- ☐ Electric clock on wall or soffit (Plan to locate the outlet behind the clock)

Bathroom
- ☐ Ceiling and/or wall lights
- ☐ Medicine cabinet with lights and shaver/hair dryer outlets
- ☐ Ventilation exhaust fan (if no window)
- ☐ Exhaust fan/light combination (wall switch turns on both)
- ☐ Ceiling sun lamp
- ☐ GFI electric shaver outlet

Consider making provisions for the following items, which are not necessarily electrical in nature, but when concealed in the wall or ceiling will enhance the appearance of the new kitchen:

- ☐ Telephone outlets
- ☐ Smoke detector
- ☐ T.V. or FM antenna wiring
- ☐ Intercom wiring
- ☐ Speaker wiring

Ground fault interrupter

The 1975 National Electric Code (NEC) requires certain circuits to be protected by Ground Fault Interrupters (GFI) in new construction; in all 120 volt, single-phase, 15- and 20-ampere receptacles installed out of doors; in bathrooms of all dwelling units including single-family, multi-family, and mobile homes; in all 120 volt swimming pool equipment and receptacles. It is important to check this.

The code also recommends GFI protection for receptacles in workshops, laundries, and kitchen circuits.

Electricity travels in circuits. For example, it may flow from a wall receptacle through a turned on appliance, and continue in a path back to the receptacle. Normally, the same amount of electricity that flows from the receptacle returns to the receptacle. But if there is a leak, a loss of current which is escaping from the normal flow of electricity, then the same amount will not return to the receptacle. This particular leak may not be significant enough to blow a fuse or trip the circuit breaker; it is a hidden electric hazard called a ground fault. The leak flows into the housing of the appliance. Touching the housing causes the electricity to flow through your body to the ground.

A ground fault shock is potentially dangerous. The ground fault interrupter shuts off the electric power within 1/40th of a second when the leak is as little as 5 milliamps. A GFI is expensive, but a worthwhile investment.

Here is how a ground fault can travel. The GFI will shut off the current before it can cause injury, though that small a leak might not blow a fuse.

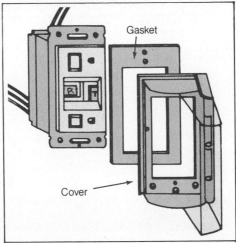

GFI receptacle fits into an outdoor box. It looks like a regular duplex receptacle with two push buttons. The one labeled "R" resets the interrupter after it has tripped, while the one labeled "T" simulates a leak so the device can be tested.

The need to check your work

A voltage tester is a must if you are going to check your home's electricity. What you will be checking is whether or not there is voltage (power) in the circuit you are working on.

The voltage tester will light when its probes touch anything that is charged with electricity. The probes are made so that they will fit into the two slots of a receptacle, thus making it possible to know whether the power is on or off without having to remove the cover plate.

A continuity tester, unlike the voltage tester, has its own source of power; a small battery that will light a bulb when there is a continuous path for current between the alligator clip and the probe. The tester must only be used when the power to a circuit or an appliance is off. Attach the alligator clip to one point and the probe to another. If the bulb doesn't light, you will know that there is a break in the line of current between the two points.

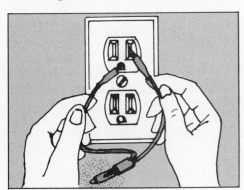

Voltage tester at work. It works in many ways, but here it tests the grounding of a receptacle when one probe is inserted into the semicircular ground slot, and the other, successively into each of the elongated slots. The device should light when the probe is in the hot slot. If the tester does not light in either slot, it means that the receptacle is not grounded, and the wiring needs correction.

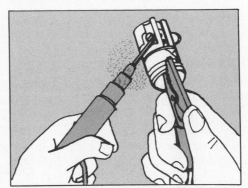

Continuity tester in action. You can check a suspected lamp socket, for example, by unplugging the lamp, removing the bulb, and taking the socket apart; then clamping the tester's alligator clip to the metal screw shell and touching the probe against the terminal. The tester should light. If it doesn't, then you will know that the socket has an open circuit, and should be fixed or replaced.

3.REMOVING CABINETS AND FIXTURES

The first step in removing fixtures and cabinets is to protect the house from debris. Remember that the length of time of the protection is increased by any delay in the construction; and so, make sure that your work schedule is being adhered to. For, while remodeling can proceed in most rooms more or less at a leisurely pace, it is usually necessary to work swiftly in a kitchen or bathroom because of family needs.

What you will be concerned with at this point is heavy dust generated by opened plaster or other types of wall structure. Although much of it may not be seen, the dust becomes airborne and can cover everything in the rooms adjoining the renovation. Rugs, upholstery, wall hangings and drapes—indeed, everything—will be affected. Unless protective measures are taken on the scene of renovation as well as in the adjoining areas, wood and plastic furniture can be scratched and dented, floors can be gouged, rugs may have to be shampooed, or inground debris may ruin the rug's fiber and shorten its life span. The odor of gypsum from broken plaster or gypsum wallboard may become so penetrating that it will be present in sofas and chairs weeks or months afterwards.

The first area to consider is, of course, the place of actual work. Resign yourself to the inevitable fact that the room you are renovating will certainly suffer from debris. The point is to minimize it. You can put down an overlay of plywood, or use drop cloths or tape down building paper. It will all help,

but only to a degree. Nothing will really keep dust and particles from slipping underneath the covering and grinding into the floor. You'd better figure on refinishing the floor.

One of the best helps is to clean up your work area as you go along, rather than wait for the end of the day or the completion of the job. Remember, too, that there is always danger of tracking as you go into other rooms, especially if you've been painting, and haven't been careful about spills.

The adjoining rooms are the really important areas to protect. Paintings and all wallhangings are to be removed and stored as far from the renovation as possible. Immovable or heavy items needing protection—for instance, rugs and carpets, furniture—are to be completely covered.

Any openings such as doors or windows that connect the renovation area to the rest of the house should be sealed and not used, as should all doors that connect to the house beyond the adjoining rooms.

It is an asset if you have windows and exterior doors in the room that is being renovated. They can be left open providing the outside air is blowing by the house and can suck out the dust. On the other hand, if the outside air is blowing into an opened doorway or window, it will force dust into the adjoining rooms. In such an instance, it would be a good idea to shut the exterior door and place an exhaust fan in a window for a flow of air outward.

Protecting floors and rugs in adjoining rooms

The best way to protect a finished hardwood floor, carpet, or rugs from debris is with wide rolls of heavy gauge plastic, rectangular fabric, or plastic cloths.

The plastic material is better suited to protect against dust, but heavy fabric cloths are less likely to tear. Any breaks, however, must be immediately covered.

Material preparation

There are two systems that may be used to protect your floors. The first calls for removal of all furniture, the second bypasses it. Regardless of which system is used, the first three steps, in the box immediately below, should be completed before continuing with the operation. It is important not to rush this job.

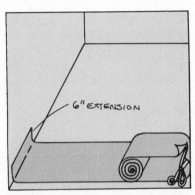

1. Allowing at least 12 extra inches, cut the floor covering to length. Use the first strip for a pattern, and cut enough strips, plus 2 extra, to cover the width of the room.

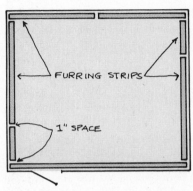

2. Cut enough furring strips to line the room's perimeter. Do not make tight fits, but leave 1 inch ends and edges of joining furring. Allow 1 inch clearance between furring and walls.

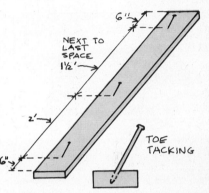

3. Starting and finishing 6 inches from each end, toe-tack an 8d finishing nail into furring strip every 2 feet. Spacing of next to last nail may be shortened. Spacing is approximate.

Covering the floors

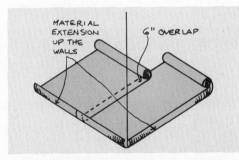

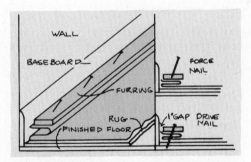

1. To thoroughly protect a floor, move all the furniture out of the room; or if that isn't feasible, move it to one end of the room. Then roll out the plastic with 6-inch overlaps, making sure that 6 inches of material extends up each wall. If using drop cloths, stretch them out with the same overlaps. 2. At the floor and wall juncture, fold the material twice to inhibit tearing. 3. Set the furring 1 inch away from the wall on top of the material.

Stationary or heavy objects: To protect the floor without moving the furniture, the same furring strip preparation must be made, as above, but with one exception. There will be no furring cut for any wall that has furniture against it. Start from an opposite wall that is bare, and stretch out the plastic rolls or drop cloths in the same way as previously indicated. Continue until the covering reaches the furniture. Cut the covering so that it will bypass sofa, chair, or table legs, or slip under them, and continue to opposite wall.

With one hand apply pressure toward the wall and downward at the same time. 4. When the material is squeezed tight to the wall and floor, drive the nails into the floor, but slanted toward the wall to insure a tight fit. After the protection has been stretched out far enough, relocate the furniture. Then, complete the rolling out of the floor protection. Be sure to clean the protection layer periodically.

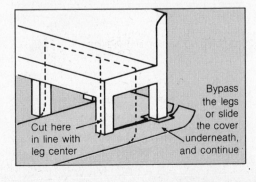

Covering the furniture

After the floor has been protected, the next step is the furniture. You will need the largest rectangular drop cloths that can be obtained. Use plastic sheets; woven cloth allows dust penetration.

You should take protective steps against heavy objects falling onto the furniture; tools for example. Use compressed fiber board as a cover.

Placement of the drop cloths over the furniture is probably the easiest part of the renovation; yet to their sorrow many people skimp when it comes to this particular task. Be generous with your drop cloths, and err, if you have to, on the side of over-abundance.

Fiber board is a good protection against heavy objects falling onto furniture. You can box a piece of furniture with it, or just cover vulnerable surfaces.

A drop cloth draped over small items and weighted at the ends with bricks or short pieces of lumber is good. Be careful about openings where dust could enter.

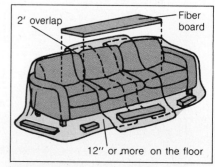

When covering large pieces, start at each end and work toward the center. Center cloth should overlap adjoining ends by 2 feet. Allow 12 inches extra at floor.

A barrier curtain

Whether it is a trimmed opening or doorway, any opening in the wall that leads to an adjoining living space has to be sealed. Again, the best material for a barrier curtain is heavy-gauge plastic sheets or rolls. With slight variations, it is hung in the opening in the same manner that you place a curtain in or over a window frame. You can support it with furring strips.

I thought I'd covered the situation—but it covered me!
I thought I had the dust and debris problem licked when I hung all that extra cloth in the doorway to my living room. But I forgot that cloth is woven, and so it's permeable. Next time I'll be smart enough to use plastic so that fine dust just can't get through.

Practical Pete

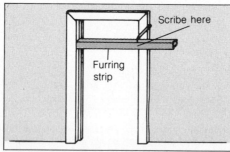

1. Place one end of the furring strip against a jamb face. Scribe a mark on the furring that is in line with the opposing jamb face. Using the mark as a guide, saw the furring to length, 1/32" to 1/16" short of the mark. Repeat the process at the bottom.

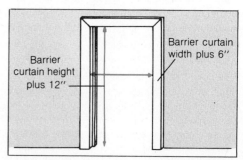

2. Cut the barrier curtain to length and width. Its length should be a minimum of 12 inches longer than the opening is high. The width of the barrier should be approximately 6 inches wider than the opening width. Staple the top and bottom ends of the plastic barrier to the furring strips.

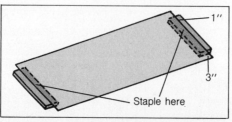

3. Expose one inch of the furring face and allow the plastic material extend to 3 inches past the furring ends. Staple the plastic to the furring every 6 inches.

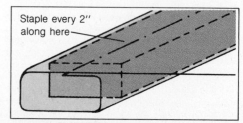

4. Rotate the stapled furring and plastic material under one revolution. Staple the two layers of plastic to the furring strip every 2 inches.

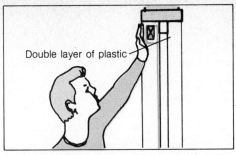

5. A friction fit is used to place the barrier in the wall opening. Hold the top end of the barrier, keeping the double layer of plastic away from your body. Squeeze the second end of the plastic-wrapped furring into the opening. Repeat at the bottom.

6. Providing that 1/32″ to 1/16″ clearance was allowed when cutting the furring strip, it should squeeze in easily. If necessary, however, place a block of wood over the plastic covered furring to prevent tearing, and tap it lightly with a hammer to squeeze it in.

Sealing doors

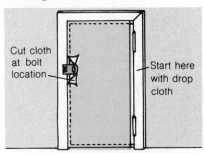

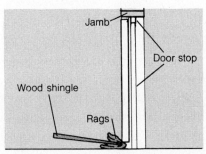

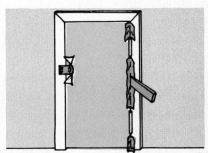

1. Place a drop cloth over the door, starting from the hinge edge and covering the lock edge. It should be a snug fit.

2. Stuff the bottom of the doorway with rags. A wood shingle will serve as a useful tool to press the rags into place.

3. Wedge a folded cloth between the length of the hinge edge of the door and the door jamb; use the wood shingle.

The daily cleanup

Just as providing a dust and debris barrier is essential to protect the rest of the house, so is the daily cleanup. It is also important for safety. Any rubbish lying in and around the work area can lead to an accident. Your best bet is to clean up as you go along, and not wait until the end of the day. As you finish working in one area, clean up, then go to the next part of the job. At the end of the day you can do a general cleanup, so everything will be ready for the next day.

Before removing rubbish, thought has to be given to where it is to be placed, and how it will be disposed of. You can stack it at the front of the house, along the sides, or in the back. When a truckload is ready, pay a commercial carter to haul it away.

Still, a load of debris at either the front or back of the house is unsightly. You may consider it necessary, but your neighbors could see otherwise. Check with them before you do anything. And check with the local authorities.

In any case, the debris will have to be placed in containers until it can be hauled off. Do not depend on the local sanitation department to handle debris.

Call sanitation headquarters to find out what the regulations are concerning construction debris.

For a fee, private sanitation companies will provide and haul away containers of varied capacities. Some of the smaller types—which hold up to 3 cubic yards—have wheels and can be located at any convenient place. The larger containers rest on steel skids, to be moved by a truck. This type is usually left in the street and this may require a special permit from the local authorities.

Remember that the trick in accomplishing a thorough and speedy cleaning is to do each part of it at its proper time. Take out the large debris first, then sweep what you can, and finally vacuum, being sure to catch any dust that has settled on top of the doors, window trim, or any other projections from the walls. After you have cleaned the work area, go into the adjoining rooms. After you have cleaned thoroughly, it will be safe to remove the seals placed around the doors, if you wish to do so at this point. Of course, if it isn't the final day of the job, you will have to seal the doors again on the following day.

What it takes

Tools and materials: Large rubbish container, between 1 and 20 cubic yard capacity, 20- and 30-gallon garbage pails, 6 cubic foot wheelbarrow, square-point shovels with 27″ and 48″ handles, 5- or 10-gallon drum vacuum cleaner, broom, gloves.

TIP: A good investment is the purchase of a drum (shop) type vacuum cleaner; 5-10 gallon capacity. It will save your expensive standard type from being damaged. Unlike a household vacuum, the drum type can suck up small bits of steel, such as nails and screws, and wood splinters with no harm to the machine.

Taking down wall cabinets

What it takes

Approximate time: To remove braces; 10-15 minutes per pair. To remove screws; depends on how quickly holes are located, and whether or not they are plugged.

Tools and materials: Saw, claw hammer, 6d nails, ruler; 1"x3" or 1"x4" wood stock; screwdriver (according to size of screwhead slot), scraper or knife, ¼" wood chisel.

As with everything else about construction and demolition (a renovation is both), a primary concern is safety. Therefore, when removing old cabinets, the hanging ones are handled first. The reason for this is that if one of the cabinets should fall, it can be stopped, or slowed, by the base cabinets. A further measure, however, is to place temporary bracing under them.

Temporary bracing

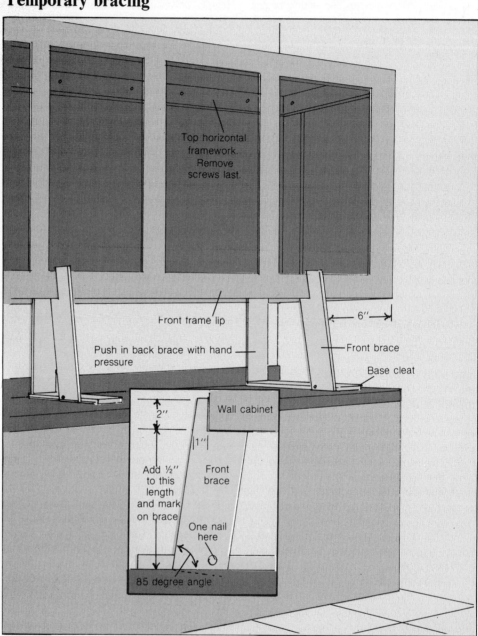

Top horizontal framework. Remove screws last.

Front frame lip

Push in back brace with hand pressure

6"

Front brace

Base cleat

2"

1"

Wall cabinet

Add ½" to this length and mark on brace

Front brace

One nail here

85 degree angle

TIP: Do not let yourself become distracted at any time you are balancing or supporting a cabinet during removal. When moving about, always look in the direction of travel. If the cabinet is over 3 feet long, get a helper.

1. Cut two 1x3 or 1x4 base cleats, 4 to 6 inches less than the depth of the base cabinet. Place each one on top of the base cabinet, 6 inches in from each end of the hanging cabinet.
2. To obtain the length of the back braces, measure from the top of the base cleat to the bottom of the bottom cabinet shelf, adding ¼ inch. Be sure to avoid the frame lip when measuring. The back and front braces will be 1x3 or 1x4 stock.
3. After you have cut the back braces, cut the bottom end of the front braces, at 85 degree angle. This is in order that the braces will lean into the hanging cabinets when they are secured. From the top of the base cabinet, measure to the front frame lip of the hanging cabinet; add ½" and mark the length on the brace. Now add 2" to the brace length and cut it to the total length. Cut a notch 1" from the front edge and at the ½-inch mark so the brace fits over cabinet lip.
4. Secure with 6d nails. The bracing will look like this when the front and rear braces are in position. Now you can loosen the holding screws.

Locating/removing screws

One of the reasons for temporary bracing is the difficulty of locating the screws that hold the cabinet to the wall. Very often a missed screw thwarts the efforts to remove the cabinets. And without the bracing the cabinet will be apt to pivot around the remaining screw making it unsafe and difficult to remove. In addition, some screws hold the cabinets to each other. The bracing keeps the supported one from tearing a piece out of the adjoining one and supplying its extra weight for you to juggle.

Front frame holding screws

Hanging cabinets are usually secured by screws because they have greater holding power than nails. Wall studs were and still are used to anchor the screws. However, some contractors install large cleats or grounds in the walls for screws to anchor into. They claim that the time spent doing so is more than offset by the speed with which a carpenter could install cabinets when he doesn't have to look for studs.

Rear frame holding screws

The screws that really hold the cabinet weight go through the back framework into the studs, cleats, or grounds. Regardless of what they are anchored to, they always pass through the highest horizontal framing member. Frequently they will also be found in the lowest member. Rarely are any found in the center framing sections. Nevertheless, they too should be looked over for screws that will have to be removed.

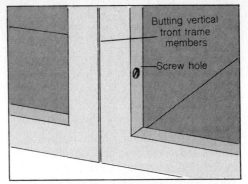

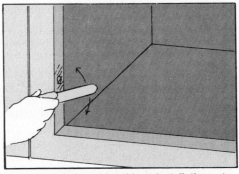

Check carefully along the inside edges of the front framework of any cabinet that abuts another. You will probably find some holes in the edges of the vertical members. These will most likely be screw holes. Using the largest screwdriver that will fit the slot, back the screws out.

On some of the old cabinet installations the screw holes have been plugged. The purpose was to provide a flush, more presentable surface when the cabinet doors were open. If the cabinet has a stained finish, the plugged holes can be located by a round discoloration that is slightly darker than the rest of the finish. Dig out the plug by first twisting a ¼-inch wood chisel part way into it; then use a screwdriver.

When the cabinet has a painted surface, it is more difficult to locate the screws. The paint must be scratched off between 2 and 6 inches from each end of the vertical framing member's edge. After the wood is bared, the round plug will be easier to locate.

You could have knocked me over with a (lead) feather!
It sure wasn't any feather that fell on me when I started removing that cabinet; but a good old tea pot that I never suspected was there.

Boy, I'll be sure to check next time for any loose items before I start taking a cabinet down.

Practical Pete

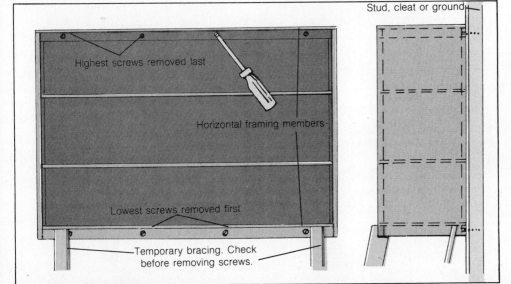

Always start screw removal in the lowest framing member, then go to the next highest. Continue until the screws are removed from the highest member. Be sure that the temporary bracing is securely in place while you work.

TIP: Stop cabinet doors from getting in the way by either removing the doors or taping them shut. On large cabinets, removal is better because it lightens the load and also provides more places to grip the cabinets while carrying them.

Removing the kitchen sink

Countertop method

What it takes

Approximate time: About 2 hours if you don't have to change the shutoff valves. Have some of the items you need ready at hand to save time.

Tools and materials: Basin wrench, water pump pliers, 10" or 14" pipe wrench, hacksaw, electric drill or hand brace, ½" or ⅜" wood bit, monkey wrench or large adjustable wrench, screwdriver, a seat wrench or ¼"·or ⅜" cold chisel (an old screwdriver would do), approx. 2 feet of ⅜" or ½" threaded rod, 2 nuts and washers for rod, about 4 to 5' of 2x4 lumber.

TIP: In some instances, turning off the valves will create a slight drip in the area of the valve handle. This can be stopped with a slight clockwise turn of the packing nut which should compress the packing around the stem. If you tighten too much, though, it will make it difficult to turn the valve handle in the future.

Begin by cutting off the water supply to the sink. Depending on the original piping installation, the shutoff valves may be located in any of several places. First check under the sink or in the sink cabinet. There should be two valves coming either from the wall or the floor, with pipes going up to the sink faucets. These are the hot and cold water lines. Turn the handles on the valves in a clockwise direction. This should cut off the flow of water. But check by opening the sink faucets.

Remember, this is a preliminary check. If those valves don't turn off the water supply, you have a number of alternatives.

Go down to the basement and see if there are two valves in the ceiling area right under the kitchen. These may be in addition to the valves beneath the sink, or they may actually be the only valves that control the flow of water.

On the other hand, the valves controlling the flow to the kitchen sink may be under the bathroom, controlling both bathroom and kitchen. This presents a problem of inconvenience since when these are turned off, the bathroom will also be without water.

If you don't find the valves in the basement, then look for two valve handles protruding from the corner of a bathroom wall or in a closet adjacent to the bathroom.

You may have fixtures with old valves and so your only recourse then is to turn off the main valve. This will be just inside the foundation wall, near the water meter if you have one. This will cut the entire water supply for the house. In fact, in some old houses the fixtures have no valves and this is the only way to cut the water off.

Once the water is turned off you may disconnect the plumbing pipes from the sink. Of course, this must be done before the sink is removed from the wall or before the countertop can be removed from the existing base cabinets.

If the plumbing is enclosed in a cabinet, you will have to crawl partly inside, and lying on your back or side, reach up to the connection between the hot and cold supply pipes and the faucet. Place the "claw" of the basin wrench on the tailpiece nut. Since the faucet is probably embedded in putty, you may have dry, crumbling putty falling into your face and eyes. Better wear goggles.

Position the wrench claw so that the tailpiece nut will turn counterclockwise. Be sure that you have a good grip on the nut; if you have the wrench on the faucet shank, locknut, or riser pipe you won't loosen the supply pipe from the faucet.

If the faucet is tied in solid, it will be necessary to cut the supply pipes with a hacksaw or tubing cutter. With copper tubing for instance, it's usual to make a solid hookup.

The next step is to disconnect the kitchen sink strainer tailpiece from the sink. Although special wrenches are available for this, such as a trap/spud

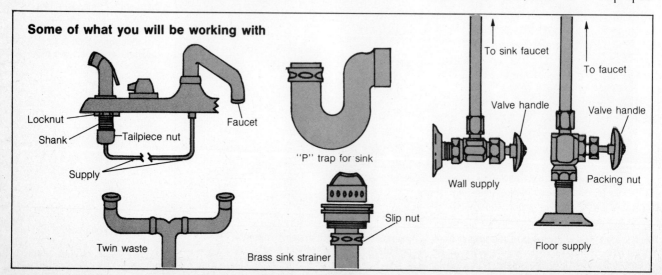

Some of what you will be working with

Locknut · Shank · Tailpiece nut · Supply · Faucet · Twin waste · "P" trap for sink · Brass sink strainer · Slip nut · To sink faucet · To faucet · Valve handle · Valve handle · Wall supply · Packing nut · Floor supply

wrench, the number of times you would use such a tool doesn't really warrant the purchase.

Actually, the slip nut(s) can be loosened with a pipe wrench, monkey wrench, or channel lock pliers. To avoid damaging the finish on the slip nut, place a piece of cardboard or cloth around the nut to protect it from the "teeth" of the wrench or pliers. A monkey wrench has smooth jaws and will not mar the finish.

Place the wrench on the nut, adjusted for a snug fit, and turn it counterclockwise. In the event that you have a twin waste (double sink) then you must loosen both slip nuts. This will free the sink strainer(s) from the waste tubing. It is not necessary to remove the strainer from the sink.

With the screws that extended up from the base cabinets into the bottom of the countertop removed, you can now take off the countertop. If the top is large and the sink heavy, you would be well advised to remove the sink from the countertop before lifting off the top.

It is difficult to lift the countertop and the sink as a unit straight up (10 to 12 inches) so that the bottom of the sink clears the base cabinet. Another difficulty that may arise is a window sill above the counter. The backsplash of the countertop will become wedged under the windowsill before the unit is raised high enough for the bottom of the sink to clear the top of the base cabinet. Realize that you may wish to use the countertop at some future time in garage or basement, and so take care to avoid damage in removing it.

Once having decided to remove the sink from the countertop you will be wise to remove the trap and any other drain pipes from under the sink. This will provide you with more room to work and will also lessen the chance of damage to the piping while the sink is being taken out. If you are able to get the top and the sink out as a unit then the waste piping can wait. Once the top is removed and the base cabinets are pulled away from the wall you will find it a whole lot easier to remove the remaining plumbing pipes.

The sink is secured to the countertop by clips in older installations, or by a sink flange and channel/lever type anchoring bolts. In either case the clips or retaining screws must be removed; and for this you will have to work under the countertop.

Again, work with goggles, but you should also secure the sink to the countertop while you are underneath it loosening the retaining clips.

Pete the Magnificent!
I figured the best way to get a tight connection was to really "sock-up-on-it," as the pros put it. So I gave it the muscle—and cracko! I was just too strong for that porcelain.

Next time for sure I'll hand-tighten first, then just snug the nut with a wrench.

Practical Pete

Securing the sink while you work

You can do this quite simply with the "sandwich" method. All you need is a short length of ⅜-inch or ½-inch threaded rod and a length of 2x4, plus nuts, washers, and a wrench.

The 2x4 should be at least 12 inches longer than the width of the sink cutout in the countertop. Center it over the sink opening, with an equal overlap on each end.

Drill a hole in the 2x4 slightly larger than the diameter of the threaded rod, and directly over the sink strainer.

Now take another piece of 2x4 and drill a hole about 3 inches from the end. Cut off a 6-inch length of the 2x4 so that you will have a 6-inch piece with a hole in the center. You must drill the hole first, before you saw, so the short piece of 2x4 will not spin on the drill bit.

Now cut the threaded rod so that it will be of sufficient length to pass through from the long 2x4 to the short piece, as shown in the drawing.

Place a washer and nut on the rod. Feed the rod through the hole and down through the sink strainer. Place

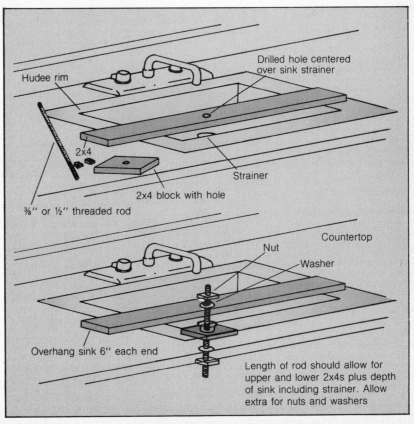

Hudee rim

Drilled hole centered over sink strainer

2x4

⅜" or ½" threaded rod

2x4 block with hole

Strainer

Nut

Countertop

Washer

Overhang sink 6" each end

Length of rod should allow for upper and lower 2x4s plus depth of sink including strainer. Allow extra for nuts and washers

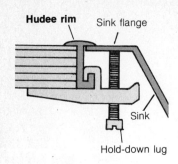

Hudee rim   Sink flange

Hold-down lug

Sink

the 6-inch 2x4 with the hole, over the rod extending below the sink strainer. Now place the washer and nut over the rod protruding through the 2x4.

Tighten the nuts, holding back on the bottom nut with a second wrench to prevent it turning while you tighten the top nut.

The countertop and sink should now be sandwiched between the long 2x4 and the 6-inch block which acts as a big washer at the bottom. Now, when all the sink retaining clips are removed the sink will not fall through the countertop opening and down into the cabinet.

If the sink has a flange-type Hudee rim, then you can lift the sink and rim up and out from the countertop. Grasp the spout of the faucet near the faucet body with one hand and place the other hand on the threaded rod directly under the 2x4. You should be able to lift the sink out. On the other hand, if it feels too heavy, ask someone to help you.

The sandwich method is ideal for heavy cast iron sinks, but a stainless steel or pressed porcelain on steel sink is light enough for one person to hold while you are working underneath. Just make sure it's someone reliable. Remember, you, not your helper, are the one who is underneath.

An older method of anchoring the sink is with clips. The top of the sink is recessed the thickness of the countertop. A stainless steel or aluminum frame covers the edges of the sink cutout. In this case, the sink cannot be lifted up and out because its length and width exceed the cutout.

When you are ready to lower the sink down and away from the countertop, have a helper grasp the threaded rod firmly just above the sink strainer. Remove the top nut and washer so that the rod can slide free from the upper supporting 2x4. The countertop can now be lifted or slid off the base cabinets.

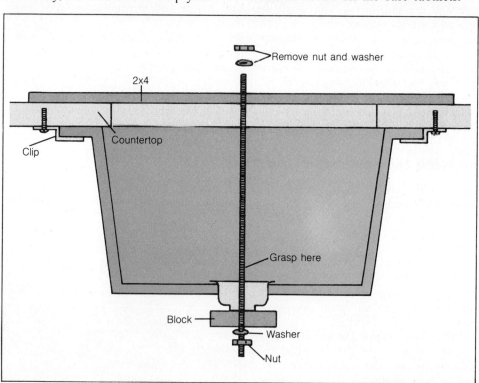

Remove nut and washer

2x4

Clip

Countertop

Grasp here

Block

Washer

Nut

Removing a small sink

Removing a small bathroom sink takes the same basic action as for a heavy kitchen fixture. Again, it's a matter of loosening nuts and bolts, and remembering where parts that have been removed will go when you reassemble.

It's always a good idea to take a hard look at old fixtures to see how they are mounted and connected to the piping. Old sinks and lavatories are mounted in a number of ways. They can be suspended from a countertop, or set on a

pedestal, or they can hang from a wall. The faucet assemblies may pass through holes in the countertop or wall, or they may extend down through holes in the fixture itself.

Remember, too, that fixtures are fragile, and if dropped or knocked with some hard object they can be damaged. You can save the parts of a fixture by removing them carefully and listing, and even sketching them before storing them in a solid container.

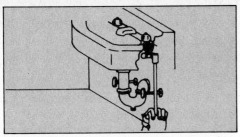

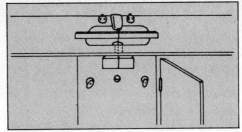

First step is to disconnect the water supply lines. Simply turn off the hot and cold valves. Unscrew the coupling nuts at the top. If the space is too tight for an adjustable wrench, use a basin wrench, as shown. If the supply lines have shutoff valves, unscrew the coupling nuts above the valves. This will free the supply lines.

To dismount this smaller countertop, lay a 2x4 across the top of the basin and tie a wire to it. Pass the wire through the drain hole to a wood block. This is essentially the same method as shown for the kitchen sink on page 23. Twist the block until it is right up against the tailpiece. Unscrew the lug bolts and lower the basin by untwisting the block.

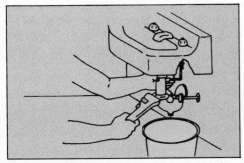

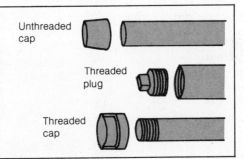

To disconnect the trap, first place a bucket beneath it and unscrew the cleanout plug so that it will drain. Unscrew the slip nut to free the trap from the tailpiece.

To remove the faucets, place the basin on its face on the floor. Put some padding under it. Unscrew the lock nuts from the faucet shanks and lift out the washers. Now turn the basin face up and tap the faucets to break the putty seal. Lift out the faucet assembly.

Capping pipes

It is necessary to seal pipes when a fixture is removed. For a supply line with a shutoff valve, just tape over the valve outlet hole. Supply lines without shutoff valves, as well as drain outlets, should be capped securely. For a threaded pipe, use a cap of the same material. Use plugs for elbows, and short pipe extenders, which have female threads. You can cement on a plastic cap if the pipe is unthreaded plastic. If the pipe is unthreaded copper, solder on a copper cap.

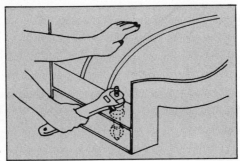

Unthreaded cap

Threaded plug

Threaded cap

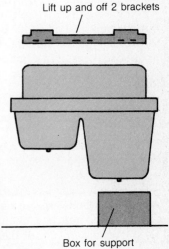

Lift up and off 2 brackets

Box for support

Wall hung sink and laundry tub

Removing this type of sink will require a helper. If the faucets are deck type, the removal of the water supply pipes is the same as the countertop method. However, older styles of sinks used swing-spout faucets with the water supplying the faucet coming out of the wall or the supply piping exposed on the surface of the wall. The faucets would then be connected at a right angle to the piping.

To remove faucets of this type, place the monkey wrench jaws on the flat surface of the faucet union. Loosen the union until the faucet is free. Be careful it doesn't drop into the sink.

With the body of the faucets off, you now must remove the faucet couplings.

They are held against the sink by nipples (short pieces of pipe) that pass through the sink and connect to a fitting behind the sink. You can use the monkey wrench to remove the faucet couplings. In some cases it will be necessary to insert a seat wrench or old screwdriver into the internal opening of the faucet couplings. The opening is "square," and the tool or device that you insert into the opening can be turned with a pipe wrench and the sink couplings removed. Disconnect the waste tubing as described earlier.

Be careful, though, if the sink has a supporting leg. Remove it, for the chances are it will fall free when the sink is lifted.

Toilet removal

In a bathroom renovation, the toilet bowl should usually be the last fixture removed. Particularly if you are remodeling the single bathroom in a home, you will not want to have the toilet out of commission any longer than is absolutely necessary.

The first step is to turn off the water supply line.

Yours is very likely one of the two standard bowl and tank setups. Either the tank is bolted to the bowl, or it is secured to the wall with several screws with a flush elbow connecting it to the bowl.

Remove the tank cover and get it out of the bathroom. The temptation is to put it on the basin or in the tub, but that might be hazardous. Eventually it will have to be moved out anyway, so you might as well do it right away.

Trip the flush tank handle, holding it down until the tank is clear of water. The small amount of water remaining in the tank can be sopped up with a rag or sponge.

The water supply line to the tank must now be disconnected. Follow the water supply pipe as it leaves the valve and enters the shank of the ballcock which extends below the bottom of the tank. There is a nut or collar below the shank which makes the connection watertight. The nut must be loosened entirely from the threaded shank. As you back off counterclockwise on the collar, using a small pipe wrench or water pump pliers, it is advisable to reach into the tank and grasp the ballcock to prevent it from turning. Failure to do so may result in damage to the float rod and float ball, as well as other working parts.

With the tank supply free from the ballcock, you can proceed to remove the tank from the bowl.

The tank is secured to the bowl by two, and in some instances, three bolts. The heads of the bolts are inside the tank. Each has a screwdriver slot. The bolts pass through the tank, and the nuts (sometimes wing nuts) are located under the upper rear portion of the bowl. A small adjustable wrench will perform nicely in this spot. An open end or box wrench will also do the trick.

Remove the nuts and washers from the tank bolts. The tank should be free to lift clear of the bowl. The easiest way to separate a wall hung tank from the bowl is to cut through the flush elbow with a hacksaw.

Locate the two or three bolts that are visible near the top-rear part of the tank. You can use a stubby screwdriver that will fit inside the tank or a long screwdriver that will allow the handle to remain outside the tank when the blade is in the screw slot. At this point, just loosen the bolts slightly. When you are sure that all the mounting bolts will turn freely, you must prepare to support the tank while the bolts are being backed out all the way.

This is best done by sitting on the toilet seat cover as you face the wall and tank. In this position the weight of the tank can be supported by your knees and legs. The bolts can now be removed completely. With the tank free from the wall and supported across your legs, you can grasp it firmly and remove it.

To remove the bowl, first take a look at the area around the base of the bowl. You will see nuts and washers protruding from the top of the base. They may be concealed by china or plastic caps. If, as is frequently the case, the caps are embedded in plaster of paris, you may have to break them off.

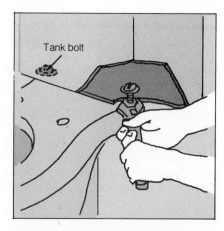

1. Disconnect the tank and bowl by first turning off the supply valve, flushing the toilet, and removing all the water remaining in the tank and bowl. The supply line should be disconnected. Should the tank be mounted on the bowl, unscrew the nuts under the rear rim of the bowl. On the other hand, if the tank is wall-mounted, take off the L-shaped spud pipe that connects it to the bowl. Loosen the slip nuts at each end and remove the bolts or screws that hold the tank to the wall. Pry off any of the caps over the flange bolts. Unscrew the nuts. Move the bowl, rocking it, in order to break the seal of putty with the flange. Finally, lift the bowl.

There are usually four caps on a toilet base. The rear pair hold the bowl to the soil pipe. The front two attach the bowl to the floor. But you may discover that the front two caps do not in fact cover bolts. It is not always necessary to bolt the bowl to the floor, and the front two caps may be there simply to cover the front holes in the bowl base.

Remove the two rear nuts and washers. If you have a problem with the entire bolt turning before the nut is removed, you can probably wedge the bolt with a screwdriver to prevent it from turning. If that doesn't work, the bolt will have to be hacksawed, directly under the nut. If the hacksaw frame will not fit, you can tape the ends of the blade and use the blade alone. Sawing these bolts is not a major effort, as they are made of soft brass. Once sawed half way through, the bolt can probably be wiggled back and forth until it snaps off.

The bowl is probably grouted to the floor with a layer of plaster of paris. There will also be a seal underneath, made of putty, wax or a felt gasket. This won't be visible until the bowl is removed, so don't be alarmed if the bowl does not move freely when all the nuts and washers have been removed. To break the seal, give the rim of the bowl a sharp blow with the heel of your hand. Repeat from the other side, and the bowl should be free to lift from the bolt.

Be certain to thoroughly scrape off the old sealer and gasket from the soil pipe to ensure a perfect join

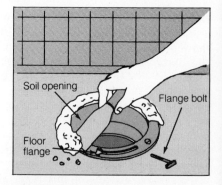

2. Take out the flange bolts and scrape the gasket with a putty knife. Check the flange closely for any cracks or other signs of wear, and if necessary, replace it. Be sure to stuff the hole with rags or paper so that sewer gas will not escape, and nothing can fall into the hole.

Removing the countertop

Large, solid countertops are heavy, yet they will still slip around on top of a base cabinet if not secured. The usual method of holding down a countertop is to screw into it from the base cabinet frame below. The hold-down screw locations vary according to a cabinet's construction. The sketches on this page show probable screw locations. Bear in mind that the framework shown is a composite of various types of construction.

The ease with which the hold-down screws can be removed depends upon how well they were put in to begin with. Another factor is the quality of wood used. Screws are more difficult to remove from plywood that is solid throughout than the less expensive type that has some honeycombing (hollow spots) within it. Another condition which will affect screw withdrawal is water damage. If the countertop wood base has been periodically soaked with water, it may have rotted to the point where the removal of the hold-down screws is unnecessary. In such a case the countertop can just be pulled up.

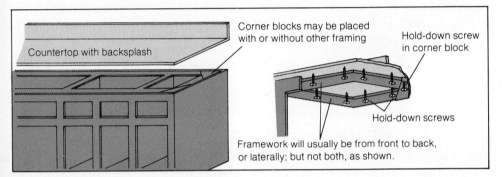

Countertop with backsplash

Corner blocks may be placed with or without other framing

Hold-down screw in corner block

Hold-down screws

Framework will usually be from front to back, or laterally; but not both, as shown.

Base cabinets

Because base cabinets rest on the floor, they are much easier to detach from the wall than the hanging kind. On the other hand, since they are bulkier and heavier, they may be more difficult to remove.

First, remove the cabinet doors, drawers, and all loose shelves. Next, locate and remove the hold-down screws, plus any screws that may hold the vertical framework of one base cabinet to another.

Locate the screws in the top rear horizontal framework or special cleat. Turn the screws counterclockwise to back them out. Should they spin and not back out, grasp the front framework and pull the cabinet away from the wall. The screws will then either come loose or tighten up enough for you to back them out.

Base cabinets can be removed by one of three basic methods. The first method would be to roll the cabinets out on pipes or rollers. When done properly this requires only average strength. It does require a bit of space to maneuver cabinets.

As a second choice of method, you can carry out the cabinets on a hand truck. This takes less time and space than the roller system. Still, you must be sure that there is adequate space to safely maneuver the hand truck, plus the cabinets and yourself without being trapped into a corner halfway through the operation. In addition, caution must be exercised when placing the cabinet on the hand truck. Both must be kept in balance, otherwise the load may pull out of your hands and fall away from, or toward you, striking items not intended to be removed and damaging them. If possible, tie the cabinet to the truck.

Finally, you can cut the base cabinet into smaller sections to ease handling.

This kickback really kicked . . .
Take a tip from a practical man! Any power saw can easily kick back when its cutting blade is pinched by the wood it is cutting.

To avoid a kickback, be sure to leave one end of any wood you are cutting free to fall or roll away from the blade. OR—use a hand saw.

Practical Pete

When screw spins, tug on the front framework and turn screw at the same time.

Locate special cleat for hold-down screws.

Cut the framework of the cabinet between partitions. The partition can then be separated easily from the bottom by hand pressure.

Taking up an old floor

What it takes

Approximate time: Allow at least one full day, depending on the area and the condition of the floor.

Tools and materials: Hammer, crowbar, circular saw, nail puller, wood chisel, utility knife, straightedge, scraper, hand iron, aluminum foil, tape, wood wedges, safety goggles.

Older flooring

Linoleum, vinyl, or ceramic tile
Construction paper
Top floor; tongue and groove
Subfloor; wide planking

Joists

Newer flooring

Finish vinyl or tile floor
Underlayment; particle board, hardboard, or plywood
Subfloor; wide planking or
⅝″ exterior plywood

Joists

A sound floor is the beginning of a sound bathroom or kitchen renovation. This means a clean, solid, and level surface that is also attractive.

A floor is usually in three layers. The subfloor lies directly on the floor joists. This can be tongue and groove lumber or exterior-grade plywood sheets. Over this comes the underlayment, which may be hardboard, particle board, or more plywood. Exterior plywood in ⅝-inch thickness is often used because it resists moisture well. The finish flooring is on top of the underlayment.

If the finish flooring is in pretty good shape you might simply lay the new one right over it. But flooring that has deteriorated should either be removed or covered with new underlayment. Of course, adding new underlayment and new flooring on top of the old will add height, and you will have to trim the bottoms of any doors. All the same, it is quicker than tearing up the existing floor and putting down a new surface.

It is important to make sure that there is no decay under the finish flooring. Check for broken tiles, loose bits of flooring, curling seams, buckling, or any signs of moisture such as dampness, discoloration, or odors underneath sinks and lavatories, and around bathtubs, dishwashers, or toilets.

Check especially at any place where the floor feels soft or gives when pushed. Remove a section and probe for rot. You may need to patch or replace the underlayment, the subfloor, or possibly both, depending on the damage.

Don't forget that susceptible area for leakage around the toilet; that is, at the ring that seals the toilet to its flange.

If your floor is in such poor shape that you need to replace it completely, start by removing the floor molding and the finish flooring. In the event that the bathtub is resting directly on the floor joists, you can leave it where it is, for the old flooring can be pulled from around it. On the other hand, if the tub is resting on the subfloor, inspect the floor underneath. If it is in good condition, leave this part intact and take up the old flooring around it. In any other situation, take the tub out of the room.

Figure out the combined thickness of the subfloor plus the underlayment, and set your circular power saw to that exact depth. You must turn off the power to any circuits that enter or pass through the room to avoid the chance of accidentally cutting a live wire.

Cut through the flooring as close to the walls as possible, and go around the entire room. Start at the side of the room which is opposite the door, prying up and taking out the underlayment and subflooring. Take out all nails from the floor joists.

With all the joists exposed, lay down two or three sheets of subflooring as a temporary work surface while you inspect each joist carefully. If you see any signs of rot, you can just cut away the area; but only if it is no more than an inch or so deep. Treat the surrounding wood with preservative. Extensive rot means you should call a professional.

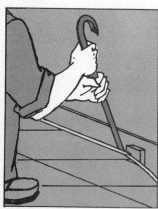

Removing the floor molding.
Your first step before you add or take away a layer of flooring is to remove the *base shoe,* the rounded strip that is attached to the floor. Start close to the center of the wall, pry with a thin blade to get it started, then insert the end of a pry bar. Work along the wall in both directions, placing small wedges as you go, so that the shoe comes off evenly and without breaking. Remove the baseboard in the same way.

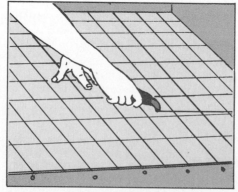

Removing continuous flooring such as cushioned vinyl or linoleum. Cut it into pieces that are a handy size, then roll or peel. If it doesn't come up easily, use a scraper with a stiff blade.

Taking out ceramic tile. You must wear safety goggles whenever you remove ceramic tile from a floor or a wall. Start at a place where you can work the edge of a cold chisel under the edge of a tile. You may have to break one of the tiles with a hammer to get a start. Chisel out the fragments, then work on the adjoining tile's edges, tapping gently with a hammer on a cold chisel.

Patching

You can take care of any minor damage in underlayment and subfloor by replacing damaged areas with solid patches. Remember to plan your patches so that the joints of an underlayment patch correspond with the joints of the subflooring. When patching the subfloor, make certain that you cut out an area of underlayment that is larger than your proposed patch of subfloor. If it is just the underlayment that you are patching, remove enough old underlayment so that the patch will span all the subfloor underneath it.

Most patching is simple work and such obstacles as a toilet flange which go through the floor are easy enough to work around.

Removing underlayment. Set your circular saw to the depth corresponding to the thickness of the underlayment, then make your cut.

Removing tongue and groove subflooring. Take out the finish flooring and underlayment from the area you wish to replace. If you're taking up the whole floor, then just proceed as shown, making your start as close to the wall as you can.

Removing and repairing damaged resilient flooring

When floor tile is cut, scratched, or damaged in any way, and you feel the need to replace it, hope that you had the foresight to save some extra tiles when it was originally installed. If you haven't done that, you'll have to buy extras. If they're unavailable or do not match, take a tile up from inside a closet or underneath an appliance where it won't be noticeable.

When removing any tile, the point is to heat the tile until the adhesive melts underneath. The quickest way to remove a damaged tile is with a blowtorch (this is not recommended for use on undamaged tiles). A slower but safer method is heating the tiles with an iron to soften the adhesive and make them more pliable. Set the iron at medium and place aluminum foil between it and the tile. When the tile has loosened, pry it out with a putty knife or similar tool.

It is also possible to remove a tile without using heat. If the tile surface is soft you can cut an X through it with a utility knife and pull the pieces out. Cold also breaks the bond. Put a block of dry ice on a tile for just a few seconds, then pry.
Caution: Don't touch dry ice with bare hands, and keep the room well ventilated.

Resilient sheet flooring. This is not as easy to repair as tile, and again hope that you have saved a scrap of it. Place the scrap over the damaged area so that the pattern matches. Cut a square piece, using a utility knife and straightedge. Tape the piece down firmly, and cut a smaller square through the top piece deeply enough so that you score the flooring underneath. It is important to hold your knife vertically. Take away the top piece and finish cutting through the score lines into the subfloor. Remove and replace the damaged section just as you would a tile. In this way you should have a perfect fit and pattern match—only the barely visible outline of the patch may remain.

TIP: When putting down new tile, make sure that the area is completely clean before spreading fresh adhesive on the subfloor with a notched trowel. Set (don't slide) the new tile in place, and go over it with a rolling pin. Weight it until the adhesive is dry.

4.REFRAMING

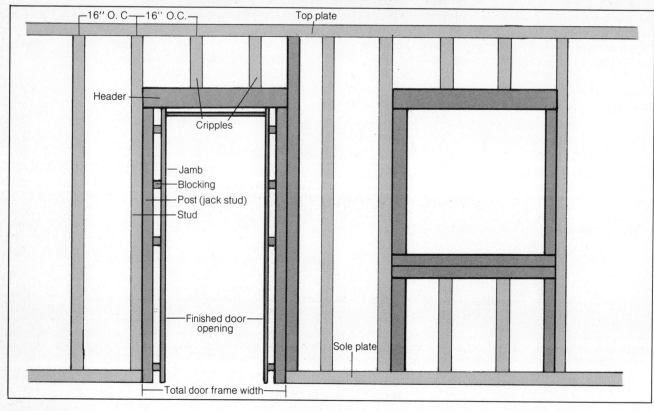

16" O. C. — 16" O.C. — Top plate

Header
Cripples
Jamb
Blocking
Post (jack stud)
Stud
Finished door opening
Sole plate
Total door frame width

What it takes

Approximate time: 15 minutes for measuring and marking; another 30 to 45 minutes for cutting.

Tools and materials: Ruler and pencil, straightedge, carpenter's level, claw hammer, broad cold chisel, crosscut saw (or reciprocating saw).

You may or may not be willing to engage in major renovation on your own, but whether you hire a contractor or do your own work, you will still need to know the procedures for cutting through walls, and

for framing a doorway, a window, or any wall opening. The important thing is to plan well. Allot your time carefully in order to minimize inconvenience to the members of the household.

Cutting an opening in an existing wall

There is a general procedure when cutting an opening in a wall. Whether cutting for a doorway, sash frame, or trimmed open-

ing, the steps are the same. Only the measurements and frame assembly may change, depending on the situation.

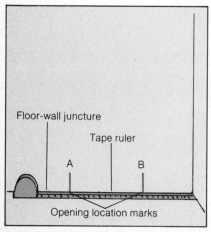

1. Mark the location of the opening on the wall at its juncture with the floor.

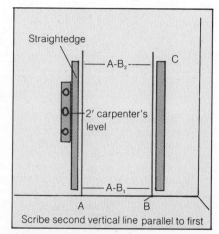

2. From Point A plumb a line upwards to obtain the first vertical line. Measure distance A-B₁ at the floor-wall juncture. Duplicate the measurement at location A-B₂, approximately one foot from the ceiling. Scribe the second vertical line with the assistance of a straightedge placed on B and C.

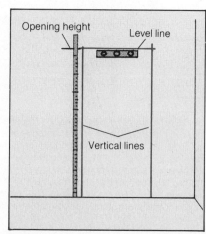

3. Measure and mark the opening height on one of the vertical lines. From the opening's height mark, scribe a level line between the two vertical lines.

Locating electrical wiring and plumbing lines

Any planned wall opening alteration must take into account the possibility of existing plumbing or electrical lines. A nearby plumbing fixture (sink, bowl, tank, etc.) definitely points to the existence of water supply and waste lines. Unless you are prepared to go through the expense of relocating plumbing lines, it is suggested that no wall opening be planned where plumbing lines may exist.

It must be remembered, however, that most plumbing lines (this includes steam or hot water heating) occur in exterior walls, or the walls between kitchen and bathroom. Electrical lines, on the other hand, may pass through any wall in the house. Consequently, they present a problem. If cut while the wall is being opened, the circuit will be useless. The chief problem is the cutting edge of the tool that goes into the wire. At the least it will be burned at the point of electrical contact. In the case of an electrical saw that cuts swiftly through a wire, that is all that may happen. On the other hand, should the tool not be properly grounded, the user may receive a severe shock. You can safely figure on any planned wall opening having an electrical wire passing through it; and so it will be necessary to open the wall with caution, and at the same time to make provision for the wire's relocation.

I really blew it!
When I opened my kitchen wall I checked all the electrical lines leading to outlets so I wouldn't cut into any of them. But I forgot about the room on the other side of the wall, which had its own outlets and wiring. I really blew a fuse!

Practical Pete

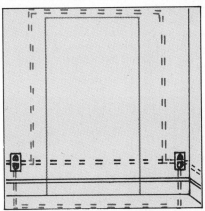

1. When electrical outlets are located as shown (in relation to the projected cutting lines), it can be assumed that there will be electrical wires running between them. Make your opening cut carefully at this point. To keep this electrical circuit intact, you will have to rerun the wiring connecting these outlets either under the floor or around and over the opening, as shown by the colored lines.

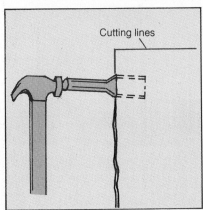

2. Score the cutting layout with a broad cold chisel and hammer—just enough to break the surface. Now go over the scored line again. This time hammer the chisel through the gypsum board or plaster. Repeat the process on the opposite side of the wall. With the hammer, break an opening large enough to put your hand in, and pull the section out. If there is much resistance, break the wall into smaller pieces.

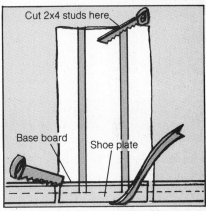

3. Cut the shoe plate and baseboard which are at the bottom of the opening. Use a hand saw. Now cut each stud at the top of the opening. Pull on the stud until it is loosened from the shoe plate. Pry the shoe plate and baseboard loose with a crow bar.

Framing a new doorway in an existing wall

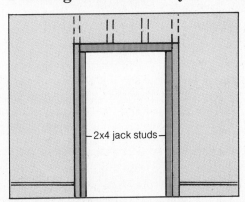

The jack stud length is determined by the door height. To figure the proper jack dimension, add 1⅝″ to the height of the door. Then cut two 2x4s to that dimension. The header length is determined by the door width. Add 4½″ to 5″ to the width of the door and you've got it. Either measurement allows clearance for squaring the door jambs. This allowance has not been codified, and diverse practices exist in different parts of the country.

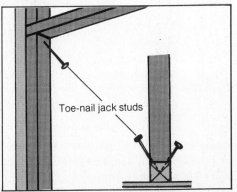

After the wall opening has been cut, it is time to assemble the framing members. 1. Slip a full-length stud into place and nail through the wall and the stud edges into the plate faces. 2. Place the header in position. Toe nail it to the cripple studs and full-length trimmer studs. 3. Toe nail the lower ends of the jack studs to the shoe plate and the upper ends to the header. When secured top and bottom, face nail to the trimmer.

What it takes

Approximate time: Allow 2 hours.

Tools and materials: Claw hammer, 8d and 10d nails; 2x4 framing stock.

Framing a window

To frame a window, follow the same method as for a door. As a rule, most windows, with the exception of kitchen pass-through openings, are in exterior walls, and so involve structural support.

Walls that run parallel to the ridge of the roof are generally supporting walls, while those running across the gable ends are not. If the window is wider than average, you will need a larger header, even if the wall is not load-bearing. Otherwise, there will be the tendency for cracks to appear in plaster or wallboard.

Base the dimensions of the window (and door opening) on the actual size of the window/door to be installed.

Framing in the bathroom

Framing details

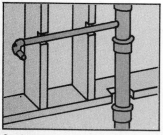

Studs notched for pipe

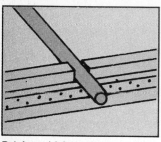

Reinforced joints

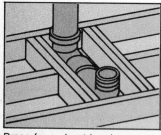

Brace for a closet bend

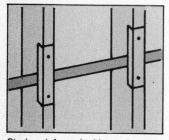

Studs reinforced with steel strips

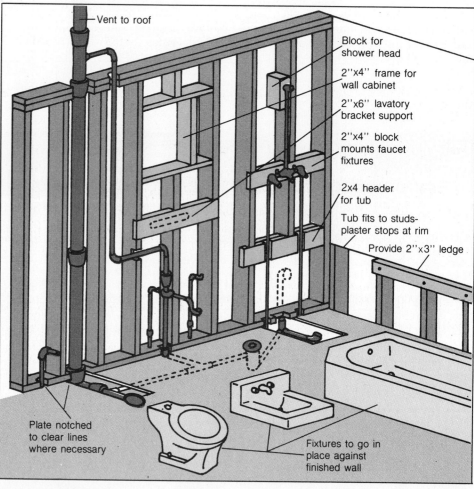

Vent to roof

Block for shower head

2''x4'' frame for wall cabinet

2''x6'' lavatory bracket support

2''x4'' block mounts faucet fixtures

2x4 header for tub

Tub fits to studs- plaster stops at rim

Provide 2''x3'' ledge

Plate notched to clear lines where necessary

Fixtures to go in place against finished wall

In any bathroom or kitchen renovation that involves plumbing, it will be necessary to support pipes and fixtures. In the kitchen, this will generally mean the sink, and as a rule this item will be supported by the countertop. In the bathroom, there are three basic fixtures requiring special supports—the toilet, lavatory, and bathtub.

The lavatory. It could be said that the lavatory is the simplest of the three. Because many lavatories are set in a countertop, special supports are not needed. Some models, however, hang from a crosspiece set into the wall.

To install a crosspiece and brackets for a lavatory, cut a 2x4 crosspiece 3 inches longer than the distance between the studs. Hold the 2x4 across the two studs at the height of the lavatory; each end of the crosspiece should overlap a stud by 1½ inches. Check with a level, and mark the top and bottom of the crosspiece on the studs. Now notch the studs within the marks, and wedge the crosspiece into the stud notches so that the front of the piece is flush with the fronts of both studs. Nail it in place, making sure you maintain your alignment. Finally, close the wall, and screw the bracket to the wallpiece, right through the surface of the wall.

The toilet. As a rule the toilet stands closest to the DWV (drain-waste-vent stack). Its waste pipe curves beneath the toilet at a part called the closet bend. This needs strong support because of the pressure of the water and wastes rushing through. If the toilet waste pipe crosses a joist, you should cut out a short piece of the joist and frame the cut section so that it is supported.

The bathtub. This is the largest of the bathroom fixtures, and strangely, in certain ways it is the easiest to support. Still, it is necessary to cut an access hole in the floor for the tub drain and the overflow pipe, and also to install cross-pieces in the wall to support the faucets and shower trim. Should the assembly for the overflow and drain rest on a joist, and you can't move the tub to a new position, then cut the joist and frame that section for support.

Now, with all the supports in place,

you can run supply pipes and drain-pipes to the fixtures. In running pipe through holes or notches, joists, or top plates, you must be sure to reinforce the cutouts. At the same time, the pitch of a long section of drain-waste pipe running along joists may require running the pipe underneath. Pipes running below joists are not very attractive, but you can hide them with an easily installed dropped ceiling.

It is important to remember that a bathtub will need an easy access to the trap in the event of emergency repairs. When you are finished connecting the fixtures and the wall surfaces are completed, go into the room that adjoins the wall next to the tub, and cut a square between two studs, directly behind the tub and at the level of the floor. Close the opening by screwing in a piece of plywood. This panel can be easily removed when necessary.

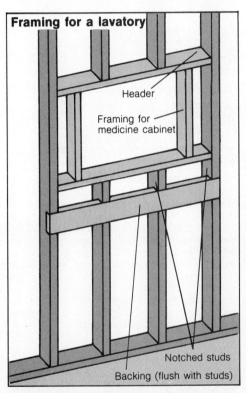

Framing for a lavatory

Header

Framing for medicine cabinet

Notched studs

Backing (flush with studs)

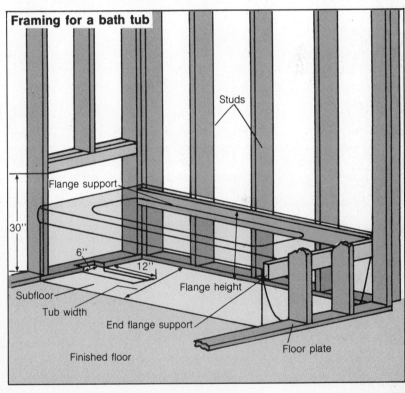

Framing for a bath tub

Studs

Flange support

30"

6"

12"

Subfloor

Tub width

Flange height

End flange support

Finished floor

Floor plate

Rules for notching

- Joists should be notched only in their end quarters; not in the center half. Notch no more than ¼ of depth of the joist.
- Drill the joists to a maximum diameter of ¼ of the joist depth. Then locate along the span, centered if possible, but not any closer than 2 inches to an edge.
- Notches on the studs should be no

larger than 2½ inches square. After installing the pipe, nail a steel strap reinforcement over each notch. If the notch is 1¼ inches square it doesn't need to be reinforced.
- For larger cutouts in framing members, it will be necessary to add a 2x4 or heavier bracing nailed on both sides of that particular member.

5.WIRING

Potential electrical problems—overloaded circuits from too many kitchen appliances working at the same time, or water-soaked surfaces in the bathroom causing shock—are easily solved by improving the existing wiring or installing new lines.

To obtain power for a single use—say, a kitchen fan or a special light fixture over a work area—you can tap from an existing box. Large appliance additions, a garbage disposal or broiler oven for instance, will require their own circuits.

While you may need a professional to connect the circuit at the house service panel, you can do a good deal of the electrical work yourself.

Wiring along foundation sills

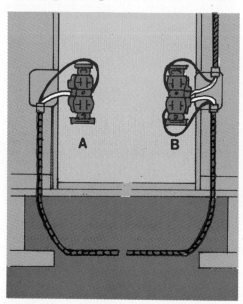

Wiring new wall outlet A from existing outlet B on ground floor is simple. Drill through the floor and then run your wire (armored or sheathed cable) across the basement ceiling. The drilling methods shown here apply to outer wall, but if either outlet is on an interior wall, you can drill straight upward between the walls. Use cable strap every three feet to secure the cable to the basement ceiling or side of joist. Connect the black wire to the brass terminals of the outlet, the white wire to the light color terminals.

For wiring from a basement ceiling light to a first-floor outlet, use armored or sheathed cable in a continuous length. 1. Select the location for the outlet and prepare the opening. 2. If the outlet is to be on an outer wall, use a long-shank bit to bore a hole diagonally (as shown) through the floor from the basement. If the outlet is to be on an interior wall, then bore straight up between the walls. 3. Push a length of fish wire up the hole from the basement; then, with wires attached to it, you can simply pull the wires through to the outlet. 4. Connect the black wire to the brass-color terminals; the white wire to the light-color terminals.

Wiring from the attic

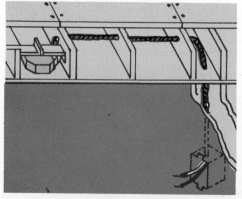

Where the attic is accessible, the attic floor boards can be raised, the joists notched and a hole bored to accept the cable. When you replace the floor boards, be careful not to nail through the cable.

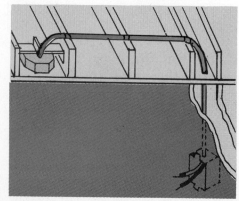

If there is no flooring, then the simple thing is to run cable across the joists and secure it with cable straps. The cable is non-metallic.

Wiring around doors

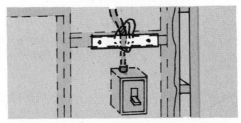

Going around a header. If the switch or outlet is to be next to a door, remove the door stop, drill a hole through the door jamb and frame above and below the header. Notch the door jamb to take the cable.

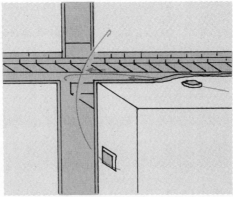

Running wire around a door frame. First remove the base board and door trim, as shown. Notch the wall and the spacers between the door frame and the jamb. Replace the door trim and baseboard.

Going past a header. An alternate method is to notch out a piece of plaster, lath and header from top to bottom, as shown. Of course, this means that you will have to patch the plaster.

How to mount a ceiling box from below

1. Cut away plaster to size of a shallow box, and cut away the center lath.

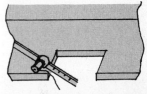

2. After removing locknut, insert hanger and put wire through threaded stud. Hold the stud above the ceiling with one hand; pull the wire with your other hand and the hanger will center.

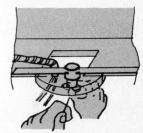

3. Connect the cable to the box. Pull the wire, from the hanger, through the center knockout and install locknut on the threaded stud.

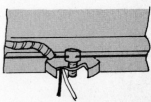

4. And this is how the completed installation will look.

How to fish wires

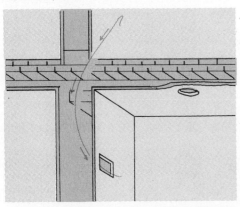

1. After drilling hole, use a fish wire (about 12 feet) with hooks on both ends. Push it through the hole on the second floor, then pull the end out at the switch outlet on the first floor.

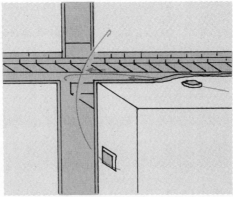

2. Push a second fish wire (20 to 25 feet) with wire hooks on both ends through the ceiling outlet as indicated by the arrows. Continue to fish until you contact the other fish wire.

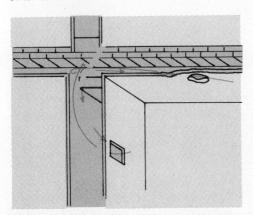

3. When the two fish wires have touched, withdraw either wire (see the arrows) until it is hooked on the other one. Then withdraw the other wire until the hooks are securely together.

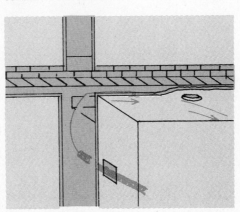

4. Finally, pull the shorter fish wire through the switch outlet until the hook from the other wire appears. To the end of this wire attach a continuous length of cable. Pull it through the wall and the ceiling.

Installing outlet boxes in an existing structure

All switch and outlet boxes should be located between studs at a spot 4 to 5 inches from the stud on either side. Make certain that you place the switches at convenient heights: roughly 48 to 50 inches from the floor. Convenience outlets can be 12 to 18 inches above the floor, or at table height in a kitchen. You should place wall light fixture outlets at about 65 to 70 inches above the floor. Never place a switch on the hinge side of a door, but rather on the opening side.

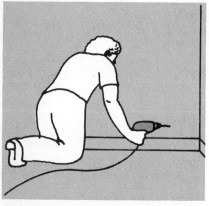

1. If you cannot locate studs by sounding the wall, then drill every 2 inches until you strike solid wood. Drill just above the baseboard so that the holes will not be noticed.

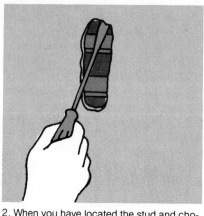

2. When you have located the stud and chosen the right place for the box, notch out plaster. Expose one full lath, but only sections of top and bottom laths.

3. Outline the position for the box with a template and soft pencil.

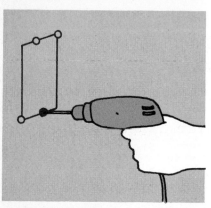

4. After the template has been outlined, drill four holes in the wall (as shown on the template) using a ½-inch bit.

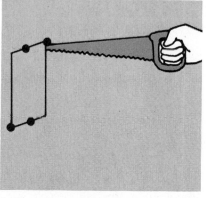

5. The holes provide space for your hacksaw. Draw the blade toward you to avoid loosening plaster. Hold your hand or a board against the plaster to prevent cracking.

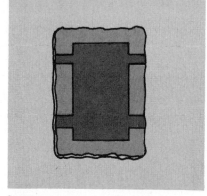

6. When you cut the opening, do not cut away two full laths. You will have a stronger mounting if you cut the center lath completely and half sections from the others.

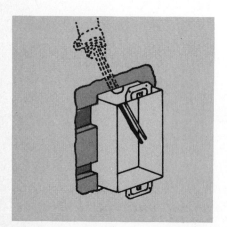

7. Draw the cable out of the hole in the wall, attach the connector less the locknut and pull lead wires through the knockout and into the box. Leave an 8-inch length on the lead wires.

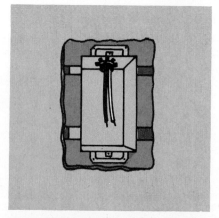

8. Now pull on the lead wires to bring the connector into place. Bear in mind that armored and sheathed cable boxes are available with built-in clamp for easier hook-up.

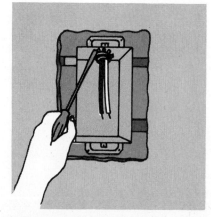

9. Finally, screw the locknut to the connector and tighten. Then anchor the box securely to laths using No. 5 wood screws.

Installing outlet boxes in a new structure

Installation in new work, directly over the bare studs, is certainly a lot easier than cutting electrical openings in old walls. In new work, your goal is to find the most practical route along which to run the wiring which connects various switch boxes and outlets.

Local regulations frequently require that new wiring be done with conduit, rather than armored or sheathed cable. The reason for this is that conduit is sturdy and makes future rewiring easier—wires can simply be pulled out of the conduit and larger load-bearing wires installed.

A conduit run is put in place before the new house or addition is finished. After the walls have been plastered, wires are run through and connected.

Handling conduit. It is important that you bend conduit gradually. Sharp bends will make it difficult, if not impossible, to insert wiring, and may potentially damage wire insulation. Be careful when running wiring from one outlet to the next

that you don't have more than four quarter bends in the conduit.

Conduit running vertically should be clamped or strapped every 6-8 feet. Horizontal conduit should be laid into notched studs or run across the subflooring.

When running wires through the conduit, make sure the wires used conform to the color code: in a two-wire circuit, one black, one white; in a three-wire circuit, one black, one white, and one red. Use the same wire from outlet to outlet; don't splice. Junction boxes must be placed where they are accessible at all times.

In a short run with few bends, you can probably push wire through a conduit. In a longer run, you will have to use fish tape, available in 50 and 100 foot lengths. If you are having trouble getting the tape past a bend, use soapstone or talcum powder as a lubricant.

Tip: Be sure to check your local electrical code before installing any wiring in your home. Regulations vary from region to region.

TIP: Take care that you punch only the knockouts you intend to run wire through so that the box will not have an unused hole at any time. Open holes in boxes are a fire hazard and should always be plugged with knockout filler.

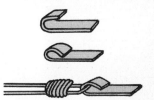

Fish tape hooks are made by heating the end of the tape over a flame and bending it with pliers.

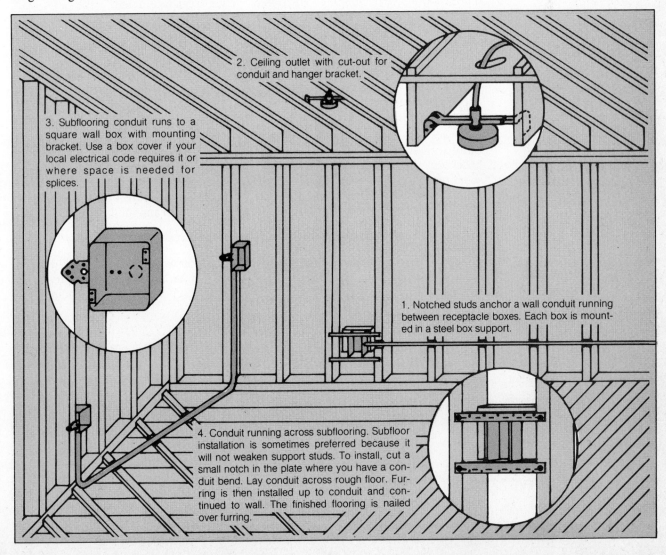

2. Ceiling outlet with cut-out for conduit and hanger bracket.

3. Subflooring conduit runs to a square wall box with mounting bracket. Use a box cover if your local electrical code requires it or where space is needed for splices.

1. Notched studs anchor a wall conduit running between receptacle boxes. Each box is mounted in a steel box support.

4. Conduit running across subflooring. Subfloor installation is sometimes preferred because it will not weaken support studs. To install, cut a small notch in the plate where you have a conduit bend. Lay conduit across rough floor. Furring is then installed up to conduit and continued to wall. The finished flooring is nailed over furring.

6.WALLS: OLD & NEW

You might decide that part of your kitchen or bath renovation will be to replace one or more of the walls. If the existing wall is solid, it can be used as the base support for new gypsum board, plastic laminate, plywood, or a combination hardboard of some type.

If the old wall is not sturdy enough to build on, it will have to be removed (see "Removing Ceilings and Walls," page 82). Furring over the bared wall studs provides an excellent base for new walls.

Durability, water and fire resistance, and easy maintenance are important considerations when choosing wall material for these high traffic areas.

Sturdy wall paneling, suitable for use in a kitchen or bath, is available in a wide range of materials, surfaces and prices.

A few of the more popular choices:

Gypsum wallboard, also known as plaster board or Sheetrock (a brand name), is flame-proof and highly resistant to cracking and shrinkage by humidity or extreme temperatures. The board is made of a gypsum core covered with a smooth glazed surface paper suitable for any decorative treatment. It is also available with a prefinished vinyl surface, or can be papered with a vinyl wall covering. Gypsum board can also be used as the backing for plastic laminate. For a kitchen or bath select waterproof gypsum board.

Plastic laminate. Probably the most rugged of wall surfaces, plastic laminate is available in a wide range of textures and patterns. Because sheets of laminate are quite heavy, the 1/32" thickness is preferred for use on walls, when backed with gypsum, plywood, or hardboard. Plastic laminate prebonded to plywood might be a practical alternative.

Prefinished hardboard. Plasticized or vinyl coated hardboard is tough, moisture proof, and available in many colors. Hardboard, like gypsum board, comes in standard 4x8-foot sheets, though longer lengths can be ordered.

Installing wallboard

Preparing old walls

If you are willing to screw or nail your new wall material to the old wall or to build wall framing first, you need not knock out the old wall even if it needs some repair. When using adhesive alone to put up new paneling, be sure that the subwall is sound. In either case, the existing wall will need some preparation.

Remove all trim and loose or poorly bonded plaster. Repair any holes (see pg. 45). Extend electrical outlet boxes to make them flush with the new wall. In general, make sure that the subwall is clean, smooth and solid.

Planning for the new

Careful planning will save you time, money, and probably give you a better looking result. Figure out how much wallboard you will need, where you want the joints to be, and for economy try to use the longest practical lengths obtainable.

Cutting wallboard

It was like living under London Bridge

I thought I'd give my battered plaster walls a face lift, so I used the best wall adhesive money could buy to put up new gypsum wallboard. What I didn't realize was that adhesive is only as good as the wall to which it's applied. If the plaster works loose, so will the adhesive and mounted wallboard. Next time I'll remember that screws or nails are the only sure way to keep a board mounted on an old wall. Nail or screw along a panel edge at intervals of 6 or 7 inches for the best result.

Practical Pete

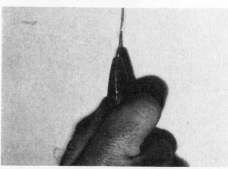

1. Using a utility knife, first score the face paper along your measured line.

2. Snap through the gypsum core, but do not tear the face paper on the reverse side. Cut the reverse face paper with a sharp knife.

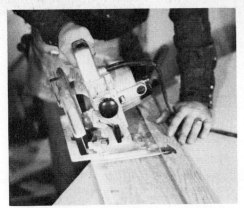

3. Use a power saw with guide for a mitered cut or one where perfect fit is essential.

4. Use a rasp to smooth rough edges, being careful not to tear the face paper.

Curved walls and archways

Gypsum can be shaped around a gentle curve with a little special handling. You may wish to use a slightly thinner board for curved surfaces than you would use on a flat wall.

First, measure the area to be covered, and cut the wallboard to size. Then score or cut through the back paper at intervals to increase its flexibility. Moistening the board will also ease the curving process. Secure one end of the board to the wall and gently bend it into the curve. Nail at closer intervals than you would on a flat wall. When completed, spread a little joint compound around the curve to guard against cracking.

When taping the edges of archway wallboard, cut notches in both sides of the tape at intervals where it will have to ease around the curve. You will probably need two or three coats of joint compound to cover this area.

Finishing wallboard seams

When wallboard installation is completed, you must finish off the seams. For joints you will want to use joint compound and drywall patching tape.

Patching tape for wallboard is available in paper, perforated paper and mesh. Paper tape is standard. It has a ridge that's easy to fold for taping inside corners. Perforated tape has holes in it to permit the compound to seep through, which is good for spreading, but it can form ridges where the holes are as it dries. Mesh tape is used where wallboard joints are particularly prone to expansion and contraction, or when joining old wallboard to new. It is also the best material for bonding a crack that keeps coming back after repair.

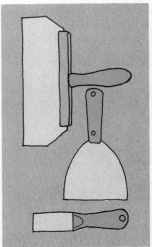

Taping knives are used to smooth the plaster compounds. They are flexible metal knives available in ½-inch to 12-inch widths. For cracks and small holes, a 2-inch putty knife is suitable. Larger areas require wider blades so the compounds can be blended with the surface of the wall.

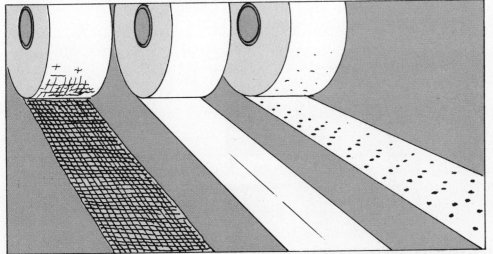

Drywall patching tape will form a permanent bond to seal patches or the seams between wallboard sections. It is 2 inches wide and is available in plastic mesh, paper, or perforated paper. The mesh is best for joining old and new wallboard or where a wallboard joint may expand or contract; for instance, where the edge of a sloping ceiling meets a dormer. Paper patching tape has a ridge in the middle that makes it easy to fold for joining inside corners. Perforated patching tape has holes in it that allow the wallboard compound to seep through.

Taping wallboard seams

1. To fill gaps between adjoining sheets of gypsum wallboard, force joint compound into the seam with a 5-inch taping knife. If the seam is very narrow, you can use spackle

2. Press mesh tape into the wet compound and run the blade of the taping knife along the mesh to squeeze the compound through. Feather the edges to blend with the wallboard. Let it dry overnight, then apply another thin layer of compound. Sand it smooth when it has dried about 24 hours.

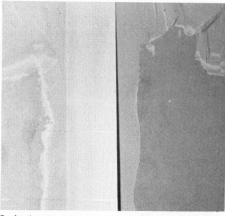

3. Apply paper tape in the same manner. Press it into the wet compound and run the blade over it in one long continuous stroke. When you put on the final coat of compound, use just enough to cover the tape. Feather smoothly outward using a 10-inch taping knife.

4. For inside corners, fold paper patching tape at the ridge that runs down the center of it to seal the gap where two sheets of wallboard make an inside corner. Apply the joint compound and feather it out from the corner as previously described. Sand when it dries.

Metal corner bead

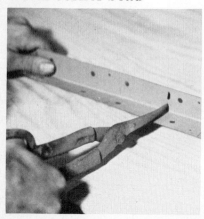

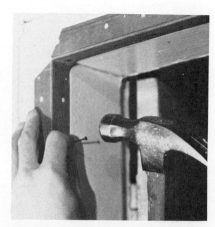

1. Use metal shears to cut a length of metal corner bead. It's easier to smooth the edge if it's cut at an angle. If the bead will turn a corner, as in a door jamb, cut out a small triangular piece from both sides, leaving the middle ridge intact.

2. Bend the corner bead to fit tightly around the corner. Attach it to the wall with screw-type, plasterboard ring nails driven into the wood of a door jamb or into the studs beneath the wallboard where two walls join.

3. Use a 5-inch tape knife to spread a generous coat of joint compound on the bead, smoothing it as even as you can to make sanding easier later. But don't fuss with it. Let it dry for 24 hours. Apply a second coat, feather the edges, and let it dry completely (about 24 hours) before sanding.

	2'	3'	4'	5'	6'	7'	8'	9'	10'	11'	12'	13'	14'	15'
2'	68	86	104	122	140	158	176	194	212	230	248	266	284	302
3'	86	105	124	143	162	181	200	219	238	257	276	295	314	333
4'	104	124	144	164	184	204	224	244	264	284	304	324	344	364
5'	122	143	164	185	206	227	248	269	290	311	332	353	374	395
6'	140	162	184	206	228	250	272	294	316	338	360	382	404	426
7'	158	181	204	227	250	273	296	319	342	365	388	411	434	457
8'	176	200	224	248	272	296	320	344	368	392	416	440	464	488
9'	194	219	244	269	294	319	344	369	394	419	444	469	494	519
10'	212	238	264	290	316	342	368	394	420	446	472	498	524	550
11'	230	257	284	311	338	365	392	419	446	473	500	527	554	581
12'	248	276	304	332	360	388	416	444	472	500	528	556	584	612
13'	266	295	324	353	382	411	440	469	498	527	556	585	614	643
14'	284	314	344	374	404	434	464	494	524	554	584	614	644	674
15'	302	333	364	395	426	457	488	519	550	581	612	643	674	705

Wallboard computation chart. Computation for square footage of wallboard required in a room with an 8' ceiling. (For net footage, deduct wall openings.)

Applying plastic laminate

Plastic laminate is applied directly to gypsum or other unfinished wallboard material with wall adhesive.

Bonded laminate hardboard does not require a wallboard base, but should not be applied directly to a plaster wall. Furring strips nailed to the wall studs will support hardboard glued to it with wall adhesive. Obviously you want as few nail holes as possible in a plastic laminate finish, but it is best to lightly nail the top of each sheet to the framing at ceiling level. Most manufacturers sell color coordinated finishing nails for this use.

The tough part of plastic laminate installation is not putting it up but cutting it out. Great care must be taken when measuring, and cuts should be carefully executed with a saber saw. Edges should then be smoothed with a router, laminate cutter or file, depending on the length and accessibility of the cut.

Plastic laminate molding

Plastic laminate is mounted in metal molding strips. On a plaster or wallboard surface, they are nailed to the wall. For use over tile, they are glued with a wall adhesive.

There are two basic types of panel molding: one-piece and two-piece. One-piece molding is installed as the paneling progresses, a strip at a time. Two-piece molding has a base strip which can be installed before any of the paneling goes up. The paneling is fitted into the base strip and glued to the wall. A decorative molding strip, which snaps into the base molding, is then laid on the outside. As with one-piece molding, there are several styles of two-piece molding. **Division molding** goes between panels and has a double flange. **Edge molding** is used to define the outside edge of a partially paneled wall and can also be used as cap molding for a wainscot installation (where the paneling only extends part way up the wall). **Inside** and **outside corner molding** join two paneled walls.

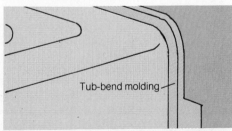

Tub-bend molding

When cutting paneling for installation in molding, remember to cut each dimension about ⅛-inch short, to allow for expansion due to climate changes. Never force paneling into a molding. It should extend into the molding flange only about half way. If the fit is a bit tight, you can bevel the back of the panel to ease it, but never nail panel edges.

Where edge and ceiling molding meet, both pieces should be mitered for a per-

One-piece molding

Outside corner molding

Inside corner molding

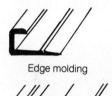

Edge molding

Division molding

Two-piece molding

Two-piece corner molding (inside)

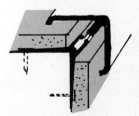

Two-piece corner molding (outside)

Decorative strip

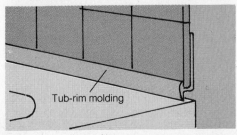

Tub-rim molding

fect fit. To mount plastic laminate panels, use some cardboard shims about 1/16 inch thick along the floor. If you are using two-piece molding, your base molding is already installed. Using panel adhesive on the wall, the panel, and in the flange of the molding, attach paneling as soon as the adhesive has reached the tackiness recommended by the manufacturer. Go over the entire surface with a hammer and wood block to make sure that the bonding is complete. When the installation is finished, remove the shims and attach a vinyl edge or cove molding along the base of the wall.

Start at a corner when installing panels with a one-piece molding. Cut and fit panels and molding strips as you go.

Cutouts and special fittings

In a bathroom or kitchen area particularly, there are a number of fixtures, appliances and outlets to work around. All panel fittings should be cut before the panel is installed. Make a template on a piece of heavy paper taped over that part of the wall where a cutout is needed. Then transfer the cutout lines to the face of the panel and cut them with a saber saw.

Electrical and plumbing control openings won't need further finishing. A face plate will do the trick. But tub and counter openings will need an edge molding. Molding strips specially fitted for curving tub edges are available, and their installation is the same as for wall molding. Before attaching molding around a tub or sink area, be sure to caulk all around the rim for a watertight seal. Do the same before attaching faucet and spout fittings.

About panel adhesives

Panel adhesive comes in bulk form or in cartridges to be used with a caulking gun. Many laminate manufacturers carry their own brand of panel adhesive, though it is certainly not necessary to restrict yourself to one adhesive.

There are two types of adhesive generally used with laminate paneling. The first is contact cement, particularly suited for bonding laminates to plywood. Contact cement bonds instantly, so care must be taken in positioning the panels before the glued surfaces touch (see page 87).

The preferred panel adhesive is epoxy. Epoxy is a two-part adhesive, one a resin and one a hardener, which must be mixed in equal parts—so measure carefully.

Since both of these adhesives are petroleum based, they are extremely water resistant, but for complete moisture protection a sealer should be used around all panel edges.

Their petroleum base also makes contact and epoxy adhesives highly flammable. Be sure that the room in which you are working is well ventilated and sustains a temperature of about 75°. Take a break every couple of hours when working and don't smoke in the area. Also avoid alcoholic beverages while working, as the combination of alcohol and adhesive fumes is toxic.

Patching plaster

Cracks, gouges, and holes in solid plaster or plaster-filled wallboard are easy to fill and smooth with one of the following compounds. These are applied with a putty knife or broad-bladed taping knife. Inside joints are reinforced with tape made of paper, plastic mesh, or metal; outside corners with metal corner bead.

Mixing tips. If you plan to be taping seams, attaching corner bead, or smoothing large areas with joint compound, you can make a terrific holder with scrap lumber.

Make a handle about 8 inches long that you can grip firmly. Nail one end into the middle of a piece of scrap lumber about 18 inches square. Carry a supply of compound on it and use the edge of the board to scrape excess compound off the taping knife.

Compounds for patching plaster

Spackling Compound

Form: Premixed in cans: easy to work with, lasts indefinitely. Powder: less expensive. Mix it with water.
Use: Filling small cracks (⅛″ max.), shallow holes, and bulges in solid plaster.
Application: Putty knife. Thin layer.
Handling: Scoop small amount out of can and mix only what you can use in 5 minutes. Doesn't shrink when applied thinly. Be sure to reseal can.

Patching Plaster

Form: Dry powder to mix with water.
Use: Filling large holes or cracks. Contains fibers for strong bond.
Application: Broad-bladed putty knife or taping knife. Difficult to apply smoothly. Let dry overnight before sanding.
Handling: Mix small quantities. Starts setting immediately. Doesn't shrink even in wide cracks or holes.

Filling a crack

The most common problem with plaster walls is the inevitable crack that forms from age or climate, or from the house settling. Small cracks can be filled with spackling compound; cracks that run the length of a wall should be filled with joint compound. If you have a crack that will not fill or that keeps coming back, apply a length of mesh patching tape with the joint compound.

What it takes

Approximate time: Half an hour or more, depending on how much patching you have, plus drying time. Sanding is a few minutes.

Tools and materials: Putty knife for small cracks or 10" taping knife for long ones, joint compound, sandpaper or, for large areas, an electric sander, goggles, and dust mask.

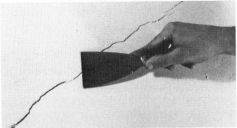

1. Scrape loose plaster from the surface of the wall with a putty knife. Don't dig into the crack—it only makes it worse.

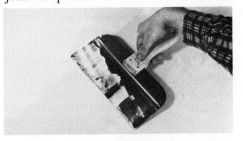

2. A 10-inch taping knife is the best tool to use to spread a thin layer of joint compound over the crack. Run the knife straight along the line in a continuous sweep.

3. To "feather" the edge of the compound so it blends with the wall surface, place the blade parallel to the line of compound and gently pull the knife towards the edge. Let compound dry 24 hours.

4. You can sand small areas with a piece of medium sandpaper wrapped around a small block of wood. For large areas or particularly rough walls, use an electric sander and wear goggles and a dust mask.

Patching a hole

What it takes

Approximate time: A few minutes.

Tools and materials: Brush or sponge, putty knife or tape knife, patching plaster, scrap piece of wallboard or plywood.

1. Holes in wallboard that are too large to fill easily with patching plaster must first be patched. The hole left after removing an electrical switch or outlet is a common example. Scrape away loose plaster and dampen the surrounding area with a brush or sponge.

2. When wood studs are visible, break off a piece of scrap wallboard small enough to fit in the hole but large enough to bridge the studs. Cement it to the studs with patching plaster.

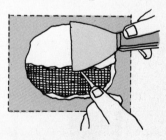

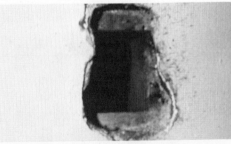

3. The patch fills the hole and gives support to the patching plaster. Starting from the bottom, use a putty knife to fill the remaining space with patching plaster.

4. Fill the rest of the hole with plaster. Let it dry for 24 hours before sanding it smooth.

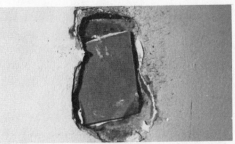

Alternative method

When there are no studs behind a large hole, cut a piece of stiff wire mesh an inch or so bigger than the hole. Thread a string through the center. Smear a thin layer of plaster around the edge. Bend it just slightly to fit it through the hole and pull it tight. It should be larger than the hole. Hold the string tight while you fill the hole with plaster. Then cut the string off flush after the plaster has dried.

Replacing ceramic tiles

What it takes

Approximate time: A couple of hours to remove tiles in a fairly small area; a full day plus drying time to lay new tile.

Tools and materials: Hammer, chisel, straight bar or crowbar, notched trowel, tile cutter, tile nippers, rubber-surfaced trowel, sponge; tiles, wall-tile mastic, grout.

Ceramic tile is a popular surface in bathrooms—it's durable, water resistant, and attractive. See page 56 on laying a tile floor; the same techniques will apply to tiling walls.

Tiles surrounding a bathtub and shower get a lot of abuse from water. When the grout gets old and begins to chip away, water can seep behind the tiles. If the tiles are not re-grouted, they loosen from the adhesive beneath. Where grout is beyond repair, it's best to replace the tiles.

Choosing new ceramic tiles can be fun. And don't forget that a variety of accessories are available to set in with the tiles.

Before you begin, protect the bathtub with a sheet of plastic so tile chips don't scratch the surface.

After removing the tiles, the first—and perhaps most important—step is to square off the area to be tiled. Walls are rarely perfectly rectilinear, and trying to line the tiles up by eye is a mistake. To mark off a squared area, start at the lowest point of the bathtub line. On the wall, measure the height of one full tile and mark. Use a level to make a horizontal mark with a straightedge or chalk line. Mark perpendicular lines on either side of the wall to site the placements of the first and last full tiles. To tile, start the work from either vertical line.

1. When ceramic tiles surrounding the tub are beyond repair, loose tiles bulge from the wall, chunks of grout have fallen out, and some tiles may be cracked.

2. Use a straight bar or chisel to loosen the top tile. Strike it gently with a hammer—the tile should come free readily.

3. Continue working down, loosening the tiles with a bar or chisel. Around fixtures, work extra carefully to avoid damage.

4. Beneath the tiles you'll find an uneven surface of old adhesive. Thoroughly remove the old adhesive, and sand the surface with a belt sander. Make sure the whole wall is clean.

5. Spread wall-tile mastic adhesive with a notched trowel, as evenly as possible. Press the tiles in place—do not slide them or you will push adhesive up into the joints. Allow 24 hours for mastic to dry before grouting.

6. A rubber-surface trowel is the best tool to use to apply grout, but you can apply the mixture with a putty knife and sponge.

7. Once all the gaps between tiles are filled, wipe the surface clean with a dampened sponge. Let it dry for at least 24 hours.

8. Ceramic tiles in a checkerboard pattern cover two walls of this bathroom. What an improvement!

Those necessary accessories

A bathroom without certain accessories—soap dish, towel bars, toilet-tissue holder—is not complete. These accessories are available in three types: flush-set, surface-mounted, and recessed.

Flush-set accessories are mounted on the wall rather like tile or paneling. They are put on at the time the wall covering is applied.

Surface-mounted accessories can be installed at any time over the wall covering. Some are glued on, but screws and mounting clips give better results. The way you fasten the accessory to the wall will depend upon whether the accessory is ceramic or metal.

Recessed accessories, which are installed either when the wall covering is applied or at the time of framing, are fitted into holes in the wall or directly into wood blocking in the framing. They are usually made to fit snugly between studs.

In addition to the essentials mentioned above, there are optional accessories available for the bath. For instance, grab bars (vertical or L-shaped) are handy. They are affixed on top of the wall covering and must be solidly mounted. Do not use plastic anchors to hold the mounting screws. Screw a grab bar directly into wood blocking which is placed behind the wall when the framing is done.

New wrinkle

Suppose you see surgery for your ceramic tile wall. Before you take down the whole wall, check your local dealer for an Easy-Set modular system that goes right over your old tiles. Each block of 9 tiles is pre-grouted to form 1 square foot of tile wallcovering. Just spread the adhesive over a good surface, put the sections in place, and grout the seams.

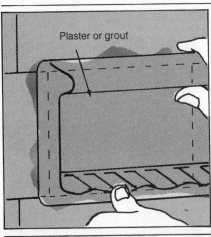
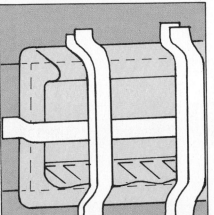

Flush-set. Mix water and plaster of paris in a bowl slowly, stirring well and continuously. The material must hold its shape but not be hard. Trowel about ¼ inch of the mixture on the back of the accessory, keeping it thinner at the edges. Set the accessory against the wall, moving it slightly to work the plaster of paris into any irregularities. Wipe off any excess. Hold in place a few minutes until the plaster of paris grips. An alternate method is to use a coating of grout consisting of white Portland cement and water. Secure the accessory with masking tape until it sets firmly.

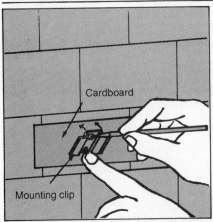

Surface-mount. First position the accessory so that its screw holes are as close as possible to the center of the tile. Using rubber cement, place a piece of thin cardboard on that tile. Hold the mounting clip against the card, and mark the screw holes. With a carbide-tip bit, drill at low speed using light pressure so as not to break the tile. Remove the cardboard. For a ceramic accessory, screw the metal mounting clip into the plastic wall anchors. Slip the accessory down over the clip until it is snug against the wall. Grout the joint between the wall and the accessory. A metal accessory is similarly installed, except that it is not grouted. A set-screw on the bottom is tightened to hold it to the clip.

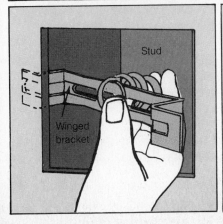
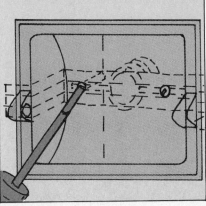

Recessed. If you planned to install a recessed accessory before the wall was surfaced, screw it right into the wood blocking at the time of framing. If you are installing it after the wall has been surfaced, cut an opening, and use a winged bracket to secure the bracket behind the wall. Mount the accessory by running a bead of caulking compound around the back of its front flange. Carefully insert it into the opening, then place and tighten the screws.

7.NEW FIXTURES

The bathroom

What it takes

Approximate time: A half hour but it is wise to allow yourself a little extra time.

Tools and materials: Wrench, screwdriver, hacksaw, putty knife/trowel, folding ruler; Teflon tape, plumber's putty, plaster of paris; fixtures.

Installing most bathroom fixtures—tubs, toilets, and sinks—is a simple reversal of the procedures used when removing old fixtures. Any pipe connections will require only the tightening of slip nuts. But be careful not to over-tighten nuts or you can damage the parts. Hand tighten first, then snug the nut with a wrench. The main thing to keep in mind is that even the sturdiest porcelain fixture will break under undue pressure or if it's dropped. Notice particularly the careful handling of the toilet bowl in the installation photographs here.

When you want a watertight seal, use plumber's putty; apply joint tape or pipe-joint compound to threaded connections, plastic as well as metal. You can check your work by turning on the water to see if there are any leaks.

Connecting a toilet

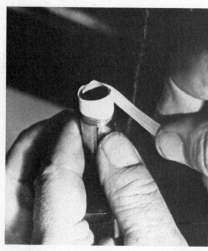

1. If there isn't a shutoff valve at the location, you'll have to install one. Cut the supply pipe 2 inches away from the wall. Wrap the end of the pipe with Teflon tape or use a little pipe compound.

2. Slide an escutcheon over the pipe and press it against the wall opening. Then slide the coupling nut and compression ring over the pipe. Slip on the valve, with its outlet hole up, and tighten the nut.

3. Remove the burlap or paper (which prevented dirt entering the pipe) from the soil opening and slip flange bolts into their slots (see page 26). (In most cases these will be replacement bolts, since the originals may have been cut when removing the old bowl.) If using a felt gasket, slip it on over the bolts.

4. If using a wax floor gasket, turn the bowl upside down and press the gasket down over the horn around the waste horn.

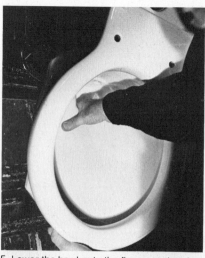

5. Lower the bowl onto the flange so that the two flange bolts protrude through the rim holes. If using a wax gasket, press down and twist firmly on the bowl to seal it.

6. Make sure the bowl is level. Use copper or brass washers to shim, if necessary. But don't raise the bowl enough to break the gasket seal.

7. Snug a washer and nut over each flange bolt just enough to hold the bowl in place. Don't overtighten. Cover the bolt ends with plastic or porcelain caps.

8. To install a bowl-mounted tank, first check to make sure that the spud lock nut is secure. Again, don't overtighten. If it seems secure, leave it alone.

9. Place the tank cushion over the spud lock nut and drop the tank bolts through either side.

10. Lower the tank onto the bowl, guiding it so the tank bolts slide into the two holes on the back of the bowl.

11. Snug a washer and nut up onto each bolt.

12. To install a flexible supply pipe, first measure for the bend needed. (1 inch here.)

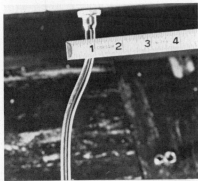

13. The copper tubing can be bent by hand. Then measure again. Mark the bent pipe for required length.

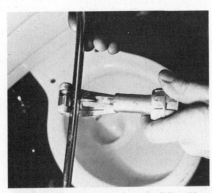

14. Cut the measured pipe carefully with a tube cutter.

15. Daub the upper end of the pipe with pipe compound.

16. Slide a coupling nut up the pipe and hand fasten it to the inlet stem.

17. Slide the valve coupling nut and compression ring onto the lower end of the pipe. Insert the pipe into the valve and tighten both nuts with a wrench.

Finishing up:

Grout around the base of the bowl with plaster of paris. Smooth the plaster with a putty knife or trowel. A coat of clear lacquer applied after the plaster has dried will ensure that it's moisture-proof. The plastic or china caps over the closet bolts can also be anchored down with plaster at this point. Connect the water and test for leaks. Finally, install the lid and seat.

Bathtub/shower combination

The bathtub is the first fixture to be installed in a new or renovated bathroom. It goes in before the floor and walls are finished, since flooring and wall material will extend to the edges of the tub fixture.

Tub positioning is a heavy chore. Even the most maneuverable fiberglass and pressed steel tub needs two men to lift it. Moving a cast iron tub is a four-man job. The three-sided tub enclosure, which is standard, affords extremely limited work space for installation. Good planning is essential.

Tub support. For a three-sided tub enclosure, nail 1x4 tub supports horizontally to each of the three walls. The height of these supports should be carefully measured and the 1x4s leveled exactly. The tub flange must rest evenly on the supports with the tub base sitting on the sub-flooring.

Pipes. Consult manufacturers' rough-in plans for the exact height of overflow pipe, faucet assembly, and shower head, as well as the prescribed location of the floor drain opening. Extend all piping horizontally as necessary. Be sure that the shower pipe is braced on a vertical 1x4 nailed between studs.

Setting in the tub. Two men can position a steel and fiberglass tub in front of its wall enclosure and slide it straight back to the rear wall, being sure to lodge the underside of the rear flange securely on the wall support. For a heavier tub you will need more help in positioning and should lay a pair of 2x4 runners on the subfloor as a track on which to push the tub. When removing the 2x4s, do so as gradually as possible, again settling the tub flange on all three supports and the subfloor.

Once the tub is in position, level it again and shim under the flange, if necessary, with wood shims. Make sure the tub does not wobble. Nail or screw the tub flange to its wall supports. A cast iron tub needs no fastening.

The walls and floor around the tub can be finished at this point.

Plumbing provisions. An access panel in the head wall behind the tub will give access to hidden plumbing. If you do not plan to install an access panel, use permanent drain connections and large enough faucet face plates to facilitate faucet repair from the tub wall. The trap installed in a no-access tub fitting should accommodate an auger through the tub drain for cleaning.

Attaching drainpipes. Remove the overflow plate, lift linkage, and strainer cap. Join the waste and overflow pipes with a slip nut and washer, and set the assembly on the waste T. Position the large beveled washer between the back of the tub and the overflow pipe. Place the large flat washer between the drainpipe and the tub bottom. Position the

Rube Goldberg was a piker!
Hear this! When ordering any flush fitting tub whether flanged on one side or three, *be sure* to specify which side will face the wall. Otherwise, you may end up—as I did!—with the water spout at one end and the drain at the other.

Practical Pete

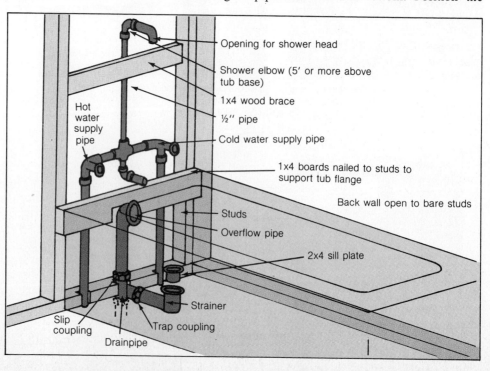

Opening for shower head

Shower elbow (5' or more above tub base)

1x4 wood brace

½" pipe

Cold water supply pipe

1x4 boards nailed to studs to support tub flange

Back wall open to bare studs

Studs

Overflow pipe

2x4 sill plate

Strainer

Hot water supply pipe

Slip coupling

Trap coupling

Drainpipe

whole assembly and tighten the slip nuts. Use a strand of plumber's putty around the underside of the strainer, then handscrew it into the drain hole.

Hardware. Slip the lift linkage into the overflow hole and attach the overflow plate. For faucet handles, slide escutcheons and sleeves onto spindles, then screw on handles. If your faucet handle requires another kind of installation, consult the manufacturer's instructions.

To install the tub spout, remove the rough-in nipple, and replace it with a nipple measured to extend from the face of the pipe behind the wall to the threads of the spout *plus* ¾-inch allowance (for threaded fitting). Daub the nipple threads with joint compound and then hand screw the spout as tightly as possible.

To install the shower arm, remove the nipple from that supply pipe. Use joint compound on the threads of the arm, fit the escutcheon over the arm and hand screw the arm to the pipe.

When installing faucet handles, spout, and shower arm, be sure to use some form of caulking or sealant around the pipe fittings before the escutcheons go on. Also be sure to caulk around all the tub edges and check for leaks before installing floor and wall materials.

Prefab possibilities

Many manufacturers offer prefabricated fiberglass shower stalls and shower/tub combinations. These lightweight units are available in one-piece packages or four-piece snap-together assemblies. A one-piece tub/shower unit is usually positioned in a new bathroom before the framing is roughed-in. Four-piece units are easier to bring in through the door frame of a pre-existing bathroom. You may want to install support framing and sound-proofing insulation. Check all specifications before purchase, to ensure getting the right unit for your needs.

Custom showers

Custom showers as a rule are more expensive than the standard ones. However, in certain cases they are the only ones that will fit into the area available.

Tiled showers are fairly expensive, and it can be a job keeping the joints clean. The use of a silicone grout will discourage the growth of mildew. The tile can be put on with mastic over gypsum wallboard or plaster, or it can be set into wet mortar. Pregrouted tile shower *surrounds* are available in sizes that will fit the most popular receptors: that is, the floor of a custom shower, be it a pre-fab waterproof unit or one constructed on the site from ceramic tile or some other suitable material. To install the shower receptor:

1. Select the appropriate size, unless it is to be custom made.
2. Measure the receptor to locate the center of the drain outlet.
3. The center of the trap inlet must be directly under the drain outlet.
4. Place a short pipe nipple in the trap.
5. Lower the receptor over the trap. If it is a concrete type receptor, it will be heavy.

6. Mark the pipe so that the mark will be even (flush) with the socket of the cast in the strainer.
7. Remove the pipe; and cut the pipe on the mark.
8. Remove the receptor.
9. Replace the pipe and tighten.
10. Apply packing, and pack firmly between the outside wall of the pipe and strainer body.
11. Run a heavy bead of caulking onto the packing; smooth for a watertight joint.
12. Place the strainer grille in place.

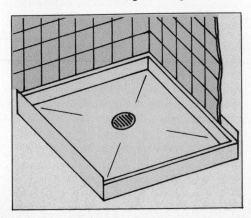

Installing shower doors

What it takes

Approximate time: 1-2 hours.

Tools and materials:
Screwdriver, pliers, caulk; shower door and frame, hardware.

Plastic panels or metal-framed glass are the usual tub-shower doors. They come in a number of patterns and fit showers and tubs of varying dimensions.

Nowadays in new houses that have shower doors, safety glass is used. This is written into the building codes as a requirement. But older houses are liable to have shower doors made of ordinary ¼-inch glass. This type of door might resist a glancing blow, but will shatter if hit with great force.

Dangerous glass can be replaced by putting approved safety glass or acrylic plastic in the existing frame; or you can install a whole new door.

Tub enclosures come in three styles. **Horizontal sliding panels** containing either plastic or tempered glass. They're simple to install, replace, and repair. The disadvantage to this type of door is that cleaning is harder because there's no smooth tub edge, and the panels block off half the tub, even when opened.

Plastic vertical panels that raise and lower like double-hung windows give you clear access to the tub. However, installation is more complicated—the panels must be exactly aligned so they don't stick. Moreover, the panels may not be as watertight as other types of doors. Since they are not as widely available as the horizontal type, there might be some difficulty in finding replacement parts.

Accordion-fold doors have a strong advantage in one respect; when folded, the panels store at one end, thus taking up very little space, which makes cleaning easier. But they often are not as watertight as sliding panels, and they have been known to wear around the hinges. They are made of plastic and consequently are not as rugged nor as long-lived as glass doors.

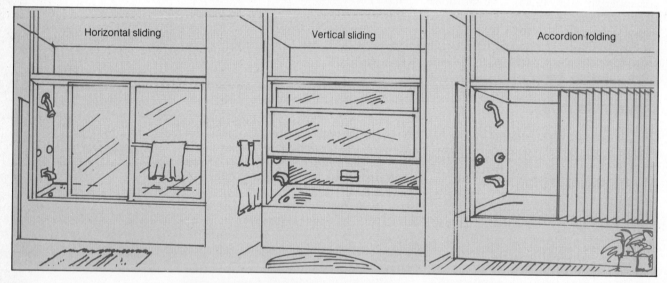

Horizontal sliding   Vertical sliding   Accordion folding

Soundproofing the bathroom

When renovating, measures to minimize bathroom noise are best done before the walls are put up. There are a number of ways to accomplish this. Gypsum wallboard folded in accordion fashion between the studs is quite effective, as is installing blanket insulation. Bathroom wallboard should be thick, and adding sound-deadening fiberboard to the back of it increases its ability to muffle sound.

The plumbing system when well planned, eliminates another source of unwanted noise. When pipes are located close to fixtures and drainpipes slanted to slow the flow of water, it is easier to achieve quiet. You can wrap noisy pipes with layers of asphalt building paper and fiberglass insulation. Remember that a steel bathtub or shower stall will make a lot of noise when water hits its surface, and you may prefer to install either fiberglass or porcelain fixtures.

The bathroom door should be solid rather than hollow core, and it should fit snugly to the threshold. Thicker glass—or even the sound control kind—will reduce noise through windows to the outside, as will weatherstripping around any doors.

There is ceiling material available that is not only moisture-resistant but also sound-absorbing. Carpeting the floor also softens the sounds.

Installing a medicine cabinet

The customary medicine chest for the bathroom is recessed into or mounted on the wall over the lavatory, and usually has a hinged, mirrored door. Other more elaborate cabinets have different styles of doors, built-in lighting fixtures, and electrical outlets. Cabinets are available in numerous sizes and styles. Of course, the medicine cabinet doesn't have to be located above the lavatory. You can hang a large mirror over the wash basin, and the medicine cabinet can be on another wall.

The inside of the cabinet consists of shelves, 4 to 6 inches apart, which hold tubes, bottles, and jars. You should allow one shelf to be taller so it can accommodate larger items.

Most homes built in the past quarter century have dry wall construction. If you have this type of wall in your bathroom, there is an easy way to install a medicine cabinet. Recessed medicine chests come ready-made to fit inside the 16-inch space between wall studs, making installation very simple. First, it is necessary to find the studs. This can be done by tapping the wall to find where it is solid, or by using a stud finder. The stud finder has a magnet that detects the hidden nails in the wall. Once you find the line of nails, you will know a stud is there.

• Locate two consecutive studs in the area where you want the cabinet to go. Hold the cabinet exactly where you want it, and draw its outline on the wall.

• Drill a hole inside the outline, and with a keyhole saw cut from the hole toward either stud. When you reach the stud, cut along the outline you drew on the wall.

• Now cut two 2x4s into 16-inch lengths. Toenail them into the top and bottom of the opening. These crosspieces should be behind the surface of the wall, but exactly at the edge of the opening. Make sure they are level.

• Place the cabinet in the opening, and drive screws into the 2x4s on all four sides. This will secure the cabinet.

Recessed cabinets are also available in greater widths which require special installation. You will have to saw out stud sections to accommodate these larger units. This installation also requires the addition of headers or crosspieces as replacement support for the missing stud sections.

However, if there's plumbing or wiring behind the wall at the place where you want to hang your medicine chest, it's better to install a surface-mounted cabinet.

What it takes

Approximate time: 1 afternoon.

Tools and materials: Stud finder, drill, keyhole saw, screwdriver; screws, nails, 2x4s, medicine cabinet.

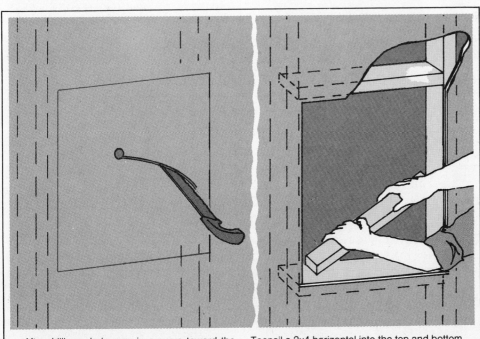

After drilling a hole, saw in a curve toward the nearest stud. Then saw out the outline you have already drawn on the wall.

Toenail a 2x4 horizontal into the top and bottom of the opening. You can drive one or two nails into each of the vertical studs to hold the horizontal 2x4s in place while securing them.

Kitchen trio

Whereas in former times the kitchen contained principally the range, icebox, and sink, many modern kitchens also have a garbage disposal and dishwasher. These, along with the sink, can almost be considered a single unit when it comes to installation, and in many new homes are treated as such. This is because the disposal is actually an extension of the sink drain, and all three appliances use the same waste pipe. Indeed, if there is proper preparation, the installations of all three consist chiefly of tightening screws and nuts.

The simplest method for mounting a sink is to attach as many fittings as possible before you place it into the countertop. Clearly, if you have the faucets, spray hose, tailpiece, and strainer already attached, it will reduce the problem of having to work in a tight space.

For the garbage disposal you will need a handy wall switch. It is a simple matter to connect the disposal with the sink, and to connect the wires, once you've installed and tested the wiring.

A dishwasher has three connections; a hot-water supply line, a waste line, and an electrical connection. These connections are made through an access panel at the lower front. This is done after the dishwasher is in position.

Sink and disposal installation

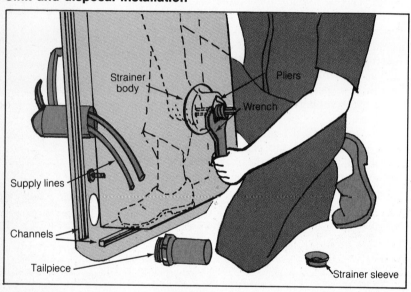

Strainer body
Pliers
Wrench
Supply lines
Channels
Tailpiece
Strainer sleeve

1. First attach the fittings. Stand the sink on its side for easier access. If the faucet body has a rubber gasket, slide it over the stems; if not, apply an ⅛-inch bead of plumber's putty around the body base and then slide the stems through the holes that are provided. If it is necessary to straighten the attached copper supply lines, bend them carefully. If there is a spray hose, follow the instructions of the manufacturer for attaching it to the faucet body and the sink opening. If the sink has no garbage disposal, apply an ⅛-inch bead of plumber's putty to the bottom of the lip of the strainer body before you place it in the drain hole. Place the metal and rubber washers plus a lock nut onto the threaded bottom of the strainer body. Tighten the locknut, carefully, by hand. Insert plier handles into the hole to keep the strainer body from turning before tightening. Assemble the strainer sleeve, tailpiece, and lock nut and attach the tailpiece to the strainer body.

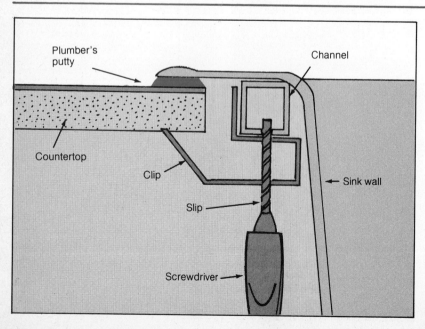

Plumber's putty
Channel
Countertop
Clip
Slip
Sink wall
Screwdriver

2. To attach the sink, apply a ¼-inch bead of plumber's putty along the top edge of the countertop opening. Place the sink into the opening. From beneath, slide 8 or 10 clips into the channels that rim the underside of the sink and position them to grip the bottom of the countertop. The clips should be evenly spaced. With a screwdriver tighten the slips, being careful not to crimp the rim of the sink by overtightening. Check the top to see that you have a good seal between the countertop and the sink rim. Adjust the level if necessary by drawing on the clips.

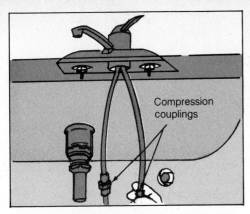

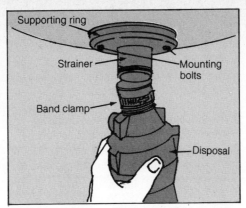

3. To connect the pipes you must first attach the shutoff valves to the stub-outs. If there are supply pipes attached to the taucet body, fasten them to the valves in the same way that you would to a toilet supply (page 48). If there are no pipes, or if they are not long enough, use compression fittings to attach copper tubing.

Add a coupling to the drainpipe, after first uncapping it. For a disposal, see the instructions in Step 4; otherwise, place a slip nut and washer on the tailpiece. Place the drainpipe so that the trap fits correctly, and cement the drain to the coupling. Place an escutcheon, slip nut and a washer over the drainpipe. Install the trap.

4. To attach the disposal, insert the disposal strainer in place of the strainer body (see Step 1). Place the rubber and metal gaskets and thread the mounting bolts loosely before you snap on the support ring. Tighten the bolts, but don't buckle the support ring. When the sink has been mounted (see Step 2), put the clamp around the disposal collar. Lift the disposal so that it locks into the sleeve of the strainer, as shown here. Install a P trap to connect the drain and the disposal waste pipe. Tighten the clamp, and connect the electricity.

Keep in mind that certain disposals require you poke in a knockout plug at the top if you plan to attach a dishwasher drain. You will have to retrieve the plug, so be sure to use long-nose pliers.

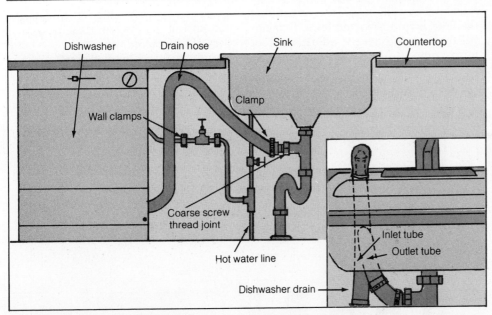

All you have to do is ask the right person!
My friend told me that our local code insists on an air gap for a dishwasher waste line. This prevents siphonage of waste water back into the cleaning chamber. So okay—only thing is *he* forgot to tell *me* to make sure my new sink had a precut hole, so I wouldn't have to cut through all that steel.

Practical Pete

In order to connect the dishwasher, you will need to prepare the space. It will also be necessary to cut a hole about 6 inches wide in the lower rear section of the cabinet wall that lies between the dishwasher space and the sink. This will accommodate a line of flexible copper tubing along with the dishwasher drain hose, as well as the electrical cable if required. Take away the access panel and kick plate from the lower front of the dishwasher before you move the dishwasher into its opening. Level the unit so that it is flush with the countertop. You can then make the connections with the dishwasher in or out of its space. To connect the copper tubing to the inlet pipe, use a compression fitting. A hose clamp connects the drain hose to the outlet pipe.

With the dishwasher in place, secure it with screws to the countertop through the precut

holes in the front. Connect the wiring and put back the access panel and kick plate. Attach the other end of the tubing to the sink hot-water pipe with a separate shutoff valve, and the drain hose to the sink tailpiece or air gap.

To provide electricity, 120 volt, 60 Hz, AC only, 15 ampere fused supply is required. It is also advisable that a separate circuit serving only this appliance be provided. *Do not* use an extension cord; grounding is also a must.

If you require an air gap, pull the stem up through a hole in the countertop or sink, screw on the plastic top and press in the outer cap. Use a hose clamp to connect the dishwasher drain hose to the inlet tube of the air gap. Use a section of hose and clamps to connect the outlet tube to the sink drainpipe.

8. NEW FLOORS

There is no question that the kitchen and bathroom floors receive the major punishment in a home. And so your choice of floor covering is an important decision when you renovate. There is a number of flooring materials to choose from: resilient sheet or tile, ceramic tile, and carpeting are the most popular. Other possibilities include wood, marble, poured, and painted floors.

Bear in mind that rarely will one floor finish have every quality that you desire. For instance, wood floors, though beautiful, need to be refinished, comfortable carpeting needs to be cleaned, and practical vinyl tile can loosen or get scratched.

Ceramic tile

For the bathroom, one of the most popular as well as durable floors is ceramic tile. It is not difficult to install, and it is certainly attractive. When properly put down, it will resist water. The tiles are generally square or hexagonal. They come in sizes from 1 to 12 inches square, and in a wide range of colors. A great variety of trim tile is also available.

Laying ceramic tile requires a smooth surface, a planned pattern, and attaching the tiles with adhesive. Make certain that the floor is firm, flat, and level. Remember that you will have to adjust the door to accommodate the thickness of the tiles.

Tile adhesives include epoxies, latex-mortar and epoxy-mortar combinations, organic adhesives, and cement-based mortars. The organic adhesives are relatively inexpensive and are easier to apply than the epoxies because no mixing is required.

When you buy adhesives make sure the product meets your needs—setting time, bonding ability, and water resistance.

As a rule, floor adhesives harden more quickly than wall adhesives. While you can spread adhesive over a fairly large area of wall before you set tile, it is better on a floor to work in small areas.

Cutting tiles

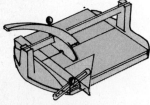

A tile cutter can be rented.

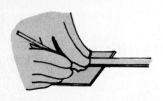

To do it without the cutter, score the tile with a glass cutter. Clamp the tile in a vise along the score line, and snap off. Another way is to lay the scored tile over a nail or piece of metal and press down on both sides.

The floor plan

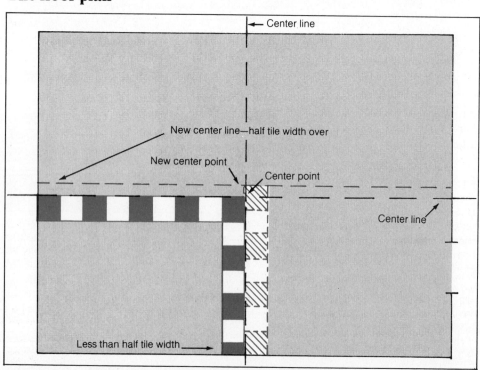

Plan the pattern well. First, lay a row of dry tile from the middle of a doorway to the opposite wall. The row will be guided by a string nailed from the doorway to the wall. Should there be a gap of less than half a tile width at the end of the run, take away the first tile and center those that are left. The spaces left for the two border tiles will equal more than half the width of a tile, which makes for a better-looking floor, and also avoids difficult cuts on very small pieces.

How to set separate tiles

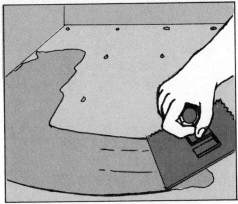

1. Spread the adhesive, using the kind that is right for your particular surface. Spread this as thinly as you can with the side of the trowel that does not have the notches. Allow the coat to dry thoroughly.

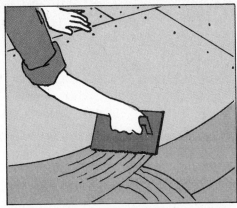

2. Spread adhesive with the notched edge of the trowel, over about 10 square feet. Hold the edge of the trowel against the surface at a 45° angle. In order that the adhesive will flow freely from the notches, use only about a cup of adhesive each time. Do not cover any lines that you have drawn on the floor for alignment or reference.

— Stopgaps and Copouts —

Keep checking the alignment with a straightedge. Do this often, because once the tiles get off line, the problem quickly worsens. If a course of tile is out of line, you can often correct it by opening the joints slightly. If the tiles do not have spacing lugs, use pieces of 1/16-inch thick wood or cardboard to keep the joints between the tiles even.

3. Set tiles by starting at reference lines near the middle of the room, and work toward the walls. Press each tile into place, carefully yet firmly, twisting it slightly with your fingertips to set it well into the adhesive. Be careful not to slide the tiles into place or the adhesive will fill up the joints, and you won't be able to grout. In the event that you are setting thick tiles that have indentations on the backs, also put adhesive on the back of each tile.

4. To "beat in" the tile, take a scrap of 2x4 about the length of three tiles, and pad it with several layers of cloth. With the padded side down, place it on the tiles that are set and tap gently with a hammer, going up and down its length several times. This beating will set the tiles more firmly into the adhesive and will help to achieve a level floor. When the adhesive has hardened for 24 hours, the floor can be grouted. If you must walk on the newly-laid tile, cover it with plywood sheets.

If you add, then you've got to subtract
I forgot that adding tile to my bathroom floor would mean I'd have to adjust the door so it could close. Remember that even a hair's thickness can make all the difference between an open-or-shut door!

Practical Pete

Grouting

The next step is to fill the spaces between the tiles with grout. This is a mortar, available in many colors, that seals out water and dirt. Since ceramic tiles have many different uses, it is best to consult your dealer to make sure you get the grout best suited to your project. For instance, the tiles used in the sunken bathtub on page 72 require a silicone grout. In other cases, such as the mosaic tiles (page 58), you can mix your own.

Mix mortar-type grout to the consistency that has been recommended by the manufacturer. This type of grout needs to dry slowly so that it can cure properly. At the same time, some floor tiles absorb water from the grout to the point where they hinder proper curing. And so, before grouting, put a drop of water on the back of a tile. If the tile absorbs it right away, then use more water in the grout.

In order to make floor grout joints flush with tile surfaces fill the joints with grout that has in it a water-retaining aggregate. Sprinkle dry grout of the same kind over the grout joints and rub the joints with a piece of burlap. Rub in a circular motion for the best effect.

After you have tiled the floor, cover it with polyethylene sheeting. If there is no sign of condensation under the sheeting the following day, remove it, sprinkle water on the floor and put back the sheeting. Allow the grout to cure for three days. In 10 days seal the grout joints. This sealer will protect the grout from dirt or mildew.

Mosaic floor tiles

What it takes

Approximate time: About half a day for a standard 5'x8' bathroom, plus underlayment and drying.

Tools and materials: ½-inch exterior grade plywood, saw, hammer, and nails if underlayment is required. Tape measure, 1-foot square sheets of mosaic tiles, mastic, spreader, grout, mixing bowl, squeegee, rolling pin, sponge.

Mosaic floor tiles are popular and easy to install. They come in 1x1-foot, or 1x2-foot sheets. Some have a paper backing to hold the sheets together; others have protective paper covering the top, and this must be peeled off after installation.

As with any new covering, the floor underneath must be leveled, all cracks must be filled, and if it's a rough hardwood floor, it should be sanded. If your floor is badly warped, you can put down a plywood or hardboard underlayment.

Mark off the floor area as you would for standard tiles. Apply adhesive with a notched trowel. Cover a 3-foot square area at a time. Place the sheets of mosaic tile lightly on the adhesive. Then slide each into its correct position, and press firmly in place.

Make certain that the spaces between the sheets are the same as the spaces between single tiles.

When the main part of the floor is done, you'll have to fit narrow pieces of tile around the edges. Cut carefully, following the pattern. Use tile nippers for cutting and shaping.

For this tile you may mix grout yourself. Mix 3 parts Portland cement with 1 part water. Continue to add water until you have a creamy consistency. Spread the grout over the tile with a rubber-surfaced trowel. Force it into the cracks. The grout should be allowed to dry for at least 12 hours before you walk on the floor.

Wipe excess grout from the floor immediately, using a damp sponge. When the floor has dried thoroughly, the cement will leave a film. This should be removed with a mixture of 1 part muriatic acid to 10 parts water. Apply with a rag, wipe thoroughly, and finally, dry with a clean rag. When working with this solution you should wear rubber gloves.

1. If the floor is at all uneven, cover it with an "underlayment" of ½-inch exterior grade plywood or heavy hardboard. Leave a ⅛-inch crack where the edges butt so the underlayment will not buckle if the wood becomes moist and swells. Offset the panels so the four corners don't meet.

2. The adhesive for ceramic tiles, called mastic, is highly flammable. Leave the windows open until it hardens. Spread it evenly with a trowel that has a serrated edge with teeth about ⅛ inch apart. Cover an area large enough to lay three 1-foot square sheets of tiles.

3. Small (½ to 1-inch square) mosaic tiles are usually sold in 1-foot square sheets. The tiles are perfectly aligned and held in place either with their bottoms glued onto a square of paper mesh or with a sheet of paper glued to their tops. Lay the squares the same distance apart as the divisions between the individual tiles on them.

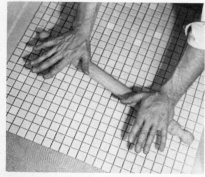

4. Imbed the tiles in the mastic, pressing them down evenly with a length of 2x4 or a kitchen rolling pin. If the tops of the tiles are attached to a sheet of paper, soak it in warm water after the mastic has dried (about 24 hours) and peel the paper off.

5. Fill the spaces between the tiles with a waterproof plaster-like material called grout. Grey is better than white for floor tiles because it won't show the dirt as much. Spread it with a squeegee, completely filling all the cracks.

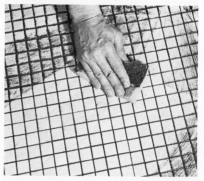

6. Wipe the grout off the face of the tiles with a damp sponge before the grout dries. Wet the sponge slightly and wipe again to smooth and remove any excess grout between the tiles. Polish the faces of the tiles with a dry cloth.

Carpet in the bathroom

It's warmer in the winter, it's softer if you drop something, and it is quieter than ceramic tile. Use washable carpeting with a non-slip back, loose-laid so it can be taken up easily for cleaning. Kitchen carpeting can be used in the bathroom, too. Indoor-outdoor carpeting is durable, although it tends to hold water. You can often pick up inexpensive carpeting at overrun outlets and remnant sales stores.

What it takes

Approximate time: One hour

Tools and materials: Washable, non-skid carpeting, heavy kraft wrapping paper to make a full-size pattern, tape measure or ruler, scissors, single-edge razor blade, masking tape, marking pen.

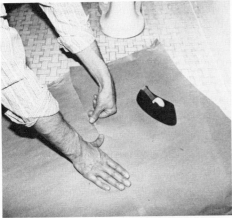

1. Make a full-size pattern of the floor with heavy wrapping paper. Overlap the seams about ½ inch and tape them together.

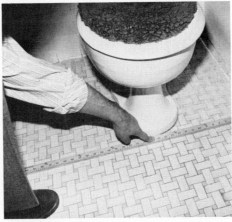

2. To cut around a protruding fixture such as a toilet bowl, measure and cut a slit in the pattern from the wall to the front edge of the bowl and another slit the width of the bowl.

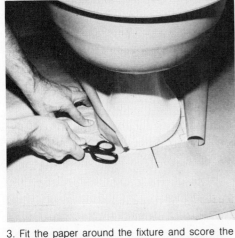

3. Fit the paper around the fixture and score the paper following the shape of the fixture where it meets the floor.

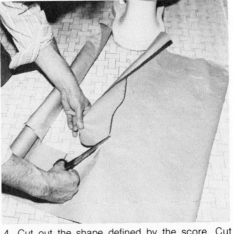

4. Cut out the shape defined by the score. Cut score and trim if necessary after refitting the paper pattern.

5. Place the *bottom* of the pattern on top of the *bottom* of the carpet, tape them together, and cut around the pattern with scissors.

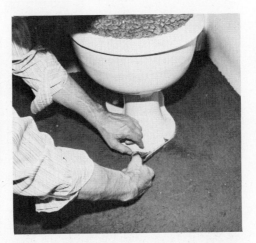

6. Trim the carpet for exact fit. Long-pile carpeting is more forgiving because the pile will hide small cutting errors.

Covering an old floor

To make sure you will have a solid tile floor, install a hardboard underlayment.
- Never butt sheets of underlayment flush together. Leave roughly ⅛" between them for expansion.
- Stagger seams to avoid having four corners meeting together at one point.
- Use annular-ring nails or cement-coated nails to fasten.

9. NEW CABINETS AND COUNTERTOPS

Single wall

What it takes

Approximate time: Allot your time in periods of no less than half a day.

Tools and materials: Hammer, saw, screwdriver, pliers, level, plumb line, electric drill and bits; screws, nails, grounds, 1x3 stock, wood shims.

First, locate the wall studs and grounds. Grounds serve the purpose of supplying an anchor to secure cabinets. They may be surface mounted or, like cleats, placed between studs. The best way is to notch them into studs. Because they will be covered by the cabinets, walls can be cut open for ground insertion without much concern about patching the wall. But level and plumb the grounds.

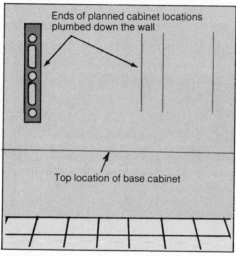

1. On the wall, lay out the left and right ends of the planned cabinet locations. Plumb these lines down the wall.

2. Lay out the top and bottom locations of the hanging cabinets. If you're planning on a soffit, or there is one already installed, then only the bottom location is necessary. Level the height locations laid out in Step 1.

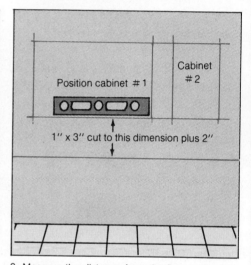

3. Measure the distance from the floor to the bottom of the cabinet. From 1x3 stock, cut two deadmen (support sticks) 2 inches longer than the measurement.

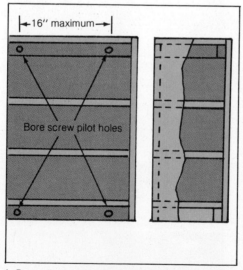

4. Bore pilot holes along the rear top and bottom cabinet framework every 16 inches (maximum).

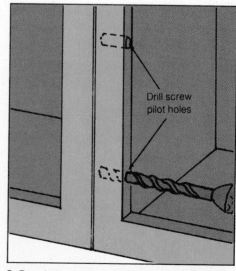

5. Bore holes so that when the two cabinets abut each other in a straight line the pilot holes will go through the edges of the abutting front vertical frames.

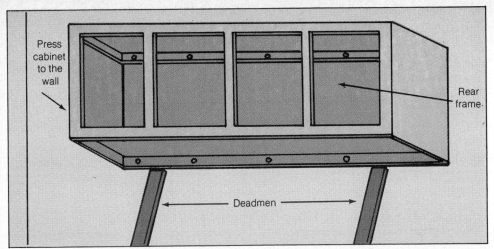

Press cabinet to the wall

Rear frame.

Deadmen

6. Place the screws in the pilot holes. Raise the cabinet to the wall layout and place the deadmen under the rear framework. Of course, you will need a helper for this operation. Press the cabinet to the wall to provide friction and avoid slippage.

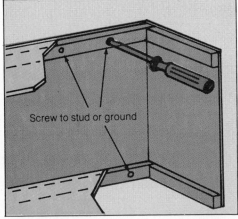

Screw to stud or ground

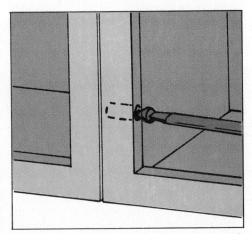

7. Anchor one top frame screw to a stud or ground. Check for level against the wall level lines previously laid out, then drive all screws into the studs and/or grounds.

8. Align the front faces of abutting cabinets and screw their front frames together.

The base cabinets

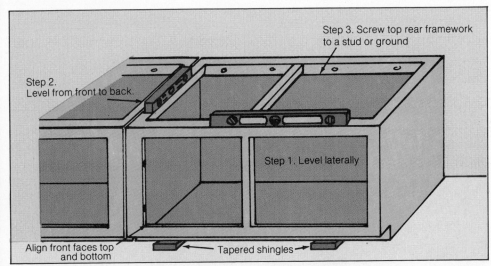

Step 3. Screw top rear framework to a stud or ground

Step 2. Level from front to back.

Step 1. Level laterally

Align front faces top and bottom

Tapered shingles

1. Place the cabinet against your marked line on the wall. Starting from the high side and working laterally, raise the cabinet until it is level. Do this by inserting tapered wood shingles underneath the cabinet, in line with the vertical frame members. Cut or break off all protruding shingles.

2. Check the cabinet for level from front to back. Shim if necessary.

3. As with the hanging cabinets, first screw the top rear framework to a stud or ground, then similarly align the front cabinet faces and screw the abutting vertical frames together.

The countertop

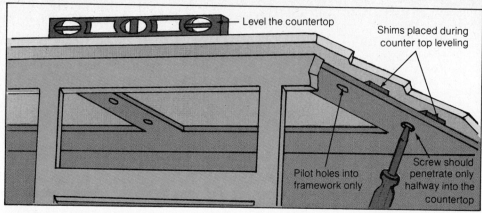

Level the countertop

Shims placed during counter top leveling

Pilot holes into framework only

Screw should penetrate only halfway into the countertop

1. Locate the high point of the countertop with a level. Place shims between the horizontal framework of the base cabinet and the underside of the countertop until it is level.

2. Secure the countertop by first boring pilot holes through the top horizontal framework which is lo-cated between the front and the back frames.

3. Screw from the horizontal frame of the base cabinet into the bottom side of the countertop. But be careful to choose the right length of screw; long enough to grip, but not so long that it will penetrate the countertop.

Multi-wall installation

Individual steps for installation of L- and U-shaped cabinet lines are basically the same as for single wall cabinet installation. As a matter of fact, if all kitchens were living room size, it would be a simple matter, for kitchens of such size rarely require this type of installation. It is the small kitchen, where wall use has to be maximized, that needs the U- or L-shaped line.

The shape in itself, were it confined to the cabinets, would present no problem. The countertop is the culprit. Because it is always desirable to have as few joints in the countertop as possible, it should be made in one piece even though U-shaped. Consequently, you will have the problem of installing a large, bulky item in a confined area.

Because of this problem, the procedure for multi-wall cabinet installation is slightly different. The countertop, though not secured first, has to be brought in first, to avoid maneuvering difficulties that would occur if the wall and base cabinets were already in place.

Completing the base units

The balance of the work on the base units is completed in the same manner as with the single-wall style. Level the cabinets while the countertop is resting on the deadmen. The top end of the sticks will be 6 inches higher than the cabinets and so will allow room to maneuver.

Fill in the missing cabinets, then level and align them with the others. Secure the top rear rail of framework of the cabinets to the wall. The countertop is the last item and is secured from the cabinet to the bottom of the countertop, the same as with single-wall units.

All a question of planning ahead

I found out the hard way—and I do mean hard! — when I did my multi-wall cabinet installation. I should have brought my countertop in *first,* even though it's put on *after* everything else has been installed.

Practical Pete

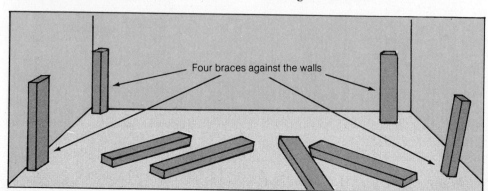

Four braces against the walls

1. Cut 8 deadmen 42 inches long. Place 4 against the wall; 1 at each corner and 1 at each end of the countertop location.

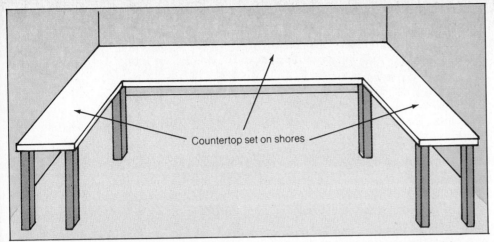

2. With the assistance of at least one person, carry the countertop in and set it on the deadmen sticks.

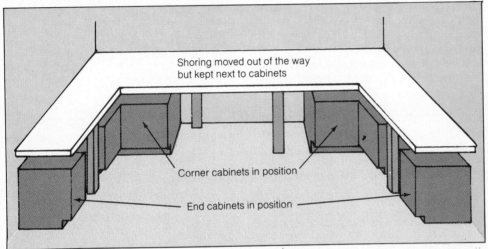

Shoring moved out of the way but kept next to cabinets

Corner cabinets in position

End cabinets in position

3. Place the corner cabinets in their approximate positions. Move the deadmen to nearby locations adjacent to the corner cabinets. Place the end cabinets in position. Move the deadmen sticks out of the way but near the cabinets.

U and L hanging cabinets

As with single-wall application, guide lines have to be laid out for U- and L-shaped hanging wall cabinets. A change occurs, on the other hand, in the makeup of the deadmen (often called shores) and the positioning procedure. See page 20 in reference to temporary bracing; remember, sound bracing is half the work.

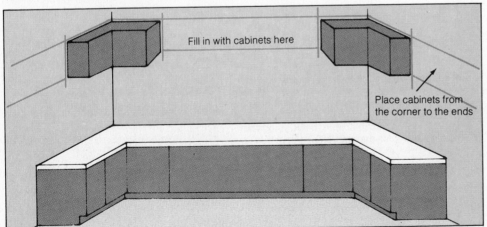

Fill in with cabinets here

Place cabinets from the corner to the ends

Cabinet placement starts in the corners as it does with the base units. The placement of the rest of the cabinets, however, is easier. The units are installed from the corners outward to the ends of the cabinet line, instead of placing the corner and end cabinets and then filling in between, as is done with the base units.

10. FINAL ELECTRICAL CONNECTIONS

You are now ready to make the final wiring installations and connections. From the planning stage through the removal operation to re-wiring, it has been necessary to understand the nature of electrical power as well as the fundamentals of wiring and the functions of various devices.

It's a good idea to keep in mind that an electrical system is very much like a pressure water system in that electricity flows from the power lines through the meter and into the switch at the entrance to your home. From this point the electricity is distributed as needed to various circuits, and to lighting fixtures and appliances.

Here's a good place to be reminded of the importance of safety:
- Turn off power in the circuit you plan to work on.
- Test wires in a box with a voltage tester to be certain the power really is off.
- Never stand on a damp or wet floor when working with wiring.
- Do not touch parts of gas piping or plumbing system when working with electricity or while using an electrical appliance.
- Before working on a lamp or appliance, be sure to unplug it.
- Check your work after you are done.

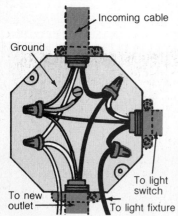

Taking power from a ceiling box.

First, take the light fixture out of a ceiling box and check the wiring. If there is only one cable, do not use the box as a source for power. If you see two or more cables coming into the box, as in the illustration here, connect the black wire of the new cable (dotted lines) with the black wire of the cable that is coming in; the white wire should be connected to the other neutral wires; and the bare wire is connected to the other ground wires.

Dishwasher and garbage disposal circuits. Run a single three-conductor cable, wired for 240 volts, from the service panel to a junction box in the kitchen. Connect the black wire coming from the service panel to the white wire of the switch cable. Either tape or paint both ends of the white wire black so that it is marked as a voltage-carrying conductor. Connect the black wire of the disposal cable to the black wire of the switch cable. Connect the black wire of the dishwasher cable to the red wire of the service-panel cable. Then fasten the three remaining white wires with a wire nut, and connect all the bare ground wires to each other and to the junction box. Finish the connections at the switch and the appliances, then cover the junction box with a cover plate which you can screw on.

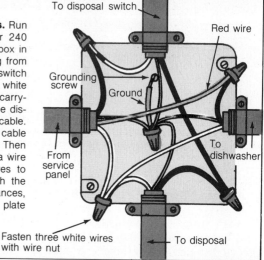

An electric range operates on 240 volts at high heat and 120 volts at low heat. It therefore requires a separate 3-wire No. 6 cable run from a 50-ampere circuit in the main entrance box to a heavy-duty wall receptacle. Check with your power company for the type of wire specified by the local code. In a good many cases, service entrance cable is used and the uninsulated wire is connected to the neutral terminal on the range receptacle.

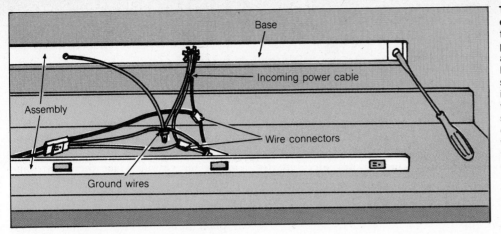

Base

Incoming power cable

Assembly

Wire connectors

Ground wires

To install a surface-mounted receptacle strip, run a two-conductor, No. 12 cable from the service panel to a spot about 8 inches above countertop. Clamp cable to knockout in base of multioutlet assembly; screw base to wall. Near incoming power cable, cut black, white, green wires of assembly; strip ½ inch of insulation from each. Join incoming black and white wires to matching assembly wires; use pressure-type wire connectors. The code forbids using these connectors for ground wires. Join the two green assembly wires, the bare cable wire, and a short grounding jumper wire; use crimp-type connector or wire nut. Fasten other end of jumper wire to assembly base with a grounding screw.

Hanging a new ceiling fixture

You may just want to exchange one simple incandescent fixture for another. Here's what to do. Turn off the power at the entry box, either by removing the fuse, or by throwing the circuit breaker. Then follow the steps as shown here.

What it takes

Approximate time: Depends upon the particular job; but allow sufficient time so you never have to hurry. From an hour to a day

Tools and materials: Hammer, ⅝-inch drill and bit, keyhole saw, hacksaw, test light, level, folding rule (6-foot), wire cutter, stripper, chisel, electrician tape, jack knife, screwdriver; fixtures and accompanying hardware.

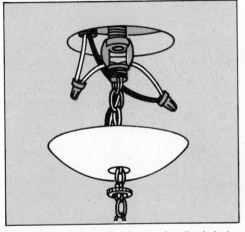

1. Remove the plate that is covering the hole in the ceiling.

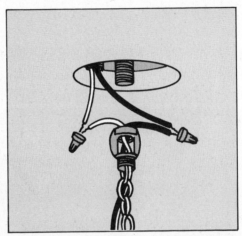

2. Disconnect the existing fixture. Note carefully how it is wired. Is there anything other than a white and a black wire coming out of the ceiling? If so, how is it hooked up?

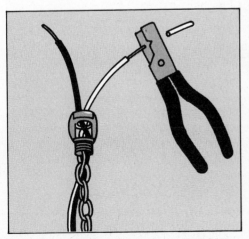

3. Peel back about an inch of insulation from the wires on the new fixture.

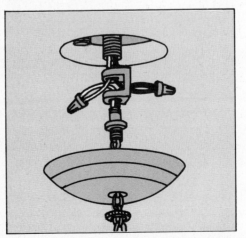

4. Connect the wires from the ceiling box to the wires from the new fixture with wire nuts—white to white and black wire to black—unless you observe some different wiring arrangement. Put the new canopy in place and turn the power on.

Fluorescents in kitchens

It makes sense to replace incandescent fixtures with fluorescent ones when you renovate, so long as they will not be turned on and off frequently.

Installation is easy. The channels of fluorescent fixtures have a number of knockouts; you can use any one for mounting. Take off the channel cover, tap the knockout with a hammer to break it free, then twist the knockout off with a pair of pliers.

Mount the fluorescent by placing the knockout over a threaded nipple and securing the fixture with a washer and locknut. Note that you can add a strap-mounted nipple to wall outlets, or a hickey and nipple to ceiling boxes that don't have nipples.

Run the black and white fluorescent power wires through the nipple and join them to the source-cable conductors with solderless connectors. The connections will be white to white, and black to black.

In large fixtures there is a mounting cutout. In order to mount these fixtures, place a metal strap inside the channel, across the cutout. Place the fixture and strap over the nipple. Hold the strap and fixture to the ceiling with a locknut.

Circular fluorescent fixtures are good replacements for the regular kitchen ceiling fixtures. With solderless connectors, connect the fluorescent fixture wires to the power wires in the box; black to black and white to white. If necessary, use a reducing nut or hickey to install a nipple long enough to project through the fixture. Fold the wires into the fixture canopy and secure to the ceiling by tightening the cap nut on the nipple.

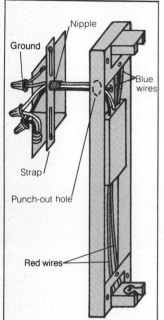

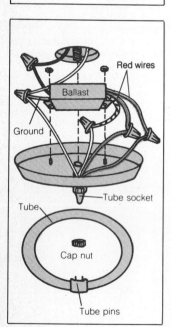

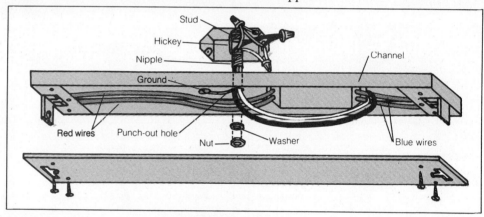

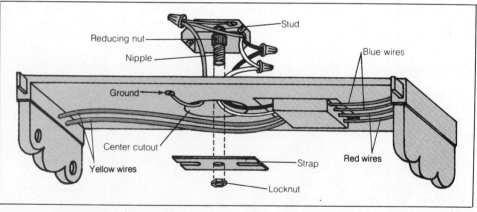

Fluorescents in bathrooms

Fluorescent lights in the bathroom are popular when it comes to putting on makeup, shaving, and so on. The fixtures can be mounted above, or on either side of bathroom cabinets.

As a rule, bathroom cabinets are recessed into the walls between studs, to which they are secured with wood screws. Sometimes they are on the outside edge of the studs. To remove the cabinet, just take out the screws on either side and lift the cabinet from the wall opening.

The opening offers easy entry to electrical connections on the interior wall. If you had an old incandescent fixture near the cabinet, the new fluorescent can be wired to the same box. Again, it is black to black and white to white.

If you find that you will need a new circuit for the fluorescent lights, install a junction box in the wall stud in back of the cabinet.

Power for a junction box is obtained by running a cable to an existing wall or ceiling box. Connect the leads from the fluorescent fixtures to the power cable in the junction box with solderless connectors.

Caution: Many local codes now require that GFIs (ground fault interrupters) be installed on bathroom circuits. If there already is a GFI on the bathroom

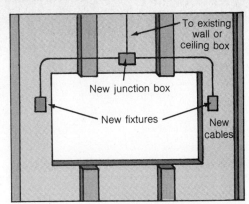

circuit in your home, be certain that you make the power connection for the junction box to a wall or ceiling box on the GFI-protected circuit. Remember that you must turn off power to the existing wall or ceiling box before you connect the new cable. Make sure that when the bathroom-circuit GFI is turned off, power is off in the box you are using for the new circuit.

Wiring cabinet lights

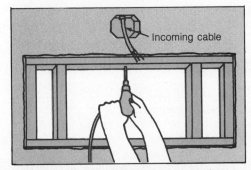

To prepare for the wiring, bring a cable from a nearby outlet box; but after you have first turned off the circuit. If there is a 2x4 header in the opening, drill a ½-inch hole through it to conform to the wiring access hole in the top of the cabinet. Lead the cable through the header hole.

To make the connections, place the bottom edge of the cabinet on the sill and draw the cable end through the opening in the top of the cabinet and into the wiring compartment. Anchor the cable with the cable clamp on the cabinet top. Fix the cabinet securely to the studs inside the opening. Using a wire nut, connect the cable's ground wire to a green wire from the cabinet. If there isn't any green wire, then connect the ground wire to a green grounding screw. Now connect the white wires from the cabinet and from the cable with a wire nut. Connect the black cabinet wire (it is sometimes red) to the black cable wire.

Installing a GFI

Wire leads instead of screw terminals are a feature of the GFI; and it is connected like an ordinary receptacle, with one big difference. The feed cable coming from the service panel must be joined to the leads marked "line," and the outgoing cable that leads to the rest of the circuit has to be hooked to the leads that are marked "load." If the GFI receptacle is the only fixture on the circuit, then connect the "line" leads in the usual way, but be sure to cap each of the "load" leads and fold them into the box. Use a wire nut for capping.

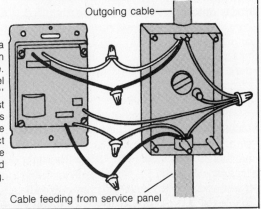

GLAMOUR BATH

After

Before

Compare this old bathroom with the way it looks above, after remodeling. Formerly, as you can see, unattractive fixtures crowded the room, while the walls and window were tacky, to say the least. On top of that, some of the pipes leaked. It was generally unattractive, and functioned poorly.

Remodeling your bathroom can also mean enlarging it. This project complete with sunken bathtub—is an example of what can be done to make your home not only practical and beautiful, but luxurious as well.

The existing bathroom and adjoining bedroom were in an old farmhouse that had been allowed to become badly run down. By adding an extension on both bathroom and bedroom, the homeowners ended up with a much larger and more practical bathroom, as well as a master bedroom which connected to it directly.

The new portion of the bathroom features a sunken tub, natural stone for one complete wall, and mirror tile on the wall opposite the stone. A glass patio door opens onto a small sun deck surrounded by a stone wall—a second project you may or may not wish to tackle later on.

The old bathroom was narrow and dark, and the old tub took up a great deal of space. The old-style lavatory offered no storage space for bath items.

The original section of the room was remodeled to include a new 6-foot vanity with lots of storage area. The 9-foot ceiling height was kept, but the sides were "cambered" so that it would appear to be lower and would blend with the low ceiling in the new section. A new chandelier

also contributed to this effect. Ceramic tile, vinyl wallpaper, and an antique mirror set off by wall sconces completed the remodeling.

The trim wood for the bathroom was done in rough-sawn white cedar to match the trim of the rest of the house. The ceiling in the new added-on portion of the bathroom was 7½ feet, just enough to allow clearance for the sliding patio door and provide plenty of header support for the new roof. Lights were recessed into the ceiling in order to show off the wall, and a heat-light-fan combination unit was installed near the tub. Instead of running new duct work out to the bathroom, an electric baseboard floor heater was installed.

First step was to lay out the room addition. The complete size of the addition was 12x18 feet, which added 10′x6′8″ to the bathroom and 10x12 feet to the bedroom. The walls took up some floor space, which accounted for the difference in dimensions. This didn't include the outer rock wall or the deck.

Once the dimensions were laid out and stakes positioned to mark the outside of the walls, a back-hoe operator was called in to dig the footing trenches. The trench for the rock wall footing was 24 inches wide and 24 inches deep. The footing trench for the rest of the construction was 24 inches wide and 18 inches deep. From here on, you could follow the same steps as the couple who built the addition.

With the footing trench dug, your next step would be to figure the amount of concrete needed to fill the trench and to order it from a ready-mix concrete firm. Normally, if you give the concrete people the dimensions of the work, they can come pretty close to the amount; however, allow for a little extra because most companies will bring a bit more than you order to insure there being enough. It's a good idea to have a small project ready for a bit of concrete in case there is some left over.

Using a trowel, smooth the footing to provide a level working surface for both the stone wall and the concrete block foundation. Allow the footing to cure for a couple of days. While it is curing you can tear off the old siding from the wall where the addition will join the building.

If the building is also covered with some sort of sheathing, cut along the inside wall dimension of the addition to remove it. At the same time, cut 6 to 8 inches above the ceiling line, or where doors or archways will enter the addition, or around any areas where walls will be removed to join the old and the new sections. This provides for header supports.

After the footing has cured, you can start laying the concrete block foundation and the rock wall. It is necessary to exercise extra care in figuring the top of the concrete foundation footing so that the concrete blocks will come out at the right height, allowing you to join to the old portion of the building properly. And so, take care that the blocks are the same height as the foundation of the old building. Remember that a concrete block normally is 8 inches high (including a ⅜-inch mortar joint), and to this height must be added the joists, subfloor, and underlayment or finished floor. If the top of the foundation of the existing house is visible, it can be used to determine the proper height of the new foundation. It then is a case of measuring down to determine where the top of the footing should be located.

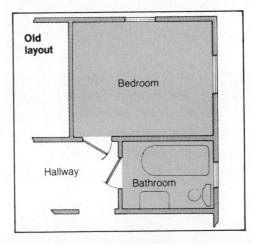

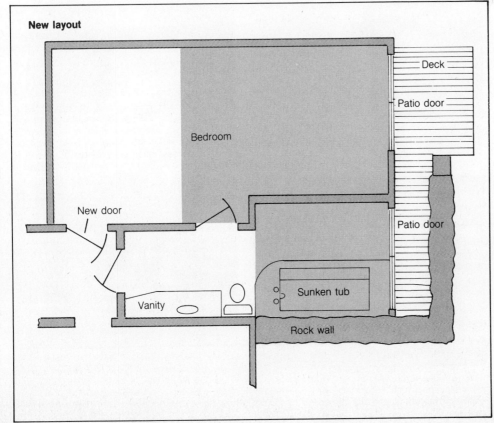

The important thing in your new layout is to avoid major plumbing work. Plan your new fixtures so that they fall within the same area as those they are replacing. This saves time and money.

Stone wall

A lot of money was saved on this project by using stone that was picked up in nearby fields. At the same time, you may not be so fortunate; you may have to buy stone. You can check local quarries to see what is available and at what cost.

Of course, you may decide simply to put up a regular stud wall with siding on the outside. Wallboard could be applied and taped inside, then covered with one of the several realistic imitation brick or

stone materials; or you could put up one of the many types of wall paneling.

If you do decide on a stone wall, however, you will find that some of the best insulation you can get is provided by sandstone, soapstone, and even flintrock and marble; that is, you can save on heating as well as cooling cost.

Laying a stone wall such as this one is both difficult and easy. The hard part is the labor. The easy part is the skill. It

What it takes

Approximate time: Depends on the weather, and if you have help; but allow a few weekends or a week if you're working by yourself, and are handy.

Tools and materials: Regular carpentry and masonry tools, plus shovel, wheel barrow, lumber for forms, mortar mix, metal reinforcing rods; finished lumber and regular building materials as needed.

Planning hints: Give plenty of time to planning your work, taking into account the weather, and the needs of members of the family. Be sure about the delivery dates of your materials; check that your order has been filled and that everything you will need is at hand *before* you start to work.

Mixing mortar

There are a number of good mixes. One of the best is as follows:
1 part portland cement
1 part lime
6 parts sand
Enough water to make the mixture smooth and creamy, yet allow it to stand up easily when placed in position.

The wall for the room addition was built from stone that was picked up around the property. The alternative would have been a regular stud wall.

The secret of a sound stone wall is the correct mortar mix. It should be troweled on heavily to fill every irregularity in the stones.

After the mortar is applied, place the stone and force it well into place, allowing the excess to squeeze out. Clean off, and smooth the joints.

Know where you will place a stone before you lift it. Don't rely wholly on the mortar to make the fit, but select stones as much as possible according to contour.

The two sides of the wall run parallel and the space between should be kept even with fill—broken rocks and mortar—as the sides go up.

While the stone wall is being constructed, floor framing for the room addition can be built on the foundation of concrete block, if you have help.

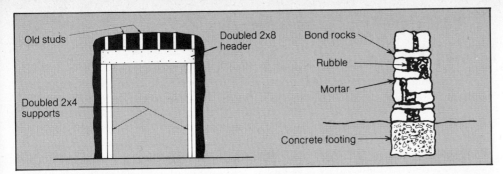

Old studs

Doubled 2x8 header

Doubled 2x4 supports

Bond rocks

Rubble

Mortar

Concrete footing

doesn't take long to learn how to find the right rock, flip mortar into place, position the rock, and then go on to the next one; but it does take some physical effort.

One of the secrets of good rock work is to mix the proper mortar. (See column at left.) Actually, the wall is two parallel walls constructed with rubble and mortar and cross-tie rocks between, as well as metal reinforcing rods.

The foundation wall of concrete block for the room addition had the top course of blocks plugged with mortar in which anchor bolts were set. The sill plate of the wall then was drilled to fit over the bolts. The anchor bolts should be about 4 to 6 feet apart, and high enough to allow you to fasten the sill plate securely in place.

Opening the wall. It was necessary to open the wall of the existing house in order to join the new addition. This operation took place in stages: first the siding was cut and removed, and then the sheathing was cut, but it was not removed until the addi-

tion had been framed and then closed in.

The opening was cut sufficiently high to allow for headers that were needed to support the wall and roof. For a span 10 feet or more, use floor jacks or shores to hold up the ceiling until the doubled 2x4 vertical supports and the doubled 2x6s, 2x8s, or 2x10s are installed for headers.

Tying in. The roof of the new structure can be tied to the roof of the existing house by first nailing a strip to the roof on which the new roof structure has been spiked. You must be sure to replace any broken or loosened shingles and install a metal or tarpaper valley at the intersection of the roofs.

The room can then be closed in, and a sliding glass door, with double-pane insulating glass, installed in the rough opening that may be sized according to the instructions that come with the door. It could take about an hour to fit the door into place, and it will be heavy enough to need at least one helper.

Bearing up under pressure

There's nothing to taking out a non-bearing partition. Removing a structural wall that's holding the house up is not an impossible job either, even for me. The problem is to find out *which* kind of wall it is before you start. All outside walls are usually bearing weight. So is an inside wall that runs down the middle of the length of the house. It usually is keeping the joists (that support the floor above) from bending or breaking in the middle. If you can't tell from the attic, cut a peep-hole in the ceiling right up against the wall. If you see a joist crossing over the wall, it's bearing. You have work on your hands—but not more than 14-feet-worth since you shouldn't remove more of a bearing wall than that anyway.

Practical Pete

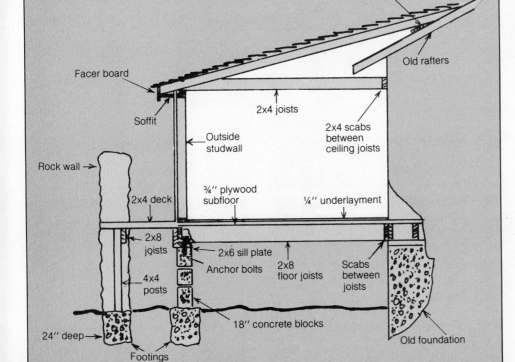

1x2 support

Old rafters

Facer board

2x4 joists

2x4 scabs between ceiling joists

Soffit

Outside studwall

Rock wall →

2x4 deck

¾" plywood subfloor

¼" underlayment

2x8 joists

2x6 sill plate

Anchor bolts

2x8 floor joists

Scabs between joists

4x4 posts

24" deep

18" concrete blocks

Footings

Old foundation

A sunken bathtub

What it takes

Approximate time: Allow 3 days, and try to have a helper.

Tools and materials: Hammer, power saw, electric drill and bits (including carbide-tipped bit), tile or glass cutter, tile nippers or pliers, screwdriver; lumber for forms, nails, screws, lag screws, anchors, mesh, sandpaper, concrete mix, shovel, trowel, caulking, grout, ceramic tile, alcohol and clean cloths; plumbing fixtures as required.

If your existing bathtub is in good condition you can install it in one of several ways to give it a "sunken" look. It can actually be recessed into the floor to project down into a basement or crawl space.

Another way to install a sunken tub would be to build a platform of 2x4s and plywood up around the existing tub, perhaps with steps; then cover it with tile.

Still one other way would be to partly recess the tub in the floor, with just a shallow platform built up around it. The method of installation would be determined by your personal preference, structural considerations, and the amount of time and money you want to spend on this particular part of the project.

The bathtub shown here is more like a swimming pool than the conventional sunken tub. However, construction is standard and will meet most building codes. If you decide to build a similar tub, check with your local code authorities to be sure you meet the requirements. One requirement, for instance, might be a waterproof membrane between the tub and the footing beneath.

The concrete tank shown here followed the detail of Fig. C.

Keep in mind that the tub was built in a room over a crawl space, which allowed it to rest on the ground.

First, a concrete footing was poured, 2 feet deep, and slightly larger than the dimensions of the tub. Because of the weight of the tub it would not be practical to set it over a basement or first floor.

With the footing poured you can start to assemble a form of 2-inch lumber. This can be built over the footing and is designed to create a wall 4 inches thick, and a bottom also 4 inches thick.

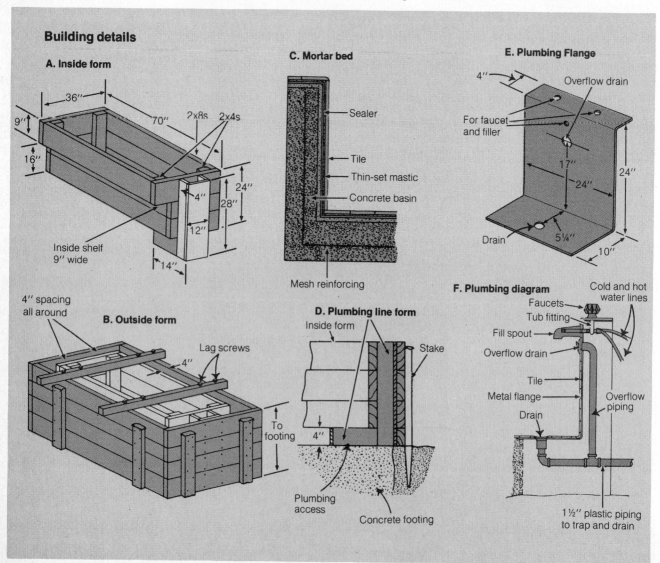

Building details

A. Inside form

C. Mortar bed

E. Plumbing Flange

B. Outside form

D. Plumbing line form

F. Plumbing diagram

The inside form may be built as shown in Fig. A. The vertical and horizontal portions of the plumbing access form can be made from ¾-inch plywood, and centered on one end of the inside form.

The outside form was built of 2-inch lumber and made 4 inches higher than the inside form. Lengths of 2x4 were sharpened on one end and driven into the soil, then spiked to the form to brace and hold it.

The inside form can then be lowered into the outside form and positioned so that there is 4 inches of clearance all the way around. Lengths of 2x2 lumber are then lag-screwed to the inside form to support it 4 inches above the outside form at the bottom. The 2x2s are also lag-screwed to the outside form so the inside form will remain in position.

For further reinforcement, a 2x4 can be spiked across each end of the inside form and the outside form. Do not use metal ties, as you would between forms used for concrete basement walls, because of the potential for water leaks.

Pour the bottom of the tub just 2 inches deep, then position reinforcing mesh the full length and width, then pour 2 more inches of concrete and compact it. The bottom, of course, extends under the sides and ends (and step), except for the L-shape form in which the plumbing later will be installed.

Trowel the exposed portion of the bottom smooth, then pour the step and trowel it. The walls are last, and they are reinforced with mesh and concrete tamped and compacted. After the concrete has set for a while (firm yet still workable) the tops of the walls are troweled smooth.

The concrete mix used here was 1 part cement, 2 sand, 3 parts pea-size gravel, water for a stiff mix.

After the concrete has seasoned for at least a week—kept damp during that time—remove the forms carefully. Any rough spots may be filled with latex patching plaster.

A sunken tub can be made any desired size. This one allows a depth of water up to 16 inches. The step was cast into the tub to make entry and exit easier. Because of the added depth, be sure to have firmly attached handholds or rails. The step and the area around the tub should have nonslip tub pads applied.

A drain must be built into the tub bottom, but the faucets and supply spout can be above and separate from the concrete form. You can locate your plumbing in an opening cast into the end of the tub. (See Fig. F). The opening can then be closed by a shaped piece of metal, as shown in Fig. E.

After the metal piece has been installed, the inside of the concrete tank may be sealed with four coats of a special sealer. In this case, "Thoroseal" was used. Check your hardware dealer. When each coat has dried, it should be sanded before the next coat is applied.

Tile mastic for use on masonry surfaces that will be submerged in water is different from mastic used for surfaces such as in a tub or shower enclosure "Thin-set" mastic is sold at most tile and flooring stores, and is mixed like plaster. The mastic is quite viscous and sticky, and is applied in a coat ⅛ to ¼ inch thick. This thickness will permit adjusting any irregularities that might appear in the concrete.

The ceramic tiles which were used come in sheets 1 foot square, with each tile 4 inches square. The tiles are pre-grouted with silicone rubber, and grouting then is required only between sheets, and tiles that have to be cut.

The grout comes in cartridges that fit standard caulking guns, and excess caulk is easily removed with alcohol and a soft cloth.

After the tiles are applied, the mastic must be allowed to set for 24 hours before the grout is applied. Any mastic that squeezes out between the tiles can be removed with a damp cloth.

With the tub finished, you can then complete the floor of the bathroom, possibly using the same tile that was used for the tub.

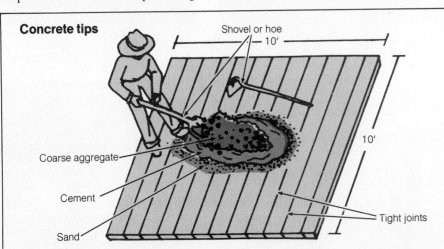

Concrete tips

Shovel or hoe — 10'

10'

Coarse aggregate

Cement

Sand

Tight joints

For this project you will not be mixing a large amount of mortar, and so you will probably be mixing by hand. You will need a clean surface. This could be a wooden platform, or a mortar box, which will have sides to it. The platform or box should have tight joints to prevent loss of mortar. And it should be level.

The desired quantity of sand is placed on the bottom and the cement is spread on the sand, and on top of this the coarse aggregate. To mix the materials—the dry first—you may use either a hoe or a square shovel with a D handle.

Turn the dry materials at least three times, or until the color of the mixture is uniform. Water is added slowly while the mixture is again turned at least three times. Add water gradually until you get the consistency you want.

Step by step

1. The first step in building a sunken tub, such as this one, is to construct a strong form. The outside edges of the inner form are the rough dimensions of the tub.

2. The bottom of the tub is poured, and it must be tamped solidly. The bottom is poured over a footing of concrete 2 feet deep, which sets before building the form.

3. The sides of the tub are poured next. It is important to tamp the mix thoroughly in order to remove all voids and to assure a continuous wall. Take time with this.

4. An opening should be formed in one end of the tub for fixtures. A metal plate was bent to shape, and then holes were drilled to accept the faucets and spout.

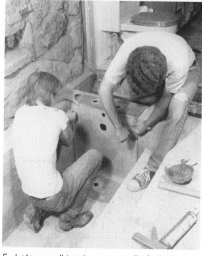

5. Latex caulking is now applied, the metal attached with screws driven into anchors set in holes that have been carefully drilled into the concrete.

6. The entire surface of the tub is then given several coats of mortar, sealer; and this includes the metal piece. This will provide a smooth surface for the tile.

7. Four coats of the special sealer were applied to the inside of the tub. Each coat was thoroughly sanded when it was dry. This takes time and care, but it's necessary.

8. After this, the tub was cleaned of debris, and vacuumed to get the dust out; then a thin-set mortar was mixed and applied with a trowel, over small areas at a time.

9. Tile mastic which is thin-set like this, is applied in a coat ⅛ to ¼ inch thick. This thickness also allows you to even out any irregularities in the concrete.

10. Sheets of tile are now pressed into the mortar, tapped smooth and flush with other sheets. Note the tile scraps; these are handy for spacing the tile.

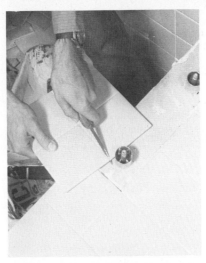

11. Cut individual tiles free from the backing with a knife along the grout lines that are between the tiles. The tiles are 4x4 inches and come in sheets 1 foot square.

12. If you need to cut an individual tile, and you will probably have to for fitting, use a glass cutter or a tile cutter. Just score along the line as for window glass.

13. Place the tile with the scored line directly over a wire, then step on either side and break the tile along the line. It should break easily and cleanly.

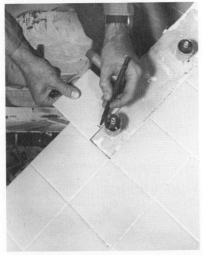

14. To fit tile around plumbing trim, you will first have to mark it with a grease pencil, allowing some clearance that will be covered by the trim.

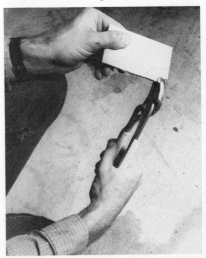

15. Some sizing of the tiles can be done by breaking away small pieces with a pliers. The water-pump type provides more leverage for this careful operation.

16. The best way to cut a hole in a tile is by drilling a ring of holes with a carbide-tip masonry bit in a power drill. Afterwards, file the rough edge smooth.

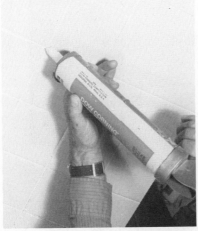

17. The tiles used here were pre-grouted with silicone rubber, and grouting then was only required between sheets and tiles that were cut. Mastic must set for 24 hours.

18. The way to clean up excess grout from the tiles is with alcohol and a soft, clean cloth. You can use the same tile for the floor of the bathroom as you did for the tub.

Vanity construction

What it takes

Approximate time: A day for construction; at least an afternoon for installation.

Tools and materials: Power saw, pipe wrench, level, saber saw, screwdriver, file, punch, hammer, plane, trouble-light, electric drill and bits, sandpaper, screws, nails and hardware, patching compound, caulk, lumber, sink, and plumbing accessories.

The design shown in the drawing is a typical construction for an extended-cabinet vanity. Your first steps should be to decide upon the exact location of your unit. Take measurements to determine the precise amount of space available, and then establish a design.

It is necessary to decide in advance on the height of the vanity; and this will be based upon the personal preferences of those who will use the room most frequently. If children and adults are likely to share the bathroom, consider the possibility of a two-level, stepped-top setup with separate sinks installed at each level.

Mark out and cut the bottom, side, divider, back and frame pieces, then build the basic framework for your vanity, and install the bottom. Cut and fit the top, add laminate and trim the edges. Follow the drawing on this page.

Remember that it is important to avoid conflict with existing electrical, plumbing, heating, or structural elements. In order that no water or drain pipes would need to be moved the vanity should be designed so that the new basin will fall at roughly the same location as the old sink.

Sink detail

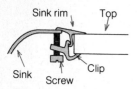

Plumbing details

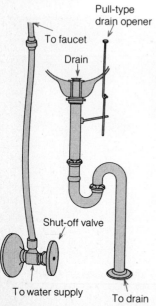

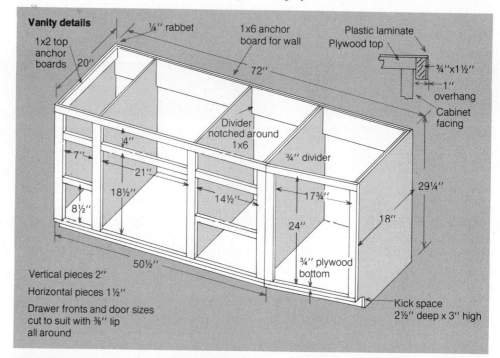

Vanity details

¼" rabbet · 1x2 top anchor boards · 20" · 1x6 anchor board for wall · 72" · Plastic laminate · Plywood top · ¾"x1½" · 1" overhang · Cabinet facing · Divider notched around 1x6 · 4" · 7" · ¾" divider · 21" · 18½" · 14½" · 17¾" · 29¼" · 8½" · 24" · 18" · ¾" plywood bottom · 50½" · Kick space 2½" deep x 3" high

Vertical pieces 2"

Horizontal pieces 1½"

Drawer fronts and door sizes cut to suit with ⅜" lip all around

Installation

1. Before you do anything else, shut the water off below the floor level. Then bleed and disconnect the hot and cold water lines. Disconnect the drain.

2. To remove the old wall-hung sink, lift up on the front edge and then lift the entire unit straight up and away from the wall. You may need a helper.

3. Next, remove the wall-mounting strip and all associated hardware; as well as any other projections. Remove electrical fixtures, reroute wiring. Fill holes, smooth the wall.

4. After the wall has been cleared and smoothed, place the vanity in position and level it. Make sure that it fits well against the wall, or walls. Use shingles or shims to level.

5. You may have to make a slight adjustment with certain pipes that project upward through the bottom of the cabinet. Best way to work here is with a trouble-light.

6. Now secure the vanity to the wall by driving nails, or large screws, through the cabinet into the studs behind the wall. Make sure that the vanity remains level.

7. Place lower part of new sink rim on vanity top, mark around lower part of rim, and then cut the sink opening with a saber saw; work slowly inside the line.

8. Punch out the holes for the clip-holding screws. Smooth with a file so that the screws will fit securely. Tighten screws no more than necessary; don't strip heads.

9. Now apply a bead of caulk to the sink rim. Don't try to scrimp here; use a quality product, because you will want years of watertight, troublefree service.

10. Place the sink and the trim ring in position, making sure they are properly aligned. Tighten the clips under the top to secure the sink in place.

11. Install the new faucets, connect the water and drain lines under the basin; and finally, clean off the caulk that was forced out around the metal trim ring.

After: A handsome marble-topped vanity provides hidden storage and requires no more floor space than the old steel legged sink.

Before: Neat and serviceable enough but a bit outdated. And not a single place to put bathroom cleaners or oversized toilet articles without tripping over them.

A bathroom renovation should be both functional and decorative. A full bath must be designed to include at the very least three major fixtures: sink, toilet, and shower or tub/shower combination. Maximum use of walls and floor for storage is crucial. These surfaces must additionally be water resistant and easy to clean. The range of decorative possibilities, beginning with color coordination of fixtures, goes on into almost limitless choices for mirrors, hardware, shower curtains, wall-covering, shelves, light fixtures, towel racks, bath mats, linens, soap dishes, etc.

The vanity and toilet shelf

The main reason for this renovation was to increase stowaway storage. Building a vanity below the sink was an obvious choice. The plastic laminate cabinet has double doors and a handy track-sliding drawer. No need to dodge sink pipes in

If your bath, as is frequently the case, has no window, you will want to make sure that a sturdy vented fan is in the plans. Shelf and storage space becomes increasingly important, as do electrical outlets, if you plan to use one or more of the electrical bathroom appliances available, including electric shavers, hair driers, heated rollers, and the electric toothbrush. This list of considerations becomes almost bewildering when the dimensions of an average bathroom are figured in. That's a lot of utility and style to arrange in a 5x8 room, no doubt the smallest in the house.

search of cleaning equipment.

The laminate is easy to maintain and plenty sturdy enough to support the molded marble sink unit above. A one-piece sink/counter is guaranteed to make cleaning easy.

A second narrower unit of molded marble extends from the edge of the sink over the toilet bowl to the wall. That's a handy resting place for any electrical appliances or toilet articles you'll be using. The join between sink and shelf units is plastered, then grouted, as is the wall/shelf join. To make tank repairs, the shelf unit can be removed, then replastered and grouted.

When installing a lighter weight counter, plastic laminate for instance, this section can be hinged to facilitate tank repairs.

The low backsplash is cast like a flange on each of the two counter sections and grouted across the top.

The overall effect of this marble topped vanity is one of elegant simplicity, easy on the eye and practical too.

The vanity and shelf unit looks like a single piece, and almost is.

The convenient roll-out shelf.

Updating—style and convenience

As is so often the case, renovating a single unit in this bath inspired additional touches. The toilet as a fixture was sound, but a colorful vinyl-covered foam rubber toilet seat was added, an improvement in appearance and comfort. A hand-held hygienic spray attachment makes a good shower better. The substitution of a light colored shower curtain gives the tiny room a brighter feeling. Flowered wallpaper on just two walls serves the same function, cheerful but not overwhelming.

TIP: To make a large bathroom cosier, use the opposite technique. A small print vinyl or treated paper on all available wall space and across the ceiling can really draw a room together.

A wall-mounted vanity shelf in tortoise plastic is handy for small items. The shelf is screwed to the wall. A matching trash basket and tissue holder complete this attractive accessory trio.

Handy over-sized plastic hooks on the back wall of the shower hold face cloths and rope soap conveniently. They are simple to mount, just peel off the protective paper over the self-adhesive and position on clean, dry tile.

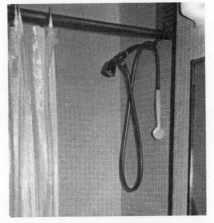

The hand-held hygienic spray loops over the shower head when not in use.

Vanity shelf and flowered vinyl wallcover—designer touches.

Handy shower hangups.

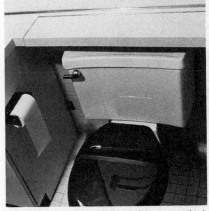

A hinged laminate toilet shelf is a practical alternative.

The careful remodeling that produced this attractive result was designed to give a visually open effect, to increase the usable traffic area, and to add counter and storage space. The major changes involved removing the wall between the old kitchen and the larger dining-working area, and breaking through their low ceilings to the roof rafters above.

This kitchen renovation is designed to take advantage of open space, with emphasis on sharp lines and planes and a contrast of surfaces.

The unique aspect is the kitchen's location—on the top floor of a three-story townhouse. Built in the 1830s, the original structure was made of brick with wood support beams. Walls were plaster over lath that had been bound with plaster and horsehair. Later, the large original rooms were partitioned, using gypsum wallboard over studs, and the house was divided horizontally into two apartments. The upstairs kitchen was probably built at that time, with existing plumbing lines dictating the placement of the 2x5-foot 1920s porcelain sink. The modern stove and refrigerator would stay, but the cumbersome sink would have to be replaced.

Electricity had been installed by stapling wires along the baseboards and around the doors. Multiple extensions lay buried in enamel paint. New wiring for outlets and soffits to hide the cables would be required.

General Planning. The original kitchen layout, with a closet, stove, refrigerator, and oversized sink, limited workable floor space to less than 50 square feet—and no counter space! The central hall next to the kitchen was useful for transit only, with five doors and no windows. Through the trap door in another room, a good look at the attic above this area revealed a roof which continued over 4 feet above the ceiling.

Inspection showed that the two walls which separated the central hall from the kitchen and stairs could be taken out without affecting the building structure. With these walls removed, the new east wall would rise over 12 feet to the roof peak—perfect for a dramatic pine board cathedral ceiling. By opening the kitchen this way and cutting back the dormer storage closet, floor space would be more than doubled.

Removing the center room ceiling would expose the attic space above the small work room behind the hall. How best to employ this high sloped space? It would hardly be convenient as a pantry. The logical solution: a loft.

Designing the new kitchen. Ingenuity was required to turn the dormer area into useful space. Cutting back the storage closet would make space for the refrigerator. Repositioning the closet door would make it more convenient. Floor space under the other eave could be filled with useful counter space—a simple plywood surface supported by wood and finished with plastic laminate.

L-shaped floor cabinets (in the area where the wall had been) would define the cooking area and create work and storage space. The new sink, installed catercorner, could connect to existing plumbing.

Before final plans were made on the cabinets, a mock-up was built of wood scraps. The sink was put into place, to be sure there would be enough room for a splash back and to measure for the angle of the corner. The counter was specifically sized to accommodate the 6x6x½-inch terra-cotta tiles.

Other considerations. There is a dazzling variety of materials available for finishing surfaces. It takes some time to explore the possibilities, but it pays off when you use the best materials to fit the design at a price that sounds right.

When you sum up the cost of materials, it's important to consider durability, waste, error, and the time needed for installation. Don't forget those gallons of paint you may need! And don't cheat. Although you may want to keep costs down, be prepared to spend your entire budget—and maybe then some. The materials used to renovate this townhouse kitchen cost $1,600 in 1978.

A showplace kitchen requires not only quality materials, but skilled labor as well. How much can you do yourself? Will you need an electrician, plumber, carpenter, or floor expert? Professional renovators may be the best investment for you. They have a variety of skills and are familiar with re-building. For this project, it took three renovators a total of 720 hours from the first blow of the sledgehammer to the last lighting fixture—total labor cost: $6,000.

The following pages illustrate the special problems and solutions in this townhouse kitchen, with specific tips and on-the-spot photographs to show you the way to do it yourself.

Floor plans

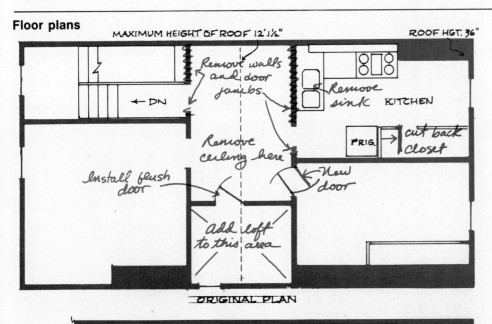

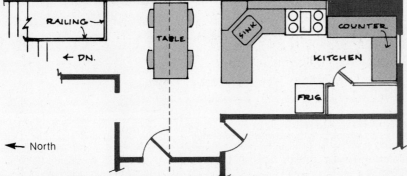

The original kitchen was 9½'x12½', but the sloping dormer cut heavily into usable floor space. The room next to the kitchen was a windowless 8'x12' box. Removing its north and south walls and ceiling created an additional 1400 cubic feet of usable space.

Material specifications

Terra-cotta tile: Carlyle Quarry Tile 6x6x½". "Navajo" Structural Stoneware Inc.;
Floor: Vinylcraft II "Yuma Clay" 12x12x⅛";
Lifetime stainless steel sink Model No. 2522. Consumer Products Corp., 1809 Bartlett Rd., Memphis Tenn.;
Walls: 5" tongue and groove pine.

Removing the ceiling and wall

What it takes

Approximate time: At least 2-3 days, depending on how much is to be demolished.

Tools and materials: Straight bar, ripping bar, 20-ounce claw hammer, 8 pound long-handled sledgehammer (or a 2 pound short-handled sledgehammer), dust mask and filters, gloves, goggles, boxes to collect rubble, plastic sheet, and tape.

Removing a ceiling or wall is a major task requiring a lot of careful planning and a good deal of energy. You should be prepared to form your own demolition team and to take precautions to protect yourself and your home from a tremendous amount of dust.

The first step is to plan the cleanup. How will you get rid of debris? Collect enough boxes to hold chunks of broken wallboard, plaster, and lathing. You may need a truck or van to haul the debris to the dump, or you can hire a metal dumpster as used on construction sites.

Before you begin, find out where electrical, gas, and plumbing lines are and turn them off. Be careful not to damage the lines when you're working. You may have to use an extension cord to an outlet in another room to supply temporary power.

Close all doors to block the dust and cover exposed archways or open doorways with sheets of plastic, taped or tacked at the side. Put a portable fan at a window to blow the dust outdoors, or at least open all windows to ventilate the room. Be sure to wear gloves, goggles, and a dust mask to protect yourself from the dirt, and change the mask filters often.

If you're removing an entire ceiling, you'll find it easier to work in a team. One person pounds through the ceiling from the attic side with a sledgehammer; the other rips down the ceiling material from the underside with his hands. If there is no space above the ceiling, work from below using a ripping bar or straight bar and hammer. To separate the ceiling from the walls, perforate the corner bonds with the end of a straight bar hammered into the join.

A good way to crack a plaster wall is with a ripping bar. Hold the straight end, and take a long swing to whack the wall with the side of the hooked end. Once there's a large crack or hole, slip the hooked end in and pull the plaster down. But watch out! Half a wall of old plaster can come down at once. If you plan to remove only a part of a wall or if you're making a pass-through, you can use a circular saw for wallboard, or a power reciprocating saw to cut right through wallboard, plaster, and wood.

While working, always know where your partner is so no one gets hurt by falling debris. And when a large area of ceiling or wall has fallen, let the dust settle so you can see what you are doing. It's a good idea to clear away debris before it piles up, so you won't be stumbling over it.

1. "X" marks a spot where there is no ceiling joist. That's where to start a hole with the sledgehammer. Hold the head near the floor between your feet and swing upwards with both hands on the handle.

2. Place the end of the straight bar in the corner of the ceiling and side wall. Use a 20-ounce hammer to pound it into the corner, loosening old paint and wallboard. Continue to perforate the corners around the perimeter of the ceiling.

3. Both the ceiling and the wall have a layer of gypsum wallboard over plaster and lathing. You can rip down the wallboard with your hands. Use a crowbar or straight bar and hammer to pry the plaster loose.

4. Clear away the plasterboard and lathing to expose the wall studs or ceiling support beams. If there is attic space, pound the ceiling through with the sledgehammer from above. If not, work from below using a crowbar or straight bar and hammer.

Boxed in again

The wall I wanted to remove *would* be the one with all those plumbing pipes and electrical wiring running inside it from floor to ceiling. I knew it was going to be trouble because the upstairs bathroom was right over it, and there were a lot of outlets and switches in it. I was not about to start re-routing water pipes myself, but I wanted to get started on the partition right away, and the plumber couldn't come for a week. He came up with the answer on the phone. "Pete," he said, "go ahead and tear out most of the old wall now, patch everything up, even paint if you want to—but leave just enough of the end of the wall standing so you don't disturb the pipes. I'll get there next Saturday and move 'em. Then you'll just have that tag end to finish up Sunday."
Sometimes I wonder why that guy doesn't run for president.

Practical Pete

5. A claw hammer will pry the lathing loose. In older buildings such as this one, the wood is bonded with plaster and horsehair.

6. Once the ceiling has been removed, there may be a rough edge at the top of a good wall. Use a straight bar and hammer to chisel away the edge; work carefully to avoid damaging the wall.

7. A power reciprocating saw will chew right through beams and wallboard. Wear goggles and a dust mask for protection, and have a partner hold the wood steady.

8. Work around electrical cables and plumbing fixtures when you tear down a wall or ceiling. The foreground of this photograph is only a portion of the square feet of floor space added to the original kitchen (shown beyond wall studs).

Cathedral ceiling and walls

With the removal of the old ceiling, roof joints and beams were exposed. Because the building was inexpensively constructed originally, the joists didn't form a uniform angle along the roof ridge and there was no main ridge beam. A new ridge would be needed to create a uniform ceiling angle.

The roof angle was 30°. The main wall sloped from the kitchen dormer, less than three feet from the floor, to the roof peak, 12 feet high. This wall area would help create a stunning cathedral ceiling.

The east wall was plaster to the height of the former ceiling and exposed brick to the roof. Usually, old brick can be restored with new mortar and cleaned up with carbon tetrachloride. But for this room it was decided that a new wall would be built over the brick.

The new townhouse kitchen ceiling was finished with 1x4 knotty pine boards nailed to a plywood base at random lengths. Random planking is less expensive than an even length design because it uses all the lumber. Also, the joins are scattered throughout and don't form an obvious line. The join lines form interesting verticals in the horizontal planking, adding to the overall effect.

The walls were covered with 5-inch tongue and groove pine boards in a vertical pattern, cut to fit the ceiling angle. The vertically planked walls make an attractive design complement to the horizontally planked cathedral ceiling.

The old crossbeams were replaced with handsome oak-veneered pine beams. These beams offer strong support for a snow-laden roof.

What it takes

Approximate time: Ceiling—It took two carpenters a total of four days to complete the ceiling. Walls—Three carpenters spent a total of three days installing the vertical wall planking.

Tools and materials: Insulation, plastic sheet, staple gun; saw protractor, power saw, electric sander, wood plane, bevel gauge, level to prepare planking; hammer, 8d and 10d cut nails, 6d galvanized finishing nails; 1x4s, 1x3 furring strips, cedar shims, 1x4 pine planking (for ceiling), 5-inch tongue and groove pine paneling (for wall).

1. Here's how the ceiling looked before construction began. New plasterboard would be joined to old below the beam. Wood planking for the ceiling would begin above the exposed beam, rising from there to the roof ridge and extending down the far side of the ridge to the top of the north wall (see plans).

2. Lengths of 1x4 board are nailed at the ridge to form the ceiling angle. Shingles are used to shim the boards so they will make a flat support for the ceiling.

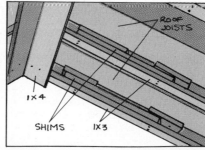

3. Strips of 1x3 furring are attached to the roof joists and shimmed to make a level nailing surface.

4. A staple gun is used to attach fiberglass insulation between the roof joists. Then the ceiling is covered with plastic sheeting.

5. Plywood is attached to the furring with 6d nails. The fit doesn't have to be perfect as long as the ceiling is covered and forms an even surface for the wood planking.

6. When preparing the wood planking, use a saw protractor to measure the boards for cutting. By taking time to measure and cut correctly you'll avoid a lot of problems when it comes to nailing up the boards.

7. The boards are butted tightly against each other and fastened to the plywood with 6d galvanized finishing nails.

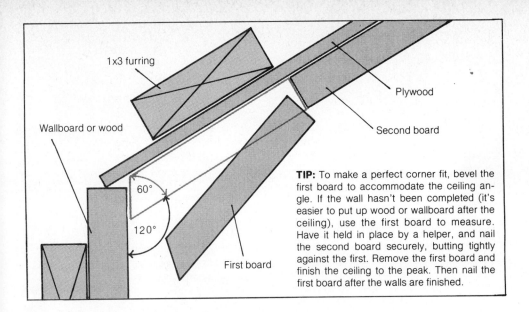

1x3 furring

Plywood

Wallboard or wood

Second board

60°

120°

First board

TIP: To make a perfect corner fit, bevel the first board to accommodate the ceiling angle. If the wall hasn't been completed (it's easier to put up wood or wallboard after the ceiling), use the first board to measure. Have it held in place by a helper, and nail the second board securely, butting tightly against the first. Remove the first board and finish the ceiling to the peak. Then nail the first board after the walls are finished.

Covering the walls

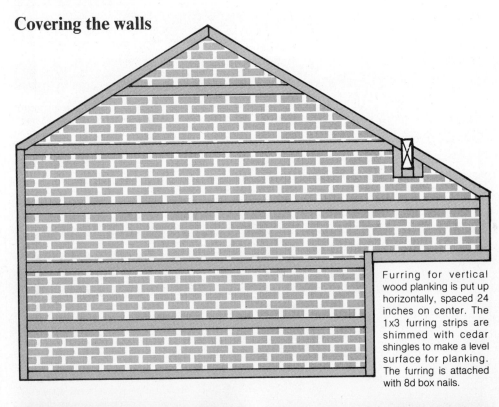

Furring for vertical wood planking is put up horizontally, spaced 24 inches on center. The 1x3 furring strips are shimmed with cedar shingles to make a level surface for planking. The furring is attached with 8d box nails.

8. Tongue and groove pine, used for the walls, comes in a variety of widths. The notched edges slip into each other to make a strong, snug fit.

9. Furring strips are attached at the base of the ceiling to form a level surface for wall framing. A bevel gauge is used to measure and cut the boards to fit snugly at the lower edge of the ceiling. Boards are then nailed to the furring with 6d finishing nails.

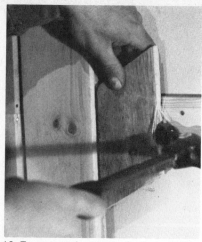

10. To prevent damage to the factory edge, a scrap piece of pine is used to hammer against when fitting one edge into the next.

11. One door is covered with planking and attached with a length of continuous hinge. The boards are matched to give the impression that the door is part of the wall.

12. Wall planking is cut to accommodate electric outlets and switches.

A

B

C

D

A. The expanse of pine board which climbs the east wall gives the room a feeling of grace. It's easy to maintain after applying a coat of varnish.

B. This photograph, taken after work had been completed, shows the east wall planking which extends into the work area, stopping just short of the stove space.

C. Ceiling planking stops just short of the beam. Plasterboard continues below the beam to the dormer wall.

D. The cathedral ceiling, so vast in feeling that it's hard to believe the roof peak is only 12 feet high.

Plastic laminate counter

Plastic laminate makes an excellent surface for kitchen counters. Laminates are easy to clean and are durable under normal use. Some laminates, however, can be damaged by bleaches or cleaners, and may be sensitive to extreme heat. Be sure to observe the manufacturer's recommendations for maintenance.

Sheets of laminate are available in standard sizes from 2x5 feet to 5x12 feet, the more durable 1/16-inch for horizontal surfaces and 1/32-inch for vertical surfaces. They come in a wide range of designs—from solid colors to abstract patterns and wood grain—and are available in matte or gloss finish.

1. Here's the difficult dormer area for which a plastic laminate counter was planned. A high, unusable shelf built previously has already been removed. The new counter took about two days to build.

2. To make a support for the countertop, fasten 1x3 boards to the wall with panel adhesive and wallboard screws. Frame out to the width of the counter and use braces for additional strength. Level carefully.

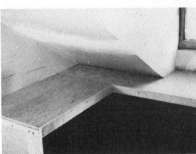

3. Use 8d nails to secure ⅝-inch plywood to the framing, fitting it to the contour of the wall. Laminates can be glued to most flat surfaces, but plywood and chipboard are the most commonly used bases.

4. A power saw with a fine-toothed blade is the quickest way to cut the laminate. It can also be cut with a fine-toothed hand saw or scored with a special laminate-cutting blade and snapped apart. Cut from the decorative side, and make the pieces slightly oversize for trimming.

5. Apply contact adhesive to the back of the laminate and the plywood top. Let it dry for about 15 minutes. Work carefully when putting the laminate in place, because the adhesive sticks instantly.

6. Clamp the edges with C-clamps. Use pieces of wood between the clamp and the laminate to protect the surface. Let the work dry in the clamps for half an hour before removing.

7. You can trim the edge with a saw and file, but the neatest edge is made with a router and a special bit made specifically for trimming laminate. Gaps between the laminate and the wall should be filled with latex caulking compound. Run your finger along the seam to smooth the caulking.

8. Clean, smooth lines define the new counter area, which adds 10 feet of working space. You can install shelves beneath the countertop and finish them the same way. The shelf here adds 18 inches of storage.

TIP: Care must be taken when laying down large sheets of laminate to which adhesive has been applied so that they will not adhere before you are ready. Lay small strips of wood between the laminate and the plywood surface. Press down, starting at an edge, moving the wood strips as you go along.

Custom cabinets

What it takes

Approximate time: Three days.

Tools and materials: Saw, hammer, screwdriver, level, sander, 8d box nails, wallboard screws, finishing nails, wood putty; 1x3s, 4x3s, ⅝-inch birch plywood.

In order to create an L-shaped area for sink and counter space, it was necessary to design and build custom cabinets. Two important considerations in figuring dimensions were the size of the sink to be installed and the height of the stove which was already in place. For ease and efficiency, the sink would be positioned catercorner, with counter space on both sides.

One potential problem was the water that would splash behind the sink (thus over the edge and down the side of the cabinet). The solution: a boxed surface of tile recessed an inch behind the sink lip, high enough to stop water. The width of the counter and height of the backsplash (which continues along the wall to hide pipes and gas lines) were determined by the size of the counter tiles (6x6x½-inch) and the space required for grout.

Storage space beneath the counter would be divided into three cabinet areas: a door and shelves next to the stove; a door beneath the sink; and a drawer, door and shelves on the end. The last 12 inches of the counter would be open beneath.

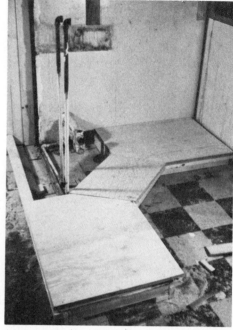

1. The base frame is made with 2x4s, nailed together with 8d box nails and covered with ¾-inch birch plywood. Notice how the bottom is recessed for a kick board.

2. The cabinets are framed with 4x3s, 1x3s, and ⅝-inch birch plywood, nailed with 8d box nails and fastened to the wall with wallboard screws. Horizontal boards are level; verticals are plumb.

3. The top is cut from a single piece of plywood, with a cutout for the sink. The edge is trimmed with 1x3 pine, attached flush to the top surface with finishing nails.

4. A box is framed and covered with plywood for the backsplash. Notice how the angle is cut back so it doesn't form a point. The side piece of plywood is cut from a single sheet.

5. Doors are attached flush to the front surface with lengths of continuous hinge. For a natural finish, nails are recessed and filled with wood putty. Hardware goes on after the cabinets are painted or varnished.

Tile countertop. Ceramic or terra-cotta tiles add a nice design touch to a countertop and sink backsplash. Available in 4- or 6-inch sizes, they are laid the same way as for floors or walls. Bull-nose end pieces are rounded to fit corners and sides.

For best results, plan the way the tiles will fit even before you buy them. You may want to place the dry tiles on the counter and tape them to the wall to be certain of the design. In this case, full 6x6x½-inch terra-cotta tiles fit perfectly because the counter was custom built to accommodate the width of four full tiles (plus grout).

The tile for this counter took about eight hours to install. The sink was put in shortly thereafter. Allow grout at least 24 hours to dry.

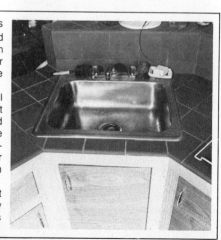

Vinyl tile floor

Choosing from the dozens of floor vinyl designs on the market can be overwhelming. One-piece vinyl may need expert fitting, but tiles are easy for anyone to put in. Some are backed with adhesive—you pull off the protective paper and stick the tile to the floor. Though less messy, it is not necessarily easier or faster to put down adhesive tile than to spread floor cement and lay the tiles in place.

Preparing the surface. Check to see that the subfloor is firmly attached. Renail loose boards and drive all nails flush. On an old tiled surface, replace missing tiles with new ones to fill the space. Larger areas can be filled with ¼-inch plywood. Smooth small gaps with floor grout or wall compound.

For best results, the subfloor should be smooth, dry, and free of dust and grease. Scrape off splatters of spackle, wax, or other material that might form a bulge.

Lining up the tiles. The placement of the tiles depends on the design and the shape of the room. Some designs combine four or more tiles to form a pattern, others don't need special attention. Rarely are rooms exactly rectilinear, and the edge pieces which are cut to fit often show the slant of a wall.

The key to laying tile so that it looks straight is to mark off the center of the room. Snap chalk lines from the center of opposite walls to determine where the room center intersects. Measure the intersecting lines. How will the tiles fit? Lay dry tiles down along the lines to check; you may need to adjust the lines.

Oddly shaped areas are more difficult to set straight. Sometimes you should go by what the eye sees as straight—even if it doesn't measure that way. For example, in this renovation, the tile at the top of the stairs can be seen first, because it opens up into the room. The tile was not laid so it would be in the middle of the top step; rather, it was done so there would be two full 12-inch tiles and an even line of trim on the wall side. Since the other side is the bannister and spindles, it is not as noticeable that the tile is not parallel to the edge at that spot.

What it takes

Approximate time: A couple of hours for a small room, up to two full days if there are repairs and a lot of special fitting.

Tools and materials: Spackling compound, wallboard compound, commercial floor grout, ¼-inch plywood to fix a bad floor, floor cement, notched trowel, tiles, utility knife.

TIP: Professionals use a grout that comes in powder form and mixes with water. Troweled onto a broken subfloor, the grout provides a strong, smooth bond for the tiles.

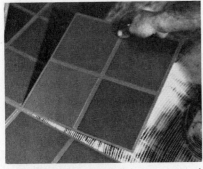

1. Large areas of missing tile can be patched with ¼-inch plywood. Fill the gaps between the wood and tile with spackling compound or wallboard compound applied with a taping knife. Let it dry for 24 hours.

2. Patch small areas with a new tile cut to size. Use a taping knife to apply floor cement to the back and stick it in place.

3. Spread floor cement with a notched trowel. Take large sweeping movements with the tool to spread the adhesive. Let it dry until it is tacky to touch before you lay the tiles.

4. Lay each tile in place, doing a quarter of the room at a time. Press tiles down gently; don't slide them, or the adhesive will ooze at the seam. Run your finger along the seams to pick up excess cement.

5. To fit the areas next to the wall, place a new tile over the first full tile from the wall. Take another full tile and butt it against the wall. Cut along the edge. The piece cut off will fit the area next to the wall.

6. Vinyl flooring is extremely durable, resists damage by spirit solvents, grease, and alkalis, and has high resiliency. The tiles are easy to lay and look great.

CASE STUDY: COMPACT KITCHEN

What it takes

Approximate time: Three days.

Tools and materials: Hammer, screwdriver, level, electric handsaw, hack saw; screws, nails, wood shims, stain, putty, cabinets and hardware.

Before: Here's how the kitchen looked before renovation began.

After: This kitchen renovation is designed to update and organize a very limited work area. The new fixtures and countertops make the fullest practical use of space.

The basic work involved is carpentry and the installation of new fixtures. The range, refrigerator, sink, and dishwasher seen in these photos are new, but they are replacements for original appliances, not additions. Thus, no additional electrical lines were required, though several outlets were added or repositioned.

For guidelines to follow when removing old cabinets and fixtures, see the pertinent chapters in the front of this book.

The work sequence described in this case study begins with the installation of base cabinets. Preparation for the reconstruction involved removal of the old fixtures, roughing in plumbing and electrical lines, and basic plastering to even out damaged walls.

Setting base cabinets

Base cabinets go in first. Leveling and setting the base or floor cabinets is the key to the entire job. If the base cabinets are not level, the entire job will be misaligned, since the splashback and top cabinets are leveled on the base installation.

If the floor is fairly level, the base cabinets can be set and shimmed. If shimming is not sufficient, lay down ¼-inch Masonite and level that. Shim the Masonite if necessary, and tack it down.

Once the cabinets are in place, they should be secured to the rear wall with four screws. To secure cabinets to each other, first countersink through the corner stiles; then drive screws through them.

1. Base cabinets should be carefully leveled, both front-to-back and side-to-side.

2. Cabinets are shimmed with angled wood shingles until they are perfectly level.

3. It was three days before the new sink and countertop could be installed. The old sink was hooked up for temporary use.

The countertop

The pre-cut, pre-finished plastic laminate countertop is installed next. It is set on the cabinets and secured by drilling through cabinet corner blocks into the countertop deck. When drilling into the underside of the countertop, be careful not to go through the laminate surface.

Once counter is secured, sink can be installed.

Appliances

With the counter and base cabinets in place, all appliances can be installed and hooked up.

Here the dishwasher fits under the counter and hooks into the plumbing beneath the sink. The refrigerator, which opens toward the kitchen, fits snugly at the end of the sink counter. On the opposite wall, the edges of the range are leveled to exactly match the adjacent 36-inch countertop.

Backsplash

There are two types of backsplash popular for use in the kitchen. The standard backsplash extends 4 inches up the wall behind the countertop and sink area. The second type covers the entire wall from the top of the counter to the bottom back edge of the hanging cabinets. If installing a standard low backsplash, the wall cabinets must be leveled before hanging. Begin the installation with an end or corner cupboard and shim to the wall until it is level. The standard measurement for the height of hanging cabinets is 18 inches from the countertop deck. The high backsplash measures 18 inches, so the cabinets rest on top, automatically level if the base cabinets have been properly leveled.

Soffits

If you are not installing top cabinets, you may want to construct a ceiling soffit even with the top front cabinet edge. Furring strips (1x3) are secured to and leveled on the top of the wall cabinet at a distance from the front edge which measures the thickness of your soffit material: ¼ inch for ¼-inch Masonite, or ⅜ inch for ⅜-inch Sheetrock, for example. Carefully measure and secure corresponding furring on the ceiling above. Furring can be a continuous vertical strip or short (2-inch) strips spaced 16 inches apart. Nail fitted Masonite or Sheetrock to the furring. What is most important is that the finished soffit be even and level with the cabinet fronts. The finished soffit can be painted or wallpapered as desired.

Hanging cabinets

The first cabinet is screwed to the back wall with four screws. When working from a corner, hang the corner cabinet first. Any shimming is done between the first cabinet and the wall, not between cabinets. The next cabinets are also screwed to the wall, and then attached to each other.

1. The corner cabinet is positioned and screwed hand tight to the wall while aligning.

2. Standing at eye level in front of the cabinet, you can check the work with a level.

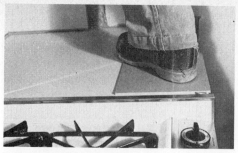

3. When working on hanging cabinets, it is easiest to stand on the countertop, but be sure to protect the surface from scratches.

4. Slender wood shims are driven between cabinet edge and wall.

A second bank of cabinets

If you are putting up a second bank of cabinets rather than a soffit, the second tier will be leveled and secured on the first bank. Installing a second row of cabi-nets is not much more difficult than building a soffit. The extra expense translates into a lot more storage.

1. A second bank of cabinets here rises to the ceiling. To reduce weight and expense, the upper bank is in fact a skeleton, hinged doors on a frame, not full boxes.

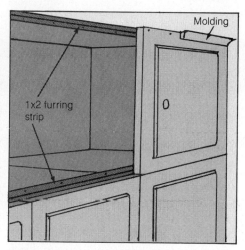

2. The door frame is aligned with and secured on two lengths of 1x2 furring. One strip is nailed across the top front edge of the lower bank of cabinets, just far enough back to accommodate the depth of the skeleton frame. The second furring strip is carefully aligned parallel to the first and nailed to the ceiling.

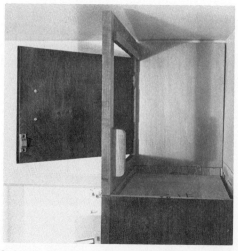

3. A right angle panel L on each end frame makes alignment easier and gives additional vertical support.

4. Here's how it looks when the work is in progress. When the installation is completed, however, it will appear as solid as a real cabinet. Those skeletons are useful for storing infrequently used items.

Molding

Molding gives a finished look to your cabinet installation. While measuring and leveling your work carefully is imperative, molding will disguise any minor join flaws and smooth the whole cabinet area into its setting.

1. Matching molding, available from your cabinet manufacturer, should be installed at all wall, soffit, and double bank intersections.

2. Countersink nail heads with nail set and touch them up with crayon or wood putty and stain mixed to match the wood.

Details and additional features

1. The cabinet-wall intersection is carefully spackled prior to wallpapering.

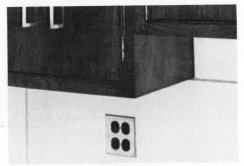

2. Cutouts for electrical outlets in a high backsplash must be made prior to installing the laminate.

TIP: Bear in mind the resale value of your home when you're planning a renovation. For instance, low counters of around 32 inches, and high ones of 39, may really limit the number of prospective buyers for your home.

3. A built-in paper towel and plastic wrap dispenser is available as a unit from various manufacturers. The backsplash cutout required, as for outlets, must be made before installation.

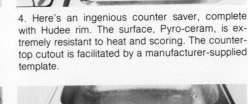

4. Here's an ingenious counter saver, complete with Hudee rim. The surface, Pyro-ceram, is extremely resistant to heat and scoring. The countertop cutout is facilitated by a manufacturer-supplied template.

5. A convenient ready-made rack for can storage. Available pre-assembled, the rack is screwed to the back of a cabinet door.

6. A bottom-hinged sponge and brush drawer in front of the sink. A drawer such as this can only be installed where cabinet doors hang flush with their frames.

Index

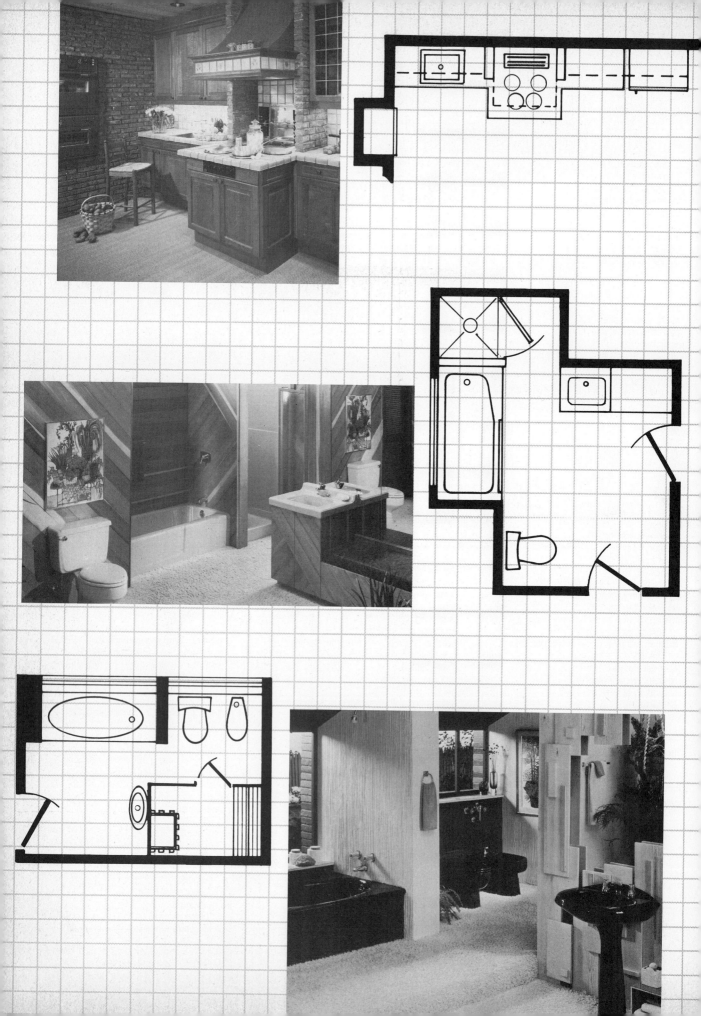

ADDING STORAGE SPACE

ADDING STORAGE SPACE

Created and editorially produced for Petersen Publishing Company
by Allen D. Bragdon Publishers, Inc., Home Guides Division

STAFF FOR THIS VOLUME

Editorial Director	Allen D. Bragdon
Writer	Tim Snyder
Art Director	John B. Miller
Assistant Art Director	Clara Rosenbaum
Text Editors	Laura K. Palmer, Hannah K. Selby, James Wyckoff
Production Editor	Eileen Bossong Martines
Contributing Photographers	J. Kenneth Boehm, John B. Miller, Tim Snyder
Contributing Artists	Pat Lee, John B. Miller, Gary Monteferante, Clara Rosenbaum
Production Coordinator	Dana P. Sephton
Production Artists	Ellen Dichner, Eleanore Fahey, Chon Vinson
Cover design by	"For Art Sake" Inc.

ACKNOWLEDGEMENTS

The Editors wish to thank the following individuals and firms for their help in the preparation of this book: S.F. Bailey & Sons; Creative Woodworking; Evans Products Co., Riviera Division; Excel Wood Products Co., Guildmark Furniture Division; Haas Cabinets; John Jackson; Minolta Corp.; National Recessed Cabinets; Poggenpohl USA Corp.; Rockwell International, Power Tool Division; Rubbermaid Corp.; Schulte Corp.; the Stanley Works, Tool and Hardware Divisions; U.S. Gypsum.

Petersen Publishing Company

R. E. Petersen/Chairman of the Board
F. R. Waingrow/President
Philip E. Trimbach/V. P. Finance
William Porter/V. P. Circulation Director
James J. Krenek/V. P. Manufacturing
Jack Thompson/Assistant Director, Circulation
Nigel P. Heaton/Director, Circulation Marketing
Louis Abbott/Director, Production
Arthur Zarin/Director, Research
Al Isaacs/Director, Graphics
Bob D'Olivo/Director, Photography
Maria Cox/Manager, Data Processing Services
Erwin M. Rosen/Executive Editor, Specialty Publications Division

Library of Congress Catalog Card No. 78-50828
Paperbound Edition:
ISBN 0-8227-8010-0

Table of Contents

1.PLANNING

ONE OF THESE DAYS WE'VE GOT TO GET ORGANIZED!

On the average, about 10% of the space in your house or apartment is used for storage. In other words, a house with 4000 square feet of floor space would have around 400 square feet of shelf, cabinet, or closet space. What is the state of storage in your home?

Take a moment to explore in your mind, room by room, all the places you have your possessions and supplies tucked away—and don't leave out the bathroom, attic, garage, or basement. (1) Are some closets nearly empty while others seem to be stuffed? (2) Can you quickly and conveniently locate things you use occasionally? (3) Can you reach frequently used items easily? (4) Are trophies, fine china, or heirlooms hidden from view when they might be displayed instead? (5) Are delicate or hazardous articles stored safely? (6) Can you reach and remove large or unwieldy items without upsetting others? (7) Is there empty space under stairs, in crawl spaces and entranceways, on walls or in overhead areas, that could be converted to storage? If your answers to these seven questions are, in order: no, yes, yes, no, yes, yes, no—and you aren't living in

an igloo—then pass this book along to a less well-organized family.

Inconvenient storage is one of those irritations that results from lack of planning and which has come to be taken for granted. Convenient, visually pleasing storage doesn't just happen—it's a true accomplishment. This book is designed to help you convert unusable living space into attractive and accessible storage space, and organize the accumulated clutter of a growing family living in a house that can't grow with it.

Reorganizing storage areas or creating new and successful storage space depends not only on careful planning, but on good craftsmanship, and perhaps even a creative and open-minded reconsideration of how you want to live. (You may, for example, decide that it's about time you held a tag-sale.)

Since constructing storage areas requires some basic carpentry know-how, it would be wise to familiarize yourself with the concepts, tools, materials, and techniques explained in the first part of this book (chapters 1-4) before you pick out a project from the second part.

Different kinds of storage

Here are a few of the words which might be used to describe good storage areas: accessible, decorative, convenient, safe, unique, flexible, protected, temporary, hidden, modular, adaptable, permanent. It's easy to see from this list of adjectives that storage space can be used in many different ways. A display case full of fine glassware and silver, a bathroom cabinet, and a set of bookshelves are vastly different storage units which serve equally different needs. Just as your storage requirements vary from room to room, or even from area to area within a room, there are quite a few ways of designing a storage unit to meet your requirements. Should your bookcase be built-in or portable? Do you want the shelves themselves to be fixed or adjustable, to accommodate some stereo components you are saving up for? Would it be more attractive or economical to buy some special shelving hardware

instead of building the bookcase completely by hand? Or do you want to buy your storage unit in kit form, and simply assemble it on the spot, using a minimum number of tools?

The questions above suggest the wide range of choices you have when facing storage problems. It's important to keep an open mind when making decisions about storage space. After you have considered some of the solutions suggested in this book as projects, you might very well come up with a better design of your own. It's a good idea to draw up an overall storage plan for your home, but don't try to execute it all at once. Start where new storage space is needed most and take it from there as time, energy, and budget will permit.

To paraphrase an old and famous saying: "A sketch in time saves nine trips to the lumber yard."

My "Fibber McGee" closet

Fibber McGee was half of a comedy team in the early days of radio known as "Fibber McGee and Molly." He had a closet full of junk that he was always going to organize "someday." I've had a closet like that for years, and by now, as Molly used to say, "It ain't funny, McGee."

Practical Pete

Open-front plywood boxes make attractive modular display storage anywhere in the house. It's easy to add and subtract units, and the whole set can be moved in minutes.

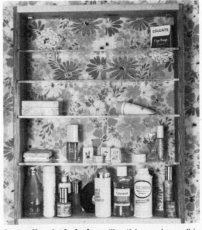

A small set of shelves like this works well in the bathroom, where many small items need to be stored. Acrylic plastic is durable here, and adds a modern touch.

Big storage projects include plans for a bed with built-in drawers.

A built-in hamper/shelving unit makes efficient use of an awkward bathroom niche and offers ample storage for towels and toilet articles.

Unused basement and garage areas can be converted to storage space with rough shelving. Here, plywood and construction grade lumber are used to keep costs down.

Two metal tracks which have adjustable support brackets hold these shelves. There are many different types of shelving hardware designed to fit a wide range of needs.

Evaluating your storage needs

Storage problems can be divided into two groups, and consequently are usually solved in one of two ways: (1) There isn't enough storage space, and more must be created, or (2) existing space is used inefficiently, and must be reorganized. Use the guidelines at right to evaluate your present storage spaces and to help plan new areas or redo old ones.

The first step in planning storage space is to evaluate your needs as far as storage goes. A good way to do this is to make a list of the items that you want to store in a given space. Number the articles according to how often they are used, giving those that are used together the same number. Isolate the objects you think will be difficult to store because of size or weight; find a place for these things first. Put a special mark next to children's things; you'll want to store these within easy reach. Look through the list for dangerous, delicate, or valuable articles that should be confined to limited-access storage and safekeeping.

Making a list like the one described above helps to define storage priorities and will enable you to use your space wisely. There are other considerations as well. How will the bookcase, cabinet, or closet you're planning be used in five years or more? Now is the time to decide how permanent, portable, or flexible you want your project to be. For example, a set of fixed, built-in shelves wouldn't be right in a child's room, since his or her storage needs will change as toys are discarded for sports equipment and stereo sets, books and trophies.

Let the location of your planned storage space help to determine the design and construction of your unit. The study or living room is a good place for built-ins. Storage needs will change little in these rooms, so flexibility is not as important as a well-made, nicely-finished structure. Display cases or cabinets which provide glass-enclosed, dust-free, storage space work well in the hallway or dining room, or in a den.

Cases, cabinets, or closets in the basement or attic can be built inexpensively from rough lumber, with less attention to detail and joinery than a kitchen cabinet would require. Remember, though, that if you plan to remodel your basement or attic within the next few years these units will probably have to be taken down.

In the kitchen or workshop, convenience is the primary consideration. Tools, utensils, ingredients, and other specialized items are used on a day-to-day basis, and should be especially easy to locate, identify, and replace. High traffic storage areas like these must be well constructed in addition to being well planned.

The bathroom is another area where convenience is important. There are many small items to keep track of here, so storage space must be arranged on a correspondingly smaller scale (see page 64). *Bear in mind that safety should be considered here. Certain medicines must be inaccessible to children, for example.*

More than any other area, the bedroom is the place where unique and highly personalized storage ideas are found. Here you can let your particular tastes and requirements determine what ideas about style, materials, and flexibility you use.

Guidelines for good storage

- Most frequently used articles should be most accessible.

- Store items where they can be easily identified and reached by the person who is going to use them.

- Tools, utensils, or other items which are used together should be stored together.

- Store large or cumbersome items where they can be reached, removed, and replaced easily and without upsetting smaller ones.

- Store dangerous, delicate, or valuable things in safe, out-of-the-way places.

- Be sure that new or reorganized storage units are compatible with the surrounding decor.

- Choose the storage plan or design that best fits the space which is available to you.

- Plan for the future as well as the present. Design shelves, cabinets, or closet space that will accommodate changing family needs.

Using space wisely

The floor plans at right illustrate an important consideration in planning new storage space. Locating a closet near the bedroom door makes good sense because it requires less "traffic" space than other locations, and steps are saved in returning clothes to the closet. However, careful planning is important to avoid blocking the door space by placing a closet too close to it. And locating a closet on the wall opposite the door creates unnecessary additional traffic "lanes." Small planning details like this add up to determine the convenience of new storage space.

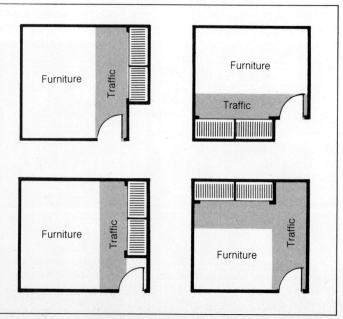

Sample houseplan of stored items

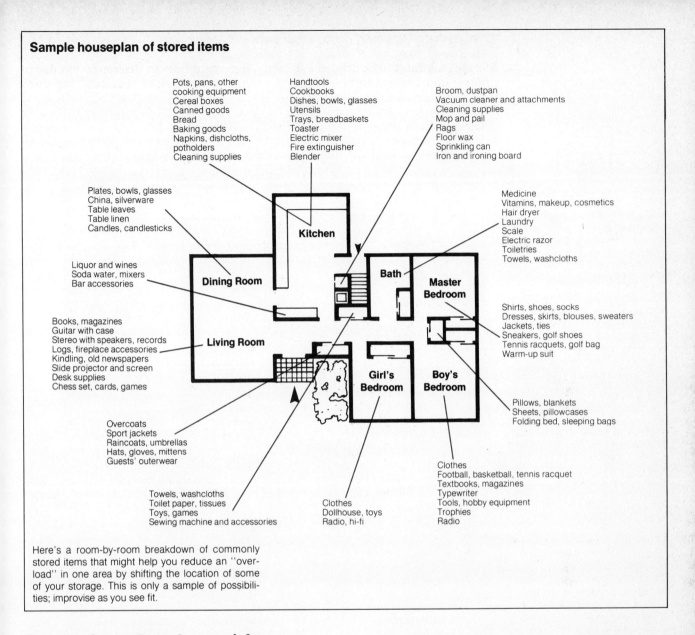

Pots, pans, other cooking equipment
Cereal boxes
Canned goods
Bread
Baking goods
Napkins, dishcloths, potholders
Cleaning supplies

Handtools
Cookbooks
Dishes, bowls, glasses
Utensils
Trays, breadbaskets
Toaster
Electric mixer
Fire extinguisher
Blender

Broom, dustpan
Vacuum cleaner and attachments
Cleaning supplies
Mop and pail
Rags
Floor wax
Sprinkling can
Iron and ironing board

Plates, bowls, glasses
China, silverware
Table leaves
Table linen
Candles, candlesticks

Medicine
Vitamins, makeup, cosmetics
Hair dryer
Laundry
Scale
Electric razor
Toiletries
Towels, washcloths

Liquor and wines
Soda water, mixers
Bar accessories

Shirts, shoes, socks
Dresses, skirts, blouses, sweaters
Jackets, ties
Sneakers, golf shoes
Tennis racquets, golf bag
Warm-up suit

Books, magazines
Guitar with case
Stereo with speakers, records
Logs, fireplace accessories
Kindling, old newspapers
Slide projector and screen
Desk supplies
Chess set, cards, games

Pillows, blankets
Sheets, pillowcases
Folding bed, sleeping bags

Overcoats
Sport jackets
Raincoats, umbrellas
Hats, gloves, mittens
Guests' outerwear

Clothes
Football, basketball, tennis racquet
Textbooks, magazines
Typewriter
Tools, hobby equipment
Trophies
Radio

Towels, washcloths
Toilet paper, tissues
Toys, games
Sewing machine and accessories

Clothes
Dollhouse, toys
Radio, hi-fi

Kitchen
Dining Room
Bath
Master Bedroom
Living Room
Girl's Bedroom
Boy's Bedroom

Here's a room-by-room breakdown of commonly stored items that might help you reduce an "overload" in one area by shifting the location of some of your storage. This is only a sample of possibilities; improvise as you see fit.

Sources for tools and materials

Your lumberyard probably has the most comprehensive supply of softwood lumber, plywood, and particleboard. Plan to look a little harder for hardwoods; most lumber dealers carry a limited supply or simply don't stock it. Cabinetmakers and millwork shops are often more reliable sources of maple, oak, mahogany, and other hardwoods. *Note:* If you're buying more lumber than you can transport yourself, ask your dealer if he makes deliveries; most do. He can also cut your larger stock down to more manageable size, usually for a small charge per cut.

Hardware stores stock nails, glue, tools, shelf supports, and other woodworking accessories. Most lumberyards sell hardware, but can't offer the variety that an independent dealer can. Your hardware dealer can also provide you with some helpful information on storage ideas, construction details, special hardware, or new items that might make your job easier.

Home decorating centers are a relatively new source for storage-related tools and materials. These stores cater to the weekend repairman, hobbyist, or home craftsman rather than the professional carpenter, so this is a good place to go if you're uncertain about designing or building from scratch. Home decorating centers specialize in track shelving, shelf supports, and other storage-related hardware designed for quick, easy assembly. You may even find prefinished wood shelves in various lengths and widths.

When you visit your neighborhood home decorating center, hardware store, or lumber dealer, bring your ideas with you and share them with the salesman or store manager. He'll save you time in your search for tools, materials, and hardware. He probably will also have some valuable advice on construction details, special equipment, or alternative materials that can make your job easier and the result more professional.

2. FIRST STEPS

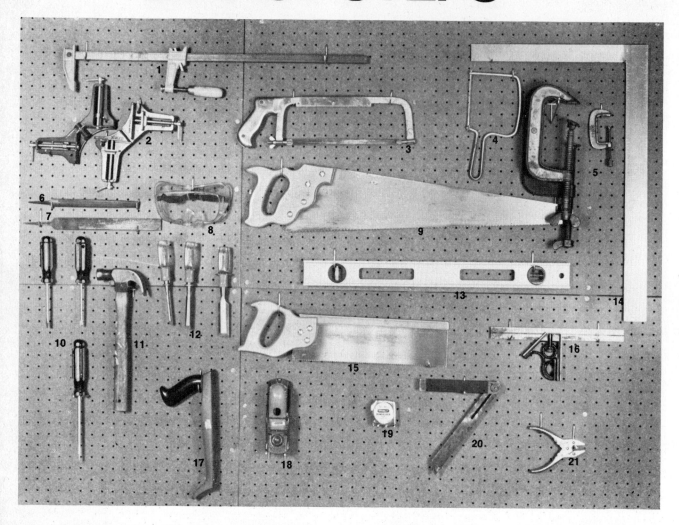

1. Bar or Pipe clamps (2' long)
2. Corner clamps
3. Hacksaw
4. Coping saw
5. C-clamps
6. Medium half-round file

7. Flat bastard file
8. Safety goggles
9. Crosscut saw
10. Screwdrivers
11. Hammer (16 oz. head)
12. Chisels

13. 2' Level
14. Carpenter's square
15. Backsaw
16. Combination square
17. Surform tool
18. Block plane

19. Steel tape measure
20. Sliding bevel
21. Slipjoint pliers

Great storage projects begin as well-planned ideas. Ideas then become designs; designs include specifications for materials as well as exact dimensions. Finally, after selecting the tools needed to do the job, work begins. This chapter describes the preliminary work, or first steps, involved in designing and building new storage space.

A good basic toolkit like the one described on the next few pages will see you through many projects, not just for storage, but for all kinds of home repairs and hobbies too. If you're just beginning to outfit your workshop, it's a good policy to buy quality tools. Initial savings on budget tools are usually offset when they wear out prematurely and must be re-

placed. With proper care good tools will last more than a lifetime. Detailed information on how to operate tools is included throughout this book as each tool is introduced; and you will also find descriptions of specialized equipment that can save time and effort.

An idea for new shelves, cabinets, closets, or other storage space becomes a design when you take measurements, make a scale drawing, and select the building materials you want to use. This sequence of events just about completes the preliminaries that help determine how smoothly the rest of the job will run. The only other first step is to estimate how long the job will take and what it's going to cost you.

Basic toolkit

Cutting and clamping tools

Saws are used for cutting material to size. They are among the most important tools in any workshop because they are used so often. With the five types of handsaws described below, you'll be able to handle just about any project.

The **crosscut saw** is for cutting across the grain of the wood; and for cutting plywood. Most crosscut saws have a 26-inch blade with 7 to 10 teeth per inch. The teeth-per-inch (TPI) count determines the speed and smoothness of the cut. Saws with fewer teeth per inch cut faster but leave a rough wood surface.

Use a **ripsaw** for making cuts that run with the grain. The TPI for most ripsaws is between 5 and 7; ripsaw teeth are larger and chisel-shaped. (Crosscut teeth look like little knives.)

Backsaws have a stiff metal spline which runs along the back of the blade. These saws have finer, denser (12-21) teeth and are used where smooth, accurate cuts are needed. Backsaws are often used with a miterbox (see page 20) for precise joinery work.

You'll need a **coping saw** to cut curves or contours in wood. It has a narrow blade which is pulled tight by a curved holder. These blades dull quickly and are liable to break when forced, so keep some replacements on hand.

If you're going to be cutting metal of any kind, you'll need a **hacksaw.** Hacksaw blades are available with different types of teeth for various metal-cutting jobs.

Keep your saws sharp, since dull blades cut less accurately and are dangerous because of the extra force required to make them work. Hacksaw and coping saw blades can simply be replaced when they dull, but all other handsaws must be re-sharpened and reset. Sharpening and setting requires a good deal of skill as well as special tools, so you're better off having a professional do the job. Prevent your saw blades from rusting by coating them with light machine oil once or twice a season.

The plane is a cutting tool with a chisel-like blade mounted at an angle in a wooden or metal body. Planes do the same fine shaping work as chisels, but over a wider, flatter area, since they are larger and can be used with more force. The blade is adjustable to control the depth of the cut. These tools can be costly as hand tools go, but the comparatively small and inexpensive **block plane** will handle most of your

shaping and smoothing jobs. An effective and less expensive alternative to the conventional plane is sold under the name Surform. Shaped like a plane, Surform tools have a sharp, finely perforated cutting surface that works like super-rough sandpaper and can be easily replaced when it grows dull.

Files are for small shaping jobs like rounding off corners, softening a hard edge, or reaching into a tight or curved area which is too cramped for a chisel. A **medium-cut half-round file** and **flat bastard file** will suffice for just about all the woodworking you'll do.

Chisels are used for the fine cutting and shaping of wood. Unless you have a dado attachment for your circular saw (see page 22), you'll need a chisel for making rabbet, dado, and lap joints. A set of three chisels (¼-, ½-, and 1-inch blade widths) should be all you need for most woodworking projects. Keep them sharp. Careless handling and improper storage of these tools will dull the blade much faster than woodworking will. Protect your chisels between jobs by covering their blades with tape, and storing them individually in a separate case or holder.

Clamps are indispensable for holding different pieces of material together while glue is setting, or to hold stock firmly while you work on it. There are many different types of clamps, and each is usually available in different sizes, so choosing your first set could be a problem. These are the three most useful types:

Bar clamps are used where a long reach is needed. Two metal feet are attached to a bar or pipe (usually between 2 and 6 feet long) and the stock is clamped tightly between them. One of the feet is fixed at the end of the bar, and the other is adjustable, with a screw-in mechanism to provide clamping pressure.

C-clamps are by far the most common for medium-sized and small work. They come in sizes ranging from an inch to a foot or more and are the least expensive of all clamps, so you can add to your selection by purchasing them as they're needed.

Corner clamps are designed to hold two pieces of stock together at a 90° angle. Using a corner clamp is the best way to make sure a shelf, cabinet, or picture frame joint is perfectly square. (See page 25.) Keep a few on hand.

Handtool checklist

- ☑ 2 Corner clamps
- ☑ 2 Bar clamps (1'-3' long)
- ☑ 4 C-clamps (two 10", two 3")
- ☑ Block plane
- ☑ Surform tool
- ☑ 3 Chisels (¼", ½", 1")
- ☑ Flat bastard file
- ☑ Medium cut ½-round file
- ☑ Hacksaw and blades
- ☑ Coping saw and blades
- ☑ Crosscut saw
- ☑ Rip saw
- ☑ 3 Screwdrivers (1 Phillips head)
- ☑ Hammer (16 oz. head)
- ☑ Slipjoint pliers
- ☑ Combination square
- ☑ Carpenter's square
- ☑ Level
- ☑ Steel tape measure
- ☑ Safety goggles

Measuring tools and how to use them

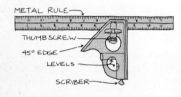

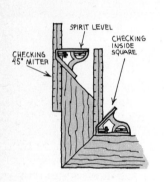

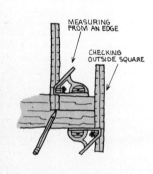

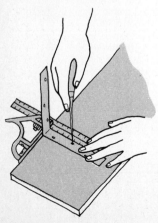

The level is an important tool whose name defines its function: to indicate whether or not a given surface is level. For putting up shelves, hanging cabinets, and other building projects around the home, you should have a level that's at least two feet long. Levels of this length contain at least two clear, calibrated tubes set at right angles to each other. Each tube is filled with liquid and contains a single air bubble. When the air bubble is centered exactly between the calibrations, you've got a level surface. The level will test for true horizontal (always read the horizontal tube, not the vertical one) or true vertical, more commonly called plumb. Don't drop, bang, or jar your level; it is a delicate instrument and rough use will make it inaccurate.

A square will tell you at a glance whether or not a square-looking corner measures a true 90°. Squares are also used for marking stock that has to be cut to smaller dimensions. The **steel or carpenter's square** is a sturdy, all-metal tool that is best used on large pieces like 4x8 panels. The **combination square** is a ruler attached to a metal edge which contains a 45° angle as well as a right angle (and sometimes a level bubble). The edge can be locked in place at any point along the length of the rule, or removed completely. It is a good first-purchase because it is compact, accurate, easy to use, and versatile enough to handle or help out on just about every measuring or marking job you do (see margin).

The sliding bevel is not an exotic animal, as some people may believe. To a carpenter, this is a tool that is used for transferring angle measurements. The sliding bevel consists of a metal straightedge (usually 1″ wide and 10″ long) which pivots and slides around a thumbscrew set in one end of a wooden handle. Tightening the thumbscrew locks the straightedge in place, "memorizing" the angle so you can transfer it to the stock. Easy to use and infinitely adjustable, the sliding bevel is an indispensable tool for custom-fit projects where odd angles are involved.

The tape measure is a compact and convenient invention that has largely replaced the folding rule as the carpenter's most frequently used measuring tool. Tape measures come in lengths as short as 6 feet, but you're better off with a 12-foot model, since measuring longer distances with a short rule is time-consuming and can cause inaccuracies. The metal tape, which comes in ½- or ¾-inch widths (¾-inch tapes are usually easier to read), is rolled into a metal container that's small enough to fit in your pocket. Unrolling the tape puts a spring inside the container under tension, and unless your tape measure has a locking mechanism, the tape will recoil itself as soon as you release it. The tapelock, although more expensive, is a worthwhile feature if you're someone who does a lot of measuring. Make sure the tape measure you buy is graduated at least to 16ths of an inch; 32nds is better. The best tapes have inches on one side and centimeters on the other.

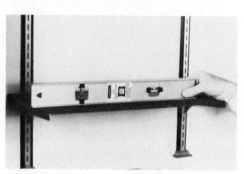

A level is an indispensable tool for hanging shelves. A true horizontal surface is indicated only when the bubble is centered exactly between the calibrations on the tube.

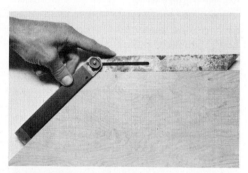

Use the sliding bevel for transferring odd angle measurements to your stock. Lock the adjustable metal straightedge in place after you've taken the angle by tightening the thumbscrew.

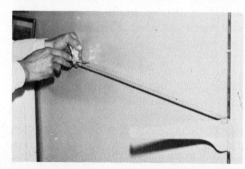

Your tape measure should be at least 12 feet long and calibrated to 16ths or 32nds of an inch. The metal lip at the beginning of the tape enables you to measure longer distances without the aid of a helper to hold one end. This model has a tapelock which will hold the tape at any given length instead of letting it recoil into the housing.

Choosing power tools

Power tools will usually enable you to work faster, more accurately, and with less effort than you could by hand. Below is a brief description of the most widely used power tools, including tips on what to look for when buying them. You'll find specific operating instructions on the pages ahead, as each tool is used.

The circular saw is a hand-held power tool that is used more often for cutting larger stock to manageable size than for precision work. With a good blade and a saw guide, however, the circular saw will do a great job of cutting wood to finished dimensions. If you're buying a circular saw, get one that will take a 7-inch blade; this will allow you to cut lumber up to 2 inches thick. Your saw should have a base that is calibrated and can be adjusted for both depth and angle of cut. Using a saw guide is the secret of straight, accurate cuts, so make sure your saw is equipped with one.

There are many types of blades available: one made especially for crosscutting, one strictly for ripping, a combination blade designed to do both (which usually comes with a new saw), special blades for plywood or for smooth finished cuts, and long-lasting carbide-tipped blades.

The saber saw, or portable jigsaw, has a thin blade that moves rapidly up and down. Saber saws are best suited for cutting curves and contours, and won't make straight cuts as true as those made with a table or circular saw. Most saber saws have a base that tilts and locks in position so you can cut at an angle.

Don't buy a cheap saber saw. They are usually underpowered and tend to vibrate at an alarming rate, which makes accurate cutting difficult. Plan to pay a little more for variable speed control, a calibrated beveling base, and a saw guide—extra features that are well worth the extra cost. Buy assorted blades.

Table saws are found less frequently in home workshops than other power tools because they are expensive and far from portable. The table saw is a real timesaver on projects where many pieces of the same size must be cut, since you can easily improvise a template or jig and thereby eliminate repetitive measuring and marking. The table saw uses the same blades as the circular saw, and the blade can be adjusted for angle and depth.

An electric drill is the least expensive and perhaps most versatile power tool you can own. With the right accessories, you can use your drill for sanding, polishing, grinding or sharpening, and driving screws, as well as for drilling holes. You can buy either a ¼- or ⅜-inch drill; this designation refers to the maximum diameter of the chuck, or bit-holder. Either model will work fine, although ⅜-inch drills are usually more powerful, especially at low speeds. Be sure the drill you buy has a variable speed trigger. Variable speed control means you can control the rpm simply by the pressure of your finger on the trigger.

Bits, like saw blades, come in several varieties. Get a set of common twist drills (bits are sometimes called drills) ranging in size from 1/16- to ¼-inch for starters, then buy them as you need them. Special bits for metal or masonry are also available.

The router is a specialized tool used for grooving and edging wood. The shape of the groove or edge is determined by the type of bit that is used. A router makes dado, rabbet, or lap joinery work a quick and accurate job, and is the best tool to use for trimming formica. Routers are adjustable for depth of cut, but not for angle.

The circular saw will make its most accurate cuts when you use it with a guide. A good circular saw has both depth and angle adjustments.

An electric drill makes holes in all kinds of material quickly and easily. Electric drills are the least expensive of the power tools, and can also be used (with different accessories) for sanding, polishing, and grinding.

Saber saws use a variety of thin blades and are designed for cutting curves. With a saw guide, however, you can also use this tool for straight cutting.

The router is used for making grooves and edges in wood. The bit you use determines the type of groove or edge effect. Using a guide is the best way to insure straight cuts.

Power tool safety checklist

☑ Keep power tools away from children and others who don't know how to use them.
☑ Read the owner's manual before using any unfamiliar tool.
☑ Never change a blade or bit, or try to repair a power tool that is plugged in.
☑ Before operating, check to make sure nuts and screws are secure; the motor's vibration will sometimes cause fittings to work loose.
☑ Make sure the blade or bit is *tightly* secured.
☑ Before you plug in, check the switch or trigger to make sure it's at "Off." As soon as you've finished using it, switch to "Off" and unplug your tool.
☑ Make sure your tool is grounded. Double-insulated power tools do not need to be grounded.
☑ Use only blades and bits that are sharp and in good condition.
☑ Exert moderate, controlled pressure; don't force the blade or bit.
☑ Examine the cut line and remove any nails, bolts, or other metal that might get in the way of the blade or bit.
☑ Clamp material securely.
☑ Wear eye protection. Under heavy dust conditions, wear a filter mask.

Drawing up plans

Inside and outside dimensions

The inside and outside dimensions for all 3 plans are identical, but the width of the horizontal piece changes according to the joint detail.

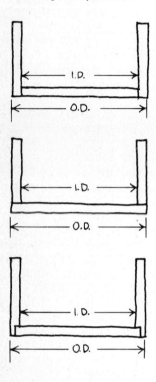

An **architect's scale** is a time-saver if you like to "blueprint" your ideas or if you find yourself making many scale drawings. Triangular in shape, it contains over 11 scales from 1/16" = 1' to 3" = 1', and each scale has exact calibrations for feet and inches.

You'll also need a **right triangle** to square up your drawings. Both instruments are available at office supply outlets or art supply stores, along with mechanical pencils, graph paper, drawing boards, and other helpful drafting supplies.

1. Get the right dimensions. Make a rough sketch of the storage space and label it with the readings you get on your tape measure. You should also take the dimensions of the articles you want to fit into the redesigned storage area. If possible, take your measurements in groups of three: height, width, and depth.

Before you start buying materials, put some rough project plans down on paper. Sketch as many ideas as you can, and use these preliminary drawings as worksheets you can refer to later. Include different ideas concerning style, size, appearance, materials, finish, and other details. **Note:** If you're designing new storage space, use the information on the facing page concerning shelf widths and human dimensions as a guide. Make sure your project is designed for the people who use it as well as for the items you want to store in it.

Take down the dimensions of the articles you want to store while you're measuring your storage space. Knowing the size of various items will enable you to allocate the right space so that the available area is efficiently utilized.

Now is also a good time to use your level and square to make sure your walls, floors, and other existing structural features are plumb and square. Your design may have to take slightly skewed or slanting surfaces into account.

When you make a scale drawing of the area you will be redesigning, you may want to draw a side view or a floor plan in addition to a front view in order to show the proper depth.

2. It's always a good idea to follow a scale drawing while you work. Establish a comfortable scale such as 1 inch equals 1 foot (small enough so it won't run off the page), then use a ruler and a right triangle to make a finished drawing exactly to scale. Now make sketches of your ideas for locating shelves, hooks, cabinets, clothes poles, etc. When you have come up with the best arrangement, make construction drawings of those elements to scale as shown on the facing page.

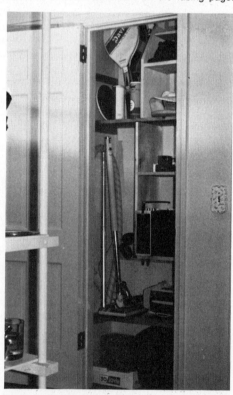

3. The finished project reflects the care that has gone into important preliminary work: sketching out rough plans, careful measuring, making a scale drawing, and designing the reorganized closet space.

Stopgaps and copouts

Graph paper offers a quick, easy alternative to the ruler and right triangle method of drawing to scale. Use the grid on the graph paper to establish your scale and square your corners.

Get the most from your drawings

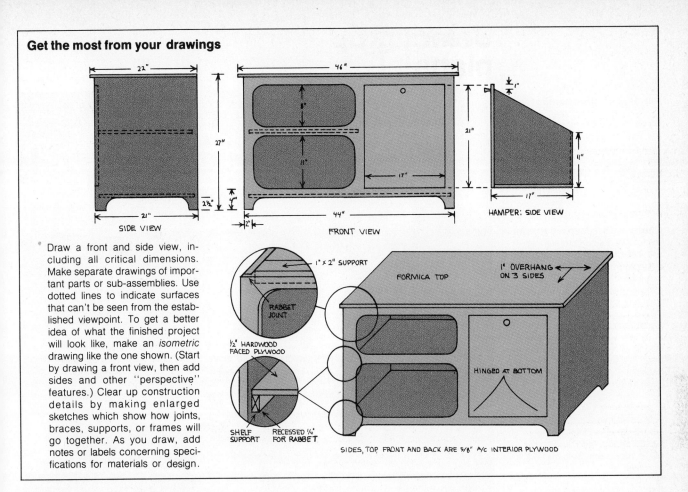

SIDE VIEW

FRONT VIEW

HAMPER: SIDE VIEW

SIDES, TOP, FRONT AND BACK ARE 5/8" A/C INTERIOR PLYWOOD

Draw a front and side view, including all critical dimensions. Make separate drawings of important parts or sub-assemblies. Use dotted lines to indicate surfaces that can't be seen from the established viewpoint. To get a better idea of what the finished project will look like, make an *isometric* drawing like the one shown. (Start by drawing a front view, then add sides and other ''perspective'' features.) Clear up construction details by making enlarged sketches which show how joints, braces, supports, or frames will go together. As you draw, add notes or labels concerning specifications for materials or design.

Using standard dimensions

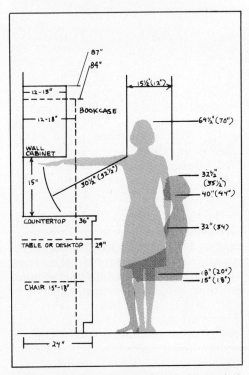

Human dimensions. The dimensions of the typical female figure shown above are followed in parentheses by typical dimensions for a 6-foot male. Adjust the standard dimensions given here for shelves, cabinets, etc., to fit the convenience of the people who will be using them most.

When deciding on specifications for length, width, and depth of shelves, cabinets, or other new storage space, there are two important factors to consider: (1) the size of the items to be stored and, (2) how convenient it will be to reach these items. Measuring articles is an easy job; usually you need only concern yourself with the larger things that will be taking up a substantial amount of space. The list at right gives standard dimensions for some common household items.

Building convenience into new storage space largely involves human dimensions: how far you can stretch or bend comfortably to reach stored goods. The standard width for kitchen counters is 24 inches because it is 6 or 8 inches less than the maximum reach of an outstretched arm. Goods stored in the cabinet space underneath the counter can be reached easily. The 36-inch standard for counter height allows the average man or woman to work conveniently. Wall-hung cabinets usually aren't deeper than 13 inches because items at the back of deeper cabinets would be difficult to identify and reach. There may also be some items that you'll prefer to store safely out of reach of children or pets.

Minimum shelf depths

Item	Inches
Books	8-14
Business papers	12-16
Cleaning supplies	4-10
Dinnerware	12-16
Glasses and cups	4-6
Infant supplies	20-24
Luggage	20-24
Magazines	8-12
Radios	8-12
Sheets and blankets	20-24
Toiletries	4-8
Tools (hand-held)	4-10
Towels and bath supplies	16-18
Trays and bowls	16-18
Turntable, records	16-18
Typewriters	16-18

Selecting materials

Grain direction

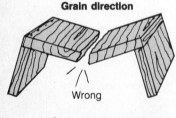

Wrong

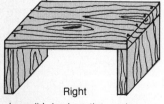

Right

In solid lumber the grain runs lengthwise.
If you cut even a short piece that must carry weight, be sure that the grain still runs lengthwise, in the direction of the legs supporting it.

Consider the materials you want to work with as you develop your design ideas. The standard thickness and rigidity of materials differ. This will effect your detailed plan for the project, as much as aesthetics and cost. For example, you wouldn't want to use expensive hardwood or acrylic for shelves that will be hidden from view most of the time. A low-grade softwood with knots will cost less and be easy to work with but it will sag and break under a load that plywood, hardwood, or glass of equal thickness could support. Metal shelving is also a possibility.

Lumber

There are two kinds of wood: hardwood and softwood. Although characteristics such as weight, knottiness, strength, coloring, grain pattern, and workability can vary from piece to piece regardless of species, the general distinctions between hardwood and softwood are important. **Hardwood** refers to lumber cut from deciduous trees. Oak, maple, birch, cherry, mahogany, and walnut are the popular hardwoods used for fine carpentry. Other hardwoods include teak, rosewood, ebony, and bubinga, but these *exotics* are extremely expensive, hard to find, and generally not used except as thin veneers covering less expensive wood.

Hardwoods are generally more expensive and more difficult to work with than softwoods. They are hard to cut, even with powertools. Don't try to nail or screw two pieces of hardwood together without pre-drilling the stock. Some lumberyards don't even carry hardwoods (cherry and walnut are much scarcer than maple and oak). All hardwoods are sold in random widths. The absence of standard lumber sizes for hardwoods means you may have trouble finding boards of matching widths and so you'll have more cutting and fitting to do.

In spite of the above shortcomings, the strength, durability, and beauty of these woods makes them ideal for certain building projects. (See margin for important characteristics of each species.) Oak or walnut shelves are set off beautifully by just about any kind of shelving hardware. Building a display cabinet or wine rack from maple or cherry will allow you to show off your woodworking talent and will also create a handsome focal point in your home.

Don't choose hardwood if you plan to paint or enamel your project; these woods are used almost exclusively where a clear, natural finish is desired to highlight the grain. Use hardwoods for projects and places in your home where you want storage space to be especially beautiful and on display.

Softwoods are used for every type of construction from rough framing to fine cabinetwork. Readily available, softwoods are a pleasure to work with because of their easy sawing and shaping characteristics. Pine and fir are the most common softwoods. Pine may have a slightly darker and more defined grain than fir, but otherwise the two are nearly indistinguishable. Construction lumber (2x4s, 2x12s, etc.), mouldings, and boards in varying dimensions are all made of softwood. For most storage projects, you'll want to use boards 4- to 10 inches wide and in ½-, ⅝-, ¾-, or 1-inch thicknesses.

Buying lumber. Lumber is sold in *board feet*, a number which you can calculate by multiplying length (in feet), width (inches), and thickness (inches) together and dividing the product by 12. You'll discover that the nominal dimensions of the stock, specifically width and thickness, differ slightly from the actual dimensions (see chart).

The grading system for lumber may vary depending on your dealer and the stock he has available. First and second grade hardwood stock is considered to be of highest quality. Select and #1 Common hardwood lumber will have slight surface defects. High quality softwood may be referred to as Select, Clear, or Supreme. To be sure you're getting the lumber you want at a price that's within your budget, do two things: (1) Describe your project to your lumber dealer. He will tell you what wood is available and may come up with some valid alternatives to your original lumber specifications. (2) Whenever possible, select the wood you buy yourself, piece by piece. Below are some important things to look for.

Make sure your wood has been fully seasoned, Green, or freshly cut lumber is full of sap and unsuitable for construction of any kind. Seasoning allows the sap and other moisture in the wood to dry out, reducing the chances of warpage, shrinking, or cracking. Wood that is sticky, white or slightly green in color, heavier than other pieces, or well-marked with pitch pockets or bubbles is not fully seasoned. Softwoods darken to a greyish tan as they season.

Examine the endgrain of each piece. If the growth rings appear as long curves across the end of the board, the stock is likely to warp (see illustration). The best pieces to buy are those that have a straight up-and-down endgrain. Plainsawn lumber, the most common, often has a circular endgrain, while quartersawn stock does not. Quartersawn lumber is more expensive, but if you want your shelves to be straight five years from now, go with the good endgrain.

The secret 2x4 ripoff
This was the first time I had tackled any fine carpentry so I drew up a very precise set of plans and measured and cut the pieces carefully. When some didn't fit properly—mostly too short—I nearly went batty trying to find my mistakes. Why? Nobody told me that the actual dimensions most lumber is planed down to before it is sold are less than what everybody calls it. A 2x4 ain't 2″x4″; same with a 1x12 and the rest of them. They are a lot less. Measure them if you don't believe me.

Practical Pete

Nominal vs. actual lumber dimensions

Nominal	Actual
1x2	¾″x1½″
1x3	¾″x2½″
1x4	¾″x3½″
1x6	¾″x5½″
1x8	¾″x7¼″
1x10	¾″x9¼″
1x12	¾″x11¼″
2x2	1½″x1½″
2x3	1½″x2½″
2x4	1½″x3½″
2x6	1½″x5½″
2x8	1½″x7¼″
2x10	1½″x9¼″

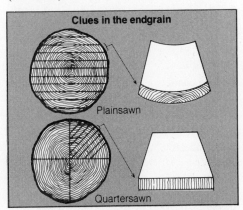

Clues in the endgrain

Plainsawn

Quartersawn

Plainsawn lumber, although economical and easily found, is highly susceptible to warpage because of the circular ring pattern that can be seen in the endgrain. Changes in temperature and humidity cause the wood to shrink or swell unevenly.

Quartersawn lumber has a vertical grain that reacts evenly to changing moisture conditions. The wood will still swell and shrink, but warpage is less likely to occur.

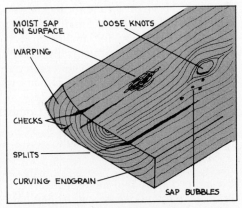

MOIST SAP ON SURFACE
LOOSE KNOTS
WARPING
CHECKS
SPLITS
CURVING ENDGRAIN
SAP BUBBLES

Characteristics of low-quality lumber. Don't buy wood that is knotty; it is difficult to cut and will split easily. Also be on the lookout for cracks and splits. Shallow, narrow cracks or *checks* in the wood are normal signs of seasoning, but deep splits that run with the grain are indicative of poor quality stock.

Plywood

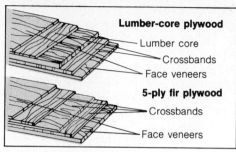

Lumber-core plywood
- Lumber core
- Crossbands
- Face veneers

5-ply fir plywood
- Crossbands
- Face veneers

Plywood is made from wood plies that are glued together so that alternating plies have their grains running at right angles to each other. This gives the material great strength in all directions.

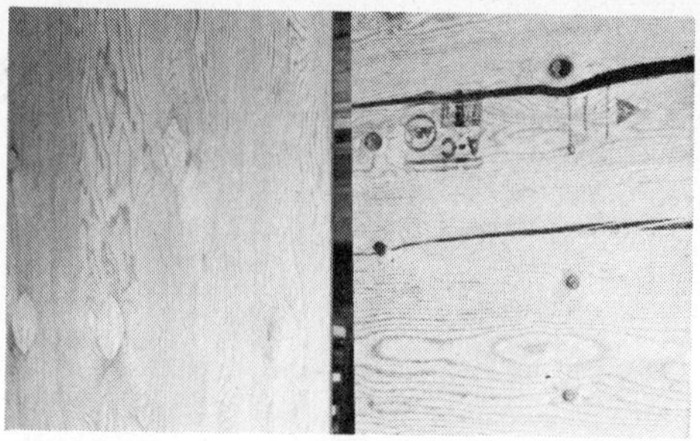

Plywood is sold in 4x8-foot sheets, in the following thicknesses: ⅛-, ¼-, ⅜-, ½-, ⅝-, ¾-, 1-inch. The sheet on the left has an A grade face veneer, while face veneer on the right hand sheet is C grade.

Plywood is a popular alternative to solid lumber. It is stronger, less expensive, and virtually immune to warps or cracks because it is made from thin wood plies, or veneers, that are glued together under great pressure. It also has exceptional strength for its weight because adjacent veneers are laminated with their grains running at right angles to each other.

Plywood is sold in 4x8-foot sheets, in thicknesses from ⅛- to 1-inch. The type of glue used in manufacturing determines whether it is interior or exterior grade. It is graded according to the quality of its two face veneers. "A"-graded veneers are smooth and free of knotholes. A "B" grade means the veneer is solid but may have knots and plugs (plugs are boat-shaped patches used to fill holes). "C" veneers have a limited number of knotholes and splits. As an example of the grading system, a *⅝-inch A/C exterior* designation would mean the plywood sheet is ⅝-inch thick, is made with waterproof glue, and has one clear, solid side and one side with knots and splits.

For most storage projects, you'll want at least one good side for painting or finishing. The lower, less expensive grades are used chiefly for tough construction, although they are great for raw shelving in garage, basement, or attic. You can also buy hardwood-faced plywood in different thicknesses. Use this more costly plywood for an especially smooth, hard surface that can take a natural finish.

Other building materials

Particle board is an economical lumber product made from wood chips that are bound in an adhesive matrix and compressed to form a hard composite material. Like plywood, particle board is sold in 4x8-foot sheets of different thicknesses. You may be able to find half sheets or particle board planks for smaller projects or "instant" shelving. Structurally weaker than plywood, this relatively new material tends to be brittle, hence more difficult to chisel and plane. It is used widely as shelving with track-and-bracket or other hardware shelving systems, but it is not suitable for general construction.

Acrylic plastic, popularly known by the brand names of Plexiglass or Lucite, is becoming a symbol of modern decor. It is unbreakable and can be cut, drilled, and smoothed much like lumber, using special blades and bits. It can also be bent to shape when heated. In clear form it is frequently used as display shelving, but is not rigid enough for large projects or heavy storage jobs. Acrylic is sold in sheet form (thicknesses: ⅛-, ¼-, ⅜-inch), and is comparable to hardwood in cost.

Particle board is a composite material made from wood chips. Warp-free because it has no grain, this material is comparable to plywood in price, but more difficult to work. It's sold in 4x8-foot sheets or in planks of different widths.

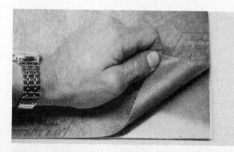

Acrylic plastic lends a modern, unique appearance for storage space that is decorative as well as functional.

Estimating costs and work time

Having to leave your work unfinished or rush through the job because you're pressed for time can take the fun out of any home craftsmanship. Changing specifications for materials in the middle of a project because of high costs is equally frustrating. To avoid these unfortunate circumstances, it's important to get an estimate of costs and work time before you begin the job.

If you have an accurate drawing of your project which includes a materials list, estimating cost is easy. Use the dimensions for each piece to determine how much lumber, plywood, or other material you'll need. When you've figured out how many board feet or sheets of plywood you require (and in what lengths, widths, and thicknesses, in the case of lumber), call up your dealer for a price quote. Remember, your cost estimate should include nails, glue, screws, sandpaper, finish, and any other tools or materials you'll need to complete the job.

Refer to the "What it takes" heading at the beginning of each project in this book for rough estimates of how much time you should allow. Even if you're planning a job not detailed on the pages ahead, you can probably find a project similar enough to yours to give you a rough idea of the time investment you'll have to make. If you have to figure out a time estimate from scratch, be generous. Remember to take drying times for glue, stain, and finish coats into account. Your estimate should also include time for cleaning up and (of course) coffee breaks.

Don't rule out readymades. If the anticipated expenses and time sap your ambition, there's a good chance you can find a set of put-together shelves that is less costly than the lumber required for a home-built unit.

Better hardware stores and home decorating centers have a variety of pre-fab shelves, cabinets and closets designed to fit a wide range of tastes. You can buy an expensive unit if your primary consideration is saving time or working with a minimum number of tools. On the other hand, there are plenty of economical alternatives to handcrafted storage space. Metal shelf supports are available at low cost, as well as track systems that require only a few wood planks to do the same job as a solid bookcase that would take more time and money to build by hand.

Consider a cutting diagram

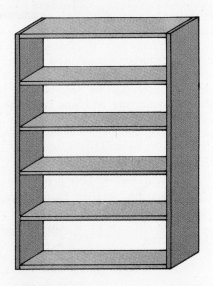 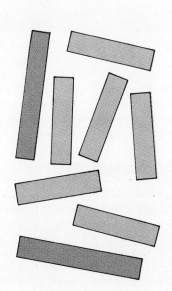 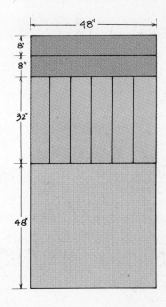

Measuring wisely before cutting larger stock to size saves money by minimizing waste material. A cutting diagram is especially important when working with hardwood, since these woods are expensive and often difficult to find. The easiest way to make a good cutting diagram is to make a scale drawing of each individual piece in your plan and cut them out. Then arrange the pieces by trial and error, like a jigsaw puzzle, edge to edge, until you get a cutting pattern that fits your stock. When transferring your dimensions to the stock, allow for the width of the saw blade; this is ⅛-inch for most power saws. A cutting diagram will also reduce the actual number of cuts you have to make. For pieces that will have to take stress in the middle, like shelving, be sure that the grain runs along the length, not across.

3. CUTTING/JOINING

This chapter explains the tools and techniques you'll be using to put your project together. Whether your plans are simple or complex, good craftsmanship will make a big difference in the way your new storage space looks and works. Developing skill with woodworking tools takes time and patience, so take a good look at the sawing, smoothing, and joining techniques on the next few pages. The information on glues, nails, screws, and other fasteners will be necessary for just about any storage or home repair work you will want to do.

Sawing straight and true

Sawing wood and other building materials is an art that takes time to master. Making accurate cuts not only determines how easily separate pieces go together—it makes all the difference in the final appearance of your project. The tips below will give you a head start on sawing craftsmanship.

- **Measure and mark accurately.** If you're cutting small pieces from a larger sheet or board, plan your cuts in a sequence that will allow you to hold the stock in place and guide your saw as easily as possible. For example, when cutting pieces from a 4x8-foot plywood panel, make your longest cuts first to divide the sheet into smaller, more manageable sections. Be sure to allow for the width of the saw blade when marking and cutting.

- **Choose the right cutting tool.** Crosscut saws are for cutting across the grain of the wood; use a rip saw to cut with the grain. If the stock you're working with is delicate or if a smooth edge is important, use a backsaw with a TPI count of 14 or more. If you're cutting with a power saw, use a blade that is designed for the work you want to do (see page 22). Make sure all blades are sharp.

- **Hold the stock securely.** Smooth, straight, accurate cutting is difficult if the material is shifting or wobbling while you work on it. Use clamps to hold it in place, or recruit a helping hand or two.

- **Use a saw guide.** You may indeed have a steady hand, but a saw guide is more reliable. You can use the guide that was made for your saw, or improvise your own. A miter box (pages 20-21) is an absolutely reliable way of making precise handsawn cuts.

- **Don't force your tool.** Cut through the material at a speed that doesn't strain your arm or the motor of your power saw. Make allowances for stock that is thick, hard, or knotty; any of these characteristics will slow down a saw.

- **Prevent binding.** The weight or positioning of the stock can cause it to bind against your blade as you saw, making cutting difficult or impossible. Support the material in such a way that the cut will remain open and not clamp on your blade.

Preventing a rough edge

Saws and other cutting tools often leave a rough edge that is undesirable for precise joinery work. The blade leaves at least part of the cut-line jagged with small splinters and torn wood fibers; usually on only one side of the stock (see illustration below). Using a fine-toothed blade will produce a smoother surface. Smooth- or finish-cutting blades are available for both circular and saber saws, and of course a fine-toothed backsaw or hand saw (14 or more TPI) will also leave a smoother cut.

Even with the best possible blade or bit you may get some splintering, but there are some tricks you can use to prevent it or keep it at a minimum, as shown in the illustrations below.

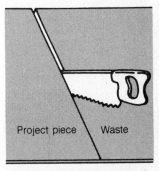

Account for the width of your saw blade. To cut your stock to exact dimensions, keep the "inside" edge of your blade on the outside edge of the cut-line. Centering the blade of the line will leave your piece too small.

Masking tape placed along the cut-line will hold the surface of wood fibers together and so prevent a rough edge. It can also be marked clearly with a pencil if necessary.

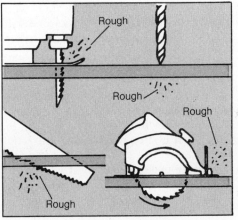

One surface or edge is always more susceptible to splintering than the other, depending on what tool or blade is used.

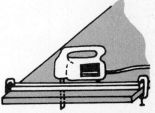

Make your own saw guide if you can't use the guide that goes with your power saw. All you need is a straight length of wood and a couple of clamps to hold it in place.

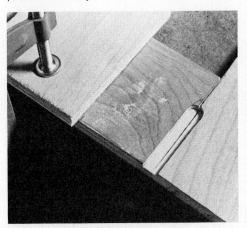

When making a rabbet joint with a router, prevent splintering by butting a scrap piece against the end of the stock.

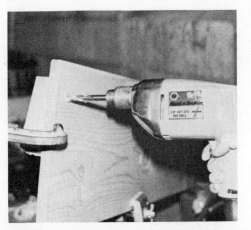

In drilling, you can avoid splintering if you clamp some scrap material to the stock, as shown. The point is not to drill straight through the stock but into the scrap wood.

Joint work

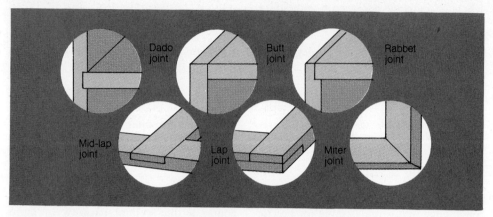

Reinforcing joints

You can strengthen joints considerably by using one or more of the ideas illustrated below.

Use screws to pull the joint together.

Glue and nail a wood cleat in place; ¼-round stock looks better than square stock and works just as well.

Use metal braces; your hardware store will have different styles and sizes.

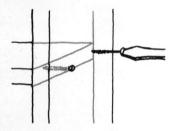

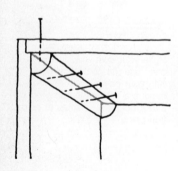

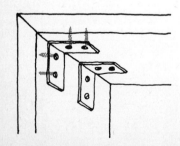

Fitting different pieces of wood together, commonly called joinery, is a crucial part of the craft of carpentry. The strength and final appearance of your work depends upon how well your joints are made.

The butt joint is the simplest joint you can make. Yet while its construction is a lot faster and easier than other joints, it is also a good bit weaker. Butt joints work well where strength or appearance isn't all that important, and you can use them if you don't have the time or tools for more complicated joints. Butt joints are always glued and are often reinforced with screws, wood blocks, or hardware for extra strength.

The rabbet joint is your best bet for corners. It is strong and has an attractive appearance. This type of joint is also fairly easy to make, especially if you have a miter box, router, and a circular or table saw. The rabbet should not be more than half the total thickness of the stock.

The dado joint is used most often for making built-in shelves. As with the rabbet joint, the depth of the groove, or dado, should not be more than half the thickness of the stock. Although most popular on projects where strength and permanence are primary considerations, dado joints add a special touch to small or delicate work, and can also be used for take-apart or adjustable shelving.

The lap and mid-lap joints are simply variations of the rabbet and dado joints, respectively.

The miter joint is nearly as weak as the butt joint and must be cut absolutely perfectly for the sake of strength and appearance. For this reason, it is used only on smaller projects, or where no corner joint may be seen.

The miter box

Here's a tool that's almost indispensable if you plan to work without a power saw. Miter boxes are really nothing more than sophisticated saw guides, but they enable you to make handsawn joints nearly as quickly and accurately as you might with power tools. There are many types, from simple wood or plastic ones that cost a few dollars to expensive metal units with calibrations for cutting any angle from 0-180°. A few of the inexpensive boxes can be used with conventional hand saws, but most require a backsaw. Generally, the more costly the miter box, the greater the number of angles you can cut.

The simplest, least expensive miter boxes are made of wood or plastic, with saw guide slots for cutting 45° and 90° angles.

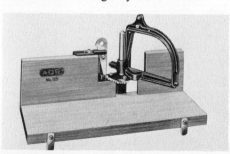

If you do a lot of joinery by hand, get yourself a good quality miter box with a metal saw guide that can be adjusted to cut a variety of angles.

Making a rabbet joint

1. After you've marked off the depth and width of the rabbet, make the depth cut as shown above. Use a backsaw whenever possible for greater smoothness and precision.

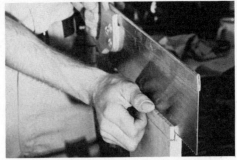

2. To make the second cut, clamp the stock firmly in place and saw along the line you've marked. Sawing "freehand" like this demands a great deal of skill, so work carefully.

3. Use a chisel to smooth the joint before fastening the two pieces together.

4. Corner clamps aren't absolutely necessary for making corners, but they do make gluing and nailing easier; you can also be certain that the corner is square.

Chisel tips

- For smoothing lap or rabbet joints, it's best to work with the bevel of your chisel facing up.

- Work with the bevel facing down when smoothing dado and mid-lap joints, or whenever the recess in the wood is completely enclosed.

- Try to work so the grain of the wood is running up and away from the blade, as shown in the top illustration. If the grain is running back towards you, the chisel blade will follow the grain down into the wood uncontrollably, leaving a rough, irregular surface.

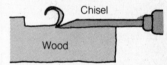

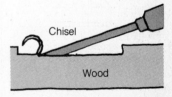

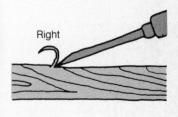

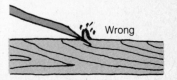

Dadoing step-by-step

1. Use a square to measure and mark before cutting. Width of dado should match thickness of shelf. Since both sides or shelf supports will be identical, you can save work by marking them both at the same time.

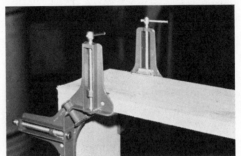

2. Make the two outside cuts first, then make a series of inside cuts; the more you make, the easier your chisel work will be. Be sure to saw to the measured depth on every cut.

3. Use a chisel to remove the waste material and to smooth out the bottom of the groove before you assemble the work.

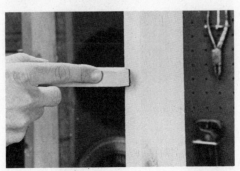

4. Dadoed shelves do not have to be nailed or glued in place, but if you want removable shelves, make the dado slightly wider than the thickness of the shelf.

Circular and table saw blades

Cross cut–for cutting across the grain of the wood.

Carbide-tipped–for cutting materials that are unusually brittle or hard: particle board, plastic laminate, masonite, hardwoods.

Plywood–also called finishing blades; for cutting plywood or making finish cuts in solid stock.

Hollow ground–for fine end grain cuts; good for fine-cutting thick, dense, or oversize stock.

Dado sets–for cutting dados in one operation. Most sets can be adjusted to cut different widths.

Router bits

Mortise–made especially for dadoing, but can also be used for rabbet joints.

Straight–for cutting slots and grooves; also for dadoing.

Rabbeting–for cutting rabbet joints.

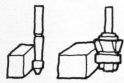

Laminate trimmers–one bit is for trimming the laminate flush; the other is used to bevel the corner where two laminated surfaces join.

Making joints the easy way with power tools

Power tools are your best bet for joint work. Cutting joints with hand tools often requires skilled chisel work in addition to careful sawing. With a circular saw or table saw, however, you can cut accurately enough so that smoothing the cut will be a quick, easy operation. Joints cut with a router hardly ever need additional work before assembly. Bear in mind that when you use a router or power saw for joinery, you must expect to spend more time on adjusting and aligning than on actual cut-ting. Cutting will be quick and precise, as long as you've adjusted the blade or bit and lined it up correctly with the marks on your stock. Use the guide that's right for your tool: for a circular saw, the adjustable metal guide or a straightedge clamped parallel to the cut-line; for a table saw, the miter gauge or rip fence; for a router, a straightedge clamped parallel to the cut-line. Some routers can be equipped with a special guide which is adjustable for straight or circular cuts.

Circular saw. 1. Adjust the baseplate of your saw so that the depth of your cut is no greater than half the thickness of the stock.

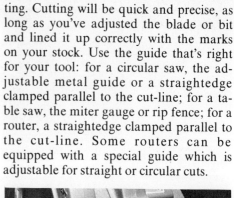

2. Adjust your saw guide and cut the dado. Saw the outside edges of the groove first, then remove waste material inside. Clean up the joint with a chisel before assembling.

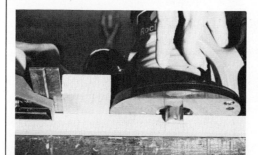

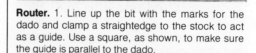

Router. 1. Line up the bit with the marks for the dado and clamp a straightedge to the stock to act as a guide. Use a square, as shown, to make sure the guide is parallel to the dado.

2. Turn the router on and let it reach full speed before applying the bit to the wood. Use steady, firm pressure. Routed joints rarely require smoothing with a chisel.

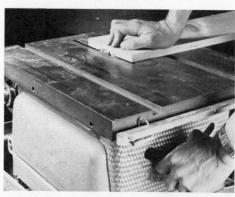

Table saw. 1. Adjust the height of the blade by turning the knob located near the on/off switch.

2. Hold the stock firmly against the *miter gauge,* making sure the gauge is set for a 90° cut, and feed it through the blade using even pressure.

Large-scale construction details

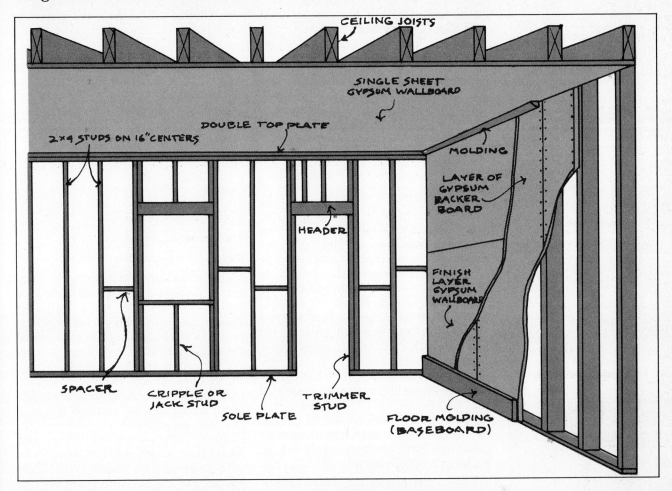

Knowing a little about how your house or apartment is built can be a big help in planning and constructing new storage space. For example, it's important to know how to locate studs if you plan to hang cabinets or shelves. Building a new closet, putting up a wall, installing hooks or hangers, and mounting pegboard are other projects that require some knowledge of the structure of your house.

Structurally, a house consists largely of a system of beams and joists joined to form a skeleton which supports both an outer and inner skin. The outer shell is of necessity thick and strong, usually consisting of several layers: plywood *sheathing*, asphalt-impregnated building felt, and exterior siding. Most interior walls are comparatively thin and delicate: sheetrock, paneling, or plaster.

Locating studs. Let's get back to our skeleton, or structural framework, known more commonly as *framing*. While you can't count on the wall itself to support a great deal of weight, the 2x4 framing joists, or *studs,* can really hold a load. The problem is to locate the studs in your wall so you can fasten into them. In conventionally framed homes, the studs run vertically on 16-inch centers (see illustration above), so if you locate one, finding others on the same wall is easy. Although you can use a stud-finder, or listen for a solid sound while knocking on the wall, the surest way to find your first stud is by drilling a small hole in the wall. If your bit stays in solid material and keeps turning out sawdust, you've found a stud. Only don't just drill randomly; measure 16 inches from a corner, door, or window frame. **Note:** An inconspicuous place for exploratory drilling is about 5 inches above the floor line; fill the hole later with spackling paste.

Old or unconventionally framed homes. Locating studs will be more difficult in these cases. It is not uncommon for builders to space studs on 24-inch centers in non-loadbearing walls for the sake of economy. In many old houses, post and beam construction was the rule: large beams set farther apart, and at random intervals. If you're having trouble locating studs and suspect unconventional framing, try removing the floor molding. Chances are you'll find an exposed nail or two which indicates solid wood underneath.

Screws, nails, and glues

Skillful cutting and fitting is only half the joinery story; choosing and using the right fasteners and adhesives is equally important. In fact, a poor-fitting joint can often be "rescued" with a good glue bond and a few screws to pull it tight. Screws, nails, and glue can be used separately or in combination, depending on the joining job you've got to do. The information on these two pages will help you to select and use the fasteners and adhesives that are best for your project. See page 26 for different types of fasteners available for mounting things on walls.

Screws

Screws are stronger and hold longer than nails, but are also more expensive and more time-consuming to "sink." For this reason, they're not used for rough carpentry such as framing a wall, or in cases where quick assembly is important. Used along with glue, screws will often eliminate the need for clamps because they can pull a joint together with great force. Screws can also be removed easily if you want to disassemble your project, although bolts are better for "take-aparts." (Bolts are available in the same variety of sizes and head types.) Use screws where an extra strong joint is needed, or on fine or traditional work where countersunk or counterbored screws are called for as shown in the diagrams, left.

Choose the length and gauge (shank diameter) of your screws according to the material you're joining. At least two-thirds of the screw's total length should extend into the base material, as shown at left. Select a gauge that's large enough for the holding power you want. If in doubt, use the smaller screw. Glue provides most of the bonding strength; screws pull the joint tight while the glue is curing.

You also have a variety of head types to choose from when selecting screws. Flat-head screws are used most often in woodworking because they are made for countersinking or counterboring, and are therefore less conspicuous.

Always sink screws in predrilled holes. Drill the pilot hole first, using a bit that's slightly smaller than the threaded section of the screw (see illustration at left). The pilot hole should be small enough so the threads bite firmly into the wood, and large enough so you don't have to strain while driving the screw in. Drill the shank clearance hole and the countersink depression next. (You'll need a *countersink bit* for this.) Special combination bits are available that drill pilot, shank, countersink, and counterbore holes in one operation without changing bits.

Nails

Nails are the fastest, least expensive fasteners. The three types used most often for construction of all kinds are illustrated above. The *d* is an abbreviation for *penny*, or length classification. (The nails above are actual labeled size.) Common nails are for rough or large scale building; you'll need 8, 10, and maybe 12d nails for framing a wall or putting up a closet. Box and finishing nails are narrower in gauge and best-suited for finer joinery work. Finishing nails are made to be *set* and covered with wood dough (see below).

To determine the length of the nails you plan to use, remember that ⅔-¾ of the total length should extend into the base material. If you're nailing into hardwood or delicate stock, you may have to predrill your nail holes to prevent splitting or use a shorter, thinner nail. Use a bit that's half the diameter of the nail or less.

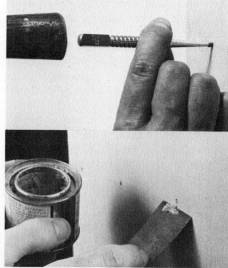

Use a special punch called a *nailset* to sink finishing nails slightly below the surface. Then fill holes with wood dough and sand the dough flush when it hardens.

Countersunk screw

Counterbored screw

DOWEL PLUG

COUNTERSINK DEPRESSION

SHANK CLEARANCE HOLE

PILOT HOLE

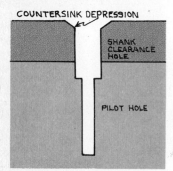

Types of screw heads

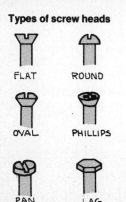

FLAT   ROUND

OVAL   PHILLIPS

PAN   LAG

Glue

Glue is a must for all permanent joints. Instead of forcing a joint together like screws or nails do, glue is a bonding agent that makes two separate pieces into one. The main types are described in the chart. *Setting time* is the time it takes for the glue to dry and form a bond. Maximum bond strength is achieved when the glue *cures*. When deciding what kind of glue you should use, consider cost, ease of application, and the conditions which the glued joint will be exposed to.

Regardless of what glue you're using, be sure to read the manufacturer's description of the product and follow the directions for surface preparation and application closely.

Here are some general guidelines to good gluing. Clean the joint thoroughly before you glue; oil, dirt, wax, and dust are all enemies of adhesion. Work the glue into the material; don't just bead it on. This is especially important when gluing porous surfaces like the endgrain of a pine or fir board. Last but not least, remove excess glue as soon as possible, using a damp rag. Glue allowed to stand even for a few minutes can leave a stain in the wood that's tough to remove.

Description/Setting time/Curing	Advantages/Limitations/Suggested use	Preparation and application
Polyvinyl acetate (PVA). Familiar white glue; usually comes in a clear squeeze bottle. Dries clear. Water soluble/3-4 hours/24 hours.	Inexpensive; sets quickly; no mixing/Poor moisture resistance; limited shelf life; discolors metal/For interior use on porous materials.	Apply generously to both surfaces; clamp securely; wipe away excess glue.
Aliphatic resin. Yellow glue similar to white glue in consistency. Dries clear or slightly amber. Water soluble/3-4 hours/24 hours.	More water-resistant than white glue; made especially for woodworking; no mixing; quick setting; economical for large jobs/Limited shelf life; not waterproof; will not bond non-porous materials/Use on wood-to-wood joints.	Apply generously to both surfaces; clamp securely; wipe away excess glue.
Resorcinol. Also known as waterproof glue; usually sold in cans, it comes in two parts/6-10 hours/24 hours.	Completely waterproof; excellent bonding strength on porous surfaces/Expensive; requires mixing; long setting time; leaves a dark glue line/Use on exterior wood-to-wood joints, or where a waterproof bond is needed.	Mix only amount needed, according to manufacturer's instructions; coat both surfaces; clamp. Heat will shorten setting time.
Epoxy. A two-part adhesive sold in cans or tubes; comes in several varieties, with differences based on setting time, opacity, and viscosity. Waterproof/¼-12 hours/24 hours.	Excellent bond strength; waterproof. (Short-setting epoxies are weaker.) Can be used as a filler/Expensive; requires mixing; offers no advantage over aliphatic resin on interior wood-to-wood joints/Use for small gluing jobs, or when joining dissimilar or nonporous materials.	Combine and mix *hardener* and *resin* according to manufacturer's directions. Use only as much as needed. Clamping is optional; avoid forcing epoxy out of the joint.
Contact cement. A specialized glue that bonds on contact; comes in cans and small tubes or bottles. There is no setting time/curing takes 24-48 hours.	Flexible; reaches 75% bond strength on contact; no clamping needed/Expensive; surfaces to be glued can't be realigned once they contact each other/Use for covering surfaces with veneer, plastic, and other laminates.	Apply generously and evenly to both surfaces (use a brush for large jobs). Allow to dry until slightly tacky. Align surfaces exactly and press together.

Tips from the gluing experts

A heat lamp can help you to cut down setting and curing times. Don't create a fire hazard by exposing the wood to dangerously high temperatures, and be sure the joint is heated evenly.

It's easy to make your own wood dough with some fine sawdust and a little white or yellow glue. Mix the sawdust into the glue gradually until you get a creamy, homogeneous paste.

Use scrap pieces of wood as clamping blocks; they will distribute clamp pressure more evenly and prevent the metal clamping feet from damaging the finished stock.

If you can't clamp your joint, use screws to pull the glued surfaces together and keep them under pressure while the glue sets. A few finishing nails will secure the joint while you drill screwholes.

The 007 bond
I got a great bond on my last glue job; so great that when I tried to remove my project from the workbench it wouldn't budge. Next time I'll use a little waxed paper to keep the glue where it belongs: in the joint and off the bench.

Practical Pete

Wall fasteners

Building new storage space often involves wall fasteners of one type or another. Whether you're hanging shelves, putting up pegboard, securing a built-in bookcase, or installing cabinets, you can be sure there's a wall fastener made for the job. Wall fasteners come in a confusing array of sizes and shapes, so if you're uncertain of size or design, ask your hardware dealer for advice. Tell him what kind of wall you're dealing with, and what you want to hang, secure, or support. **Note:** Don't make your wall-joining job more difficult than it needs to be. You may not need special fasteners at all if you can locate a stud or joist to nail or screw into. The wood framing behind your gypsum, panel, or plaster wall will always hold more weight than the wall material itself, so try locating studs before shopping around for wall fasteners.

If your wall is concrete, brick, tile, or some other solid, non-wooden material, or if you can't locate or utilize the framing, the information below can help you out. The most frequently used wall fasteners are listed below. Suitable wall types for each fastener are indicated in italics.

Installing standard fasteners

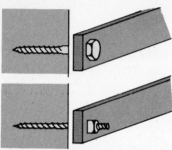

Lag screws and hanger bolts *for solid wood, studs, or other wood framing members.* Sink these heavy-duty hangers into studs or joists for holding loads of 20 pounds or more. (See hints on locating studs in a hollow wall, page 23.)

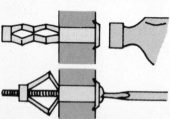

Mollies *for gypsum wallboard, wood paneling, plaster, and hollow walls.* Available in different sizes, these wall hangers consist of a threaded, collapsible metal housing and a matching bolt. To install a molly, first drill out a hole no larger than the molly's diameter. Then hammer the unit into the hole. Make sure the teeth on

Plastic expansion anchors *for gypsum wallboard, plaster, tile, hollow walls.* These inexpensive anchors come in several designs and sizes, but all operate on the same principle: driving a screw into the hole in the installed anchor forces

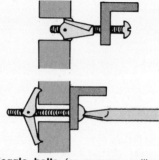

Toggle bolts *for gypsum wallboard, wood paneling, and hollow walls.* These fasteners come in a variety of different sizes, and are easy to install. Make sure the bolt is long enough for the spring-activated toggle to open up. The hole should be just large enough to accommodate the toggle assembly.

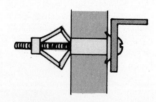

the lip of the molly are firmly embedded in the wall (first illustration). Turn the bolt clockwise with a screwdriver to collapse the molly and lock it in place. Make sure the lip doesn't turn with the bolt. Now you can remove and re-insert the bolt for mounting.

two plastic feet out against the hole, wedging the anchor in place. Most anchors are labeled with the correct bit diameter for installation; if not, use the bit that gives you the snuggest fit.

Metal expansion shields *for brick, concrete, stone, marble, and other solid walls.* These anchors expand as bolts or screws are turned into them, exerting pressure against the walls of the installation hole which wedges them in place. Although available in different styles and sizes, metal expansion shields are only suitable for use in hard, solid walls.

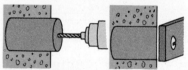

Wooden dowels *for brick, concrete, stone, marble, and other solid walls.* You can make your own wall anchors from wooden dowels. Your installation hole should be at least an inch deep and must match the diameter of the dowel so the wooden plug fits *very* snugly. **Hint:** A generous dab of epoxy glue will help hold the plug in place and compensate for an oversize hole. Drill out the pilot hole for the screw after you've hammered the dowel into the hole.

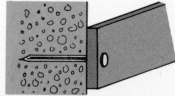

Masonry nails *for concrete and cinder block walls.* Because of the thick gauge of these nails and the shock transmitted to the stock, it's advisable to drill a pilot hole in the material you're fastening to the wall. Masonry nails are notorious for bending and won't penetrate concrete that is extremely hard or fine. *Caution: Always wear eye protection when nailing into hard materials like concrete or cinder block.*

Building the basic box

1. Working from a simple drawing like the one shown at right, transfer your measurements to the stock. Use a carpenter's square to make sure your cut-lines are true. Take the width of the saw blade into account when marking out adjacent pieces.

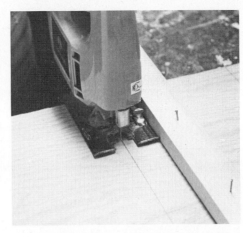

2. Use a saw guide to assure a straight cut. In this case a straight length of wood is clamped parallel to the cut line. To prevent binding, make sure the waste side of the stock is supported while you saw.

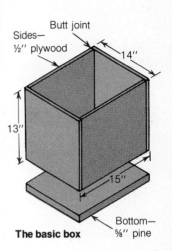

The basic box

Butt joint
Sides— ½″ plywood
14″
13″
15″
Bottom— ⅝″ pine

3. Glue and nail the sides together. For this box, a butt joint is used for the sake of speed and simplicity; a rabbet joint is stronger but takes longer to make. If you improvise a support like the one shown here, joining the sides is easier.

4. Square up the box using a square and a diagonal brace as shown. Nail one end of the brace to a side about midway between the corners. Then force the corner against the square and nail the free end of the brace to the adjacent side.

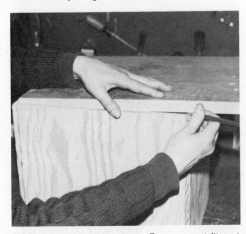

5. Measure and cut the base. For an exact fit, cut the stock to measured width, then fit it into the bottom and mark the length for final cutting.

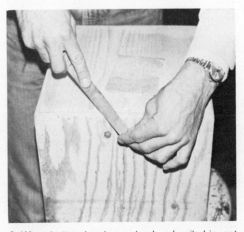

6. When bottom has been glued and nailed in, set all nails and fill the holes with wood dough. When wood dough dries, round corners with a file and smooth sides and bottom with sandpaper. Finish as desired.

7. Make a group of boxes and you can stack them as shown. An advantage of *modular* storage such as this is that it can be taken down, relocated, or rearranged quickly and easily.

4.FINISHING

Now that you've planned your new storage space, drawn up design details, selected materials, cut parts to size, and assembled the whole project, you're ready for finishing. Although the main function of finishing is to preserve and protect the wood or other material, a good finish really shows off the craftsmanship involved in the design and construction of your project for years to come.

Finishing means more than just applying paint or varnish. The three steps involved in surface preparation (to be described) are essential for a good finish. You may also decide that you want to stain the wood or apply wood filler before putting on the finish. Finishing decisions depend on a number of important factors: how much time and money you want to spend, the size of your project, the type of wood or other material you're dealing with, the surrounding decor, application details, drying time, and durability. Apply these considerations to the information on the following pages to determine how you want to finish your project, then do it!

Getting the surface set

Step 1: Fill holes

Fill all cracks and holes with wood dough. Clean up cracks or holes before you fill them by removing loose splinters and sawdust. Use a putty knife or any knife with a flexible blade to apply the dough. Always overfill depressions so they can be sanded flush. You can make your own wood dough by mixing sawdust with some white or yellow glue. Take some fine sawdust from the stock you're filling for the most inconspicuous patch. Mix in the sawdust gradually until the consistency is creamy, not stiff. Fill deep holes in stages, letting each layer of wood dough dry before applying the next.

Step 2: Make it smooth

Use sandpaper to smooth all surfaces to be finished. Sanding your project down before applying the finish is one of those jobs that is easy to neglect, but it really pays off, since any irregularities are always accentuated by finish coats. Sanding also improves absorption and adhesion by removing surface wood pores that may be clogged with dirt, wax, or oil.

Smoothing work will go faster and easier if you use sandpaper of the right abrasive strength (see chart below). Always work from coarse to fine grades. For example, a 100 grit followed by a 150 grit smoothing schedule works well on most lumber. Sandpaper will eventually wear out as abrasive particles become dull or clogged with sawdust, but you can get more "life" from each sheet if you use sanding blocks (see margin).

Don't forget to round off edges and soften corners slightly while you smooth to prevent chips and blemishes. You can use sandpaper for this job, but a *medium-cut bastard* file will work much faster.

Sandpaper		
Grit	**Classification**	**Common uses**
600 500	super fine	wet or dry polishing
400 360 320	extra fine	
280 240 220	very fine	dry sanding between finish coats
180 150	fine	final sanding on bare wood before applying finish
120 100 80	medium	general wood sanding, preliminary sanding on rough wood
60 50 40	coarse	rough sanding, paint and finish removal

Always sand with the grain of the wood. Start with a medium grit and finish with a fine grit. The best way to sand flat surfaces is to use a sanding block, as shown above.

Round off sharp corners and edges with a file. For best results, keep the file at an angle to the edge, as shown. It's a good idea to give filed areas a once-over with some sandpaper.

Put power tools to work for you. Sanding discs are available as an accessory for your electric drill, and make quick work of sharp edges. An orbital sander is a good investment if you really want to speed up smoothing operations.

Sanding Blocks

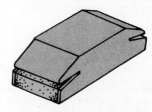

1. Commercial sanding blocks are easy to "load." You'll find them in most paint and hardware stores.

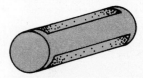

2. Use a length of dowel rod to make a sanding block for curved surfaces.

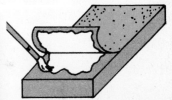

3. You can bond your sandpaper permanently to a wood block with some contact cement. Coat both surfaces, allow glue to get tacky, then press wood and paper together.

Step 3: Remove dust

Sanding leaves a thin layer of fine sawdust on the wood surface. Remove it with a tack rag. You can buy one at most paint and hardware stores, or make one by dampening a piece of cheesecloth in some varnish and allowing it to get tacky.

For large projects, save time and effort by using a vacuum to remove sawdust. Make sure the attachment you use has soft bristles, like the one shown, so there's no risk of scratching the wood.

Wood filler: how and when to use it

Open or coarse-grained woods like oak, hickory, mahogany, and teak will not take a smooth, even varnish or lacquer finish unless their large and irregularly spaced pores (see margin) are filled beforehand. To do this, you'll need some wood filler, a preparation made specifically for this job. Wood filler comes as a paste and usually requires thinning before application (check instructions on can). Most fillers work best on wood that has been sealed with a wash coat (thinned-down) of shellac or lacquer. When the sealer coat has dried completely, mix up your filler and brush a thick coat onto the stock. Work the filler into the pores of the wood with your brush.

Note: Wood filler comes in different colors, or it can be custom-colored by using a wiping stain as the thinning agent. When the filler begins to dry out or dull over (5-25 minutes), wipe it off with a coarse rag. Always wipe across the grain so you don't remove the filler that's lodged in the wood pores where it belongs. Don't stop until you have wiped it all off the surface. If it dries hard it is difficult to remove. You will have to soak a rag in turpentine or benzene to soften it enough to wipe away. Wait 24 hours for the filler to dry, smooth the surface with extra-fine sandpaper if necessary, and you're ready for stain and finish coats.

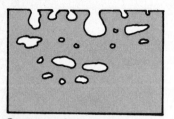

Coarse-grained woods have irregularly spaced pores.

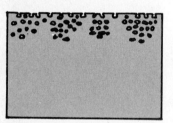

Fine-grained woods have small, evenly distributed pores.

1) Thin wood filler according to manufacturer's instructions, then brush it onto the wood generously. Work the material into the pores of the wood with the bristles.

2) When the filler starts to dry out or dull over, wipe it off with a coarse rag. Always wipe across the grain to fill the pores and clean off excess.

Staining wood

There are three reasons for staining wood: to make it look like another type of wood, to give it an older appearance, and to make it blend in better with surrounding wood or decor. You may want to make a major tone change by staining a light-colored wood like birch to look like walnut. On the other hand, you may have several oak boards to use with track shelving that are slightly different in color. In a case like this, only a subtle stain is needed. It's even possible to spot-stain a piece of wood to make its color more uniform. Once the wood has been stained, the next step is to apply a clear finish to show off your work and to protect the wood from moisture, abrasion, undesirable stains, and general wear.

There are several different types of stains. Consult the chart at right to determine which one is best for the job you have in mind. Stains are available in a wide variety of wood tones. Don't rely on the name or color designation alone when choosing; all stain manufacturers have samples of each stain as it looks on different kinds of wood. You'll find these displays wherever stains are sold. As a final check, you should test your stain out on a scrap piece of wood identical to the stock in your project.

Staining wood is easy but very important as far as final appearance is concerned. Here are some tips that will help you to do a good job: If more than one can of stain is to be used, mix all the stain together in a large container before application to assure consistent color. When removing excess stain from the wood surface, dampen your cloth with stain first. A dry cloth is likely to remove pigmentation from the surface wood pores and leave lint behind. The end grain on any piece of wood is extra absorbent, and will "drink" enough stain to make it noticeably darker than the rest of the wood. Control end grain stain absorption by applying a limited amount of stain to these areas.

Stain samples

The grain-raising story

You've sanded the bare wood to a satin-smooth texture in preparation for staining and finishing. The stain goes on well and gives you just the color and highlights you'd hoped for. The only problem is that the stained wood surface seems to be rougher than it was before you applied the stain.

There's no need to be alarmed; the surface actually is rougher than it was after the final sanding. This is because the stain has caused the surface wood fibers to swell and stick out unevenly. Water-base and penetrating oil stains will always raise the grain to some degree, especially on softwoods. Wiping stains and non-grain-raising stains will not.

A raised grain can get in the way of a good finish, and should be smoothed "flat" when the stain has dried. Use a new piece of extra-fine steel wool for this job. Go over the wood lightly, so that you only remove the protruding wood fibers. **Note:** Some finishing experts raise the grain purposely *before* staining by wetting it down with a damp cloth. When the bare wood is smoothed again, it can be stained without raising the grain noticeably.

Comparing different kinds of stain

Description	Use	Application
Non-grain-raising (NGR) stains. Also known as quick-drying or alcohol-base stains, these preparations are more expensive than other stains but do have several advantages: they dry quickly enough so that finish can be applied within 3 hours, and they can be sprayed on to save time with large projects.	Use NGR stains on hardwoods like oak, maple, or birch. These woods don't need a "transforming" stain to make them resemble some other wood type, but rather a slight shading to accent their already distinctive grain. NGR stains don't work well on softwoods.	Wipe or spray on; avoid brushing. Don't worry if the coloring isn't as dark as you want; just reapply the stain at 15 minute intervals for darker effects. Don't flood NGR stains onto the wood; additional tone is achieved by reapplication, not penetration.
Water-base stains. These stains are available in ready-to-use liquid form, or as a powder dye that must be dissolved in water before use. You can save money by mixing the stain yourself, adjusting the color simply by varying the concentration. Drying time: 24 hours.	Use these stains on hardwoods or softwoods, for either subtle or dramatic changes in tone. On absorbent woods like pine, water stains will raise the grain considerably, so don't use this type of stain if you want to avoid additional smoothing work before applying a finish.	Apply the stain generously, making sure to keep the surface wet until the wood is saturated. Wait a few minutes, then remove all excess stain with a cloth that has been slightly dampened in stain.
Nonpenetrating oil stains. Characteristically thick and paint-like, these stains have a linseed oil base and are heavily pigmented. Drying time: 24 hours.	Effective for darkening pine, fir, and other light woods; the best stain to use if you want to hide the grain of the wood rather than highlight it.	Apply generously, using a brush. Wait several minutes for the pigment to settle, then wipe the surface down, removing excess stain with an absorbent cloth. The harder you wipe, the lighter the final color of the wood will be.
Penetrating oil stains. These are the most popular stains for use on softwoods, and come in a wide variety of wood tones. Because of their mineral spirit or turpentine base, these stains penetrate deeply into the wood, and do a good job of sealing and protecting in addition to staining. Drying time: 24 hours.	Use mainly on softwoods, including plywood. Penetrating oil stains can be used effectively under a paste wax finish because of their protective quality.	Apply liberally, using a brush, sponge or rag. The intensity of the stain depends on how long it is allowed to penetrate into the wood, so wipe off early if you want a lighter shade. Reapply to achieve darker coloring or let the stain stand longer before wiping.

Using finishes

Putting a finish on your project serves two purposes: 1) to protect the wood or other material from general wear, and 2) to enhance the appearance of the project. Al-

though there is a variety of wide finishes available, those described here offer a range of choices, and are more durable and easier to use than less popular finishes.

Paints and enamels, for sure results on any surface. Finishing with paint or enamel is a great way to transform a drab-looking project into something special. Compared to clear finishes, paints and enamels give more reliable, predictable results because they don't depend on the grain of the wood for good looks. Used as a cover-up, these finishes enable you to use inexpensive building materials (plywood, particle board) without worrying about the final appearance of your project. Use rustproof formulas on non-wooden materials like metal and gypsum wallboard.

Because of the confusing variety of products available, deciding what paint or enamel to use can be pretty frustrating. Choosing the right color, and deciding whether you want a flat, gloss, or semi-gloss finish are the first (and the easiest) decisions. Other considerations are cost, durability, drying time, and ease of application and clean-up. All this information is on the paint can, and your paint dealer can give you additional information and specific rec-

ommendations. Paint is less expensive than enamel, but enamel finishes are comparable to varnish as far as durability goes. Used often in high traffic zones like the kitchen and bathroom, enamel will stand up to hard use, won't stain or spot, and can be wiped clean with a damp cloth. If you're putting up a wall, constructing a built-in shelf or cabinet space, or finishing new storage space to blend in with the room, paint will give you the best results. Painted surfaces lack the hard brightness of enamel.

Whether you're painting over bare wood or wood that has been previously finished, at least two coats are required for a first-class job. The first coat, often referred to as the *base, primer,* or *undercoat,* must seal the wood, cover all stains or irregularities in the grain, and provide a smooth, uniform, and adherent surface for subsequent finish coats. Although the paint you use for finish coats can often serve as a primer (consult manufacturer's instructions), you're usually better off using a *primer-sealer.*

1. Use a primer-sealer as the base coat on bare wood or over an existing finish. Because of their short drying time and sealer/stain hiding qualities, commercial primer-sealers are ideal undercoaters.

2. Once the undercoat has dried, paint on the finish coat. Use a clean brush, dipping only the bottom third of the bristles into the paint. Always paint from the top down.

Combine oil and turpentine in a three-to-one mixture and soak this into the wood by pouring or brushing. Let finish penetrate for 15 minutes; remove excess; then buff wood surface with a clean, lint-free cloth.

Oil, for the traditional, hand-rubbed finish. Boiled linseed oil, turpentine, and elbow grease are all you need for this finish. One of the oldest and least expensive finishes, rubbed oil protects the wood from stains of all types and gives a warm, soft luster that is most beautiful on dark-grained hardwoods. Light woods like pine or maple can be stained before they are oil-finished, but never apply oil over filler or sealer coats.

Begin an oil finish by thinning your linseed oil with turpentine; one part turpentine to three parts oil is about right. (Later coats will be at full strength.) Flood the wood surface with this mixture, let it soak in for 15 minutes, then remove the ex-

cess and buff the wood until you get a dull glow. It's important to rub the surface vigorously, either with a lint-free cloth or your palm, to drive the oil deep into the pores of the wood. Additional applications (ten or so, no kidding) and rubdowns will produce an even deeper, richer glow. Wait at least 24 hours before reapplying the linseed oil, and rub in a little at a time, instead of flooding the whole surface.

The traditional rubbed-oil finish really takes a great deal of time and effort, and now there are several finishes available which will produce nearly the same results after one or two applications. Ask your dealer for "easy" oil finishes if the traditional method scares you off.

Varnish and polyurethane, for durability and beauty. These are far and away the most popular clear finishes. Available in either gloss or satin, these finishes will show the wood grain and protect against moisture, stains, and abrasions.

Old-fashioned varnishes took hours and sometimes days to dry completely—a major drawback, since dust and other particles would dry into the finish. Modern varnishes are made largely from synthetic resins (polyurethanes) and

will dry in 4-6 hours. When buying varnish, read the product description on the can to make sure you won't have to deal with extended drying times. All the synthetic varnishes (known by different brand names, but usually labeled as urethane or polyurethane) are quick-drying. Two coats of varnish are normally required for a complete finish. All varnishes are made to be used over bare wood, so check your finish for compatibility if you plan to use stain or wood filler.

Apply varnish generously, but avoid bending or slapping the bristles of your brush, since this can cause bubbles.

Spraying on a lacquer finish is usually easier if you hang up your project so that you can move around it freely. Keep the nozzle moving and build up at least three thin, even coats for a durable, good-looking finish.

Lacquer, the alternative to brush-on finishes. Lacquer is a fast-drying, multiple-coat finish which can be applied with an air compressor/spray gun unit, but is most often used in spray can form. Most hardware, paint, and home decorating centers have a wide selection of colors as well as clear lacquer. You'll also find *acrylic* finishes in spray cans; they apply and dry just like lacquer, but tend to be less durable.

Because of its quick-drying and spray-on application, lacquer is convenient and easy to use. It's great for

finishing curved, contoured, or large projects which would involve an undesirable amount of brushwork. (You won't have to clean any brushes either.) **Note:** Lacquer shouldn't be used over an oil-base stain. Follow the manufacturer's instructions pertaining to staining, sealing, and filling under a lacquer finish.

As far as spray finishing technique goes, just remember to keep the nozzle moving to avoid bubbles or runs. Build your finish up in thin layers, coat by coat.

Penetrating resin, for protection and durability without covering the wood. Unlike varnish, paint, or lacquer—surface finishes which protect the wood by covering it—penetrating resin is an in-the-wood finish that leaves the wood surface exposed. The synthetic resins that make up this finish penetrate deep into the wood and harden, making the wood surface strong and extremely resistant to water damage, stains, heat, and abrasion. A penetrating resin finish will darken the wood slightly and highlight the grain considerably, although in a softer, subtler way than varnish or lacquer. It is used

most often on walnut, mahogany, cherry, oak, and other hardwoods which have distinctive coloring or grain patterns. There are really only two drawbacks to penetrating resin finishes: They're expensive; and they won't do much for wood with an even, uninteresting, or light grain. Penetrating resin can be applied over a non-grain-raising stain.

This is one of the easiest finishes to apply; just let the liquid finish soak into the wood and wipe off the excess that remains on the surface. Most brands recommend two separate applications. Allow at least 4 hours between "coats."

Keep the wood surface horizontal, if possible, and pour the finish onto the wood, spreading it out with some extra-fine steel wool. The object is to saturate the wood pores, then wipe off excess finish with a rag.

Four clues to a fantastic finish

1) Study the information on the can or container before using the product. You'll find the manufacturer's recommendations for surface preparation, thinning agents, companion products (like stains, fillers, and sealers), application tools and techniques, and clean-up, to name a few.
2) Make sure the different preparations you use sequentially are compatible with one another. Never apply oil over sealer coats, for example. Compatibility infor-

mation should be on the can.
3) Prepare the surface. Any finish coat is only as good as the surface it covers. If you're working on bare wood, follow a filling, sanding, and sealing *schedule* that will really show off the finish. Wait for each coat to dry *completely* before applying another. You can speed up drying time by using a heat lamp.
4) Don't apply anything under damp or humid conditions, and make sure the surface you're treating is dry; otherwise absorption and adhesion are incomplete.

5. PROJECTS

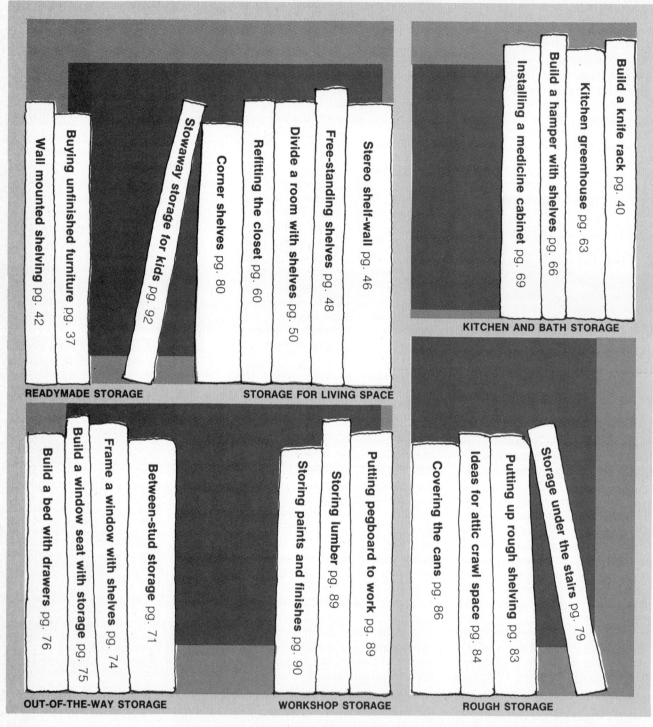

READYMADE STORAGE

Wall mounted shelving pg. 42

Buying unfinished furniture pg. 37

Stowaway storage for kids pg. 92

STORAGE FOR LIVING SPACE

Corner shelves pg. 80

Refitting the closet pg. 60

Divide a room with shelves pg. 50

Free-standing shelves pg. 48

Stereo shelf-wall pg. 46

KITCHEN AND BATH STORAGE

Installing a medicine cabinet pg. 69

Build a hamper with shelves pg. 66

Kitchen greenhouse pg. 63

Build a knife rack pg. 40

OUT-OF-THE-WAY STORAGE

Build a bed with drawers pg. 76

Build a window seat with storage pg. 75

Frame a window with shelves pg. 74

Between-stud storage pg. 71

WORKSHOP STORAGE

Storing paints and finishes pg. 90

Storing lumber pg. 89

Putting pegboard to work pg. 89

ROUGH STORAGE

Covering the cans pg. 86

Ideas for attic crawl space pg. 84

Putting up rough shelving pg. 83

Storage under the stairs pg. 79

In the 60 pages that follow you will find a full two dozen storage projects you can build yourself, plus practical advice on a range of storage ideas—from fasteners and hardware to how to hang cabinets; from readymades to pegboard and track/ bracket bookshelves. (Did you know that wall track has top and bottom ends?)

Most of the projects are designed to be easy enough for non-carpenters to construct without special tools—and still look good. Many of the designs are original (including some take-apart shelving units you can knock down when you move and reassemble in your new home). Nearly all of the plans are drawn so you can change the dimensions to fit the area you have available. Try a simple one first, the knife rack on page 40 or the basic box on page 73, for instance, before you tackle the big jobs like the platform bed with storage drawers on page 76.

Readymade storage

There is a good chance that many of your storage problems can be solved with a quick trip to your hardware store or home decorating center. Instead of buying hardware, tools, nails, glue, and building materials, you may find a set of put-together shelves, some quick-mount fixtures, a hang-up rack, or other *readymade* storage unit that fits your needs exactly. There are plenty of readymade storage ideas that are not only easy-install storage solutions, but they are actually less expensive than a comparable built-from-scratch project. Adding new storage space with readymades may not give you quite the satisfaction of completing a project you've designed yourself, but the time and money saved can go toward a special project that you really want to put your energies into.

This set of shelves is supported by screw-on spindles. Both shelves and spindles are prefinished and can be combined in a variety of ways to make an attractive, free-standing set of shelves. Made by the Cranmere division of Kirsch Co., you'll find these and similar shelf systems at hardware stores and home decorating centers.

Nuts, screws, washers, bits, pencils, and many other small and easy-to-misplace items in your workshop are most effectively stored in a small set of drawers like this. Made especially for work and hobby-shop storage, the clear plastic drawers can be completely removed. Most models can be labeled on the front of each drawer.

A metal shoe stand keeps your footwear in good order. Most models are inexpensive and come at least partially assembled.

Here's a bright idea for stashing paper bags. This tough plastic unit can be screwed to the inside of any cabinet door.

Pegboard and free-standing plastic shelves like the one shown here are good readymade solutions to storage problems. Each shelf unit has holes in its top that are handy for cataloging grouped items. Shelves can be used individually or stacked to form larger modular storage area.

Another convenient readymade holds common containers for plastic wraps and aluminum foil, as well as paper bags. This unit is also designed to be screwed to the inside of a cabinet door.

These bent-wire shelves (made by Shulte Corp.) are designed for easy installation and can create new storage space wherever you've got an "empty" door. Building a similar set of shelves would take hours, and materials costs would probably exceed the cost of this readymade unit.

Pegboard for a storage quick fix

What it takes

Approximate time: One hour or less, to cut and hang a 3x6 foot panel.

Tools and materials: Crosscut saw or power saw with fine-toothed blade, drill with bits, screwdriver, plus: 2-inch or 2½-inch round-head screws with washers, rubber pegboard spacers or furring strips.

Sad sag story

You wouldn't believe how fast I put up a sheet of pegboard in my T.V. room. From bare wall to beautiful storage area took just half an hour. A couple of weeks later though, things didn't look so good. Because I had only put in screws around the edges, the pegboard was starting to bow and sag. Luckily I spotted the bend just in time and managed to save the board. Next time I'll space my screws at more frequent intervals and I won't forget that middle sections need support too.

Practical Pete

With just a few tools and perhaps an hour of work time, you can transform an empty wall into an impressive storage area with the help of pegboard. Pegboard, technically called perforated hardboard, is easy to work with, inexpensive, and offers flexible, quick-change storage space. The vast array of pegboard fixtures on the market can handle all kinds of storage chores and can be removed or rearranged for changing storage needs. Pre-finished pegboard, available in several colors and wood tones, lends a fine decorative look.

Pegboard is sold in standard 4x8-foot sheets, though you may be able to find 4x4 sheets at some home decorating centers. Standard thicknesses are ⅛- and ¼-inch. The ¼-inch pegboard, which has larger holes and requires heavier-gauge fixtures, is only necessary if you have very weighty implements to hang. For storing most hand tools and general household items, ⅛-inch pegboard will work fine.

Pegboard is easy to cut but tends to fray at cut-line edges. To prevent this, use a fine-toothed plywood or finish cut blade with your power saw. If you're cutting by hand, use a crosscut saw. An equally important preventive measure is to support the board very securely along the cut line. Don't let it flop or vibrate while sawing.

When hanging pegboard, be sure to allow clearance for fixtures, at least ⅜-inch airspace is required between the pegboard and the wall. This means that if you are putting up pegboard over paneling, sheetrock, plaster, or masonry, you will have to use special rubber spacers or furring strips to get the proper clearance. If you're covering exposed studs, clearance behind the pegboard is built-in.

When fastening pegboard to any wall, it is important to give the board all-over support. Without a screw to secure it every 16 to 24 inches, sooner or later your pegboard will bow out from the wall—not a happy prospect. Use 2-inch round-head screws with washers to secure it.

An alternate anchoring method is to construct a sturdy frame on the back of your pegboard panel, using wood strips at least ½-inch thick. Once the frame has been glued and nailed in place, you can fasten it to the wall in several places along the top and bottom edges. This method is good for working on masonry or any hollow wall with irregularly spaced studs.

It's a good idea to round pegboard edges slightly with medium-grit sandpaper. Pegboard can be painted or clear-finished just like wood. It isn't waterproof and has a tendency to deform and weaken when wet. A protective finish is advisable if the board will be exposed to moisture.

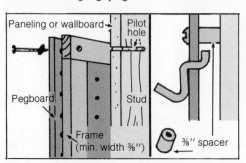

Mount rubber spacers, or build a frame between pegboard and wall to provide clearance for fixtures and good support.

You can give pegboard a finished appearance to complement the decor of your den, kitchen or bedroom. Here the addition of molding strips will frame new hang up space nicely.

Buying unfinished furniture

An unfinished cabinet or bookcase can be a very attractive readymade solution to storage problems. With a little creativity and as much elbow grease as you are prepared to supply, your own finishing work can give any piece of raw furniture a custom-built look.

Before you go to a raw furniture store, write down the minimum and maximum dimensions for the bookshelf or cabinet you want to buy. While shopping, pay attention to construction. There should be no cracks, discolorations, or loose joints in the piece you're thinking of. You should also know in advance whether you want to stain or paint the piece. The same unit is generally available in two or three grades of lumber. Clear lumber will cost a bit more, but may be worth the price if a smooth finish is desirable.

Highlighting: for a light, clean look that doubles as a wood sealer. Working on one surface at a time, brush on white pigmented stain in a full, flowing coat. Allow the stain to stand for ten minutes. Then use a soft cloth to wipe it down, moving against the grain. Wipe the stain off evenly and as completely as you can. The look you want is a white luster only. Allow 24 hours before using the piece.

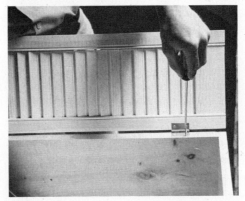

Louvered doors, purchased separately, can be attached to the front of an unfinished bookcase. Mortise the hinges to the doors and bookcase frame, then hold temporarily in place while screw holes are pre-drilled. Position each hinge exactly square with both the bookcase and the door frame and drill the holes exactly on center. Add magnetic catches and handles after finishing the piece.

TIP: Most raw furniture stores offer lists of their factory-standard dimensions. If one store does not have the exact dimensions you want, check another store. Custom built raw furniture is not cheap, and each manufacturer's standard dimensions list will vary slightly. You may find the additional shelf inch you need on someone else's standard sheet.

Molding strips added to a cabinet door give the piece a finished look. Select your favorite half-molding. Measure and mark molding and door, aligning carefully. Use a miter box to angle the corner cuts for perfect fit. Nail the molding to the door using brads at 4-inch intervals. Set and putty nail holes before finishing the piece. (Molding can dress up a plain pre-finished piece too. If you can't match the finish exactly, try an accent tone.)

Antiquing your unfinished readymade will give it the look of a valuable heirloom. This process involves applying an accenting *glaze* over an enamel finish. (The glaze should always be darker than the base enamel.) Give the wood an enamel finish and let it dry overnight. Then brush on a generous coat of glaze, let it sit for a few minutes, and wipe it off with a piece of cheesecloth. The effect is enhanced if a little extra glaze remains in cracks and corners.

Hangups and racks

Before you hang something on a wall or ceiling, from a picture hook to a cabinet, you have to find out what the surface covering on the wall or ceiling is made of; what, if anything, is behind it; how much weight the fastener must support fully loaded; and what type of fastener can support that weight without pulling out. See page 26 for a description of standard wall fasteners and how they work.

Fasten to a stud or a joist if you can

The easiest reliable way to attach anything weighing over five pounds per square foot to an interior wall is to nail or screw it into one of the wood or metal studs behind the wall surface. Studs are 1½-inches wide and run from floor to ceiling every 16 inches. Since they are spaced exactly 16 inches apart (unless your house is very old), you will always find one within eight inches of the spot at which you wanted to hang something anyway.

Wooden joists that support the floor above are usually spaced 16 (sometimes 12, 20 or 24) inches apart and are two inches wide. They generally run across the width, not the length, of the house.

Fasten light objects (up to five pounds per square foot) into wood studs with a 4d finishing nail, 6d common nail, or No. 6 wood screw driven at least one inch into the wood. Increase the nail sizes by 50 percent to support objects weighing about 10 pounds per square foot. Objects weighing much over that should be held by No. 8 wood screws or ¼-inch lag bolts driven at least 1½ inches into the wood.

If you cannot locate a stud where you want to hang something on wallboard, you can use a 4 to 8d finishing nail or ⅞-inch plastic anchor with a No. 4 to 8 sheet metal screw to fasten objects weighing up to five pounds per square foot. Over that, use a molly hollow wall anchor, or stronger still, a ¼-inch diameter toggle bolt. Beware of attaching very heavy objects only to hollow wallboard or thin plaster because they can collapse. If you make a cross of sticky tape over the mark on the plaster or wallboard before you drive or drill a hole for the fastener, the tape will keep the surface from chipping or crumbling around the hole.

I made more holes than a woodpecker—and with less result!

My exploratory holes near the bottom of the wall brought out solid wood, but when I drilled on a plumb line farther up, all I got was hollow wall. Frustration! Then I realized I was drilling into the horizontal sole plate instead of the vertical stud. Every exploratory hole was bound to be in solid wood, regardless of actual stud location. Now I do my stud searching at least 4 inches above the floor, and when I hit solid wood, I'm sure it's the real thing.

Practical Pete

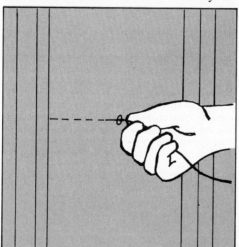

To find the nearest stud, tap with your knuckles lightly along the wall until you hit a dead-sounding spot, and tap up and down floor to ceiling to be sure it is a stud. Drill a tiny hole where you want to hang the fastener. If you hit wood shavings, it's a wood stud; hard resistance and metal shavings indicate a metal stud (usually hollow). If you can't locate a stud by tapping, drill a small hole through the wall covering at an extreme angle. Push a straight length of coathanger wire along the inside of the wall until you hit something. Pinch the wire at the hole with your fingers and pull it out of the wall. Measure the distance between the end of the wire and your fingers. Add ¾-inch and mark that total distance from the hole. The mark will be pretty close to the center of the stud, but drill a tiny pilot hole to be sure.

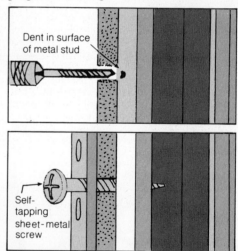

Dent in surface of metal stud

Self-tapping sheet-metal screw

Metal studs are hollow. To fasten something through a wall and into a metal stud, drill a small hole through the wall covering, but not into the metal. Make a dent in the metal by tapping a finishing nail or center punch so the drill tip won't slip around (top). Drill a hole one half the thickness of a No. 4 self-tapping sheet-metal screw for light objects; No. 8 for heavy objects over 10 pounds per square foot. Drill a hole almost the same thickness as the screw in the object you are hanging, and drive the screw through the object, through the wall, and through the metal side of the hollow stud (bottom).

How to find out what the wall is made of

When you drill a test hole into	You will find . . . .
Wallcoverings:	
Wallboard or plaster only	White dust, little resistance, quick breakthrough
Thick plaster	White dust, some resistance, no breakthrough
Thin plaster over wood lath	White dust, then gray powder, then breakthrough
Behind-wall materials:	
Wood stud	Moderate resistance, light wood shavings
Metal stud	Heavy resistance, silver shavings
Cinder block or concrete	Very heavy resistance, gray-brown dust
Brick or hollow tiles	Heavy resistance, red dust
Mortar between bricks/blocks	Moderate resistance, gray dust

Attaching things to solid concrete, brick, etc.

If you want to hang something heavy on a solid brick, concrete or cinder block surface, you generally have to drill a hole in it to receive an insert that you can then drive a screw or other fastener into. For light, rough work masonry nails and cut nails can be driven directly into concrete with a hammer. (These and inserts for wall fasteners are shown on page 26.) Whatever type of insert you use, be sure that the screw or bolt you drive into it is long enough to pass through both the thickness of the object you are attaching to the wall and the insert in the wall. Check before making any holes.

When you drill holes in concrete, blocks, brick or stone, wear goggles and gloves because chips and powder will fly around.

The mortar between cement blocks and bricks is easier to nail or drill into, but it is more likely to crumble, so the fastener is more likely to pull out if you hang something heavy from it.

How to drill the holes

Power

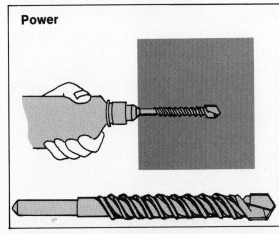

A power drill with a carbide-tipped bit is the easiest and fastest tool. Most home-shop electric drills have ¼-inch or ⅜-inch chucks. These spin too fast and may not have enough power to drive a big bit into solid concrete or brick. A drill with a ½-inch chuck is ideal. If you don't have one, try drilling a small hole first, then a larger one.

Carbide-tipped bits range in size up to one inch in diameter. If your drill has a variable-speed trigger, use a low speed and stop if it begins to stall so you won't burn out the motor in your drill. Slide the drill bit back and forth in the hole as it rotates rather than pushing hard continuously.

Hand

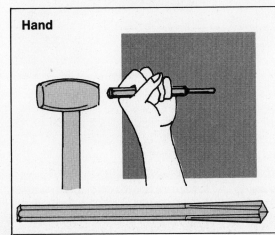

A hand Rawl drill has interchangeable bits that make holes up to ¼-inch in diameter. The bit fits into one end of a steel shaft. Place the tip of the bit against the wall surface and hit the drill with a hammer, rotating the drill slightly between blows.

A Star drill makes larger holes, ¼- to one inch in diameter. It is a heavy duty tool and needs a strong arm wielding a light sledge to drive it into solid concrete or brick. Rotate it after each blow and blow out the dust from time to time.

---New wrinkles---

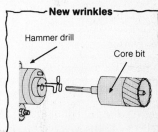
Hammer drill

Core bit

Electric hammer drill
These pound a carbide-tipped bit into concrete, brick or stone at the rate of about 3000 blows a minute. For holes over one inch in diameter, use a core bit that cuts a plug out of the masonry.

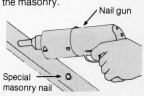
Nail gun

Special masonry nail

Masonry nail gun
Specially hardened masonry nails can be loaded into a gun that fires them, with .22-caliber blank cartridges, into cement blocks and concrete. This is a quick way to put up 1x3 furring for example, so you can attach rough shelving to it. Rent these gadgets if you can. They are too expensive to buy for a one-time project.

Build a knife rack

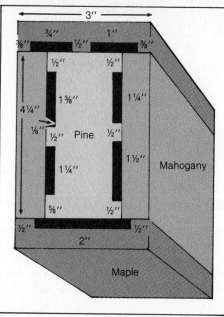

What it takes

Approximate time: 2-3 hours, not including drying time for glue.

Tools and materials: Basic cutting tools, assorted clamps, plus the following materials: 2 pieces of maple ¾"x3"x9", 2 pieces of mahogany ¾"x4¼"x9", 1 piece clear pine 1¼"x4¼"x9", waterproof glue (e.g., Resorcinol).

Don't hide your favorite knives in a drawer; store them safely out in the open with a knife rack like this one. It's made from left-over pieces cut from mahogany, maple, and pine lumber. The different woods give the project a unique appearance. You can use just one type of wood if you wish and adjust the size of the slots to accommodate your own knives.

1. Cut all five pieces of wood to size, then measure and mark cut-out areas as shown.

2. Cutouts for knife blades are ⅛-inch deep, made just as you would a dado groove (see page 21). You can use a router, a table saw, circular saw, or backsaw to make cutouts.

3. Clean out the slots with a chisel after sawing. You'll have to do a good amount of chisel work if you used a hand saw for making slots, as was done here.

4. Use a waterproof glue to join pieces together. Large C-clamps and several bar clamps positioned as shown will hold the parts securely until the glue dries.

5. Improvise a scraper like the one shown to remove excess glue from inside of the slots.

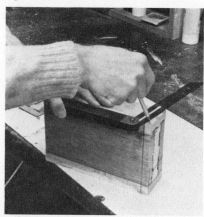

6. When the glue has dried, cut off the top at a slight angle, then sand all surfaces smooth and give your project an oil or satin-style varnish finish.

Other hang-up projects

Increasing the storage space in most kitchens requires some creativity. Wall space is largely filled with cabinets, and floor space unoccupied by fixtures, furniture and base cabinets is generally needed for traffic. If there's no place to go but up in your kitchen, you might consider a design like the hanging rack at right. Or try putting up a clothes pole over the window. The addition of a few S-hooks makes that a handy spot for storing frequently used utensils. The wine glass rack detailed below is another convenient storage suggestion. The rack can be wall-hung or can stand on an open counter. Each of these projects serves two functions: to ease the space squeeze in storage, and to make an attractive display area for serving and cooking wares.

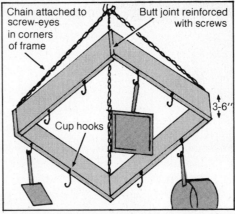

Chain attached to screw-eyes in corners of frame

Butt joint reinforced with screws

Cup hooks

3-6''

If you've got the ceiling space, this square rack is great for keeping pots, pans, and utensils within easy reach. Use ¾- or 1-inch lumber, cut between 3 and 6 inches wide. The frame dimensions can be as large or small as you wish; 1½ or 2 feet square is a good size.

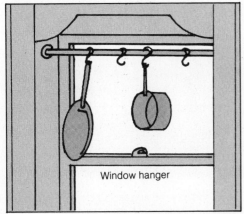

Window hanger

Take your clothes pole out of the closet and put it to work in your kitchen. Position it above the sink or stove, between cabinets, using the plastic holders shown on page 62. With a few S-hooks you can quickly and easily make new storage space for pots, pans, mugs, and other kitchen items.

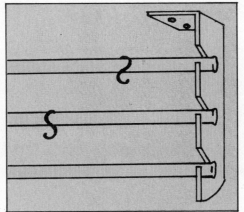

If you need more hang-up space than one pole can provide, try this simple design. You'll need some ⅛'' sheet metal, as well as a hacksaw or saber saw (use a metal-cutting blade) to cut it. Fasten each slotted metal support to a ceiling joist with two round-head screws.

Wine glass rack

Here's a nice-looking project you can build in an afternoon. You'll need 1x6 pine lumber (which actually measures ¾''x5½''): 4 pieces 15'' long and 2 pieces 30'' long.

Temporarily nail the shelf pieces together, then measure, mark, and drill out 1'' diameter holes as illustrated at left. Once the holes are drilled, saw out slots piece by piece (all at once if you have a table saw). Then make dados in the side supports, and join sides and shelves. Sand your project smooth, give it a stain or natural finish, then christen it with a few glasses of wine.

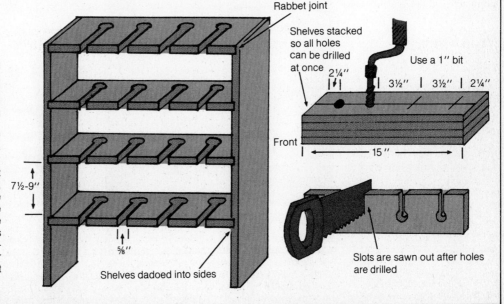

Rabbet joint

Shelves stacked so all holes can be drilled at once

Use a 1'' bit

2¼'' | 3½'' | 3½'' | 2¼''

Front

15''

7½-9''

⅝''

Shelves dadoed into sides

Slots are sawn out after holes are drilled

Wall-mounted shelving

The quickest, easiest, and least messy way to convert unused wall space into useful shelf storage is to put up individual shelf brackets or track-and-bracket shelving (technically called "standards"). Hardware for both is widely distributed in a variety of styles, sizes, and materials which makes it easy to fit them into the space you have available. The following pages provide some of the most popular options and instructions for easy installation.

If you're putting up only a few shelves, it's practical to buy them pre-cut and pre-finished. Ready-to-use shelves are available in different widths and finishes at most hardware stores, lumber suppliers, and home decorating centers. For larger projects, you'll save money by buying unfinished lumber in standard dimensions and cutting it to size yourself.

Shelf brackets, left, are made in sizes ranging from three inches to eighteen inches. They are usually packaged in pairs and range in decorative appeal (and price) from flat angle irons to handmade wrought iron or finely finished wood. Track-and-bracket "standards," right, are equally easy to put up and preferable if you need more than one or two adjustable shelves.

Individual angle brackets

The quickest way to put up built-in shelves is to use metal angle brackets. These shelf supports have been around for a long time and are great in places where only one or two shelves are needed. Their only limitations are that they're permanent and non-adjustable, and they must be securely anchored to the wall. This means you usually have to locate studs to fasten into.

Shelf brackets in a variety of styles can be found at any hardware store or home decorating center. Wrought iron brackets go well with paneling or an antique decor, while brushed aluminum supports give a more modern appearance. You'll also find inexpensive angle irons which can be used in the workshop, garage, basement, and other parts of your home where storage space needn't be stylish.

In addition to appearance, you'll also have to select brackets according to the load you want to support and the shelf width you want to use. The longer side of the bracket should be installed vertically, against the wall. The shorter, or horizontal support should be at least three-fourths as long as the width of the shelf. The heavier the load on the shelf, the longer the vertical side of the bracket should be.

What it takes

Approximate time: Only a few minutes per bracket after you have located and marked the studs.

Tools and materials: Drill with bits to pre-drill screw holes, screwdriver, carpenter's level, pencil, crosscut saw and combination square for cutting shelf lengths, shelving lumber, bracket hardware.

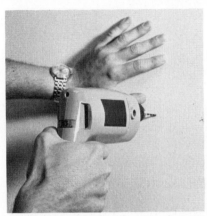

1. Locate and mark the centers of the studs (usually spaced 16 or 24 inches apart) by tapping the wall and drilling a row of ⅛-inch holes until you hit one. Use a level to draw vertical guidelines for attaching the brackets.

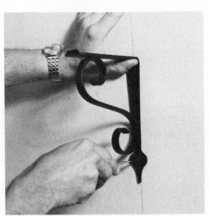

2. Determine the best height for your bracket, and anchor it through the wall and into the stud with screws. Remember that at least ⅔ of the screw's length should be in the stud.

3. Use the level as shown to line up accompanying brackets, then anchor brackets as in step 2. Now you're all set to lay down the shelving itself.

Shelving hardware

Pilasters and clips. These slotted metal tracks are used in groups of four inside cabinets and bookcases. They are screwed in place (sometimes dadoed flush), and accept metal clips which act as corner supports for the shelves.

Pins are used in groups of four, with each pin supporting one corner of the shelf. Available in either *spade* or *angle bracket* styles, they fit into holes drilled in the side shelf supports.

Shelving standards are the most popular type of shelving hardware, mainly because they are versatile, easy to install (see page 44), give a weightless, contemporary effect, and can accommodate heavy loads. The shelf brackets that fit into the slotted tracks are made in several sizes so you can install shelves of different widths. The tracks themselves are available in different lengths and styles, from plain aluminum to enameled or wood-grain vinyl. Shelving standards should be fastened through the wall surface into studs for maximum holding power.

Angle brackets are attached to the wall in a horizontal row with screws that pass through the wall and into studs. They are available in a wide range of sizes and styles and are commonly used where only one or two shelves are needed.

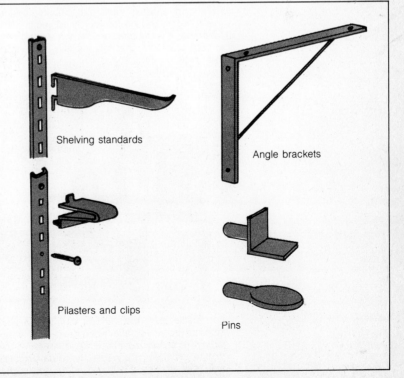

Shelving standards

Angle brackets

Pilasters and clips

Pins

Track-and-bracket shelving standards

Upside down and bowlegged
There are at least three ways to foul up the job when you install track-and-bracket shelving standards—and I managed to combine all three in one go. First, a lot of those wall-mounted metal tracks are made with no holes for the brackets at one end. *That* end should be at the *top* so you can put the last shelf at the very bottom of the track. Second, don't cut corners by skipping screwholes on those metal tracks. With any weight at all on the shelves, the track will bow away from the wall where it isn't held by a screw. Third, shelves full of books will sag in the middle unless you have a bracket for every two feet of shelf length. The studs inside most interior walls are spaced 24 inches apart anyway.

Practical Pete

Since conventional shelving standards are relatively inexpensive, easy to install, and able to support heavy loads, they can readily solve storage problems all around the house. Here an entire wall has been converted to shelf storage with the track and bracket system.

Here's an unusual track and bracket system that's elegant enough for your finest room. Made from teak, it is designed so that the slanted pegs in each bracket fit precisely into the holes in the teak track.

For a little extra money, you can buy a shelf standard system with a wood-grain vinyl finish. *Cranmere* shelves by Kirsch Co. (Sturgis, Mich.) feature decorative standards and shelf brackets, along with shelves of different widths, as shown.

1. Locate the stud you'll be fastening into, then sink a screw through a hole near the middle of the standard, into both the wall and the stud behind it. Drill a pilot hole out as usual before sinking any screw. If you're not fastening into a stud, use a wall fastener that's suited for your type of wall (see page 26). Don't tighten the screw completely.

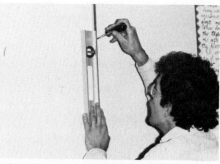

2. Using the screw as a pivot point, plumb the standard with your level, mark locations for pilot holes with a pencil or awl, as shown here, and sink screws through the remaining holes.

3. Use your level to mark a vertical line for the adjacent standard. For maximum shelf strength, fasten through the wall and into a stud, as you did for the other standard.

4. Insert brackets in corresponding slots on both standards, then use your level and a shelf as shown to position the adjacent standard. Fasten the standard to the wall as in steps 1 and 2. Insert brackets as desired and lay down shelves.

Get fancy with the shelves themselves

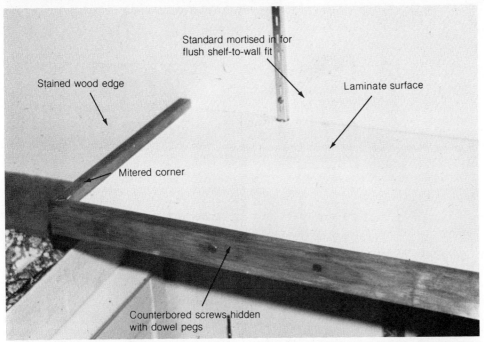

Stained wood edge

Standard mortised in for flush shelf-to-wall fit

Laminate surface

Mitered corner

Counterbored screws hidden with dowel pegs

You don't have to be satisfied with conventional shelves when using standards. Here are some ideas that will give your new shelf storage space a unique, eye-catching appearance.

Off the wall ideas

Most shelving standards are made to be used on the wall, but you make a free-standing unit by mortising the standards into upright supports which are secured to the floor and ceiling. Use angle brackets or screw-in casters as shown below to secure the supports.

The easiest way to give your shelves a fancy look is to buy them pre-cut and pre-finished at your hardware store or home decorating center. You'll find them in a variety of sizes and surfaces.

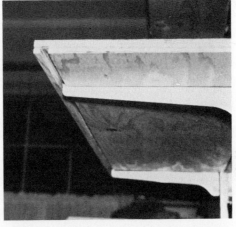

Hide the front lip of the metal bracket by dadoing a groove or making a depression to fit with your drill—but don't drill all the way through!

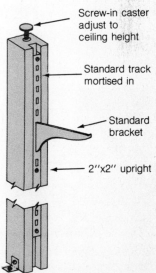

Screw-in caster adjust to ceiling height

Standard track mortised in

Standard bracket

2"x2" upright

Angle bracket secures upright to floor.

How about adding a built-in bookend? It will keep books from falling off the end of the shelf.

Give your shelf a special edge treatment with half-round molding. Miter the corners as shown.

Stereo shelf-wall

What it takes

Approximate time: Plan on spreading the work out over two or three days. Taking and transferring measurements is time consuming, especially where an odd angle or contour copying is involved.

Tools and materials: Basic cutting and joining tools, sliding bevel, level, plus the following materials: 2 sheets ¾" A/C interior plywood, 16 shelf supports (optional), 10d common nails, 10d finishing nails.

This stereo/record shelf-wall was built in three evenings. Notice how the side support at left was angled to give the small adjacent window a better chance to brighten up the room.

These are the important points to remember when you're working on new shelf space for your stereo components: Give your set room to breathe. The fit of the enclosing shelves and side supports should allow for at least 1″ of airspace on all sides. If possible, cut component-supporting shelves so that there's an inch of open space between the back shelf edge and the wall. If you intend to replace your present system or any part of it at some point in the future, don't nail or glue the shelves for these units. Use pilasters and clips or shelf supports so you can make adjustments for any size discrepancy.

1. Measure, mark, and cut three side supports, then fasten them to the wall and floor, starting with the corner support. Nail the left support to window molding. Notice how the back edge of the support has been cut out to accommodate the molding.

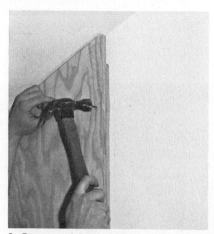

2. Because of floor molding or an out-of-plumb wall, you may have to slip *shims* between the corner support and the wall, as shown above. Drive a 10d nail in at an angle to catch the nearby stud.

3. Use cleats as shown to secure the two remaining supports to the floor; then install a kick-plate along the bottom front as shown. Don't worry if the center support is slightly shaky; it will firm up as you nail shelves in place. Nail a cleat to the molding to support the back edge of the bottom shelf.

4. Mark locations for shelf support holes, then drill them out. Start each hole with an awl to keep your bit exactly on center.

5. Press the shelf supports into holes, then cut and install the shelves. For this project, shelf supports are used for corner shelves; the longer center shelves will be glued and nailed in.

6. Cut the longer shelves to size, then glue and nail them in place. Angled window support means you'll have to custom-fit the shelves, so measure carefully.

7. Even with expert measuring and cutting, you may get an imperfect fit. Use a plane, file, or surform tool to trim all edges flush.

8. Cut and install trim along the front edge as shown.

9. Set all nails, fill holes with wood dough; sand your work smooth, remove the sawdust, and apply finish. Don't skimp on finishing touches; they make a big difference.

Construction guidelines

When creating wall storage, your design is limited only by the dimensions of the empty wall you have to work with. As the step-by-step instructions for the design on these pages suggest, your wall-work can be as simple or as complex as your needs and abilities allow—given the dimensions of your wall. Here are a few guidelines that apply to all built-in wall storage projects:

1. Before you start building, locate and mark all studs along the section of wall where you'll be working. Fastening into a stud is *always* better than just fastening into the wall. If possible, plan your design so that at least a few shelves or supports will be secured to studs.

2. Establish your vertical supports before you decide on definite shelf lengths and locations. The stability of the uprights will determine the steadiness of the entire wall unit.

3. It's usually best to begin in the corner and work out toward the middle of the wall. Your corner shelves and supports are the easiest to square, plumb, and join firmly. Remember that you don't always have to work *on* the wall. It's easier to construct the bulk of the framing on the floor, then tilt it up and fasten it to the wall.

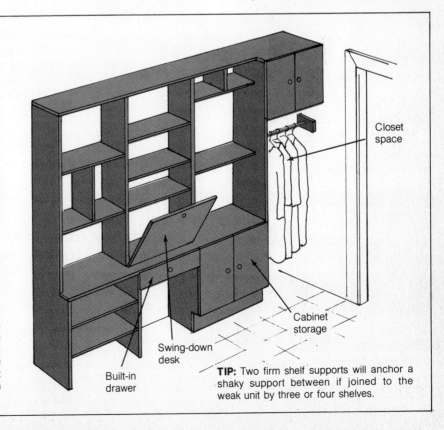

Closet space

Cabinet storage

Swing-down desk

Built-in drawer

TIP: Two firm shelf supports will anchor a shaky support between if joined to the weak unit by three or four shelves.

Free-standing shelves

Take-apart book shelves

What it takes

Approximate time: 1-2 hours, not including finishing.

Tools and materials: 1 4'x4' sheet ¾-inch A/A plywood, crosscut saw, table or saber saw, and ½- or ¾-inch chisel.

If you're a frequent mover, you've probably had to leave plenty of shelves, cabinets, or bookcases behind because they've been too bulky, built-in, or just too inconvenient to take along. Here's a project for pull-apart shelves that will enable you to take some storage space with you when you move. You can take them apart in a minute or less, carry them easily under one arm, and put them back together just as fast.

Plywood is the best building material to use for this project, since the slotted design demands strength in all directions. For extra stability, attach a diagonal brace to the back of your shelves, using screws on both sides and on at least two shelves (see step 7).

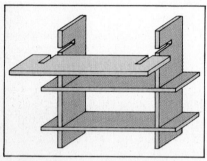

1. Start with a simple design labeled with dimensions and specifications for materials and construction details. Make sure the depth of the slots can be reached with your saw.

2. Cut out all shelf pieces. Here's where a table saw comes in handy, since the rip guide sets the width and eliminates the need for repetitive measurements.

3. Join shelf pieces together with finishing nails (don't hammer them all the way in). Measure and mark slot locations, then saw out slots as shown. Use a back saw or a saber saw with a long blade.

4. If you're using a handsaw or saber saw to cut slots, saw all the way to both corners first. Then square up the slot to make two curved cuts to opposite corners. Chisel away any remaining waste.

5. Cut both sides in the same way you cut the shelves. Joining sides together before marking and cutting the slots makes the job go twice as fast.

6. Assemble your new shelves. The slotted parts should have a snug, but not forced fit; use a file to smooth out any tight joints.

7. Adding a mortised-in, diagonal brace not only makes these slide-together shelves steadier, it gives your project a unique appearance. Screws can easily be removed for quick take-apart.

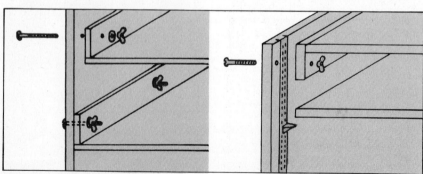

More take-apart ideas Build your shelves with a lip on both ends so they can be fastened to the side supports with two bolts and a couple of wing nuts. For extra stability, dado the lips into the sides as shown above. As an alternative, you can use the lip joint for the top and bottom shelves only, and either dado the middle shelves, or install pilasters and use clip supports for the shelves.

Build yourself a bookcase

What it takes

Approximate time: 3-4 hours.

Tools and materials: Basic cutting and joining tools plus the following materials: 3 8'x1''x8'' pine boards, 16 shelf supports, 4d finishing nails, 8 No. 6 gauge flat-head screws (1½'' long), 4'x4' paneling, plywood, or hardboard for back.

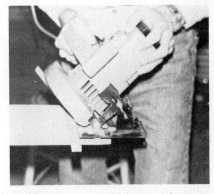

1. Cut sides, top, and bottom pieces to finished size. Mitered corners must be cut precisely, so use a saw guide. Set the blade for a 45° angle cut.

2. Mark sides for shelf support insert holes, then drill them out. Use a depth gauge on your bit (here a piece of adhesive tape) so you don't drill all the way through the board.

3. Join sides, top, and bottom, using two 4d finishing nails in each corner (and glue, of course). Corner clamps make the job easier. Set all nails, then fill holes with wood dough and sand it smooth.

4. Miter joints should be reinforced with metal angle braces and screws. Counter-bore screws and fill holes with dowel plugs. Glue plugs in place, then cut and sand them flush when glue dries.

5. Put the back on. Here paneling is used for appearance, but you can also use wallboard or ¼'' plywood.

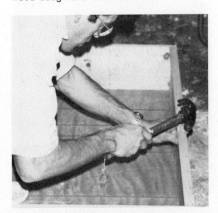

6. Glue and nail molding to front of bookcase, using number 18 gauge ¾-inch nails. Miter the top corner joints.

7. Cut shelves to size, push shelf support inserts into their holes, slide shelves into place, and it is ready to be finished.

Divide a room with shelves

What it takes

Approximate time: 2 hours, not including finishing.

Tools and materials: Basic cutting and joining tools plus the following materials: Five 1″x12″x8′ #1 common pine boards, one 4′x8′ sheet pegboard.

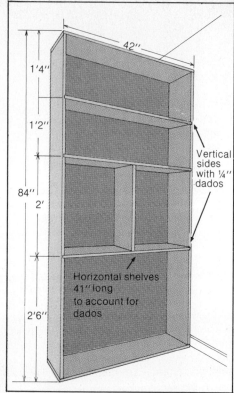

Here's an idea for new storage space that doubles as a room divider. The divider is nothing more than a set of free-standing shelves backed with pegboard. It can be built in the proportions that best fit the area. The drawing, far right, gives the dimensions of the unit pictured here.

1. Cut sides, top, and bottom to size. Then mark locations for dados as shown, using a tape measure and combination square.

2. When cutting dados, be sure to groove the supporting shelf board no more than half its thickness. A dado does not have to be deep to make a strong joint.

3. Assemble the outer frame with 8d finishing nails. Then glue and fit shelves into the dado grooves. Use a scrap of wood between the hammer and the shelf when you're tapping in.

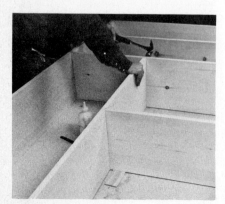

4. Add vertical dividers and other shelves according to your design for shelf size and location.

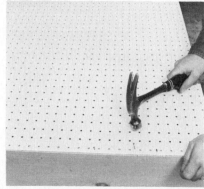

5. The true edges of the pegboard backing will help you align the sides of the cabinet. Fractional adjustment of the cabinet edges can be done by hand. Don't drive nails home until the frame is aligned with the pegboard all the way around.

6. Countersink the nails and fill all holes prior to giving the assembly the finish you have selected.

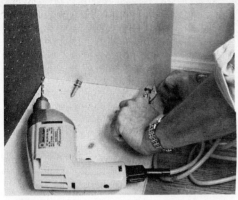

7. Fasten the completed divider to the floor with lag screws and washers. One screw in each corner will do the job.

8. Two separate units, bolted across the top, will divide larger rooms and offer extensive storage. You can get a combination of shelf and hang up storage on both sides by bolting them front to back.

Building a wall to divide a room

1. Measure and mark the location for the 2x4 sole plate, then nail it in place. If you're nailing through linoleum or asphalt tile into cement, you'll have to use masonry nails, as shown above.

2. Cut the first stud to size (the distance from the sole plate to the ceiling), then nail it to the wall, using a level as shown to make sure it's plumb.

3. Nail the 2x4 top plate to the ceiling, making sure it aligns with the sole plate. Then start toe-nailing the studs in place. Studs should be spaced 16 inches on center.

4. Cut the sheetrock to size and nail it to the studs. After the sheetrock is in place, install molding along the floor, wall, and ceiling.

Don't fuss with it!
You should see a professional wallboard seam taper zip around a room after the wallboard panels have been nailed up. One 8-foot seam after another—plaster-tape-plaster—zap! Fifteen seconds each, smooth as paper.
It's enough to make you cry.
When I try to smooth taped wallboard seams, it's like trying to keep my checkbook balanced. The more I fuss with the compound after a point, the worse it gets. I learned to leave it rough after the first couple of tries and sand it smooth after it dries.

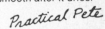

5. Spackle the nail depressions, and tape the joints as shown above. When the spackle has dried, sand the new wall smooth. For more details on sheetrock work, see page 58.

6. A couple of coats of paint, some track and bracket shelves, and a table complete the job. Good work!

Cabinets

Solid oak frames and doors give a real feeling of substance to this pair of base cabinet banks. Cathedral-shaped door dados would be difficult for even the experienced home carpenter to duplicate.

Readymades

Constructing a cabinet from scratch can be a tough job. There are plenty of dado, rabbet, and lap joints to make, and precision is essential. Building special-design doors like those shown above is nearly impossible without an extensive (and expensive) assortment of shop equipment rarely found in home workshops. Even accomplished carpenters often choose to buy readymades rather than build comparable cabinets from the ground up. (If you're really eager to build your own, turn the page.)

Factory-made cabinets aren't just for use in a kitchen. Readymades like the ones shown here would add attractive new storage space anywhere in the house. And the basic installation techniques certainly don't vary from room to room.

If you do decide to invest in cabinets, ask your lumber dealer for brochures which describe the various cabinet lines he carries. There's such a range of sizes, styles, and prices to choose from that you shouldn't rely solely on display models when making your choice. One other thing to think about is that most base cabinets don't come with tops. If that's true of the model you've selected, you should decide on the color and composition of the top you want at the same time. **TIP:** Sales on cabinets or sets of cabinets aren't uncommon. Discontinued styles and slightly damaged cabinets are always sold at considerably lower prices. Shop around and you're sure to turn up a few bargains. *Unfinished* factory-made cabinets are available in certain styles at substantially lower prices than identical cabinets pre-finished.

Storage space dominates this kitchen design. Cabinet doors are made of melamine low pressure laminate. Cabinet ends are a matching wood grained embossed vinyl.

Slatted oak fronts give these cabinets a country feel. Note refrigerator, concealed at the right.

Cabinet installation

Installation is remarkably easy compared to the work involved in cabinet construction. Detailed manufacturer's instructions generally accompany each set of cabinets. Those specifics will supplement these general guidelines.

The most important part of the job is laying out the location of each cabinet before it is positioned and fastened in place. Use a tape measure, pencil, level, and chalk line to mark cabinet outlines on the wall as shown. You should also mark stud locations within cabinet areas before installation begins. That way you won't have to hunt for them at the last moment, just as the cabinet is ready to be fastened to the wall.

When putting up either wall or base cabinets, install the corner or end cabinet first. Adjoining cabinets should be bolted together through their corner stiles using 3/16-inch diameter round-head bolts. Fasten them together as they are being installed, but don't tighten the bolts fully until each cabinet has been leveled.

TIP: Another support suggestion is to temporarily nail a cleat along the lower side of the line where the back bottom edge of the cabinet will go. Use the cleat as you would dead men (see photo 6, this page) to support the cabinet while you level it. Then screw through the cabinet back and into a stud. Remove the cleat once all the cabinets have been secured to the wall and to each other.

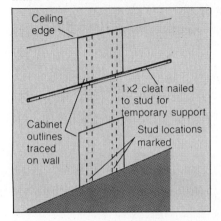

Ceiling edge

1x2 cleat nailed to stud for temporary support

Cabinet outlines traced on wall

Stud locations marked

Screw through top frame into studs.

Screw to studs after leveling.

If floor slants use shims.

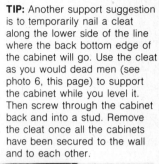

1. Measure and mark the base cabinet height from the floor. (The standard height is 36 inches.)

2. Use a level to mark a second point parallel to the first.

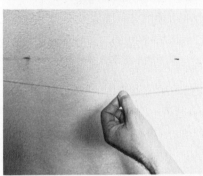

3. Aligning between your two measured markings, snap a chalk line across the wall.

4. Once the base cabinet line is set, measure and mark for the height and width of the hanging cabinet, using the same technique. Hanging cabinets usually sit at a height of 18 inches above the countertop.

5. Move the base cabinet into place and check the leveling again. If necessary, shim to level with wood shingles. Once level, screw the cabinet to the back wall at the four corners.

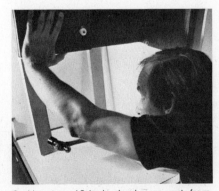

6. Use two 19-inch dead men cut from 1x2 to prop your top cabinet while checking the alignment. Here the cabinet is supported on both sides, by the range on the left and the wall on the right. If your cabinet is going on a flat wall, have another pair of hands to hold it.

7. Once the top cabinet is leveled, screw through the back into wall studs at each upper and lower corner.

Cabinet construction

Cabinet-making involves more time, skill, and tools than other storage-related projects. The drawings below are *basic* designs for a wall and base cabinet appropriate for a kitchen, den, bedroom or bath. You can make design and dimension changes to fit your taste and space requirements. If you want a more elegant look and are willing to pay for it, an expensive hardwood-faced plywood can be used for cabinet sides. Doors or drawer fronts can be made from solid wood.

What it takes

Approximate time: 4-5 hours.

Tools and materials: Basic cutting and joining tools; router with dado, rabbeting, and rounding-over bits; plus the following materials: 6' length 1"x12" clear pine board, 4'x4' sheet ¼" hardboard, 2 drawer pulls, 2 offset semi-concealed hinges, 3'x3' sheet plastic laminate (optional), 2'x2' sheet ½" A/C plywood, 4'x8' sheet of ¾" hardwood faced plywood, 1 drawer guide assembly.

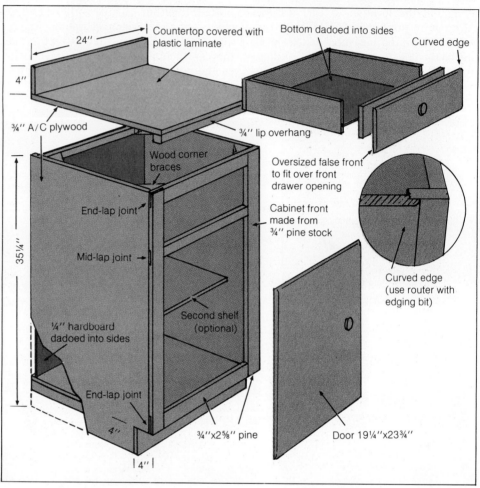

Countertop covered with plastic laminate
24"
4"
¾" A/C plywood
Bottom dadoed into sides
Curved edge
¾" lip overhang
Wood corner braces
Oversized false front to fit over front drawer opening
End-lap joint
Cabinet front made from ¾" pine stock
35¼"
Mid-lap joint
Curved edge (use router with edging bit)
Second shelf (optional)
¼" hardboard dadoed into sides
End-lap joint
4"
¾"x2⅝" pine
Door 19¼"x23¾"
4"

Building the base cabinet

1. Assemble the cabinet front from ¾" pine or birch stock. Use end-lap joints at the corners and a mid-lap joint for the middle divider (see page 20). Glue and clamp the pieces together and let the assembly stand until the glue has set.

2. Measure, mark, and cut the sides. Then join them together by installing the kickplate across the front and a brace across the back. Slide the hardboard back into dadoed grooves on each side.

3. Glue and nail the front frame in place, using 6d finishing nails. Notice here the kickplate assembly detail.

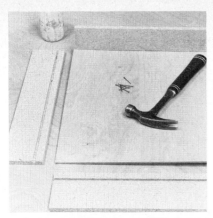

4. Construct the drawer, using ½″ plywood or particle board for the sides, back and front. Use ¼″ hardboard or plywood for the bottom. Dado for the bottom panel in front, back, and side pieces as shown. The drawer front can be made from two pieces of ½″ plywood or a single ¾″ piece that has been edged and rabbeted. **Note:** Buy a drawer guide assembly at your local hardware store. There are several varieties available, and all come complete with detailed installation instructions.

5. Reinforce the corners by gluing and screwing wood blocks in place at the top and bottom.

6. Cut doors to finished size. Use a router with a rounding over bit to put curve on the front edges. Then cut a lip along the inside of the door edges with a router or table saw. **TIP:** It is important to rout before rabbeting the door since the router needs a solid edge to guide it.

7. Attach offset, semi-concealed hinges to the door as shown. Then position the door in the front opening and screw the hinges to the front frame.

8. Attach a catch assembly to the door and the front frame of the cabinet. Then fasten a pull or handle to the door.

9. Construct a top and attach it to the top of the cabinet with glue and finishing nails. Use flat-head screws in the corners for extra holding strength.

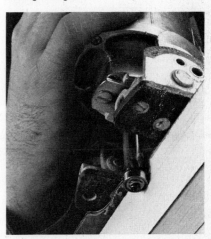

10. Cut the laminate for the top slightly oversize (¼″), then coat the back of the laminate and the plywood top with contact cement.

11. When the contact cement has dried to the touch, place kraft paper between the laminate and the top while aligning the laminate. Then slide the paper out and press the laminate against the top.

12. Trim the laminate overhang with a router and laminate trim bit.

Closet storage

Before

Cutting wallboard

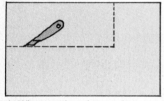

1. When cutting sheetrock or any other gypsum-core wallboard, first score the face paper along your measured cut line, using a utility knife.

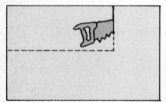

2. Use a saw to cut all the way through the panel along the shorter line.

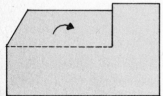

3. Fold along the second score, snapping through the core. Then cut through the back paper with the utility knife.

Building a closet from scratch is a big job involving careful measuring, designing, and planning, large amounts of expensive building materials, and lots of time. If your proposed closet site looks something like the room-end pictured above left, you've got your work cut out for you. This site was plagued with a curved, slanting ceiling, out-of-plumb walls, and irregularly-spaced studs. A heating vent located on the left meant the closet could not extend all the way across the wall. In spite of such problems, a major project like this is fun to undertake. You'll want to spend time considering designs and materials (door types, paneling vs. sheetrock, shelf and clothes-pole locations) before you begin building. The reward is a closet that's custom-built to fit your needs.

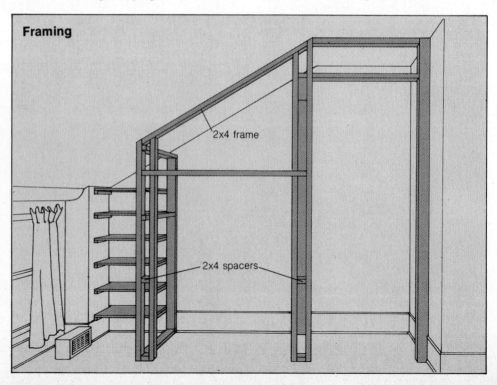

Framing

2x4 frame

2x4 spacers

Step-by-step construction

1. The first step is to pull up the wall-to-wall carpet and expose the bare floor where the new closet will go. Carpeting can be refitted after the closet is complete.

2. Working from the wall out, frame in the closet door. Installation instructions for this bi-fold door call for an opening 2″ higher and 3″ wider than the door dimensions.

3. Continue framing in the closet front. A curved, slanted ceiling and out-of-plumb walls mean you'll have to spend extra time measuring and custom-fitting.

4. Here's the completed front frame. For additional stability, vertical studs should be toe-nailed to the floor.

5. Because this closet doesn't extend all the way across the room, the end must be framed in. Here molly bolts are used to fasten the stud to the wall.

6. Cut door jambs to size and nail them in place. The front edge of the jamb should extend ½″ out from the rough frame to allow for the width of the sheetrock.

7. Jambs for the bi-fold door must be *shimmed* as shown so that they're plumb and the finished width of the doorway matches the width of the door. This is a job where patience and precision pay off.

8. Cut sheetrock to size (see margin opposite), then nail it to the studs with sheetrock nails. For this particular project, it's best to install the vertical panels first.

9. Horizontal sections require careful measuring and cutting. **TIP:** Don't put in more nails than you need: you'll make your spackling job harder that way.

10. Measure, mark, and cut molding to fit over the front edge of the door jamb and the sheetrock. To assure a good fit at mitered corners, cut joints on a miterbox with the saw guide set at 45°.

11. Nail the molding in place. Use 1¼″ *brads* (small finishing nails) and nail through the thickest part of the molding to minimize the chance of splitting the wood.

12. Use a block plane to smooth the edge of the molding flush with the jamb where necessary.

Spackling

A paint job is only as good as the spackling job it covers. Depressions in the sheetrock around nailheads, corners and other areas where the gypsum edges of the sheetrock are exposed, and joints between separate pieces of sheetrock, must all be filled with spackling compound and sanded smooth before painting.

If you haven't used spackling compound before, don't worry. It doesn't take long to get acquainted with this special preparation. Spackle, or spackling compound, is a dough-like substance which adheres readily to gypsum wallboard, plaster, wood, and other porous materials. It dries in 1-3 hours, becoming hard and brittle, but is easily shaped and smoothed with sandpaper.

The real art to spackling is learning how to use your putty knife as quickly and effectively as possible. For dishing out spackle, filling small depressions, and working in narrow areas, you'll need a 1-1½-inch-wide putty knife. For taping, corner work, and wide areas, use a knife at least 3 inches wide.

TIP: Deep or extensive depressions should be filled in stages; apply a layer of spackle, let it dry, then apply another layer until the hole is filled. Once a can of spackle has been opened, its shelf life is shortened considerably. Keep this in mind when you're buying and using it. Don't open a large can for a small job. Spackle is also fine for filling holes in wood. It can be stained and clear-finished, but won't blend in with the wood as well as wood dough.

1. Using a putty knife to apply spackling compound, fill the depressions around nailheads and smooth the filled area flat.

2. Cut corner bead to length and nail it in place as shown. Angle the nails slightly to get a good hold in the corner stud.

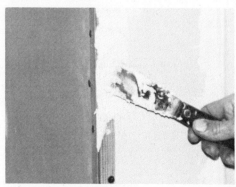

3. Spread spackle generously along the edge, covering both metal and sheetrock.

4. Use a wide putty knife as shown to smooth spackle and create a uniform edge. Keep one edge of the knife on the metal bead and use firm pressure, working from top to bottom.

5. Joints where two pieces of sheetrock meet should be taped as well as spackled. Spread spackle over the joint, press the tape in place over the joint line, then cover the tape liberally with spackle.

6. Using a wide putty knife, force the tape firmly against the joint, work the surface flat, and remove excess. When the compound has dried, go over the spackled areas with medium-grit sandpaper until the surface is smooth enough to paint.

The door

When the closet door goes on, the job is nearly done. Actually, the door should be removed before you paint the rest of the closet, finished separately, and then reattached. It's a good idea to temporarily install the door before you start painting, since you may have to make some small adjustments for a better fit (planing down a jamb or door edge, for instance).

You may decide that a sliding door or simple hinged door is better for your closet. Modern hardware for both folding and sliding doors makes installation easy. The door used in this closet came completely assembled, with hinges and pivots already attached. Lumber retailers and builders' supply outlets have different models to choose from. These ready-to-install doors come in standard dimensions.

The crucial factor in hanging a door is the doorway itself. Are the jambs plumb and square? Does the width of the doorway equal the width of the door? Is the doorway high enough to accommodate the track? The manufacturer's instructions that accompany each set of doors or door hardware contain specifics regarding dimensions, construction, and installation, so your best bet is to be guided by them while planning, measuring, and building.

1. Screw the track for the folding door in place. Follow the manufacturer's instructions concerning the position of the track on the top jamb.

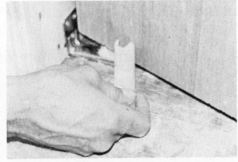

2. Align and screw the bottom pivot in place according to installation instructions.

3. Lift the door into place. For most doors, whether they are sliding or folding, the top edge of the door is positioned first, then the bottom.

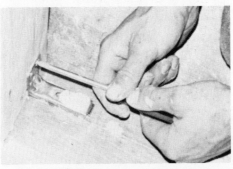

4. Adjusting a threaded peg attached to the bottom edge of the door locks the door in the pivot assembly. A special wrench for this job is enclosed with other door hardware.

Other options

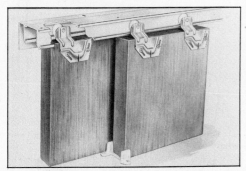

Sliding doors are easy to install. Most sliding door hardware consists of an aluminum track, rollers that are attached to the top door edge, and a simple plastic guide assembly that screws to the floor.

Louvered doors are more expensive than flat or raised panel doors. Use them where ventilation is important, or where you want to have a distinctive appearance.

Refitting the closet

There's no need to despair over a closet that defies all attempts at organization (see below left). A little imagination combined with the basic cutting and joining tools and some lumber can result in an attractive storage area that uses the available space well and meets your particular storage needs (below right).

Before. The stuff-stack-and-cram look

After. Same space, same gear, but what a difference!

First steps: cleaning out, measuring, planning

The first and most dramatic part of the job is the complete clean-out. Remove the old clothes pole and the shelf, but leave the pole-holding cleat; you can use it as a shelf support later. Once everything is out, take measurements and make final plans. For this re-fitting job, the limited space in a single closet is to be divided and reorganized for two people.

You'll be surprised at how much space you have to work with once you've completely emptied out your closet. The clothes pole and single shelf arrangement found in most clothes-storing closets leaves a great deal of space unused and makes the storage situation haphazard. Shoes, bags, boxes, and other closet items are all left on the floor, and the shelf above the pole is almost always over-crowded.

A more practical way of organizing closet space for clothes is to remove the single eye-level pole and replace it with one or more shorter poles at different locations in the closet. The object is to confine hang-up storage for shirts, pants, or dresses to smaller, well-defined areas of the closet in order to gain space for new shelves, dividers, or even additional poles.

After you've gutted your closet and have started measuring and planning, take a moment to locate a few studs in the closet wall. You can always count on studs in corners, but finding one or two in the back wall will make it easier to nail in new cleats, shelves, and upright supports.

The finished job, before refilling, is used here to illustrate construction sequence. The center unit, which acts as a divider, was installed first, after being completely assembled in the workshop. With the divider in place, both lower clothes poles were installed, then new shelves were added between the divider unit and the side walls. Construction was completed with the addition of the upper clothes pole.

Relocating the clothes pole

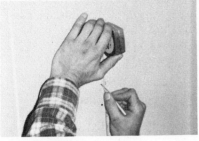

1. The lowered clothes pole should be about 40 inches above the floor, but you can adjust this height according to how much hanging room your clothes need.

2. Since the pole holder will also serve as a shelf support, make sure it's level. Use your two-foot level to mark a horizontal guideline for installing the holder.

3. Use stock one inch thick and 4 to 6 inches wide for the pole holder. Cut the stock to fit the depth of the closet, then drill out a hole for the clothes pole. (Here two identical pieces are being drilled out together to save time.)

4. When the hole is made, saw out a slot in the top of one holder so the pole can slide into place.

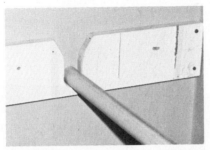

5. Nail the holder in place, using 8d-10d common nails. The top edge can be used to support a shelf.

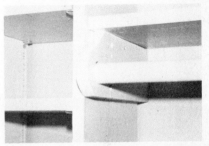

6. The companion pole-holder should remain closed to reduce wobbling. If a closet pole isn't going to extend all the way across, as is the case here, a custom-built holder like this one adds a nice touch.

Building in more shelves

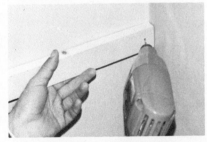

1. Cut the cleats for new shelves from one-inch stock, then pre-drill holes for 10d nails in corners as shown. Drill in at a slight angle so you're sure to nail into a corner stud.

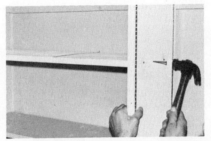

2. Cut new shelves to size, position them with a level, then nail through the center upright into the shelf edge as shown here to complete installation.

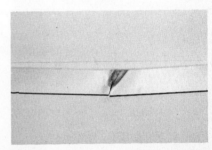

Caution: Don't use a knotted cleat; it's bound to split sooner or later. Knots are structurally weak, especially in narrow pieces like this one.

Finishing touches

Once the construction is over, the only job left is applying a finish. Before you apply stain or finish, however, take some time to soften sharp edges, round corners, and give all shelf surfaces a once-over with medium-grit sandpaper.

If you're going to paint, use a quick-drying primer, followed by a gloss or semi-gloss enamel. A flat coat won't stand up to everyday use like enamel, and can't be dusted or wiped clean as easily. **Note:** Your finishing plans should include a new coat of paint for the inside of the closet; now's the best time to do it.

No matter what finish you use on your closet, make sure you allow *more* than enough time for the final coat to dry before moving your stuff back in. Let the closet air out completely; otherwise, your favorite shirt may pick up the odor of the finish—a not too desirable cologne.

Before you paint, stain, or finish your work, remove sharp edges with a plane or surform tool. For this refitting job, lumber from some dismantled shelving was recycled to make new shelves and supports.

Because previously painted lumber was used in this project, new shelves will have to be painted rather than stained or clear-finished. Use a quick-drying primer, followed by a gloss or semi-gloss enamel.

Refitting tips and ideas

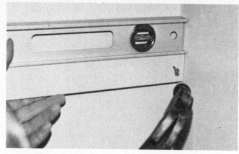

The quickest way to put up shelf supports in a closet is to hammer your nail just part way in, hold the support in place, and use your level as shown while nailing the support to the wall. The nail is hammered in at an angle to catch the corner stud.

The uppermost shelves in your converted closet may have to be made narrower, like this one, so you can reach up and in easily.

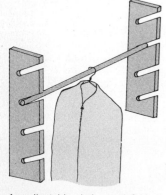

An adjustable clothes pole? It's a great idea if you've got a fast-growing child or if a change in seasons demands a higher (or lower) pole. To make this unit, drill out holes first, then use a saber or crosscut saw to cut slots at an angle, as shown above.

Hammer a few nails into a shelf support and you can convert an empty closet corner into storage space for belts.

How about refitting your closet with a tie rack? This one slides in and out; ties hang on a double row of ¼-inch dowels.

Special closet hardware

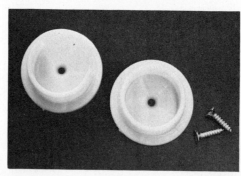

You can buy plastic clothes pole holders like these at most hardware stores. They are screwed in place as shown, and one holder is open so the pole can be removed.

Stanley Hardware makes a metal *Pin Strip* which serves as both a pole holder and shelf support. The strip is fastened to the closet side-wall by driving screws through two or more holes in the strip.

Refitting a clothes closet usually involves relocating the clothes pole and combining multiple pole locations with new shelf space, as shown in the photo above.

Your hardware store may also have adjustable metal clothes poles like the one shown above. Available in different extendable lengths, these poles are sturdy and easy to install.

A combination shelf bracket/pole holder is made by Stanley Hardware and can make your refitting job easier. The bracket is fastened into a wall stud.

Kitchen greenhouse

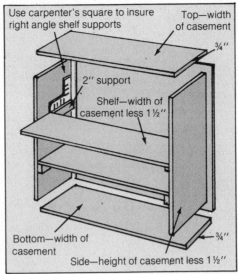

Use carpenter's square to insure right angle shelf supports

Top—width of casement

2" support

Shelf—width of casement less 1½"

Bottom—width of casement

Side—height of casement less 1½"

What it takes

Approximate time: 2-3 hours.

Tools and materials: Basic cutting and joining tools, carpenter's square, tape measure, electric or hand drill with two bits—one the size of the screw shank and one slightly smaller, 12 brass or galvanized metal screws about 1¼" long, 3d and 6d galvanized finishing nails, waterproof wood glue, ¾"x¾" wood strips, caulking compound; 1x12 lumber (redwood and western cedar stand up well to weather), one sheet ¼" clear acrylic measured to the outside dimensions of your 1x12 frame.

Here's a handy, heated greenhouse for your kitchen window which provides attractive display storage for your favorite plants and can double as a year-round herb garden.

Calculating lumber. To figure lumber requirements, measure the inside width and height of your open window casement. If you cannot or do not wish to open your window to the full size of the casement, build the frame to fit that portion of the casement you can reach through the open window.

1. The horizontal frame boards top and bottom extend the full width and sit outside the vertical frame boards. Cut them to the exact inside width of your window casement.

2. Cut the two vertical frame boards to fit between the horizontal boards. Subtract the combined thickness of the horizontal boards (1½") from the inside height of your window.

3. The shelves extend the full width inside the frame. Subtract the combined thickness of the vertical frame boards (1½") from the inside width of the window casement to determine shelf length. (We subtracted an extra ¼" from each shelf measure for easy sliding.)

4. Each shelf support is a 2-inch strip cut lengthwise from a 1x12 board. Allow another 12 inches of 1x12 for the four shelf supports.

5. Add together the inch lengths calculated in steps 1-4 and divide by 12 to get a rough idea of the lumber footage you'll need. Remember to allow for some waste and keep in mind that lumber is sold in foot lengths only (i.e., 1 ft., 2 ft., 3 ft., etc.).

Constructing the frame

1. Measure and cut your lumber to the lengths calculated above. Be sure the ends are square.

2. Glue and fasten the shelf supports into each of the sides with 3d nails. (Consider the projected height of your plants when positioning supports.)

3. Glue and nail the frame pieces together to form a box.

4. Lay the frame box down and place the acrylic sheet on top, squaring the edges all the way around.

5. Drill 12 screw holes through the acrylic sheet, around all four edges, with a bit the same size as the screw shank. Change to a smaller drill bit and drill about ½-inch into the outside edges of the frame lined up with the holes in the acrylic.

Installing the frame

1. Insert the assembly in the window casement from outside. Tap the edges with a hammer to snug the frame in place.

2. Nail through the frame into the casement on all sides using 6d finishing nails 6 inches apart. You will not need angle iron support if you have at least two inches of casement to nail into on all sides.

3. Screw on the acrylic sheet.

4. Caulk around the edges of the acrylic sheet, inside and out, and around the inside of the frame where it meets the window. Glue and nail ¾-inch wood strips around the outside of the frame, overlapping the edges of the acrylic sheet.

5. Insert the shelves from inside the house. Put your herbs and plants inside and watch them grow.

Greenhouse viewed from outside

Bathroom storage

Putting the space in your bathroom to work can really make life easier. By making more storage space, you can separate functionally different items that are now crowded together: shaving cream, make-up, dental floss, and band-aids, for example. The many small items you keep in the bathroom demand similarly small storage spaces so they can easily be grouped and identified. The shelves in your medicine cabinet are ideal for this type of storage. (For instructions on how to install a medicine cabinet, see page 69.) If your cabinet is overcrowded, transfer some articles to a small set of shelves like the one below. You can gain extra wall space for shelves by removing wall-mounted towel racks and reinstalling them on the back of the bathroom door.

Larger articles like hair driers, cleansers, soap, and tissues can often be stored under the sink. If your under-sink space isn't being utilized, put it to work by building in some shelves or a cabinet, as detailed on the facing page. What about towels and dirty clothes? There's a good chance you might be able to find space for a hamper/shelving unit like the one on page 66.

Build a small set of shelves

A small set of shelves like this is always helpful for storing toiletries and other bath items. The dark mahogany sides contrast nicely with the pine top and bottom pieces. Any satin-style polyurethane or penetrating resin finish will work well here. Shelves of clear acrylic plastic will lend a unique and attractive appearance to your project.

Tools and materials: Basic cutting and joining tools; plus: one mahogany board (¾″x2′x8″); one pine board (¾″x18″x8″); 12 6d finishing nails; and 4 acrylic plastic shelves (¼″x18″x3⅞″). Have your glass dealer cut the plastic to size.

Approximate time: 2 hours, including finish coats.

Easy to make: 1) Measure, mark, and cut rabbets (¾″ wide) and dados (¼″ wide) in mahogany board, then rip board in half. Rip pine board into two identical pieces at the same time. 2) Glue and nail sides to top and bottom, square the frame up and brace it. 3) When glue has set, remove brace and finish as desired. 4) Insert acrylic plastic shelves and install.

Storage under the sink

Custom-made shelves. A quick, easy, and effective way to convert an empty undersink area to storage space is to build in some shelves. To get the most out of the existing space, measure carefully and custom-fit your design around the plumbing fixtures and corner leg supports.

Measure and cut the three side supports first, then cut shelves to size; each shelf is cut at a 45° angle at one end. Glue and nail shelves to center support, then add side supports. Offset shelves as shown above for easy nailing through center piece.

Cabinets. Building a cabinet under your bathroom sink isn't a difficult job. You should be able to make the entire cabinet from a single 4'x8' sheet of ⅝" or ¾" plywood. If your sink has legs, try to remove them and use the cabinet sides to support the sink. Cut the sides and front first, then fasten the shelf supports to the sides and join the front to the sides. (Use white or yellow glue and 4d finishing nails.) Measure, mark, and cut the shelves, then install them. Cut the doors to size, then hinge them to the sides of the front opening. Before sanding and finishing, attach two magnetic catch assemblies to the doors and the front edges of the shelf, as shown in the final illustration. Finish knobs separately and install them when cabinet finish is dry.

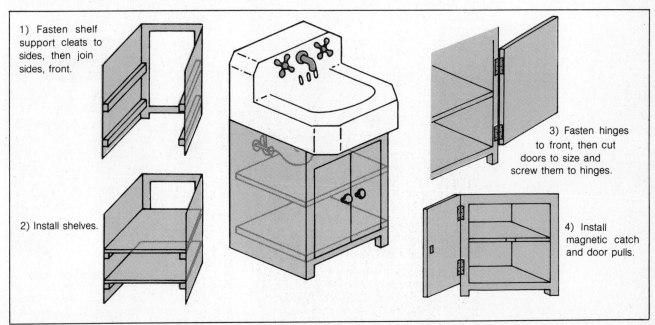

1) Fasten shelf support cleats to sides, then join sides, front.

2) Install shelves.

3) Fasten hinges to front, then cut doors to size and screw them to hinges.

4) Install magnetic catch and door pulls.

Build a hamper with shelves

What it takes

Approximate time: 8-10 hours, including primer-sealer coat and laminating top.

Tools and materials: Basic cutting and joining tools plus these materials: two ⅝"x4'x8' sheets A/C plywood, white or yellow glue, contact cement (1 quart), 1 lb. 4d finishing nails, 1 wooden knob, with ¾" screw, and a 2'x4' sheet of plastic laminate.

Cutting diagram

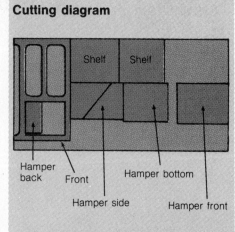

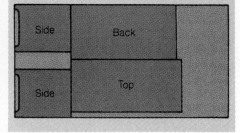

Why keep dirty clothes in a corner or stuff them in a laundry bag when you can build a combination hamper/shelving unit like the one shown here? With its formica top, this combination storage unit can endure the spills and heavy traffic common to busy bath areas and still look like new. The enamel finish on the front, which is applied over one coat of primer-sealer, is also highly resistant to wear and staining and can be maintained with the swipe of a sponge.

The model you see above, only partly visible because of cramped bath space, was designed to fit a particular bathroom niche, but you can adjust height, width and depth for the space you have available.

Note: You may also want to choose a patterned formica to give your project a more lively look; there is a large variety of colors and patterns available.

A **cutting diagram** can save both work and material. Arrange the elements from a scale drawing of your own design on 4x8-foot sheets of ⅝-inch and ½-inch plywood as shown top and bottom in the diagram above.

1. Cut out and label the parts to be assembled. A saber saw makes quick work of both curves and inside cuts. Start inside cuts by drilling out ⅜" holes along the cut-line, as shown above.

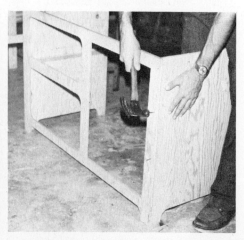

2. Fasten shelf supports to left side and join both sides to front, using white or yellow glue with 4d finishing nails. Then square up corners with a carpenter's square, using two lengths of scrap lumber as diagonal braces.

3. Glue and nail shelves in place. You can get away with shelf supports on only one side by nailing through front and back panels into shelf edges. Now is a good time to seal, finish, or prime-coat the interior, before the top goes on.

4. Glue and clamp stops in place for hamper front in top corners of hamper opening, as shown. Use scrap lumber for these small pieces, and make sure they'll allow the hamper to open and close freely.

5. Put the hamper together. The easiest assembly sequence is to join back and sides first, nail in bottom, then attach front. When you've put the hamper together, square it up with a diagonal brace, and allow glue to set.

6. Install the hamper. First fasten hinges to bottom edge of hamper front, then position hamper as shown, drill out pilot holes, and screw hinges to front panel. Screws should be at least 1" long, and hinge plates no wider than ⅝".

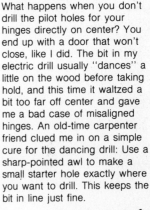

Don't get unhinged over a simple problem.

What happens when you don't drill the pilot holes for your hinges directly on center? You end up with a door that won't close, like I did. The bit in my electric drill usually "dances" a little on the wood before taking hold, and this time it waltzed a bit too far off center and gave me a bad case of misaligned hinges. An old-time carpenter friend clued me in on a simple cure for the dancing drill: Use a sharp-pointed awl to make a small starter hole exactly where you want to drill. This keeps the bit in line just fine.

Practical Pete

7. Glue and nail top in place. Allow for an even overhang on sides and front; back should fit flush if it's going to be against the wall.

8. Set nails, then fill all exposed holes and cracks with wood dough. When dough dries, sand the wood smooth and remove sharp edges and corners. The final step before the first coat of paint is to remove sawdust with a tack rag or vacuum cleaner.

9. Paint on primer-sealer. You can varnish the inside shelves, as we've done here, or paint them the same color as the outside. Remove the hamper and paint it separately. For step-by-step instructions on how to put on the plastic laminate top, turn the page.

10. Almost forget the knob. Find the center of the hamper front and drill out a hole a couple of inches from the top for the screw-in knob. Finish the knob separately, then install it when final coat on hamper front has dried.

Putting on plastic laminate

Bathroom and kitchen areas are favorite places for plastic laminate surfaces. Although only 1/16-inch or less in thickness, this material is smooth, hard, and exceptionally resistant to heat damage, abrasion, and stains of all kinds. In other words, gluing laminate down over plywood, as detailed step-by-step below, will give you a nearly indestructible, no-maintenance surface.

Plastic laminate comes in sheet form, and is sold by the square foot. Most lumber yards and builder supply outlets will cut it roughly to size for you. You can also choose from a wide variety of colors and patterns.

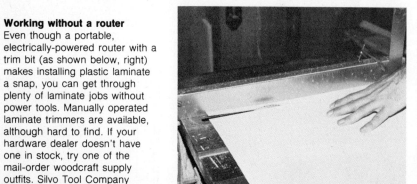

1. Cut plastic laminate roughly to size (about ⅛" oversize), using a carbide saber or circular saw blade, or one with fine teeth, as shown. The key to cutting thin laminates successfully is to brace them securely while sawing. Keep the underside of the laminate *down* when sawing with a table or hand saw; *up* when you're using a saber or circular saw.

2. Glue edging for sides first. Coat the plywood edge and the back of the laminate evenly with contact cement. Allow the cement to dry (5-15 minutes), then align both surfaces and press the plastic in place, working from one end to the other as shown.

3. With a laminate trim bit, use a router to trim the plastic flush. Work with controlled, moderate pressure, and keep the router moving. Repeat steps 1-3 to apply laminate to front edge.

4. Use a large brush to coat plywood top and underside of laminate with contact cement.

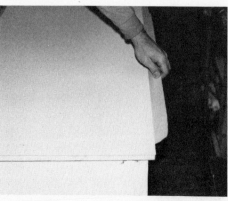

5. When cement is dry to touch, place a paper *slipsheet* between both surfaces, align them as shown, and carefully slide the slipsheet out. Use a roller to force laminate against top.

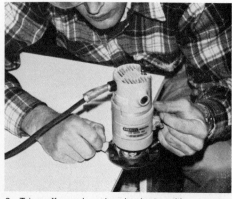

6. Trim off overhanging laminate with a router, using the edge-trimming bit. Once you've trimmed the edge flush, bevel it slightly with a file, or use an edge bevel bit with your router.

Installing a medicine cabinet

1. Locate the inside corner of the stud that will be the cabinet side support. You can use a stud-finder, drill exploratory holes, or use a keyhole saw as shown.

2. Once you've found the inside corner of the stud, use a level to mark a cut-line running along the inside edge.

Need more space than a normal-sized medicine cabinet can give you? National Recessed Cabinets (Miami, Florida) sells several different models of over-sized cabinets. They are installed just like conventional ones, but provide you with considerably more storage space.

3. Draw the outline of the cabinet box, starting from the line you've just marked. In a conventionally framed house, the opposite side of the box should line up pretty closely with the adjacent stud (see insert).

4. Cut out the hole for the box, using a saber saw or a keyhole saw.

On the wall, not in the wall
What if your bathroom wall is brick or plaster, or you don't have the time or energy to cut out a custom-fit recess between two studs for a medicine cabinet? Don't worry. With a little looking around, you can locate several types designed to be mounted on the wall using conventional wall fasteners. These cabinets can be installed in a few minutes, and are available in many different styles, some with built-in lights.

5. Install horizontal supports for top and bottom of box. Cut 2x4 stock to inside dimensions and *toenail* the two pieces in position as shown.

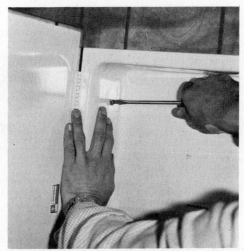

6. Position the cabinet and sink the screws through the holes in the side of the box into the support framing.

Out-of-the-way storage

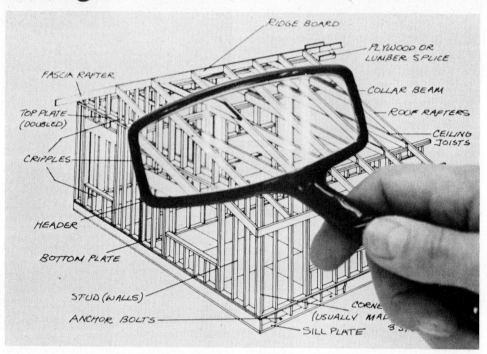

It's not always easy to find room in your home for new storage space. If you already have a lion's share of storage space and can't find room for more, don't give up. A closer look around your house or apartment is sure to unearth potential storage areas that haven't yet been taken advantage of. (See the illustration above.) The projects and ideas on the next twelve pages can help you make use of these hidden storage areas.

Between-stud storage: a readymade solution

Readymade cabinets of metal and wood are available in various lengths but built to a standard width that fits exactly between the studs (usually 16 inches apart) in interior walls. The readymade model shown below is metal.

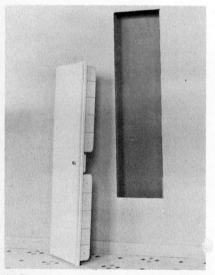

1. First locate the studs that will bracket your installation. Measure the exact dimensions of the recessed cabinet frame, not the facing. Determine the desired wall height of the cabinet, then cut away the wallboard to the studs on each side.

2. The recessed part of the cabinet will probably be a little narrower than the distance between the studs. If so, cut spacers out of scrap wallboard and nail them to one of the studs so the cabinet will slide in snugly.

3. Lift the cabinet into place and screw it to the studs on both sides through holes on the inside. The molding around the face of the cabinet will cover the edges of the cut wallboard even if the cuts are a little ragged.

Doing the job yourself

1. Cut out and remove wallboard or paneling between the studs as shown on page 69, using a keyhole or saber saw. Then nail cleats for the bottom shelf in place; they should be flush with the bottom edge of the wallboard.

2. Cut a sheet of hardboard, paneling, or ¼″ plywood to the dimensions of the opening, then glue and nail it into place, using cleats to support the bottom corners, as shown above.

Push-pull click-click

Oops! I got a bit too enthusiastic with my keyhole saw when cutting out the wallboard between a couple of studs, and ended up cutting through two walls instead of one. Luckily I caught the mistake before the cutout was complete, but the subsequent repair could have been avoided if I'd kept my sawstrokes shorter.

Practical Pete

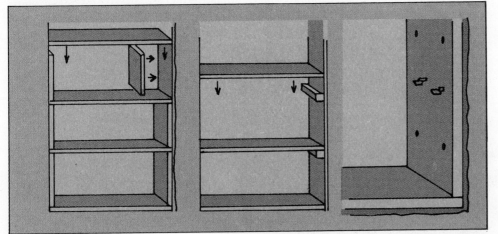

3. Install shelves, following one of the designs shown above. Be sure to cut and fit all shelves so that the front edge of each shelf is flush with the wall surface, not the stud behind it.

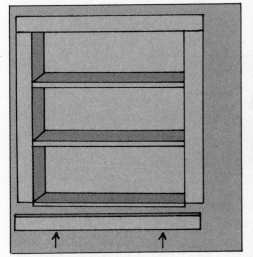

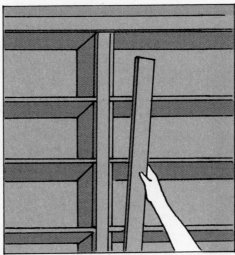

4. Measure, cut, and nail the trim in place. You can use either straight lumber or casing molding.

Note: For more extensive between-stud storage, remove the wallboard between several adjacent studs and build in new shelves as shown above. Install molding over the center studs to hide both the studs and the shelf support cleats.

Build a coatrack with an antique look

What it takes

Approximate time: 1-2 hours, not including finish.

Tools and materials: Hammer, back or crosscut saw, drill with ⅜″ and ¾″ bits, plus the following materials: pine board 1¼″ x 8″ x 6′, pine board ¾″ x 8″ x 4′, 3′ length of ¾″ dowel rod, 1′ length of ⅜″ dowel rod, 7d finishing nails, white or yellow glue.

Here's a project that can do a handsome job of converting an unused entryway wall into storage space for hats and coats. It's simple in design, easy to build, and attractive as well. Adjust the length and number of dowel pegs to suit your wall space, but keep the pegs at least 6 inches apart. They should also be at least 65 inches from the floor to hold long coats.

For this project, you'll need a drill guide so all the dowels will go in at the same angle. Many hardware stores carry both 90 degree and adjustable drill guides, but it's very easy to make your own.

Select a small, thick piece of scrap wood such as a 2x4. Then drill out a hole at the angle you want your dowels to incline, using the same bit you'll use for sinking the dowels (¾″). The drill guide is then clamped over the rack back at premeasured locations.

1. After the rack back has been cut to size, mark the locations for dowel centers. Then align your drill guide over each spot, clamp it in place, and drill out the dowel holes.

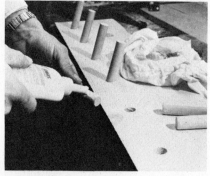

2. Coat the dowels and holes lightly with glue, then hammer the dowels in place. Tap them in gently, bit by bit, until the dowels protrude 2-3 inches.

3. Join the top to the rack back. Keep a rag nearby so you can wipe off any excess glue immediately.

4. Cut angled side braces to size and join them to the top and back of the rack. Use a couple of finishing nails in each side, followed by one or two dowel pegs for decoration.

5. Round off the dowels with a file and medium-grit sandpaper, then soften the corners and edges of the rack. Sand the surface smooth before finishing.

6. Apply a penetrating oil stain to the wood. When the stain dries (24 hours), give the wood extra protection with an oil or satin style varnish finish. Fasten the coatrack to the wall by screwing it into three studs.

Fancy treatment for the basic box

What it takes

Approximate time: 2-3 hours.

Tools and materials: Basic cutting and joining tools plus the following materials: 4'x4' sheet ½-inch A/C interior plywood, 18' casing molding, 1 piece (13¾" x 16") ¾" A/C plywood for top, ¾" x 1¼" x 6' clear pine for top lip, foam pad 3" x 13½" x 15½".

Types of molding

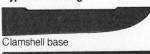

Clamshell base

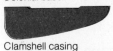

Colonial base

Clamshell casing

Colonial casing

Band molding

Clamshell stop

With a few additions and special touches, the basic box becomes an attractive seat or footrest with a hinged top and storage space inside. This box was made to hold records, but you can adjust the dimensions to make this portable piece of furniture any size you want.

1. Begin by building a simple open-top plywood box, using either butt or rabbet joints at the corners. (See page 20.)

2. Edge each side with molding as shown. Measure and cut mitered corners carefully so you get a good fit. The molding used here is called *colonial casing*, but you can use whatever type you wish. (See margin.)

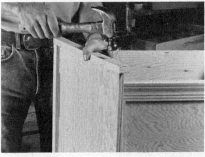

3. Cut the top from a piece of ¾" plywood, to 1½" less than the outside dimensions of the box. Then glue and nail a lip around the edges of the plywood as shown, using clear pine ¾" thick and 1¼" high.

4. Mortise a latch into the top, then hinge the top to the box, also using a mortise. When the top is hinged securely, attach the remaining part of the latch to the box.

5. Cover a cut-to-size foam cushion with fabric, then drill out a pair of holes in each corner of the box so the cushion can be tied on. Drill holes in both ends of the box for rope handles and attach them when the finish is dry.

6. Before applying a stain or finish, give your project a more authentic antique look by *distressing* the wood. Use a hefty set of keys or a chain to make decorative nicks and scars on the top and sides of the box.

Frame a window with shelves

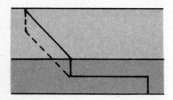

TIP: You may not be able to find a piece of lumber long enough for the top shelf. If this is the case, *splice* two boards together with a lap joint, as shown above, to get your shelf the right length.

Don't bypass the space around windows in your search for more storage area. Framing a window with shelves will give both the room and the view a new personality.

If you've got room and really need to make as much shelf space as possible, frame the window completely instead of just part way, as was done here. Extend your side supports all the way down to the floor and build shelves in below the window sill. You can also increase the length of the shelves all around the window area.

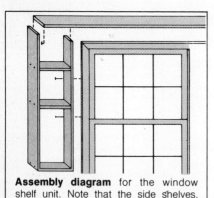

Assembly diagram for the window shelf unit. Note that the side shelves, shown here in color, are constructed before they are mounted on the wall.

1. Assemble both side shelf units completely before attaching them to the wall. Leave the upper sections open, as shown, to accommodate the top shelf. Use screws or 6d finishing nails to assemble the pieces.

2. Drive screws or 6d box nails through the vertical side supports into the window molding. The top edge of each inner side must be flush with the top edge of the window molding.

3. Measure and cut the top shelf, then fasten it to the top window molding and side shelf units. Glue all bare wood joints.

4. Nail or screw through the outer shelf sides into the top shelf as shown. Set all the nails, fill holes with wood dough, and sand before finishing.

5. For extra stability, or to keep the outer edges of the shelf securely on the wall, use small angle braces or toe-nail into a stud, as shown.

Build a window seat with storage space underneath

What it takes

Approximate time: 4 hours.

Tools and materials: Basic cutting and joining tools, plus the following materials: 3 eight-foot 2x4s, 1 sheet ⅝" A/C interior plywood, 1 pair ⅝" butt hinges, 6d finishing nails, 10d common nails.

Here's a plan for a sturdy window seat that doubles as a storage area. If your window isn't recessed from the wall like the one above, you can still use the same design and just add sides. Putting a bottom on is optional.

Constructing the seat is a simple but satisfying job that can be done in an afternoon. The first step is to measure, mark, and cut the front panel, top, and framing pieces. **Note:** Make your seat ¼" narrower than the width of the alcove. The drafts and temperature changes common to window areas can cause the wood to swell, making it difficult to open the seat.

Assemble the frame first, using 10d common nails and beginning with the top. The lap joints will give extra strength and make nailing easier. (Toenailing gives a much weaker joint and often splits the wood.)

When the frame is together and you've tested it for fit, glue and nail the front in place. Here you'll want to use 6d finishing nails, since they can be easily set and hidden with wood dough. The front should be high enough to hide the seat or top and provide a slight lip to keep the cushion from slipping off.

Installing the top is the last step. Fasten the hinges to the back edge of the plywood, position the top, then screw the free wings of the hinges to the back frame member. Make sure the back edge of the top is at least an inch from the back edge of the frame (see design detail below).

Now all you need to do is finish your project and give it a cushion.

TIP: If you don't want to take the trouble to apply a finish to the front, use a piece of pre-finished paneling instead of regular plywood.

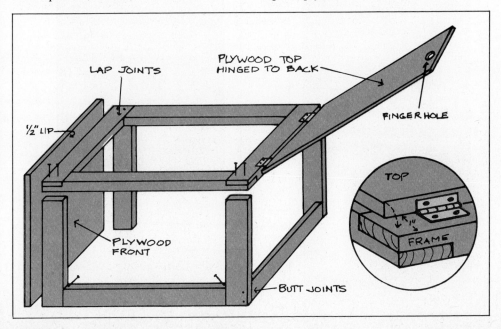

Build a bed with drawers underneath

What it takes

Approximate time: The bed shown took one long afternoon and a couple of evenings to complete, not including the finish; you should allow at least 6 hours.

Tools and materials: Basic cutting and joining tools, plus the following materials: 2 6' 2x6s, 6 3' 2x4s, 2 6' 2x4s, 1 sheet ⅝'' or ¾'' A/C exterior plywood, 1 sheet roughsawn plywood or other siding and drawer front material, drawer pulls (2), 8 rollers for drawer bottoms, 12 4-inch bolts, with nuts and washers, 10d common nails.

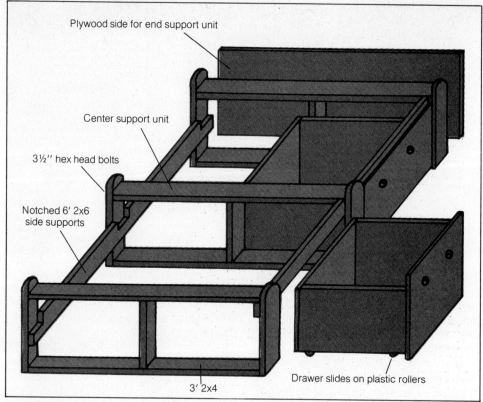

Plywood side for end support unit

Center support unit

3½'' hex head bolts

Notched 6' 2x6 side supports

3' 2x4

Drawer slides on plastic rollers

Assembling the frame. Here's a super design for a bed with loads of storage space built in underneath. The entire bed can be taken apart and put back together easily so you can build it in your workshop instead of on the spot. Construction-grade lumber keeps materials cost down and gives the bed a rugged, rustic look. (When buying your lumber, choose 2x4s and 2x6s that are straight and as free of cracks and knots as possible.) The drawers slide out completely for maximum accessibility. **Note:** Because this bed had to go against the wall, drawers were built into one side only. If your bed is going to be in the middle of the room, you can build an identical set of drawers for the other side. (Each drawer must be no more than 17'' in length.)

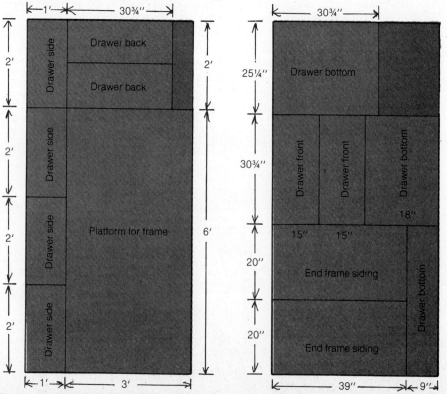

Cutting diagrams. To get the most from your plywood and siding sheets, use these cutting diagrams.

Building the frame

1. Build end and center support units, working from the design opposite. Glue all joints, and use 10d common nails for fastening.

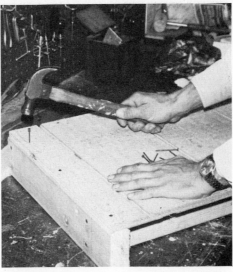

2. Glue and nail sides to end support units. Here you can use plywood, paneling, or rough lumber, depending on the style and appearance you want.

3. Cut 2x6 sidepieces to correct length (6', in this case), then measure, mark, and cut notches as shown. File or chisel notches to final dimensions.

4. Temporarily secure completed 2x6 side supports to the three frame units with clamps as shown, then drill out bolt holes and install bolts.

5. Cut and fit platform in place.

6. Round off the six upright frame members. Use a saber or coping saw to cut curves and a file or surform tool to soften edges.

Drawers for under the bed

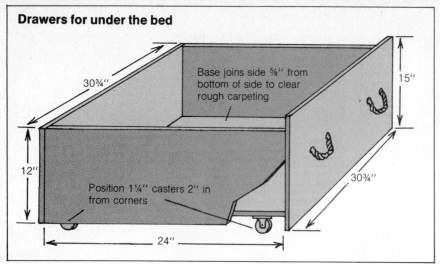

30¾″

Base joins side ⅝″ from bottom of side to clear rough carpeting

15″

30¾″

12″

Position 1¼″ casters 2″ in from corners

24″

1. Measure, mark, and cut the back, bottom, sides, and front for each drawer according to the design above. If the finished bed is to go against a wall, as is the case here, then only two drawers are needed. If the bed is to be located in the middle of the room and both sides are accessible, you can build four drawers. But each drawer should be no deeper than 18 inches.

2. Join the sides to the bottom. Here a rabbet joint is used for extra strength.

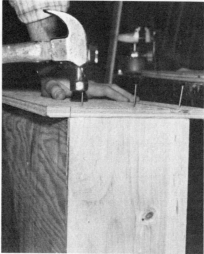

3. Glue and nail the back in place. The bar clamp forces the back against the bottom.

4. Join the front to side and bottom edges. Position the front panel so that roller clearance is at least ¼″ for bare floor; ⅝″ if the drawer must roll on a thick pile carpet.

5. Screw one caster into each corner of the bottom as shown. Make sure your screws don't stick through to the opposite side. If they do, file them flush.

TIP: When you've got the bed frame assembled, label the joints where the different parts meet, using either a permanent felt-tipped marker or a soldering iron, as shown above. Since holes for the bolts are slightly different for each joint, labeling will make it easy to realign parts when you reassemble the bed.

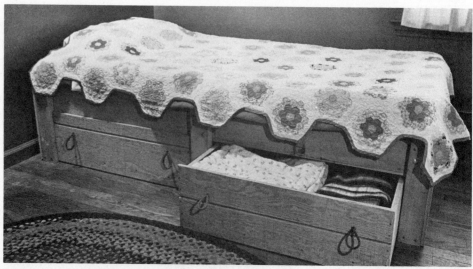

6. Now you are ready to put a finish on the bed and slide in your new storage space. Here two coats of polyurethane varnish (satin-style) were applied, to protect the wood and accent its natural beauty.

Storage under the stairs

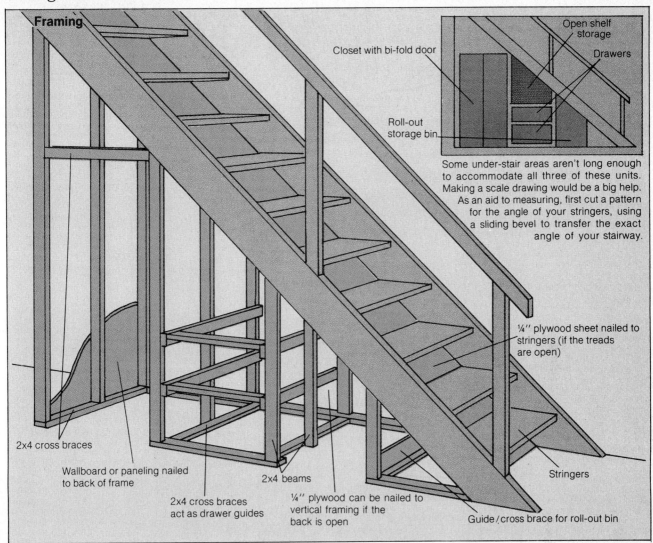

Framing

Closet with bi-fold door

Open shelf storage

Drawers

Roll-out storage bin

Some under-stair areas aren't long enough to accommodate all three of these units. Making a scale drawing would be a big help. As an aid to measuring, first cut a pattern for the angle of your stringers, using a sliding bevel to transfer the exact angle of your stairway.

¼" plywood sheet nailed to stringers (if the treads are open)

2x4 cross braces

Wallboard or paneling nailed to back of frame

2x4 cross braces act as drawer guides

2x4 beams

¼" plywood can be nailed to vertical framing if the back is open

Stringers

Guide/cross brace for roll-out bin

Nail ¼-inch plywood to the stringers if necessary (see **TIP:** this page). For framing, begin by nailing the 2x4 vertical frame members to the stringers. Then complete framing with 2x4 horizontal crossmembers both front to back and side to side between verticals.

Nail front to back supports for the drawer/shelf verticals at a height that they can be used for runner guides. Should your stairs be accessible from both sides, you will want to close in the back side of your storage space. Fit ¼-inch plywood or sheetrock in

under the stringer on that side and nail it to the vertical supports. Then nail on your pre-cut and measured front paneling (⅝-inch plywood or sheetrock), including a small triangular piece at the low end. (For more information on framing, see page 57.)

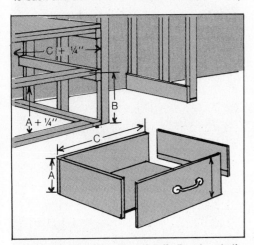

Drawer and shelf framing detail. For the shelf, nail a sheet of ¾-inch plywood over cross braces measured for the top drawer height. The cross braces serving as runner guides must be level.

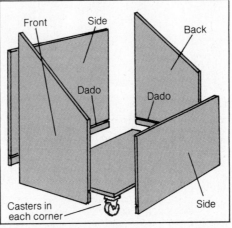

Front

Side

Back

Dado

Dado

Side

Side

Casters in each corner

Roll-out storage bin detail. When measuring for the roll-out bin, be sure to leave clearance of about one inch on both sides to allow for easy sliding. The bin bottom should be inset 3" to make room for the 3½" casters.

TIP: If your flight of stairs is open-backed (just treads, no risers), dirt will fall down into the storage area unless it is protected. Nail a fitted sheet of ¼-inch plywood across the underside of the stairs, from stringer to stringer, to eliminate the problem.

Claim that empty corner

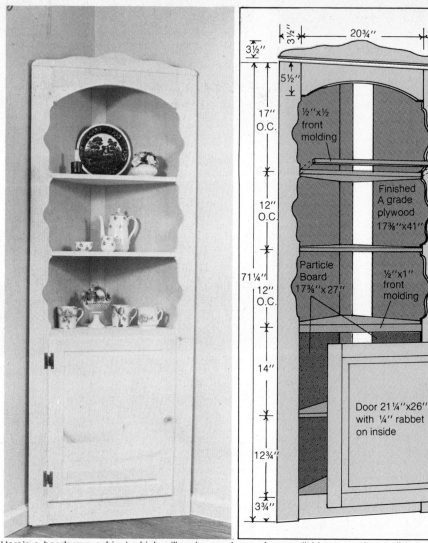

Here's a handsome cabinet which will make good use of an available corner in any living space. The assembly diagram above and the photo sequence below will help you build it yourself. This same cabinet is available preassembled from S.F. Bailey and Sons, Clarks Summit, PA. Other styles are also available from the same manufacturer.

1. After making dados for the sides and shelves, assemble the decorative front frame, using glue and wood braces as shown to secure joints.

2. Fasten triangular shelves to the front frame. Dados in the frame combined with glue and screws anchor shelves firmly.

3. Glue and nail the back support to the shelves, using 2 nails per shelf as shown. Dadoing these joints isn't necessary, but does make the cabinet stronger.

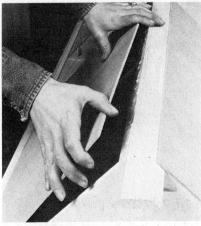

4. Fasten the back panels to the back support, shelves, and front. Use glue generously, but be sure to wipe off the excess as soon as the joint is closed.

5. Nail molding to the top three shelves to bring the front edge of each shelf flush with the front frame. Wide molding goes on the third shelf from the top.

6. Screw hinges to the door first, then position it squarely in the front frame opening and fasten the hinges to the cabinet.

7. Fasten the two-part magnetic catch assembly to the door and front frame.

8. After rabbeting the decorative top piece, glue and screw it to the top of the cabinet as shown. Now you're ready to show off your work with a good finish. (For finishing suggestions, see page 37.)

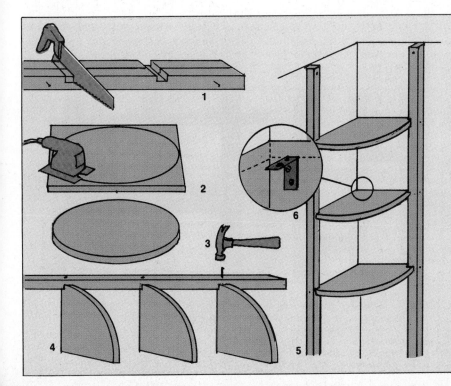

Stopgaps and copouts

1. Temporarily join the side supports together with finishing nails, then measure, mark, and cut out dados as shown above.

2. Use a saber or coping saw to cut out a circle from ¾-inch A/C plywood.

3. Cut the circle into quarters.

4. Join the shelves to side supports, using white or yellow glue and 8d finishing nails.

5. Install assembled shelves by fastening side supports to wall as shown. If you can't screw into a stud, use the wall fastener designed for your wall type (see page 38).

6. Check shelves to make sure they're level, then join back corner of each shelf to wall corner with an angle brace. Keep angle brace close to wall corner so you can fasten into corner stud.

Rough storage

This chapter contains ideas and how-to information on rough storage projects. Every house or apartment has some garage, attic, basement, or utility room space that is unfinished or in some way not usable as living space. Studs and framing are usually exposed; the area is unheated, not easily accessible, or poorly lighted. Until you decide to remodel these areas, you might as well exploit their storage potential. Here there's no need to get fancy; materials should be economical and easy to work with. Use C/D plywood, particle board, and cheap grades of lumber whenever possible. If you do plan to remodel in the future, make sure your rough storage project can be dismantled or removed without much trouble.

There are quite a few ready-made rough storage ideas. If you're working with exposed studs, using pegboard is hard to beat. It's inexpensive, and you don't need to build a frame or use spacers to install the board; just fasten it directly to the studs. Heavy-duty shelf brackets work well too, and you'll also find a variety of specialized hardware "hang-ups" for garden hose, bicycles, rakes, shovels.

A 6'' plastic-sheathed hook for each wheel safely supports a bicycle hanging frame down on a garage wall. A hole for the hook threads (which are about 2'' long) is drilled into the joist, using a drill bit slightly smaller in diameter than the hook. The hook is then handscrewed into the joist.

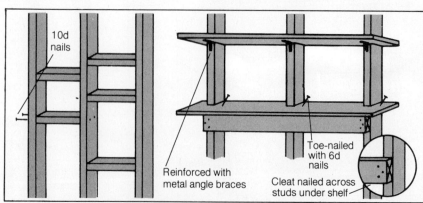

Shelving between the studs: Utilize between-stud space by putting up shelves as shown above. Nailing short lengths of 2x4 stock between the studs is the quickest way to make more storage space in exposed framing. If you need wider shelf space, slot your shelves to fit over studs, as shown at right. Toe-nailing alone won't make the shelf strong enough, so get extra support by using metal angle braces or nailing into a cleat that's been fastened firmly across the front of the studs.

Putting up rough shelving

What it takes

Approximate time: 2-3 hours.

Tools and materials: Crosscut saw, level, drill, pliers, plus the following materials:
1 sheet ¾″ C/D exterior plywood, 2 six-foot 2x6s (rip them in half lengthwise to make 4 vertical supports), 24 4-inch bolts, with nuts and washers, 24 crosspieces (18″ long) cut from 1-inch lumber.

In general, rough shelving should be inexpensive, easy to install, and very sturdy. The shelves you see here were put up in the corner of a garage, but they would work equally well in the basement, attic, or utility room. Because they're held together with bolts (use finishing nails just to position the supports for drilling and bolting), you can relocate them if you decide to remodel. **Note:** If your shelves are going to be exposed to outdoor conditions, treat the lumber with wood preservative.

1. Join the horizontal crosspieces to the vertical supports as shown, using just one finishing nail. Don't put the nail in the center of the crosspiece; that's where bolt will go.

2. Use a level to position the crosspieces on the wall framing, then nail them in place. Allow 16″ between the wall stud and the vertical support to accommodate the shelf.

3. Once you've positioned the support with finishing nails, secure each joint with a matching bolt as shown. Drill out holes for the bolts with a slightly larger bit.

4. Repeat steps 1-3 for each support. Four supports, positioned 32 inches apart (skip 1 stud, for 16-inch center framing), will make a shelf 8 feet long.

5. Cut and install plywood shelves.

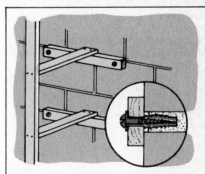

TIP: If you're putting up rough shelves against a cement wall, fasten 2x4 cleats to the wall with bolts and expansion shield anchors made for masonry walls. You can also use 2x4 stock for vertical supports and crosspieces, as shown above.

Ideas for the attic

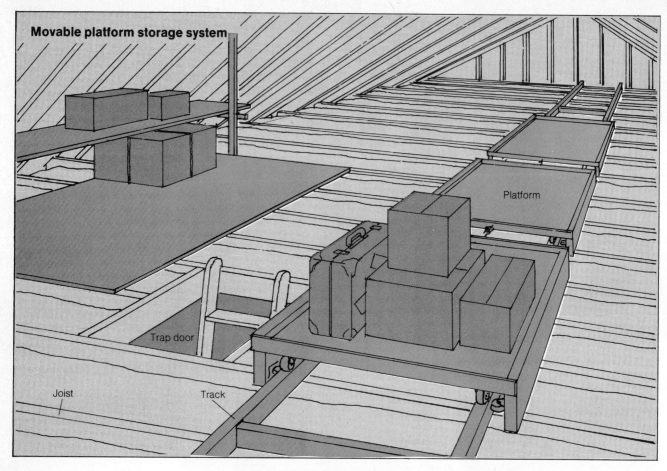

Movable platform storage system

Platform

Trap door

Joist

Track

Building storage space into an unused attic or crawlspace can substantially reduce the storage load in other parts of your home. Out-of-season clothes, sleds, suitcases, folding beds, camping equipment, any articles that are used on a sporadic or seasonal basis, are candidates for attic storage. Storing such items in the attic keeps them out of the way but accessible, so they're not taking up valuable space in the main living areas of the house.

If there's room to stand up in your attic, lay down a rough plywood floor before you start building new shelf or closet space. Use C/D exterior grade plywood to keep costs down. Over joists spaced 16″ apart, ½″ thickness is good; use ¾″ thick plywood over joists set on 32″ centers.

If your attic or crawlspace has no room to stand, building a movable platform storage system like the one detailed here is an excellent way to squeeze space out of this otherwise useless area. **Note:** A movable platform system will only work in crawlspaces where the access door is centrally located, as shown above.

I put my best foot forward—and look what happened.

I was up in the attic taking measurements for some shelves I planned to build, and the next thing I knew my foot was sticking through the living room ceiling. I was so intent on my tape measure that I lost my footing on the ceiling joist and stepped through the sheetrock. Calling on my constantly reliable hindsight, I realized that the first step should have been to lay down a rough plywood floor in the area around my planned shelf space.

Practical Pete

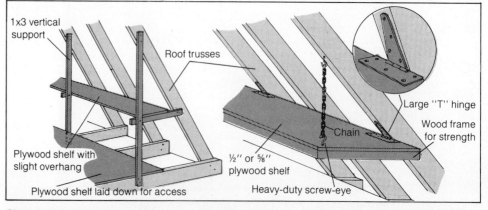

1x3 vertical support

Roof trusses

Large "T" hinge

Wood frame for strength

Chain

Plywood shelf with slight overhang

Plywood shelf laid down for access

½″ or ⅝″ plywood shelf

Heavy-duty screw-eye

Shelves and the slanted ceiling. You can build shelves in your cramped, slant-roofed attic with one of the designs illustrated above. Cut a sheet of ½″ or ¾″ plywood lengthwise for long shelves. The slope of the roof and the amount of headroom in the attic will determine the size of your shelves.

Building the platform

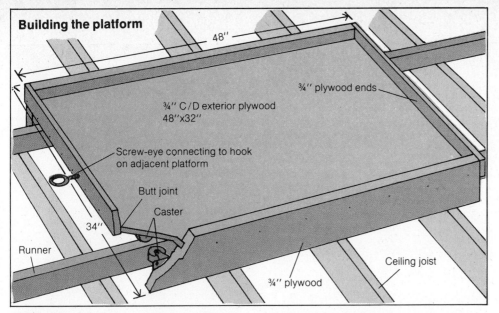

48″

¾″ plywood ends

¾″ C/D exterior plywood
48″x32″

Screw-eye connecting to hook
on adjacent platform

Butt joint

Caster

34″

Runner

¾″ plywood

Ceiling joist

What it takes

Approximate time: 4-5 hours, for building and installing 3 platforms and two 16′ runners.

Tools and materials: Router with ¾″ dado bit, crosscut saw, hammer, screwdriver, plus the following materials: one sheet ¾″x4′x8′ C/D exterior plywood, 6 4′ 2x6s, 2 heavy-duty screw-eyes, with matching hooks, 24 small-wheel (1″), screw-on casters, 32′ of straight 2x4s for runner assembly.

1. Working from the drawing shown above, build the platform/runner assembly from ¾″ C/D exteri- or plywood and 2x6 lumber. Cut three 48x32-inch platforms from one 4x8-foot sheet of plywood.

2. Attach the side casters to the 2x6 platform supports as shown. Locate each caster several inches from the corner, and place it high enough to allow for good runner contact.

3. With a length of 2x4 stock held against the side casters and the platform bottom (top photo), mark the runner outlines. Then screw the top casters in place, making sure that the caster wheel is centered between runner outlines (bottom photo).

Installing the runner assembly

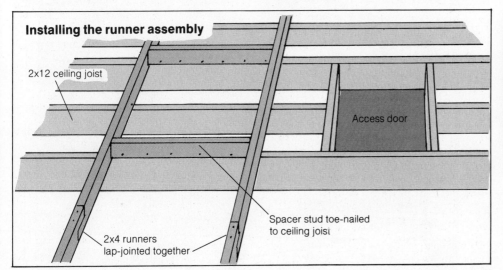

2x12 ceiling joist

Access door

Spacer stud toe-nailed
to ceiling joist

2x4 runners
lap-jointed together

This endview shows the alignment of track and casters on one side of the storage platform. When measuring the track fitting, be sure to allow ⅛″ clearance on both sides between runners and side casters.

4. Using the straightest 2x4 lumber you can find, make two continuous runners by joining shorter lengths with a lap joint (above). Line the runners up and join them together with 2x4 *spacers,* as shown. Position the spacers about six feet apart, directly over the ceiling joists, then toe-nail them in place to secure the runner assembly. Put the platforms in place, and connect them with heavy-duty hooks and screw-eyes.

Covering the cans

What it takes

Approximate time: Plan to spend a long afternoon on this one if you're building from scratch. (Two hours if you use a kit.)

Tools and materials: Tape measure, square, crosscut or circular saw, hammer, drill, screwdriver, four strap hinges with screws, two butt hinges with screws, one hook and eye fastener, four cement blocks, plus the following materials: 34' of 2x2 lumber, two 4x8 sheets of C/D exterior-grade plywood (¾'' thick). **Note:** The grooved plywood used for the shed pictured here is a special exterior siding called *Texture III*.

A small shed like this one for concealing trash containers can be free-standing because it has a back and bottom. It's a great way to keep overflowing cans out of sight and to protect garbage from possible upset by animals or wind.

Some home centers and builders' supply outlets sell sheds pre-assembled or in kit form, but you can usually build one much cheaper from scratch in about half a day. This design is for a completely enclosed shed that holds two 32-gallon cans.

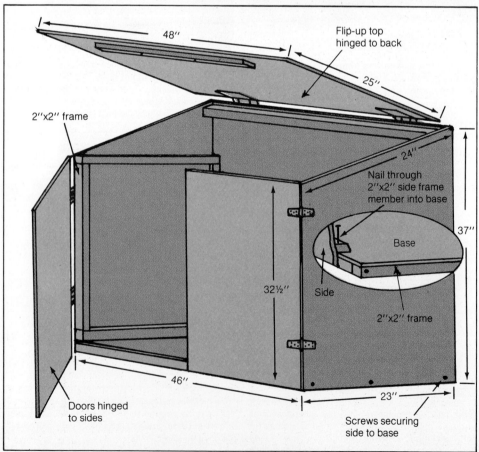

48''

Flip-up top hinged to back

25''

2''x2'' frame

24''

Nail through 2''x2'' side frame member into base

37''

Base

32½''

Side

2''x2'' frame

46''

Doors hinged to sides

23''

Screws securing side to base

1. Shovel out a depression about 6 inches deep, two feet wide, and four feet long.

2. When your hole is uniformly deep and level to the eye, pack the bottom flat with a tamper or the back of your shovel.

3. Fill the flattened depression about half way up with pea gravel. You'll need about two wheelbarrow loads to do the job.

4. Spread gravel evenly over the bottom of the hole, using a rake to make the surface roughly level.

5. Position cement blocks to support corners of base, then seat blocks in gravel bed as shown. Use a level and straight length of 2x4 to make sure the blocks are level.

6. Place the base on the block foundation, then nail the sides to the base as shown. Here double-headed nails are used so that the shed can be disassembled easily.

7. Attach the back to the base by nailing through the bottom 2"x2" frame member and into the base.

8. Fasten sides to back with screws. Drive screws through plywood sides and into back frame member, as shown. Screw sides to base for additional strength and stability.

9. Attach the front doors to the sides. Have someone hold the doors in place while you attach the hinges.

10. Hold the top in place, then hinge it to the back as shown.

11. Keep the front doors closed with a simple hook and eye latch. Screw the hook in place first, then the eye.

12. Even though exterior grade materials have been used throughout, a coat of wood preservative will make it weather-proof.

Workshop storage

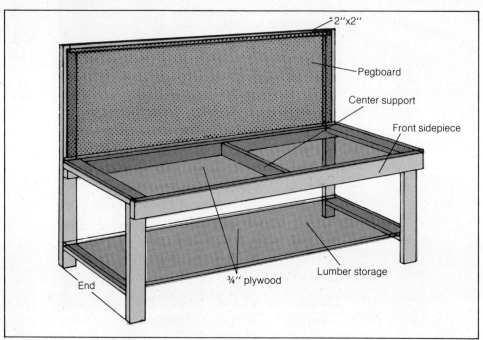

2"x2"

Pegboard

Center support

Front sidepiece

Lumber storage

¾" plywood

End

Here's a plan for a workbench with built-in storage space for tools and lumber. It's sturdy, as well as easy to build. The ends of the bench are assembled first, then joined with the front and back sidepieces. The rear corners are lap-jointed for strength. The center support is nailed in place, then the workbench top is installed. The top is screwed rather than nailed in place because it may have to be replaced in the future. A 2x2-inch horizontal support is fastened to the rear uprights and the pegboard attached, then the bottom shelf is installed. Adjust workbench dimensions to needs.

Your workshop may be the best place to start building new storage space. It's a good first choice because a well-organized workshop makes subsequent projects go smoothly and pleasantly; you can concentrate on building instead of on locating tools or materials.

Whether your workshop is large or small, extensively or minimally equipped, there are several important items you should have on hand. Keep a fire extinguisher within easy reach. You should also have a first aid kit nearby. Your power tools should be out of reach if your workshop is accessible to children. You might even want to lock these tools up or, if that's not possible, construct a small box around the electrical outlet in your work area and put a lockable latch on it.

Once you've got these safety precautions out of the way, you can go ahead with the ideas on the next few pages.

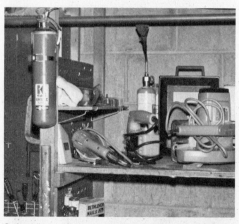

Safety first is the rule when it comes to workshop storage. Keep a fire extinguisher and a first aid kit within easy reach. Notice that safety goggles and a filter mask are stored right along with power tools.

Metal sawhorse brackets are inexpensive and surprisingly handy to have in your workshop. With a few 2x4s and a sheet of plywood, you can put up additional workbench or storage space in a matter of minutes to help you cope with a large project or a sudden case of storage overflow.

Putting pegboard to work

Because of its low cost, universal availability, and easy installation, pegboard is the perfect wall material for work areas of all kinds. It also helps you create an incredibly adjustable storage system. Making room for new tools or accommodating special tools and materials for a particular project is a quick and easy job.

When planning pegboard storage space in your workshop, remember that you can choose either ⅛″ or ¼″ thickness. Use the heavyweight perforated hardboard if you plan to store heavy items (axes, power tools, bar clamps) or install shelf supports.

Hand tools and pegboard were made for each other (see page 36 for pegboard installation instructions). If you or your fellow workers have trouble returning articles to their proper locations, trace the outline of the hanging tool, then paint in the silhouette, as shown above.

TIP: It's easy to go overboard with pegboard storage. Even ¼″ pegboard is not suitable for long term storage of heavy items: after several weeks it starts to bow away from the wall; the shelves become slanted, and the clips start to pull out of their holes. To prevent this from happening, fasten your hardest-working shelf supports and hangers into the wall behind the pegboard.

You can really get the most from your pegboard by using both sides of it. Here one side faces the workbench, while the other faces a shelf storage area. There is one important limitation to getting double duty from pegboard: it's easy to overload, so use it only for lightweight items.

It's hard to beat this system of storing screws, nails, and other small items. The screw-on tops of these clear plastic containers are fitted with pegboard clips. Your hardware store or home decorating center should have them in stock.

Storing lumber

Having ample storage space for building materials means fewer trips to the lumber yard since you won't have to stop work in the middle of a project to go out and get more wood. Making more room for lumber will also enable you to take advantage of sales or special prices on building materials. Unfortunately, storage space for wood is often neglected in favor of tool and workbench space. To keep your wood supplies in top condition, all lumber should be stored away from moisture. This usually means you'll want to keep it off the floor.

Here's a good way to store plywood, paneling, and other sheet material. Suspend two five-foot lengths of 2x4 stock from the ceiling joists as shown. Using a chain enables you to adjust the height of your sheet storage area or remove it entirely.

With two pairs of large angle braces, you can convert unused ceiling space between the joists into storage space for boards.

Make a separate storage area for scrap wood. Longer stock that can still be used for building is stored on two horizontal supports which are nailed to studs and strengthened with a diagonal brace. Small kindling is kept in the box on the right.

Storing paints and finishes

It doesn't take long for the space you've allocated for stain, varnish, wood filler, paints, and enamels to become a disorganized array of cans and containers of all sizes (see photo). A secondary shelf for smaller cans will utilize your storage space more efficiently and prevent your quarts, pints, and half-pints from being hidden by the "big boys."

Separate your finish-related preparations into these groups: Thinners, solvents, brush cleaner solutions; wood stain and filler; sealers and clear finishes; paints and enamels; waxes and polishes; spray products. **TIP:** Keep a supply of empty cans near your thinner, solvent, and brush-cleaner section so you won't have an excuse for not cleaning your brushes right after you're through using them. You'll also need cans whenever you use finish, since it's bad policy (see margin) to apply straight from the original container.

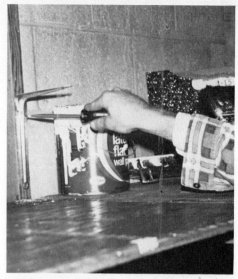

Separate small cans from large ones by putting up a narrow secondary shelf. This is a quick, easy job with inexpensive shelf brackets like the one shown. Make sure your shelf is at least 8½ inches high so gallon cans can fit underneath.

Before

After

An open and shut case

I got on the wrong side of a paint expert friend of mine recently. He stepped into my workshop just as I was putting the lid on some enamel and really got an eyeful of my can-closing technique. To make a long story short, I ended up buying him a new shirt and he ended up giving me some important pointers:

1) Paint cans are made to be opened and shut gradually, not by prying or pounding in just one or two spots. Open the can by working all the way around the lip with a screwdriver or can opener. Close it in the same way, tapping the edge in place bit by bit. Once you've deformed the lip with a heavy blow, you can forget about getting a good fit.

2) Don't apply paint or finish straight from the container it comes in unless you'll be using the entire can. The original can is for mixing, storing, and pouring. Use a clean coffee can to hold the paint or finish while you're applying it.

3) Keep the lip clean. Before you start applying the paint or finish, use your brush to remove the excess from the groove around the top of the can. Keeping the groove free of dried finish makes reclosing the lid a simple and airtight job.

4) Sort through your paints and finishes at least twice a season. Give inactive paints a good mixing and throw away finishing preparations that have dried out or become too concentrated or contaminated to use.

Practical Pete

Other workshop storage ideas

A handy nail-file can be created in an empty drawer by building in small bins. Shallow drawers like this one are well suited for small item storage.

Screw-top jars and lids fastened to the underside of a shelf as shown make see-through storage space for nails, screws, bolts, and other small items.

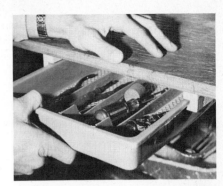

A plastic dish tub functions as a drawer when slid on two pieces of U-shape wood molding nailed to the underside of a workbench or shelf.

Build a carry-all toolbox

If you and your tools have to do a lot of traveling, a simple tote/storage box like the one shown above will come in handy. You can make it in about an hour, using spare or scrap lumber, some 6d box nails, and a length of 1½'' dowel rod. Toolboxes should be built to take a beating, so use ¾'' exterior grade plywood if possible. Both sides of the interior should, for safety's sake, be slotted to hold and protect handsaw blades.

1. Cut the bottom and end pieces, drill out holes for the dowel rod, and cut an opening for your 2-foot level in one endpiece. Then join as shown above. A toolbox 19 to 21 inches in length will be long enough to hold most handsaws.

2. Cut the sides to size, then cut a slot for the saw blade near the top edge of each sidepiece. Locate and bevel the slot so it lines up with the top endpiece edge as shown, then join the sides to the ends and the bottom.

3. Divide one end of the box to hold nails, screws, tape measure, and other small items. When planning the divider, make sure you leave room for your level to lie flat. Also keep in mind the importance of evenly balanced weight in the toolbox, if you plan to be carrying it frequently.

4. Secure saws by driving a round-head screw in on one edge or endpiece. Sink the screw in just far enough to hold the blade. Tie down the handle at the other end with a length of leather cord secured to a screw-eye. Slide the dowel rod into place and lock it in position with a small nail. Finally, give your toolbox a coat of varnish for durability and easy cleanout.

Stowaway storage for kids

What it takes

Approximate time: About half a day.

Tools and materials: Carpenter's square, electric circular saw, electric or hand drill with ⅞-, ½-, and ¼-inch bits, hammer and a nail set, sandpaper, 6 dozen ½-inch finishing nails, 3 feet of ½-inch rope, two washers with holes at least ⅞-inch in diameter, acrylic enamel paint and/or stain; one sheet ¾-inch 4x8 plywood, 6 feet of 1x8 board, 40 inches of ¾-inch dowel.

Planning hints:

- It is very important when constructing the two basic boxes involved in this project that your measurements allow for easy sliding of the engine box into the garage.
- Measure all corners with a carpenter's square to ensure right angles.
- Pieces should be glued as well as nailed for extra support.
- For a more finished looking product, use dowels to cap the exposed nailing. Drill holes ¼ inch in diameter about ¼ inch deep where nails will go. Set the nails deep in their holes, and hammer glued pieces of ¼ inch dowel into the holes. Sand the tops flush.
- When cutting the ends and sidepieces for the boxes, be sure to compensate for the various dimensional fractions lost to kerf (the width of the saw cuts, that is). Add the width of the saw cuts to your finishing strip measurements as you go, tailoring them to the large panels.
- When cutting finishing strips as diagrammed, it's a good idea to make all lengthwise cuts before sawing crosswise measures.

Do all toys come complete with 50 losable parts, or does it just seem that way? And how do you keep open-shelf playroom storage from looking like the baseball toss in a penny arcade? Short of instituting martial law, why not try building an eye-catching closed storage box?

Here's a combination toy box/work table which kids will enjoy. The fire engine rolls in and out of its garage on wheels, holds all kinds of toys, and is sturdy enough for a small child to ride in.

To begin

Finishing strips and wheels. To be cut from 1x8x6 lumber. Each strip should be ¾″ in width.

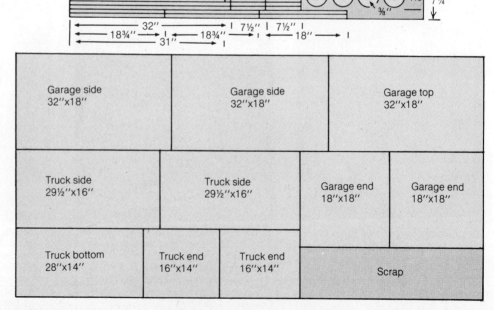

1. Cut the measured pieces of plywood as shown. Use a circular power saw.

2. Cut out wheels and finishing strips. Remeasure. Use the larger panels as a guide.

Assembling the garage

1. Glue and nail the two 32-inch finishing strips to the top edge of each of the side pieces. Then glue and nail horizontally through each of the strips into either side of the ¾-inch edge of the top piece to hide the exposed laminations.

2. To make the back of the garage, glue and nail an 18¾-inch strip on each vertical side edge of the 18x18 plywood back end. The strips will stick up ¾-inch above the top. Fit and fasten one 18-inch strip along the top edge of the back. Then glue and nail through the strips into the exposed ends of the top and sides of the garage.

3. Attach the two remaining 18¾-inch strips to the top of the 18x18-inch plywood front. Lay this assembly aside. It will be painted and nailed to the front of the fire truck later when the body has been assembled.

Assembling the truck

1. Drill ⅞-inch holes through the bottom corners of both side pieces, 2 inches from the bottom and 4 inches in from the ends.

2. Glue and nail the truck pieces together as shown. Be sure to set the floor piece at least 3½ inches up from the bottom so that it will clear the axles.

3. Cut the two 17½-inch axle dowels and insert through the holes. Slip on the washers and hammer the wheels on flush with the ends of the dowels. If they are too loose smear glue on the end of the dowel.

4. Paint the truck as you desire. Carefully nail the front panel onto the truck so it will fit exactly into the open end of the garage when the truck is backed in all the way. We painted the truck red inside and outside, with gold grille and bumpers, white headlights, and black coats and hats on pink-cheeked firemen.

5. Round off the sharp rear corners of each 31-inch strip for the sides of the two ladders. Glue and nail them to the rungs as diagrammed here. Nail each ladder to a side of the truck, square ends facing forward.

6. Drill holes ½-inch or ⅝-inch in diameter through the front of the box, centered. (Here each is the center of a headlight.) Run the ends of a tow-rope through the holes and knot them inside.

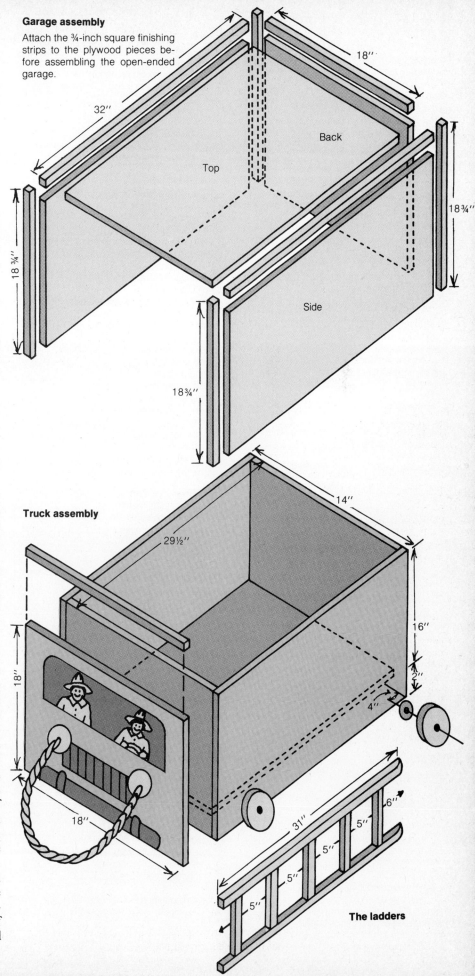

Garage assembly

Attach the ¾-inch square finishing strips to the plywood pieces before assembling the open-ended garage.

18″

Back

Top

32″

18¾″

18¾″

18¾″

18¾″

Side

Truck assembly

14″

29½″

16″

2″

4″

18″

18″

31″

6″

5″

5″

5″

5″

5″

The ladders

Index

WINDOWS, DOORS, SECURITY & INSULATION

WINDOWS, DOORS, SECURITY & INSULATION

Created and editorially produced for Petersen Publishing Company
by Allen D. Bragdon Publishers, Inc., Home Guides Division.

STAFF FOR THIS VOLUME:

Editorial Director	Allen D. Bragdon
Managing Editor	Michael Donner
Art Director	John B. Miller
Text Editor	James Wyckoff
Production Editor	Jayne Lathrop
Contributing Artists	
	Clara Rosenbaum, Jerry Zimmerman
Contributing Photographers	
	Monte Burch, John B. Miller, Tim Snyder
Cover design by	"For Art Sake" Inc.
Technical Consultant	Monte Burch

*Monte Burch contributed much of the specialized information in this
book, drawing on years of practical experience in general contracting
and cabinetmaking. He is the author of many how-to articles and more
than 15 books written during and after his years as Associate Editor of
Workbench magazine.*

ACKNOWLEDGEMENTS

The editors wish to thank the following individuals and firms for
their help in the preparation of this book: Abloy, Inc.; Adams
Rite Manufacturing Co.; American Plywood Assn.; Andersen
Windowalls; Armstrong Cork Co.; Biltbest Windows; BRK
Electronics; Caldwell Manufacturing Company; Consolidated
Edison of N.Y., Inc.; Fedders Corp.; Federal Chemical Co.,
Inc.; Fichet, Inc.; General Aluminum Products, Inc.; Home
Center Institute, National Retail Hardware Association; Hon-
eywell Inc.; Johns-Manville; K-S-H, Inc.; Kwikset Sales and
Service Company; Lafayette Radio Electronics Corp.; Madico;
Medeco Security Locks, Inc.; Mortell Company; NuTone Divi-
sion, Scovill Manufacturing Co.; Owens-Corning Fiberglas
Corp.; Plaskolite, Inc.; Quaker Window Channels; Radio
Shack; Reynolds Metals Company; Schlage Lock Company;
Stanley Tools, Division of the Stanley Works; United Press
International; U.S. Department of Agriculture; U.S. Depart-
ment of Housing and Urban Development; United States
Gypsum Company; Westinghouse Security Systems.

Petersen Publishing Company

R. E. Petersen/Chairman of the Board
F. R. Waingrow/President
Alan C. Hahn/Director, Market Development
James L. Krenek/Director, Purchasing
Louis Abbott/Production Manager
Erwin M. Rosen/Executive Editor,
Specialty Publications Division

Library of Congress Catalog Card
No. 77-076138
Paperbound Edition:
ISBN 0-8227-8003-8
Hardcover Edition:
ISBN 0-8227-8015-1

Table of Contents

1. OPENERS

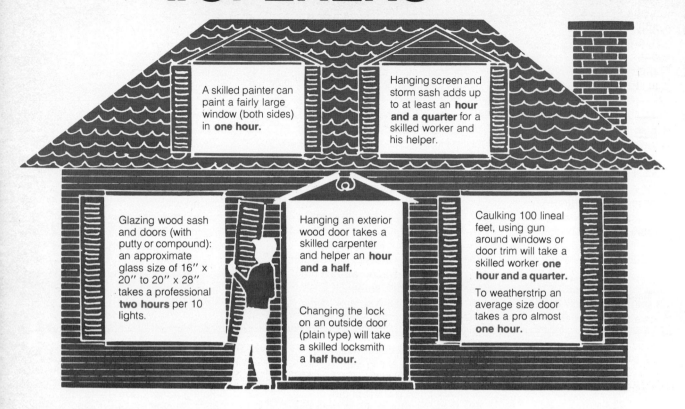

A skilled painter can paint a fairly large window (both sides) in **one hour.**

Hanging screen and storm sash adds up to at least an **hour and a quarter** for a skilled worker and his helper.

Glazing wood sash and doors (with putty or compound): an approximate glass size of 16″ x 20″ to 20″ x 28″ takes a professional **two hours** per 10 lights.

Hanging an exterior wood door takes a skilled carpenter and helper an **hour and a half.**

Changing the lock on an outside door (plain type) will take a skilled locksmith a **half hour.**

Caulking 100 lineal feet, using gun around windows or door trim will take a skilled worker **one hour and a quarter.**

To weatherstrip an average size door takes a pro almost **one hour.**

Above are a few of the jobs you will be doing around your house, along with the estimated time it takes skilled workers to do them, including travel and set-up time. Estimate the labor cost of a project by finding out the local pay rate for professionals and applying it to the above time estimate.

A house without doors and windows is about as useful as a solid sieve. Your house is 40-70 percent holes and it is the holes that make a house work. They let in what you want in, and keep out what you want out.

Taking care of those holes is essential to the appearance and well-being of any house—to keep it snugly insulated, to save on fuel and electric bills, and to be free of pests and secure from criminal entry.

Maintenance and repairs, even new window and door installations, are not difficult or dangerous because they seldom involve the structural strength of the house. So you don't need a lot of experience or technical knowledge to do them yourself. If you do have to call a professional carpenter to do these jobs, he must bill you at the same hourly rate for replacing a broken window pane, say, as he would for building a new garage. His bill could even be higher because, while these small jobs don't take much time in themselves, he must include his travel time to and from your house as well as his general overhead.

Partly for this reason it is sometimes difficult to persuade a carpenter to come and fix something *when* you need it. Although it may take you twice as long to replace a broken window pane or install a deadbolt lock, the alternative may be many days of drafts or insecurity before a profes-

sional can get to it. So try it for yourself.

This do-it-yourself manual has been written, illustrated—and organized—to show exactly how to do each of the jobs that is necessary to maintain, repair, and install things in those crucial holes in your house. All you need to know about how to handle each project is in this book—even if you have no experience yet in carpentry or other manual skills and are not familiar with the tools and terminology. This book is built for beginners, with even the simplest steps included. It is organized into specific projects each with its own list of tools, recommended materials, planning hints and step-by-step illustrated instructions in ordinary language. Just look up the job you need to do in the table of contents or index, turn to that page—it's all right there in one spot. You will even find an estimate of roughly how much time you should set aside to do the job.

The drawing of the house, above, shows some typical jobs you could do yourself, along with the number of hours a carpenter or handyman would take. Multiply that time by the hourly rate carpenters and handymen charge in your area (don't forget to include overhead and travel time). The result will show how much you could save by doing the job in your leisure time—not to mention the satisfaction.

Your maintenance calendar

Your maintenance check can of course continue all through the year. The calendar is simply a reminder of certain specifics. For instance, storm and screen windows and doors are always checked as the season changes. And the best time to inspect your furnace is *before* the cold weather arrives. But you can always keep an eye out for broken panes or insulation leaks, squeaking door hinges or termites.

It's useful to read the literature on new products for there are often stopgaps and new wrinkles that you can call upon which will save you time, trouble, and money.

	Northern	Temperate	Dry-hot	Wet-humid
January	Keep a close watch on heating equipment, such as your furnace, and radiators if you have them. Check temperature control systems. (Page 60)	Inspect furnace operation; see if fan motor is in need of oil. Change filters. Check temperature control systems. (Page 60)	Check all window screens. Repair or replace those in poor condition. (Page 22)	Check for windows that are loose, or tight; and for screens that may be torn or loose in their frames. (Pages 14, 22)
February	Recaulk any drafty areas you can find. Check around outside doors and windows. Change weather stripping if necessary. (Page 56)	Maintain a monthly checkup on heat outlets. Also check humidifiers. (Page 60)	Start a pest control program. Check for termites especially. (Page 90)	Take a look at dehumidifiers. See that they operate at highest efficiency and are in the best locations in your house. (Page 60)
March	Check all window glass for cracks or leakage due to loose or broken putty or compound. It's also spring cleaning time, a good moment to check drapery and windowshades. (Pages 10, 32–35)	Make sure everyone in household knows local tornado precautions. Oil and adjust door and window hardware. (Pages 14, 89)	Make sure that all airconditioning equipment, including wiring is in good condition. Be sure that your electrical circuit is not carrying too heavy a load. (Page 64)	Inspect for pests. It's a good idea to keep up with the literature on pest control. Keep in touch with your hardware dealer on this. (Page 90)
April	A good time to check for leaks. Inspect paint on inside of windows. And check airconditioning, fans, etc. (Pages 30–31, 64)	Check for evidence of termites. Look in basement and in crawl space, but also in other parts of the house. (Page 92)	Clean out vents, removing old bird and wasp nests. Cover any open vents with wire screening. (Page 63)	A good time to paint doors and windows, and of course to do any reglazing that might be needed. (Pages 10–11, 30–31)
May	Check for termites in basement, especially crawl spaces. (Page 92)	Check your storm windows and repair or replace any that may need it. (Pages 28–29)	Make it a point to inform all members of your family on local tornado precautions. (Page 89)	Patio and other sliding doors will require attention, especially checking tracks and hardware. (Pages 44–45)
June	Replace, repair, paint (if necessary) storm doors and windows, and screens. Check fit on all of these. (Pages 22–29, 46, 48)	A good moment to start any major carpentry that may require cutting through an outside wall (such as for a new door or window). (Pages 16, 38)	Replace any broken or cracked glass panes. See if any windows need to be reglazed. (Page 10)	Take a look at how well your garage doors are operating. Also check cellar door and windows for leakage, as well as security. (Pages 47, 68)
July	A good time to inspect the operation of all sliding doors and windows, as well as garage and other exterior doors. This includes a check on weather stripping. (Pages 44, 56)	See that all locks are working properly, and oil them lightly. (Pages 72–81)	Are humidifiers working properly? And are they in the most advantageous areas? (Page 60)	Clean and oil all locks and make sure they are working properly. Consider the possibility of changing locks, especially if you have given out a number of keys over a period of time. (Page 68)
August	Take a look at insulation and also check and, if necessary, clean any exhaust fans. (Page 50)	Start your pest control program by cleaning any nests out of openings such as vents or fan ducts. Keep to your program. (Page 90)	If you have any plans to cut a new window or door, now is a good time to do it. (Pages 16, 38)	Make sure vents are clear and in good condition. (Page 62)
September	Oil furnace motors. Clean what parts you can. Check temperature control systems. (Page 60)	Add insulation where needed. Check weather stripping. (Page 56)	Check all locks and catches on doors and windows. Clean, if necessary, oil them. (Page 68)	Check again for termites. Familiarize yourself with ways of preventing their entry; don't wait until they are already present. (Page 92)
October	Recaulk any areas that need it. Check your fuel bills carefully and prepare a record for the coming months. (Page 58)	Recaulk where you find it necessary. Clean or replace furnace filters. Make sure that storms are in good condition. (Page 58)	Clean window and door frames, storms, screens. (Pages 22, 28)	Make sure the whole family knows local hurricane precautions. (Page 89)
November	Now is a good time to check your attic insulation; also inspect all vents. (Page 53)	Adjust and maintain all window sash, drapery hardware, venetian blinds. (Pages 14, 32)	Paint windows, storms, screens as needed. (Pages 30–31)	Replace or repair window sash as needed. But be sure before you actually replace; maybe repair is all that's necessary. (Pages 16–18)
December	A time for inside carpentry, such as repairing interior doors. Check how these doors hang, and inspect all hardware on them. (Page 36)	Build any outdoor projects you might wish to install later such as window boxes or maybe a bird feeder. (Page 20)	Take a good look at drapery, hardware, blinds, and all hinges. (Pages 32–35, 36)	Recaulk any areas that need it. Check insulation, weather stripping. (Pages 56–59)

2.THE TOOLS

Basic tools for measuring and cutting:

1. Tin snips
2. Crosscut hand saw
3. Wood chisel
4. Hacksaw
5. 24" Carpenter's level
6. 6' Wood extension (zigzag) rule with metal slide extension
7. 16', ¾"-wide metal tape measure with locking button
8. Metal "rafter" square with standard 24" and 16" legs

Basic tools for drilling, fastening, smoothing, and filling:

9. Electric drill with ¼" chuck, variable speed, and reversing switch
10. Chuck key
11. Twist metal bits
12. Circle cutter
13. Screwdriver bit
14. Spade bit
15. 16-oz. curved-claw hammer
16. Caulking gun and correct type of caulking compound
17. Ratcheted push drill with screwdriver bits and hole drilling attachment
18. Brace and bits
19. Putty knife
20. Slip-joint pliers
21. Phillips-head screwdriver
22. Small and large slot screwdrivers
23. 8" Smoothing plane

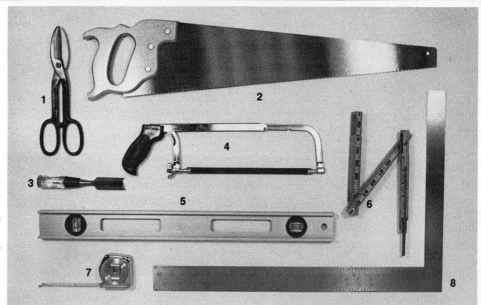

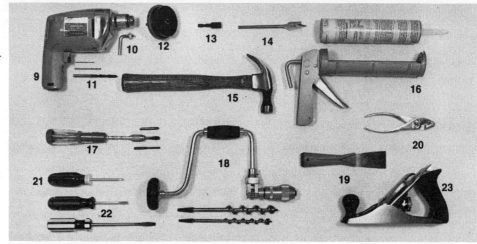

Selection and use

When you can lay your hand on the tool you need, if it is sharp and operating smoothly, you can greatly reduce the frustration factor potentially lurking in even simple jobs. This section is a guide to the selection and use of the tools you will need to maintain, repair and do light installation work on the doors and windows in your house, as well as most other light carpentry jobs.

Generally, a professional carpenter carries fewer different tools to a job than an inexperienced beginner thinks he might need to do the same job. The pro knows exactly which ones he is likely to need, his experience lets him do more jobs with a basic tool and he doesn't need mistake-preventing attachments.

Compare your own inventory of tools with the ones shown here. If yours are dull, have them sharpened. When you plan to tackle a job, check the "What it takes" section that appears in this book at the head of each job entry to see what tools and materials will be needed. Especially if you need to invest in a variety of tools or expensive ones, try looking in the classified want ads for used tools. But don't hesitate to pay for quality. Poorly made or designed tools don't hold an edge, are inconvenient to operate, and, under stress, handles break or metal parts give way. Try out a new tool where you buy it to be sure you know how to operate it; see that all its parts and advertised features work; make sure it is not so heavy and awkward to hold that it will be needlessly tiring to work with over a long stretch.

The following descriptions of the most useful tools to have in your house (shown in the photographs opposite) are grouped by their use into categories that parallel the four steps involved in most carpentry projects: measuring, cutting, fastening (including drilling) and smoothing. Painting and decorating tools are not included since they vary so much with the job.

Measuring tools

A tape measure is used for curved surfaces on long distances especially when you can hook one end over the edge of a board. A 16-foot long metal tape, ¾-inch wide, and with a locking device to hold it open at any length, will hold up well and handle all kinds of jobs. A 12-foot tape, ½-inch wide, is a slightly less expensive alternative. Metric measure alongside the inches printed on the tape will become an increasing advantage in coming years.

A folding (zigzag) rule may not be quite as accurate as a metal tape measure, but it extends 6 feet and is stiff enough to measure across horizontal openings. Get one with a 6-inch metal extension that slides out of the first section so you can take an inside measurement in one operation.

Squares are like two rulers joined at their ends to make an accurate 90° angle. They are used to measure right angles, especially for marking a cutting line across a board at an exact right angle to the sides of the board.

A steel square sometimes called a rafter or framing square, is shaped like an L with the body 24″ long and the tongue 16″ long. These are the standard distances between the studs in, respectively, the interior and exterior walls of a house. It is handy as a straightedge for drawing cutting lines as well as measuring an accurate right angle. You can lay out a 45° angle with it by drawing a line from a number on the body to the same number on the tongue where a parallel line (or other side of the board) crosses it.

A combination square (optional) is more compact. The body is usually 12 inches long, and the tongue, which slides along it and hooks over the edge of a board, usually has a level bubble set in it. It can be used to check an inside or outside right angle, measure depth, and draw a 45-degree angle as well as a right angle cutting line.

A carpenter's level is two or three feet long and has at least two, usually removable, vials in it full of liquid. A bubble floats in the exact center of the vial when the horizontal (window sill) or vertical (door jamb) surface you hold the level against is itself level.

Measuring and leveling

The metal extension that slides out of the first section of a folding rule allows you to measure across hard-to-reach inside dimensions in one operation.

If the framing around a door or window is not level, both vertically and horizontally, the opening will not be perfectly square and the door or window won't fit.

Remember that you must add the width of the case to the reading on the tape when you use a steel tape to measure an inside dimension. Note the lock button on the case.

When one leg of a try square hooks over and lies flat along the edge of a board, the other leg makes an exact right angle across it so the cut end will be square.

It wasn't exactly my fault
Even when I measured carefully and cut the board along the waste side of the line, the dang piece *still* wouldn't fit the way it should. Why? Because the ends of a board are not always sawn exactly at right angles to the sides, even when you buy new ones from the yard. So I learned to always put a square against the end I'm measuring from and, if it was cut off at an angle, to trim it square before I measure.

Practical Pete

Cutting tools

A hand crosscut saw has 8 points (7 teeth) to the inch filed like alternately beveled knife points so they cut and crumble away a strip through the wood, called the kerf, as the cut progresses. A crosscut saw is designed to cut *across* the grain (grain runs parallel to the natural lines in the wood). A rip saw's teeth are shaped like a row of chisels to cut parallel with the grain. A crosscut saw can also manage comfortably for short ripping.

Grip the handle with your pointer finger and thumb extended on either side to help hold the blade perpendicular to the surface of the board.

Start a crosscut saw at right angles to the board and pull upward in short strokes. Change the angle to 45 degrees and push, pull in long easy strokes almost the full length of the blade. Twist the handle to one side if the saw cut begins to wander away from the line.

The saw will bind partway through unless the board hangs free on one side of the cut, but support that end a little before you get near the end of the cut or it will break off.

Hacksaw cuts metal with a removable blade set into an expandable frame that can also tip the blade at right angles to the frame. A general-purpose blade has 18 or 24 teeth to the inch—32 for very thin metals. Install the blade so the teeth point toward the front of the frame away from the handle, and screw it tight so it is stretched rigid in the frame. Press hard on the downstroke; otherwise the blade won't bite into the metal. Work at about 50 strokes per minute; less for very hard metals.

Tin snips are useful for cutting thin metal flashing around windows and wire screens.

Chisels must be kept razor sharp and free of nicks. The two most useful sizes for general use, such as cutting insets for hinges and lock plates in doors and door jambs, are ¼- and ¾-inch wide. Good-quality ones have the metal tang running right through the length of the handle to the butt, so you can safely tap it with a hammer without splitting the handle. Lay the flat side next to the wood, tip it up at a very slight angle and push it with the heel of your hand to sliver away a slice in the same direction the grain runs.

Sawing

1. Start a cut with a crosscut hand saw held almost at right angles to the edge of the board. Rest your thumb against the blade to hold it next to the cutting line and pull upward to start the cut.

2. When the notch is deep enough to hold the blade in it, change the angle to 45 degrees and push and pull through the full length of the blade. Don't bear down on the wood; a sharp saw will cut straighter with its own weight.

Planing

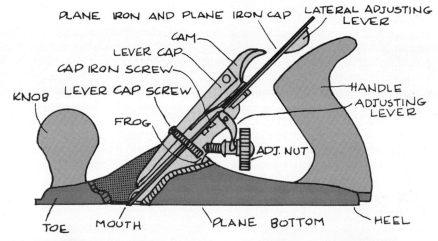

1. To take the plane apart, lift the cam so that the lever cap can be slipped out of the large hole under the screw. Note that the iron and blade underneath is inserted bevel side down.

2. The lateral adjusting lever moves left and right to tip the cutting edge of the blade horizontally in the open throat across the bottom of the plane.

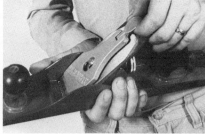

3. Turn the round, serrated adjusting nut so it moves out toward the handle in order to push the blade out further in the throat so it makes a deeper cut.

4. Hold the plane flat and firmly on the surface of the board with two hands (one hand on knob). Turn it at a slight angle, across the grain during the forward cutting stroke so the blade cuts the fibers of the wood with a shearing action.

Drilling/fastening tools

A portable electric drill is so convenient, powers so many useful accessories, and is now so inexpensive that it has become a basic household tool. You can handle most household projects with one that has a ¼-inch chuck (the maximum diameter of the shanks on the bits and accessories that will fit it), spins at 2000 to 2500 top rpms, and has a trigger that controls the speed (slow speeds are for driving screws and drilling metal or concrete). Other useful features are a switch to reverse the direction of spin (for removing screws and clearing the bit from a tight hole), a double-insulated housing, and a two-pronged plug.

Tips for safe, effective use of an electric drill: Unplug it when changing accessories. (One way to remember is to fasten the chuck key to the plug end of the cord.) Center punch an indentation in the work, especially metal, so the bit won't slip as you start the hole. If it slows down, reduce pressure; if it stalls, try reverse, or remove the bit, but don't keep clicking it on and off. Go easy at the end of the hole (so you don't stall the bit or splinter the wood) and keep the bit turning as you remove it to clean the hole. Use a lubricant when drilling metals except brass or cast iron (bacon grease will do); use kerosene with aluminum. Don't leave a locking switch on when you unplug the drill. A long, too-thin extension cord may slow the rpms and damage the motor sooner or later. It's unlikely, but if you hit a live wire when drilling into a wall, don't touch any of the metal parts on the drill.

The bits and accessories for electric drills that are most useful for the jobs in this book include a set of twist metal bits for wood, especially the smaller sizes for predrilling screw holes. Use a spade bit for drilling wide (¼" holes and up). A hole saw (sometimes called a circle-cutter) looks like a saw blade bent into a circle. It is used for cutting very large holes. Most standard lock sets need a 1⅜-inch diameter hole, for example. Use high-speed twist drill bits for metal or, better still, carbide-tipped bits which can also handle brick or cement. A screwdriver bit with a spring-loaded housing keeps the blade from slipping off the screw.

A ratcheted push drill, sometimes called a "Yankee" drill is used for pre-drilling screw holes and driving or removing screws. It leaves one hand free to hold the screw while the other hand pushes the drill and the ratchet rotates the blade. Bits store in the handle. Get a small and a large screwdriver bit for slot screws and at least one Phillips-head bit (the kind for screws with deep crosses in the head instead of a slot).

A brace and bits. Though an electric drill with spade bits and a push drill for small work can do most of the necessary boring jobs, a brace delivers tremendous turning power for removing screws that are paint stuck or corroded.

Screwdrivers should have blades that closely fit the exact length and width of the slot in the different size screws you will be using, so you will need more than one. If the blade extends out beyond the slot it will chew up the wood; if it is too short it may bend or strip the screw head. A tip-off of good quality is that the blade is shaped so the flat sides are nearly parallel, not gradually tapered down to the tip. Under pressure, the blade is less likely to ride up and strip the slot of the screw. The three most used sizes will be ⅛-, ¼-, and ⅜-inch blades. Add at least one Phillips-head screwdriver because many metal windows and lock-and-hinge sets use them.

A 16- or 20-ounce hammer (with a curved claw for pulling nails) is the correct weight for adults using it for general household repairs. A 16-ounce hammer will be easier for someone of slight build to control. The striking face of the hammer's head should be very slightly rounded so it won't dent the wood when the nail drives flush. Wood or fiberglass handles tend to absorb the impact more than steel and may be somewhat easier on the wrist and elbow if you have to drive a lot of nails. The head should be drop forged—cast iron may chip—and it should be absolutely solid on the handle. If it is even a little bit loose, the head can fly off and turn into a lethal weapon.

Slip-joint pliers are the standard gripping tool. An 8-inch size with serrated jaws and a wire cutter next to the pivot is the most versatile. Don't use them to turn tough nuts if you don't want to bark your knuckles. Pliers are not wrenches.

Smoothing/filling tools

Jack planes come in lengths of 11½ to 15 inches and they are surprisingly expensive. An 8-inch smoothing plane with a 1¾-inch wide blade will do typical light repair and maintenance jobs such as trimming down the edges of doors or window sash or removing a light layer of paint on a window sill. A dull or incorrectly set blade turns this tool into a frustrating, even destructive monster. Practice with it on scrap, moving it along, not into the lay of the grain. Hold it flat on the wood but turned at a slight angle so the blade shears the fibers rather than attacks them head on.

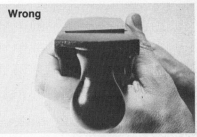

If the edge of the blade is not exactly parallel to the flat surface of the plane's bottom it will cut irregular grooves in the wood. Adjust it by moving the lateral adjusting lever to the left or right.

A putty knife with a flexible blade 1¼ inches wide is the right tool for smoothing glazing compound around window panes, breaking paint seals on stuck windows, filling holes in wood, smoothing spackle into cracks and scraping flaking paint (wear safety glasses to keep flying paint chips out of your eyes).

A caulking gun holds replaceable tubes of caulking compound and squeezes it out of the nozzle on the tube. They cost very little but be sure that the metal head and plunger are solidly attached; cheap ones tend to break off when you first put pressure on them. Before you buy a tube of compound for caulking around exterior window frames to eliminate drafts, read the label carefully to be sure it is made for that purpose and is the color you want.

3. WINDOWS

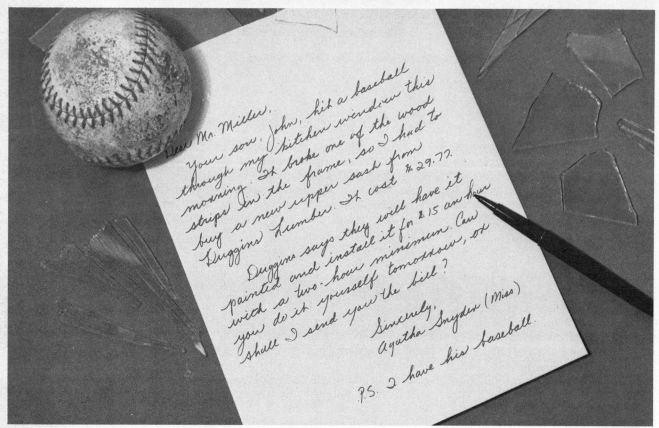

Dear Mr. Miller,

Your son, John, hit a baseball through my kitchen window this morning. It broke one of the wood strips in the frame, so I had to buy a new upper sash from Duggins Lumber. It cost $29.77.

Duggins says they will have it painted and install it for $15 an hour with a two-hour minimum. Can you do it yourself tomorrow, or shall I send you the bill?

Sincerely,
Agatha Snyder (Miss)

P.S. I have his baseball.

Replacing panes

What it takes

Approximate time: About 30 minutes per average-size glass pane.

Tools: A sharp chisel, but one you don't use for fine work. Hammer, screwdriver, putty knife, ruler, heavy work gloves, goggles, wire brush. A felt-tip pen and a glass cutter—if you plan to cut the glass yourself, rather than have it cut at the store. A glazier's point driver is worth the investment if you are going to install more than just a few panes. It works like a staple gun to drive the metal glazier's points into the wood frame to hold the glass in place.

Materials: Glazing compound, light oil, linseed oil, rust preventive paint.

Obviously, a broken pane of glass must be replaced right away, not only because broken glass is dangerous and unsightly, but because it lets all that expensively heated or cooled air escape. Cracked and loose window panes also let the outside air in.

Check the windows of your house from the outside. Even if your home is fairly new you may discover a crack or two that you didn't notice before, or places where the glazing compound has dried out and is cracked or has fallen out. By doing the reglazing yourself you can save money and even time.

Wear heavy work gloves as you carefully remove all broken glass from the frame. If you find it necessary to pry or tap the glass and dried putty loose, wear safety goggles. Gather up and dispose of any glass slivers immediately. Paint inside the glass channel of the frame (after it is thoroughly clean) with a thin coat of primer or linseed oil to feed the wood.

It is easier to work when the window is lying flat, so if you are working with a wooden sash window and can take it out easily, do so.

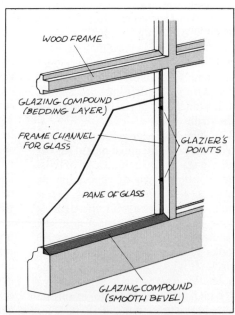

WOOD FRAME

GLAZING COMPOUND (BEDDING LAYER)

FRAME CHANNEL FOR GLASS

GLAZIER'S POINTS

PANE OF GLASS

GLAZING COMPOUND (SMOOTH BEVEL)

1. Remove broken glass from wood frame. 2. Clean old putty and points out of channels. 3. Smear thin layer of compound along channels. 4. Press pane down carefully but firmly so it is well seated. 5. Fix pane into channels with new glazier's points. 6. Fill each channel in turn with compound and smooth with putty knife.

Wood sash windows

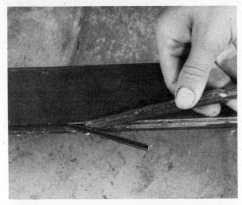

1. An old chisel with a fairly sharp edge is the best tool for removing old glazing compound. You have to clean the glass channel right down to the wood, and the old bedding putty can be hard to get off with just a putty knife or a screwdriver. You must be careful not to cut into the wood frame.

2. Pry out the metal glazier's points. Sand the glass channel smooth and use a whisk broom or vacuum cleaner to pick up the sawdust, bits of glass, and other debris. Paint the channel to match the frame. After the paint has dried, put down a thin layer of glazing compound along the channel.

Don't flip your lid.
I finally learned to put the lid back on my new can of glazier's compound right away and *tight* to keep out air. Tapping the lid back down all around with a hammer is all it takes (if I had had enough sense not to bend the lid when I pried it off the can). This stuff is a nice, gooey white putty when it's new, but it dries rock-hard in about a week when it is opened to air.

Practical Pete

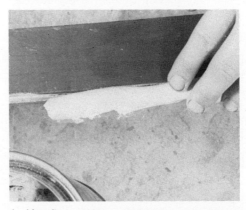

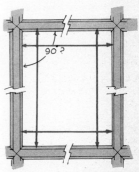

3. Place the glass firmly into the frame opening, pressing down against the squeezed-up layer of glazing compound. Push the metal glazier's points into the side of the channel, tight against the glass. Space them about 6 inches apart. If you don't have a glazier's point gun (a *very* handy tool), position the point with your fingers, lay the flat tip of a screwdriver on the top of the point and push or gently tap it halfway down.

4. After first making sure that the glazing compound is thoroughly mixed (no oil on top), use a putty knife to dig out a glob about the size of a golf ball. Work it between your hands until it has a good consistency, and then roll it into a ball. Twist this into a long rope a little thicker than a pencil. Lay it along the channel next to the glass and press it down gently with your fingers so it fills the angle between the channel and the glass.

Measure the opening of the frame inside the channels. Old frames, especially, may not be exactly square, so you can check by measuring the length of the channel on all four sides. Cut the new glass 1/16 inch smaller all around than the frame, to allow for bedding compound and irregularities. For an extra-tight seal, spread a very thin layer of glazing compound along the channel before inserting the glass.

5. Place a clean putty knife, polished smooth with steel wool, against the compound so the edge of the blade is angled and lying on the wooden edge of the frame and one corner of the blade is riding on the glass. Pull the putty knife toward yourself in one long, smooth stroke, from one end of the frame side to the other. This should push the compound down into the joint and leave a smooth beveled surface. This technique requires practice.

6. If the compound pulls out or doesn't fill the joint, just take it all out, roll up another rope and start again. When you have made the joint as smooth as you can, use the blade of the knife to remove excess compound from the frame and the window glass. The compound should take a week to dry hard enough to paint.

Metal casement windows

The procedure for replacing these panes is the same as for wood sash windows (page 11), except that the glass pane is held in the frame by metal spring clips instead of glazier's points. These clips hook under a lip along the metal channel, or their tips fit into holes in the channel.

After you remove the old glass, wire-brush away any rust that may be in the channel. Wipe it clean and spray lightly with rust-preventive paint.

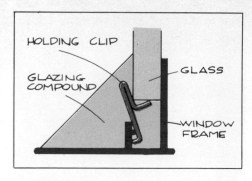

Metal sliding and storm windows

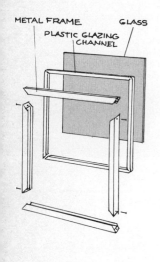

No glazing compound is required. The frames of metal sliding windows are taken apart by removing screws at the ends of the top and bottom rails, or pins at the corners. The glass is held by a plastic bead or a channel that runs around the edge.

The pane in a metal storm window is held tightly in its frame by a removable plastic gasket which you must pull out. The ends usually meet at one of the corners. When you have put in the new pane, press the gasket back in place with your fingers. Start at the corner where the ends meet and work around the frame carefully.

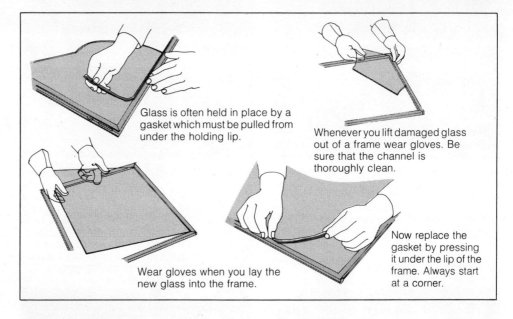

Glass is often held in place by a gasket which must be pulled from under the holding lip.

Whenever you lift damaged glass out of a frame wear gloves. Be sure that the channel is thoroughly clean.

Wear gloves when you lay the new glass into the frame.

Now replace the gasket by pressing it under the lip of the frame. Always start at a corner.

Glass cutting

Especially if you live in a house that has irregularly shaped windows, as many do, you will save time and money by doing your own glasscutting.

One of the most important things to know about cutting glass is that you must have a flat, clean surface to work on. A table top, workbench, anything will do, as long as there are no globs of paint, bits of wood or other debris that might crack or scratch the glass while you are working on it. If you can find a table with a smooth square edge, so much the better.

It is very important that you work with clean glass. If it is not clean your cut will not be smooth. Any sort of grit or even dust on the surface can impede the accu-rate movement of your glass cutting wheel, causing it to skip. It's wise to brush some machine oil along your cutting line.

A word of caution about handling glass in general. Work slowly and, especially if you are handling broken or cracked glass, use gloves. Whenever you do the actual cutting be sure that you are facing your work as though the cut you will be making is directly in front of you.

A pro scores the glass and snaps it off along the line in two lightning moves. The glass is more likely to break evenly if the glass molecules are still in movement from the scoring stroke. So snap it right away, but move carefully until you have had a lot of experience.

1. With the glass lying flat on the work surface, measure and mark it for the first cut. The best marker is a felt-tipped pen. Do not use a grease pencil; it will clog the cutting wheel and cause the cutter to skip.

2. With the cut marked, position a straightedge (one of the best straightedges is a shop T-square) held firmly in place with one hand so that it doesn't move as you make the cut. Lubricate the wheel of the glass cutter with machine oil.

3. Position the cutter with the cutting wheel down on the glass. Hold the cutter handle straight up and tightly against the straightedge. Grasp the cutter and push down firmly, but not so hard that you break the glass. Now make a smooth stroke along the straightedge from one edge of the glass to the other. Do not repeat the scoring stroke. This is important for you will only chip the glass and may cause it to fracture or break out when you intentionally break it along the scored line.

4. After you have scored the glass, snap or break it off along the scored line. Most experts simply position the glass with the scored line just over the edge of the table. They hold the glass on the table with one hand and with their other hand give the piece to be removed a quick downward snap. Most of the time this works, but not always. Try this technique on some pieces of scrap glass until you perfect it.

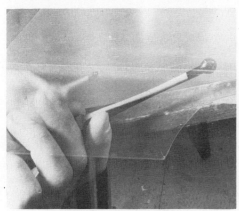

Most glass cutters have slots at one end, and these can be used to break off those small sections. However, pliers work best in most cases.

5. A safer method is to position the glass on the table so the scored line protrudes about an inch, then using the heavy ball on the end of the cutter, gently tap on the underside of the glass, following the line exactly. As you do this you will notice the crack starting along the line. Sometimes it will shoot along the line for several inches. Gently tapping on the underside causes the crack to follow the score, and the piece of glass will simply fall off on its own. Finally, you can smooth the edge of the glass with a fine wet-dry sandpaper.

6. In some instances you may have a piece of glass that will break out of the line, for instance where a skip in the score occurs, or the glass piece to be removed may be extremely narrow. Because the small piece isn't large enough to fall by its own weight, tapping on the underside may not cause the glass to fracture. In this case you will have to break it off. Using wide-jawed pliers, grasp the glass piece and quickly snap downward. Make sure that the jaws of the pliers don't extend over the scored line.

Sash repairs and hardware

Unsticking a window

What it takes

Approximate time: Minutes.

Tools: Hammer, wide chisel, small pry bar, screwdriver (Phillips or regular slot head for removing storm window if necessary), plane, wide putty knife.

Materials: Sandpaper, soap, candle, or paraffin, lightweight oil or silicone spray.

Louis Cyr, who in an earlier day was billed as "The strongest man in the world," still failed what was considered the acid test for any man of muscle; he was unable to raise and lower every window in a regulation-length Pullman train. You may appreciate this the more when you come up against that window in your house which has stuck fast and will not budge.

There are a number of reasons why a window will stick. Paint or dirt may have gotten into the channels or onto the edges of the various stop moldings. Humidity may have caused expansion or swelling of wood parts. Or, the weather stripping may fit too tightly. This can easily be loosened. But the most common reason for jamming is dried paint.

As a rule this disaster occurs when the window is in the down position and the inside or lower sash will not come up. At this point some homeowners resort to physical assault by delivering a series of karate chops to the sash in the hope of loosening it. But this can result in loosening the glazing around the window, or you may knock out a pane of glass and cut yourself in the process.

First of all check to see that the window is not locked. Work the blade of a wide putty knife between the window sash and the parting strip. Use a hammer to tap the handle of the knife if necessary. Check the tracks above. If paint is too thick in the track, remove it with a chisel or sandpaper. Lubricate the track with a candle or a bar of soap or paraffin; use lubricating oil or silicone spray if it is metal. If the window is still fast, try prying it open with a pry bar, gently, and preferably from the outside.

Is it still stuck? Then tap around the sash with your hammer and a block of wood. You might loosen the window through vibration. The block of wood is necessary so you won't dig hammer tracks into the sash. Finally, you can tap the frame with the hammer and wood block, edging the frame away from the window.

If the window is badly swollen you may have to loosen or remove and reset the stops. If you do remove the window you may find that planing or sanding will do the trick. But be careful not to remove too much wood or the window will rattle.

TIP: When painting a window position the sashes an inch or two from the top and bottom. When you have finished painting, and before the paint sets, move the window up and down. In this way the seal will not form and you will have avoided a stuck window.

1. Place edge of small pry bar under one corner, or down rail of window, and tap in place. Being careful not to gouge the wood, gently pry window open—but work at corners only. If possible use a piece of cloth, heavy cardboard or wood shim between the bar and the window.

2. But you may have to move the stops. This is a simple operation with hammer and chisel; but again, be careful not to gouge. When you nail the stops back into their new position be sure they are in alignment with the window itself, permitting free, but not too loose, passage.

3. If your window has metal channels, you can spray with lightweight oil to prevent sticking. For wood you can rub in paraffin or soap. But remove excess carefully as you go.

Securing a loose window sash

Of the inconveniences we suffer due to malfunctioning windows, the loose sash is high on the list. Loose window sashes are often caused by poorly working old-fashioned sash weights. Or the sash weights may be gone completely—the rope supporting them having disintegrated through age or rot—and you end up the victim of an inside sash that will not stay up in place.

There was a time when this created a not-small dilemma, for it meant taking out the entire window; professional work which could be costly and time consuming. We now have an almost instant-answer through the application of *sash holders*. These marvels are available at any building supply, and you can fix them to a window in no time at all, at the same time saving yourself some money.

Push the lower or inside sash all the way up. With prongs toward the inside, spring the metal supports and push them until they are covered by the sash. At a stroke, you have probably saved enough energy to read a short novel.

Push lower or inside sash all the way up. Holding the metal supports with the prongs toward the inside, spring them a bit and push all the way up into the window channel until they're covered by the sash. Do both sides in this manner. Now simply lower the window to embed the prongs in the wood and secure the sash holders in place.

What it takes

Approximate time: 10 minutes per window.

Tools and materials: Sash holders, available at any building supplier.

Crank handles and other hardware

The casement window—except for broken panes of glass—seldom needs repair beyond tightening a loose hinge now and then, and cleaning and lubrication of the operator crank and arm.

You may have difficulty in opening and closing the window, and the thing to do then is to inspect the gear mechanism. This is concealed, and in order to get at it you must remove the screws from the crank assembly. If the gears are worn it may be necessary to replace the whole assembly. If old and hardened grease is causing the problem, wash it out with solvent and then lubricate.

The operator arm should slide easily in its tracks as you open and close the window. But there may be rust or hardened grease that has accumulated, or the arm could be bent. Remove the operator arm and straighten it, clean out debris and apply fresh grease when you reassemble.

What it takes

Approximate time: A few minutes.

Tools and materials: Screwdriver, household oil or silicone spray.

1. The first step is to lightly lubricate all moving parts of any hardware with a lightweight household oil. At the same time check to see that the piece of hardware is properly secured, neither loose nor too tight.

2. It should be a simple operation to remove any bent or broken crank handle by loosening the holding screw and sliding the handle off the shaft. If the handle has rusted, or the screw slot is stripped, you may have to take it off with a hacksaw; but this is rare. The chances are that oil or silicone spray will help any sticking.

Replacing double-hung sash windows

Some "Golden Rule"!

My daddy *told* me. "Pete," he said, "measure twice, cut once." But I measured our old window casement once, very carefully, and ordered the new sash window to fit it. It had to be specially made and cost $54. It didn't fit. I had read the markings on the tape measure wrong. The feet are printed on the top half—continuous inches on the bottom half. I read the closest foot mark "2 feet," looked down and read the total inches "25¼ inches," added them together and ordered a 49¼-inch window—two feet too wide! Look at your tape measure; you'll see what I mean.

Practical Pete

TIP: It's much easier to prime, paint, or stain units before installing them permanently in place.

TIP: Save the old units; they make great cold frame covers.

TIP: Sash weights make good boat anchors for drift-fishing, weights for holding down tarps, or pulley counterweights to keep a bird feeder high out of reach until you want to lower it to fill it again.

As windows age, not only do the sash cords deteriorate, but the sashes themselves often rot through in so many places that they can't be caulked enough. In this case they should be replaced altogether.

The question at this point is whether or not you need a whole new frame. Will the new window fit into the old frame? Consider, first of all, how your house is covered. If it's brick veneer, stucco, solid masonry, or cement, you'll more than likely *only* be able to put in the exact same size of new window. These wall materials are difficult to remove in order to allow for a larger window. In fact, it's easier to put in a smaller one by building a new framework inside the old.

At the same time, if your house is built with wood shingle, or clapboard or asbestos siding it's not hard to remove pieces of the siding and then put in a new frame. But for the present, let's consider an exact replacement of the old window. This will be an easy job. All you have to do is buy a new window to match the original. The important thing is to make absolutely sure that your measurements are correct when you order your new unit from your local building supply dealer.

1. Remove the old window stops with a large chisel; these hold the window sashes in place.

2. With the old stops removed, cut the sash weights and allow them to drop down inside the wall. If you are reframing, or redoing the entire wall, then you can remove the window trim and also remove the sash weights.

3. Using a hammer and chisel, remove the sash weight pulleys. Chisel out any other stops holding the window sashes in place and remove them.

4. Try the two metal strips which you will have purchased from your window dealer. Probably they'll be just a bit long. Take a pair of tin snips and clip off their bottom ends to get an exact fit.

5. Now position the two side strips over the window units. Remember that the top window is the outside one, while the bottom window (the one with the slanted edge) is the inside. The slanted edge is positioned down. The units must fit down over the top of the spring-loaded T-bars in the metal guides.

6. Press the window units down until the top of the upper unit is flush with the metal guide strip; then gently push the entire assembly in place. If the units are a bit wide, remove them and look for any old paint lumps that may be keeping them from fitting securely. Scrape and chisel away any obstructions that may be in your way. If the units are still a bit wide, remove them from the strips and plane their edges, using a hand plane. The point is that the units should fit snugly, but not bind.

7. With the units positioned in place, put a carpenter's level against their outside edges and make sure the units are plumb. If they are not plumb, the units will not only not seal properly, but will be difficult to operate, so check very carefully.

8. With the units properly positioned, drive a couple of flat-head brads through the top and bottom of each strip and into the window casing. Replace both inside and outside stops, caulking the edge of the metal strips on the outside before installation of the outside stops.

1. First step is to take off the old window stops on the inside. These are what hold the window sash in place. Use a chisel with a wide blade and a hammer to pry them loose.

2. Now, with the old stops gone, cut the sash weights and let them fall down inside the wall. You don't need them. At the same time, if you are redoing the entire wall, or if you're reframing, then you can just take out all the window trim and save the sash weights.

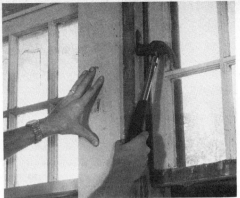

3. Remove the sash weight pulleys. Best implements for this action will be hammer and chisel. Also chisel out any other stops that are holding the window sashes in place and remove them.

4. Check the two metal strips. If they are long, and chances are they will be, cut the extra off with tin snips. Try to get as near perfect a fit as you can.

5. Now you're ready to put in the unit. You'll most likely have to do some juggling. The thing is to make everything level, a fit which will be snug but at the same time will allow the windows to open and close smoothly.

The spring-lift alternative: You can recognize this type of sash window by the tube that runs from the top of the window casing channel. A spring mechanism in the tube allows the window to be raised or lowered easily.

The tube type is the most popular. Inside it is a spring attached to a twisted rod which keeps the spring tight so the sash will remain stationary. The tension allows the sash to move up or down with little pressure. Adjust the spring tension after a little use.

The spring type is a steel trap design where one looped end is fastened to the window sash and the other to the casing. This type is not adjustable.

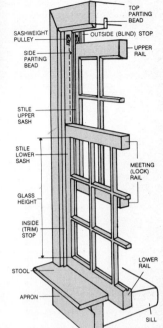

Parts of a double-hung window frame

TOP PARTING BEAD
SASHWEIGHT PULLEY
OUTSIDE (BLIND) STOP
SIDE PARTING BEAD
UPPER RAIL
STILE UPPER SASH
STILE LOWER SASH
MEETING (LOCK) RAIL
GLASS HEIGHT
INSIDE (TRIM) STOP
LOWER RAIL
STOOL
APRON
SILL

Window channels

Maybe the answer to that loose or tight window lies simply in replacing the channels. Measure the vertical distance occupied by glass on one sash from inside the meeting rail (lock) to inside the upper or lower rail. Double the measurement; add 6 inches. (On Boston windows add 5.)

Remove all stops; take out the window.

Try-fit the channels in the window opening. Trim with tin snips if necessary.

Now try-fit the windows in the channels, then position them in the opening.

When the channel units fit, remove and paint the old windows, fit them back into place and tack the channels at top and bottom with brads.

What it takes

Approximate time: 15-20 minutes.

Tools and materials: Tin snips, hammer, chisel, and replacement channels.

1. After carefully measuring your window, take out the stops. Remove the window and place it to one side. Then try fitting the window channels in the opening. If they need to be cut use your tin snips.

2. Try-fit the window in the channels; then position it in the opening. When the window-channel units fit properly, remove and paint the old window; then fit it back into place. Finally, tack the channels in place at top and bottom with small brads.

Replacing sash cord

What it takes

Approximate time: Under an hour.

Tools and materials: Hammer, screwdriver, single-edge razor blade, putty knife (wide blade), replacement cord.

Parts of a sash cord window

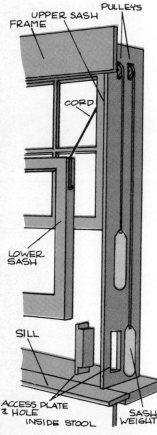

The double-hung sash window has been used in houses for centuries. It is called double-hung because the upper, or outside sash (the frame holding the glass that moves up and down) and the inside or lower sash are both "hung" movably inside the window's frame.

Some double-hung sash windows are aluminum, but most are wood. The older style sash windows operate with ropes, weights, and pulleys which are concealed in the construction. The ropes are attached to the sash; they pass along the same tracks in which the window frame moves, up to a pulley which is at the top of the track. The rope passes over the pulley, fitting in the groove, and is tied to the hidden sash weight which acts as a counterbalance permitting the window to stay at the height to which it has been raised or lowered. It is marvelously simple.

But the rope can become frayed and will eventually break, and the weight will fall inside the frame. The consequence is that the window will no longer do what you want it to do—stay where you put it.

But it's a simple problem to cope with. Here's what to do:

1. Remove the inside stop strip from the side where the broken cord is. If you have to break the paint seal to get the strip out without breaking it, slice the seal with a sharp single-edge razor blade. Then, with a putty knife blade (not a pry bar) pry the stop strip out.
2. Now pull the sash away from the frame.
3. Untie the knot and remove the rope from the sash frame.
4. Do the same on the other side, and remove that rope. But wait—knot this rope so that it will not disappear into the wall, thus requiring removal of the frame.

5. Set aside the entire sash and look for the access plate located in the lower part of the track. It may have been painted over, in which case you will have to find it by tapping with a hammer or the handle of a screwdriver. You can then cut around its outline with a razor blade, and finally unscrew it from its place. Take the weight out. Note: Older windows do not have access plates. If you find yourself in this predicament you will have to take out the whole window frame to get at the sash weight and broken cord.
6. Untie the old cord. The two broken pieces can be used to measure your new cord. Tie a small weight onto the new cord, small enough so that it will feed in over the pulley. Now feed in the new cord. When the cord has come down to the level of the access plate opening, pull it through.
7. Now take the small weight off and tie on the regular window weight and put it back into the access hole.
8. Take the cord which is opposite to the one you have worked with and tie it to the sash; then put the sash back in the track.
9. Tie the new cord to the sash and hold the sash against the parting strip as you raise it to the top.
10. Check the weight at the access opening. It ought to be about 3 inches above the sill as you hold the sash at the top. If it isn't, adjust the rope. When the weight is correct, put back the access plate and the stop strip. The same procedure is followed if the broken cord is in the upper sash, only you must remove the lower window and parting strip before taking out the upper sash. That's all there is to it.

But while you're at it, you could just as easily replace it with a sash chain and so avoid a broken cord in the future.

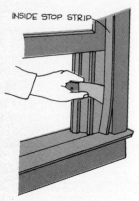

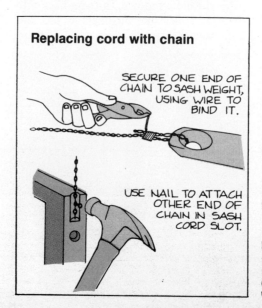

Replacing cord with chain

SECURE ONE END OF CHAIN TO SASH WEIGHT, USING WIRE TO BIND IT.

USE NAIL TO ATTACH OTHER END OF CHAIN IN SASH CORD SLOT.

New wrinkles

Sash balances are sold in easily installed kits to replace sash weights, cords, and pulleys. The hardware fits into the hole left in the frame after you remove the old pulley. It has a spring-loaded tape inside a revolving drum—like a steel measuring tape. The tape hooks onto the bottom of an L-shaped bracket, screwed to the top corner of the sash, and rides inside the old sash cord groove.

Closing in a window or doorway

There was a time when buildings were taxed according to their number of windows. And so, enterprising landlords, chagrined over this invasion into their source of revenue, hit upon the clever idea of closing some of those taxable windows. That is to say, they bricked them in. And one can today see on certain buildings those places where the newer brick is of a different color and so reveals the outline of what had once been a window.

You may wish to close in a window for other reasons. Perhaps you've just had it with that particular window; its vagaries of behavior, the way it allows the light to strike your eyes, its seemingly unfixable draughts. Or it could be a doorway; the principle is the same. You may be remodeling your garage, for instance. In any case, the operation requires little in the way of tools or expense; nor does it take much in time or expertise.

What it takes

Approximate time: It shouldn't take more than a couple of hours.

Tools: Hammer, chisel with wide blade and/or a pry bar, sharp knife, saw, square, ruler.

1. After removing the outside trim, pry away the inside window stop, using either a small pry bar or large chisel. The inside stop is recessed into the frame and takes a bit of work to get out.

2. When you have lifted out the window sash remove all inside trim.

3. Now drive the frame out from the inside. Carefully discard the frame, making sure there are no old nails sticking up for somebody to step on.

4. Fasten a 2x4 stud in place and now you are ready to cover the wall. But remember that the stud is essential for support.

Special window treatments

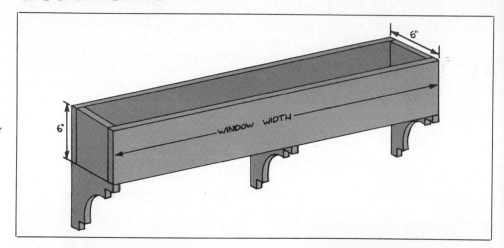

What it takes

Approximate time: One to two hours.

Tools and materials: Hammer, handsaw, coping or saber saw, screwdriver, lumber, sandpaper, galvanized nails, screws, stain or paint.

How to make a window box

One of the great things about windows is that you can look out of them. This may sound obvious, yet the fact is that the view is important. You could be looking at the side of another building, or at someone shaving, or you could be looking at a lovely lawn, a lake; or if these are not available you could look at your own garden—your window box.

Indeed, window box gardening is one of the easiest and most enjoyable ways of having flowers around your home. For one thing this form of gardening requires less weeding and other hard garden chores. The important thing is to make sure your windows are low enough to allow you easily to water and otherwise care for the plants once they are in the boxes.

Here's what to do. Purchase the boards you will need already ripped from 1x12s at your local building supply dealer.

Using galvanized rustproof nails, nail

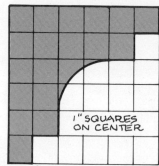

the sides and ends together. Nail the bottom in place and cut the three supports using a saber saw or coping saw.

Sand thoroughly and fasten the supports to the bottom of the box with screws.

Sand the remainder of the work thoroughly and stain or paint to suit your taste.

To fasten your new garden to your house, drive screws through the top of the backboard into the house wall studs; and follow with screws through the bottom of the supports.

Make your own frosted glass

What it takes

Approximate time: One hour.

Tools and materials: Silicon carbide powder, block of wood, epoxy cement.

Frosted glass may be just the ticket for you if you want a door or window which will allow you the benefit of light coming in, but will also give privacy.

But why not make your own frosted glass? You can do it easily enough right on the kitchen table. All you need is a block of wood, a piece of glass glued to the block with epoxy cement, and a bit of silicon carbide powder. Here's what to do:

Glue the glass to the block. Mix up a bit of silicon carbide powder with water so that you have a kind of thick soup.

Now use the carbide soup as an abrasive between the two pieces of glass to grind down the glass surface. As it loses its cutting power, add grit and water. Rinse.

How to create your own stained glass window or door panels

For centuries the stained glass window lay within the province of religion and royalty. It appeared principally in church windows, depicting religious figures or scenes.

Today it is possible to create your own stained glass windows without undergoing the exigencies of long-term apprenticeship; nor is it required that you spend a fortune.

Leaded glass is the traditional method of joining pieces of stained or clear glass between lead channels called lead "came." The leading outlines the glass pieces and is an integral part of the design. The places where the strips of came join one another are soldered on both sides to hold the construction together.

Make an exact, full-sized drawing (called a "cartoon") of the finished design on a sheet of craft paper. Number each section and note the color of the glass you will use.

Place another sheet of craft paper underneath the cartoon, interleaved with carbon paper. Tape it down and retrace.

Cut the carbon pattern into individual template patterns for cutting each piece of glass. These must be 1/16 inch smaller, all around, than the pattern to allow for the thickness of the lead came that will separate adjacent pieces of glass in the finished design. Use special pattern scissors, or instead, tape single-edge razor blades to each side of a piece of cardboard as a cutting guide.

Position the templates on the pieces of glass and fasten the backs of the templates to the glass with coils of masking tape.

Use a metal-edged ruler and glass cutter to score the straightedge pieces, and immediately snap them apart with your fingers. If they don't break, tap the back of the glass along the scored line with the ball on the glass cutter handle, and try again. Do not retrace your score. Tip: It's a good idea to keep your glass cutter in a cup of kerosene between cuts to lubricate it.

Make a right-angle wood frame with strips of wood. Use a carpenter's square to be sure you nail them onto your work surface at an exact 90-degree angle.

Cut the U-channel and H-channel lead came to the necessary lengths. The H-channel will join the glass pieces inside the design, the U-channel will frame the outer edges.

Begin assembling the glass pieces and the lead came. Insert a ¼-inch wood dowel in the other side of the channel to carefully push the lead came against each piece of glass, so the edge of the glass fits snugly all the way into the channel. Hold the assembled pieces in position as you go by temporarily tacking small nails or push pins into the work after each new piece is added.

When the design is completed, place more boards along the other two sides to complete the frame. Tap them to fit tightly, then nail them in place. Use oleic acid as the flux (applied with a small brush) and a spool of solid 60/40 wire solder. Keep a small sponge in a dish of water to clean and cool the soldering iron. Always return the iron to its stand when it is not in use. Be sure the tip of the iron is clean and properly tinned.

Start in one corner and brush each joint with a generous amount of flux.

Put solder on the heated iron until a small bead forms; roll this bead onto a joint. Do not touch the lead with the soldering iron, as it can melt the lead came and ruin your work. Pause until the solder starts to set; then quickly roll the bead of solder with the tip of the iron to cover the joint.

It's a good idea to brush the tip of the heated iron on the wet sponge to cool it before rolling the solder over the joint. This will help prevent melting the lead came.

After all the joints are soldered, remove panel, turn it, and solder the other side.

Leaded glass using lead "came" of various widths is soldered only where the edges meet.

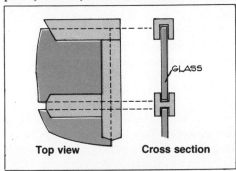

Top view **Cross section**

GLASS

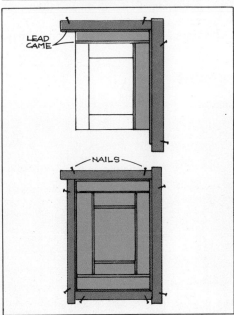

LEAD CAME

NAILS

Nail two strips to your work surface at right angles. With temporary nails hold the pieces firmly together as you go along. Finally, enclose the finished design with two more strips.

What it takes

Approximate time: About four hours for project shown; working time varies widely, depending on size and number of pieces.

Tools and materials: Heavy craft paper, lead pencil, carbon paper, masking tape, and scissors (or two single-edge razor blades and a piece of cardboard) for making the pattern and templates; pieces of colored glass, metal straightedge, glass cutter, and small cup of kerosene for cutting the glass; strips of scrap wood, carpenter's square, hammer, and 6-penny finishing nails for making an assembly frame; U- and H-channel lead came, craft knife with replaceable blades, and ¼-inch wood dowel for assembling the glass pieces; and oleic acid flux, small brush, spool of 60/40 wire solder, and small sponge in dish of water for soldering the pieces together.

Screens—installing, replacing, maintenance

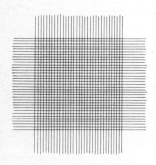

To repair a large hole, make a patch out of scrap screening.

The modern screen, unlike its ancestor of not so long ago, will last for years. If it has a fine enough mesh it will keep even the very small insects out of the house.

Today, screening is made of rustproof materials such as bronze, copper, plastic, and aluminum, and there is also a fiberglass screen and one of anodized aluminum that has a baked-enamel finish. In addition, there is a louver type of either aluminum or brass.

But even with these improvements holes will appear. It is important to repair them before they get out of hand and you have to replace the whole screen.

You can patch a small hole in a metal screen with a quick-drying waterproof glue (for plastic use acetone-type glue).

For a large hole first make a patch by cutting a piece from scrap screening which is larger than the hole in your screen. Bend the free wire ends of the patch and push them through the mesh around the hole. Then bend the ends back so that the patch holds. Plastic ends should be cemented.

Or you can mend small holes by weaving or darning strands from screening scraps; or even use wire.

Maintenance of screens is important, and this includes keeping them clean.

Keep wood frames painted. This isn't just for appearance but to keep away moisture which would cause the wood to swell and even rot. Aluminum frames can suffer from oxidation. Clean them and then coat with wax.

If joints become loose on wood frames,

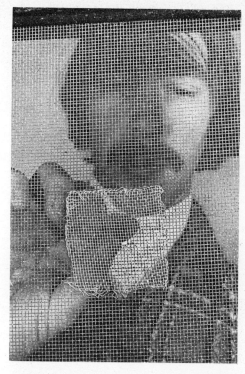

reglue them or reinforce them with corner plates, mending plates, T plates, corrugated or chevron-type fasteners, wood screws, or glued-in dowels. At the same time, it's sensible to inspect the hangers now and again—both the brackets on the house itself and the hooks on the screen.

After you have cleaned both sides of the screen (you can use the round brush attachment on a vacuum), apply a thinned screen enamel, varnish, or paint to both sides with a brush or a piece of carpet.

Taking care of those screens

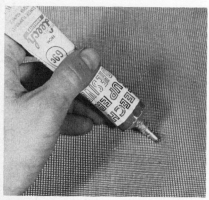

1. Fiberglass is the easiest to repair. If there is nothing more than a pinhole in the screen, use a touch of household cement to fill. Make sure the cement doesn't run down the screen and cause an unsightly appearance. You may wish to lay the screen down.

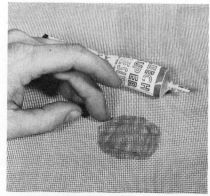

2. A larger tear or gouge can be repaired by merely cutting a tiny patch of fiberglass screening to match and gluing it in place. Again, use household cement and make sure you blot the cement carefully, to remove any excess that might run down.

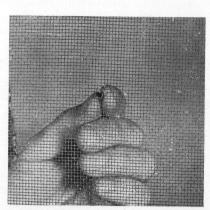

3. A tiny hole in an aluminum screen can be patched by pushing the wire back in place with a sliver of wood such as a toothpick.

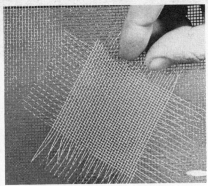

4. A larger hole or tear should be patched with a piece of aluminum screening laced to the hole.

5. Cut a patch about 2 inches larger all around than the hole. Remove a few outside cross threads, fold down the sides and push the threads through the wire, pushing the patch up against the damaged portion.

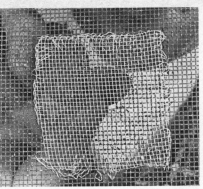

6. From the opposite side bend the protruding wires down flat against the screen and clip off any extra wires that stick out.

Replacing aluminum storm screening

One of the most put-off, but easy-to-do jobs is replacing damaged storm window screens. The screens are normally made of either fiberglass or aluminum, and you can purchase the material either way, plus the required screen retainer strips.

What it takes

Approximate time: An hour.

Tools: Screen installation tool (special purpose), hammer, tin snips, utility knife, replacement screening material.

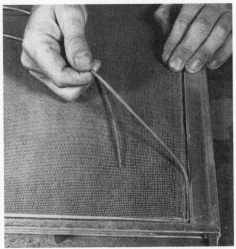

1. Place the aluminum screen on a flat work surface such as a table. Using the end of a screwdriver, pry up the retaining strip and remove it entirely.

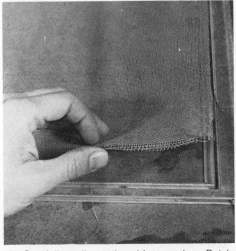

2. Carefully pull out the old screening. But be careful whenever you handle wire screening. It can cut; it can scratch.

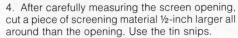

3. With a soft cloth wipe the screen retainer channel in order to remove any debris or bits of old screening, or dust.

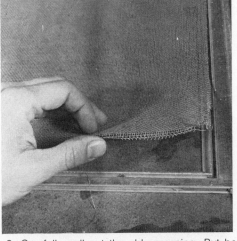

4. After carefully measuring the screen opening, cut a piece of screening material ½-inch larger all around than the opening. Use the tin snips.

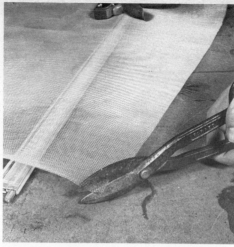

5. Lay the screening material in place and mark the exact corners of the screen. Now cut a ½-inch diagonal for each corner. This allows the material to be fitted down in the screen retainer slot without warping or buckling.

6. Using the convex roller on a screen retainer installation tool, gently roll the screen down in place. It's best to use short, light strokes, while holding the screen carefully to prevent buckling.

Leaving out the leftover can be a mistake.

After making sure the frame was perfectly square, I measured and cut my new aluminum screening to the exact size. Only I should have cut it ½ inch larger all around in order for the leftover screening to fit down into the retainer groove.

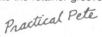
Practical Pete

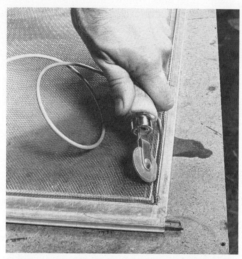

7. Choose a spline or screen retainer strip of the right size, and starting at one corner, force it and the surrounding screen down in the retainer groove. Push firmly now but with short strokes.

8. Use your finger to gently crease the screen on the inside edges of the retainer strips.

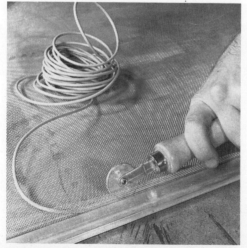

9. And again lightly push the screen on the next side down into the groove. Follow with the retainer strip, seating it firmly in the corner before starting around the next side.

10. After installing all sides, use a utility knife to cut away excess screening on the outside edge of the retainer strips.

What about fiberglass?

A man's home is his castle; but it is also a signal of his genius for improvisation. And high on the list of man's improvisations is that of fiberglass, a product of such present ubiquity that the word itself has acquired the status of place in the language.

Fiberglass is particularly useful when it comes to screening. It is easy to maintain, and moreover, it is attractive. The old screen door and window with their sagging, rusty wire are history.

Fiberglass screening, furthermore, offers the appealing feature of ease in repair. For instance, it is not necessary when replacing fiberglass screening on windows and doors to remove the panel itself. This is a sure bonus if you happen to be limited for time and space.

1. With fiberglass screening you can make your replacement on doors or windows without removing the panel, although it is easier to work with the panel on a flat surface.

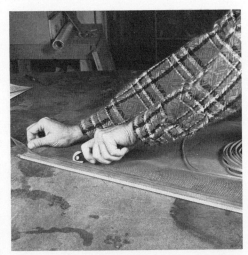

2. To replace with fiberglass screening: again, measure and cut screening material ½ inch larger all around than the screen retainer opening. Starting at one corner, gently push both the screen and retainer down in the channel at the same time, using concave side of a screen-retainer roller tool.

3. As you reach the corner, merely turn the tool and start down the next side. You won't have the problem of buckling as you would have with aluminum screening, so no need to cut away the corner.

4. The last step is to cut excess screening material away from the outside edge of the retaining strip. You can use a utility knife.

Some handy tips

- Aluminum oxide is a good cleaner for aluminum screens.

- Have a few weights to hold down corners of the screening while you're working with it, so that it won't roll up on top of your work area.

- Any time you handle screening it's a good idea to wear gloves. For those who like to work without gloves, the suggestion is that you exercise special caution against cuts and scratches.

- One of the best ways to work with screening—or for that matter, any material—is to be thoroughly prepared with a clean and orderly work surface before you start. Plan, prepare, and then you can produce.

Replacing a wood-frame screen

What it takes

Approximate time: An hour.

Tools and materials: Piece of replacement screening, hammer, two C-clamps, wide wood chisel, staple gun, small pieces of wood or cloth to go between C-clamps and screen.

TIP: Know that old screen wire can cut your hands, so be extra careful when removing it. Also make sure you don't pop any of the tacks off and lose them in an area where you might step on them or run over them with a bicycle.

TIP: Dispose of old screen wire and tacks in a tight cardboard box that you can leave for the garbage collector.

TIP: For this type of work—prying out nails, removing molding—use an old chisel, but keep the tool for that purpose. Never use one of your new, freshly sharpened chisels for such work.

There does come the time when you find you must replace a screen on a window or door. The hole is too large to patch, or repeated blows from a variety of objects have caused the screen to take on a sag which is not only unsightly but has caused an opening or tear at the edge of the molding. Or, if it's a galvanized metal screen it may have started to rust.

Using a large wood chisel, remove the screen molding that is covering the edge of the old screen wire. Be careful not to damage the molding.

Gently pull the old screen wire up, pulling out the tacks as you go. You may have to loosen some of the tacks with the chisel before removing the screen. In this event, slip the chisel under the screen wire next to the tack and pry up both wire and tack. With the old wire removed, cut a new section of screen, larger than the frame.

Now it is necessary to bow or arch the frame in order to get the screen taut. Place two 2x4s on sawhorses or a flat surface, and place the screen on it; then put a 1-inch strip under each end of the frame. Use C-clamps to draw down the center edges of the frame. This bows it. If you don't have C-clamps you can use a heavy weight to hold down the center. But place a thin piece of wood between the clamp and the screen frame.

Position the new piece of screening in place and staple one edge down securely. Then proceed to the opposite end and staple the edge down. Release the clamps and allow the screen to resume its normal shape. Then staple the sides down, making sure you start in the center and work toward the ends, pulling out any buckles that may form. Now, with the wire firmly stapled in place, retack the screen molding into place. Finally, using a sharp utility knife, cut away excess screening.

Installing screen wire on old wooden screens

1. With a large wood chisel, take off the screen molding along the edge of the old screen wire.

2. Gently pull the old screen wire up, pulling out tacks as you go. You may have to loosen some of the tacks with the chisel before removing the screen. In this case, slip the chisel under the screen wire next to the tack and pry up both wire and tack. With the old wire removed, cut a new section of screen, larger than the frame.

3. Place a couple of 2x4s on sawhorses or a flat surface, lay the screen down, then place a 1-inch strip under each end of the frame. Place C-clamps (with protective wood strips) over the center edges of the frame and under the 2X4s, and draw the frame down to bow it a bit. Now position the new screening in place and staple one edge.

4. Proceed to the opposite end and staple the edge down there.

5. Release the clamps and allow the screen to return to its usual shape. Now staple the sides, making sure that you start in the center and work toward the ends, pulling out any buckles that may have formed.

6. With the wire firmly stapled in place, retack the screen molding.

Instant fix with hardware for screen doors

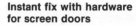

Pneumatic screen door closer.

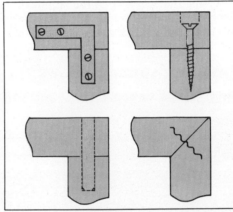

7. Using a sharp utility knife, cut away any screening that may be sticking out beyond the screen molding.

8. Corner bracing can save a screen. You can use a metal angle plate, a hardwood dowel, a long wood screw (countersink, fill with wood dough); or reinforce mitered joints with corrugated fastener.

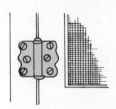

Spring hinges keep screen door tight.

Tight-locking screen door catch.

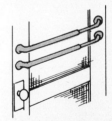

Screen door guard supports door and also acts as push bar.

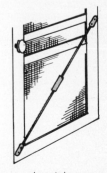

Brace on door takes up sag.

How to bow a screen frame

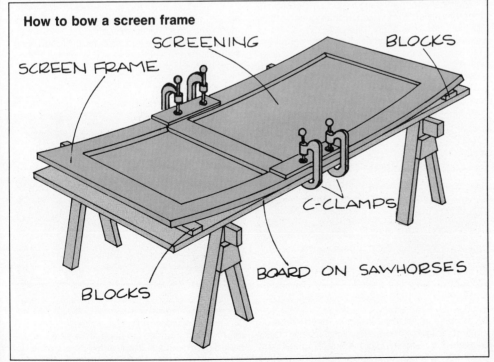

SCREENING

BLOCKS

SCREEN FRAME

C-CLAMPS

BLOCKS

BOARD ON SAWHORSES

Place screen on board with blocks at each end and draw center down with C-clamps.

Installing storm windows

Probably the most simple job you can do to help combat high energy expenses in your home is to install storm windows. The easiest for the homeowner to put in, and the most practical as well, are aluminum combination windows. These come in all standard sizes to fit standard windows. Indeed, they can be ordered custom-made in case you have non-standard windows.

The really nifty thing about these windows is that once up, the job is done. No more does the homeowner have to take down the storms and lug them to the basement or attic and then put up screens, reversing the operation in the fall; he now benefits from year-round units that keep out insects or cold air as the case may be.

The combination storm window and screen units are available in both two-track and three-track, but for most uses the two-track unit is best. Moreover, some brands of storms tilt inward to facilitate cleaning the inside of the glass.

By pressing on the locking tabs on the sides of the windows you can raise or lower them to provide ventilation in summer or cold protection in winter.

A second advantage to these combination units is that they normally fit more tightly than the old-style storm units. Because they are in the window permanently, they can be caulked to provide even more protection from drafts and air leakage from a warm room.

Installing storm windows

1. The most important thing in good installation of storm windows is to measure properly when ordering the units. There are basically two styles of window, each requiring a slightly different measurement, although the screens will be the same. The most common storm windows overlap the outside window casing and you merely measure the window frame opening in width and height. The width is between the side casings and the height is from sill to bottom of top casing.

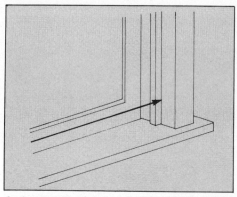

2. A measurement for a window unit that fits against a blind stop is made in exactly the same manner, except the storm window fits back inside the window casing and against the blind stop. Naturally, storm windows to be used in this manner must be measured extra carefully.

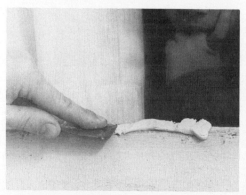

3. Examine the window to see if it needs recaulking and reglazing. It probably will if it hasn't been protected by storm units before. Reglaze and caulk any openings or cracks. This is also a good time to repaint the entire window.

4. Turn the window unit over on its front and slip the metal strip under the clips. This strip can be pulled down to adjust to any unevenness in the sill, giving an absolutely tight, weatherproof fit.

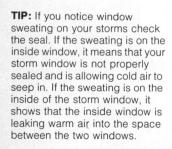

TIP: If you notice window sweating on your storms check the seal. If the sweating is on the inside window, it means that your storm window is not properly sealed and is allowing cold air to seep in. If the sweating is on the inside of the storm window, it shows that the inside window is leaking warm air into the space between the two windows.

Your own do-it-yourself storm windows

You can create a pretty snappy looking storm window out of plastic sheets and trim. The plastic is clear and rigid and can be bought in standard window sizes. Wood trim or molding can be purchased according to measure. The sheets are placed in the window from the inside, and the molding tacked or screwed in, to hold it in place. This sort of storm window assembly can be purchased in kits or you can make up your own. One of the beauties of it is the fact that you don't have to be climbing up and down ladders outside the house.

The weather conversion

You can turn your window screens and screen doors into storm windows and doors simply by covering them with a clear plastic film. You'll need fiber strips for holding the film in the frame. You can either assemble these materials yourself, or buy a kit. While this system is not as good as a real storm window or storm door, it will save heat and energy.

TIP: Try putting a bit of caulking around the inside lip of the storm unit before screwing it in place, or you can apply a bead around the outside edge after you have finished. This gives even more protection from the winter winds.

5. Place the storm unit in place against the window and make sure it will slide easily in place. Do not force it, the soft aluminum bends quite easily and you'll end up with a distorted frame. If it doesn't go in, there may be a lump of paint or a bowed casing. Examine and carefully cut off what is needed to allow the unit to slip in place.

6. The screws furnished with these units are normally quite small Phillips head screws, so instead of using a drill to make the starting hole, just use an 8-penny nail, tapping it in about ¼ inch with your hammer. Then drive the screws in tight.

The great paint-out.
I didn't actually paint myself into a corner, but I did paint over the key numbers on some of my storm windows, and so I lost track of which sash they paired with. Next time I'll stick a piece of masking tape on the glass and write the number on it.

Practical Pete

Maintaining wood sash storm windows

While aluminum storms may be easier as far as maintenance goes, you could very likely have wood storm windows in your house. They are just as efficient, but there are certain points to watch for. See that they fit snugly in their frames. Put on weatherstripping so that the seal is even more tight. Periodic removal of the storms for repainting is necessary; this prevents swelling and distortion as a result of moisture absorption. Be sure to key the window and the frame with an identical number so that you'll know where it goes after painting. Also inspect every now and again for bent hooks or hangers, loose joints, loose screws, dried-out or missing putty.

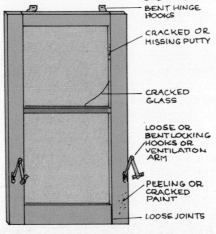

CHECK FOR:
BENT HINGE HOOKS
CRACKED OR MISSING PUTTY
CRACKED GLASS
LOOSE OR BENT LOCKING HOOKS OR VENTILATION ARM
PEELING OR CRACKED PAINT
LOOSE JOINTS

Painting professionally

What it takes:

Approximate time: About one hour each for painting.

Tools and materials:
3″ brush.
1½″ sash brush with the bristles cut at an angle.
Single-edged razor blade scraper.
Sandpaper and block.
Wire brush, putty knife, broad knife, and spackle for badly chipped paint.
Wood primer paint for new wood.
Metal primer paint for steel surfaces.
Safety glasses if you are chipping or scraping old paint.

Preparing surfaces

Chipped paint. After many coats have built up they may crack and begin to chip in spots. Slide the corner of a putty knife blade into the chip and force away as much loose paint as will come away. Sand the edges of the open area to feather them gradually into the old paint around them. Or, if the paint buildup is very thick, smooth premixed spackle into the hollows to even them up with the surrounding paint. Use your finger tip for filling chips in contoured moldings. After the spackle dries white (it looks gray when it's still wet), sand it smooth. Wear a kerchief over your nose, like a bandit, and cover your hair to keep the flying spackle dust out. Wipe the surface with a tack rag or dampened cloth.

Flaking paint. Usually this turns up on sills exposed to lots of sun or moisture. Perhaps the last painter did not clean off greasy soot first. A wire brush will remove the flakes, but don't dig grooves in plaster or old wood with the brush. Sand the area smooth and wipe off the dust. Put a primer coat on bare wood or metal.

Molding cracks. In old houses the molding strips sometimes warp or separate from the wall, leaving a crack that can't be closed. Fill it with spackling compound, draw a wet finger (or a rubber spatula) along it to make a smooth contour. Wipe off any excess, on either side of the crack, with a moist sponge.

Planning hints:

- Old surfaces with chipping, cracks, and many coats require a lot more preparation time (to scrape down, spackle, touch up, and sand smooth) than they do to paint.
- Plan preparation and painting as two separate stages. Clean up after the preparation is done and start again with fresh newspapers, stamina, and patience.
- If you are using a specially mixed color, get enough for all the windows, doors, and trim in that color. Figure at least a quart for one side of a door or two windows.
- Check the rain forecast before starting to paint out-opening casement windows.
- Plan to paint one whole side of a door, especially flush doors, without stopping. A line may show where you stopped because the fresh paint can't flow into the dried paint.
- When painting doors, wedge them open and slip newspapers under them so you don't build up paint in the cracks and splatter on the frame or wall.

Painting sequence. The sequences given here for painting the parts of a door or window will produce a better result for two reasons: Most wooden doors and windows have vertical sides running top to bottom and horizontal pieces butted inside them. If you paint the horizontals before the verticals, the paint strokes will run with the grain of the wood in the same pattern as the door or window was constructed. These sequences also allow you to do the job in the shortest time without overlapping fresh paint on dried paint where it will be noticeable.

Paneled door: First do the panels, around the molding, then the flat part working from the edges of the panel toward its center; do the horizontal surfaces next, left to right; the vertical surfaces come last, top to bottom. If you are painting the panel moldings a darker, contrasting color, paint them first with a 1-inch angled trim brush and let that paint dry completely before painting the rest of the door.

Flush door: Use a 3-inch brush or roller. Paintbrush jobs should be done in foot-high strips across the width of the door. Start in the upper left corner and lay the paint on about halfway across the door, first with down-up strokes and then back-and-forth strokes; then do the same with the other half of that strip; smooth the full strip first up and down, then back and forth across the full width of the door. Repeat that procedure in foot-high strips until you reach the bottom of the door.

Frame and joint: Paint the edge of the door that opens toward you the same color as that side of the door. Also paint the door frame and jamb, including the section that has the lock striker plate in it, so that when you stand back into the room a little with the door open, everything you see on the frame and jamb is the same color.

New door: Take it off the hinges so you can paint the bottom and hinged edges to keep the wood from swelling (you won't have to paint them ever again). Lift out both hinge pins with pliers or drive them free with a spike nail set, bottom hinge first. Lift the door off both hinges simultaneously so one hinge never carries the full load and bends out of shape. If it is new wood, give it a primer coat first *all over*. If you paint only one side of a new wood door it will probably warp. Sand the primer lightly to smooth tiny bumps. And remember to wipe it off well.

Painting windows and screens

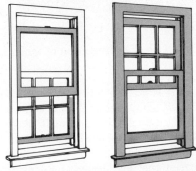

Double-hung windows. Push the inside sash almost all the way up and pull the outside sash almost all the way down. Paint all of the inside sash with a 1½-inch sash brush, cross pieces first, then vertical pieces, but don't paint the top edge of the sash yet. Then paint as much of the outside sash as you can reach. Don't paint the bottom edge of the lower sash (so you won't get paint on your fingers when you push it up), unless you can't reach it later.

Push the outside sash up almost to the top, and push the inside sash almost all the way down. Paint the parts of the sash you couldn't reach before, plus the frame, but not the inside and outside channels. Let the paint dry; then lower both windows all the way, paint the jamb and top halves of the inside channels lightly with a thin coat. After it dries, raise both windows and paint the bottom half of the inside channels. Lubricate the unpainted metal parts.

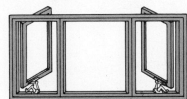

Casement windows. Swing the window out and lock it open. Paint the parts of the window in the following order: The strips surrounding the glass, horizontal first, then vertical; the sill; the frame, starting with the hinged side. If they are steel, rust will bleed through most interior paints. So after you have wirebrushed off loose paint or rust, touch up the bare spots with a metal primer paint. Sand the primer lightly before the finish paint job.

Painting metal screens. Tack a piece of short pile carpeting onto a small block of wood that you can hold comfortably in one hand. Dip it in the paint and wipe it across the screen. Then paint the frame. Use rust-preventive paint for protecting old steel mesh screens.

Painting doors

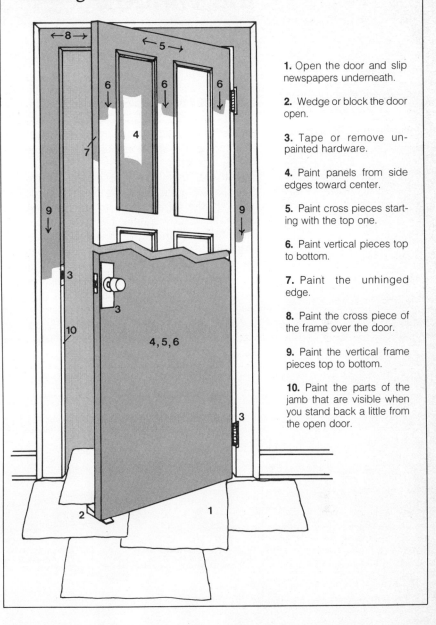

1. Open the door and slip newspapers underneath.

2. Wedge or block the door open.

3. Tape or remove unpainted hardware.

4. Paint panels from side edges toward center.

5. Paint cross pieces starting with the top one.

6. Paint vertical pieces top to bottom.

7. Paint the unhinged edge.

8. Paint the cross piece of the frame over the door.

9. Paint the vertical frame pieces top to bottom.

10. Paint the parts of the jamb that are visible when you stand back a little from the open door.

Cleaning paint off glass and hardware. Use a single-edge blade to scrape the paint off glass after it has dried a little. First, score along the edge where the glass meets the wood strip, then scrape the blade flat along the glass, and the unwanted paint will come off like a banana peel.

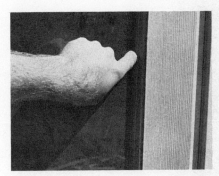

Another trick. Smear some petroleum jelly (Vaseline) on the glass with your fingers where the glass meets the wood. Also smear it on hardware. When the paint has dried, it scrapes off easily where the paint went over the jelly.

What goes with the window

Installing drapery hardware

What it takes

Approximate time: Under an hour.

Tools and materials: Hammer, screwdriver, 8-penny nail, Yankee drill, measuring tape or ruler, portable electric drill and bits, plastic wall anchors or expansion bolts, drapery or curtain rods, with fasteners provided by the manufacturer.

It is the easiest thing in the world to put up drapery rods that will be uneven. This is not only unsightly, it is perilous, for it can all fall when you open the drapes.

But this sad situation can easily be avoided. A bit of care in measuring and leveling, and a small amount of patience will do the trick.

The two main types of installation to consider are: concealed and exposed hardware. If the hardware is to be installed inside the window frames, merely measure, mark for position and then fasten in place either with screws or the small brads that are usually furnished when you buy the rod. Some of the smaller hardware, such as for small cafe rods, is furnished with tiny brads which you simply drive into place.

The simplest type of drapery rod is an extension rod with a spring inside it. Measure to allow for the contraction of the rod. Slip the drapery on the rod and squeeze the rod to fit in place. Regardless of what type of hardware is used, if it is to be placed on the window trim, measure, position, and screw in place. Incidentally, a small Yankee screwdriver can start screw holes, but don't bore too deep, or the screw won't hold.

Draperies that are designed to remain more or less stationary may be hung on poles or rods that are fixed; but if you require your draperies to open and close frequently, then a traverse rod is the best bet. This piece of hardware can be operated by hand or by an electric motor. The beauty of the traverse rod is that when your draperies are hung in this manner, no matter how wide the area that they cover, you can open both sides with a single motion, and just as easily close them.

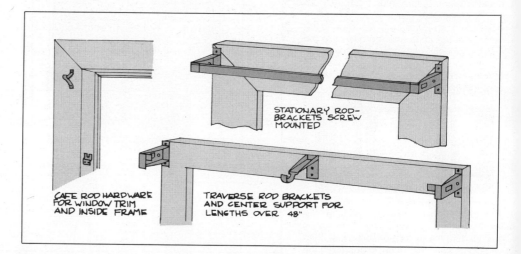

STATIONARY ROD-BRACKETS SCREW MOUNTED

CAFE ROD HARDWARE FOR WINDOW TRIM AND INSIDE FRAME

TRAVERSE ROD BRACKETS AND CENTER SUPPORT FOR LENGTHS OVER 48"

TIP: If any curtain rod is over 48 inches long make sure it has adequate support between the two ends.

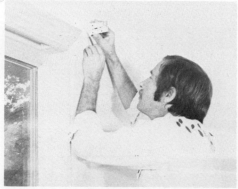

1. In most cases the hardware won't be placed on the trim. The first step is to mark the location of the hardware. Drive an 8-penny nail at one of the screw hole locations to determine if the hardware will be located on a stud. If the hardware is located on a stud, predrill holes with a Yankee drill and fasten hardware in place.

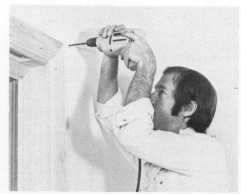

2. If the nail goes through the wall, indicating the absence of a stud in the area, you'll have to use wall anchors. The first step is to bore a ¼-inch hole.

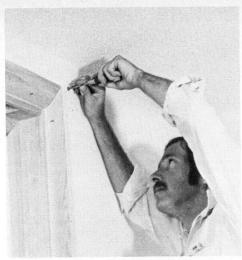

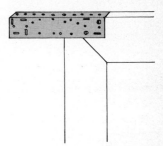

TIP: Should you want to hang draperies beyond the window frame to take full advantage of light you can use extender plates which are mounted directly on the window casing so that no wall mounting is required.

3. Next step is to position the wall anchor in the hole; then turn the screw in the anchor to pull it in place. Remove the screw.

4. Position the hardware over the anchor and re-place the screw to hold the hardware securely. Remember that you will have to do this for two screws on each piece of hardware.

5. In many cases the rod will be supported by a center support. Fasten this in the same manner.

6. Do the end supports in the same way. Then snap the rod in place. Be careful that you have not pushed any of the hardware out of level.

More ain't better

I had no trouble at all putting up my new drapes; but the rod began to wobble after I had opened and closed them a few times. Luckily I figured out what the problem was before the whole shebang fell on top of me. I had drilled too deep and the screws didn't have enough to hold to. So I just got longer screws and the problem was solved. Next time I won't drill deeper than the length of the screw.

Practical Pete

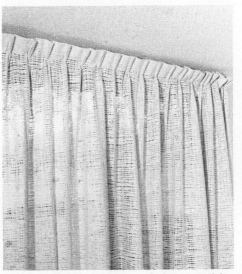

7. Loosen the adjusting screw on the center sup-port and move the support arm into the right posi-tion. Then snap the rod in place on the support, and tighten the adjusting screw.

8. Your final step is to fasten the drapery material to the rod, using the hooks.

Installing and maintaining window shades

What it takes

Tools and materials: Hammer, screwdriver, Yankee drill or portable electric drill and bits, sandpaper.

Standard inside bracket

Inside extension bracket

Sash-run bracket

Outside bracket

Combination bracket

Ceiling bracket

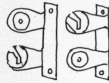
Double bracket

One of the most alarming—not to say noisiest—of those necessities of civilized living with which the homeowner must deal is the malfunctioning window shade. But what a deceptively simple mechanism it is. A plain-looking wooden roller, one end of which is hollow and holds a coil spring within. At either end of the roller is a pin. The one at the spring end is flat. It rotates, winding or unwinding the spring. When you pull down the shade the spring winds tight. The moment you stop pulling, a small lever, called a pawl, drops into place against a ratchet at the spring end of the roller. It is the pawl that prevents the spring from winding the shade back up.

When you want to raise the shade, you pull down slightly on it, thus moving the pawl away from the ratchet and so permitting the spring to take the shade back up.

The fasteners for installing shades are similar to those used for drapery hardware: brads and small screws in a wooden frame, and wall anchors when there is nothing in the wall to grip.

There are seven types of brackets.
Standard inside bracket. This is the most commonly used, and it is used any place that has enough depth inside the window frame to accommodate a roller.

Inside extension bracket. Also mounted inside a window frame, it requires less space than the standard inside bracket.

Sash-run bracket. A special bracket that is used with an all-wood, double-hung window. The bracket is mounted at the top of the sash rung.

Outside bracket. This type of bracket can be mounted on either the trim or the surrounding wall. It is commonly used where there is no space on the inside of the window frame. Shades wider than the window can be used with these brackets to block out the light.

Combination bracket. These dual purpose brackets hold both a window shade and a curtain rod.

Ceiling bracket. Useful on high windows, these brackets are mounted on the ceiling. They can also be used to give a standard window the illusion of extra height.

Double bracket. These are designed to utilize two shades at one time. As a rule, one is translucent, the other opaque.

While installation is fairly simple, it is the actual maintenance of the window shade that is one of the prime concerns of the homeowner.

If the shade does not want to stay down, it means that it is not catching. Check that the brackets are not interfering with the roller. A roller should have 1/16" to 1/8" clearance. Make sure that the flat projection of the roller is vertical in the slot in the bracket. Never, by the way, use oil in a shade mechanism.

If the shade pulls up too strongly, it means that the spring is too tight. Roll the shade up to the top and remove it from the brackets. Unroll two revolutions of cloth and replace on the brackets. Repeat until the spring has regained the proper position. Do not unroll more than half way.

If the shade refuses to return, this means that it lacks sufficient tension. In order to increase the tension, pull the shade down about two revolutions; then remove the flat pin from its bracket. Roll the shade back up by hand. When it is all the way up, put the pin back in its bracket and test for tension. If the shade still won't go up far enough, repeat the procedure until it does.

If the shade wobbles when it goes up or down, this probably indicates a bent roller pin. Straighten the pin with pliers, but with gentle pressure. If the pin is dirty or rusty you can clean it with sandpaper.

If the shade cloth is worn, on the bottom edge, the shade can be salvaged. Just trim off the damaged part; remove the cloth from the roller and remount it by tacking or stapling the cut bottom end of the cloth to the roller. Be careful that you keep the bottom of the shade absolutely straight.

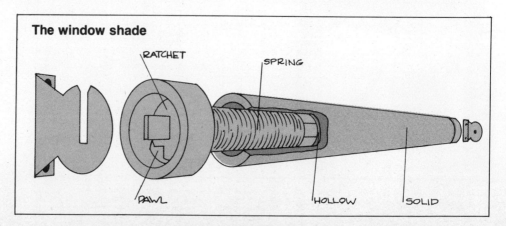

The window shade

RATCHET

SPRING

PAWL

HOLLOW

SOLID

Venetian blinds—repair and maintenance

The two chief problems with any venetian blind are concerned with the webbing (the ladder tapes) and the cords. These can—and they do—become frayed or broken.

First of all you will see that there are two sets of cords. One set, known as the "lift cord system," raises and lowers the blinds. The other set is called the "tilt cord system," and it controls the amount of light by altering the angle of the blinds.

Some experts suggest that you make a drawing of your blinds so that you will more easily get the cords back to their right places. It's a good idea. After all, you simply need to replace the old with the new *in exactly the same way.*

Open the blinds. Starting with the lift cord, take a look at the knots under the tape at the base of the bottom rail. The tape might be held in place by a clamp, if the rail is metal, or if it is wood it may be stapled.

Untie the knot on the side that has the tilt cord and join the old cord to the new cord by butting the ends and wrapping them with transparent tape.

Now feed the new cord from the bottom up through the openings in the slats; and on through the entire route of the old cord until you reach the knot on the opposite end. You must make certain that the cord threads alternately back and forth on different sides of the ladder tapes—the webbing—as you feed it in.

You can change the tilt cord at the same time. Run it over the pulley and back down.

If you wish to replace the tapes, remove the blinds from the window and place them either on the floor or on a large table. Remove the cover from the bottom slat. Untie both ends of the cord and pull free. This releases the slats so that you can pull them out for washing and painting.

When you purchase new tapes be sure that they have the same number of ladders as the old tapes and that they are for the same width slats. Install them by securing them to top and bottom; now thread the lift cord through the tapes.

What else can you do in the way of maintenance? Check the gears and pulleys; these pick up lint, affecting their operation. Clean and lubricate with silicone spray.

What it takes.

Tools and materials: Scissors, pliers, replacement webbing, replacement cord, silicone spray.

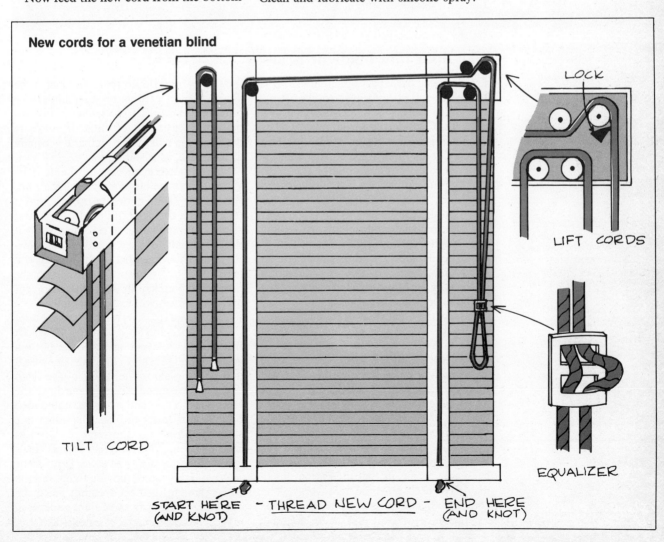

New cords for a venetian blind

LOCK

LIFT CORDS

EQUALIZER

TILT CORD

START HERE (AND KNOT) — THREAD NEW CORD — END HERE (AND KNOT)

4.DOORS

The door that binds or is loose

What it takes

Approximate time: Varies with the job from minutes to a couple of hours.

Tools and materials: Hammer, plane, screwdriver, carpenter's square, file, wooden toothpicks, glue, plastic wood, shirt cardboard, chalk, wooden wedges, and penetrating oil.

TIP: To keep the door upright while planing, anchor it with a C-clamp to a large wooden box.

The door is a basic part of any house. It is both entry and exit, it leads to other rooms, it leads to closets, basements and attics, hallways. Considering the simplicity of its shape, it is striking how many different kinds of doors there are. Yet, the point for us is the proper functioning of the door. Simply put: will it open and close without shoulders, tools, or a professional carpenter being brought to bear?

The principal door problems are binding and looseness. Why does a door stick? It could be because the hinges are loose or poorly mounted; possibly the wood has swollen, or the house may have settled, and so the door frame is out of shape.

Inspect the hinges and strike plate. If any screws are loose as a result of the holes being enlarged try longer screws, or you can fill the holes with wood plugs or plastic wood and reset the old screws. If the door still binds, try locating the places where it rubs by slipping some stiff but thin cardboard between the jamb and the edges of the closed door.

Suppose that the door is free near the bottom but is sticking near the top on the latch side. It means that the bottom hinge may have been mortised too deeply. The approach then is to open the door and place a wedge under it to make it secure. Remove the screws from the bottom hinge leaf in the jamb, place a cardboard shim under the hinge leaf, and reset the screws. This will move the lower part of the door out from the jamb and will push it so that it is square in its frame, as it should be.

On the other hand, should the door be sticking near the bottom on the latch side, you can put a shim under the upper hinge in the jamb. If the door still binds, then sand or plane off some wood at the point where it rubs. You can do this without taking down the door. But remember that whenever you take off wood you must put finish on the raw wood to match the door and to prevent moisture which will cause swelling.

If the door is now binding at the top, wedge it open and sand or plane the wood. But should the binding be at the bottom you will need to remove the door; likewise if it is sticking along the whole of the latch side. Remove it and sand or plane down the *hinge* side. This method is recommended because it is easier to plane the hinge side since you don't need to remove the lock; also, the hinge side is not so noticeable as the latch side and may be easier to refinish.

What if the door is moving freely and the latch, though lined up does not reach the strike plate? You can put a shim under it to move it out far enough toward the door so it will hold. Should the door open by itself when it is not latched, then put a narrow cardboard shim under half the hinge leaf on the pin side of each hinge on the jamb.

The recommended way to remove a door—if it has loose pins—is to drive the pins up and out with a hammer and screwdriver or nail set. Take out the bottom (and middle) pin first and then the top hinge so the door won't fall while held with only one hinge. If the door is held by hinges that don't have loose pins, remove the screws from one leaf of each hinge on the door's jamb side. Do it with the door wide and with a wedge supporting its outer corner.

However, before you start this operation mark the place or places where it binds. Plane down to these marks. Be very careful.

If it is the hinge side you have planed, you may in certain cases need to deepen the hinge mortises so that the position of the door in the frame will remain as it was.

To plane the bottom of the door you will have to prop it so that the bottom is vertical to the floor. Plane from the top corner toward the center. Turn the door over so that it stands on the other long edge, and plane from the other corner toward the center. It is important when planing the side always to cut toward the edges. Remember that the latch side is slightly beveled to prevent the door edge from striking the frame when the door closes. And so if you do have to plane the latch side make sure that you don't lose the bevel.

A door will not stay closed if the latch tongue does not go into the strike plate opening. You can file the opening to make it larger. But if the strike plate is too much out of line you will have to move it. Remove the plate, cut the mortise to the new place, fill the exposed part with plastic wood, and plug the screw holes.

In some cases you can position wood shims under a threshold to bring it up into position and prevent door looseness.

In all cases doors should have at least ⅛-inch clearance on top and at each side to allow for shrinkage and expansion. In areas of high temperature and humidity changes, you may even wish to make this ¼ inch, and use weatherstripping around the opening.

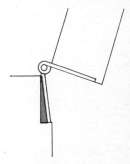

If the door is too tight, place a small piece of cardboard shim on the front side of the hinge.

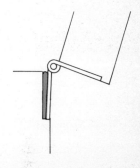

If the door is too loose, then place a shim on the back side of the hinge.

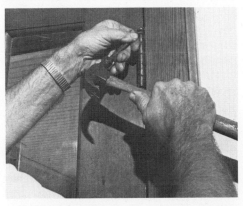

1. In some cases you'll have to remove the door and so start by tapping out the hinge pin. Use a nail set or a screwdriver and hammer. After the door is down you can plane or sand it as needed. Remember, though, before taking the door down, to mark where it needs planing.

2. Use a jack plane and make sure the blade is in good condition. It's best to remove wood on the hinge side, but you may have to plane on the latch side; if so, make sure you leave a bevel edge.

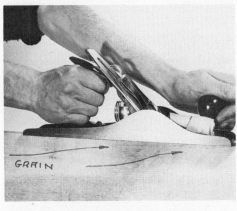

3. Plane with the grain, never against it. Also, make sure that the work is secure and won't wobble or move in any way while you are planing.

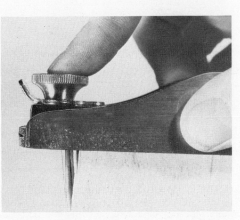

4. When planing across the edges of doors, work from the end toward the center in order to avoid splintering as shown here.

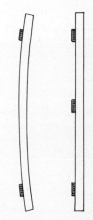

If a door becomes warped, one easy remedy is to install a third hinge centered between the other two.

Cutting a new doorway

What it takes

Approximate time: One day.

Tools and materials: Hammer, saw, pry bar, level, square, large wood chisel, large utility knife, hacksaw (optional), plumb bob and chalk line, portable electric saw, and portable electric drill.

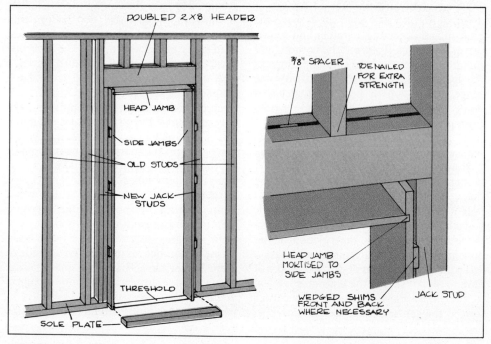

Decide the general position of the door opening. This will include the framing you will add. Tap the wall or drill small holes to locate the studs; use a ⅛-inch bit. Make sure that you aren't running into any heating ducts or pipes. You can check in the basement for this. Electrical wiring is easy enough to relocate.

Now mark the inside of the wall, using a straightedge or chalk line to make certain the lines are straight. Use a plumb bob or carpenter's level to make sure the sides of the opening are plumb.

Using a long bit on a portable electric drill, bore through the wall at the top corners of the marked opening. This should give a rough location of the opening on the outside wall. Now measure outside to make sure it is positioned properly, and drop a plumb bob chalk line down to mark the locations of the side cuts. The opening must be cut 5 inches wider on each side and 9 to 12 inches higher on top to allow for the new framing and door facings.

With both the inside and outside cut marked, the first step is to remove all nails from the cut lines on the outside, and then, using a general-purpose blade in a portable electric saw, saw out the outline on the outside. If you plan to install new siding, you can make the corner cuts larger. However, if you intend to save the siding, cut

1. After marking both the inside and outside cuts, remove all the nails from the cut lines on the outside; then, with a general-purpose blade in a portable power saw, saw along the outline from the outside. Here, a window is being removed so that a door can be installed in its place.

2. Remove all lath, plaster, or sheetrock from the inside of the opening lines. Make sure you remove all nails before making any cuts with your saw. Before removing the studs you should preassemble the framing so it can be placed in position quickly after the last stud is removed.

just barely past the corners, leaving enough so that the trim on the door will cover. Set the saw blade so it will go only through the siding and boxing and not into the 2x4 studs. Remove the siding from the opening.

With all the siding and boxing removed from the outside, go back inside the house and use a brick chisel or large wood chisel to score around the rough opening lines through the lath and plaster, if that is what's covering your wall. If the inside wall is covered with sheetrock, you can use a large utility knife. After scoring along the lines, remove all plaster or sheetrock from the inside of the lines. If the wall consists of lath and plaster, use a hacksaw or portable electric saw to cut the lath around the edges. Then pull the lath away.

You should now have only the studs left in the opening. Before removing them, assemble the framing. It can then be quickly placed in position after the last stud is cut away and removed.

The framing comprises two 2x4s on each side and a double header consisting of at least two 2x8s on end with a ⅜-inch spacer between to make the header the proper wall thickness. Make sure that the ⅜-inch spacer is right for your wall.

With the new frame completed, cut the 2x4s loose first at the bottom and then at the top. Leave the center 2x4 until last. Then cut it away at both bottom and top and quickly position your framing. Toenail it at the bottom, and toenail the existing studs into the header at the top.

Hanging a new door

The first decision is to pick the door that fits your requirements. The door will be either interior or exterior, either flush or sash, and there are also louver doors.

Be sure that your measurements are precise. Either you will have to cut an opening or the opening is already there; but in either case you will order the door from the lumber yard to fit your measurements.

First measure for height from the floor to the headpiece of the frame. Then measure for width. More than likely you will need a 6-foot-8-inch or a 7-foot door. But it will have to be cut to allow for the thickness of the saddle or threshold piece. As a rule the saddle will be ¾ inch, though this is variable. The point is to buy a door that will have ⅛-inch clearance at the top and on each side. But this is the maximum; more than that and the door will be too loose. It is important, especially for an exterior door, to see whether you need to paint the bottom and top edges to seal them against moisture and warping.

When you are ready to hang the new door, first saw off the two horns, the protective ends that are extensions of the vertical members or stiles. Measure the door and mark it for height and width. Cut it to size. With a plane, trim the edges of the hinge, latch stiles and bottom rail. Be careful not to lose the bevel on the latch side.

Place the door in the opening to try it for fit. Put wedges (wood shingles are good) under the bottom rail so that it is raised ¼ inch for clearance. If there is a rug or carpet over which the door is to open or close, then increase the clearance to ⅞ inch. To ensure the proper clearance around the door insert wedges; hammer

these in on all four sides to hold the door in its proper position.

Select your hinges. Depending on the size and weight of your door you will have either two or three hinges. Locate the top hinge 6 inches from the top of the door, and the bottom hinge 10 inches from the bottom. If you are using three hinges you can space these out a bit and locate the third hinge halfway between. Take the door away, and with a try square extend the hinge marks onto the jamb. Lay the hinge

Figure labels: CASING, STOP, HEAD JAMB, TOP RAIL, LATCH STILE, HINGE STILE, JAMB, PANEL, LOCK RAIL, THRESHOLD (OR SADDLE), BOTTOM RAIL, STILE EXTENSION (TO BE SAWED OFF), WEDGES

What it takes

Approximate time: 4 hours.

Tools and materials: Saw, tape measure, plane, sandpaper, chisel, screwdriver, hammer, try square, level, plumb line, wedges, nails, hinges, cardboard shims, door.

The time I really got into a "jamb."

Sometimes it's the easiest thing in the world just to forget something. I forgot to bevel the latch edge of my new door when I planed it to size. And so it didn't clear the jamb as it was supposed to. Luckily it only splintered the edge a little and I was able to fix it. But next time I'll remember.

Some doors come with one edge beveled at the factory. In that case you'll have to remember to hang the door with the bevel on the latch side.

Practical Pete

Knock wood for good luck?
But that wooden door knocked me. I goofed and took the pin out of the top hinge first. Next time I remove a door for planing, I'll remember to take the bottom pin out first so the door can hang until I'm ready.

Practical Pete

leaf down on the hinge edge of the door as a guide, and outline it with a pencil. The barrel of the hinge should lie beyond the inner face of the door. Mark the thickness of the hinge on the inside of the door face.

Use a chisel to score the outline of the hinge inside the pencil line. Hold the chisel vertically, keeping its beveled face toward the opening, and drive it to approximately the depth of the hinge. Make scoring marks inside the mortise outline and cut these out to the depth line. The chisel's beveled edge should be held downward. It is better to make several small cuts than a few large ones. You'll have a cleaner mortise. You can shave off your scored cuts by holding the chisel along the depth line and tapping it lightly against the grain of the mortise opening. The beveled side of the chisel

should be facing up. Place the hinge to see how it fits. If it lies too deep in the mortise, shim it up with cardboard until it lies flush. Drill or punch holes for the screws; then drive the screws home. The hinge must be absolutely flush with the door edge.

You will have separated the hinge leaves to make it easier to attach them to the jamb and door. Now bring the door with the hinge leaves attached to the jamb. Engage the pairs of leaves, top hinge first, and insert the hinge pin. Repeat for the second pin, and for a third if there is one. Tighten all the screws. Now cut the doorstop to size and attach it with finishing nails (see diagram, page 39). The stop should contact the door on the latch side and at top, but there can be a slight clearance on the hinge side. Finally, check your door swing.

Mortising a hinge

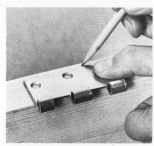

1. Use the hinge leaf as a guide to outline the mortise. Let the hinge barrel extend beyond the edge of the door.

2. With a chisel, score the hinge outline inside the pencil mark. Keep the beveled face of the chisel toward the opening.

3. With beveled edge down, clean the mortise to the depth of the hinge leaf, using shallow feather cuts.

4. Holding the chisel on the depth line, tap across the mortise grain to shave off the cuts. Keep the bevel facing up.

5. Drill or punch holes for the screws, being sure to go straight down and not at an angle, nor too deep.

6. Drive the screws home Check that the hinge leaf is flush with the edge of the door Use a shim if cut is too deep.

Doorstop

Now is the moment to nail the doorstop in place. This essential door part consists of two vertical side pieces and one horizontal head piece (see illustration, page 39). Cut all the pieces of stop you need to their approximate length, with one end of each cut square. Hold the head piece in place at the top of the door, mark the other end at the edge of the jamb, and cut to length. With the door closed and latched, install

the head piece, being careful not to force the stop against the door. Nail it with 1/16 inch of clearance between it and the door.

Now install the stop piece on the hinge side. Don't force it, make sure you have clearance, and try the door after you nail each piece in place. In this way if the door binds you will know right off which piece of the stop needs adjustment. Finally, nail the stop piece on the latch side.

Casing

The casing is the flat molding that goes around the door (see illustration, page 39). It's simple enough to nail up; chiefly it is a question of cutting accurate miter joints.

This takes care and it's a good idea to practice first on scraps. You will need a miter box so you can cut a 45-degree angle, and a backsaw with which to make a flat cut at the molding end.

The door casing consists of two legs and a head piece. Stand the leg that fits against the hinges in place. It should be the thickness of a hinge away from the edge of the jamb. Try to keep this distance all around the door as you install the casing. Casing is always installed with the wide part away from the door. Its bottom edge rests on the floor, not on the baseboard.

Start by cutting the miter in the leg, put it in place and tack it there temporarily. Cut a matching miter for the head. Tack this in place. If the joint doesn't fit perfectly you can work on it with a sharp block plane, or a sharp, fine-tooth saw (10 point), or sandpaper. Finally, cut the remaining leg to an exact fit.

When you have the fit, use 3-penny finishing nails through the thin side of the casing into the jamb, and 6-penny finishing nails through the thick side into the studs. Countersink the nails and fill the holes with wood filler.

Door accessories

Installing a mail slot

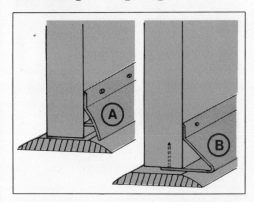

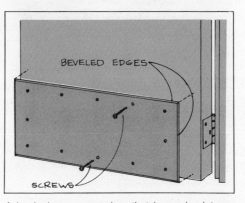

A mail slot should be set at least 30 inches above the floor, and in the thicker part of the door. It should not be set in a panel, and if the door is hollow core, you will need a metal chute between the inside and outside plates. Place the inside plate (the one without a flap) on the *outside* of the door in correct position and outline its opening. Remove the plate and enlarge the outline by at least ½ inch to allow the flap door on the outside plate to open. Bore starting holes with a drill, and cut out the opening with a keyhole or saber saw. Finally, screw the plates to both the inside and outside of door.

What it takes

Approximate time: Under an hour for all.

Tools and materials: Level, electric drill and bits, saber saw, screwdriver, pencil, and parts as illustrated.

Installing a drip cap

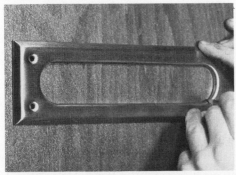

A drip cap keeps rainwater from draining or blowing under the door. It may be made of metal or wood and is easy to install, usually requiring only screws. One type is installed on the outside of the door over the threshold (A); another extends under the bottom of the door (B).

Installing a kick plate

A back door, or any door that is used a lot can benefit from a kick plate. Made of plastic or metal, it can be screwed to the bottom of any door to protect its surface. As a rule, the plate measures a couple of inches narrower than the door width; this allows clearance for the door stops.

Replacing a threshold

What it takes

Approximate time: One hour.

Tools and materials: Small wrecking bar, hammer, chisel (optional), awl or punch, screwdriver or electric drill and bit, hacksaw, backsaw (optional), square, portable electric saw or handsaw, and replacement saddle.

While the door itself is opened and closed with a frequency that you don't notice, it is actually the threshold that receives the most wear. There will come a time when you will want to replace the threshold, or saddle. Chances are your old saddle will be of wood; saddles are generally made of hardwood—oak as a rule—but you may wish to replace them with aluminum.

Swing the door wide; you may find it necessary to take it down. You may even have to remove the door stops from the jamb. Lift the old saddle with a pry bar or the claws of a hammer.

If the saddle is in bad shape it might be simpler to split the wood with a chisel and take out the pieces. The saddle may even extend under the jambs; if so, try first to remove it in one piece. But if you can't, cut it into three sections with a backsaw, take out the center piece and then the other two. Use the old saddle as a pattern for the new one. If you can't do that, take careful measurements. Cut the new saddle so the protruding ends fit neatly against the door casing. Drill holes and sink nails, or countersink screws to secure the new saddle to the floor. Fill holes with putty.

1. The first step is to remove the old saddle. You can use a pry bar. If this doesn't work, then try cutting the saddle out with a backsaw, or taking it out in pieces with hammer and chisel. **TIP:** When purchasing a new threshold, make sure you buy one at least as long as the opening. It can be cut to fit, but one that is too short will let in cold air and pests.

2. If you install an aluminum saddle (which we recommend), you will first have to remove the rubber sealing strip. Then, with the threshold held in position, mark for length and for any notches that might have to be cut out. Use a carpenter's square or straightedge to mark straight across the threshold. Cut the aluminum piece with a hacksaw. You can remove any burrs formed by using a small file on the corners and wherever else you made cuts. Position the saddle in place and use an awl to mark for screw holes; then bore with an electric drill.

TIP: If you bore too deeply, the screws will not hold the threshold down snugly. Wrap tape around the drill bit to let you know when you've reached the depth of your screw shanks.

3. Using the proper size screwdriver, screw the threshold down snugly. Many builders like to run a bead of caulk on the outside edge before installing the threshold, but this is optional.

4. After installing the metal portion of the threshold, replace the rubber grommet. Squeeze the edges together and slip them into the metal grooves. You may have to use a screwdriver with a thin blade to help push the rubber down properly.

Installing a prehung door unit

The prehung door is a great convenience for home handyman and professional alike. The unit comes with the door already hinged in a factory-assembled frame. All you do is order the right size, slip it into the door opening, square it up, and nail it into place. This not only saves a great deal of time but also eliminates much fuss, irritation, and uncertainty. Few tools are needed; just a bit of time, very little experience, and some plain common sense.

Position the door in the opening; be sure not to remove any diagonal packing strips or blocking. It is important that you have the door plumb as well as square. Shim it if you need to do so.

Fasten the door in place with 10-penny casing nails, but don't drive them all the way in. Remove the corner block from the upper corner. This holds the door square in the frame until you have installed it. Check for squareness again and if all is well then finish driving the nails into place. Last step is to install the knob.

What it takes

Approximate time: One hour.

Tools and materials: Hammer, 10-penny casing nails, level, square, screwdriver, and prehung door. Scrap cedar shingles make good shims. Doorknob, and lock hardware if desired, can usually be purchased with the door.

1. First position the door in the opening. Be sure not to remove any blocking or diagonal packing strips. The door shown will open onto a deck that is yet to be built.

2. Make certain that the door is square and plumb. Shim with pieces of wood shingle if necessary. Use both square and level on the top and both sides to make sure the door is in the correct position. Remember that there will be an opening at the bottom for a threshold, or saddle.

3. Fasten the door in place by driving 10-penny casing nails through the casing into the door framing. Do not drive the nails all the way in, but leave the heads protruding.

4. Remove the corner block from the upper corner. This holds the door square in the frame until it has been installed.

5. Again check to see if the door and frame are square. Realign if necessary and finish driving the nails.

6. Install the doorknob as per the instructions which are packed with the door.

Installing a sliding patio door

What it takes

Approximate time: A full day's work.

Tools and materials: Hammer, level, screwdriver, circular saw or handsaw, Yankee screwdriver, electric drill and bits, caulking gun and caulking compound, tape measure or folding rule, pencil, 2x4 for wedge, 10-penny casing nails, 8-penny finishing nails, Number 8 flathead screws (1 inch long), lumber for two 2x8 headers and for 2x4 studs, wood shims, and sliding door unit of your choice with accessories.

Here's a job that would seem a huge undertaking but can actually be quite simple. It all depends on the type of door you buy and how it is installed. The essential thing is to pay careful attention to leveling and plumbing the door to insure that it will work properly on the slide rails.

Basically, there are two steps: first the framing and then the actual installation of the door. For the first step follow the diagrams below and the accompanying instructions. The installation procedure is shown on the opposite page.

The framing sequence consists of measuring for the opening, constructing a header and jack studs, and sheathing the exterior. Installation involves several aspects of weatherproofing in addition to securing the door unit in place.

The corner you cut may be your own.

I read the instructions carefully about keeping everything level and square. Only I didn't realize that the square I was using was itself not square. I'd bought a cheap one thinking I could save. I know now that a good carpenter relies on good tools.

Practical Pete

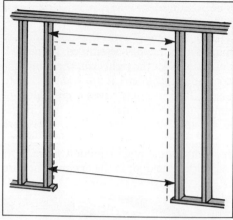

1. Lay out the door opening width between the regular studs to equal the width of the sliding door rough opening *plus* the thickness of the two regular studs, shown in dashed vertical lines. (Standard door widths conform to standard stud intervals.)

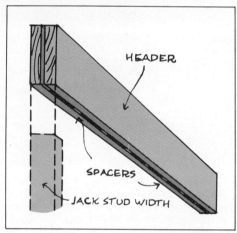

HEADER

SPACERS

JACK STUD WIDTH

2. Build the header (two 2x8s) to equal the rough opening width of the door plus the thickness of the two jack studs. Nail the header together with adequate spacers so that the header thickness will equal the width of the jack studs.

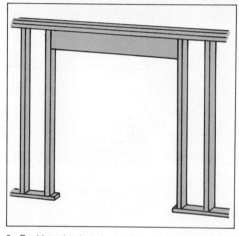

3. Position the header at the proper height and between the regular studs. Nail through the regular studs into the header in order to hold it in place until the next step.

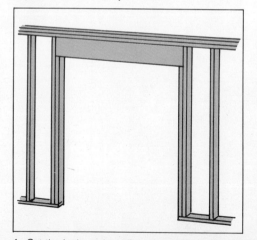

4. Cut the jack studs to fit under and support the header; then nail them to the regular studs.

EXTERIOR SHEATHING

5. Apply the outside sheathing flush with the header and jack stud framing members. It is important at this point to make sure that the rough opening is plumb and square and that the floor is level.

The installation

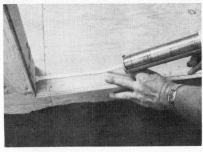

1. Run a bead of caulking compound across the bottom of the opening to provide a tight seal between the door sill and the floor.

2. Position the frame in the opening from the inside. Apply pressure to the sill to properly distribute the caulking compound. The door frame sill must be level. Shim if necessary.

3. Secure the sill to the floor by nailing along the inside edge with 8-penny finishing nails.

4. Temporarily secure the jamb in the opening with 10-penny casing nails through each side of the opening. Make sure the jamb is square and plumb by providing shims between the side jambs and the jack studs. Nail through the casing into the framing.

5. Position the flashing on the head casing and secure it by nailing through the vertical leg. The vertical center brace may now be removed but be sure to save the head and sill brackets for later use.

6. Apply the treated wood sill under the protruding metal sill facing. Fasten this tightly to the underside of the metal sill with 10-penny casing nails.

7. Position the stationary door panel in place in the outside run. Be sure the bottom rail is straight with the sill. Force the door into the run of the side jamb with a 2x4 wedge. Check the position by aligning the screw holes of the door bracket with the holes in the sill and the head jamb. If the door happens to be a triple door, repeat the procedure.

8. Note the mortise in the bottom rail for the bracket. Secure the bracket with Number 8 flathead screws, 1 inch long, through the predrilled holes. Position the head bracket in the top mortise; drill and secure in place. Align the bracket with the predrilled holes in the head jamb and secure with screws. Repeat the procedure for any other panels.

9. Install the security screws through the parting stop into the stationary door top rail.

10. Place the operating door on the rib of the metal sill facing and tip the door in at the top Then position the head stop and fasten in place with screws.

11. If the door sticks or binds, it is not square with the frame. Remove the caps from the two adjusting sockets on the outside of the bottom rail. Insert a screwdriver and turn to raise or lower the door.

12. Your final step is to install the hardware.

A new storm door is an easy job

What it takes

Approximate time: One hour.

Tools and materials: Hammer, screwdriver, electric drill and bits or Yankee push drill, caulking gun and cartridge, chisel, carpenter's square, and door unit plus accessories provided in kit.

TIP: If you're planning on repainting the door jamb and trim, now's the time for the job, before installing the new door unit.

One of the simplest jobs you can do is install a new storm door. This one task can save a tremendous amount of money on heating and cooling bills.

The most popular units are aluminum and combine both the glass for winter protection and screening for summer use. You can also purchase storm doors in wood, or even in fancy metal shapes that will complement any front entry way.

Simplest and fastest is to purchase a prehung door. These are available in all standard sizes at most building supply dealers. Before you shop, measure the inside of the door opening from casing to casing. A prehung door unit fits inside this measurement, while the outside aluminum flange fits over the outside of the casing. If your dealer doesn't have your size in stock, he can normally get it within ten days.

Remove the old storm door, or if you are making your installation on a door that does not already have a storm, then take off any fancy door trim.

See how the unit fits in the opening. It may be necessary to cut down the inside corners of the casing somewhat so the door rests flush on the sill. On the other hand you may find that the unit doesn't fit because the jamb is out of square, or there may be old paint in the way. In this event, a little chiseling will do the trick.

Try the unit again. If it fits this time remove it and run a bead of caulking compound along the inside edge of the outer flange; then push the unit into place permanently. Bear in mind that the unit has to fit the opening with the hinge side tight against the wooden jamb.

With the unit in proper position, bore pilot holes for the holding screws through the screw holes in the outside flange—but not too large, or the screws won't hold.

Fasten the flange in place securely with the screws that come with the unit; then remove the retainer clips. Install the catch, the automatic door closer, and the spring chain unit. Push down the bottom expander strip until the vinyl sweep touches the door sill; drive the screws in place to hold the strip.

Finally, you will need to adjust the closure and spring unit so the door will close tightly but without banging.

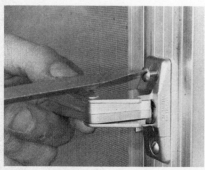

1. As soon as you have your new unit, remove the old storm door. If you are putting in your new storm door where there was no storm previously, then remove any fancy trim that might be in the way.

2. Try the new door in the opening. You may have to cut off some of the inside corners to allow the door to fit flush on the existing door sill. Or the opening itself may be out of square, or there may be old paint blocking a neat fit. In this case, try a bit of chiseling.

3. Once the unit is positioned well, bore pilot holes for the holding screws through the guide holes in the outside flange. Be careful to bore these to proper size.

4. Carefully read the instructions packaged with the door on how to install the catch, and follow them exactly. This is a simple job, but it must be precise.

5. Still following instructions, install the automatic door closer and the spring chain unit.

6. Adjust the closure and spring unit so the door won't bang shut, yet will close tightly each time. On many units this simply means turning the outside knob on the closure unit.

Maintaining a garage door

Nowadays, most garages are built with overhead doors; at the same time, a number of older structures still have hinged or folding doors. All require maintenance.

Hinge-mounted garage doors tend to sag, and so opening and closing can become difficult. The problem of loose screws or hinges can be dealt with by first tapping wood wedges under the corner that has dropped and raising the door until it is level. At this point tighten all the screws in the hinges. If this isn't possible, perhaps because the hole is too loose, use longer screws that will grip; or it may be necessary to reposition the hinges so that the screws can meet solid wood. Of course, if a hinge is damaged in any way it should be replaced. Hinges should be kept oiled.

Suppose the door sags, but its hinges are tight. It means that it is probably not square. To correct this problem, place wedges under the door until it is hanging straight. Reinforce the corners with right-angle metal mending plates, and attach a metal door brace with a turnbuckle. It is also possible to brace the door with a 1x4 piece of lumber, attaching it diagonally across the door face with flathead screws.

The most popular garage door, the overhead, comes in two basic types—the swing-up and the roll-up. Both use a heavy spring, or springs. The roll-up has a track; the swing-up may or may not.

Swing-up doors do not as a rule require much maintenance, except for their moving hardware. This should be kept lubricated with powdered graphite or oil. Lubricate the hinges and rollers when the door is in the down position. If there are tracks, check that they are clean because oil collects dirt. Any nicks that you notice in the tracks should be straightened out.

Most of the binding or dragging in the case of a roll-up garage door is the result of poor track alignment or the need for lubrication. The vertical tracks need to be plumb, and the two curved sections must be at the same height. When you inspect the track, make sure the overhead part slants slightly downward toward the rear of the garage so that when the door is raised it will stay up. Crimps in the track can very likely be straightened, but more serious damage of course means replacement.

When you have tried everything else as the possible source of trouble, you can check the spring. Perhaps you have the sort of roll-up door with a spring on either side. Try shortening the cable while the door is up. The cable is knotted to a hole in a plate above the door. Move the holding knot inward to shorten the cable.

The other type of roll-up door has a torsion spring in the center. This type really requires a professional, for the torsion is tremendously strong. You could get hurt.

But the springs on a swing-up door hook into holes or notches. These can be adjusted by moving the spring hook from one notch or hole to another.

Garage doors sometimes cause problems when they become too heavy. A wooden door for instance, can easily absorb a lot of moisture. You can prevent this situation by painting the door. Paint both sides, as well as the top, bottom, and side edges.

What it takes

Approximate time: Most check-ups and repairs take less than an hour.

Tools and materials: Hammer, screwdriver, carpenter's square, level, adjustable wrench, machine oil or powdered graphite, grease, paint, cleaning solvent, and wedges are among the items you may need, depending on the type of job you have to do.

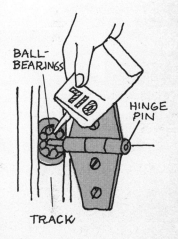

BALL-BEARINGS · HINGE PIN · TRACK

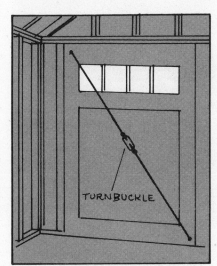

To eliminate sag in a swing-type door you can use a metal brace or wire with a turnbuckle. Install it diagonally from the top at the hinge side to the opposite corner.

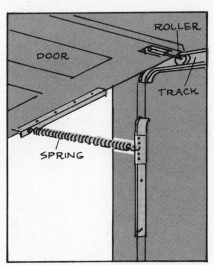

A swing-up garage door of this type has a track. It is important to check that all hardware is tight. (There is another type of swing-up door that does not have a track.)

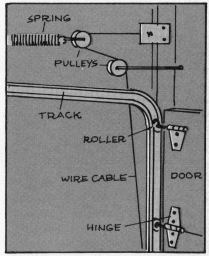

This type of door rolls up, has two springs, one at each side. The track, as well as the roller bearings, must be kept free of dirt and well oiled.

Safety glazing

What it takes

Approximate time: Half an hour.

Tools and materials: Screwdriver, hammer, acrylic cutting tool, ruler, straightedge, heavy gloves, and sheet acrylic to fit.

Glass can be a hazard around the house, especially where active children are present. The places to watch carefully are sliding glass doors, storm doors, and shower and bathtub enclosures. Many states have adopted safety glazing rules as part of their building codes. Even though these new codes may not be in effect where you live, you might wish to replace breakable glass in these particular locations with safety glazing materials.

Safety glazing materials include tempered glass, laminated glass, wire glass, and certain rigid plastics approved by the American National Standards Institute. There are drawbacks to some of these. Tempered glass cannot be cut to size after it leaves the factory. Laminated glass lacks impact resistance and is not available thinner than 1/16 inch. Wire glass lacks breakage resistance, is not optically clear, and is difficult to install.

The most effective and easiest safety glazing material for the homeowner to install is a rigid-plastic material such as acrylic sheet. In ¼-inch thickness this material is 17 times stronger than glass, and it does not break in the dangerous manner of ordinary glass; fragments are larger, have relatively dull edges, and seldom cause laceration injury.

Installing acrylic sheet in storm windows, doors, or even shower doors is a very simple operation that can be done quickly.

Storm doors

1. The first step in storm-door glass replacement is to take out the sash. Carefully remove the rubber retainer gasket and broken glass. Clean off all dirt and glass fragments. Wear leather gloves.

2. Before starting to cut be sure your measurements are exact. One method of cutting acrylic sheet is to use a straightedge as a guide and score with a sharp cutting tool.

3. After scoring, place scribed line on a wooden dowel and press down to snap off.

4. Remove protective masking paper and place in frame. Press rubber gasket in place.

5. Reinsert the repaired sash in the storm door frame.

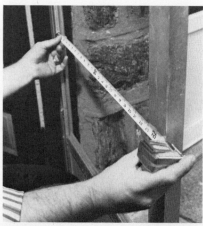

6. Another method is to discard the sash frame. (This is your best option anyway if it's at all bent out of shape). Then measure the opening exactly.

7. After cutting acrylic sheet to an exact fit, place it directly into opening.

8. Rotate the frame clamps into place and tighten them. It's a good idea to caulk around the glass if you use this no-gasket method.

Shower doors

What it takes

Approximate time: One hour.

Tools and materials: Screwdriver, hammer, sheet acrylic cutting tool, straightedge, ruler, leather gloves, sandpaper, and plastic panel to fit (⅛-inch thickness usually works best).

1. Remove the shower-stall door, usually by loosening screws in the hinges.

2. Remove the screws on all four corners of the shower door frame. Save the screws. Disassemble the entire frame. Take care that you don't produce burrs on the metal edges.

3. Wearing leather gloves, carefully remove glass. Clean the rubber gasket and the frame. Measure the opening and cut plastic to fit. Cut 1/32″ per foot less than the measured dimensions to allow for thermal expansion of the material.

4. Fit the gasket around the plastic sheet. Gently sand the edges of the plastic smooth and carefully press the frame over the rubber gasket on all four sides. Replace the screws and rehang the door.

5.INSULATION

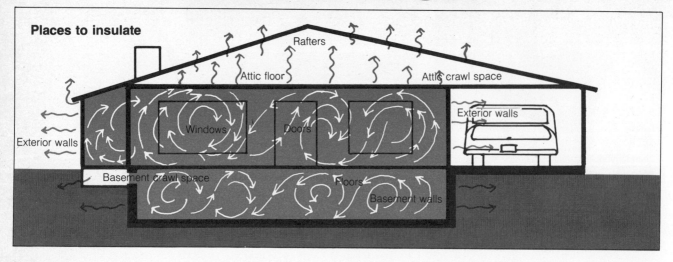

Places to insulate

Rafters
Attic floor
Attic crawl space
Exterior walls
Windows
Doors
Exterior walls
Basement crawl space
Floors
Basement walls

The best way to save money on your heating and cooling bills and to live comfortably in your home is to insulate the large, flat areas exposed to outside temperatures. With proper insulation, the average house (15% window area, two outside doors, and exposure to only light winds) can retain 75% of the heat that would pass out through uninsulated floors, walls, roof, and windows.

Heat enters or escapes not only through cracks but by radiation through the various materials your home is sheathed with. It travels through metal and glass quickly, through plaster and wood less quickly, and slowest of all through pockets of dead air sealed around with some other material. Commercial insulating material is like wool and feathers because it contains millions of these tiny air pockets.

The effectiveness of various insulation materials is rated in "R" values. The R value indicates the material's resistance to the flow of heat through it. The higher the R value the lower the loss of heat and the greater the saving on heating and cooling costs. The first inch of insulation has a much higher R value than the next inch, and so on.

Insulating the exposed areas of a house is a job anyone can do. It requires very little physical strength, simple tools, and no carpentry skills. Although the work area is awkward to reach sometimes, it is easier than painting. The one major exception is putting insulation in the spaces between interior finished walls and the outer skin of the house. It must be blown in by machine.

Insulation also absorbs sound, and many of the new materials will resist or retard fire. But a word of caution: read any safety warnings in the instructions for indications that gloves might be required, because the fibers can work into your skin; likewise, check to see if you'll need goggles or a mask.

Rigid

Batt

Blanket

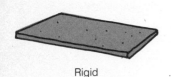

Loose-fill

Where to check for heat loss

The attic is where a great deal of heat can be lost because hot air rises. Check between the floor joists in the attic to see if old insulation has settled. Be sure that you have insulation material between the rafters and/or on top of the attic ceiling. Insulating your attic can lower heat loss by as much as one-quarter in many cases.

The basement. Insulate interior walls between heated and unheated rooms. Where the basement is not heated, or in crawl spaces, insulate the underside of the overhead flooring. The place where the building meets the foundation walls and any outlet ducts should be sealed tight.

Exterior walls, especially on the windy side of the house, are extremely critical sources of heat loss because of their large area. Most houses have insulation blown between the interior and exterior walls when they are built. If you are in doubt about your house, check it by looking down between the wall studs from the attic, or bore a hole into the space between an interior and exterior wall. If you don't see insulation, then you can have it professionally blown into the walls.

Doors and windows often develop cracks, as the house settles, between the units and their framing, or between the framing and the interior or exterior walls. Glass conducts heat, so if you use double or triple pane windows, the air locks between the panes will provide good insulation. On the same principle, storm windows and doors can reduce heat loss by up to 15%. And you should also see that your house is caulked.

Types of insulation

There are four general categories of home insulating materials.

Blanket insulation comes in long rolls of different widths and thicknesses. You use it in the long spaces between floor joists and rafters or wall studs.

Batt insulation is almost the same as blanket except that it is cut or perforated into lengths of about 48 inches and 96 inches. Its outside covering can be of paper, or foil which will act as a vapor barrier.

Loose-fill insulation can be poured into walls and between floor joists. It is the least expensive form of insulation, but it does lose efficiency as it settles over the years and needs to be added to.

Rigid insulation comes in boards of various composition. It can be used either inside or outside the house. There are new forms of this type which look like decorative paneling. These are great if you're planning to turn your basement into living quarters.

	Insulation type	Packaging	Where to use	Installation	Pros and cons
BLANKETS	Mineral wool	Slag; rock; glass wool.	In ceilings; between studs in walls; between rafters.	Staple or tack between studs or rafters; bow in to form air space between wall and blanket.	**Plus:** Cheap; gives continuous vapor barrier. **Minus:** Can irritate eyes, skin, nose; must be cut to size.
	Cotton	Fireproof blanket.	In ceilings; between studs in walls; between rafters.	Staple or tack between studs or rafters; bow in to form air space between wall and blanket.	**Plus:** Clean; lightweight; efficient. **Minus:** Must be cut to size; can irritate eyes, skin, nose.
	Wood-fiber matt	Paper-enclosed rolls.	In ceilings; between studs in walls; between rafters.	Staple or tack between studs or rafters; bow in to form air space between wall and blanket.	**Plus:** Comes in many widths; efficient. **Minus:** Inconvenient for small jobs, as it must be cut to length.
	Fibrous blanket	Compressed roll.	In ceilings; between studs in walls; between rafters.	Expand by pulling to full length; then staple or tack between studs or rafters; bow in to form air space between wall and blanket.	**Plus:** Easy to handle; compact; does not irritate; can be cut to desired width. **Minus:** May require added vapor barrier.
BATTS	Mineral wool	Rock; slag; or glass.	In ceilings, walls, and roofs, where framing interval can accommodate standard batt width.	Lay between attic floor joists, or nail or staple to studs.	**Plus:** Inexpensive; handy size; built-in vapor barrier. **Minus:** Barrier is discontinuous; loose batts shed irritating particles.
LOOSE-FILL	Mineral wool	Sacks of rock, slag, or glass.	Spread on attic floor between joists; pack into areas around pipes and within walls.	Pour between joists, raking level.	**Plus:** Cheap; easy to install. **Minus:** No vapor barrier; irritates skin, eyes, sinuses.
	Vermiculite	Bags of shredded mica.	Spread on attic floor between joists; pack into areas around pipes and within walls.	Pour between joists, raking level.	**Plus:** Easy pouring; good for filling in masonry walls. **Minus:** No vapor barrier; on the costly side.
	Wood fiber	Bales.	Spread between attic floor joists.	Pack between joists; add vapor barrier if necessary.	**Plus:** Fills wall space; retards fire. **Minus:** Not widely sold; creates no vapor barrier.
RIGID	Compacted	Asphalt-impregnated fiber board; cellular glass.	Fasten to masonry walls; wedge against exterior foundation.	Cement to masonry or insert around foundation and then backfill.	**Plus:** Stiff; moisture-resistant; can be used in many places where other types can't. **Minus:** Expensive; limited insulating power.
	Board	Plank, board, or tile built into structure.	Additions; basements or attics to be converted to living space.	Fasten with staples, nails, or specially made clips.	**Plus:** Cheap. **Minus:** Insufficient in some climates.

The vapor barrier

A vapor barrier is actually a material that will neither absorb moisture nor allow moisture to pass through it. Thus it prevents the insulation from becoming wet or matted and losing its effectiveness.

Plastic, metal foil, and asphalt between layers of brown paper are commonly used as vapor barriers. While the main purpose of the barrier is to keep insulation from getting wet, it is also a way of retaining moisture in the air inside the house. Moist air is warmer than dry air. When the vapor barrier is made from a material with a shiny surface, such as foil (reflective insulation), it can reflect heat back toward its source.

The vapor barrier may completely enclose the insulation, as in blanket insulation, or it may be attached to one side of the batts and installed with the barrier toward the inside of the house. Another method is to place the insulation material where you want it and then cover the inside surfaces with a vapor barrier, perhaps polyethylene, before putting on the wall finish.

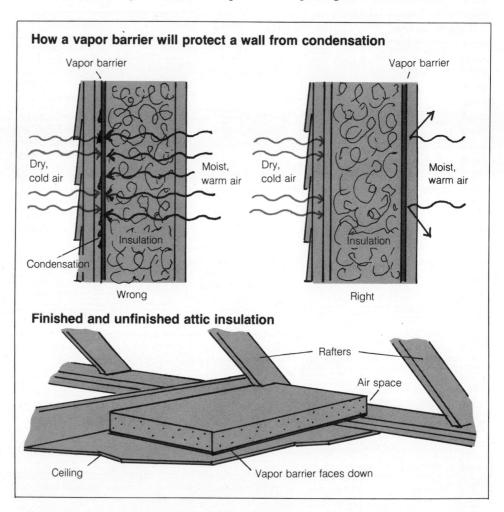

How a vapor barrier will protect a wall from condensation

Vapor barrier

Dry, cold air

Moist, warm air

Insulation

Condensation

Wrong

Vapor barrier

Dry, cold air

Moist, warm air

Insulation

Right

Finished and unfinished attic insulation

Rafters

Air space

Ceiling

Vapor barrier faces down

When you install a vapor barrier the rule is to place it as close as possible to the inside or warm surface of exposed ceilings, walls and floors. There is an exception to this in the case of insulation used with concrete floor slabs, where a barrier is put underneath the insulation in order to protect it from ground moisture that would otherwise rise.

When insulating a floor, place the insulation with the vapor barrier up except where you are using vapor-barrier paper in place of the building paper over the subfloor. In such a case, it may face down.

In reinsulating—your attic, for example—it is best to use unfaced insulation only. The facings are vapor barriers, and since they prevent moisture in warm air inside your house from rising to condense as it hits the cold air in the attic, you are creating a problem if you add one vapor barrier to another. If you find that you do have to add a faced batt to existing insulation then be sure that you slit the facing on the new material with long gashes.

In the case of insulating an unheated attic for the first time, you may dispense with a vapor barrier so long as you have proper ventilation. You can check with your local building supplier on what the adequate ratio of ventilation to attic area may be.

Insulating an unfinished attic

Your attic is a good place to start, first because heat normally rises and escapes through the roof and unfinished walls; second, because no carpentry or special skill is needed to lay or staple insulation between exposed floor joists, rafters and studs. Even if the area is partly finished with a floor and interior walls, but unused, you can attach blanket insulation right over them in a few hours. If the attic floor has insulation that has settled and matted down with age, destroying most of its effectiveness, simply lay new insulation right over it.

If there is no insulation, you must lay vapor barrier (polyethylene sheeting) material on the floor under the insulation. This will help prevent moist warm air from condensing into water when it hits the unheated attic air. Some types of batt and blanket insulation are sold with vapor barrier material on one or both sides. Face it down on the floor; out toward the room on the walls and overhead areas.

On the floor spread loose fill insulation to an even depth between the floor joists and on top of the vapor barrier material; or simply roll out blanket insulation between the joists without attaching it. It is sold as rolls in widths that fit between joists, beams and studs, so you need only cut them to the length you need. Cut scraps to fit irregular areas. To leave ducts, pipes and wiring accessible, cut the blanket at the obstacles and pour loose fill around them.

Rafters and walls. Blanket insulation can be fastened or batts stapled at 8-inch intervals between the rafters or studs on the walls, keeping the vapor barrier toward the inside of the house. Leave an inch or more of space for ventilation between insulation and roof sheathing when you staple the insulation to the rafters. Do not cover any vents, exhaust fan motors, wiring or lighting fixtures. Stuff the insulation between them and the exterior wall. Before you order insulation sold in rolls to fit between rafters, joists or studs, measure the distance between these wooden supports (usually 14 inches), as well as the total area you must cover in length.

If you wish to insulate under the floors of your home, go down to the basement or crawl space and staple insulation batts to the joists. If you can't staple the insulation, special gadgets are made for holding insulation in place. The most common are sheets of wire mesh, to be nailed to the bottoms of wood beams, or stiff wires precut to the right length to jam between rafters or joists, bowing upward to hold the insulation in its proper place.

Don't forget to attach insulation to the cold side of doors leading from unheated rooms into heated areas.

What it takes

Tools and materials: Staple gun and staples, or other support hardware, for blanket or batt insulation; knife or scissors, gloves, blanket, batts and/or loose-fill insulating material, wide boards (to walk on so you don't step through the ceiling of the room below); polyethylene sheeting if the insulation material does not have vapor barrier attached.

If there is no insulation on the attic floor, lay the insulation with the vapor barrier side downward. If you are using blanket insulation without a vapor barrier attached to it, or are spreading loose-fill insulation, lay polyethylene sheeting down first.

To make a rake for spreading loose-fill evenly, cut the blade out of ½-inch plywood about 4 inches wider than the distance between the floor joists. Notch the ends so that they will ride along the tops of the joists and cut the bottom of the blade flat so it will clear the floor below by the depth of fill you want.

To insulate and vent a crawl space

Attic and crawl space ventilation are mandatory both in summer and winter to keep condensation from collecting inside the house. In winter leave the louvers open; and always provide at least two vent openings. An exhaust fan is useful in areas that are difficult to ventilate. In an unheated crawl space, ground cover is required to keep down humidity and to protect the living area overhead from moisture.

Stapling batts to rafters or studs is one of the quickest methods of putting insulation on unfinished ceilings or walls. Batt insulation has flaps on each side to make stapling easy.

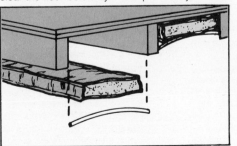

Wire fasteners can be used instead of staples on blanket insulation when it is used in attic, or in basement ceiling or crawl space. Simply jam the two ends between the wood beams at intervals that will keep the insulation firm. The tension will hold them in place and support the insulation.

How to calculate how much insulation to buy.

To determine the total floor area to be insulated, measure the distance between the joists as well as the length and width of the attic. You must account for space taken up by the joists, and so if your attic is built on 24-inch centers, multiply the area by 0.94. If it is on 16-inch centers multiply by .90. The insulation packages will have printed on them the amount of square feet of material, so it's easy to figure how many packages to buy.

Insulating around openings

Windows and doors

What it takes

Approximate time: Fifteen minutes for insulating an untrimmed window; two hours for removing and replacing trim, plus time for painting.

Tools and materials: Hammer, pliers, wide chisel or stiff putty knife, pry bar, flat piece of wood for paddle, insulating and vapor material, paint, spackle or putty, sandpaper.

Most old houses, and some new ones, lack insulation around windows and doors. Even if the rest of the house is thoroughly insulated, these areas can lose a good deal of heat, or cooling, through simple leakage.

If your house or addition is still in the process of being built you may consider putting in triple-pane windows, which lock air between the panes and provide good insulation. Glass is one of the areas through which heat escapes in winter and enters your house in summer. Another thing you can do is to make sure there is insulation around your door and window frames. You can also check for insulation around your attic windows, which may still not be trimmed even though your house is otherwise complete. Pack pieces of insulation into the cracks between the window and door frames and the rough framing. Remember that all insulated cracks should be covered with a vapor barrier.

1. Tear off pieces of insulation material and stuff them in between the window unit and framing. Wear gloves to protect your skin. Use a scrap of wood, as shown, to push the insulation in tight. The principle is the same for doors as for windows.

2. All areas that are insulated should be covered on the *inside,* or next to the living area, with a vapor barrier, as shown here. Staple it in place.

Removing trim

If you find that your windows and doors were installed and finished without adequate insulation, you will have to remove the trim to get at them. This isn't difficult, but it does take patience and care. If you are the type who likes to rush, then forget it and hire a professional. But if you wish to try for yourself, then allot a good amount of time for the job—at least a couple of hours. Try to work with patience.

Score and cut the paint line between the trim and the surface it joins. With a wide chisel or stiff-bladed putty knife, ease out the trim. Go very slowly, working from the corners toward the center of each strip. You can use a pry bar as a lever to reach under the trim. Be careful not to force the trim beyond its ability to bend, and also take

---

New wrinkles

In the effort to save energy, one of the most easily applicable devices is a transparent insulating window film. The film is actually a shield that reduces heat transmitted through windows, while maintaining a satisfactory level of visibility. An added advantage is that it turns ordinary glass windows into safety glass. Ask your hardware dealer about it. It's a simple procedure to attach the film.

The first step is to clean the window. Make a soapy mix with a teaspoon of liquid dishwashing detergent and one pint of water. Put it in a spray bottle and thoroughly spray the glass you wish to cover. Use a single-edge razor blade, if necessary, to clean off any debris that sticks. The important thing is to start with a window that is completely clean, dry, and free of lint.

Place the film on a clean, flat surface and cut it to ¼ inch larger all around, than the desired size. To separate the film from its backing, place a small piece of masking tape at one corner. Place a second piece of tape on the same corner, but on the opposite side, without letting the two pieces touch each other. Pull the tapes apart and the backing will separate from the film.

Wet the side of the film that was next to the clear plastic backing. You can put it under the water faucet or spray it. The film must be completely wet, even the edges. Then wet the glass thoroughly; it should be soaking wet, right to the corners.

Lift the film by the corners and place the wet side on the glass. Move it until you have it positioned exactly. You will see now why it was necessary to use so much water. With the film positioned, spray the other side with water. Make sure it is completely wet.

Squeegee out all the excess water that has gathered under the film. Work from the center toward the edges of the glass. Use vertical and horizontal strokes only, but do not squeegee to the edges until you have trimmed the film. To trim, use a utility knife or single-edge razor blade and a straightedge. Leave a border of clear glass about 1/16 inch wide. Then squeegee to all the edges.

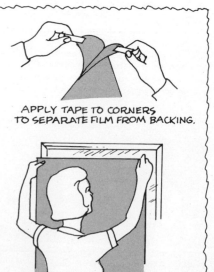

APPLY TAPE TO CORNERS TO SEPARATE FILM FROM BACKING.

LIFT FILM BY CORNERS AND LAY WET SIDE AGAINST GLASS.

care not to chip the wall. (This is why it was necessary to score and cut the paint line.)

When you have the trim partly raised, push it back in place so the nail heads protrude; then draw them all the way out. Use pliers, not a claw hammer or nail puller, to prevent scarring the wood. If you do have to use a hammer, be sure to place a piece of cardboard between the claw and the wood for protection against scarring.

With the trim off, remove any nails that are left. Clean off chipped paint and sand away any hard bead of paint that may remain between trim and wall surface.

After installing the insulation, replace the trim exactly as it was. You may have to use slightly larger nails. Spackle or putty, sand, and paint.

Insulating the basement

The basement is sometimes a living area but more often simply a space for storage, laundry, carpentry, or painting. Whether or not you wish to convert your basement into a usable living quarter, you will still require proper insulation on the ceiling and in any crawl space, as well as around windows and vents. On the other hand, if you do intend to convert your basement into everyday space, you will have to insulate the walls as well; and they will very likely be of concrete block.

Masonry walls may be insulated either with blanket insulation material and a vapor barrier, or foil-backed gypsum board which requires no barrier. If you plan on gypsum board, 1x2 furring strips should be used. Rigid insulation also can be purchased in the form of paneling to serve double duty as finished wall.

Ceilings may be insulated with batt or blanket material placed between the joists. This can be stapled to the joists, or it can be set tightly against the floor above and supported with wire fasteners made for that purpose. Or you may use crossed wire which will allow the insulation to rest at the bottom edges of the joists. It makes for better insulation if the material is snug against the upper floor. If there is bridging or any other obstruction, insulation must go under it; the vapor barrier must be placed at the top, and the ends of individual pieces must overlap.

Another way to cut heat loss is to install an acoustical-tile ceiling. This not only saves heat but insulates against undesirable noise as well.

The basement floor can of course be insulated if you are converting to living quarters, though this will probably require laying a whole new floor over the existing area. Insulation would be the same as for other floors in the house except if you have concrete floor slabs. In this case lay the vapor barrier under the insulation in order to protect against ground moisture.

Crawl space floors need as much insulation as the walls, plus a vapor barrier under the subfloor if the crawl space is unheated. There should be at least two inches of insulation around the walls of crawl spaces to reduce cold air from rising through the floors and walls.

Piping and ducts require insulation around, behind, or under them. It should be firmly secured, on the cold side of plumbing pipes, not in front on the warm side. Any pipe in an unheated basement or crawl space should be wrapped with insulation and then taped. Some companies sell special pipe and duct insulation which comes in various sizes, shapes, and styles. Insulation should be placed around electrical outlets but should not cover any outlet or hot-air vent.

Heaters and chimneys also need to be insulated; special covers can be purchased for heaters; a chimney needs insulation between the flue and any wood, such as rafters or floor joists or flooring. Make sure no paper backing is stuck to the pieces.

I almost got a real slow burn. I insulated carefully throughout my house, and even stuffed pieces of insulation down around the edges of my fireplace flue where the rafters and floor joists meet the chimney. This would have been a good idea, except that I left some paper backing on a few of the pieces and almost had a fire. Next time I'll remember that when you light a fire the chimney gets hot, and placing paper next to it is risky business.

Practical Pete

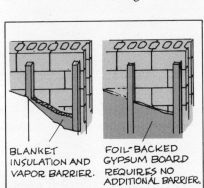

BLANKET INSULATION AND VAPOR BARRIER.

FOIL-BACKED GYPSUM BOARD REQUIRES NO ADDITIONAL BARRIER.

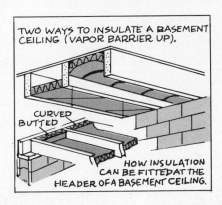

TWO WAYS TO INSULATE A BASEMENT CEILING (VAPOR BARRIER UP).

CURVED BUTTED

HOW INSULATION CAN BE FITTED AT THE HEADER OF A BASEMENT CEILING.

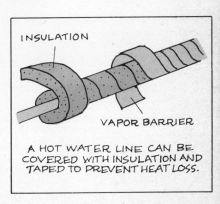

INSULATION

VAPOR BARRIER

A HOT WATER LINE CAN BE COVERED WITH INSULATION AND TAPED TO PREVENT HEAT LOSS.

Weather stripping

What it takes

Approximate time: For an average door, one to two hours, depending on the material used; a window will take less time.

Tools and materials: Staple gun and staples, hammer, tinsnips, hacksaw, handsaw, weather-stripping material of your choice.

One of the essential energy savers is weather stripping. If you live in an old house, you should weather-strip the windows and doors so that cracks and openings are sealed against the escape of costly heat or the intrusion of wintry air. Weather stripping can be purchased by the yard, or in kits with rustproof tacks for installation.

The way to check whether your doors (or windows) need weather stripping is to direct a portable hair dryer against the areas where the door itself meets the frame. Move the stream of air along the door while a helper, on the other side of the door, holds his hand against the crack between the door and the frame and marks any place where he feels air coming through. If you have just a few leaky places, you can perhaps fix the present weather stripping, but it might be the moment for a complete replacement.

Doors

Felt stapled all around the inside edge of the stop is the quickest and easiest method of weather-stripping a door.

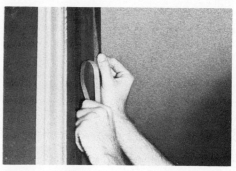

Adhesive-backed foam provides a somewhat tighter weather stripping. Just peel off the protective tape and adhere it to the inside of the door stop.

Foam-edged metal or plastic weather stripping can be purchased in kit form. It has two pieces for sides and one for the top. It is simply tacked in place on top of the stop and against the closed door.

Flexible metal weather stripping fits inside the door channel and behind the stop. The edge springs out and the door meets it to force it in place.

Foam-backed wood-molding weather stripping is also available in shapes similar to a doorstop. It can be applied over the door stop or instead of it. The same materials and methods of weather-stripping may be used on patio and roll-up garage doors.

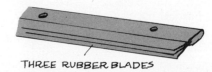

THREE RUBBER BLADES

Door sweep has triple blades of vinyl to close the gap that admits drafts under the door.

Aluminum strip with tubular vinyl (left) and **wood strip** with foam seal are both used for swing doors.

Windows

For double-hung windows the weather stripping is essentially the same as for doors: thin spring-metal strips, adhesive-backed foam, tubular vinyl as a covering over a sponge core. All of these attach to molding and fit neatly against sash. And the installation is simple.

Casement, jalousie, or awning-type windows which are metal-framed may be weather-stripped with a transparent vinyl tape which covers their edges, or with an adhesive-backed foam installed at the joints. Also available is an aluminum strip made especially for casements.

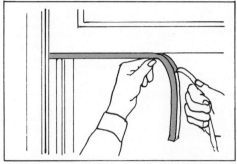

Adhesive-backed foam strip is applied to exterior of upper sash bottom rail, exterior of parting strips, and bottom rail of lower sash.

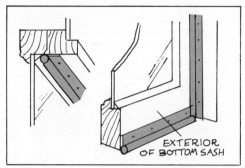

Vinyl weather stripping, either sponge or tubular kind, is nailed to exterior of upper sash bottom rail, and to exterior of parting strips and bottom rail on lower sash.

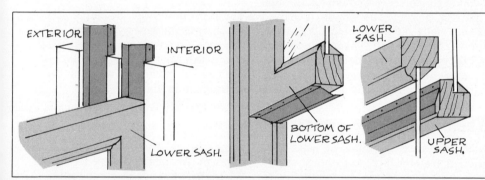

Spring-metal type is nailed to sash channels; be careful not to cover pulleys in upper channels. Nail a strip the full width of the sash to bottom of lower sash bottom rail; attach a strip to inside edge of upper sash bottom rail.

Insulation locks

Insulation locks are similar to regular sash locks but have the added advantage of pulling the sash together to prevent leakage between them. The secret in a good installation is to position the halves of the lock so they draw the windows tightly together, yet don't cause them to bind.

Stopgaps and copouts:

You don't necessarily have to mount a major campaign against that drafty door or window. Sometimes a fast application of a clay weather stripping will do the trick. It comes in rolls and looks like rope, but it acts like clay. Press it into place with your fingertips. It's self-adhering, yet comes off easily. And it can be used again.

Another quickie is the door-stripping kit—two 7-foot lengths and one 3-foot length, plus nails. Cut the pieces to length and hammer home.

Caulking seams

What it takes

Approximate time: A few minutes for small patching jobs; a full day or so to completely caulk an average house. Professionals figure it takes 1¼ hours to cover 100 lineal feet.

Tools and materials: Wire brush or scraper; mat knife or single-edge razor blade; cartridge of caulking compound and gun, or a squeeze tube; cleaning solvent and a clean rag.

Planning hints: The best time to caulk is in the fall, in preparation for winter. Work in warm weather—above 50°F. If that is not possible, warm the caulking cartridge before you apply its contents. In extremely hot weather—above 90°F—the caulking can get too runny. Place the tube in a refrigerator for an hour or two to slow it down.

A cartridge of caulking compound will cover approximately 100 lineal feet if you spread an average bead—about ¼ inch.

TIP: Before you apply caulk, it's a good idea to try a practice run on a scrap of wood so that you get the feel of the gun.

Caulking compound is one of the most potent weapons in guarding your home against winter attack. It works two ways, serving not only as a barrier against cold drafts, insects, and moisture, but it also eliminates heat loss during winter and so contributes toward a lower fuel bill.

Caulking is a compound of a semisolid substance and a binder of natural and synthetic oils to keep it resilient and elastic. It comes in five basic types, and it can stick securely to wood, masonry, and metal. It is able to expand and contract along with the surrounding surfaces that will shrink or swell according to the weather.

Caulking comes in bulk form and in disposable cartridges which are used with an applicator gun. (It can also be purchased in squeeze tubes and in rope form.) The caulking gun forces compound out through a narrow nozzle. The nozzle is moved steadily along the joint being filled, overlapping it on each side. There are two basic types of caulking guns: the full-barrel type, designed for bulk filling, and the half-barrel (drop-in type) which is used with

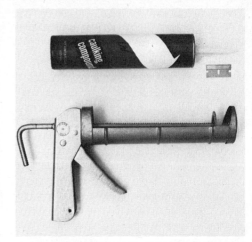

disposable cartidges; this is really handy.

Cartridges do cost a little more than bulk caulking, but they are more convenient. You just throw away the empty cartridge, which saves you a messy cleaning job on the gun each time you use it. Another advantage is that you can change color without cleaning or having to wait for the first cartridge to be finished.

Where should you caulk?

Caulk wherever two different parts (two different materials) come together with a crack in between. Here is a sample list of places to caulk:
1. Wherever wood meets masonry, for instance at the line where the house joins the foundation; 2. Around windows and doors where the framing and house siding join; 3. Where the chimney meets the roof; 4. At the place where porches or steps and the house itself come together; 5. Where plumbing vents come through the house;

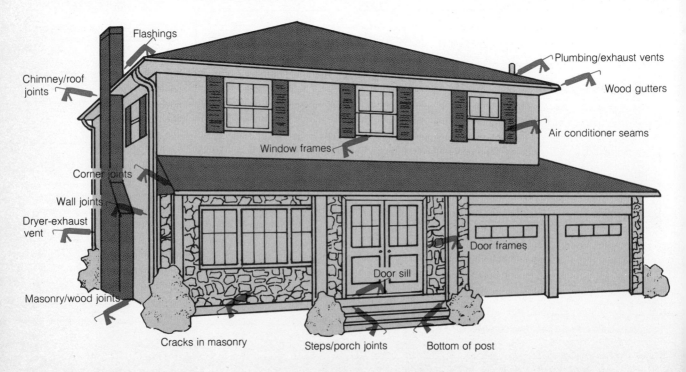

Flashings

Chimney/roof joints

Corner joints

Wall joints

Dryer-exhaust vent

Masonry/wood joints

Cracks in masonry

Steps/porch joints

Bottom of post

Door sill

Door frames

Window frames

Air conditioner seams

Wood gutters

Plumbing/exhaust vents

6. At corner seams where trim and siding meet; 7. In the space between an air conditioner unit and the window frame; 8. Between dormer cheeks and roof shingles; 9. Around the exhaust vent for a clothes dryer; 10. Around flashing and in the gap between flashing and shingles.

How to caulk

1. Clean out old caulking. This is important. Use a wire brush or scraper. Then clean the area with solvent so that it is quite free of dirt, oil, wax, or any dust. If it is not clean, the new compound will not hold.

2. With a mat knife or single-edge razor blade, cut the tip off the nozzle at a 45-degree angle. Make your cut at the place where it will allow you the proper size bead for the work at hand. The bead should overlap onto both surfaces.

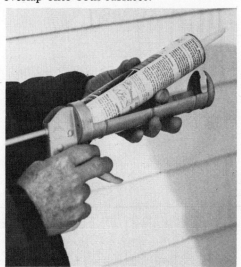

3. Load the half-barrel caulking gun by inserting the cartridge, rear first and with the nozzle opposite the trigger.
4. Break the plastic inner seal by pushing a nail or screwdriver back into the tip of the nozzle as far as the cartridge base.

It is best not to seal every seam in the house. A house needs to breathe and so you should allow some openings for moisture vapor to escape from inside the walls. Pick spots where strong drafts or water cannot enter, for instance where the bottoms of window sills and siding come together.

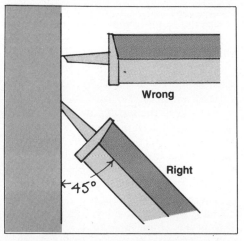

5. To apply caulk to a seam, hold the gun at an angle of 45 degrees, tilted in the direction of movement. The slant on the tip will help guide this.
6. Squeeze the trigger with an even, gentle pressure and the caulk will flow out.

7. Move it slowly and steadily along the crack, pressing lightly with the tip of the gun as you go. On vertical seams work from top to bottom; on horizontals, move across from left to right, or the reverse, depending on which hand you work with.
8. When finished, quickly lift the gun from the joint and twist the plunger rod so that it disengages and so stops the caulk from coming out. You can clean with solvent, soap, and water.

If you have very wide cracks to fill, you can put in oakum, then apply one or more beads to cover.

The trick to a smooth bead is to try to finish a seam without having to stop in the middle of it.

Caulk won't grip? Made a mess?
I have found that just cleaning out the old caulking may not do the trick. Sometimes you have to scrub the area with solvent and clean up dirt, oil, and mildew as well. Caulking won't stick to damp surfaces either. If you make a mess, don't worry. I scrape it up with a putty knife first, trying not to spread the caulk any further in the process. Then I wipe off what's left with a clean rag soaked in solvent and start over. Take your time, keep your eye on the bead, and keep the pressure of your trigger finger steady.

Practical Pete

Humidity and temperature control

Good insulation includes more than prevention of simple heat loss in the winter and cooling loss in summertime. It is also a question of controlling the kind of air inside your home. Comfort in your home is only partially dependent on temperature. There is also the factor of moisture content in the air. At 70 degrees, moist air feels warmer than dry air at 75 degrees. The lack of moisture in the air can make you feel cold even though the thermostat registers a comfortable temperature. And so, if you take steps to keep the air in your house moist, you can operate it at a lower temperature and with less cost. Low humidity also causes physical discomfort, and it dries out the furniture, so you may invite permanent damage if you don't take corrective steps.

There are a number of things you can do to raise the moisture level in your home during the winter months. If you are heating your home with hot air, you can add to the moisture content of the air by installing an automatic humidifier in the heating system. If your home is heated by hot water, you can fill containers with water and hang them or place them behind the radiators.

But if your home is heated by steam, the air is probably already moist enough, because even a well-maintained air-release valve will leak a little steam.

It is sensible to turn down the thermostat for short periods, even for a few hours. There is no gain in leaving the thermostat at 70 degrees all day when the house is empty. It can be pushed up during breakfast time, lowered when everyone leaves for work or school, raised for an hour at lunch, if necessary, and set down again until supper and the evening hours.

While it is true that if the whole house cools down to 60 degrees, it's going to take a long time to heat it back up to 70, nevertheless, it will actually feel warmer in the house while the temperature is rising than when it has become stabilized. This is because radiators put out most of their heat while the furnace is working. When the temperature has reached its goal of 70, the radiators cool down and there isn't much radiated heat in the room. Actually, when you raise the temperature for just a short time you are doing the most good, because you are warming the people rather than the house.

Humidifiers

The type of humidifier you may add to your central heating system will depend upon the type of heating in your home. If your central heating system cannot accommodate a built-in humidifier unit you can purchase one or more freestanding humidifiers.
Maintenance of a humidifier is simply a matter of keeping it clean and maintaining the fan motor as you would any other. Your best guide for maintenance will be the owner's manual. The most common problems arise from the fact that the water leaves mineral deposits after it evaporates. These mineral deposits form a scale which can hamper the unit's operation. With some humidifiers a fungus forms, and an odor may even develop. (See opposite page.)

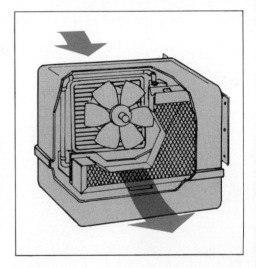

Dehumidifiers

On the other hand, too much moisture in the air can make you feel uncomfortably hot during the summer. Most excesses of humidity are brought on by cooking, taking showers, doing laundry, running a dryer, washing floors. The way to handle high humidity levels in the home is to install an attic fan or one or more dehumidifiers.

A dehumidifier consists of a fan that pulls air into the unit and passes it over refriger-

ated coils, causing the air to condense on the coils. The condensation then drips into a tray and flows through a hose to a drain. It may be that you cannot hook up the dehumidifier conveniently to a drain, and in such an event it must be emptied by hand.
Maintenance of a dehumidifier involves simple cleaning, especially the coils. To clean the coils you can use a bristle brush or a vacuum cleaner with a brush attachment.

TIP: Winter colds are aggravated and prolonged by dry air. So keep an inexpensive, portable humidifier handy and, when illness occurs, run it continuously in the sickroom with doors closed.

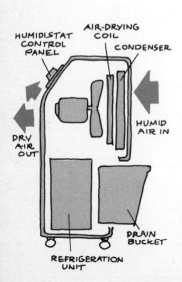

HUMIDISTAT CONTROL PANEL
AIR-DRYING COIL
CONDENSER
HUMID AIR IN
DRY AIR OUT
DRAIN BUCKET
REFRIGERATION UNIT

Hallmarks of a quality dehumidifier

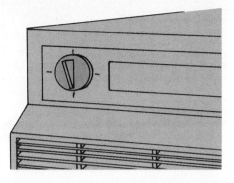

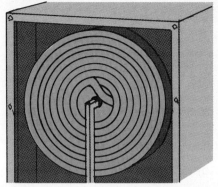

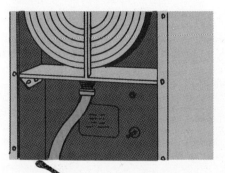

An adjustable humidistat automatically activates the unit as necessary to maintain desired humidity level.

Air-drying coils are exposed to simplify cleaning process.

A water catch bucket, holding up to 2½ gallons, can be easily removed and emptied.

A threaded connector for a garden hose alternatively allows direct removal to a nearby drain.

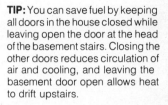

TIP: You can save fuel by keeping all doors in the house closed while leaving open the door at the head of the basement stairs. Closing the other doors reduces circulation of air and cooling, and leaving the basement door open allows heat to drift upstairs.

The mildew problem

Moisture in excess brings another problem in the form of mildew. Mildew is a fungus which feeds on moisture and dirt. Bathroom walls are one of the likeliest places for this household scourge. The soap dish at the sink is another.

The cure for mildew is to cover all the spots you see with household bleach. A plastic squeeze bottle is a good way to apply the bleach, for with it you can get into cracks, crevices, and grout lines between tiles. Be very sure that you follow all the caution notices on the label of the bleach bottle.

Most of the spots of mildew will disappear in a few minutes, but some will need more bleach and maybe a scrub. An old toothbrush is a handy tool for getting into corners and between tiles. When the mildew has gone, *rinse the area thoroughly with water. When you are satisfied that none of the bleach is left on the walls, wash the walls with household ammonia. This will kill the spores of the fungus and will prevent the swift return of the mildew. But it is very important that you do not mix bleach and ammonia. The two together release deadly chlorine gas.*

Unless you eliminate the conditions that encouraged the mildew in the first place, it will return. Find out what caused it. If mildew occurs in the kitchen, bathroom, or laundry, you know where the moisture came from. A dehumidifier or exhaust fan may be the best way to cope; or you may first want to try regular airing of the room. If the moisture comes from a leak under the house or faulty drainage, you will need to correct the problem to eliminate any return of mildew.

Mildew can also form outside your house. To get rid of fungus on exterior walls mix one quart household bleach, ⅓ cup of powdered detergent, and ⅔ cup of TSP—trisodium phosphate (get it at the paint store). Make a gallon of the solution by adding warm water. Scrub the area with a stiff brush; then hose it thoroughly.

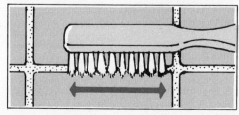

To get rid of mildew, scrub corners and between tiles with a stiff brush.

What it takes

Approximate time: Depends on the area involved; about 10 minutes per square foot.

Tools and materials: Old toothbrush, stiff hand brush or broom, garden hose, household bleach, household ammonia, plastic squeeze bottle, powdered detergent, and trisodium phosphate; for persistent problems, a dehumidifier or exhaust fan.

TIP: Trim back any foliage that prevents air and sunlight from reaching the problem areas.

When moisture accumulates

What it takes

Approximate time: Depends on the area involved and the extent of the problem. For cracks, figure about 15 minutes per square foot. For seepage, allow an hour per wall for waterproofing in an average-size basement; your outside work might involve a day or two. Condensation may be a matter of purchasing and plugging in a dehumidifier, a half hour, or installing an exhaust fan and/or louvers or vents, which can take up to a day or two for the average attic or basement.

Tools and materials: Among the items you may need are a hand mirror, hammer, stone chisel, garden hose, mason's trowel, stiff brush or broom, patching compound, waterproofing compound, louvers, dehumidifier and/or exhaust fan.

One of the more irritating household complaints is the damp basement. This usually results in a tremendous amount of wasted space in the house: a dry basement could be used for any number of purposes, whereas a basement that is damp becomes a liability.

The first thing to check out is where the moisture originates. Is it the house plumbing? If so, this may require professional attention. If the problem is not the plumbing, then the dampness must be due to leakage, seepage, or condensation.

Leakage is simply water that comes in from the outside through cracks. Seepage is also water from outside, but it travels through the pores in the concrete. Condensation is inside water which is actually humidity in the air until the moment it condenses on the cool masonry walls or cold water pipes.

It's simple enough to tell when the problem is leakage because you will see that the moisture is only present around cracks. But condensation and seepage are sometimes hard to differentiate. In order to find out which is present, attach a hand mirror to the wall in the center of a damp spot. Leave it overnight. If the mirror is fogged the following day, it means that there is condensation. If there is no fogging, then you have seepage.

Leakage can be dealt with by patching. You can buy hydraulic cement for this purpose. It sets quickly and in fact can actually set up while water is coming through the crack. Any crack that is more than a hairline should be undercut. You must make the crack wider beneath than it is on the surface. This is done best with a hammer and chisel. It will allow the cement to lock itself into place. Clean away all debris and wash out the opening. Use a hose

to force out loose material. Mix the patching compound, following the directions exactly. Work the mix into the crack, making certain it fills. Use a trowel. Finally, smooth the surface and let it cure as the instructions indicate.

Seepage may be dealt with further by coating the inside of your basement with waterproofing compound.

Waterproofing your basement walls is a simple job. Clean the walls. Wet them thoroughly. After mixing the compound as per directions, apply it with a stiff brush. Be sure to cover the walls thoroughly. If necessary put on a second coat. Of course, no matter how good the compound it will not reduce or eliminate your problem unless you handle the drainage situation outside the house.

The situation will simply recur, whether it is due to seepage or an outright leak. How did the water get to the crack in the first place? Check gutters and downspouts. They should be free of foreign materials and they should be pitched at an angle to carry the water off. The ground on which the downspouts spill should be sloped so that the water will flow away from the house. It's a good idea to put down concrete splash blocks.

Check the ground around the house to make sure it slopes away. If it doesn't, fill it until there is a proper run off. Roll and seed to prevent the soil from washing away. At the same time, be sure that walks and patios butting against the house also slope away. Check the joints to see that they are properly sealed and that they curve properly.

You may have a serious drainage problem outside the house which can be dealt with only by digging down around the foundation and laying drains. This may

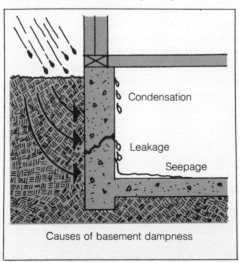

Causes of basement dampness

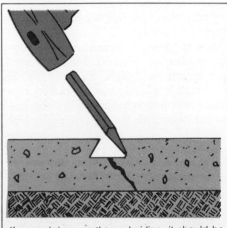

If a crack is more than a hairline, it should be undercut to let the cement lock itself in place.

require a professional hand, but it is possible to do it yourself if you are enterprising. Dig down below the basement floor, although not below the footing. Set a drain along each wall, and extend the drain out to carry the water away. The drain should consist of sections of clay tile pipe covered with about two feet of gravel. It's a good idea, while the outside wall is exposed, to coat it with waterproofing compound.

There are also companies that will pump a special sealing compound into the ground under pressure.

Condensation in your home simply means the transformation of water from vapor to liquid. This can be an all-too-familiar problem for the owner of even a well-insulated home. It is especially prevalent in the attic and in basement crawl spaces.

A house needs to breathe. In normal living, four people will produce 10½ pints of water vapor in a day. This will result from cooking, bathing, laundry, and breathing. This water needs to escape. When condensation shows on windows, it means the relative humidity is too high, and the moisture can't get out of the house. If you have water on your windows then you will know that there is water in your walls. Ice on the windows means ice in the walls. The first winter in a newly built home is the most troublesome as far as condensation

goes, for the building is still drying out. Condensation should not continue into the second heating season, however.

Attic condensation is best dealt with by louvers. Louvers should be placed at gable ends or under the eaves. The ratio of the louver area to the attic floor area should be about 1:300 to properly ventilate the attic, allowing humid air to escape but without losing a lot of heat. If your attic area is about 600 square feet, for example, the total louver area should be at least 2 square feet. (This figure should be doubled if you have screens on the louvers.)

Of course, if the attic is being used, then it should be insulated with a vapor barrier between all rafters, with adequate air space between vapor barrier and roof boards and venting at the eaves or ridge.

Crawl space condensation is equally a problem. Adding a ground moisture seal over the bare earth will help keep crawl space humidity at an acceptable level.

Attic and crawl space ventilation are as necessary in summer as in winter. Keep the louvers open in winter, and provide two vent openings as well. Try to face them so that air can flow in one and out the other, having traversed the insulated area or ground surface. If it is not possible to ventilate by natural means, then an exhaust fan can be the answer.

An attic fan

The attic fan's purpose is not to reduce temperature, but the air movement it causes will help cool the human body by evaporating perspiration. Because it replaces hot indoor air with cooler night air drawn in from outdoors, it will eventually reduce temperature and humidity.

There are two basic types of attic fan. One type is installed in the ceiling beneath the attic, and it draws air from the living area below into the unused attic space above. The air then moves outdoors through louvers, which are customarily in the gable ends. It is important that the louvers be big

enough to accommodate the volume of air that the fan will set in motion.

The other type of attic fan is installed in an opening that is cut in the gable end. The rest of the attic is sealed, with the exception of a louver through the ceiling to the living area downstairs. The indoor air moves into the attic as the fan draws out the attic air.

These fans come in a variety of sizes. It is the size of the blades and the speed of revolution that decide how many cubic feet of air can be moved per minute. Your building supplier can help you determine which size fan is best for your house.

Tips for keeping dry

- Turn off the humidifier.
- Ventilate wherever possible.
- Be sure the laundry dryer exhaust is vented to the outside.
- If you have a fireplace, open the draft.
- When cooking, turn on the exhaust fan; turn on the bathroom fan when bathing. Make sure that both of these exhaust outside.
- Remove inside screens in winter to allow more air circulation around windows. Open drapes and curtains.
- If you have a bow window and a condensation problem, make certain you have heavy insulation under the seat board as well as over the head board.
- Use one or more dehumidifiers.

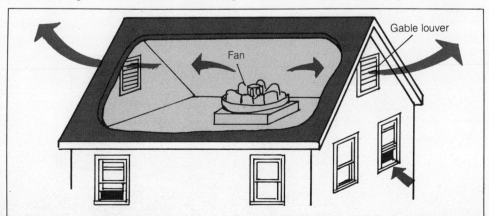

Gable louver

Fan

Air conditioners

What it takes

Approximate time: One or two hours.

Tools and materials: Screwdriver, mounting frame or cradle plus installation kit with necessary parts, weather stripping, heavy rubber gasket, and caulking compound.

Planning hints: It is important to check the wattage and amperage ratings on the unit you are planning to install against the electrical circuit in your home. Otherwise, you might overload the circuit. Your electrical supplier can help you with this.

Ways to lower your cooling load

- If your house has no shade trees close by and the outside walls are of a dark color, you might consider painting the house white next time around. White paint reflects a lot of heat and helps to cut costs.
- Likewise, if your house now has a dark-colored roof, switch to a lighter-colored shingle when you need to replace the roofing.
- Vent your clothes dryer to the outdoors.
- If you don't have a dryer, then hang wet laundry outdoors, never in the house.
- If you like to take a lot of showers, use a plastic shower curtain or a glass enclosure around the shower. Don't use a fabric shower curtain, because it will absorb water and add humidity to the air.
- If your house has awnings, keep the top edge of the awning an inch or so away from the house wall. This gap will let heated air escape from beneath the awning and so reduce the heat load on the window.

Cooling it in the summer can be as important as heating it in winter. For this, of course the basic requirement is air-conditioning. There are two general air-conditioning systems: *central air-conditioning* which cools the whole house, and *individual room units* which cool only the room where they have been installed. With central air-conditioning, you will more than likely have a contractor do the installation. But the individual room or window unit you can put in yourself.

How the individual unit works. Whether it is mounted in a wall or in a window, the individual unit functions by venting hot air from both the fan motor and the condenser to the outside. Some air conditioners have more power than others and can cool more area than just the room in which they are installed. A couple of such powerful units could cool several rooms. The room air conditioner passes warm air from the room over the cooling coil; the cooled air is then circulated by a blower or fan. The heat from the warm room air causes the cold liquid refrigerant which is flowing through the evaporator to vaporize. The vaporized refrigerant carries the heat to the compressor, which in turn compresses the vapor and increases its temperature to a point higher than that of the outside air. In the condenser, the hot refrigerant vapor liquefies and gives up the heat from the room air to the air outside. The high-pressure liquid refrigerant then passes through a restrictor which reduces its pressure and temperature. The cold liquid refrigerant then re-enters the evaporator, and the cycle is repeated indefinitely.

Mounting a room unit is not a difficult procedure. Many window air conditioners come with a do-it-yourself installation kit. Instructions should be followed carefully to save time and trouble later. For installation of larger models you would probably need a professional. Check with your dealer.

The procedures of installation differ a good bit, because room units can be mounted a number of ways. It's best to take into consideration what mounting is most suitable to the conditions of your home and the local building codes. The most common methods of mounting are:

Inside flush: the interior face of the conditioner is approximately flush with the inside wall.

Outside flush: the outer face of the unit is either flush or just beyond the outside wall.

Upper sash: the air conditioner is mounted in the top of the window.

Balance: the unit is installed half inside and half outside the window.

Interior: the conditioner is completely inside the room, and so the window can be closed or opened at will.

There is also a special mounting designed for horizontal sliding and casement windows. Installation procedure is similar.

Location of the air conditioner. It is best to locate the unit as far as you can from exterior doors. This will help prevent drafts from interfering with the cooled air. Be sure there are no obstructions in front of the conditioner, especially draperies or furniture. See that the vents are directed upward so that the cool air will rise. Later it will drift to the floor.

Exterior windows and doors should be thoroughly weather-stripped; otherwise you'll overwork the unit.

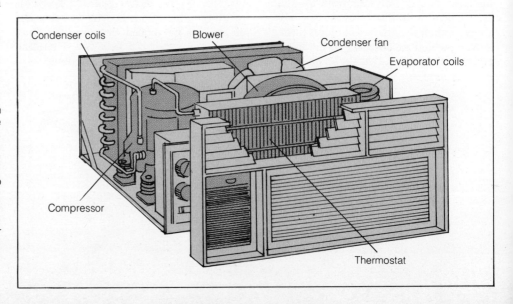

Condenser coils — Blower — Condenser fan — Evaporator coils — Compressor — Thermostat

Maintenance

Filter. Clean it often. Follow the directions in the service booklet. Vacuum, wash in warm water, dry, and replace.

Grille. Clean with warm water, soap, soft cloth. Do not use any cleaners. And do not allow any insect spray on it, for solvents may cause corrosion. Keep it well dusted.

Grille condensation. The grille may collect moisture when it is first turned on because of high humidity in the room. Close the doors and windows in the room to lower the humidity to let the moisture evaporate.

Installing a window unit

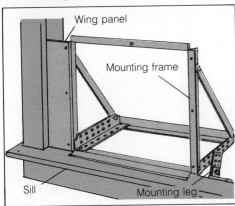

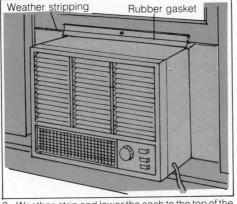

1. First assemble the mounting frame that comes with the unit. It must be centered in the window. Screw small mounting legs to the sill near the outer edge. A slight pitch to outdoors lets water run off.

2. Weather-strip and lower the sash to the top of the frame. Then slide the air conditioner into the frame until it is flush with the window. Tuck it in place with a heavy rubber gasket all around. This seals the space between the frame and the unit.

Installing a unit through the wall

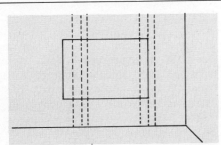

1. Mark an area and cut it out with a keyhole saw. Remove the outside wall and insulation.

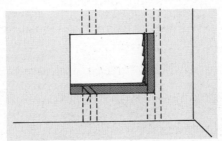

2. Saw out the center stud and take it away.

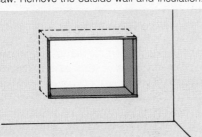

3. Insert a preassembled wooden frame. Its purpose is to act as buffer against vibration.

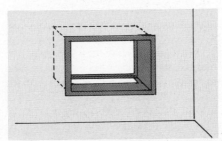

4. Insert metal sleeve that comes with unit.

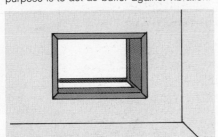

5. Put on molding, and caulk where needed.

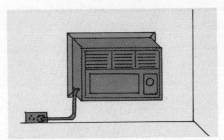

6. Place the air conditioner in the frame.

What it takes

Approximate time: Three hours.

Tools and materials: ¼" drill and bits with long shank to pierce wall, insulation, siding, keyhole saw, handsaw, hammer, wood chisel, screwdriver, caulking compound, weather stripping, and lumber for frame.

I was cool till I took a look at my electric bill.

I figured I'd beat the electric company by turning my thermostat way down at night and throwing open all the windows. Everyone knows it's cooler outside at night. Trouble was, this let moisture into the house because nighttime humidity can be high. As I learned later, this made my air conditioner run overtime during the day, just to reduce the humidity.

Practical Pete

Soundproofing your home

Noise is unquestionably one of the great problems of our time, especially for those who live in or close to urban areas. While there is little that the individual can do about environmental noise pollution, there are some steps that can be taken to eliminate a great deal of unwanted sound in and around the house.

Soundproofing a new home. If you are planning to build a new house, you might consider the following quite simple measures beforehand:

Specify double studs for walls instead of the usual single-stud construction. The studs are placed on two 2x4 sole plates instead of one (or on a single 2x8) and staggered. This permits weaving insulation between them to help deaden sound. See illustrations below.

Certain types of wallboard—and acoustical wall tile—are also available to reduce the passage of sound. Both are ideal for a rumpus room. Acoustical ceiling tile is also a good means of controlling sound, and it comes in attractive styles, is durable, and easy to install.

In planning your new home, try to place bedrooms toward the back of the house, away from street noises. Use solid-core doors throughout the house, and position closets as buffers between areas of noise and bedrooms. Use carpets wherever possible. It is also a good idea to avoid long, straight stairways and halls, because they act as channels for sound.

Soundproofing an existing house. Outside noise can be checked by the use of insulation, including storm doors and windows. See that all cracks are caulked and all doors and windows have weather stripping. Judicious planting of shrubs and trees will help check the invasion of your peace and quiet. High, solid wood fences, provided they do not conflict with zoning laws, will be a wise addition. The interior walls of your house which face the direction of the annoyance can be covered with heavy materials such as lined drapes. As a last resort, the wall itself can be furred out, and a second, inner wall put up. This will create an air pocket to trap sound.

Plumbing noises. The roar and crash of household plumbing can frequently be lowered by such simple acts as wrapping pipes, replacing washers on faucets, securing loose pipes.

Ticking in pipes is caused by hot water flowing into a cold hot-water supply pipe. The pipe expands, and this produces a ticking sound. The cure is to make sure that the pipe has room to slide on its hangers.

Whistling comes when water which is under high pressure must flow past a restriction. The whistling toilet inlet valve is a sound familiar to countless homeowners. Some toilets are graced with an adjusting screw that allows you to reduce the flow to below the whistling level. If your toilet does not have this useful feature, you can turn the tank's shutoff valve to the point where the rate of flow decreases and the whistling stops. But this is an exception to the general rule: it is a good idea to check all the valves in the water-supply system to be certain that none of them are partially closed.

The gurgling drain, like the whistling toilet, not infrequently proves a major source of irritation. The customary causes are wrong drainage-pipe size and improper venting. The remedy might be an anti-siphon trap, an inexpensive hardware-store item that comes in a kit for easy installation.

Water hammer is a hard, knocking sound in the piping when a faucet or an automatic-washer solenoid valve turns off quickly. Water which has been moving quickly through the pipes while the valve is open will come to a dead stop as the valve is shut, with the result that heavy pressures are put on the whole water-supply system.

The problem in this case is improperly operating air chambers, or even a complete lack of them. Air chambers allow rushing water to bounce gently against a cushion of air when a valve closes, thus taking the strain off the pipes. Installing air chambers may be something you would pass on to your plumber.

Wallboard / Sole plate

Staggered studs

The view from above shows how studs can be staggered for the best effect.

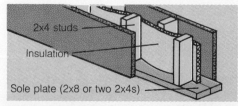

2x4 studs

Insulation

Sole plate (2x8 or two 2x4s)

Soundproof a frame wall by placing staggered 2x4s on a single 2x8 sole plate, or on two 2x4 sole plates. Then weave insulation through the studs, leaving air locks to trap sound.

Acoustical ceiling tile

One of the easiest ways to dampen sound inside the house is to install an acoustical-tile ceiling. There are two ways to put up ceiling tiles: either with adhesive or with staples. It is important, right off, to gauge the condition of your existing ceiling. If it is a clean, firm surface of wallboard or plaster, then it should take adhesive or staples well. But if a plaster ceiling is not smooth, then you will have to put up furring strips and staple or adhere the tiles to these.

While there are a number of systems for joining tiles together, depending on the manufacturer, the principles of installation are essentially the same. First of all, find out how wide your border tiles should be. The borders at each end should be the same width. To do this, measure each wall, but in your calculation pay attention only to the leftover inches. For example, if a wall measures 9 feet 4 inches, then what counts is the number 4. Starting from this number, the rule is: Add 12 and divide by 2. This will give you 8, in the example given, which will be the width of the border tile on each end. If the other wall measures 13 feet 10 inches, the borders along the other sides will be 11 inches (10 plus 12 divided by 2).

Start at a corner, measure out the width of the border tiles, and snap a chalk line across the room in each direction.

Stapling. If you intend to staple the tiles, then cut the corner tile first with the staple tabs aimed toward the center of the room. For cutting, use a fine-toothed saw or sharp fiberboard knife, and always cut with the face of the tile up.

Place the corner tile carefully against the chalk line and staple it. The back edge of the tile can be nailed in place because it will be covered by molding later on. The exposed part of the staple will be covered by the interlock of the following tiles.

Staple a whole course of cut border tiles along one wall, nailing the back edges in place. Then run the border tiles along the other wall. And now work in rows with the full tiles, stapling them in place. At the other end, the border tiles will have no staple tabs. They will be held in place with nails and the interlocks.

Adhesive. You may wish to put up your ceiling tiles with adhesive rather than staples. Apply four dabs of adhesive to the back of a tile, about 1½ inches in from each corner. Don't put on too much—about the size of a silver dollar is good. Place the tile near the chalk line, and slide it into place. On later courses, slide each tile onto the tongues of tiles already in place.

Press each tile firmly with your hand to make sure that it holds well to the ceiling (but be sure that your hands are clean). If the tile seems not to be level, take it down and adjust the amount of adhesive to compensate. Don't forget to cut holes for light fixtures and other obstacles, and bear in mind that a fixture's outer rim will cover the opening. After all the tiles are up, finish off with molding along the edges.

What it takes

Approximate time: A good day's work, provided the original ceiling is in good condition.

Tools and materials: Measuring tape, chalk line, either adhesive and putty knife or staple gun and staples, fine-toothed saw or fiberboard knife, hammer and nails.

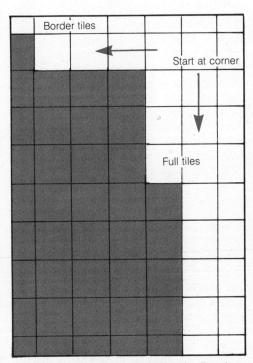

1. Start from a corner and install border tiles along two walls. Then work out into the room in both directions with full-size tiles.

Staple here

2A. Attach staples near the edge of the long inner tab on the two grooved sides of each tile. Then slip the tongue of the adjacent tile into the groove, covering the exposed staple. Use four staples per tile, one at each end of each tab.

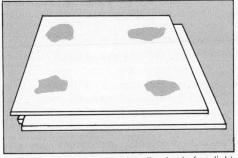

2B. Alternate method: apply adhesive in four light dabs spaced 1 to 2 inches from each corner.

6.SECURITY

A burglary takes place every 15 seconds.

There is a fire every 58 seconds.

Protecting your home

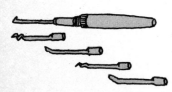

Lock pick set looks like a fountain pen. It is available only to locksmiths.

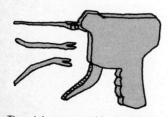

The pick gun, used by locksmith and burglar, vibrates pin into position within the cylinder. The tumbler core is then turned with a tension wrench.

It takes only one small match to start a four-alarm fire, one unlocked window to admit a burglar to your home. Carelessness is without question the principal contributor to accident, fire, and theft in the American home. Your carelessness, perhaps.

It is reported that in the United States a burglary is committed every 15 seconds. No target is beyond the range of today's thieves and vandals, and their numbers are rapidly multiplying along with their cunning and boldness.

The determined burglar can get into anything. The question is how much time and risk he wishes to take. For, though a tight house with strong locks may not stop every thief, it can stop a good many and will slow all of them down. Time is your ally in the battle with burglars. Your home's security should be geared to delay, foil, and discourage the intruder.

How a burglar operates

When the professional burglar really wishes, and has the time, he can defeat just about any lock or alarm system. Only there aren't a great many professionals about, and those who do merit top seeding are selective with their targets. They will only mount a strike after much casing and planning, and when assured of a brisk haul.

The pro does a lot of research. He will chat in neighborhood bars, with mailmen and repair and service personnel such as plumbers and carpenters, with shopkeepers and gas-station attendants. His effort is to learn who has bought valuable items, where they are kept, who is going on a trip and when, what sort of locks and security systems are popular in the area, who has dogs, and which dogs bark?

His target is not just your house, but you. He needs to know a great deal about you—your schedule of arrival and departure each day, for example. He will note such details as deliveries, how many people live in the house, and how many are at home during the day. The professional burglar notices if your lawn is well kept, if your house needs painting, whether the catch basin in your driveway is plugged up. Small things, but he needs to know who you are: a dilettante, or a generalissimo who double-locks even his toothbrush.

To really understand the burglar and your own vulnerability, why not try an exercise for yourself? Study your own home, and see how you would go about robbing it. Plan to burgle yourself! How would you enter your house as a burglar? When? How would you work without anyone noticing? And how would you make your getaway? In that game or exercise you might discover weaknesses in your home protection that you had no idea existed.

How the burglar enters

Burglary depends upon opportunity, and so a burglar will very often walk right into a house through an unlocked door or window. Failing that, he will resort to that marvelous tool, the jimmy, with which he can open almost any window or door. It is simply a common pinch bar with one end flattened sufficiently thin so that it can enter a very narrow space. In the hands of a pro it is a sophisticated tool.

Many burglars favor the use of the plastic credit card. This they slip between the door and the jamb to open ordinary beveled latches. To the trade, this operation is known as "loiding," from the time when the cards were made of celluloid.

A further talent is that of the lock picker. Yet the jimmy is faster, and so for the homeowner it is less important to have a lock that is pick-proof than to have a deadbolt latch, a heavy-duty door, and a tight and solid frame.

At the same time, the professionals are in the minority. Many thieves are amateurs, drug addicts, or kids looking for thrills. They are dangerous in the way that a dull knife is more to be feared than a sharp one, for they are usually quite ignorant in regard to sophisticated security equipment, and they frequently panic and resort to unnecessary violence.

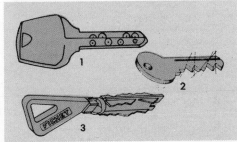

The unpickables. Each of these keys operates a cylinder which is supposedly pickproof. The Sargent Keso (1) has a radial pin arrangement. The Medeco (2) has V-shaped cuts crisscrossing the key, allowing millions of noninterchangeable key combinations. The Fichet cylinder (3), with each groove in the key cut to 10 possible depths, has 10 grooves, offering billions of combinations.

Preventing burglary

Without doubt the best way to secure your home is to protect its perimeter. This means sturdy doors, windows, locks, good outdoor lighting, and even fences and hedges. Above all, it is best to avoid confrontation with any hostiles, and so keeping them at a distance is only sensible.

Make it difficult to enter your house. Solid doors, strong locks, locked windows, lights, alarms, plus security habits such as locking up even when you go out for a short time all tend to discourage thieves. The burglar casing your house will appreciate the sort of person he is dealing with and will think again about invading your privacy.

Keep your life private. Do not attract burglars by letting neighbors or tradespeople know that you have a valuable coin collection, or that you are planning a trip. Don't let the contents of your house be seen through lighted windows. If you have an expensive hi-fi, keep it away from viewers who might be passing by. Also make your daily schedule erratic. Don't always arrive home from work at exactly the same time, if you can help it.

Let your house appear occupied at all times. Use timers to switch lights off and on and switch radios on when you're not at home. Have a neighbor pick up your mail and newspaper whenever you're away on a trip. Do not cancel your subscriptions with the announcement that you won't be at home for a month; but do notify the police. Keep garage doors closed and locked when cars are not there. Lock up even if you're just going next door for coffee.

Be suspicious, stay alert. Be careful about anyone posing as a salesman or pollster who wants to see the inside of your house. Watch out for strange cars parked near your home. It could be the burglar casing his next job. Never let anyone inside until you have checked them through your front door peephole and talked to them with the door on the chain, and you are fully satisfied. Be in touch with your neighbors whenever you see any suspicious-looking person hanging about the neighborhood.

He didn't even leave me a drink! That security-system salesman seemed like one of the nicest fellows I ever met. I took him all through my house and showed him how my door alarm worked. He even said he'd come by and have a drink with me in a couple of weeks after I got back from vacation. Next time I won't let anyone into my house until I check out his credentials. *Practical Pete*

About watchdogs

Any dog can be an excellent alarm system. A dog will almost always bark when a stranger approaches, or when it feels or smells something out of the ordinary. Even a very small dog can be effective in this regard. A large dog, such as a German shepherd, is an even greater help, for not only would its bark threaten the burglar, but so would its bite. In fact, when casing a neighborhood the sensible crook will pass up a home with a dog.

Doors and windows: first line of defense

Doors

Security isn't only a matter of locks and bolts. It is also doors and windows. And although a locked door will offer a psychological deterrent to certain amateurs, it will seldom put off a seasoned burglar. He knows very well that a lock, no matter how strong, is only as good as the door of which it is a part. A strong lock on a hollow-core door, a door with loose hinges, or a rotting frame is useless. A kick, a vigorous fist, and the intruder is within.

There are three types of doors: solid wood, hollow core, and paneled. Of these the solid wood is the most reliable. It is simply thick, hard wood. All exterior doors should be of this type, at least 1¾ to 2 inches thick.

A paneled door is only safe if the panels are of heavy wood and are well set. If the panels are glass, they should be replaced either with strong wood or with plastic panes. Otherwise the invitation to the burglar is irresistible. He will simply break the panel, reach inside, and open the door.

The hollow-core type should never be used as an exterior door. Hollow-core doors offer a measure of privacy, but they are no security for the homeowner. They are strictly for the interior of the house, blocking little more than other people's curiosity. A determined shoulder or boot is all that's needed to get through one of these.

Your first task in any home-protection program is to check what your burglar will be checking—the condition of your outside doors and windows.

A rotting door or frame. It's easy for any burglar to pry his way through rot. Your best action would be to replace either the rotted area or the entire door and/or frame with new, solid wood.

A poorly constructed door. It could be too thin, or it could have thin wood or glass panels. All the thief has to do is make an opening with his elbow, knee or fist, reach in and open the door from the inside. Get a new door or fortify this one.

A door with loose hinges or with outside hinges. In either case you're in trouble. Even the callow apprentice would find it easy. Your remedy is to sink longer screws. But check that the wood isn't rotten. If it is, you'll need solid blocks or strips of wood so that the screws will hold. The screws should be nonretractable. Put glue on the threads before sinking; or you can purchase special screws which can be screwed in, but not out.

Many old houses have door hinges on the outside. All the thief has to do is knock out the hinge pin, and it's payday. The best approach here is to take down the door and reset the hinges inside, if possible; or put up a new door and frame.

A door with too much space between the door and its frame. This is a loud-and-clear invitation for the burglar to use his jimmy. Remember, the jimmy can get into very small crevices. If the thief can't jimmy the lock so that it pulls away from the frame and causes the bolt or latch to pop out of the receiver, he can make a large enough space to insert a hacksaw and cut through the bolt. To thwart him, allow no more than 1/64th of an inch space between the door and its frame.

Don't be fooled into thinking that modern construction techniques will see to it that you have sturdy door frames on your new house. Too often, modern construction is concerned with haste and there is a gap around your door frame which is simply filled in with small wedges and plaster. Time and frequent door slamming soon loosen this. It's a breeze then for the pro and his jimmy bar.

The clever thief will sometimes use a method that will bamboozle not only you but your insurance company as well. He can stretch the frame just above the lock with an automobile jack. As the jack expands, the frame stretches, and eventually the bolt can be pulled out of its place in the lock strike. The thief opens the door, loads up and departs without a trace. The frame returns to its original position and there will be no sign of forced entry. Try and collect on that one.

Reinforcing an outside door. You can easily do this yourself by attaching a panel of ¾-inch plywood or a piece of sheet metal

How to share the wealth
I put my Christmas bonus into the best stereo I could get for the price. And it was great sitting in my picture window listening to music and watching the sunset. Trouble was, I didn't know that others were watching me—and my stereo. Next time I'll either keep my curtains drawn or put my valuables in another room where they can't be seen. At least they didn't steal the view.

Practical Pete

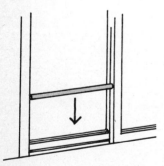

TIP: A good way to block entry through sliding glass doors is with a metal bar placed along the tracks.

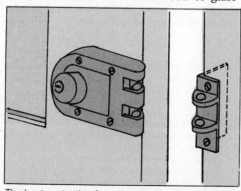

The best protection for a door with glass panes is a locking door bolt. Even if the glass is broken it prevents entry.

to your door. It won't be necessary to take the door down. Be sure that the existing hinges will bear the added weight. If there is any question, get heavier hinges with longer screws.

If you live in a rented house and the landlord won't allow you to reinforce or change the door, then install a double cylinder lock which requires a key to open it from inside as well as outside. If a thief breaks through a panel and reaches in, he will find he has a lock to contend with rather than just a knob.

Sliding doors. The problem is that sliding doors have very narrow stiles and can be jimmied. Moreover, there is very little room in the door to mount the traditional horizontal latch or throw bolt.

There is a special lock, however, with a cylinder-operated deadbolt and tamper-proof screws; it is lightweight, inexpensive, and easy to install. Another lock has a pivoted latch which, when it is not in use, lies vertically in the housing, thus allowing for a long throw bolt within a small space.

Windows

The burglar will usually look for a window that has been left open. Failing that, he will try to defeat a window lock or, as a last resort, will take a chance on breaking or cutting glass. To protect your windows you will need one or more of these devices:

- A good window lock.
- Iron grilles or window gates.
- An alarm system on the window.
- Burglar-resistant glass.
- Windows with many small panes rather than a large area of glass.

The sash lock is actually not a lock at all but a latch made of a curved metal arm and a receptacle. The two pieces are supposed to draw the windows tightly together. Unfortunately, because of poor construction,

poor installation of the lock, or warping of the window, the device is often useless.

Some homeowners favor the wedge lock which has a rubber tip and is mounted on the upper part of the lower window frame. It holds the windows shut, but it does so by spreading them apart. All the burglar has to do then is slip a knife blade between the windows and cut off the rubber piece.

Your best protection is a window lock with a key. Even if the burglar breaks the window he must then cope with your lock.

Put window locks on all the windows in your house. It is wise to have all locks keyed alike and to give each member of the family a key; keep a key near the window, where children but not a burglar can reach it. (This is highly recommended as a fire-safety precaution.)

The window lock is customarily installed with self-tapping screws on the lower window frame. Drill a hole in the upper frame into which the bolt can slip. A second hole may be drilled a few inches higher in order to secure the window in a ventilation position when desired. Never leave the window opening wider than 6 inches when ventilating. Thin burglar arms and tools can pass through anything wider than that.

For the sake of economy, it is not necessary for every window in the house to have the same level of protection. Some windows are more accessible than others, and so their defense merits more time and money. Other windows, which can be reached only with difficulty, require less protection. Windows which you never use, basement windows for example, should be nailed shut. They are among the most vulnerable target areas in any case. Trees which are located near windows and from which a burglar may gain access, and shrubs around the house which can shield him from view as he attempts to break into your house, are major weaknesses in your line of defense.

TIP: After installing a window lock, drip some solder onto the screw heads. This will stop a burglar from unscrewing the lock after he cuts a small hole in the windowpane (a common means of entry).

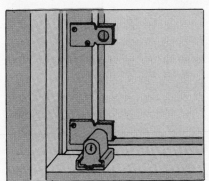

It's a good idea to put an auxiliary lock-pin on windows so that nobody can simply break the glass, reach in and open the window. At the same time, a steel pin can hold the window open for ventilation. Bore two holes for the pin—one in the closed position, and one so that the window can be open no more than 6 inches.

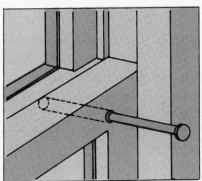

All downstairs windows should be securely locked so that even if the glass is broken they cannot be unlocked. Upstairs windows may not require prime security, but pins or bolts would not be amiss with these in any case.

Sometimes it is a problem to lock an aluminum sliding window in a ventilating position. A locking, sliding window bolt allows you high security as it foils entry even if the glass is broken.

Lock options

Locks may be classified into two basic groups: surface locks, and locks which are installed within or through the door. Surface locks include sliding bolts, bars, safety chains—or any other locking device which is fixed to the surface of the door. The disadvantage of surface locks is that they can be ripped off. You can forestall this by fastening the surface lock in place with long, heavy screws coated in glue before driving them into the wood.

Door locks consist of three common types: key-in-knob, mortise, and rim lock. **Key-in-knob locks** (including tubular and cylindrical locks). These are quite common, and they range from the flimsy to the fairly secure. They are easy to install and come in standard sizes. There are certain disadvantages: the locking mechanism is in the knob, which puts it *outside* the house. A sledgehammer could dismantle the lock without much trouble. Also, these locks have a tapered latch which can be opened in a matter of seconds by an adroit "loid" user. Finally, the latches as a rule are pretty short and therefore easy to jimmy. To deal with these problems, some manufacturers have added longer latches or trigger bolts.
Tubular locks are of the same type as key-in-knob locks. They are used on interior doors. Some have a push button in the knob or a small lever or button on the interior side. Tubular locks are most commonly used on bathroom doors.
Cylindrical locks are similar to the tubular, only larger and stronger. They can be used on exterior doors. They are locked by a key in the outer knob or with a push button or

lever which is located in the inner knob.
Mortise locks are installed in the edge of a door. They cannot be installed in a door that is less than 1⅜ inches thick. The mortise lock has a spring-loaded latch and a deadbolt. When the key is fully turned in the lock, the deadbolt will double-lock the door, thus offering top lock security.
Rim locks are actually auxiliary locks. They add clout to the security you get from your key-in-knob or mortise lock. Rim locks are mounted on the inside face of the door. Some have deadbolts, while others have a spring-loaded latch that locks automatically when the door is closed.

Buying a lock

When you buy a lock, it comes already assembled. Bear in mind that the lock and the cylinder are two separate entities. You can take out the cylinder and replace it without replacing the entire lock. Some locks that are almost impregnable in the face of physical assault may have cylinders that are child's play to the experienced pickman. Yet there are cylinders that are nearly impossible to pick. On the other hand, the truly professional burglar is not without resource, and in answer to a difficult cylinder he will simply reach for his large, heavy set of pliers and yank the cylinder right out of the door. The cylinder puller needs only to get a grip on the cylinder. Protective cylinder plates are available which cover the cylinder and the surrounding area, leaving space only for the key, and so baffling the burglar.

Which lock to use

The locks which you can buy are almost without limit. To keep out the casual burglar you may use one or several. Much depends on what you wish to protect. If you have valuable paintings and jewels, for example, then you'll want a high-security system. The point is to decide how much you wish to invest in security. For basic security against the average thief, however, the cost is not high.

Spring-latch lock

Deadbolt lock

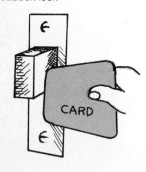

The spring-latch lock is highly convenient for the burglar who is adroit at "loiding"—slipping a plastic credit card against the latch tongue to depress it and unlock the door. The deadbolt, on the other hand, defies any attack. It is only vulnerable when the door has enough space from its frame so that the intruder can bring power tools or a hacksaw to bear. But that takes time, which is to his disadvantage.

A tubular lock has very few springs and working parts. Its basic action is contained in a small area, sometimes just in the latch itself. This type of lock often lacks the strength and smooth action you would find in a more sophisticated cylindrical lock. It is not for use as a keyed lock, but more for bathroom and passageway doors.

A cylindrical lock has a large chassis. It is strong, designed with precision, and highly serviceable. It may be used on exterior doors.

Primary locks

Key-in-knob locks and mortise locks are called primary locks because they are the locks that usually come with your house or apartment. These locks are really for keeping the door shut and do little to exclude the burglar.

If you are building your own home, or even if you are buying a home already built, it would be wise to put in a mortise lock. Get one that has a protective faceplate for the setscrew and an angling plate to cut down on the distance between the frame and the door. Unless you get these features you could be asking for trouble; mortise locks have a tendency to encourage the jimmy bar because the homeowner often forgets to deadlock the door and relies only on the regular latch. This makes him easy prey for a burglar who, posing as a fund raiser, will surreptitiously loosen the setscrew while your back is turned, and then return later to complete the job.

If your builder puts in a key-in-knob lock, make sure that it is made of pressed steel rather than zinc casting so as to be more resistant to physical attack. Also, make certain that it has a trigger bolt to prevent "loiding"; and get a latch that protrudes at least ½ inch.

Secondary locks

Though called "secondary" because they are added on, in terms of hard security they are the truly primary locks. Your heavier artillery may be anything from a vertical deadbolt to those locks which brace the door against the floor or deep into the door jamb. Don't forget that in deciding what lock you need you should first check the physical condition of both jamb and door.

A very strong wooden door or metal door can probably be protected best with the vertical deadbolt lock. With solid mounting this lock is usually as strong as the door itself. When buying, ask the salesperson for a jimmyproof deadlock.

Even if your wooden door is not in the best condition there are a number of locks which can help keep the burglar outside. With a wooden door that opens inward you can install a brace lock or police lock. It locks the door into the floor. A long steel bar fits into the lock mounting on the door and into a metal socket in your floor, so the would-be intruder will be pressing against the floor itself.

Another superb lock is the Fichet Vertibar. This bolts into the door frame in seven places. It is said to resist all physical attacks, while its ten-lever cylinder is considered pickproof. It's expensive.

Mortise locks are not as popular as they used to be, since the development of the cylindrical lock. Installation can be costly, and it is of course necessary to mortise out fairly large sections of the door and jamb.

Rim locks are usually installed above existing locks, and are therefore auxiliary. They are an additional security. Mounted on the inside of the door, some have deadbolts, and others have a spring-loaded latch that locks automatically when the door is shut.

A bored lock looks like this when you remove it from the door. Removal and replacement is a simple operation requiring little time and few tools.

Double-locking security is what can thwart even the most determined burglar. 1 and 2: Combination of a ½-inch throw deadlocking latch and a 1-inch throw deadbolt in which is concealed a hardened-steel roller that resists sawing or just about any other attack. 3: Armor plate protects the lock mechanism from piercing, sawing, drilling. 4: When the door is locked, the outside knob is free-spinning, making it impossible to get any leverage on it to force or twist it. 5: Forceful entry is discouraged by the recessed cylinder. The lock is also panicproof for safety. Both the latch and the bolt retract simultaneously, permitting instant exit, with a simple turn of the inside knob or thumb turn.

About keys

Just as a lock without a key isn't much good, so a lock with a lot of keys is also of no use to your security. Be careful about the disposition of your keys, and change the cylinder on your lock from time to time, just in case someone has gotten hold of a key or has made a copy of a key you or a member of your family left lying around. If you lose your key, change the cylinder immediately.

Open sesame

The future of locking devices will very likely be determined in the field of electronics. Today, there is the "invisible keyhole" whose lock is operated by a hidden control. The "key" resembles a plastic credit card, and it is simply held near a sensor unit. Radio frequencies read it, and providing it is the correct key, the door is released. Furthermore, a door can be made to appear as part of a wall, adding even further security. Perhaps one day not very far from now, all that will be necessary will be for you to utter a special password and the door will open for you.

How to replace a broken or worn-out lock

It is an easy job to replace a lock, even if some door preparation is necessary. For the most part, no special tools are required. First of all, check the lock you are replacing. Make a list of the pertinent facts so that you can show them to your hardware dealer, and he will be able to help you.
- What type of lock are you replacing? Is it a bored or mortised lock, for instance.
- Name of manufacturer.
- What is the thickness of your door?
- Measure the lock hole diameter, latch-bolt hole diameter, latch unit faceplate, and the distance from the edge of the door to the center of the lock hole.

The parts of the lock that you will need to know are:

The strike. Located in the jamb, the strike can practically always be left where it is. Just check the hole that is mortised into the jamb to be sure it is deep enough to receive the new latch bolt. It should be in the correct position to depress the plunger on the deadlocking latch. If you find it necessary to lessen the gap between the frame and the door, you can shim the strike from behind with a small piece of cardboard.

The latch. Currently, there are two basic latch types in use. The standard, or traditional latch has a faceplate which is fastened to the door with two screws. The drive-in latch has a circular front about an inch in diameter in the edge of the door. It will either have spring clips that grip into the full length of the bore, or raised ribs that hold by friction. You can usually install a drive-in latch without additional mortising.

The lock mechanism. Using the template that comes with the new lock, you will be able to tell if the hole is of the right diameter to receive the new lock. If you need a larger hole, use a wood rasp to enlarge it to the necessary measurement. If you are replacing more than one lock, you will find a boring jig helpful. Ask your dealer about lending or renting you one.

Changing a bored lock

Full-lip strike   T strike

Proper installation of strike

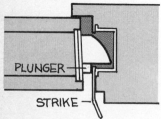

Plunger on latch bolt should fit exactly against strike so latch can't be forced when door is closed.

Replacing a bored lock—whether cylindrical or tubular—is a simple job if you have average mechanical ability and the usual home-shop tools.

1. Remove the worn out or broken lock.

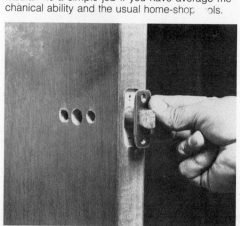

2. Remove the latch. It should come out easily.

3. If necessary, use the symmetrical, reversible template to outline a new hole.

4. If you have the use of a jig, as shown here, use a hole saw to enlarge the area so it can accept the new lock mechanism.

5. With a chisel, cut away excess wood in the edge of the door, if necessary, to accommodate the new latch plate.

6. Put in the new latch plate. It is important that your mortise and bored holes be precise. If you have mortised too deep, shim out with cardboard.

7. Insert the lock mechanism from the outside of the door. If you find that the hole requires only minor enlargement, you can use a wood rasp.

Deadlocking latch with standard faceplate.

Drive-in latch with circular front.

8. Attach the mounting plate on the inside of the door and finally put on the trim and knob. It is important to achieve precise alignment of the knob.

9. The completed installation looks as though a professional had done it. But the job isn't over. You must keep a maintenance check on all locks.

Replacing an old lock with a deadbolt

What it takes

Approximate time: Three hours.

Tools and materials: Measuring tape, adjustable square, portable electric drill, hole-saw attachment (or saber saw), paddle bits, putty knife and putty, hammer, wood chisel, replacement lock set with template and instructions, sandpaper, and stain and/or paint as needed.

While the exchange of similar locks is a relatively simple affair, the replacement of an old lock by a new security lock equipped with a deadbolt is a little more time consuming, though still within the reach of the home handyman.

The old mortise lock in the photo sequence below had been on the door for a number of years and was loose. The door was also loose on its hinges and would not shut tightly. First, the hinges were repositioned so that the door fit snugly in its frame, and then the homeowner addressed himself to the door lock. His purpose in installing a deadbolt was to correct a serious weakness in the locking mechanism. The solid metal bolt spanning the gap between door and frame is called "dead" because it has no springs to operate it, and so cannot be loided (see page 72).

1. After removing the door so it will be easier to work, take out the old lock pieces; then cut a plug to fit into the mortise cut.

2. Using the installation template supplied with the lock, mark the locations of the various holes.

3. You can use a hole saw in an electric drill, or a saber saw to bore the large-diameter holes.

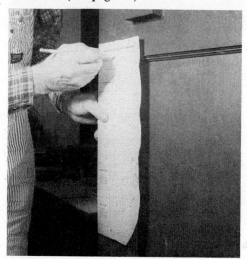

4. Bore the deadbolt hole, as well as the latch lock hole, with a drill and paddle bit.

5. Fit the new handle and latch in place.

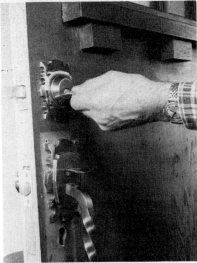

6. Install the deadbolt, latch, and their respective plates, with the plates mortised in flush to the edge of the door; then fit the deadbolt key and escutcheon.

7. Now it is simply a matter of mating the pieces from each side and checking the lock and knob operation.

8. Fill any holes left from the old lock, and then paint or stain.

9. Mark the locations of both the deadbolt hole and the regular latch hole, and mark around the plates.

10. Bore the hole for the deadbolt, using a paddle bit.

11. Mortise for the deadbolt plate and fasten it securely in place.

12. Mortise and bore for the latch plate and fasten it in place.

13. Your final step is to install a new doorstop and paint it to match the rest of the door trim.

Invisible patching

In this and the following project, you may need to cover tracks left by old hardware. The best way to hide a cylinder hole is with diamond-shaped patches. Cut a patch from scrap wood for each side of the door. Pencil the outlines of the patches on the door; then chisel recesses. Bevel the sides of the recesses and the patches to ensure a snug fit. Glue the patches into the recesses and clamp for 24 hours. Fill any spaces, and when the filler is dry plane or sand the whole area smooth. Then give the entire door a coat of paint.

Installing a mortise lock

The heavy-duty mortise lock is one of the better security locks, chiefly because it is made of strong metal and rests within the actual door. Since it is fitted with a deadbolt and is not accessible from the outside, it is that much more effective. It is not difficult to install this type of lock. Just follow the manufacturer's instructions, which are basically similar to any other lock installation. The main concern will be cutting the mortise. For this operation it is best to take down the door.

Cutting a mortise

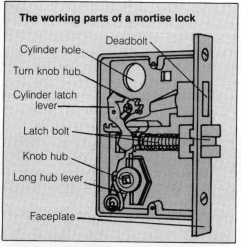

The working parts of a mortise lock

Cylinder hole
Deadbolt
Turn knob hub
Cylinder latch lever
Latch bolt
Knob hub
Long hub lever
Faceplate

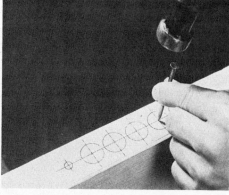

1. Start by taping the template which comes with the lock set to the edge of the door. With a sharp tool, such as an awl or nail, mark the centers of the areas to be drilled.

2. Drill on your center marks. The template will indicate how deep to go and what size bit to use.

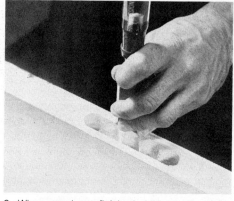

3. When you have finished drilling, cut out the remainder of the mortise with a sharp chisel. Start by outlining the area to be removed with chisel cuts ⅛ inch deep. Then chisel out between the holes.

4. Chisel the ends and sides of the mortise so they agree precisely with the dimensions of the new lock. The cuts are for the ends of the faceplate, which will receive the screws to hold the lock to the door.

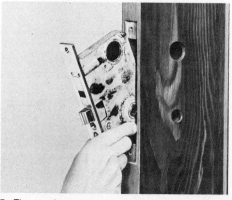

5. The mortise cut must be exactly centered, and the lock must fit snugly. Remove excess wood if necessary. Fasten the plate with screws and insert knobs and key cylinder.

What it takes

Approximate time: One long afternoon.

Tools and materials: Hammer, chisels, screwdriver (regular and Phillips), electric drill and bits, nail (optional), lock set with template and installation instructions.

Putting up a chain lock

One of the most popular extra security locks is the simple chain door guard. Although the chain door guard can be defeated by a knowledgeable burglar, it will offer pretty good protection against the more pedestrian crook.

Installation is simply a matter of positioning the device on the door and jamb in such a way that the door can open only slightly when the chain is latched, and the chain can be freed from the inside only.

Position the chain door guard with this in view; mark for screwholes. Predrill the holes with a hand drill; then insert screws.

There is also a new electronic door chain that can be put on when you *leave* your home. It has a battery-powered alarm.

There are many styles of chain door guards, but the principle, as shown here, is simply to allow an opening for viewing and conversation, without permitting entry until the homeowner frees the chain.

What it takes

Approximate time: About twenty minutes.

Tools and materials: Screwdriver, hand drill, pencil, chain door guard, and screws.

A handy one-way viewer

A door peephole, or one-way viewer, is essential to the well-protected home. With this device you can observe any caller before you open the door.

Some peepholes are just a swinging cover over a hole in the door. A better version comes with lenses that give you a wide-angle view of what is outside. It is sensible to purchase the best-quality viewer even if it costs a little more. The difference between viewers is the range of vision they give you from the viewing side. Low-cost viewers have a limited range. One-way viewers are easy to install. All you do is drill a hole of the proper size, insert the viewer, and tighten it. Just make sure that the viewer is at the appropriate height.

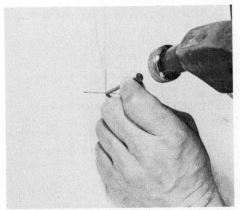

1. Figuring the eye level of the shortest member of the household who is likely to be answering the door, mark a point on the door.

What it takes

Approximate time: About twenty minutes.

Tools and materials: Electric drill with ⅝-inch bit (for most viewers) or a keyhole saw; one-way peephole hardware.

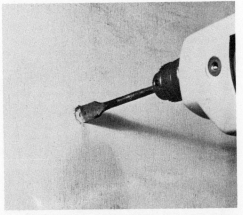

2. Depending on the type of viewer, you can either drill or saw a hole. If you drill, be sure to bore a small pilot hole and then drill from each side to prevent the door from splintering out. A better way is to clamp a piece of wood to each side of the door and bore through these.

3. Thread the two parts together, making certain that the proper viewing side is to the inside.

Installing a rim lock

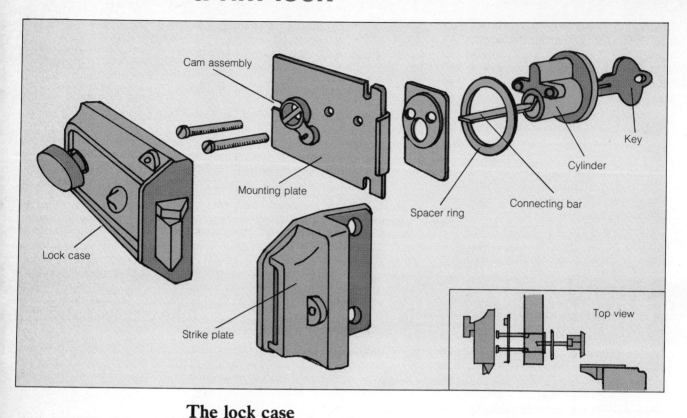

Cam assembly

Mounting plate

Lock case

Strike plate

Spacer ring

Connecting bar

Cylinder

Key

Top view

The lock case

The rim lock is the easiest door lock to install, since it is surface-mounted and requires drilling only one hole through the door. Make the hole at the height you want the lock to be. The manufacturer will specify the size of the hole and its correct distance from the edge of the door. The lock cylinder goes on the outside of the door, and the connecting back-up plate on the inside. Secure the back-up plate with the bolts provided in the package, and fasten the lock in place with wood screws (also provided). This completes the installation of the larger portion of the lock; the strike plate is installed next on the door jamb opposite the lock.

The strike plate

With the door closed, mark the position that the strike plate must occupy to line up with the lock. Open the door. Position the strike plate in the marked area and trace its full outline with a pencil. Using a hammer and chisel, mortise (recess) the strike plate so it falls flush with the inside of the door jamb and with the door trim. Secure the strike plate with the screws provided. Try the key to make certain there is no binding, and check to see that the strike plate is in exact relationship to the lock.

What it takes

Approximate time: A couple of hours.

Tools and materials: Electric drill and bits, hammer, screwdrivers (regular and Phillips head), wood chisel, combination square, and lock set.

TIP: Inexpensive locks have strike plates that need only to be mortised in the door jamb, while the more expensive locks need to be mortised in two places. If you're going to do this job at all, then pay a few dollars more and plan to spend a little longer on the installation. It's your security that's at stake.

Instant crime-stopper

A plain 2x4 with some sponge rubber or felt glued on one end and a metal T-bracket attached to the other end can prevent unwanted entry through a hall door.

Saw the 2x4 so it just reaches from the closed door to the wall facing it in the hallway. The felt on one end will prevent damage to the wall, while the metal T-bracket will prevent it slipping out from its purchase on the door. It's a good device for night-time when you're not so concerned about decor. Come the morning, stick it in the closet, out of sight.

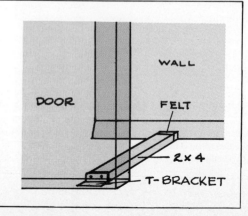

WALL

DOOR

FELT

2 x 4

T-BRACKET

Lock maintenance

One of the most important maintenance jobs with locks is to keep them properly lubricated—and too much lubrication is no better than too little. One of the best lubricants is powdered graphite. It is sold in tube form at most hardware stores. The tip is inserted into the lock and the tube squeezed a couple of times. Apply some graphite to the key while you're at it.

Lock problems

- **Broken key.** If the key has broken off in the lock, you may be able to take the broken piece out with tweezers or a pair of long, needle-nose pliers. Failing that, loosen the setscrew and unscrew the cylinder from the lock faceplate. Hold it face down and tap gently to dislodge the broken piece.
- **Stuck lock.** If the key fits into the lock but will not turn, use penetrating-oil lubricant around the key to try to loosen the lock, working the key gently to allow the oil to move around it. If this doesn't work, the cause of the problem may be that the cylinder has shifted in the lock faceplate, making it impossible for the cam to throw the bolt. Loosen the setscrew and turn the cylinder back to its

A light penetrating-oil lubricant can also be used. This type comes with a long, thin tube spout which can be placed in a keyhole for more exact servicing. Never use a heavy oil in the cylinder because it will gum up the tumblers. Lubricate the latch with light oil, wiping away the excess. If you wish to clean a mortise lock, wash it well in a grease solvent or paint thinner; then lubricate it.

correct position. A third possibility is that a wrong key has recently been used and has damaged the tumblers, in which case a new cylinder will be in order.

- **Stuck bolt.** When the key partially turns in the cylinder but the bolt does not move, check the door alignment to see if the bolt lines up with the strike plate. Depending on how far out of line it is, it may be necessary to realign the door on its hinges, change the location of the strike plate, or enlarge the bolt opening.
- **Frozen lock.** When the key will not enter the cylinder, chip away any ice that may be apparent, and then hold a heated key or lighted match to the cylinder entry. Turn the key gradually and with care to avoid damaging the tumblers.

Use a lock lubricant applicator with an insertable spout or tip. Go easy; be careful not to overlubricate.

When a key has broken off in the lock, try to retrieve the fragment first with tweezers, then with needle-nose pliers.

Key control

It is essential that you maintain control of all the keys to your house. This means that you should know who has keys, and which ones they have. Moreover, other key holders should be instructed in key security. For instance, if a key is stolen, or simply lost, change the lock cylinder immediately. Keys left lying around offer too great a temptation; it takes only a moment to make an impression of a key and return it so that the owner will be none the wiser. For example, never keep your house key on the same ring with the key to your car; when left in a parking lot, it will offer a delightful opportunity to some unscrupulous person.

When you move into a new (or an older) house, there is always the possibility that extra keys are in the possession of others—the workmen, former owners, their relatives, or their friends. It is also not unlikely that master keys used by tradespeople and contractors are still around. It would be easy for any of these keys to fall into the hands of a burglar, professional or neophyte. So why encourage temptation?

It is a simple matter and a great convenience to have all your doors keyed alike. It is also possible to extend the range of the master key to include such areas as a hobby room, workshop, boat, or vacation cabin.

Automatic garage-door opener

Thanks to a push button inside your car, you will be able to open your overhead garage door as you approach your house and drive right into a lighted area. The lights will go on as the door opens. The door will also close automatically after you are inside. You will have avoided any prowlers who might have been lurking, and in the event of rain you'll keep dry. Installing an automatic garage-door opener is not generally considered a do-it-yourself project. Many retailers install the system for you. When shopping for your unit, check that it has an automatic return switch to reverse direction if the door encounters an obstacle, and a light-delay system which turns the lights off several minutes after you pull in. When you go away on a trip, remember to set the door so that it cannot be opened by remote control, but only by a switch inside the garage.

Changing locks

When it is possible, take off the lock which you want to replace and bring it to your hardware dealer or locksmith. If you don't wish to do that, take a photograph or make a sketch or two of the lock. At the same time collect the following information and give it to your locksmith or hardware dealer: door thickness, name of lock manufacturer, distance from edge of door to center line of

lock, diameter of the lock mechanism hole, height and width of the faceplate.

Whenever you make changes in your security system, it is a good idea to check for any security provisions of the local building codes and ordinances. You should meet their requirements. It is also sensible to check with your insurance company's minimum standards for your home.

Lighting for security

Fences are very effective burglar deterrents. It isn't that a fence will stop the determined invader, but it will give him pause. He will note that you are telling him this is your place. He will see that you are not a careless homeowner. He will wonder whether the fence might impede his getaway. He will reason that if you take the trouble to put up a fence, then you will very likely take care of security inside your house, with good locks, alarms, and so forth. Yet, the fence must not be too high. Three feet is high enough. You want to make a difficulty for him, not offer him cover.

Another excellent homeowner ploy is a good hedge, especially if it includes thorn bushes.

What it takes

Approximate time: Under an hour per unit.

Tools and materials: Electric drill and bits, hammer, screwdriver, pliers, floodlight assembly, and a ladder.

A strong deterrent to burglars, prowlers, and undesirables in general is good exterior lighting. This may appear a rather droll statement in view of the fact that more than half of all burglaries take place in broad daylight. Yet thieves are naturally at an advantage in the dark. Moreover, lighting in and around your house can be helpful not only to your family's security but to their safety as well.

Outdoor illumination

The best lighting for a house that is centered on a lot and a bit removed from neighboring houses is a system which can cover the whole house with light. As a general rule, this type of lighting can be handled by a dozen or more floodlights mounted in clusters of two or three.

Floodlights are easy and also inexpensive to install. They are usually mounted on the eaves at the corners of the house. You can place additional lighting at ground level, and direct it toward the house if you wish. But it's a good idea to locate ground-level lights in planted areas where they are out of the way of general traffic.

If you cannot, or do not wish to illuminate the entire house, then at least make certain that the vulnerable areas are well lighted—for instance, the front and rear entrances, walks around the house, low windows, and the garage door.

It makes good sense to have most of your outdoor lighting controlled by one centrally located panel. This might be located in your bedroom as a matter of convenience. Entrance lighting—the one exception—can be handled by switches just inside the door. You can also have your exterior lights wired into any burglar alarm system so that when the alarm is tripped, lights suddenly flash on. The sudden wailing of the alarm plus the bright lights will rout even the most resolute marauder.

Plastic-covered cable makes underground wiring installations easier and less expensive than the older conduit wiring. It is also waterproof and will resist acids and alkali almost indefinitely.

Remember that all electrical installations must conform to local codes, so check before you start. If you should forget that, you also run the risk of voiding your insurance in the event of an electrically caused fire. Don't take a chance.

Eave lighting

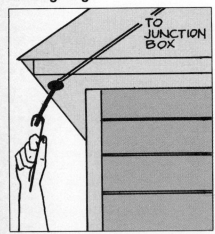

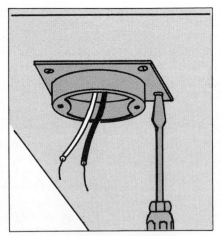

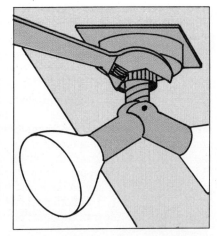

1. To install an eave light, drill a 1-inch hole in the soffit. Connect one end of the electrical cable to a grounded junction box inside the house; then pass the cable through the hole to the outside.

2. The outside end of the cable must now be secured with a locknut to a special outdoor box which is weatherproof. At least 4 inches of cable should be left hanging in order to connect the light fixtures.

3. Connect the two white wires (cable wire to fixture wire) and the two black wires. Secure the fixture assembly with the hardware provided for that purpose.

Indoor lighting

The lights within your house can also be a line of defense against burglars. The point is to give the impression that your house is occupied, even when you are not there. One way you can do this is by setting an inexpensive timer to turn on certain lights and radios at times you have decided on. Experts say it pays to vary the routine of the lights you use and the hours of illumination. It will confuse possible intruders.

Burglar alarms

There are three basic types of electronic security systems in popular use: (1) self-contained alarms which cover a single door or window; (2) motion-sensing units that cover a single room; and (3) perimeter systems which have a central unit connected to each entry in the house.

Self-contained alarms are easy to install and inexpensive. They are generally battery operated and are attached to the inside of a window or door. Some types can be set when you lock up. The fly in the ointment is that they don't make very much noise. If you are at home, you will hear the alarm, but the next-door neighbors probably won't. The alarm might consist of a siren, horn, or bell, and it may well be enough to spook a nervous burglar. But because the alarm is right where the burglar is, he may figure out that you are not at home. All he has to do is execute an adroit snip with his pliers and the alarm will go off. Another problem with self-contained alarms: the larger your house, the more costly they will be, because each window and door requires a separate installation.

Motion-sensing units are usually set in a corner of the room and are plugged into the house current. The system works by sending ultrasonic waves across the room. If anything disturbs the waves, the unit senses it and triggers the alarm. The units are expensive and can only guard the room they are in; you may have to reconsider your financial involvement if you want total house protection. Moreover, nothing takes place until the burglar is actually within the premises. At the same time, pets or family members headed for a midnight snack can easily set off the alarm. This kind of alarm is generally best for a garage or outbuilding, though it is useful in the main house if you go away for days at a time.

The perimeter-alarm system is a sophisticated arrangement which not only announces unauthorized visits to your home, but it even can be connected via centralized control to sensors for smoke or fire (page 86). Most any homeowner will be capable of installing this system. Usually the units at each entry consist of two parts. One is attached to a fixed object, such as a door frame, and the other is on a movable object—in this case the door itself. When the door is shut, the two parts make contact. When it is opened, the circuit is broken. This will send a signal to the central control, and an alarm goes off.

An outside alarm is a useful addition to any system, for it will alert the neighbors to the situation at your house. Make sure the alarm is out of reach of the intruder.

A further deterrent is to show physical evidence that you have electronic security. Most manufacturers furnish stickers or decals, and these can be clearly posted.

A number of extra features can be worked in with your electronic system. You can add dialers that call the police or fire department and play a taped message. Or you can work out an arrangement with the neighbors so that an alarm will go off in their house when a burglar enters yours.

This is all very clever, yet your alarm system will never work unless you activate it when you want it on. Remember that if it uses batteries, you should check them and keep spares on hand.

Jimmy Valentine I was not!
I read that the best way to check my home security was to see how I would go about burglarizing the place myself. I found that the weak spot wasn't in my alarm system but in my neglecting to tell the police what I was up to.

Practical Pete

Installing your alarm system

The various components for alarm devices can be purchased from mail order houses, radio supply stores, and hardware stores. Some systems are available in complete kits. The units which are generally available include these components:

Panic buttons. Resembling regular doorbell buttons, they can be placed at strategic points such as front and back doors and in the master bedroom. When you press them the alarm is activated.

Magnetic contact switches. Installed on windows and doors, they sound an alarm when either is opened.

Sirens, bells, and screamers. These are the sound-shockers of the alarm system. Most experts go for the screamers, since the sirens tend to burn out, and bells don't have a great deal of effect.

Foil tape and foil block connectors. Apply these to windows to set off the alarm if a pane is broken.

Motion detectors. Monitoring the space in front of it with ultrasonic rays, the sensor in a small box sets off an alarm if anything in front of it moves.

Master control panel. The central unit around which an alarm system will be assembled, the master control can be hooked up with *heat sensors* (that trip the alarm when the temperature reaches 135 degrees Fahrenheit) and *smoke sensors*, both of which are excellent fire detectors.

Bear in mind that wherever you are, there will be a local electrical code with regulations that must be followed.

TIP: For the most effective system conceal all wiring. A burglar will be looking for any place where he can disconnect your security system.

Window burglar alarm

It's possible to run up a pretty stiff bill if you go all out for a sophisticated home-security system. This may include such items as ultrasonic motion detectors, window and door alarms, pressure-sensitive mats, and photoelectric beams. And unless you are an electronic whiz, you will need to engage the services of a professional to install it. Note: in some areas, it is possible to *rent* the more elaborate alarm systems.

In shopping for a system and in having it installed, you must exercise extreme care. Check out the company and the sales and service people before you commit yourself. It is no mere jest that today's salesman might be tomorrow's burglar. After all, who would know your security system better than the person who sold it to you?

Where to place the most protection

When designing your alarm system try to see where you need the most protection and where you need the least. Certainly, even the most simple alarm system would include the front door and any other exterior door. And of course ground floor windows should be protected, especially if they are concealed by shrubbery or are in the back.

Remember that no system offers absolute protection. The self-contained alarm is limited in not making a tremendous noise, but it is without question a discouraging factor in a good many cases. The master burglar, of course, will not be foiled by foil on your windows; he knows how that type of alarm works and he will cope accordingly. But how often is one visited by a master? More often than not it is the inept semipro, the crass amateur, the brute who seeks entry, and because of the lack of quality in his craft he will very often pass up anything that suggests a challenge and will move on to greener pastures. A simple burglar-alarm system like the one shown below is not difficult for the average do-it-yourselfer to install. In this system, a thin electrical wire is taped to a window in such a way that when the window is broken the tape breaks. An electrical circuit is thus broken, and this causes the alarm to sound.

Foil and wire devices

Burglarproofing a window begins by washing the interior glass with a solution of alcohol and water. The surface must be absolutely free of dirt, grease, and lint to insure proper adhesion of the foil. Do not use regular window-cleaner solutions; they leave a residue, and this will cause problems with your foil.

Use a straight-edged block of wood 3 inches wide as a guide for drawing lines around the border of the glass. Make the lines with tailor's chalk or a felt-tipped pen.

What it takes

Approximate time: About an hour for foiling and installing the foil connectors. The time for wiring the alarm circuit will vary with the job but will generally be less than an hour.

Tools and materials: Drill and bits, hammer, screwdriver, utility knife, block of wood or other straightedge, matchbook cover (for smoothing tape), foil tape, and connectors. (If you don't use connectors, then you will need a soldering gun and solder.)

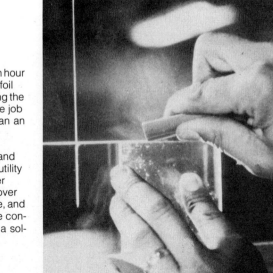

1. Mark lines 3 inches in from the window edge on all four sides. Use a block of wood or other straightedge to guide your tailor's chalk or felt-tipped marker.

2. To make the right-angle turn, lift the tape up and then back down over itself, as shown in this sequence. Repeat for all 90-degree turns. To insure good contact at the turns, prick the foil with a pin four or five times.

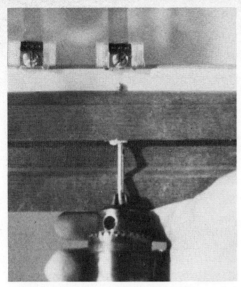

3. It is important to bury the wiring—simply a matter of drilling holes so that it is out of sight and away from the hand of any burglar.

4. A finished window might look like this, with foil connectors on both upper and lower glass.

Run one edge of the wood block along the window frame as you scribe against the opposite edge with your marker. Make the marks on the outside of the glass, the side that will not have the foil. In that way you will be able to clean off the markings once you have completed your foiling.

The tape must be stretched as it is applied and must of course run in a continuous strip. You can smooth the tape as you go, using a matchbook cover. The corners should be right-angle turns. When you reach a corner, lay your tape back over itself at a 45-degree angle. Crease it at the bend with your fingernail, and fold again to complete the right-angle turn. The sticky side of the tape must of course face the glass at all times. Pierce the corner four or five times with a pin to insure proper contact.

Attach connector blocks to the window frame to join the taped portion of the circuit to the alarm wiring. The leads of the connector blocks can be attached to the foil by simply laying the contacts of the block beneath the foil. Alarms without connector blocks require a soldered connection.

Your final step will be to apply a coat of varnish to the tape. This not only protects the tape but is also an aid to severing it should the glass be broken.

Playing it safe

The best place for your valuables is of course the safe-deposit vault in your bank. Yet there are items you may want to keep at home—certain papers, for instance, which might clutter a small deposit box, or jewelry, which you don't want to have to withdraw from a bank each time you wear it to dinner. The best place for such things as these is in a safe at home.

Most heavy-duty safes will thwart the amateur burglar. They can be placed in any room in the house. You could even build your safe into a floor or wall. The bedroom is a good place to have a wall safe. There are many safes on the market, some of which resemble ordinary furniture such as bedside tables. Others look like light switches. When you buy a safe, make sure it is fireproof as well as burglarproof.

Outwitting the burglar

Though a good safe will stop most burglars, the real pros rejoice when they find a safe; it tells them where the valuables are, and they can usually break it open or haul it off with them. So if you have a safe, hide it just the same; and if you don't have a safe, you need a good hiding place all the more. Look around your house. Can you think of clever hiding places? Here are some:

A false closet ceiling is simple to make. Cut a piece of ¾-inch plywood the same size as the closet ceiling. Fasten containers for valuables to the tops of the walls. Then nail molding on two opposite walls a foot or two down from the actual ceiling. The plywood panel will rest on top of the molding but will slide out easily whenever you want to get at your valuables. Paint the panel so it matches the rest of the closet.

An acoustical-tile ceiling can provide a good hiding place. Remove a tile and restore it to place with a magnetic fastener or similar device which you can get at any hardware store. Be careful not to leave finger marks on the tile.

Hollow legs on a table or chair make good hiding places for small objects and are easy to create. Drill from the bottom and then cap *all* the legs with rubber tips.

Fireplace logs can also be hollowed out. This little trick is best done in a nonworking fireplace. Other good places might be the underside of a desk top, the linings of drapes, underneath insulation in the attic, inside a lamp, and so on. Avoid the obvious: mattresses, drawers, figurines on the mantelpiece, picture backs, and under carpets.

Money to burn
Last summer I figured a great hiding place for my extra cash was a drilled-out log in the fireplace. And it sure worked! Someone broke in while I was on vacation and didn't find my money. Trouble was, when it got to be cold weather again, I forgot and lighted a fire. Next time I hide something, I'll tell someone I can trust or write a note to myself for sure.

Practical Pete

Fire precautions

Fire exacts its greatest toll on the physically weak, the inexperienced, and those who become confused and panicky in a moment of crisis. The majority of fires happen between midnight and dawn, when most people are asleep, and so the danger is multiplied. Furthermore, there are more fires during cold weather than warm, which poses an added difficulty. It is estimated that once a fire actually breaks into flame a person will have about four minutes in which to escape before being overcome by noxious gases or superheated air. In many cases people who are sleeping do not awaken in time to escape smoke and gases—which reach them long before the flames.

Fire action plan. For greatest security, start this four-point program immediately:
1. Know the causes of fire.
2. Eliminate fire hazards.
3. Train your family how to react to fires.
4. Have an escape plan ready in case of fire.

Knowing and eliminating causes of fire

One of the major causes of fire is cooking. Grease fires can easily start while food is being fried, especially if the stove has not been kept clear. Pot holders, paper napkins and towels, curtains, and long hair worn loose can easily catch fire. Care of your clothing and the things you are handling—hot grease for instance—is essential when you are working in the kitchen, especially when alone.

Another prime cause of fire is heating appliances. Electric heaters in bedrooms and basement heating plants located near combustibles can be dangerous. If your furnace, for example, hasn't been properly serviced, it can give off sparks or flames which could catch on something and ignite.

Cigarette smoking is infamous as a fire hazard—especially smoking in bed. Fires frequently start, too, when someone empties an ashtray into a wastebasket just before going to bed. Electrical appliances are also a possible hazard. If you overload your circuit with appliances or if wiring is frayed, there is a risk of fire. Rags soaked with grease or paint can cause fire by spontaneous combustion. Flammable fluids, faulty chimneys, overloaded and unscreened fireplaces, and children playing with matches are other common causes.

Fire equipment

Fire-alarm systems can be tied into burglar-alarm systems or can operate on their own. It makes sense to get a two-in-one installation, but in any case, the fire alarm *must* sound differently than the alarm for burglary.

Detectors. The heat detector is a widely used sensor in fire-alarm systems today. It consists of a thermostat that trips an alarm when the temperature around it reaches about 135 degrees Fahrenheit. A heat detector is very useful but is best used in conjunction with a smoke detector, for smoke is usually detected sooner than heat.

The smoke detector is available in both electric and battery-operated models. An electric detector can of course operate only near an outlet, while a battery-operated detector can work anywhere, even during a power stoppage. Of course, you must always have fresh batteries on hand.

Some of the best detectors have an ionization chamber in which a current flow has been created. This flow is disrupted when

Security closet

Why not create a special closet for combustible materials, poisonous substances, and dangerous tools that you don't want children to play with? Put a good lock on the door and a heat detector inside to alert you to any danger of fire.

For maximum security, install a smoke detector outside each bedroom and at the top of stair wells, and heat detectors in other enclosed areas.

The guts of your alarm system—burglar and fire—will be your master panel. Label all wires clearly.

visible or invisible combustion particles enter the chamber. As a result, the alarm goes off.

The detector is battery operated and easy to install, requiring two screws, two mounting anchors, and less than 5 minutes work. With normal use, the battery will last over a year. Maintenance involves a monthly check and yearly vacuum cleaning.

If you mount the smoke detector on the ceiling, place it as close as possible to the center of the room. If your ceiling is sloped, gabled, or high peaked, the smoke detector must be mounted no more than 12 inches and no less than 6 inches from the highest point of the ceiling.

If the unit is wall mounted, it should be no closer than 6 inches and no farther than 12 inches from the ceiling. Check your local code, however, because in some areas wall mounting is not approved.

In any case, the detector must not be mounted in or near:
• The kitchen. Smoke from cooking might trigger the alarm inappropriately.
• The garage. When you start your car, combustion products are present and can set off the alarm.
• Bathrooms. Steam from a shower could set off an unwanted alarm.
• The very peak of an A-frame or gable type of ceiling.
• The front of forced-air ducts used for your house heating or air-conditioning.
• Unheated buildings. Smoke detectors are unreliable below 40 degrees Fahrenheit.

Extinguishers. It is wise to keep fire extinguishers at key points around your home. These are the weapons that will keep little fires from becoming conflagrations.

It is essential to know which type of extinguisher to use. Few people realize that extinguishers are rated according to the type of fire they can handle. According to the Underwriters' Laboratories (whose seal on an extinguisher guarantees that it meets certain minimum standards) there are four designations for fires:

A. Ordinary combustibles such as paper, cloth, wood.
B. Grease, oil, gasoline, and all other flammable chemicals.
C. Fires that involve electrical current.
D. Fires that involve combustible metals.

Although water can be used to put out a Class A fire, water may cause a Class B fire (grease) to explode. And if water is used on a Class C fire involving a live electrical line, it could prove fatal to the fire fighter. When you buy fire extinguishers look for the letter classification on them; the size will be indicated by number, with 2 being the smallest and 10 the largest. Fire extinguishers must be serviced at times stipulated by the manufacturer, usually twice a year, or they may lose their effectiveness.

Operation and deployment

Most fire extinguishers are easy to operate; usually it is only necessary to compress a squeeze valve. The commonest types of extinguishers are pressurized containers with carbon dioxide or dry powder charges. The former simply smother the fire by cutting off its supply of oxygen, while the latter work by spreading a powder which turns the heat into an inert gas. A third group, water extinguishers, are not recommended for the home because they are bulky, heavy, and for some people difficult to handle. Keep at least one Class B and one Class C extinguisher in or near the kitchen, and distribute others in other key areas throughout the house, such as bedrooms, the workshop, and the garage.

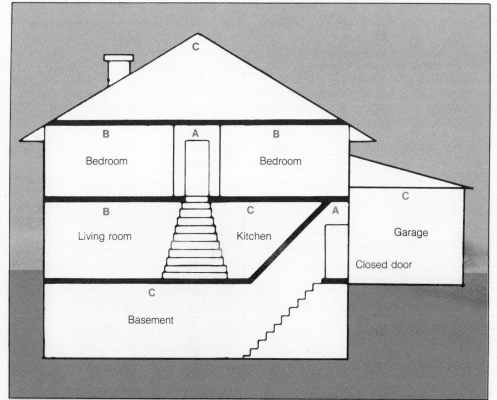

For basic protection at minimum expense, locate one detector in the hallway near each separate sleeping area. More complete protection calls for a detector on every level of your home. Shown here are locations in a typical two-story house. A: Smoke detectors for basic minimum protection. B: Smoke detectors for additional protection. C: Heat-activated detectors.

Lightning protection

Lightning is one of the most destructive forces in nature, and it poses a real threat to your home and family. It is an electric current with tremendous voltage and amperage. By way of comparison, ordinary house current is 110 to 240 volts, with 100 amperes available at the main service panel. One-tenth of an amp is enough to kill, should the current pass through the body, or to start a fire if there is a short in wiring. But a lightning bolt's amperage is 2,000 times greater than that of a typical house, and its voltage is in the millions.

Your house current consists of electric impulses which are continuous and which follow a controlled path of low-resistance wires. Lightning, on the other hand, is a tremendous, uncontrolled, instant surge of electric current that could lift a large ocean liner 6 feet in the air in a split second.

Lightning strikes trees, buildings or any other objects which consist of materials that are better electrical conductors than the air. Homes are among the most vulnerable targets because they usually stand out from the surrounding terrain, and their wiring and plumbing systems provide an ideal path to ground for an electrical charge. There are four ways lightning can strike:
1. By direct hit.
2. By following a power line or an ungrounded wire fence.
3. By flowing down the metal television attachments on a house after it has struck the antenna.
4. By leaping to a building after striking a tree to find a better path to the ground.

As a rule, lightning follows a metallic path to the ground, and sometimes even from the ground up. The bolt may leap from the metallic path to plumbing or wiring and so may cause fire or burn out electrical appliances.

A lightning-protection system should therefore offer an easy, direct path for the bolt to follow into the ground and thus prevent injury or damage while the bolt is traveling that path. Proper lightning protection should include the following:

Air terminals should be installed on the highest points of the roof and on all projections. These can be of copper or aluminum, at least 10 inches in height and no more than 20 feet apart. It is important that the terminals and their placement meet the requirements of the National Fire Protection Code and Underwriters' Laboratories. Chimneys should have separate terminals.

Main conductors are special cables made of heavy aluminum or copper that interconnect all the air terminals on the roof. In addition, there should be a minimum of two conductors on the ground.

Branch conductors connect into the main conductor system all antennas, gutters, plumbing stacks, water pipes, air conditioning, telephone grounds, and any other major metal units within 6 feet of the conductors. These lengths of cable are like those in main conductors, except smaller.

Lightning arresters are small devices mounted at the points of entry of overhead electrical service wires and also on television antennas. They connect to the system's grounding and provide protection against the smaller power surges produced by distant lightning strikes.

Grounding rods (at least two for small houses) should be placed at opposite corners of the house. Larger houses will need more than two grounds.

Special protection is also necessary for tall trees less than 10 feet from the house.

Lightning protection systems should be installed professionally; a faulty installation would be hazardous.

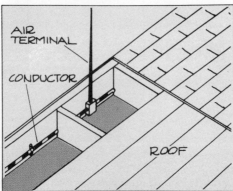

Air terminals are the only parts of a concealed lightning-protection system that are visible. They should be spaced a minimum of 20 feet apart along the ridges, and within 2 feet of the ridge ends.

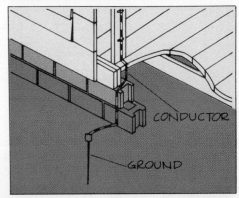

A ground connection is made through the base of the building wall. Your system should be inspected each year for loose or bent terminals, loose connecting clamps, and broken conductor cables.

Storm warnings

Whether you live in a high-wind area or just have to put up with an occasional hurricane or northeaster, you'll be wise to give some thought to storm problems before they arise. Glass may crack or shatter, shingles may blow off your roof, trees may fall dangerously. When the weather threatens, check storm warnings with your local weather bureau. If you are buying a house or planning to build in a high-wind area, inquire whether many trees have been blown down in earlier storms. Keep an eye on large trees—even healthy ones—that could damage the house if they ever fell. Cut them back as necessary.

Glass. In areas where wind is a chronic problem, local building codes set standards on the strength of glass that should be used. Depending on the prevailing wind velocity and also on the size of the window, plate glass, tempered glass, or double-strength glass will be designated. Storm doors and windows must also be glazed with either tempered glass or acrylic plastic. Be sure to check with your local code before you do any remodeling.

When a major storm is imminent, close shutters, board windows, or tape the inside of larger panes with an X along the full length of their diagonals. Even a light material like masking tape may give the glass the extra margin of strength it needs to resist cracking. Exception: When a tornado threatens, leave windows slightly ajar.

Shingles. To avoid having your shingles go like a deck of cards in the wind, check that they are adequately nailed or have proper adhesive. A lot of homeowners use self-sealing asphalt shingles in which short strips of adhesive are lined up to meet the underside of the shingle tabs in the strip above. The weight of the shingles together with the sun's heat, which softens the adhesive, produce a firm bond.

On a roof with shingles that are not the seal-down type, you can apply a little dab of roofing cement under each tab. This will give you good security in a storm. Again, check your local building code as to the best shingles for your area, how many nails should be used, and what sort of adhesive. The size and number of nails for each shingle strip are usually specified in the manufacturer's instructions. As a rule, this will be one nail on each end plus one above each slot. But in high-wind areas the Housing and Urban Development Department's minimum property standards specify six nails per strip. The nails should be large-headed roofing nails, a minimum of ¾

inch long, and galvanized. It is important to follow the requirements, not only to save your roof—but in the event of wind damage your insurance claim will be affected if you did not follow legal specifications.

Remember that structural damage can result from high winds which are less than the velocity of a tornado. Your house needs to be secured to its foundation by bolts or special steel anchors. The roof can be secured to the wall framing by special metal tie straps.

Tornadoes

A tornado is a violent, destructive windstorm of short duration. When a tornado hits a building, its winds rip and twist at the outside while the abrupt pressure reduction in the tornado's "eye" creates tremendous suction inside the structure, with the result that windows burst and walls crumble. When a tornado approaches, seek cover and stay low.

An ideal tornado shelter would be one that is constructed under the ground, outside your house yet near it. It must be far enough away so that if walls fall your shelter will not be affected. It's not a bad idea to dig your shelter into a small hill if there happens to be one; but the shelter should have no connection with the house gas or sewer pipes, drains, or cesspool. This is why the basement of the house isn't a good shelter.

The size of the shelter will of course depend on the number of people who would be using it. Figure on at least 10 square feet per person. Reinforced concrete is the best material, but split logs, hollow tile, brick, and cinder block can be used. The door must be hinged to open inward, and must be made of heavy material. The roof must of course be strongly reinforced and should slope so that water will drain off. The floor, too, should slope for drainage. And you will need a vertical ventilating shaft.

Equipment. Store a lantern, pick, shovel, crowbar, hammer, screwdriver, and pliers in the shelter; if your exit should get blocked you will have to dig your way out. Store canned food and bottled water.

Hurricanes

Though the force of hurricanes is not so concentrated as that of tornadoes, winds often exceed 100 miles an hour, and flooding is an added danger. In general, don't go out unless you have to, but seek high ground if flooding threatens, and follow instructions of civil defense personnel. Store drinking water, candles, and a radio.

I almost made it to the Land of Oz!
I figured I'd win first prize at my camera club contest if I could get a quick shot of that tornado before it really hit. But I forgot that you're supposed to get low and stay low. One minute the funnel was on the horizon, the next minute it passed right by me. The point is, you don't have as much time as you may imagine. Next thing I knew I was up a tree!

Practical Pete

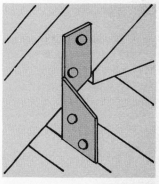

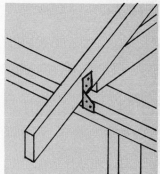

Metal tie straps for roof

7. PEST CONTROL

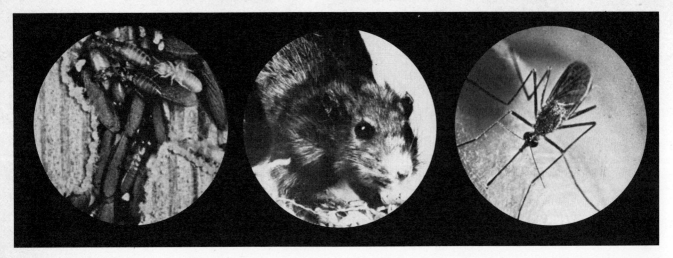

You are settled in your home, master or mistress of your castle, which is insulated, caulked, painted, weather-stripped, screened, storm-doored, locked and bolted, activated with temperature controls and alarms against fire or burglar; you feel secure in the knowledge that you can handle whatever exigency might arise.

But are you truly secure? What about those small, often hardly seen visitors who come singly or in armies wreaking damage, leaving fury in their wake; the ubiquitous cockroach, the insistent mosquito, the voracious termite, to mention but three of the more unpopular visitors? And let's not forget houseflies, squirrels, rats and mice, moths, snakes, birds, your neighbor's pets, lice and bedbugs, spiders, bats, and raccoons.

Some of these unwanted visitors are relatively harmless, but others, such as the termite, can be a severe annoyance, creating damage as well as anxiety.

Defense

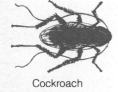

Cockroach

Happily, the homeowner is not without recourse. At his disposal are means to cope with invaders from the animal world. The most useful step is to seal any potential point of entry. Put screening behind louvers, over roof ventilators, inside cupolas and other areas of ventilation where animals could enter, including crawl-space vents and flue liners on top of chimneys.

Check all screening on windows and doors. Seal any area that requires caulking, and fill in with mortar any openings in the foundation masonry. It goes without saying that all doors and windows in the house should fit snugly.

Moisture control is important in order to deter infestation by wood insects. These animals attack damp wood, especially around foundations and crawl spaces. Crawl spaces should be thoroughly vented, and you should position the vents to allow cross ventilation. Keep a check on dampness throughout the house (see pages 60-63), and keep all exposed wood painted.

Offense

Mosquito

There are over 86,000 varieties of insects in North America, and man's battle with these persistent creatures has been going on since the earliest days. Yet experts say that no insect is a pest in and of itself; it only becomes so when excess numbers get to be bothersome to their host. On the other hand, a single mosquito, carrying who-knows-what lethal payload in its warhead has more clout for the sleepless victim than an army of termites gorging on the house foundation. The damage may be less, but the emotional embroilment of the host still justifies the word "pest."

The solution to your insect problem lies at least partly in the correct choice of weapon. The insecticide you choose may do the job, or it may be the one from which a particular pest enjoys immunity. Your best bet is to call your county agricultural agent whenever you have any doubt about the potency of a given pesticide or what method would be most effective in a particular situation. The general guidelines that follow will solve most problems with any of the pesky pests.

Fly

Insecticides

The commonest pest killers are available as surface sprays, powders, and chemically treated strips. Surface, or residual sprays are applied by brush, aerosol bomb, or spray gun to surfaces where insects travel or breed. Surface spray liquid leaves a film that kills insects on contact up to several weeks after application.

Space sprays are dispensed in an aerosol bomb or spray can, and though they kill flying insects, they have little residual effect. Insecticide powders are dusted in feeding and breeding areas.

In handling any insecticide, it is most important to read the label for instructions on how often to use it, when to use it, in what strength to use it, and what to do if any of the compound should get in your eyes or mouth. Since the hazards of misuse are numerous and very real, look for special precautions on the label and keep the following general guidelines in mind:

1. Make sure that the product you are using is for the pest you are after.
2. Avoid contact with any pesticide, and do not inhale the fumes.
3. Keep the spray away from food, pets, dishes, cooking utensils, and children.
4. Do not smoke while using pesticides, and wash your hands before handling a cigarette afterwards.
5. Use only the amount required for the job. Overkill is dangerous.
6. Never spray near a flame, a furnace, lighted stove, or pilot light.
7. Do not reuse insecticide containers. Rinse and dispose of them. If there is leftover insecticide, leave it in the same container. Keep it well covered.
8. Never use residual insecticides where children will be playing.
9. Change your clothes after spraying, and store insecticides in a safe place.
10. As soon as you have used a space spray (bomb), leave the room; close the room tightly for at least a half hour, and then ventilate it.
11. Never hang a chemically treated strip in any room where people will be present for any length of time, especially sick or old people or infants.
12. When you dispose of insecticides make sure that they will not injure the environment. Never flush them down toilets, sewers, or drains.
13. If you should feel any ill effects after you have used an insecticide, contact your doctor immediately.

Ant

Wasp

Bedbug

The six least welcome visitors

The list of insect pests is long. The more notorious household invaders are described below, along with the key facts about their habits, habitat, appearance, and extermination methods.

The cockroach. He is tough, seasoned, and aggressive. Centuries of warfare have only honed his resistance to the onslaughts of determined householders. He is brown in color, ½ to 1 inch long, and nocturnal. He eats garbage, food, starch, and glue. He is immune to chlordane. Use a residual spray with malathion, ronnel, diazinon, lindane, or baygon. Spray wherever you think he and his fellows might hide. This means cracks, crevices, and areas around water pipes and the stove. Cleanliness is one of your major weapons. Get rid of any piles of newspapers and brown paper bags. Especially in apartment buildings, where cockroaches are free to hit and run, your attack must be relentless.

The ant. He lives in colonies. His trail is easy to follow. Interrupt it with residual dust (outdoors) or spray (indoors) containing lindane, malathion, diazinon, or baygon.

The bedbug. He feeds on blood—chiefly man's—and has an elongated beak which enables him to pierce the skin of his victim. He travels on clothing and luggage, on laundry, secondhand bedding, beds, and other furniture. The mature bedbug is brown and has no wings. His size depends upon the amount of food (blood) his body contains. A bedbug that has not fed is between ¼ and ⅜ inch long. Bedbugs feed mostly at night but will also eat during the day if the light is dim. They favor the hours when their victim is asleep. Bedbugs are found in seams, tufts, and folds of mattresses and crevices in the bedstead. Lindane, malathion, ronnel, and pyrethrum are effective against bedbugs. But many household sprays are not suitable for use on mattresses, so do not use any insecticide on a mattress unless the label states specifically that you may.

The mosquito. He is one of man's most redoubtable adversaries. Not only his bite but even his sound alone has driven generations of otherwise normal humans into massive retaliatory strikes with swatter, magazine, fist, and club. The mosquito grows from larvae deposited in stagnant water. His diet consists of animal and human blood. To cope indoors, spray in a closed room, keeping people and animals out for at least 30 minutes. Outdoors, see that all stagnant water is either drained or covered with a thin layer of oil. You can also spray your grounds with foggers, which are available at home centers and hardware stores.

The wasp. He is the B-29 of the flying insects. No one who has ever been stung by the wasp will ever forget it. Inside the house, squirt with a spray can which you can buy at any home center or hardware store. Act swiftly to level any nests. Use a freezing spray for this operation, and work at night when the inhabitants are not as lively as in the daytime.

The fly. He breeds in garbage, in food, in decaying organic matter, and he spreads a number of diseases injurious to man and animal. Screens are your initial line of defense. Kill flies indoors with spray or fumes from a chemically treated strip. Outdoors, make sure that you seal garbage in sanitary containers; spray inside the containers with residual pesticide.

Termite control

What it takes

Approximate time: Indeterminate. It depends on the extent of the job; but allow a minimum of one afternoon.

Tools and materials: Ice pick or other sharp instrument, shovel, power drill with masonry bit, garden hose, watering can or soil-injector tool, chlordane (liquid or cartridge), concrete patch mix, and caulking compound and gun.

Reproductive termite

Soldier termite

Worker termite

Tiny as he is, the termite is mighty enough to bring down a house. He is silent, virtually invisible, and does not advertise himself by biting people. Often his presence is realized only when the foundation of your house has reached a terminal stage.

Termites do about a half billion dollars in property damage every year. But because they work so unobtrusively, many people fail to acknowledge the need to cope with them. The only sensible approach is determined vigilance.

Extermination is not usually a project for the do-it-yourselfer; if you believe you have a problem, you'll be wise to consult a professional exterminator immediately. But whether you do your own exterminating or not, you should know what signs to look for, and what methods are best to stay ahead of the game.

There are dozens of different species of termites, but the most destructive is the subterranean termite. The termite is frequently called a white ant. But this is a misnomer; the termite's appearance differs considerably from that of the ant. The body of the termite is more or less equally thick along its entire length, unlike the ant's hourglass figure.

The termite lives on cellulose, which he obtains from rotting plant material, dead trees, and such wooden objects as furniture, house timbers, and fence posts. In colder areas, the subterranean termite can live for up to 10 months without cellulose.

Because the destruction caused by termites is not visible and takes place over a long period of time, it can be very thorough indeed. Termites believe in team work, large teams, and they eat just the inside portion of a piece of furniture or a timber, leaving a hollow shell. No opening ever appears on the surface, and nothing is known until the gutted member collapses.

Wherever the termite finds a source of wood in the soil he sets up a colony. The colony is comprised of three groups: reproductive termites, soldier termites, and worker termites. Each group has its function, as the names imply. The reproductive termites leave the nest to mate and start a new colony, the soldiers defend the colony against enemies, and the workers provide food for the colony. It is they who do the damage. Because the workers cannot tolerate exposure to light, they build tunnels from the ground up, to reach the new source of food. The width of one of these tunnels will be ¼ to ½ inch, while the length may be several feet.

What to look for

1. The termite mating season is spring through early summer. Look for large numbers of flying insects. They are seeking a place to start a new colony. Also watch for discarded wings. Look in crawl spaces, at basement window sills, and around the foundation of your house.
2. At any time of year, look for grayish mud tubes or tunnels that lead from the ground to wooden parts of your house. These are usually found on the foundation, on piers beneath the house, or on basement walls. Check around the openings where pipes enter the house. Seal the openings with caulking compound.

3. Wood trellises and fences that connect with the house are possible entries for termites, as are scrap lumber, firewood, and low wooden structures.
4. Check crawl spaces that have dirt floors, thresholds, wood stairs, paint that has blistered or peeled on a low wood structure.
5. Use a penknife, awl, ice pick, or other sharp-pointed instrument to probe any wood that may be suspicious to you. Try the underside of porches, window boxes, the lower steps in a basement. If the point of the instrument goes into the wood easily, with only hand pressure, to a depth of about ½ inch, it's a strong indication of trouble.

Preventive measures

The best way to deny termites access to your house is to install copper termite shields where the foundation meets the wood. The shields should extend 3 or 4 inches beyond each side of the masonry and should be anchored to the top of the foundation every 3 feet. These are best installed while a house is still under construction.

Another method of control (illustrated opposite) is to create a poisonous barrier around your home. The chemical chlordane is frequently used for this purpose. But chlordane must be used with great caution for it is also toxic to humans. It comes in concentrated form and must be diluted with water to produce the exact solution specified by the manufacturer's directions. Some states have certain restrictions in the use of chlordane, and so check with your county agricultural agent before you apply this chemical around the house.

You can use a watering can to pour the mixed chlordane. Remove the sprinkler head and pour the chemical into a shallow trench dug close to the foundation all the way around the building. Don't skip any areas, because termites are adept at finding gaps and so will still reach your house. The barrier will trap some of the colony; others will be unable to cross the barrier and so will look for other places to feed. Still others will carry the poison back to the colony.

You should also apply chlordane inside your house, around and into any visible cracks where a concrete floor joins a foundation wall, near the foundation wall of all crawl spaces, and in other areas that have a soil floor.

Remember that chlordane is poisonous, so ventilate when you use it indoors. After application leave the room right away, and close it off for several days.

Dig slanting trench outside and inside foundation walls. Pour chlordane solution carefully into trench.

Creating a termite barrier

Because chlordane can be harmful to humans if it is used carelessly, it is advisable that you follow these instructions as well as any others specified by the manufacturer.
1. Dig a slanting trench about 6 inches wide and 2 feet deep all the way around your house foundation. Do not dig below the footing.
2. Pour the diluted chlordane into the trench. Be sure you pour at the rate specified in the instructions.
3. Fill the trench and mix extra chlordane solution with the dirt.
4. Trench around all pillars that support any porch, and treat in the same way with the chlordane.
5. Treat the ground under all slabs such as patios, walks, garage floors, if they are near

foundation. The way to do this is to drill holes 6 inches out from the foundation and a foot apart. You'll need a power drill and masonry bit. Pour the chlordane into these holes at the suggested rate. Use a funnel. Then patch the holes with concrete.
6. Inside your house will be next. If your house is on a slab or the floor of the basement is concrete, then drill as you did for your garage floor or patio, and treat in the same way, using a funnel. Then patch the holes with concrete.
7. If you are working in a crawl space, trench inside along the foundation wall and, of course, around each pier.
Important: Any kitchen containers or utensils that you may use should be permanently retired from service.

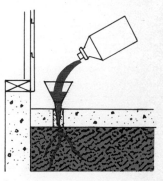

Pour chlordane into drilled holes in concrete slabs.

Soil injection

There is another method of exterminating termites that is much easier than the liquid chlordane method. You can shoot chlordane into the soil with an injector. No digging is necessary. The soil injector uses cartridges; it mixes the pesticide with water fed into it by a garden hose; the water forces the mixed chlordane into the soil. The injections are made inside the house as well as outside, in the same way as described above. The injector application costs more than the liquid method, but it is cleaner, easier, and less hazardous.

If you decide to call in a professional, be careful. Rates can vary widely. Do a lot of checking. Get several estimates on the job.

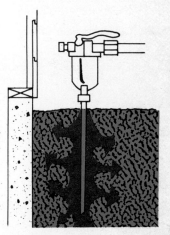

Soil injector, powered by garden hose, shoots chlordane into ground from surface.

Rodent control

When you hear "rodent" you immediately think rat or mouse, and it is these two rodents with which the homeowner is chiefly concerned. There are two ways to get rid of rats and mice in your house—with traps and with poisons.
Poisons are the most effective means. The problem is that they pose a danger to children and pets. (There is also a chance that a poisoned rodent could expire within the house and later produce an odor.) If it is possible, use poisons only where rats or mice can get them but children and pets cannot—for instance, under the house or in the attic. *Warfarin* and *red squill* will dispatch most rodents. But some rat communities have developed defenses to certain poisons, so check with your county agricultural agent or local hardware dealer.
Traps can certainly catch rats and mice; but if you have a great many pests, there is the possibility that they will reproduce more quickly than you can catch them. Be sure that the traps you buy are for the particular type of rodent you are after.

Rat traps should be baited with strong-smelling cheese, raw or cooked meat, fish, or bread. Mouse traps should be baited with peanut butter, raw bacon, or cheese. At the same time, it is important to seal all cracks or openings where rodents may enter your house. Maintain a check.

Index